Wealth and Power in Provincial Mexico

Wealth and Power in Provincial Mexico

Michoacán from the Late Colony to the Revolution

MARGARET CHOWNING

STANFORD UNIVERSITY PRESS

Stanford, California

1999

Stanford University Press
Stanford, California

©1999 by the Board of Trustees of the
Leland Stanford Junior University

Printed in the United States of America

CIP data appear at the end of the book

To Fred

CONTENTS

MAPS, FIGURES, AND TABLES

In the long and sometimes untidy evolution of this book I have incurred many debts. Research for the dissertation upon which the book is loosely based was supported by generous grants from the Social Science Research Council and the Fulbright-Hays dissertation fellowship program. Post-dissertation research was funded by the American Council of Learned Societies, the National Endowment for the Humanities, the California State University at Hayward, and the University of California at Berkeley. The National Endowment for the Humanities also supported a semester of leave during which I began the process of completely rethinking, restructuring, and rewriting the dissertation. An extra semester of leave for write-up was provided by the University of California, whose especially humane family medical leave policy I would like to take this opportunity to acknowledge.

In graduate school John Johnson took me on as a student though he was near retirement, nagging me to think logically and to finish expeditiously, all the while encouraging me unfailingly. In Michoacán the staffs at the Registro Público de la Propiedad, where the notary archive was then housed, and at the Casa de Morelos, the judicial archive, the archive of the state congress in Morelia, and the municipal archives of both Morelia and Pátzcuaro were always helpful and cheerful, especially Professor Xavier Alfaro Tavera at the state congress, whose own two-volume study of Morelia during the Restored Republic was an invaluable resource. Heriberto Moreno García, Carlos Marichal, and Luis Murillo lent their support at a crucial moment, on short notice. Gabriela Pickett, Francisca Escobedo Pérez, and Kalé Haywood provided invariably intelligent research assistance, and David Deis (Dreamline

Cartography) was a dream to work with on the maps. Permission was graciously granted by Fimax Publicistas in Morelia for the use of the photographs in the text, taken from *Familias y Casas de la Vieja Valladolid* (1969), and the cover painting is reproduced from *Historia General de Michoacán* (1989) with the permission of the Instituto Michoacano de Cultura. Fernando Corral and Enrique Bautista not only made my two years in Morelia supremely enjoyable but also helped in practical ways to keep the project on track. In a different way, so did my wonderful and (mainly) patient twin daughters, Polly and Sarah, who made sure that I had a life outside of the book, as a result of which the book is surely better, even if it was slower to coalesce.

My colleagues at Berkeley have picked me up in all kinds of ways. I owe special thanks to Tulio Halperín, Linda Lewin, Paula Fass, Reggie Zelnik, Peter Sahlins, and Jan de Vries. Richard Salvucci, Steve Haber, Eric Van Young, Charles Hale, and John Kicza have also helped me to clarify my thinking in important ways, as did one anonymous reader for the Stanford Press. I never quite understood the conventional disclaimer included in most books — to the effect that despite all the help and support one has received, the problems with the book are the author's own doing — until I came into the final stretch and realized that I simply could not incorporate all of the excellent advice offered by my friends and colleagues, either because someone else had suggested something quite different, or because I simply ran out of the steam required for yet more research. I recall wondering in the past why some people who have asked me to read their work did not take *my* suggestions more to heart. Now I know.

By far the largest intellectual and personal debt I owe is to Frederick P. Bowser — my teacher, my colleague, and my husband. This book, which I began to write at the beginning of his long struggle with cancer and which I finished a month after his death, would have been much better if he had been able to give it his usual rigorous and keen review. It is a small thing to dedicate it to his memory, but it is the best I can do.

M. C.

The following list is not a complete family tree; the children of individuals not mentioned in the text are not included. The numbers represent generations of descent from Isidro Huarte and birth order (approximate) within sets of siblings among generations.

1.1. Isidro Huarte m. Ignacia Escudero (1769)
1.1. Isidro Huarte m. Ana Manuela Muñiz y Sánchez de Tagle (1771)
  2.1. Br. José Antonio Huarte Muñiz
  2.2. Lic. Isidro Huarte Muñiz
  2.3. María del Carmen Huarte Muñiz (m. Pascual Alzúa, 1796)
    3.1. Dolores Alzúa Huarte (m. Cayetano Gómez, 1818)
      4.1. Lic. Juan Bautista Gómez Alzúa (m. Jesús González Solórzano, 1844)
        5.1. Juan Bautista Gómez González (m. María Maillefert, 1882)
        5.2. Manuel Gómez González (m. Dolores Pliego)
        5.3. Dolores Gómez González (m. Carlos Maillefert)
      4.2. Juan de Dios Gómez Alzúa (m. Josefa Basauri, 1846)
        5.1. José Gómez Basauri (m. Soledad Arrieta; m. Andrea López Pimentel)
        5.2. Ana Gómez Basauri (m. Rafael Linares)
        5.3. Concepción Gómez Basauri (m. Adalberto Vaca)
        5.4. Francisco Gómez Basauri
        5.5. Javier Gómez Basauri
      4.3. María de Jesús Gómez Alzúa (m. Dr. Luis Iturbide, 1844)
        5.1. Luis Iturbide Gómez (m. Guadalupe Chávez, 1871)
        5.2. Francisco Iturbide Gómez (m. María Dávalos, 1874; m. Soledad Macouzet López, 1883)
        5.3. Eduardo Iturbide Gómez (m. Carmen Plancarte Menocal, 1878)
        5.4. Felipe Iturbide Gómez (m. Soledad del Moral, 1882)

5.5. Concepción Iturbide Gómez (m. José del Moral, 1883)

5.6. Pilar Iturbide Gómez (m. Joaquín Macouzet López, 1884)

5.7. Paz Iturbide Gómez (m. Luis Macouzet López, 1890)

5.8. José Iturbide Gómez (m. Celine Reygondaud, 1898)

5.9. Ma. Dolores Iturbide Gómez (m. Manuel Macouzet López, 1892)

4.4. María del Pilar Gómez Alzúa (m. Francisco Román, 1847)

   5.1. Guadalupe Román Gómez (m. Ignacio Erdozain, 1867)

   5.2. Francisco Román Gómez

   5.3. Luisa Román Gómez

   5.4. Dolores Román Gómez (m. Manuel Montaño Ramiro, 1877)

   5.5. Angela Román Gómez

   5.6. Soledad Román Gómez

4.5. María Josefa Gómez Alzúa (m. Santiago Sosa, 1858)

4.6. Cayetano Gómez Alzúa (m. Paula Solórzano y Mata, 1862)

4.7. María Trinidad Gómez Alzúa (m. Luis Sámano, 1863)

4.8. José Ignacio Gómez Alzúa (m. Consuelo Castillo, 1866)

4.9. Teresa Gómez Alzúa (m. Francisco de Sales Menocal, 1861)

3.2. Luisa Alzúa Huarte

3.3. Manuel Alzúa Huarte

3.4. Juana Alzúa Huarte (m. Cor. Andrés Oviedo, 1822)

3.5. Macaria Alzúa Huarte (m. Ignacio Montenegro, 1827)

2.4. Ramón Huarte Muñiz (m. Josefa Domínguez)

2.5. Teresa Huarte Muñiz (m. Juan González Castañón, 1803; m. José Antonio Arce, 1804; m. Juan Vergara, 1809)

2.6. Ana Manuela Huarte Muñiz (m. Agustín de Iturbide, 1805)

2.7. Joaquín Huarte Muñiz (m. Francisca Guerra, 1815)

1.1. Isidro Huarte m. Ana Gertrudis Alcántara y Arrambide (1804)

2.1. María Dolores Huarte Alcántara

2.2. Manuel Huarte Alcántara (m. Antonio Izasaga, 1833)

2.3. Mariano Huarte Alcántara (m. Abelina Domínguez, 1839; m. Leonor Caballero, 1848)

2.4. María Francisca Huarte Alcántara

Wealth and Power in Provincial Mexico

Introduction

Few authors of Mexican history textbooks are able to resist underlining the ironies of Porfirio Díaz's elaborate centennial celebration of the Hidalgo Rebellion on the eve of the Revolution of 1910. The picture of magnificent ostentation in the midst of great poverty is riveting enough. That the festivities were (on the surface of things) staged to commemorate a massive, angry uprising against injustices that were in some ways not so very different from those that the 1910 revolutionaries would soon target makes for a doubly effective and affecting image. But it is an image that cannot help but imply that little of fundamental significance changed in the century between the Revolution of 1810 and the Revolution of 1910.

The authors of such textbooks would quickly protest, of course, that such an implication was not their intention. But their protests are necessarily based on a combination of intuition and the thinnest and most compartmentalized historiography of any of the Mexican centuries. There are more or less separate issues, conventions, sources, and traditions for historians writing about the late Bourbon period, the insurgent decade and independence, the Federal Republic and the so-called "age of Santa Anna," the Reform and the Restored Republic, the Porfiriato, and, of course, the Revolution.

Moreover, even within these subperiods, there is not a high degree of thematic coherence. There are relatively few studies that fall into the category of political economy, in the sense that an attempt is made to bring together elements of political history and economic history, at least for the period between the outbreak of the wars for independence and the Porfiriato.[1] A handful of useful but fairly narrow works has helped clarify the intersection between private business practices and politics, of which David Walker's work on the Martínez del Río family stands out.[2] Other studies have focused on the development of certain economic institutions, with attention to the political context in which they operated;[3] while a slightly larger number have explored the connection between national politics and national government finances.[4] In general, however, and no matter how useful these studies are in other respects, the link between Mexico's dismal pre-Porfirian economy and its messy pre-Porfirian political history has been fairly unimaginative: the chronically depressed economy contributed to the chronically unstable political system, and vice versa.

If historians with a stated interest in politics and economics have not been able to get much beyond this truism, students of politics and political thought have generally been even less tempted to do so. Finding little of irresistible relevance to their own work in an economic historiography whose main concerns have been issues of development (what went wrong? why did Mexico fall farther and farther behind?), many of these historians have skimmed or, occasionally, even ignored the social and economic dimensions of the Mexican experience in the nineteenth century, a tendency that also, almost programmatically, characterizes the handful of cultural studies that have begun to appear in the last few years.[5]

All things considered, the studies that have most effectively analyzed how political, economic, social, and ideological change fed off each other in the nineteenth century have focused on a particular social group in a particular region. Recent fine examples include Florencia Mallon's work on peasants and politics in Puebla and Morelos; Guy Thomson's work on the sierra de Puebla; Peter Guardino's book on peasants and politics in Guerrero; Andrés Lira's study of indigenous communities in Mexico City *barrios*; and Rodolfo Pastor's treatment of campesinos in the Mixteca. For elites, the best recent work is the series of articles on landowners and merchants in Puebla by Juan Carlos Garavaglia and Juan Carlos Grosso. Older but still very successful regional social histories include the excellent essays in Mario Cerruti's edited volume on Morelos, Monterrey, Yucatán, Jalisco, and Puebla; Guy Thomson's study of industry and society in Puebla; David Brading's work on miners and merchants in Guanajuato, and hacendados and rancheros in León; and Stuart Voss's on Sonora and Sinaloa. In a variation on the theme, John Tutino's ambitious and useful book takes up the question of the social bases of agrarian violence in various regions from 1750 to 1940. All of these books and essays evoke a nuanced sense of time and place for a period whose daily routines and relationships remain, nonetheless, shadowy.[6]

With the relative success of these approaches in mind, but with a keener interest than most of the authors (with the exception of Tutino) in changes across the entire long nineteenth century (roughly 1780 to 1910), I began my own inquiries. I hoped that by narrowing my focus to the actions and voices of a well-defined social group (the wealthy) in a well-defined region (the state of Michoacán), and by using local archives rarely employed in systematic fashion by historians of the nineteenth century, I would be able not only to unearth new data but also to untangle the shifting and unpredictable connections between politics, economics, and ideologies as they came into play in the lives of well-to-do provincial Mexicans.

My choice of Michoacán as a regional focus was inspired by several considerations. First and most obvious, when I began this project there were very few studies of any aspect of the state's history during the nineteenth century. Since then quite a few articles and monographs have appeared, most of them produced by researchers at the Colegio de Michoacán in Zamora or the Universidad Michoacana in Morelia. The majority of these studies are either more limited in time or geographical focus than my own, or have different goals (for example, the nineteenth-century volume of the *Historia general de Michoacán*, edited by Gerardo Sánchez Díaz, which was published in 1988). But all of them have enriched my own understanding of the history of nineteenth-century Michoacán; indeed, in retrospect, it is hard to see how this book could have come about were it not for the blossoming of history writing in the higher institutions of the state.[7]

Second, Michoacán offered a chance to study a political entity that contained great social, cultural, and economic diversity. In a fairly broad band along its northern borders, beginning in the northeastern corner of the state near Maravatío and reaching as far south as Morelia in the center and Zamora in the west, the state shared many of the characteristics of the Bajío region, Mexico's "bread basket" even today (see Map 1). A mixture of small, middle-sized, and large livestock and grain-producing haciendas occupied broad, fertile valleys, with the largest estates occasionally exporting cattle or wheat to Mexico City or the northern mining centers (during which times they were largely reliant on nearby Indian villages for seasonal labor), but more characteristically producing for relatively local markets and renting out their surplus lands to tenants or sharecroppers.

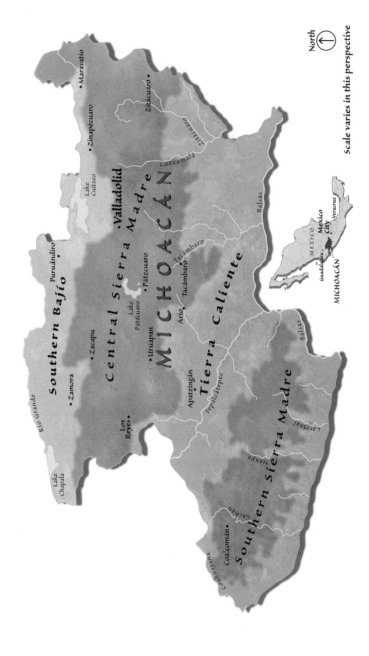

Map 1. Regions of Michoacán.

In the southern part of the state was a sparsely populated *tierra caliente* in which great, often highly capitalized haciendas, mainly devoted to production of sugar, rice, or indigo, dominated the rural landscape. Outside of the irrigable parts of the haciendas, cattle ranching provided income of another sort. Here the social makeup of the population was quintessentially multiracial, with people of African descent, indigenous peoples, mestizos, mulattoes, and poor whites linked in varying degrees to the out-of-region export economy centered on the haciendas.

In parts of both the western and eastern sierra (around Jiquilpan and Sahuayo in the west and Zitácuaro in the east), yet another pattern of economic and social organization prevailed, with a few scattered large haciendas coexisting with much more numerous small, family-run rural enterprises. Here, most Indian villages were relatively isolated from the Hispanic, hacienda-rancho economy, so there was much less ethnic cross-fertilization, and, in the west at least, a less exaggerated social hierarchy than in other parts of the state.

Third, Michoacán was an attractive candidate for study from the point of view of a political historian, with its strong liberal tradition in the east and in the capital city of Valladolid/Morelia (Hidalgo, Morelos, Abad y Queipo, Ocampo, and many others come to mind), and its equally strong conservative tradition in the west. Bishops and Conservative leaders Pelagio Antonio de Labastida and Clemente de Jesús Munguía had roots in or near Zamora, a city that built a cathedral in the late 1860s, when other parts of the country were stripping theirs. The western part of the state was also a center of *cristero* movements in the 1870s and, most famously, the 1920s.

Finally, the history of Michoacán in the nineteenth century seemed to have a flow, a movement that is not so readily apparent for most other regions. The province had been relatively rich and important in the colonial period, but by the end of the Porfiriato it had been eclipsed by all of its neighbors and by most of the other states in the Republic. The "why" of Michoacán's decline seemed not only a useful organizing principle for a book about the state, but it promised to tell us, implicitly at least, much about the history of Mexico in the nineteenth century, for only by reference to the national history was it likely that this decline could be understood.

The other important choice of focus I made was to write about the wealthy. The backlash against "elitist" history, beginning in the 1960s, led to a number of innovative social histories of what were then thought of as "voiceless" actors, to wit, indigenous peoples, peasants, workers, and so on. By the time I undertook my project in the early 1980s it often felt as if we knew more interesting things about these groups than we did about groups with a different kind of voicelessness, say, wealthy cattle ranchers in the Mexican *tierra caliente*, for whom middle-class Mexico City intellectuals were, somewhat bizarrely, presumed to speak. (The family whose history I follow across five generations in the prologues to each chapter of this book, for example, left no written trail — and surprisingly few portraits or photographs — other than their signatures on mostly formulaic legal documents.)

Why the rich, rather than, say, merchants, or landowners, or priests, or lawyers? It is easy to envision excellent books on any one of these groups, but a study of the wealthy does have the advantage of capturing the interactions and changing dynamics among individuals with these and other occupations and interests. A study with priests at its center, for example, might miss or downplay the extent to which priests were supplanted by lawyers in nineteenth-century society. Why the rich, rather than a status elite (defined, perhaps, by a combination of birth and occupation), or a power elite, defined by office-holding or political position? It seems to me that a strong case can be made for the argument that by the late colonial period, status and power followed wealth more often than not — the core of the evidence would be the political power wielded by newly rich Spanish merchants in provincial city councils and in the viceregal court of Mexico City. But this ordering of the relative importance of wealth and position is even easier to defend for post-1810 Mexico. In the wake of the economic disaster of the insurgency, if you were wealthy, you had status and power; conversely, status without at least modest wealth was a cold bed.

The well-to-do men and women who are at the core of this study comprise a fairly numerous group — intentionally so. Defining "wealthy people" as members of households with gross assets of at least 20,000 pesos makes for a larger target of study than identifying them as members of an "oligarchy" or of a set of "great families" would.[8] On the other hand, the group I focus on is smaller than the one that is sometimes implied by the term "elite" in the colonial and nineteenth-century context, where the word is often understood to include all educated people (notaries, clerks, small-time lawyers, journalists, and the like) and/or propertied people (no matter if their property consisted only of a modest residence): the *hombres de bien*, the *gente decente*, the "respectable classes."

As it happens, on many occasions in this book I *do* have reference to this more inclusive group. Sometimes it is important as a social group into which upwardly mobile people who earned their way into the economic elite may have been born. Other times its importance is more as an idea; that is, at different times and under different circumstances it was convenient or natural for either the wealthy and/or the middling elites to emphasize the common bonds that tied them to each other. One factor affecting the closeness of the bonds between the wealthy and the middle classes was their almost constantly changing relationship with popular groups, whose presence is a key part of my story in much the same un-nuanced way that the "dominant class" is important in some of the newer studies of peasants and "subalterns."

But my assumption is that under many circumstances wealth mattered. There were significant differences between people with assets of over 20,000 pesos and people with no assets other than their residence and a few uncollected bills, beginning with the fact that these members of the "respectable classes" were usually (though not always) in a position of at least mild subservience to the truly wealthy: they were their lawyers, notaries, accountants, administrators, and so on. The reader may object that there must have been significant differences between people with wealth of 20,000 pesos and people with wealth of 500,000 or a million pesos. This is true. But, in general, the income from assets of 20,000 pesos seems to have been sufficient through most of the period to allow a person to support a lifestyle that everyone would recognize as "decent," if not luxurious, without having to enter trade or a profession. Thus, though I insist on the diversity of this group, the vast potential for intragroup dissension, and the impossibility of something like a single elite discourse, at the same time I do think that in many contexts the distinction between wealth and mere respectability was an important one.

With these choices behind me I planned to pursue two related lines of inquiry. One was to establish a material context in which to understand the behavior of the men and women in whom I was especially interested. That is, I intended, first of all, to interweave a Michoacán-centered account of political events (wars, rebellions, invasions, constitutions, reforms, retrenchments) with a discussion of changes over time in factors such as distribution of wealth; the movement of land, labor, and capital markets; and the development of mechanisms to streamline these markets (e.g. banks, railroads, commercial codes).

The second line of inquiry was to explore ways that elites were able to manage and manipulate these and other aspects of their worlds. Surely the most crucial dimension of their power to manage and manipulate was their wealth, without which maintenance of their social status and political influence was not impossible but difficult. The absence of wealth on the part of other significant actors (members of the state congress, for example) was itself a characteristic that went far toward defining their identity. Thus, in a certain sense, to examine strategies for accumulating and protecting wealth — including not just decisions people made about managing their businesses, about choosing careers for themselves and their children, and about where to invest their money, but also about marriage partners and political affiliation and service — was to identify some of the most important means available to these individuals for controlling their own lives and the lives of others: to exercise power. Discerning these strategies eventually required me to piece together the lives of over 1,000 individuals in some six generations who either gained, lost, or inherited at least a modest fortune. Using wills, estate inventories, hacienda accounts, business contracts, state government reports, parish records, and cases brought before the ecclesiastical, municipal, and state courts, I asked simple questions with complex answers: who got rich and how? Did they stay wealthy and why or why not?

Another key means by which economic elites exercised power after independence was through their ability to express themselves in new public forums such as newspapers and the state congress. I envisioned a certain symmetry between my exploration of this kind of power, through which the wealthy sought space and maneuvering room within a larger discursive arena only partially determined by themselves, and my treatment of the exercise of power through wealth. Here I would be looking not only for patterns of behavior but also for the meanings that actions communicated. My richest and most consistent source — since most copies of the output of the regional press before the 1870s have been lost — was the transcripts of the state congress, in which the words of the wealthy and middle-class politicians who dominated that body were closely paraphrased and sometimes recorded exactly as spoken in debate. I was especially interested in how the debaters pressed their positions: what figurative buttons were pushed, and what symbols were employed in the course of argument?

So I set out to write a detailed and archival social history, with elements of economic history, political history, and intellectual history, that covered over a century. Even at the level of a dissertation grant proposal — a peculiar form of writing whose primary aim is to make the difficult look easy and the flawed look seamless — this was a very ambitious project; if the transition from proposal to monograph had gone smoothly, it would nonetheless have required more time than most Ph.D. candidates and assistant professors have at their disposal. But of course everything did *not* go as anticipated. There were two major complications.

The first was my unexpected discovery of a fairly impressive economic rebound in the state, beginning in the late 1820s and peaking at midcentury, after the terrible devastation of the wars for independence. Perhaps because it was largely unremarked by contemporaries this recovery has gone unexplored by historians, most of whom adopt the conventional view that Mexico was in full economic retreat from 1810 until the Porfiriato.[9] To develop this argument required me to abandon the notions that establishing the "economic context" for my actors would be easy, and that I could rely on secondary material for most of this part of the book. I found myself not only having to enter into an unresolved debate among economic historians over the long-term effects of the wars for independence, but also having to think through the multiple implications in the political arena of replacing the motifs and metaphors of decay and apathy and decline (which have dominated not only economic history but also political and cultural history) with those of vigor and animation, however fragile and unenduring. I was now forced to ask why many politicians — especially those associated with varieties of liberalism — were publicly despairing about the state of the economy, even as they and others privately thrived. Clearly, the widespread bemoaning of Mexico's lack of "progress" on the part of contemporaries should be seen as a discursive strategy meant to prepare the ground for political reform at the expense of the church and the Indian communities, rather than as prima facie evidence that Mexico's economy was profoundly depressed. But to make this argument as powerfully as possible diverted my attention, it is fair to say, for months, if not years.

My "discovery" of what was, after all, an entirely predictable economic rebound (it does not make sense to suppose that the economy experienced *no* ups and downs over a seventy- or eighty-year period) changed the way that I had conceptualized the book. Instead of developing a storyline that would endeavor to explain Michoacán's century-long marginalization (which I now saw as unsatisfyingly linear and limiting), it seemed essential to recognize, and to probe, the implications of the cyclical or pendulum-like pattern of the state's economic history: growth in the late eighteenth and early nineteenth centuries; collapse in the 1810s and early 1820s; more-or-less full economic recovery by midcentury; another depression in the 1860s and 1870s; and, finally, the Porfirian boom.

But the unexpected difficulty of establishing an "economic context" for the actions of the wealthy was not my only problem. The second complication was that as I went along, the "well-defined social group" that I set out to study seemed more and more slippery. For one thing, the composition of "the wealthy" changed frequently. Each rise and fall of the economy brought down some families and elevated others, for different reasons at different times. The label "economic elite" conjures up the image of a closed and solid group, but at least in nineteenth-century Michoacán, this elite was unstable, heterogenous, full of contradictions, and changeable to the point of fickleness in its ideological predilections. Obviously a sort of linear, Buddenbrooks model of social change (in which families with "traditional" values and aspirations were inexorably supplanted by more "modern" and entrepreneurial families) was inadequate, though at the same time this opposition was clearly not entirely absent: throughout the century one of the many tensions within the group I had targeted, and between that group and others, was the contest between what contemporaries called "aristocratic" and "progressive" values.

Beyond this, it turned out that I had presumed much more overlap between political elites and economic elites than the historical record warranted. From the premise that wealth bestowed political power I was lulled into the corollary assumption that the wealthy would choose, where possible, to exercise power directly, that is, through government and bureaucratic office-holding. Indeed, for the first two decades after independence, this seemed to be the case: wealthy people *did* participate widely in post-independence government. With the resurgence of liberalism in the 1840s, however, the easy association between political elites and economic elites began to break down. Many of the wealthy found important parts of the liberals' agenda of reform to be quite appealing, but others, fearing that the proposed reforms might jeopardize the wealth and power that they had largely regained after the post-1810 disasters, joined the church in resisting the liberals' project. This ambivalence on the part of the upper classes — combined with an explosion of political activity on the part of both the middle classes and a variety of popular groups — led them, with very few exceptions, to abandon politics, which they had dominated since independence, in the wake of the wars of the Reform and the French Intervention. Thus, even if I had been so inclined, it would have been impossible to talk about the wealthy as a "class," in the sense of a group capable of concerted political action in defense of its "interests." Certainly one of the things that stands out about the collection of rich people studied here is their *lack* of "consciousness," that is, their inability to act (more or less) as one in the political arena. There is, however, one sense in which the concept of "class" is extremely useful, and that is as an idea. In this book the image of an unproductive and backward "aristocracy" is a key element of liberal ideology in the nineteenth century, and this image becomes more and more powerful as an *actual* group of people becomes richer and richer in the middle of the nineteenth century, and again toward the end of the Porfiriato. But for the most part this study is as much devoted to plumbing the complexity of a group of people who happen to be wealthy as to discerning the characteristics and habits of behavior that they shared.

The organizing principle of my narrative, then, would not be the century-long decline of the regional economy and the regional elite in the national context (though both the national importance of the region's economy and its elite did decline over this period). Instead, it would be the almost-but-not-quite-cyclical ebb and flow of events and phenomena whose "cause" was not exclusively ideological or political or cultural or economic, but was all of those things in different and shifting combinations, as new circumstances required adjustments on the part of the historical actors, which in turn created new circumstances. At an abstract level, the chief advantage of this organizing principle may be that it permits the unexpected and the unpredictable to play a part in creating history. More practically, this view of the nineteenth century in Michoacán restores the Reform period to its proper role as a watershed in the history of the state, since it seems clear that both in terms of economic patterns and of patterns of political participation, the decades bookending the 1856–57 Reform were turning points in the lives of the upper classes.

The chapters in this book are ordered chronologically, and each chapter is preceded by a short treatment of the experience of the Huarte-Alzúa-Gómez family during the years covered in the chapter itself. The family is introduced in the prologue, where I examine the life and career of the patriarch, Isidro Huarte. Chapter 1 is a sort of snapshot of the lives of the wealthy at the turn of the nineteenth century. It paints a picture of a thriving late-colonial economy, viewed narrowly from the point of view of the economic elites, and an equally lively intellectual climate, though the philosophical ferment was mainly confined to salons and was not well connected to everyday issues. Late-colonial elites were self-confident and self-satisfied, largely unaware, I argue, of some of the flaws in the economic and social system that had served them so well. They were easily capable of absorbing into their ranks, through marriage and patronage, the most promising middle-class men and women. Accordingly, by far the most important social divide in their minds was between the "humble classes," largely Indians and workers on their own haciendas, and the *hombres de bien* or *gente decente,* among whom they counted not only themselves but also worthy members of the middle classes.

Chapter 2 sketches out the unlikely (and ultimately short-lived) alliance between poor and rich Americans against Spain and Spaniards and examines the collapse of the economy after 1810. The chapter links this collapse to a new kind of cross-class political consensus around the appropriateness of independence that began to emerge in about 1815. Chapters 3 and 4 trace the shifts in the key elements of this consensus from independence to federalism and liberalism, and from federalism to centralism, emphasizing the underlying similarities of elite/middle-class response and alignment across the period from independence to the early 1840s. They also tell the parallel story of painful economic recovery after the disasters of the insurgent decade, mounted for the most part by men and women whose social origins were distinctly middle class but who ended their lives as rich or richer, on balance, than the affluent late-colonial merchant/landowners.

Chapter 5 covers the culmination, the miniboom phase, of the economic recovery, and also the resurgence of liberal activism, now very clearly the province of self-consciously middle-class professionals and politicians whose language and political positions were decidedly anti-"aristocratic." Here I argue that the economic recovery and the reemergence of liberalism must be seen together in order to be fully comprehensible. When the conservative statesman Lucás Alamán wrote about the state of the economy and society at midcentury, he emphasized how good things were — a view that ran completely counter to the liberals' picture of a Mexico whose backward economy and "degenerate" society cried out for change and reform. By the 1840s, in other words, rhetoric about Mexico's economic well-being or lack thereof had become thoroughly politicized.

Chapter 6 outlines the extremely disruptive short-term effects of the Reform and the wars of the Reform on the economy and politics of the state, but also argues that while the wealthy suffered losses after 1860, they rarely lost everything — as had been so frequently the case during the post-1810 depression. In fact, in the long run the Reform benefited them. But by the time the economy in general and their own fortunes in particular began to improve, they had already abdicated the direct political roles they had assumed after independence. The epilogue concludes by painting a picture of growing divergence between these apolitical elites and their descendants, and the handful of aggressive Mexican-born capitalists linked to the state government, the national government, and foreign investors in the late Porfiriato.

Prologue: A City, a Province, and a Patriarch

From Mexico City to Valladolid at the Turn of the Century

In almost any season and no matter where you were going, travel in late colonial Mexico was hazardous, wearisome, and slow.[1] The trip from Mexico City to Valladolid, capital of the intendancy of Michoacán, was no exception. Just beyond Tacubaya (now fully part of Mexico City's urban sprawl), about two or three leagues out of Mexico City and still well within view of its environs, the road turned steep and stony as travelers made the long, arduous climb out of the valley of Mexico into the mountain forests that separate it from the valley of Toluca. Because of the near-impossibility of defending against bandits on this narrow, twisting stretch of road, most travelers tried to make it that first day to the town of Lerma, a distance of about twelve leagues — most of them quite miserable — from Mexico City (one British traveler later wrote that they seemed at least forty).[2]

Lerma, like many basin towns (including, most famously, Mexico City itself), was built on land that was still being reclaimed from ancient lakes, and was surrounded by extensive morasses that coalesced at this point into the Río Grande or Lerma River, which the road would follow off and on for the next several days. After a night in one of Lerma's *mesones*, the next day began with an easy four-league trip along the new, tree-lined, raised causeway that connected the town to Toluca, an important city where coach travelers who needed to catch their breath and recover from the first day out, or those with business in the city, often spent the remainder of the second day and night.[3]

Leaving Toluca, the road crossed the barren plains of the valley floor;

13

TABLE P. I
Itineraries from Mexico City to Valladolid, ca. 1800

Fastest itinerary			Slowest itinerary		
Day 1: Mexico City-Lerma	12 leagues		Day 1: Mexico City-Lerma	12 leagues	
Day 2: Lerma-Istlahuaca	13 leagues		Day 2: Lerma-Toluca	4 leagues	
Day 3: Istlahuaca-Tepetongo	15 leagues		Day 3: Toluca-Istlahuaca	9 leagues	
Day 4: Tepetongo-Maravatío	9 leagues		Day 4: Istlahuaca-San Felipe	7 leagues	
Day 5: Maravatío-Zinapécuaro	10 leagues		Day 5: San Felipe-Tepetongo	8 leagues	
Day 6: Zinapécuaro-Valladolid	10 leagues		Day 6: Tepetongo-Maravatío	9 leagues	
TOTAL	69 leagues		Day 7: Maravatío-Acámbaro	10 leagues	
			Day 8: Acámbaro-Indaparapeo	9 leagues	
			Day 9: Indaparapeo-Valladolid	7 leagues	
			TOTAL	75 leagues	

many travelers complained of cold and monotony, but it was not an especially difficult journey, and most who had not stopped in Toluca easily made the thirteen or so leagues from Lerma to Istlahuaca on the second day out. Those who had stayed the second night in Toluca usually spent the following at San Felipe el Grande, seven leagues beyond Istlahuaca, where they would sleep at the *mesón* of the hacienda of San Felipe. Thus it was not until the third or fourth day of the trip, after a steep climb off the Toluca valley floor, that travelers entered what is now the state of Michoacán through a wooded mountain pass, at the western end of which was the vast hacienda of Tepetongo (now a resort/water park).

The transition from the scrubby and dry valleys of Mexico and Toluca into Michoacán never failed to impress first-time visitors. As one English traveler put it,

> from a glaring expanse of plain, with scarcely a tree to be met with for leagues, we found ourselves transported into a delightful region abounding in forest trees . . . inexpressibly refreshing to look upon after a lengthened sojourn in the valley of Mexico, from which the traveller escapes with a painful craving to look upon trees once more. . . . [Were] Michoacán divided by a whole ocean from the state of Mexico, instead of by a mountain wall which may be passed in an hour or two, its configuration and scenery could hardly be more widely different.[4]

This part of the province lay in the southeast corner of the Bajío, a region of forested hills sloping into broad, well-watered, and fertile valleys whose large estates supplied both Mexico City and the mining centers with much of their fuel and grains in the eighteenth and nineteenth centuries. Tepetongo, accordingly, was only the first of several large and rich haciendas whose lands the road would cross over the next few days.

From Tepetongo the road wound around a ridge on which were situated the silver mines of Tlalpujahua, but only those with a special interest in the mines would make the two-league detour to reach them on a path passable only for horses and mules. Although the local mining economy was relatively strong, on the order of a million pesos a year, still the majority of travelers skirted Tlalpujahua and reached Maravatío, a small and prosperous Bajío town of about 1,000 residents, in the late afternoon, and spent the night there.

From Maravatío the shortest route to Valladolid was almost straight west through the little town of Ucareo, with its magnificent Augustinian convent and its pine and cedar plank houses, toward Zinapécuaro, only about ten leagues distant, but they were ten leagues that many travelers sought to avoid.[5] The spectacularly beautiful but steep road ascended for four or five hours, coiling around the mountains with the town visible but seemingly always just out of reach. As one impatient traveler put it in 1825: "none but those who have travelled in a country like this, hungry and fatigued, having been constantly disappointed in the estimate of distance, and with expectation about to give way to a species of despair, can have a true conception of the nervous irritability which it produced."[6] Most travelers chose to continue northwest on the Zacatecas road as far as Acámbaro, and then to turn sharply south to Zinapécuaro, even though this route was a good six leagues longer. In Acámbaro they would be joined by travelers bound for Valladolid from the Bajío cities and towns along that road and its feeders: Salamanca, Irapuato, Silao, León, Guanajuato, Celaya, Querétaro.

From Zinapécuaro the road to Valladolid was relatively straight and good, in places almost an avenue lined by willow and *peru* trees, and travelers who had spent the night in Zinapécuaro had no trouble reaching Valladolid the next day. Those who had stopped in Acámbaro, however, might have to spend a night along the way at an hacienda *mesón* or, if they were especially desperate or poorly advised, in either Indaparapeo or Charo, both considered by experienced travelers to be sad, dusty, dirty, bandit- and dog-ridden towns that were best avoided.[7] The speediest travelers from Mexico City would thus reach Valladolid on the fifth or sixth day out; for the coach travelers it was

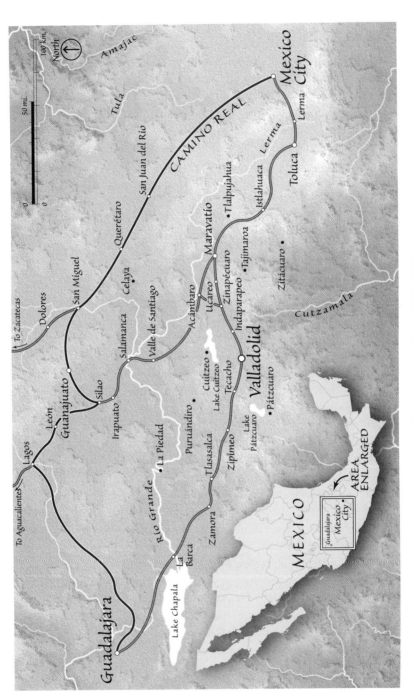

Map 2. Route from Mexico City to Valladolid, ca. 1800

probably the seventh or eighth or even the ninth day of a trip that today takes forty minutes by plane and three to four hours by bus (see Table P.1).

The first glimpse of the city, as travelers topped the last of the low hills beyond Charo, was of the spires of Valladolid's thirty churches, the highest of which were the twin towers of the cathedral.[8] Approaching the walls of the city they crossed a sturdy stone bridge over the Río Grande and continued along a wide, walled stretch of the *camino real* to the city gate. Here began the *calzada de México*, the paved causeway that fed at a diagonal into the *calle real* that was (and still is) the city's main street. The *calzada* formed a dividing line between two of the several Indian communities that clustered around the city — on the left was the *barrio* of Guadalupe and on the right that of San Juan. Here the orchards and gardens and maize patches of the indigenous residents were increasingly encroached upon by the summer houses of the wealthiest of Valladolid's residents, the gardens of which were not walled, as were gardens in the city itself, but which were open to the street.[9]

Near the Plazuela de las Animas, where the causeway ended and the *calle real* began, the road passed under the high arches of the city's impressive aqueduct, which had been almost completely rebuilt at the expense of the bishopric in the late 1780s.[10] If, before continuing west along the *calle real*, a traveler were almost to double back at a sharp angle under the arches of the aqueduct, he or she would be looking down the entrancing *calzada de Guadalupe*, another straight, broad walk paved with flagstones and bounded on either side by low stone walls and benches and by straight rows of ash trees planted about a decade earlier. The branches of these trees would, in a few years, join in the center to shade passersby.[11] This avenue led to the Sanctuario de Guadalupe on the outskirts of the city, one of many sanctuaries built in imitation of the Basilica de Guadalupe in Mexico City, even to the pilgrim path connecting the city to the church. Paralleling the *calzada* was the *paseo* of San Pedro, a wide road paved in the late 1780s — about the time that the aqueduct itself was rebuilt — which was suitable for carriages. In front of the Sanctuario and the adjacent convent of San Diego, the *paseo* branched off to the south, eventually circling the *bosque* of San Pedro, another Indian *barrio*. Toward evening the "respectable classes" of the city would stroll along the *calzada de Guadalupe* or promenade in their carriages on the *paseo*.[12]

If, instead of exploring the *calzada de Guadalupe*, travelers continued west along the *calle real* toward the center of town, they might catch a glimpse of the city cemetery in the Indian *barrio* of San Juan, just beyond the Plazuela de las Animas and two blocks off the *calle real* to the right. Nearby were the *can-*

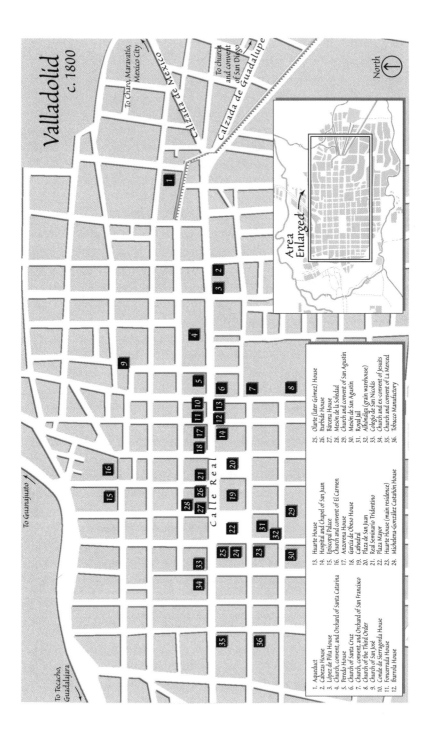

Valladolid
c. 1800

To Guanajuato

To Tecacho,
Guadalajara

To Charo, Maravatío,
Mexico City

Calzada de Mexico

Calzada de Guadalupe

To church
and convent
of San Diego

Calle Real

Area
Enlarged

North

1. Aqueduct
2. Cabezas House
3. López de Piña House
4. Church, convent, and Orchard of Santa Catarina
5. Perado House
6. Church of Santa Cruz
7. Church, convent, and Orchard of San Francisco
8. Church of the Third Order
9. Church of San José
10. Conde de Sierragorda House
11. Foncerrada House
12. Ibarrola House

13. Huarte House
14. Hospital and Chapel of San Juan
15. Episcopal Palace
16. Church, convent, and Orchard of El Carmen
17. Anzorena House
18. García de Obeso House
19. Cathedral
20. Plaza de San Juan
21. Real Seminario Tridentino
22. Plaza Mayor
23. Huarte House (main residence)
24. Michelena-González Castañón House

25. Olarte (later Gómez) House
26. Iturbide House
27. Bárcena House
28. Mesón de la Soledad
29. Church and convent of San Agustín
30. Mesón de San Agustín
31. Royal Jail
32. Alhóndiga (grain warehouse)
33. Colegio de San Nicolás
34. Church and ex-convent of Jesuits
35. Church and convent of La Merced
36. Tobacco Manufactory

Map 3.   City Map of Valladolid, ca. 1800

Figure 1.   Calzada de Guadalupe and Morelia Aqueduct, 1870. Painting by
Mariano de Jesús Torres.

teras, where the pink-hued stone used for the substantial houses and public
buildings of the city had been quarried so extensively that the northern edge
of the *barrio* dropped off dangerously, forming a natural defense for the city
and obviating the need for a city wall along this stretch.[13]

Past the *barrio* of San Juan, continuing along the *calle real*, were the first
of the "good houses" so often remarked upon by visitors. On the left was
María Josefa Cabezas' extravagant new two-story residence, and on the western corner of the same block was a substantial house that belonged to the
canon José Antonio López de Piña and his sister, owners of the hacienda of
Santa Clara near Acámbaro and benefactors of a new chair recently established in the seminary for the study of the Tarascan language.[14] But sharing
the block with these houses were a couple of quite modest one-story stone
masonry houses and a number of commercial *accesorias* and *casitas* of small
value. This block and the next, then, constituted something of a transition between the well-built, mostly two-story houses of the center city, and the
Indian *barrios* of San Juan, Guadalupe, and San Pedro to the east. The patch-
iness and occasional shabbiness of this part of the *calle real*, dominated on the

right by the orchard, church, and convent of the nuns of Santa Catarina, was probably linked to a striking pattern of female ownership of the houses in a three-block stretch across from the convent property. Of the fourteen houses in these three blocks, twelve were owned in 1800 by unmarried women, widows, or unmarried sisters. The other two were owned by priests who later left them to women in similar circumstances.[15] Many of these women lived on very restricted incomes — some from manufacture of the *dulces* for which Valladolid was renowned, others from renting out to retailers street-access rooms in the houses — and did not have the means to embellish or even to maintain their houses.

Beyond Santa Catarina, the residences along the *calle real* began to present a more uniform aspect of established wealth and architectural unity. In the block just west of the convent four large houses crowded against each other, all but one of them two story, all valued in the range of 10,000 pesos and all with the solid, sober-minded architectural symmetry typical of the eighteenth-century baroque. The cut-stone, flat-roofed house next to the convent, for example, which was owned in 1800 by María Josefa de Peredo (a wealthy heiress and another unmarried woman), was dominated by a massive wooden front door that was framed by a simple carved stone facing and flanked on each side by two shuttered windows that reached almost to street level. The upper floor had three windows with wrought-iron balconies, one directly over the front door, and the others spaced between the two downstairs windows.[16] Variations on the facades of late-colonial houses in Valladolid were not wide-ranging. Windows might be grouped together, sharing a common balcony, or they might be placed directly over the downstairs windows for an especially symmetrical effect. Above the main portal there was often a space for a discreet stone-carved crest. Besides the standard and functional gargoyles, there might be a decorative false front to break the flat horizontality of most rooflines. Several houses had carved horizontal axes (perhaps added when the second story was built) across the front, dividing the top from the ground floor. Occasionally, especially in the newer houses whose second floors were part of the original design, decorative vertical axes divided one set of top and bottom floor windows from the next. Even more rarely, a particularly wealthy owner would add a *galería*, a sort of second-floor garden patio with arches open to the street. But these variations did not produce the somewhat jarring (though also oddly pleasing) architectonic effect that the jumble of neoclassical and frenchified nineteenth- and early-twentieth-century decorative add-ons later created in the city's downtown. Instead, there was a consistency of style, and most of the variations derived from the size of the residences and the subtle elegance (or lack thereof) of their proportions.

On the other side of the street from the Peredo house, at the west end of the block, was the church of Santa Cruz. Looking south, new visitors would become aware, perhaps for the first time, that the center of the city was built on the crest of a gentle hill: down the hill from Santa Cruz were the convent, church, and orchard of San Francisco and the small church of the Third Order of Franciscans, and still farther beyond was the church/convent of Capuchinas, which traditionally served daughters of the Indian elite. Looking north, travelers would see the side entrance to the new church of San José, founded in 1760 and rivaling the cathedral in the beauty of its matching towers.

The next two blocks of the *calle real* contained some of the most splendid residences of late colonial Valladolid. On the north side of the street was the block-deep residence of the Conde de Sierragorda, who had spent over 15,000 pesos adding a second story and a delicate *galería* to a house he bought for 12,000 pesos in 1775. An outsider would probably not be lucky enough to catch more than a glimpse of the grand front patio through open doors, but he or she would surely hear stories of the fabulous furnishings and fixtures, whose appraised value in 1815, at the time of the conde's death, was an astonishing 22,000 pesos.[17] Next to the Sierragorda residence was a spacious old house worth about 12,000 pesos, one of two owned by José Bernardo de Foncerrada y Ulibarrí, owner also of the rich hacienda of San Bartolomé, through which the Mexico City road had passed between Zinapécuaro and Indaparapeo.[18] Across the street were a sprawling, one-story house that the Ibarrola family had owned since 1753 (and which would stay in the family until the end of the nineteenth century), and an impressive two-story house, one of several belonging to Isidro Huarte, the wealthiest and most powerful man in Valladolid.[19]

On the left, in the last block before the *calle real* opened up to the Plaza de San Juan and the cathedral, were the surprisingly palatial Hospital of San Juan and the convent, chapel, and buildings connected to it. These buildings were originally meant to serve as the bishop's residence. Their luxury and beauty, however, were criticized as unseemly, so the episcopal palace had been moved north two blocks to more austere quarters, near the convent of El Carmen, and the buildings were turned over in 1700 to the hospitaler order.[20] On the right-hand side of the street was another house belonging to the Foncerrada family, this one owned by Mariana Foncerrada y Ulibarri, José Bernardo's sister and the wife of José María Anzorena, whom Hidalgo would name intendant of the province in 1810. This house, which occupied the whole block in the north-south direction, had been appraised at 27,033 pesos in 1782, making it one of the most valuable residences in the city around the turn of the century, along with the principal homes of the Conde de Sierragorda, Isidro Huarte, the merchant Juan González Castañon, and the archdean of the cathedral, Dr. Manuel de la Bárcena.[21] It formed a kind of bookend with the grand house on the other corner owned by the merchant and *regidor* Gabriel García de Obeso, who had bought it in 1781 for 7,000 pesos and in remodeling had doubled its value.[22] This house would serve a few years hence as a meeting place for the Valladolid conspiracy of 1809.

But by now the eye was drawn forward to the cathedral, built over a period of 84 years beginning in 1665, and as a result a blend of (mainly) seventeenth- and eighteenth-century baroque with a smattering of eighteenth-century churrigueresque, especially notable in the fabulously busy silver-covered altars and carved pulpits. As Philip II had decreed, the cathedral was an "island" whose physical and spiritual centrality was emphasized by being surrounded by open spaces, the Plaza de San Juan on the near side and the Plaza Mayor on the far.[23] Its towers stretched almost 200 feet toward heaven, and the sense of splendid verticality was repeated inside, where soaring pillars supported a ceiling peopled with angels high above the wooden floor. The light of the sun flooded obliquely into the three naves, creating the effect of serene otherworldliness so prized in baroque architecture.[24]

In front of the cathedral loomed the massive Seminario Tridentino, until 1760 a vacant lot on which two bishops had collected the building materials that finally, in that year, under Bishop Pedro Anselmo Sánchez de Tagle, began to come together into this stately building with its Moorish towers and pinnacles at the roofline. Not even a longtime resident of Valladolid could have known that several of the students milling about in the large courtyard, including José María Morelos, Mariano Michelena, Ignacio Rayón, and Agustín de Iturbide, would rise to prominence just a decade later as leaders of the independence movements.

The solemn aspect of the cathedral and seminary stood in counterpoint to the swirl of commercial activity in the Plaza Mayor on the other side of the cathedral. All along the streets of the *calle real* there were peddlers and small *pulperías* (one observer noted with hyperbolic disgust that no block of the city had fewer than six or eight "mosqueritos" all offering the same limited selection of goods), but they had not been a defining feature of the urban landscape to this point.[25] In the Plaza Mayor, however, the commercial rhythms of the city became apparent.

A hierarchy of sellers in and around the plaza was easy to detect. At the bottom were the transient peddlers: Indians, *castas*, and poor whites who came in from their pueblos or sharecropped plots for the day or, sometimes, the week. Over 300 of them set up in the open spaces of the plaza, especially on Thursdays, selling goods they had manufactured or gathered or harvested in the region: lime, firewood, wooden beams, shingles, sugar cane and cane juice, chickens, eggs, fish, fruits, vegetables, sweets, medicinal herbs, salt, soap, wooden trays, trunks, barrels, saddles, shoes.[26] One observer described the plaza as a "an indecent jumble" of "dog-ridden, Sodom-esque mini-rancherías,"[27] but to foreign visitors the scene was picturesque:

> A crowded market is held here, and the venders display their goods, as is the general custom, beneath the shade of rude mat umbrellas. Fruits and vegetables are tolerably abundant; and amongst other luxuries, the *pescado blanco* [white fish] is brought from the lake of Pascuaro. The night market . . . is extremely pretty; each little shop having a bright blazing pile of the fragrant ocote (red pine) in its front, so that from an elevated window the scene is very lively and peculiar.[28]

Local peddlers and craftspeople who operated all week long had more or less permanent spots (for which they paid the city three reales a week) in which to display their wares around the edges of the plaza and underneath the *portales*, the broad piazzas whose roofs were supported by stone arches along all five of the blocks that surrounded the plaza.[29] The names by which some of the *portales* were popularly known came from the kinds of sellers who congregated there: Portal de las Dulceras, named for the women who manufactured and sold sweets; Portal de las Frutas, for the fruit sellers; Portal de la Nieve or de la Nevería, for the ices made with frozen snow from a peak to the west.[30]

Finally, the wealthy local retailer-wholesalers, at the top of the commercial hierarchy, maintained *locales* in the ground floors of the houses beneath the *portales*. Most downtown houses had at least two *locales*, and several had three.[31] Usually the houses in which the wealthiest merchants operated their retail trade were their own: 14 of the 21 houses under the five *portales* were owned by merchants (including, appropriately, all 5 houses under the Portal de los Mercaderes on the west side of the plaza).[32] A fifteenth, technically owned by El Carmen, was rented to the merchant Gaspar de Ceballos until his death and then sold to another merchant in 1802.[33] (By contrast, merchants owned only about 18 percent of the city's finest houses — those worth at least 5,000 pesos — that were *not* located around the Plaza Mayor.)[34]

Owning the houses in which their businesses were established meant central location, low overheads, and the opportunity for every improvement and ostentation to be noted by the public and to serve as a kind of advertisement for the merchandise itself. As a result the merchant-owned houses around the Plaza Mayor were among the flashiest in the city, and in the last years of the eighteenth and the first years of the nineteenth century the plaza must have seemed something of a construction zone. During this time at least six of them were being remodeled or completely rebuilt, reflecting the rapid pace of economic activity around the turn of the century. The standard for center-city elegance had been set by Isidro Huarte in the late 1780s, when he completely rebuilt the house that was to become his residence on the southwest corner of the plaza.[35] The house in the Portal de Mercaderes belonging to the Michelena brothers — who would later figure in the 1809 Valladolid conspiracy — was sold in 1801 for 12,500 pesos to the merchant Juan González Castañón, who leveled it and erected in its place a magnificent residence on which he spent at least 30,000 pesos; in 1803 it was said that the house was worth an astonishing 43,707 pesos; there would not be a higher house appraisal for almost a century.[36] Next door, on the corner of the *portal* and the *calle real*, another house had just undergone major reconstruction in 1797, when its new owner, the merchant José Manuel de Olarte, who had purchased it in 1794, added a second floor.[37]

In the block of *portales* in front of the cathedral, José Joaquín de Iturbide, father of the future emperor, had recently replaced the old wooden pillars that supported the piazza roof in front of his residence with stone arches and added a second story to the house he had purchased a decade earlier for 12,000 pesos.[38] At the west end of the same block was the house that Dr. Manuel de la Bárcena completely rebuilt in the last years of the eighteenth century; the previous owner (at whose bankruptcy sale, which took place sometime after 1793, Bárcena purchased the house) had paid 10,000 pesos for it in 1774; by 1821, after Bárcena's project was completed, it was said to be worth 35,000 pesos.[39]

All this construction was not limited, of course, to the Plaza Mayor: we have already noted the dramatic refurbishings and new construction of the houses of Gabriel García de Obeso, the Conde de Sierragorda, and María

Josefa Cabezas. Cabezas' 12,000-peso house on the *calle real* east of Santa Catarina had been built on a lot purchased for 600 pesos in 1795.[40] One of the most impressive reconstructions took place one block off the Plaza Mayor to the north, in the building known as the Mesón de Ulate. In 1804, after having been neglected for years, the inn was sold to Capt. José María Peredo for only 6,000 pesos. He completely rebuilt and reappointed it, also adding a second story; in 1808 it was appraised at 38,951 pesos. It remained in the Peredo family until 1864 and is still known as the Mesón de la Soledad, a name it was given in that year.[41] Meanwhile, another new inn, intended to accommodate an increased flow of traders and visitors, was in construction in the early years of the nineteenth century: the Mesón de San Agustín across from the convent/church of the same name, one block to the south of the Plaza Mayor, past Isidro Huarte's principal residence, the Alhóndiga (the municipal grain warehouse), and the city jail.[42] And in 1805 nearly half a block of small houses and *cuartos* four blocks west of the plaza was torn down so that a tobacco factory could be built.[43]

Continuing west along the *calle real* past the plaza, in the first block on the right, was Valladolid's other well-known college, the Colegio de San Nicolás, where Miguel de Hidalgo had served as rector from 1787 to 1792. Just past San Nicolás was the church of La Compañía, attached to the former Jesuit convent and the now-shuttered Jesuit college of San Javier, where Clavijero had taught. Beyond the Jesuit church was one more block of houses owned by wealthy people, but the church/convent of La Merced served as the effective boundary between the solid dwellings of the center city and the spotty suburbs. The most likely reason for a well-to-do person to venture beyond La Merced was that he or she was heading for Pátzcuaro.

Into the Interior: South, North, and West from Valladolid

SOUTH

Pátzcuaro was among the first Spanish settlements in Michoacán, and although it had declined in importance since the sixteenth century as Valladolid grew, as late as the 1780s it remained officially the administrative capital of the province, and at the end of the colonial period it was still the home of many wealthy Michoacanos. Although it was just a day's ride to the southwest, Pátzcuaro had a very different physical and cultural feel from Valladolid. At 1,000 feet higher in elevation, it was colder and wetter. A short remove from the lovely village-ringed lake of the same name and from the ancient Tarascan capital at Tzintzuntzan, Pátzcuaro seemed (and still seems) a more Indian city than Valladolid was. Indeed, for a radius of some 25 to 30 miles around the city in most directions, the indigenous population was quite dense. This was the part of the province to suffer most acutely the overcrowding and pressure on village lands from expanding haciendas that is often associated with the late colonial period.[44]

Because of its position on the slope of one of the hills around the lake, Pátzcuaro's streets were narrow, steep, and crooked — a combination that delights tourists today but was viewed with frank disdain by contemporary observers, who usually found the city disagreeably cold and forlorn (a quality that derived partly from the sense of faded prosperity, but probably equally from the strong Indian presence). This was despite a tranquil and spacious main plaza, surrounded on all sides by excellent, mostly two-story residences.[45] Many of the wealthy families who lived in these houses were connected, either as owners or as merchants who traded in sugar and *piloncillo*, to the sugar haciendas to the south. The identification was so close in the minds of contemporaries that Juan José Martínez de Lejarza could write in 1822 that almost all the sugar-mill owners lived in Pátzcuaro, though he himself, a Valladolid resident, was part owner of the sugar hacienda of Tipitaro, and so many Valladolid merchants had purchased sugar haciendas since 1770 that they almost certainly outnumbered the sugar planters still resident in Pátzcuaro.[46] Other Pátzcuaro elites were connected to the copper mines of Inguarán, Oropeo, and Churumuco, or to the *real de minas* in Santa Clara del Cobre, a bustling small town just south of Pátzcuaro; still others were owners of the handful of mostly modest haciendas in the highland valleys around the city.[47]

To get to the hot country from Pátzcuaro there were several alternatives. The easternmost route went through Tacámbaro (also accessible from Valladolid), a small entrepôt town in the foothills of the last range of sierra before the vast plains of the Balsas River Depression opened up. From Tacámbaro it was a short distance to several important sugar haciendas; one could even walk — at a steep descent — to the famous hacienda of Puruarán, where a pivotal battle during the insurgency would be fought, just below the town. The second and most frequented route to the *tierra caliente* followed the royal road that passed through Santa Clara del Cobre and Ario, another entrepôt town on the very edge of the Balsas Depression. Beyond Ario the *camino real* led almost due south through some of the finest sugar haciendas in the province, then on to the coast through the mountains of what is now the state of Guerrero. As the road approached the coastal sierra, which rose up right across the Balsas River, the humidity of the prime sugar lands diminished and the climate turned even hotter and dry (one town was named, appropriately, Sinagua). But though the cane fields grew fewer and less productive, this was prime cattle country, and huge tracts of land along the banks of the rivers and streams that fed the Balsas, including the 42 mainly cattle-raising haciendas in the parish of Churumuco—a town that, like Sinagua, was just on the Michoacán side of the Balsas—had been bought up by prominent families and individuals living in Valladolid or Pátzcuaro over the last decade or so.[48]

A third route from Pátzcuaro to the *tierra caliente* went through Taretan, a small town on the outskirts of the huge Augustinian-owned sugar hacienda of the same name, and Uruapan, another town on the fringe of the sierra noted for its lush natural beauty and prosperous Indians, whose neat huts and gardens were often praised by visitors.[49] From Uruapan it was possible to continue on to Apatzingán, at 40 leagues away from Valladolid the most distant of the major *tierra caliente* towns and a newly prosperous region of rice and indigo fields as well as of the traditional sugar and livestock. But it was not an easy trip. The terrain was forbidding to say the least; it was a landscape of treeless mountains, rocky roads, horrifying gorges, and no vegetation or water except the Río Orejón, which carved so swift and deep a path that there was no possibility of using it for irrigation.[50] Worse, the road led through the treacherous Paso de los Caracoles, where (as one visitor described it) "the cliffs are so sheer that one is constantly terrified the mule will lose its footing, which would send the rider tumbling, or rather flying, thousands of feet to the bottom." "In the most difficult parts of the pass," he continued, "the path is so narrow and twisted that one has to whistle or shout before attempting to go round a bend, because there is no room for two riders to pass each other."[51] By the turn of the century, rather than brave the Paso de los Caracoles, most travelers got to Apatzingán and other towns in the Tepalcátepec valley (Pinzándaro, Tepalcátepec) from the *camino real* that connected Ario to the coast, by way of a new bridge over the Río del Marqués.[52]

Apatzingán, like most of the true hot-country towns and haciendas, was inhabited by a handful of Spaniards, a few Indians, and many *castas*—most of them mulattoes.[53] Visitors, no doubt with the memory of a recent rebellion centered in Apatzingán fresh in their minds, were dismayed by the "degradation" of the entire population. "The general aspect of . . . almost all the residents, is most disagreeable. They have dirty complexions, and go about in shameful states of undress; the women have enormous bellies and goiters, and all display the most pernicious habits: they are restless, insubordinate, treacherous, perfidious, drunken, lazy, and inclined to the most uninhibited lechery."[54] Implicit in this evaluation was the writer's belief that there was a close connection between climate and inhabitants. Like most of the rest of the *tierra caliente*, which was known for its magnificent haciendas but also for its stifling heat, outsized insects and scorpions, and poisonous snakes, Apatzingán was a place where the wealthy invested but did not live.[55]

There were two other entries to the *tierra caliente* of Michoacán, neither from Valladolid or Pátzcuaro. One was to the east, through Zitácuaro, a rapidly growing city in the late colonial period which, like Tacámbaro, Ario, and Uruapan, was situated on the cusp between the sierra and the Balsas plains. Not far to the south of the city was a region of huge sugar haciendas: Laureles, Tiripitio, and La Barranca all had late-colonial populations of over 800, and there were numerous haciendas less impressive only by comparison with these three.[56] But this was also a region in which small independent farmers and tenants abounded, many of whom grew cane that was processed on one of the larger estates.[57] In this respect the Zitácuaro sugar districts resembled those around Los Reyes, the other *tierra caliente* region that did not have strong connections to Valladolid or Pátzcuaro. In Los Reyes, whose natural orientation was toward Zamora, as in much of the rest of the western part of the province, small farmers — rancheros — seem to have been more numerous than in either the central *tierra caliente* or in the central highlands. This is not to say that there were no large sugar estates in the Los Reyes region: the hacienda of Santa Clara, for example, with sales of 10,000 pesos a year in 1808 and 1809, was an important producer. But it had twice the sales of any of the other sugar haciendas in the district, and interspersed with the cane fields were numerous ranchos whose owners' income came more from raising grains and livestock and muleteering than from sugar.[58] The surface similarities between the Los Reyes and the Zitácuaro districts may derive from the fact that sugar could be grown in these areas only because of special microclimatic conditions; here it was not the consistently hot, humid climate of the central *tierra caliente* that made production possible, but a combination of moderate temperatures and warm soils, which were often heated by underground hot springs. This implied a greater variety of crops and of social

structures in a relatively small subregion than were present in the *tierra
caliente* proper.

The rest of the south of Michoacán — the coastal sierra and the coast itself — was out of the orbit of all but a handful of Michoacán elites. No wealthy
residents of Valladolid or other highland cities owned land in these vast areas;
indeed, there was not a single hacienda in the region.[59] The only significant
connection between highland elites and coastal or sierra residents was a trading relationship, principally in cotton, which was farmed by smallholders or
sharecroppers along the coast and bought up and marketed by Valladolid merchants, especially Isidro Huarte and his partners. The key importance of the
coastal sierra and the coast to the residents of the highlands, even in the late
colonial period, was as an idea — a forbidding frontier, sparse in population,
with much unfenced land rich in natural resources and claimed only by
Indians — and as a locus of rebellion and unrest. Coahuayana was known
in this period as "Motines" (rebellions), in reference to the long-unsubdued
Indian populations of the region, and throughout most of the nineteenth century the sierra would shelter renegades and rebels who would strike out at the
haciendas of the *tierra caliente* and even at major population centers with terrifying frequency. It is no coincidence that in the post-1810 period the many
assaults on Valladolid/Morelia almost always came from the south.

NORTH

The principal northern city of the intendancy was Puruándiro, a sizable entrepôt town with a thriving commerce in domestic manufactures, situated a
relatively easy two days' journey from Valladolid. It was surrounded by the
huge hacienda of Villachuato — owned by the Marqués del Apartado — and
shone in the reflected glory of nearby nobility: Puruándiro's population was
reputed to be especially wealthy and cultured.[60] The city had been one of
many subordinated to the *alcaldía mayor* of Huango, a backwater town that
centuries earlier happened to be the residence of the *encomendero* Juan de
Villaseñor y Orozco; but in 1787, like many interior towns, Puruándiro finally gained the municipal autonomy that its economic importance would
seem to have justified long before. After the late Bourbon administrative reforms, then, the city came into its own, developing as the subregional hub of
a thriving agricultural area as new lands were opened up by small farmers trying to take advantage of proximity to markets, especially for wheat and livestock, in both the mining centers and in Mexico City.[61]

WEST

The road west out of Valladolid toward Zamora and Guadalajara was the least used and most poorly maintained of any of the outlets to the interior. Beyond the stone causeway that led west out of Valladolid, the *camino real* quickly deteriorated into what one traveler described as "only a narrow footpath, winding in and out among rocks and patches of stunted cactus and *palo bobo*, sometimes losing itself altogether."[62] Western-bound travelers would sleep the first night at the hacienda of Tecacho, one of several owned in 1800 by Br. Juan José Pastor Morales, a very wealthy priest who would play a key role in early postindependence state politics.[63] The second night would be spent at another hacienda, Zipimeo, a huge property that, like most in this part of the province, contained acres and acres of marshlands. These wet, grassy plains, today almost completely drained and converted to crop land (thanks in many cases to projects initiated during the Porfiriato), were immensely valuable for cattle ranching, but they made life exceedingly difficult for travelers. The approach to Zipimeo was described as a path "intersected by deep muddy ditches, which are impassable in the rainy season, and in which your horse sinks up to his belly in the dry."[64] Even Zamora itself, a city of some 10,000 inhabitants, was almost inaccessible during the rainy season. Despite numerous improvements since the 1790s — a bridge over the Río Duero, canals intended to channel water away from the roads, pavement of some city streets, and a new raised causeway connecting the city to the Indian town of Jacona (like the Indian *barrios* to the east of Valladolid, a summer home of affluent Zamorans) — in 1826 one traveler could still write of reaching Zamora only "after weary wadings through deep morasses, and over useless little bits of causeways and bridges."[65] It is clear that travelers in the first half of the century were willing to try just about anything to avoid the bogs and boiling mud pits of the western part of the province. H. G. Ward, for example, coming from Guadalajara, decided to bypass Zamora in order to reach Valladolid a day sooner, as he had been led to believe the detour would allow him to do. But near Tlasasalca his party ran into a "succession of inclosures, through which it was necessary to force our way by opening breaches in the thick stone walls large enough to admit the carriage." ("Fortunately," he cheerfully continued, "Mexicans have a great talent for demolition.")[66]

In part, this route was difficult because there was not much incentive to improve the links between the central highland cities and the cities in the western part of the province. While Valladolid and Pátzcuaro looked north to the silver mines, south to the commercial agricultural possibilities of the *tierra caliente*, and east to Mexico City, the towns and haciendas of the west were most powerfully connected to Guadalajara, a market (along with the silver mines of Durango and Zacatecas) for some of the region's sugar and wheat and livestock, and a more desirable residence for the wealthiest of the landowners than still-sleepy and often-flooded Zamora, or tiny, out-of-the-way Jiquilpan. There was a small core of well-to-do Zamora and Jiquilpan families at the end of the colonial period: the Jaso, Morales, Dávalos, Jiménez, Plancarte, de la Parra, Márquez de la Mora, and Villaseñor. And the number of wealthy westerners would increase significantly over the nineteenth century, as Pacific ports were opened and Guadalajara's hinterland, broadly defined, experienced rates of growth that surely outpaced those of the central regions of the nation. But for the time being, with notable exceptions, it was wealthy merchant-landowners of Valladolid, and to a lesser extent of Pátzcuaro and Puruándiro, who dominated the economic activity of the province. And none was wealthier and more powerful than Isidro Huarte.

The Patriarch

Isidro Huarte was born in the town of Goizueta in the province of Navarre, Spain, most likely in the early 1740s. He is said to have lived in Valladolid "since his youth," which probably made him one of the many young Spaniards to have been brought at an early age to the Americas to help in a relative's mercantile enterprise. Since Huarte's first independent business transaction did not occur until 1772, however, by which time he was already a *vecino del comercio* and an official in the Valladolid city council (*alcalde ordinario de segundo voto*), the particulars of his early career, when he was surely under the wing of an already established merchant, are a mystery.

In 1769, probably when Huarte was in his late twenties, he married Ignacia Escudero, about whom little is known. She died shortly thereafter, perhaps in childbirth, and in 1771 he married Ana Manuela Muñiz y Sánchez de Tagle, an orphan related to Michoacán's great bishop, Pedro Anselmo Sánchez de Tagle. A year later Huarte purchased a fairly expensive (8,715 pesos) house on the southwest corner of the Plaza Mayor, which he later demolished, constructing in its place one of the finest residences in the city (today the Museo Michoacano), valued at almost 30,000 pesos.[67] Meanwhile, in 1773, using his wife's small dowry as security, he borrowed 4,000 pesos from a Valladolid priest, presumably to stock his own store on the ground floor of his new residence.[68] This was the last time that Huarte would be a borrower until well after the wars for independence broke out.

In 1778 he formed an association with José Manuel de Olarte to manage a second store; among other things, Olarte was responsible for purchasing *efectos de China* at the trade fairs at Acapulco for sale in Huarte's emporium.[69] In 1787 he formed a similar association with Santiago Loperena, in which Huarte invested 10,000 pesos. Unlike Olarte, who in 1795 branched out on his own, Loperena remained Huarte's *dependiente* his whole life.[70] Later Huarte formed several other trading associations, including one with Domingo Malo and Francisco Iturbe for the specific purpose of buying cotton along the Pacific coast (and presumably selling trade goods to the cotton farmers). Iturbe, who later became a prominent Pátzcuaro merchant in his own right (and whose son was a famous *agiotista* in Mexico City in the 1840s), contributed thousands of pesos worth of mules and was the partner actually responsible for making the long trips to the coast.[71] In the meantime, in 1784 Huarte had sent for a second cousin then living and working in Pamplona, Pascual Alzúa, to assist him in his main import business. Alzúa worked for Huarte for eighteen years before he became a one-third partner with him in 1802; this partnership continued until Huarte's death.[72]

Huarte's main business interests continued to revolve around trade for the rest of his life; at his death in 1824 over two-thirds of his 600,000-peso estate consisted of merchandise and store credits.[73] This emphasis on trade does not mean, however, that he was uninvolved in agriculture. As his mercantile profits accumulated he frequently put them to use in loans to landowners, usually not at interest but in return for a share in their business, or for an agreement to repay the debt in kind; thus, for example, if he loaned working capital to a sugar producer he would be repaid in sugar at an advantageous price and would then sell it in one of his retail outlets or to other traders.[74]

An early example of Huarte's expansion beyond the marketing of foreign merchandise was a 22,110-peso loan made in 1778 to Nicolás Gregorio Castañeda, the recent purchaser of the indigo-producing hacienda of Jongo and two contiguous properties, Calunga (sugar) and Cacanguio (cattle). The haciendas had been sold to Castañeda by the Pátzcuaro Augustinians for 35,000 pesos. Within a year, however, Castañeda died. Huarte and Castañeda's heirs agreed that they would hire an administrator to run the hacienda and that Huarte would continue to invest 12,000 pesos a year until the operation became profitable and he could recover his investment. Though by 1780 the haciendas were appraised for over 81,000 pesos, this *refacción* (rehabilitation arrangement) continued until after Huarte's death, despite furious recriminations by the Augustinians against "un poderoso de esta ciudad" for his delays in repaying their principal.[75] In another case Huarte virtually supported an hacendado named Angel Bernardo González (whose sons and grandsons would be very active in Michoacán politics) for two years from 1807 to 1809, paying all his expenses — including his sons' tuition at school in Morelia, his daughter's *licencia* to enter a nunnery, 200 pesos for two crosses he had ordered from Mexico, his tithe, the clothing and supplies sent to his hacienda in Apatzingán, and the operating expenses of the hacienda. When this account was liquidated in 1809 González owed Huarte 34,979 pesos, which amount he pledged to repay in indigo at 14 *reales* a pound.[76]

Perhaps Huarte's most lucrative coinvestment in an agricultural enterprise, however, was his partnership with the heirs of Juan Manuel de Michelena in their sugar hacienda of La Parota. Beginning in 1800 Huarte invested over 100,000 pesos in the hacienda during the five years that the company was in existence, and was rewarded with profits of over 110,000 pesos.[77] The success of this venture probably inspired a similar partnership with the financially troubled owner of the enormous Zitácuaro sugar hacienda of Laureles; this association, like many others, lasted beyond Huarte's death.[78]

By 1790 the eldest of Huarte's children were approaching adulthood, and he began to make provisions for their futures. In classic fashion his oldest son, José Antonio, trained for the priesthood; his second son, Isidro, became a lawyer, and his third son, Ramón, prepared to enter the military.[79] Huarte also began buying the haciendas that he would turn over to them as they came of age. In 1791, for example, he bought the hacienda of Urundaneo for 12,100 pesos, and there he established a thriving mule-breeding business (useful for his trading activities); the hacienda was worth 60,000 pesos at his death, by which time his son Isidro had long since taken it over.[80] In 1794 he bought the small hacienda of Sindurio, which would eventually belong to his son Joaquín, and in the same year he bought the hacienda of Guadalupe for José Antonio.[81] He also purchased numerous urban properties during this period, sometimes with an eye to business opportunities but chiefly for his children to live in; he eventually came to own thirteen houses.[82]

For his daughters, good marriages were the key to a secure future. The choice for his eldest daughter, Carmen, was easy: Pascual Alzúa, who had worked for Huarte for twelve years by the time of their 1796 marriage, and who had the additional advantage of being a (distant) member of the family. The choice for his next eldest daughter, Teresa, who married in 1803, was Capt. Juan González Castañón, a fellow merchant and Spaniard who had recently built an elaborate mansion on the Plaza Mayor. His third daughter, Ana, made in 1805 what was probably the least financially advantageous match of the three (though later, of course, it became the most famous), in marrying Capt. Agustín de Iturbide, son of a prosperous though not fabulously wealthy Valladolid merchant-landowner.[83] The wealth of his future sons-in-law, however, was probably not an all-consuming consideration, since by this time Huarte's own fortune, calculated in 1805 shortly after his third marriage to Ana Gertrudis Alcántara y Arrambide (a young woman from a moderately well-to-do Puruándiro family) was over 643,000 pesos.[84]

Huarte's enormous wealth gave him equally enormous power. By 1781 he had purchased the office of Alcalde Provincial Mayor, a position that he held to the end of the colonial period, and he cultivated close relationships with Michoacán's two intendants, Juan Antonio de Riaño and Felipe Díaz de Hortega. Díaz de Hortega dined frequently at his house, took the air along the *paseo* in Valladolid in one of Huarte's four carriages, and served as a *padrino* at Huarte's third marriage.[85] Huarte was accused at least twice of misconduct in municipal affairs and of stacking municipal elections with his own friends, relatives, and associates — with good reason, since at the time of one complaint (1805), the city council members included, besides himself, his son Isidro, a close in-law (Joaquín de Iturbide), and three of his business partners (Pedro and Juan Bautista de Arana, and José Manuel de Olarte). By this means, in a relatively small city like Valladolid, he could and did effectively control city affairs, including grain purchases, the rental and usufruct of public lands, bullfights, the release of grain from the warehouse, and licenses for retail trade, all of which he was accused of manipulating for his own gain.[86]

Huarte was said to have a "martial aspect," and it is certainly true that a willful, even ruthless personality shines through the documentary record.[87] One might dismiss as exaggerated or malicious the remarks of his 1805 accuser (even though he called himself "Ruperto Verdad," loosely translated as "I tell the truth"), were it not for the fact that after Huarte's death his own family, while stopping short of referring to him as a "tyrant" and a "despot," as Verdad had done, generally confirmed the picture that emerged from his complaint. Huarte's in-laws (the family of his third wife, Ana Gertrudis de Alcántara y Arrambide), held him responsible for the loss of almost all their income from their mother's modest hacienda.[88] His daughter Teresa complained that after he lost his case before the viceroy to prevent her second marriage he found ways to keep her maternal inheritance out of her hands until after his death almost twenty years later. Her third husband reported that Huarte had "constantly fought to keep from fulfilling his legal obligation [to give Teresa] her *maternas*, only turning over tiny amounts designated specifically, by paternal authority, for food, rent, and a cook's wages."[89] But the bitterest of all his relatives was his son-in-law, Pascual Alzúa, whose story of ill treatment at Huarte's hands began when Huarte sent for him in 1784:

> I was summoned by [Huarte], who asked me to join him, promising me that . . . he would protect me and help me, as he had done for others, and this offer induced me to abandon the good business I had in Pamplona and to come to Mexico in the middle of March, 1784. . . . In 1788, as I was by now well acquainted with the business, he sent me to Veracruz on a buying trip, and when I asked him on what terms I would be compensated for my efforts, he said we would talk about it when I returned, but this conversation never occurred, neither on this trip nor on the second, third, and fourth trips I made for him; I was always sent away with the same promises, with always the same results. There was no human means of making him pay me for my services, which were considerable, since the whole weight of the *casa* was on me, as none of his other *dependientes* was willing to endure such a close association. And in the end he died without ever paying me for the eighteen years of service I gave him between 1784 and 1802 [when they finally formed a partnership], during which time I was responsible for earning him profits of at least 200,000 pesos. . . .
>
> After the death [in 1808] of my wife María del Carmen, and on the occasion of my second marriage, I outlined all the reasons why it was no longer possible for me to continue to manage his [Huarte's] *casa*, and why it was imperative that he turn over the sums belonging to my children as heirs of their mother, but he was deaf to all my demands, and he forced me to continue in charge of his business affairs . . . ; my inability to separate from him without a lawsuit, which I was unwilling to bring against my own father-in-law, greatly prejudiced my own interests.[90]

Alzúa's resentments, and those of Teresa and her second and third husbands, were expressed the most clearly, but all of Huarte's children from his mar-

riage to Ana Manuela Muñiz had some complaints about their father's unwillingness to part with their *maternas*. Admittedly, at over 250,000 pesos,
their mother's share represented a huge proportion of his assets, and to turn
it over to his children would have required the restructuring and scaling back
of the whole business, the more so if Alzúa had been successful in his own
campaign to separate himself from the Huarte *casa*, taking with him the one-
third of the profits he earned from 1802 forward. Narrowly considered, then,
Huarte's stonewalling might be seen as a way to get around inheritance laws
that worked to fragment estates. But it is probably safe to assume that it was
in his character to run roughshod over others if it suited him to do so, given
that animosity toward him transcended his family circle. Those who had been
crossed by Huarte included not only the Pátzcuaro Augustinians, but (according to "Ruperto Verdad"), a significant proportion of the Valladolid
elite. Among them was the Michelena family, whose resentment toward what
they thought was Huarte's disproportionate benefit from their partnership in
the early years of the nineteenth century led to a feud between the two families that lasted even beyond Mariano Michelena's vigorous opposition to
Mexico's first emperor (and Huarte's son-in-law), Agustín de Iturbide.[91] In
sum, it is entirely in keeping with his other arrogances that he might, as
"Verdad" claimed, have refused to attend city council meetings unless something of interest to him was on the agenda, on the grounds that "wearing a
wig hurt his head."[92]

PART ONE

Toward Independence

CHAPTER ONE

"El jardín de la Nueva España":
Michoacán Before 1810, Through the Eyes
of the "Upper Two-Tenths"*

If you were traveling the roads of what is now the state of Michoacán in the last decades of the colonial period, you were probably headed for the city of Valladolid. As the seat of the bishopric of Michoacán, the city attracted a stream of pious supplicants, restless priests, visiting friars, young girls destined for convents, tithe payers and tithe collectors, would-be borrowers from full church coffers, and providers of the goods and services demanded by a complex and multifaceted institution, from organ masters to architects to property appraisers to sellers of beeswax.[1] As the capital of the intendancy of the same name, Valladolid was the posting for a constantly circulating population of royal officials and bureaucrats, including the intendant and his staff, local magistrates-cum-administrators, treasury officials, managers of the lottery, and tobacco monopoly factors.[2] As the site of two highly regarded colleges — the Colegio de San Nicolás and the Seminario Tridentino — the city was a magnet for young men with an aptitude for letters or ambition for a career in the priesthood or the law. Valladolid was also a base of operations for the collectors of information so much associated with the late Bourbons, engaged in gathering statistics, in mapping and tapping the region's presumed abundance of natural resources, and in recommending reform measures to the Crown.[3]

Mule trains converged on Valladolid from all directions. From Veracruz

---

* The full quotation, from the transcript of José María Morelos's interrogation before his execution in 1815, is: " . . . donde yo nací fue en el jardín de la Nueva España," quoted in Morales García, 1:132. The phrase "upper two-tenths" is Bishop Manuel Abad y Queipo's, as the author of "Representación a nombre de los Labradores y Comerciantes de Valladolid . . . ," in Sugawara, ed., p. 61.

and Mexico City came a variety of European imports: paper, wine, iron, and most of all cloth, much of which was resold by the city's wholesalers to smaller provincial merchants or to itinerant traders.[4] From Puebla, Celaya, Guadalajara, and Querétaro came pottery, textiles, hardware, and other domestic manufactures. From Acapulco came oriental luxuries: silk, spices, porcelain. And from the hot country to the south came mules laden with sugar, *piloncillo*, rice, cotton, and indigo, mainly destined for markets in the northern mining and textile centers.

Finally, for at least part of the year, Valladolid (with nearby Pátzcuaro) was home for wealthy owners of rural properties in a broad swath from Puruándiro in the north, on the border with the intendancy of Guanajuato, to the coastal sierra. This meant that sharing the highways with all the other travelers headed to Valladolid were absentee hacendados returning to the city after an inspection of their properties, and hacienda residents and their families making one of their frequent and sometimes extended trips to the city.[5] The roads leading to Valladolid at the end of the colonial period were, in short, busy with a disparate population of travelers.

At the same time, Valladolid was not, for the most part, a place through which people passed on the way to somewhere else. As the prologue to this book illustrates, travelers with a destination anywhere in the intendancy of Michoacán had to make a special effort. Though viceroy after viceroy talked about improving the road from Mexico City to Guadalajara via Valladolid, not much was ever accomplished, and travelers continued to prefer the easier (if longer) northern route through Querétaro and Salamanca.

Valladolid was, then, well visited and yet isolated, an administrative and ecclesiastical capital and yet on the margins of New Spain's political and economic core, the center of a bustling regional economy and yet not a place, as is clear from the vantage point of the late-twentieth century, destined for economic ascendancy. What did all this mean to the merchants, hacendados, and other well-to-do people for whom Valladolid was the chief point of orientation? Did they feel keenly and bitterly their distance from the economic, political, and cultural centers of power?

The conventional answer to this question is affirmative. An especially eloquent and persuasive case was made by Ernesto Lemoine Villicaña in his *Morelos y la revolución de 1810* (first published 1979). Lemoine points out that Valladolid owed its foundation neither to the logic of trade patterns nor to the need for a Hispanic city to anchor and control a large indigenous population (since one already existed in Pátzcuaro), but to a sixteenth-century political feud between Viceroy Antonio de Mendoza and the Bishop of Michoacán, Vasco de Quiroga. Quiroga had already designed and begun work on a cathedral in Pátzcuaro when Mendoza, initiating a long and inconsistent policy of royal curtailment of ecclesiastical power, and leery of Quiroga's godlike status among the *naturales* of Michoacán, moved the seat of the bishopric thirty miles away to Valladolid. The city thus had an artificial, "ex-centric" existence from the beginning, and Lemoine argues that this fact made for an atmosphere that was increasingly "hermetic" over time.[6] The image of a sleepy cathedral town well off the beaten track is also conjured up (often approvingly) by foreign travelers to Valladolid, especially in the early decades after independence. Fanny Calderón de la Barca, writing in 1843, put it this way: "[i]t has a singular effect, after travelling for some days through a wild country, seeing nothing but a solitary hacienda, or an Indian hut, to enter a fine city like [Valladolid], which seems to have started up as by magic in the midst of the wilderness."[7]

It seems likely, however, that Valladolid's relative inaccessibility mattered less in the late colonial period than it did later, or at least was perceived differently by late colonial elites than by their children and grandchildren. Even when asked directly to think about the problems of communication and transport, local officials were not always mindful of any pressing need for improvement. As late as 1813, for example, in response to a questionnaire about roads, bridges, canals, and other public works related to transportation, the intendant Manuel Merino nodded favorably in the direction of a proposal to improve the road between Valladolid and La Barca (on the western border with Jalisco) but emphasized that before the 1810 insurrection the producers of a wide range of goods in the intendancy had gotten along quite well, managing efficiently to export an increasing agricultural surplus to Mexico City and Guanajuato.[8] More important than new roads, he concluded, were new laws to promote resettlement of dispersed and "more savage than civilized" peoples (including *castas*) into communities with a priest, a magistrate, and a school.[9] This view — that the fundamental problem was not so much the province's isolation from the rest of the colony, but the indigenous population's isolation from Hispanic society — echoed the analyses of earlier enlightened critics and reformers, most famously Bishop-elect Manuel Abad y Queipo, whose views will be examined in more detail below.[10] An anonymous official visitor around the turn of the century implicitly concurred; obviously having been requested to provide information about the state of the roads, he labeled the vast majority as good or very good, and concentrated his attention on other problems, which he saw as more urgently in need of redress, including the rapaciousness of the local clergy and the local hacendados, who (he argued) combined to deprive Indian communities of the means with which to progress.[11]

Why were provincial elites in the decades before independence not overly concerned with the problem that would become so glaringly obvious to their descendants? For one thing, while getting to and from Valladolid was never a simple matter, it was nonetheless much easier in the waning years of colonial rule than it had ever been, and those born before 1780 had seen striking improvements during their lifetimes. Fray Francisco de Ajofrín, for example, writing in the late 1760s, had described the approach to Zinapécuaro from the Mexico City-Querétaro road as "peñosísimo"; and between Zinapécuaro and Valladolid, a distance of about 25 miles, the road was so bad that he got lost two or three times: "were it not for a poor Indian whom I met after nightfall, no doubt I would have become mired in one of the many mudholes, or drowned in a watery pit."[12] By 1803, however, the road was passable for four-wheeled carriages all the way from Mexico City to Valladolid; causeways and bridges had been constructed across the most difficult parts, and the whole of the road was well marked and at least roughly paved.[13]

Furthermore, contemporary perceptions of Valladolid's isolation were surely colored by the fact that difficulty of access was the rule rather than the exception in New Spain. Humboldt, for example, makes much of the horrors of the trip from Veracruz to Mexico City on a road that "is frequently nothing but a narrow and crooked path."[14] Valladolid was physically and politically distant from the center of royal power in Madrid, it is true, but not so much farther in a relative sense than Mexico City itself, and no farther than many other provincial capitals (Guadalajara, Querétaro, Guanajuato).

But the key to understanding the complacency and optimism of well-to-do Michoacanos around the turn of the century — with regard not only to their geographical isolation but also to the economic problems that this isolation implied — surely lies in an appreciation of the way the many economic, political, and intellectual changes of the late colonial period played out in this particular local context.

Elites and the Economy

One of the most powerful influences on the way provincial elites saw themselves in relation to the rest of the colony, and even to Spain itself, was the rapid late eighteenth-century expansion of Michoacán's economy. Increases in production, investment, imports, and out-of-region exports in the last two or three decades before the outbreak of the wars for independence are attested to by virtually all available measures. In fact, the province of Michoacán probably experienced brisker economic growth in the late colonial period than did any other part of New Spain, with the possible exception of the region around Guadalajara.

One underlying factor was the high rate of population growth, especially from in-migration. The droughts and epidemics of the mid-1780s had brought a wave of returnees to Michoacán from the crowded northern Bajío and the mining districts, as men and women who had left the state earlier in the century to form the laboring backbone of the mining and textile booms now came back. They settled in farming communities either as small independents, tenants, or day laborers on haciendas, especially in the vast, relatively vacant parts of the *tierra caliente* and in the fertile and well-watered valleys around Puruándiro and Zamora.[15]

This southward population shift and one of its presumed corollaries — increased agricultural production in the migrants' destinations — are reflected in the growing proportion of tithe revenues in the bishopric of Michoacán (which included the modern states of Michoacán and Guanajuato and parts of Jalisco, Colima, Guerrero, and San Luis Potosí) that was supplied by the intendancy of Valladolid. In the 1730s the districts that would later form the intendancy contributed under 28 percent of the bishopric's totals. By 1761 these districts' share of the total had increased to 35.5 percent, and by the 1805–09 *quincencio*, it was roughly 42 percent.[16] In other words, tithe collections in Michoacán province rose even faster than those in the rich Bajío, a region noted for its rapid eighteenth-century growth.[17]

Much of this increased agricultural production was necessary, of course, to feed the growing population. Nonetheless, a fairly significant proportion was destined for markets outside of the intendancy. According to one report, two-thirds of the sugar produced in the intendancy was exported out of the region, mostly to markets in the north: Guanajuato, Zacatecas, Durango, Chihuahua.[18] Other hot-country products, especially rice, indigo, and cotton, were also mainly marketed outside the province, as were salt from the rich beds around Colima, copper from the mines south of Ario and Tacámbaro, the tropical fruits (melons, tamarind, oranges) grown on many haciendas as a supplement to their main activities, and much of the beef consumed in the highland cities of the intendancy (whose surrounding haciendas had shifted much of their lands into the production of more profitable crops) and in Mexico City, Guanajuato, and even Puebla.[19] Moreover, while the *tierra caliente* was the main exporting region, it was not the only one. Just one hacienda in the district of Valladolid — San Bartolomé, near Zinapécuaro — sent over 9,000 *cargas* of wheat to Mexico City each year in the 1770s, well before the substantial late-colonial investments in irrigation and storage systems that permitted even stronger increases in wheat production.[20]

Virtually all of this out-of-region trade was conducted by means of well-equipped mule trains that were hired (and sometimes owned) by long-distance merchants. In one year (1800) in Valladolid, 76 different muleteers registered cargos with the sales tax office, often hired by groups of prominent merchants to transport huge cargos from Veracruz or Mexico City.[21] Muleteers from Uruapan, in the employ of three or four merchants, covered the coast of Zacatula, buying cotton directly from the (mainly small) producers, and selling them the manufactured and imported goods they needed (or were persuaded they needed).[22] In Tangancícuaro, Francisco Victorino Jaso maintained some 80 mule trains that carried goods produced in western Michoacán to Chihuahua and other places to the north and brought European imports purchased at the famous trade fair at San Juan de los Lagos to sell in Michoacán. The volume of his operations in the 1780s was between 50,000 and 80,000 pesos a year, and when he retired to the extensive hacienda of Guaracha, which he had purchased in 1791 with profits from his mercantile operations, his son-in-law Lázaro Morales continued to generate trade at roughly the same level into the 1800s.[23] Whole towns, especially in the western part of the province, were said to be engaged in muleteering, either as independents or as more-or-less permanent employees of large merchants.[24]

In light of all this activity it is not surprising that sales-tax receipts, like tithe receipts, show strong increases during the late eighteenth and early nineteenth centuries. The average *alcabala* collection for the intendancy of Michoacán from 1795 to 1801 was 120,400 pesos; but in the period 1805–09 receipts jumped over 40 percent, to 173,800 pesos.[25] The sales tax records confirm the subregional patterns displayed by both population and tithe data; that is, there were powerful increases in the western (Zamora) collection and in the south (especially in Pátzcuaro, which was the collection point for many of the *tierra caliente* haciendas). But throughout the province the pace of commodity exchange was clearly gathering force before the turn of the century.

If it is clear that the last decades of the colonial period saw more vigorous markets in agricultural commodities and trade goods, the same can also be said of the markets for purchase and rental of large rural properties. The number of haciendas sold in the province increased from an average of 1.2 a year in the 1770s and 1780s to 3.2 a year in the 1790s and 1800s, while sale prices climbed from an average of 27,500 pesos in the 1770s and 1780s to 36,700 pesos in the 1790s to 43,200 pesos in the 1800s.[26] Whole-hacienda rents (as opposed to partial rents, on which there is little surviving data) almost tripled, from an average 1,200 pesos a year in the 1770s through the 1790s to 3,275 pesos in the period 1800–10.[27] Partly these trends were a function of across-the-board inflation in land values, reflecting the perceived new opportunities for profits in agriculture that accompanied higher food prices and falling wages.[28] The fact that rents rose even faster than sale prices in the first decade of the nineteenth century especially suggests that people wanted not just to own land (for which there can be many motivations, not all of which have much to do with turning a profit), but to take advantage of good market conditions to increase production over the short and medium term. Contemporaries occasionally commented on these inflated land values. Noting that she had purchased her hacienda in 1791 for just 5,500 pesos, one church borrower claimed in 1805 that it was now worth 10,291 pesos. She attributed this near doubling of the value of her property in part to "natural" inflation in rural land values.[29]

But she also observed that in part the increase was due to money she had spent on the property since purchase, and it is clear that in investing in improvements on the hacienda, she was not alone.[30] In many individual cases property value increases are clearly the result of improvements introduced by the owners. The capital investment required to double sugar production in the southern part of the province, for example, was substantial, and huge jumps in the value of some hot-country haciendas were the result. In 1778 Pátzcuaro Augustinians sold the hacienda of La Parota to Juan Manuel de Michelena for 45,000 pesos, but by 1809 it was worth at least 185,000 pesos. The inventory carried out in that year showed over 30,000 pesos worth of permanent improvements (e.g. mills valued at over 6,000 pesos, *casas de calderas* worth over 7,200 pesos), and another 60,000 pesos in mules, equipment, and cane plantings.[31] The sugar-producing complex composed of the haciendas of Tipitaro, Tipitarillo, and San Vicente, worth around 60,000 pesos in 1793, was sold in 1801 for 130,000 pesos.[32] Another sugar and livestock hacienda, Pedernales, which had been purchased for 33,000 pesos in 1795, was appraised in 1805 at 240,000 pesos.[33]

A growing number of owners of cereal-zone haciendas also invested significant sums in developing sometimes-elaborate hydraulic systems, delineat-

ing and protecting their properties with stone fencing and building the warehousing and processing facilities (especially flour mills) that were required to
avert the necessity of selling too soon or on unfavorable terms. Morin estimates that by 1790 between one-fourth and one-third of cultivated lands
were irrigated. If that figure is correct the proportion must have been considerably higher by 1810, given the large number of loans requested in order to
build dams, aqueducts, and *sanjas* after 1790.[34] Virtually all haciendas
around the larger urban areas (Valladolid, Pátzcuaro, Zamora) and many
that sold their products out of region in either Mexico City (especially in the
valleys around Maravatío) or the mining north (especially around
Puruándiro) boasted substantial irrigated acreage, flour mills, extensive fencing, and good storage facilities. The middling hacienda of Guaraparío, for example, near Valladolid, had been purchased in 1791 for 17,500 pesos by
Dionisio García Carrasquedo, who built fifteen miles of stone fence, an aqueduct valued at 4,000 pesos, a dam valued at 3,000 pesos, and a building complex with ten structures, including a chapel, a grain warehouse, and a fine residence; he also planted 7,000 magueys. By 1810 the property was appraised
at over 68,000 pesos.[35] On the hacienda of Rincón, also in the environs of
Valladolid, the 1789 buyer spent some 24,000 pesos building a grain warehouse with nine *arcos de cantería*, a flour mill with two grindstones, a glittering new residence, and fourteen miles of fence. He also stocked the hacienda with some 1,000 head of cattle, an astonishing 2,500 oxen, and over
200 mules.[36] The vast hacienda of Guaracha, near Zamora, more than doubled in value as a result of improvements and stocking between 1791, when
it was purchased for 209,000 pesos, and 1808, when it was appraised at over
500,000 pesos.[37] Even church-owned haciendas rented out to individuals
were often improved by the renters, if granaries, storehouses, and irrigation
systems were not already in place. The hacienda of Coapa, for example,
rented for 2,600 pesos a year in 1779, 3,500 pesos in 1788, and 7,000 pesos
in 1806, and in large part the increased rent represented investments made by
José Manuel de Olarte, a wealthy Valladolid merchant, and carried out by his
administrator's widow, María Manuela Arias Maldonado.[38] In general, then,
the last decade before 1810 saw capital investments in hacienda agriculture
at a peak; in eleven hacienda inventories for the period 1800–10 an average
of 27 percent of the appraised value of the estates was comprised of porta-
bles — seeds, animals, tools, and so on — and another 18 percent of structures
like dams, bridges, canals, and buildings. This was to be the highest such proportion for half a century.[39]

Wealthy landowners, then, were optimistic about the economic future, and this translated into unprecedented activity in rural real estate markets and an almost unquestioning willingness to invest large sums in their often recently acquired haciendas. But at the same time their optimism was tempered by several factors. One of the most vexing problems, from the point of view of both hacendados and merchants, was high taxes and other forms of fiscal extraction. Although sales tax rates had come back down to 6 percent in the 1790s and 1800s, having risen to 8 percent for much of the 1780s, this was still perceived as a high rate historically, since a 4-percent sales tax was within the living memory of many. Moreover, like the tithe, the sales tax was collected more efficiently under the meticulous late Bourbon administrators than at any earlier time. When the sales tax burden was added to that of the tithe, the result was a significant reduction in the profitability of estate agriculture, which was felt especially keenly in this era of increasing competition and out-of-region export. Not even counting the new or increased fees levied for licenses to produce, say, *pulque* or *aguardiente*, or to establish a flour mill, the difference between actual hacienda profits in the range of 6 to 8 percent, which seem to have been the average in most of Michoacán, and the 9 to 11 percent that they would have been in a taxless and titheless world, was well understood by producers.[40]

Another problem of which the wealthy were keenly aware was the inadequacy of the credit system, on which virtually all of them depended, whether they were merchants or hacendados. Despite some expansion in the second half of the eighteenth century, this system, for a variety of reasons all associated at least indirectly with Spain's involvement in expensive European wars, became less rather than more capable of financing growth after 1800. But even before 1800 there were structural problems linked to the church's domination of the system (and to the state's unwillingness to permit the establishment of alternative institutional sources of credit). The church, of course, was not in the business of promoting economic growth through capitalizing risky and innovative businesses. Instead, its primary economic goals were to maintain the flow of interest income necessary to support and encourage both church activities and church personnel, and to be sure that charitable funds were available to promote the general welfare of society and the individual welfare of clergy and their families. The highest levels of church lending occurred during catastrophes such as the severe droughts of the mid-1780s, when the Juzgado de Capellanías and the cathedral chapter emptied their reserves and even borrowed from their own personnel in order to step up loans, which doubled over the averages of nondrought years.[41] In ordinary times, to protect its interest revenues, the church was notoriously cautious about lending to people who were not property owners, and it funneled much money into nonproductive ends if borrowers had good collateral and need, as defined — broadly — by the church. A survey of the purposes for which money was borrowed from the church in 1804, for example, included a trip to Spain, a trip to Orizaba for the health of the borrower, the costs of a long illness, purchase of government office, the living expenses of several families with financial problems, repayment of other debts, and purchase of the house of a neighbor who was dumping sewage into the property of the borrower.[42] Meanwhile the demand for loans from those looking to invest in productive enterprise grew.[43]

Furthermore, even if the church had been more willing to risk its capital, it was inherent in the ecclesiastical credit system that there were rarely enough funds in the system at any one time to finance more than a relatively primitive irrigation system, say, or a new fence. It is no surprise, then, that these were the very sorts of improvements landowners most often made. Church capital ordinarily became available when people either redeemed outstanding debts, or, more rarely, when they made cash bequests or payments, such as the dowry required to place a daughter in a nunnery, to the church. When those funds — which were almost invariably modest in size, given their provenance — came into church coffers, they were immediately snapped up. In 1804, for example, Francisco Ruiz y España went to the Juzgado stating that he had heard that Isidro Huarte was about to redeem 4,000 pesos that Huarte presently recognized on a certain house, belonging to a certain chaplaincy, and he asked to borrow it the moment that Huarte paid off the debt.[44] As numerous contemporaries attested, such requests were commonplace. Supplicants for church loans far outnumbered those who put money into the system, which made it necessary to have good contacts within the church and within the ranks of the already indebted (that is to say, propertied) classes, in order to have the right information to act at the right time. If one did not have those contacts, one could employ someone who did: there were *corredores* who earned a living scouting out redemptions and foundations of new pious works and alerting their clients to the prospects for a loan.[45] In short, it was extremely difficult to borrow large amounts of capital from the church in any but a piecemeal, wait-and-see fashion.[46]

Increasingly since the 1780s, some of the unmet demand for capital had been supplied by private lenders, who frequently found ways to get around the strictures against usury, especially by use of *habilitación* contracts.[47] According to these arrangements, the lender, almost always a merchant, agreed to finance an agricultural enterprise in return for a monopoly on the estate's production and fixed commodity prices. Producers sometimes complained bitterly about this system. José María Solórzano, for example, borrowed large sums from a Pátzcuaro merchant to meet the rent on the sugar hacienda of Acúmbaro, which was owned by the Augustinian order, and to pay the wages and tribute obligations of his workforce. He had agreed to repay the debt in kind, that is, in sugar, at the price of fourteen reales per *arroba*. This price, he later claimed, was "usurious and as such contemptible and morally wrong" ("indigno y reprobado"); he was chagrined because he was able to sell (in violation of the contract) to independent muleteers for seventeen reales, and dreamed of being able to sell the whole crop at this price.[48]

This sort of *habilitación* contract was favored by long-distance merchants, since it permitted exclusive access to raw materials (e.g. sugar, cotton, indigo) at what they hoped would turn out to be below-market prices, and it made the producers dependent on them. In fairness, however, it should be noted that some hacendados were grateful to merchants for supporting their weekly operations when there was nowhere else to turn, and for providing a ready, indeed assured market for their production at set prices, which could, of course, turn out to be *higher* than free-market prices. Gregorio Espino y Elisondo, for example, who rented the haciendas of Chupio and Magdalena, stated in 1813 that Isidro Huarte had been his sole source of support during the period 1805–10; without Huarte's cash advances, he said, the hacienda's "opulent and flourishing state" in 1810 would have been impossible.[49] That is, monopoly over a producer's crop by a single merchant could be seen as a convenience and a safeguard for the producer and as a boon for the merchant.

Despite the occasional happy customer, however (and as it happened, Espino went bankrupt in spite of Huarte's ministrations), the impression remains of a credit situation that worked distinctly to the disadvantage of frustrated hacendados, and in general was simply not meeting the demand for capital. Although the dimensions of the problem are not easy to appreciate, since the true interest rate commanded by private lenders cannot be known (all loan contracts on paper carried the same nonusurious interest rate as that charged by the church, 5 percent), it appears that the supply of credit peaked in the 1790s and diminished markedly in the first decade of the nineteenth century, with a concomitant rise in real interest rates. The system, which was at first merely inadequate (in the 1790s), entered something like a crisis in the

1800s: after averaging well over 200,000 pesos a year in the 1790s the total of private and ecclesiastical loans dropped off in the 1800s to less than half that amount.[50]

Though the structure of the credit system was relatively inflexible and un-responsive, the primary blame for this inopportune constriction of credit (at a time when even greater supplies of capital were desperately needed if agri-cultural production was to continue to increase) lies with the government de-cree known as the Consolidación de Vales Reales. From 1804 to 1809 this policy of requiring the church to call in outstanding loans — and then to lend the money to the Crown — called a halt to any further church lending and forced property owners to come up with funds to which very few of them had access. Even though the government quickly revised the policy to allow for a drawn-out schedule of repayment, it was still exceedingly difficult for many property owners to comply. The consolidation exposed and exacerbated the worst aspects of the credit system: the perennial shortage of capital, the per-sonalistic lending policies of both church and private creditors, and the lax re-payment policies of the church, which had allowed debts to accumulate over decades. As chapter 2 argues in more detail, there was probably no single part of the Bourbon legislative program more obnoxious, more unsettling, than the Consolidation.[51]

High taxes and fees, and inadequacies in the credit system — which fea-tured not only a shortage of lending capital but high levels of debt — were far from the only constraints on economic growth in the late colonial period. Economic historians differ as to the relative severity of other problems, but all agree that New Spain's grotesque inequities in income distribution (making for a very narrow base of consumption), high transport costs, and low profit rates, combined with a state that intervened where it should not have (espe-cially in creating state monopolies) and that failed to intervene where it should have (by effectively protecting property rights, for example), created massive obstacles to anything like self-sustaining economic growth.[52]

But we must question which of these bottlenecks and structural contra-dictions were understood by wealthy men and women and figured in their calculations about the future and, therefore, in their behavior. I have argued that elites *were* anxious about some aspects of the late colonial economy. Almost daily they battled high taxes and credit shortages, and they were surely aware that the rate of indebtedness and even bankruptcy was histori-cally quite high, a feature of the late colonial economy that the Consolidation had highlighted. But these problems, all of which could be and probably were

blamed on the policies of the state from which many of them would soon declare their independence, were the only ones that we can be certain were
clearly understood as obstacles to continued growth.

A handful of elites understood the long-term implications of the falling
wages, which had paved the way to higher profits, but it is unlikely that many
saw the warnings posted by enlightened churchmen and bureaucrats about
the need to reduce poverty as more than an entirely appropriate expression of
church and state paternalism and concern for the poor. Indeed, it is possible
to read even the analyses of Manuel Abad y Queipo, the most vocal, articulate, and far-seeing of the social critics, as rhetorical devices meant as much
to defend the institutional power of the church as to warn about the dangers
to economic growth of social inequities. When Abad characterized New
Spain as a land in which "everyone is either rich or poverty-stricken, noble or
infamous," we should not forget that the point was made in support of his
self-interested argument that the northern reaches of his bishopric of
Michoacán could not afford to support a proposed new bishopric of San Luis
Potosí.[53] In any event, it is unrealistic to suppose that hacendados, who so obviously benefited from falling wages, were especially open to the suggestion
that their still-fragile profits were endangered in the long run by the very
thing that made them possible in the short run, even if this is what Abad
meant to convey. They surely saw the isolation and poverty of the Indian majority as a moral and even a social problem (to the extent that poverty was associated with unrest), but it is most unlikely that more than a few saw it as a
serious economic problem.

Other obstacles to growth that historians have described as embedded and
enduring, wealthy contemporaries (by contrast) must have seen as in the
process of being resolved. This was no doubt true of profit margins, which,
while still uncomfortably thin, were improving with the trends toward higher
commodity prices and lower wages. It was also true, I have argued, of high
transport costs posed by poor roads and geographical isolation, limited supply networks (which had broadened markedly, as sales tax receipts demonstrate, with the 1789 policy of *comercio libre*), and inadequate information
about prices and markets (which improved in a formal sense with the publi-
cation, beginning in the late 1780s, of the *Gaceta de México*, and in an informal sense with the geographical expansion of investments made by the
wealthy). In general, it seems plausible that the dominant element of elites'
economic identity in the last decades before 1810 was neither their isolation
from economic centers — however real *we* might find it to be — nor a sense

that they were significantly disadvantaged by geography or political distances, nor a fear that their economic future was compromised by abiding
structural problems, but their full and increasing participation in the pattern
of colonial growth in the last decades before 1810. The most nagging, daily-
evident problems were, significantly, those that might have been most easily
resolved by replacing the current government (which was capable of such destructive policies as the Consolidation) with one more sympathetic to their
own needs. That is to say, with a government organized and administered by
themselves.

Institutional Affiliation and Social Identity

There were other factors besides changes in the late colonial economy that
worked to obscure elites' perception of their isolation and to increase their
sense of themselves as significant figures on the larger canvas of New Spain.
One was the centralization and strengthening of provincial government that
accompanied the inauguration of the intendancy system in 1786.[54] Some of
the Bourbon reforms, of course, tended to disempower creoles, including —
most notoriously — the Gálvez-era restrictions on creole office holding. And
it is also true that the intendant was a stronger advocate for royal administration in the region than the *alcaldes de partido* had ever been, that he played
a powerful role (which included the exercise of veto power) in the city council of Valladolid, and that the new system took away from merchants and
property owners the customary right to collect their own sales taxes and
other government fees, turning over the responsibility for collecting these
taxes to a new royal treasury office in Valladolid.

But insofar as the new system meant that provincial taxes were collected
and judicial matters decided in the capital city of the intendancy rather than
in Mexico City, provincials gained a certain autonomy and self-importance.
This was especially true in light of the fact that well-to-do provincials were
generally quite successful in establishing close ties and working relationships
with the intendants and other royal officials. Michoacán's second intendant,
Felipe Díaz de Hortega (1792–1809), was very well-connected to — one
might even say absorbed by — Valladolid society. He served as *padrino* for
several prominent weddings; his son became a canon in the Valladolid cathedral; his daughter almost married into the Huarte family; and he had a financial or business relationship, perhaps something like a silent partnership,

with Coronel Francisco Menocal, owner of the sugar hacienda of Araparícuaro.[55] Wealthy Michoacanos also succeeded, after the death of Gálvez, in filling many of the *subdelegado* positions in the province: José María Abarca y León and Agustín Barandiarán in Pátzcuaro, Lic. Nicolás de Michelena in Zamora, Luis G. Correa in Zitácuaro, Fernando Cos in Tacámbaro, Dionisio Fernández de la Torre in Urecho; Manuel Diego Villavicencio in Uruapan.[56] Though not all of these men were creoles, many of their bondsmen were Mexican-born property owners.[57]

Perhaps even more important than the new sources and relationships of power associated with the intendancy system was the expansion of the officer corps that accompanied the late colonial military reforms, especially under the regime of Viceroy Branciforte (1794–98).[58] Like provincial elites elsewhere, wealthy men in Valladolid eagerly made generous donations to the formation of the two new local regiments, the Provincial Infantry of Valladolid and the Provincial Dragoons of Pátzcuaro, in return for which they expected to receive a commission. The appeal of a relationship to the military in the late colonial period was partly the practical advantages that came with membership in any corporate body that had its own regulations, its own courts, and its own esprit: the church, the government bureaucracy, the mining guild, the *consulado*, or the army. But the army had a special position among the other corporations. First, unlike the church, its rights and responsibilities were being expanded by the Bourbon monarchy, which saw the military as a more suitable bulwark of royal power than the church. Second, unlike the royal bureaucracy, a military career was open just about equally to creoles and Spaniards alike. Many prominent families, including most in Valladolid itself, sought commissions for themselves and their sons. I have identified 62 wealthy Michoacano officers, about evenly divided between peninsulars and creoles, with a slight edge to the former for older men who had been among the first generation of officers recruited beginning in 1780, and to the latter for the second generation of officers who entered the military in the late 1790s.[59] Whatever the problems and resentments and jealousies aroused in the process of naming officers (and these were clearly not insignificant), to occupy high positions in an institution so clearly favored and relied upon by the Crown surely gave provincials a sense of their own importance that combined with the changes brought about by the intendancy system to make elites more confident of their own power or access to power.

The political and institutional changes initiated from Madrid, as well as the economic patterns sketched earlier, were closely related to a phenomenon that some scholars have referred to as the formation of a provincial "oli-garchy" in Valladolid.[60] What these scholars have in mind is a relatively small group of individuals whose activities and interests interlocked more and more over time, and who excelled at using institutions such as the military and the city council to promote those interests.

There is no doubt that in the last decades of the colonial period wealthy provincials in and around Valladolid were more connected to each other in more ways than ever before. In the economic sphere elites simultaneously pursued profits in trade, finance, agriculture and (to a lesser extent) mining. Following a well-known pattern, much of the new enthusiasm for purchasing and improving rural estates came from merchants; in fact, there was scarcely a prosperous merchant in Valladolid or Zamora or Pátzcuaro at the turn of the century who had *not* recently purchased an hacienda. Merchants also provided loan capital for agricultural and mining enterprises in which they did not invest directly. But the decision to diversify into agricultural invest-ments was not limited to capital-rich merchants. Even soon-to-be bishop-elect Manuel Abad y Queipo got into the act by buying the expensive (105,000 pesos) sugar hacienda of Puruarán in 1799, and there were a fairly significant number of other churchmen who bought haciendas (though the more com-mon pattern was for wealthy clerics to invest in urban properties).[61] In short, any attempt to categorize the late-colonial upper class by occupation or in-vestment must begin by creating numerous overlapping categories, only the most obvious of which is merchant/landowner.

These multiplying economic interests naturally led elites to cement their ties to institutions with important political and economic functions, especially the church and the *ayuntamiento*. By serving their town or city as a *regidor* on the city council, they put themselves in good position to influence con-tracts with suppliers, municipal tax policy, and regulatory legislation that might have a direct effect on their businesses. By serving the church as, say, a tithe collector for the district to which their haciendas belonged, not only could they earn a profit on the sale of tithed goods, but, by pacing the sale of these goods, they could also affect the prices they would receive for their own crops. On another level, membership in church organizations or family ties to churchmen smoothed access to church loans.

Indeed, before the late 1780s, it is fair to say that the most important in-stitutional affiliations for the wealthy were those associated with the church, and not only for narrow economic purposes. The political and cultural power of the church was simply unmatched by anything the state could muster. This was especially true in Valladolid, where dozens of male and female religious and some 77 priests resided, including the 27 members of the cathedral chapter; where numerous lay institutions like the confraternity of the Preciosa Sangre de Cristo and the Third Order of St. Francis provided opportunities for wealthy laymen to organize in association with the church, and where, as one historian put it, "the city's daily rhythms were set by the church."[62] It is true that by the last decades of the colonial period the church's influence in local society and politics was no longer so exclusive as it had once been, in part because of the strong push by the Bourbon state to establish its own institutional presence in the province, and in part because of internal philosophical and factional conflicts within the church itself.[63] But one source of these intrachurch disputes was the presence of a group of strong-minded, progressive churchmen who renewed the church's role of leadership where social and intellectual change was concerned. The shape of the changing ideological climate in Michoacán will be taken up in more detail below, but here it is worth noting that one member of the cathedral chapter, José Pérez Calama, led the push to establish in Michoacán a chapter of the Sociedad Vascongada de Amigos del Pais, a liberal-minded group devoted to finding "enlightened" solutions to pressing economic and social problems. The membership list of the Sociedad shows that this was yet another new institutional setting in which the upper classes came in contact with and forged new ties to each other.[64]

Besides associating themselves with the right institutions, it was important for elites to solidify their ties to one another. Because they operated within a legal culture that emphasized personal honor and deemphasized impersonal guarantees of property rights, astute businessmen necessarily enlisted the support of other wealthy and influential people. One usually needed to have well-connected cosigners, for example, who were willing to offer their own property as collateral, in order to borrow money from the church or to make a bid to collect the tithe. One needed trusted associates to name as executors of one's will or to serve as one's power of attorney in an age virtually without lawyers. One needed honorable business partners, preferably also connected by blood or marriage or at least *compadrazgo*, because there were no special laws to limit personal liability in the case of bankruptcy. In short, the ties that bound upper-class society show up not only in institutional settings but also in the repetition of names in testaments, contracts, loan documents, and guardianship designations.

A brief sketch of the career of Francisco de la Riva will suffice to illustrate this uncontroversial portrait of a social group that was deeply intertwined. De la Riva, a Spaniard, came to Valladolid to work in his uncles' store, which he later inherited from them. He continued to run it until his death in 1806, purchasing his inventory in Mexico City and Veracruz, where he maintained accounts with several large houses. But, unlike his uncles, whose 50,000-peso fortune was almost entirely mercantile, de la Riva diversified into agriculture, purchasing the nearby hacienda of La Huerta in 1796 for 28,000 pesos, stocking it with over 50,000 pesos in livestock, and building two modern flour mills. He also partnered a business in the *remate de metales* with the *corregidor* of Zitácuaro, made numerous loans to other businessmen, and served as the syndic for various convents, including San Diego in Valladolid.[65] In 1781, when he was just 28 years old, he joined the militia unit at Valladolid as a sublieutenant, eventually rising to the position of captain. At about the same time he began serving on the city council, where he distinguished himself as something of a visionary and a philanthropist during the 1785–86 crisis by purchasing 10,000 *fanegas* of corn with 14,000 pesos of his own money, a move which was said to have greatly reduced the impact of the crisis on the city and which earned him the title of honorary *regidor* and city treasurer.[66] Naturally such a highly respected, wealthy, and enterprising man had close ties to other prominent families and individuals: his wife's uncle was Dean of the Cathedral Chapter and left her a sizable fortune; one son became a priest; his daughter married into the prominent García de Obeso family; he himself was one of the *padrinos* at Isidro Huarte's third marriage. Another well-to-do merchant/landowner, Manuel Valdovinos, was the *curador* for his minor children after his death in 1806. The nephew of a member of the Cathedral Chapter was his *dependiente* and one of his executors, and he served as executor for several other prominent individuals.[67]

But if the fabric of Valladolid elite society was very tightly woven, was it also a closed society obsessed with minute gradations of status, impervious to penetration from those outside the group? Was it a "hermetic" group, to use Lemoine Villicaña's adjective? One of the best ways to assess the extent to which the habits of association traditionally attributed to elites — hierarchy, exclusivity, endogamy — were reinforced during this period is to examine marriage patterns.

In many ways the marital choices made by wealthy families in the late eighteenth century and the first decade of the nineteenth do suggest a relatively closed social group. Most obviously, they tended overwhelmingly to marry within the region, to establish connections with families who lived nearby. (The well-known pattern of marriages between creole heiresses and Spanish merchants is borne out in Michoacán, but those marriages almost always took place after the Spaniard had lived in the region for many years.) There are a handful of cases in which marriages linked geographically distant families. Captain Felipe Robledo, for example, a Valladolid merchant/ landowner, married Francisca Jiménez, from one of the most prominent families in Zamora; Juan José Martínez de Lejarza y Unzaga married María Ana Alday, the daughter of the famous Querétaro textile entrepreneur, Francisco Antonio Alday; Josefa de Iturbide, sister of the future emperor, married a wealthy man from Durango in 1797.[68] But these were the exceptions in a pattern of elite marriages in which partners were most often sought from within families living in the same town or city, and, where the Valladolid upper classes are concerned, rarely outside the central part of the province.

But close scrutiny of elite marriages suggests that some kinds of "outsiders" did achieve upward social mobility through marriage. The conventional picture is one in which land-rich and capital-poor creole families married their daughters to wealthy Spanish merchants. But, somewhat surprisingly, men with little or no wealth and no prospect of inheritance often succeeded in marrying women who did enjoy such prospects. This was especially true in the last decades of the colonial period: in almost one-third of all eventually wealthy marriages between 1770 and 1810 the man had no money, compared to just 11 percent in the period 1710–69. Poor men who married wealthy women were, in fact, the largest category of elite marriages after 1770, ahead of the elite-consolidating marriages (in which both partners expected to inherit at least 1,500 pesos) that had predominated earlier in the century (see Table 1.1).

It is true that some of these marriages between a poor husband and a rich wife involved men who were partners in an ongoing enterprise, so that while technically they had no personal wealth, they had a good income from their business and they would eventually receive a share of the profits when the partnership was dissolved. But, in other cases, it is clear that what these men mainly had to offer at the time of marriage was ambition and promise, not income. And sometimes they did not seem (to the woman's parents, at least) even to possess those qualities. There are several cases in which wealthy patriarchs or matriarchs tried to block their daughters' marriages to men of whom they disapproved. Isidro Huarte, the reader may recall, vigorously opposed the marriage of his daughter Teresa to José Antonio Arce, and it cost her thousands of pesos to defend her rights before the viceroy.[69] Similarly,

TABLE 1.1

Amounts Brought by Husband and Wife to Households
That Eventually Became Wealthy, 1710–1810

Amount Brought	Date of marriage	
	1710–69 (n = 45)	1770–1810 (n = 57)
Both ≥ 1,500 pesos	44%	28%
Both < 1,500 pesos	11%	17%
Husband < 1,500, wife ≥ 1,500 pesos	11%	30%
Wife < 1,500, husband ≥ 1,500 pesos	33%	25%

SOURCES: ANM, AHCP, AHMM, AMHCR, AHPJ.
NOTE: For convenience I have used the symbols "≥" for "at least" ("greater than or equal to") and < for "under" ("less than").

María Josefa Ponce de León, who inherited two haciendas from her parents, and her husband José Mariano de Torres, whose worldly goods consisted of four horses and four mules, had to spend 2,000 pesos to defend themselves against a *pleito* initiated by her mother to stop the marriage.[70] But both marriages went ahead, and contributed to a pattern of modestly increasing upward social mobility for middle-class men.

In fact, even if neither partner had any wealth at the time of the marriage, upward social mobility was somewhat easier to achieve in the late colonial period than it had been earlier in the century. From 1710 to 1769 only 11 percent of eventually wealthy couples involved partners who were both poor, but this figure rose to 17 percent after 1770. This does not necessarily mean, of course, that these families were viewed as social equals by older, more-established families, but it does mean that the outer trappings of eliteness (a carriage, a good house in the center of town, a piano, good clothes and numerous jewels, imported wine on the table, etc.) were accessible to a greater number of middle-class men and women than they were before.

Moreover, if the upper classes in the late colonial period still tended to be geographically insular when it came to selecting marriage partners, this does not mean that they did not pursue allies and contacts outside of the region, and certainly outside the city of Valladolid. In fact, the geographically expanding nature of their investments required them to do so. Out-of-region business relationships took numerous forms: connections between Valladolid merchants and their suppliers/associates in Mexico City and Veracruz, between Valladolid merchants and their customers in Querétaro and Guanajuato and Durango and San Luis Potosí, between Valladolid merchants and their agricultural business partners/clients in the *tierra caliente*, between large hacendados and mercantile houses in urban centers of demand, and between partners in the farming of the tithe. It was fairly common for Guanajuato miners or merchants, for example, to serve as *fiadores* for Valladolid tithe farmers, and vice versa.[71] It was especially important for people living far from Valladolid to cultivate a relationship with someone living there, in case they might need the Valladolid resident to act on their behalf before the ecclesiastical and civil authorities of the city.[72] A very significant proportion of legal transactions at the end of the colonial period were arranged and signed by men who held power of attorney for the principals.

The picture that emerges from all this is of a regionally bounded elite, tied together by economic interest, institutional affiliation, and marriage; but not precisely an oligarchy, at least to the extent that the word implies a tiny, closed social group. It was a group that could be penetrated by men with certain essential qualifications: whiteness (a category that included many nonelites and no doubt some people whose identity as "Spaniards" was as much social as biological); and either education or exceptional promise of financial success.[73] As a result there was considerable diversity within the upper classes along lines of wealth, occupation, portfolio structure, place of birth, and education. In short, by the quantifiable measures historians can produce, this was an upper class like Valladolid itself: inward-looking, interconnected; yet dynamic and in some ways increasingly open, increasingly a part of broader trends and institutions and events outside the province.

As far as can be discerned from the handful of rhetoric-rich documents generated by Michoacanos during this period, their own self-image conformed to the picture of a relatively inclusive and mobile elite that we have pieced together by analyzing patterns of behavior. The most useful of these documents are the petitions sent by various groups in the province to the king in 1805 and early 1806, urging him to suspend the 1804 Consolidación de Vales Reales. These petitions will be analyzed in the context of developing Mexican patriotism in chapter 2, but here it is worth noting that in each of them, wealthy petitioners assigned themselves to a group that also included modest property owners, artisans, and merchant/mule drivers. In other words, in an era in which the number of truly wealthy Michoacán families was no more than 150 to 200, the authors chose to emphasize their identification with a much broader segment of the population, what we might today call the middle class. Of the 537 signers of the petition sent by the "labradores y comerciantes" of Valladolid and its surrounding district, for example, I can certify only 42 as heads of households with assets of at least 20,000 pesos.[74] In all of New Spain — in which there were perhaps 1,000 wealthy families — the Cathedral Chapter warned that "over 10,000 families who today live in comfort and decorum, will lose their patrimonies and will be reduced to indigence."[75] "Ten to twelve thousand honorable families . . . will be ruined," worried the city council of Valladolid.[76]

Obviously, the decision to emphasize the fact that the direct impact of the Consolidation would extend well beyond the minuscule, rich minority to a much more numerous (though still relatively small) strata of modest property owners was meant to influence, to persuade, and certainly cannot be understood to mean that wealth was not an important element of the self-image of economic elites. Nonetheless, having invited middling merchants, owners of modest ranchos, midlevel bureaucrats, teachers, and prosperous artisans to sign the petition, to join them in a cause that affected them all, the wealthy petitioners acknowledged a degree of commonality with the merely "decent" people of Valladolid that had been mainly subliminal before. Put another way, though social mobility between the middle and upper levels of wealth was greater in the late colonial period than it had been earlier in the century, as we have seen, this was probably not something elites could have articulated, or recognized as a pattern or trend. But when they signed their names alongside those of the *gente decente*, they could see before them a visual representation — several pages of signatures, randomly arranged — of a collectivity that had never been concretized before. The significance of this bond for elites was great, and for the middle classes, in light of later events, it may have been even greater.

The Challenge of the Enlightenment: Elites and Ideological Change

One night in July 1787 a conversation between two high church officials — Dr. José Pérez Calama and Dr. Manuel Vicente Yáñez — turned to the "anti-intellectual miasma and political lethargy" that pervaded the intellectual life of Valladolid. They agreed that the weekly billiard and card games attended by prominent churchmen and civil authorities were a symbol of the problem.

Why not transform them into a literary salon in which the former gamesmen would discuss books with religious, historical, and political themes? The next day, the always-energetic Pérez Calama sent Yáñez a proposed set of ground rules for the new gatherings:

> The participants will be able to wear whatever they wish and to come and go as they please; all will be free to smoke and otherwise behave with the same frankness, freedom, and familiarity formerly observed in the *tertulias* of billiards. There will be no seating arrangements; people will take seats as they come in the room, and no one will be expected to rise or pay any other obeisance to anyone else.[77]

Calama's lament and his proposed solution reveal some of the changes in the intellectual and cultural climate of late colonial Michoacán. It is doubtful that a generation earlier the city's "anti-intellectual" tone would have been noted by even the most bookish scholar — it was the willy-nilly influx of "enlightened" ideas (many of them introduced by Calama himself) that highlighted and challenged the "antiquated" culture and intellectual style known as the Mexican baroque. The impact of the Enlightenment on Mexico was concentrated in time (having scarcely stirred a ripple before the 1760s) and powerful in effect: it altered the way people thought about the relations between themselves and God, between themselves and the church, between themselves and the state, and between themselves and the rest of society. This process has been the subject of several excellent studies and will not be examined in detail here, but it is important to place these elements of change alongside the economic, political, and social changes outlined above.[78]

As is suggested by the fact that the Valladolid salon was first proposed by one churchman to another, the Michoacán clergy took the lead in reforming not just the church itself but religion and society in the province. This activism exacerbated fissures within the clerical hierarchy, as progressive clergy introduced new curricula to replace the outmoded reliance on Aristotle and St. Thomas, founded new seminaries with new kinds of chairs to promote new areas of learning, and in general scorned the old teachers and the old ways of thinking.[79] At least equally important, deep wedges were driven between the hierarchy and its reform-minded allies outside the church on the one hand, and, on the other, those elites and non-elites who for a variety of reasons did not wish to change the way they worshipped God, much less the way they went about their daily business.

The hallmark of enlightened Christianity was its emphasis on "simple, interior piety and good works," as against the emotional, extravagant displays of collective public devotion to miraculous images that characterized baroque Catholicism.[80] Enlightened bishops and priests tried to ban as many processions and other "spectacles" as they could, and reacted with disgust to the popular inclination for "uproar, puerile ostentation, and pernicious meetings."[81] They strongly supported the Crown's push in the 1760s and 1770s to turn over to the bishopric the missions of the regular orders, in part because of long-standing rivalries between the friars and the secular church, but in part because they associated with the orders the mysticism, asceticism, and other baroque devotions that they so disdained.[82]

The actions of the enlightened church leaders were at once more palatable and more revolutionary when it came to their emphasis on social activism as a supplement to (or even replacement of) traditional charity and good works. During the severe drought of 1785 to 1786 the bishop and canons personally distributed food to the hungry, as they had always done, but the crisis also spurred a church-sponsored program of public works that included massive road repairs, tree plantings, and rebuilding of the Valladolid aqueduct — all of which were intended primarily to provide work for the unemployed.[83] Even before the crisis, church authorities had explored the idea of promoting industries such as tanneries and cotton and wool workshops to relieve vagrancy, mendicancy, and other "problems" of the poor (and especially of the "weaker sex"). In these proposals, condemnation of the inequities of Mexican society was mainly implicit, and idleness was still seen more as a cause than as a symptom of the problem of widespread poverty, but the solution — creating more jobs — was a new twist on traditional charity.[84]

By the turn of the century, the social criticism was more explicit and more trenchant, and the solutions much more far-reaching. In Manuel Abad y Queipo's well-known analyses, New Spain was depicted as a land of profound inequality. Worse, this inequality was perpetuated by laws that celebrated hierarchy as a key principle of social stability, and locked Indians and other nonwhites into inferior positions by legal enforcement of ethnic difference. Abad's promotion of social mobility and legal equality had been foreshadowed by Calama's rules for his proposed salon, in which he insisted that everyone must be treated the same and should enjoy the same rights as others. But in Abad's hands these rules were linked to proposals much more radical than an open seating arrangement at gatherings of the wealthy: abolition of caste distinctions, division of communal lands, redistribution of some hacienda lands. Abad's assumption was that once a framework of legal equality had been created and private ownership of land made easier, "every individual, no matter what his race or history, would respond to economic incentives" and the result would be enhanced growth and prosperity for all.[85]

Obviously not all wealthy landowners and merchants were willing to follow Abad and other enlightened figures down this road of radical social reform any more than they could all accept the enlightened critique of traditional religious practices. Even Abad himself displayed a certain ambivalence toward full legal equality, most notably in his defense of clerical privilege published in 1799, a tract in which he was forced to defend the right of all "distinguished classes" to enjoy their respective *fueros*.[86] This awkward, partial embrace of the principle of hierarchy had been present in Calama's work as well, when he argued against breaking up wealthy parishes on the grounds that they were needed in order to attract priests of "illustrious birth and fine breeding, of polished ideas and eminent knowledge."[87] It even turned up later in the insurgent priest José María Morelos' insistence on corporate privilege (though Morelos was firmly opposed to ethnic distinctions).[88]

These intra-elite disagreements on the need for or desirability of reform were complicated by a different kind of fissure: the antagonism between peninsulars and creoles that had bubbled to the surface most recently in the 1770s, with the Bourbon policy of preferring peninsular-born Spaniards over Americans for the occupation of public office. It would be a mistake to suppose that philosophical splits always followed ethnic lines. Many Americans, as well as peninsulars, were "enlightened." The close relationship that the creole Hidalgo enjoyed with the Spaniards Pérez Calama and Abad is well known, and it is clear that many other creoles shared the enlightened clergy's penchant for reform. This was perhaps especially true among those creole sons educated at the Tridentine seminary in Valladolid, where they were often taught by activist churchmen.[89] Moreover, some Spaniards as well as some creoles were known to oppose the social engineering advocated by the most progressive of the clergy and Bourbon officials; in fact, the most vigorous opposition to Pérez Calama and Abad within the Cathedral Chapter actually came from other Europeans. And among Spaniards — including most merchants — outside of the church and the royal bureaucracy, there cannot have been universal admiration for the more extreme "enlightened" proposals, especially as so many of them owned rural property that was threatened by the vague proposals for redistribution of hacienda lands, and (along with wealthy creoles) enjoyed privileges conferred by their whiteness that were threatened by a movement toward legal equality.[90]

But there is no escaping the fact that the enlightened project was identified with Europe and Europeans. The strong role played by the peninsula-born clergy in the push to modernize Christianity, the church, and society; the strong role played by the Bourbon state in promoting and legislating new social arrangements; and the European (especially French) philosophical underpinnings of the new currents of thought all contributed to that impression. The most progressive clergy were peninsulars: Pérez Calama, Abad y Queipo, Bishop Antonio de San Miguel, Dr. Manuel de la Bárcena, and others in what Brading describes as a "tight circle of [European Spaniards] who all prided themselves on their enlightened ideas and their practical competence in governing the diocese [and who] dealt easily with the leading merchants of Valladolid . . . who were also from the Peninsula."[91] And the incompatibility of European-inspired reformism and Mexican patriotism was underlined by the fact that the "modern" religious style, with its rejection of cults and miracles and popular display, included an attack on the most potent symbol of American-ness, the Virgin of Guadalupe.[92] I will argue in chapter 2 that it is important not to imagine political and social thought as exclusively defined by the creole-peninsular split, but at the same time it is useful to note that there were patriotic overtones to the philosophical differences of the period. In the end, as Brading points out, both Abad and Hidalgo would subordinate their shared social principles to loyalty to their respective *patrias*; the split between the old friends was symbolized by Abad's excommunication of Hidalgo in 1810.[93]

Perhaps the most important feature of the enlightenment in New Spain is that it called into question traditional alliances (between church and state, among wealthy individuals wherever they were born, between the church and these elites), and helped to define new ones (among those born in America and those born in Spain, among those embracing social change and those who feared it — predilections that later earned them labels like "liberals" and "conservatives"), bringing tensions within institutions like the church to the foreground. All of these new identities were being forged during a period of rapid change in the material world, and were at once sharpened and confused by the examples of the North American Revolution and the French Revolution. The changing attitudes toward France in the wake of the Revolution, for example, hint at the uncertainty and flux that characterized elite ideological positionings and repositionings. In 1793 the European-born bishop Fray Antonio de San Miguel turned away from enlightened ideas that he had previously embraced, when they became associated with the French attack on religion and monarchy. A vigorous advocate of the abolition of caste distinctions and legal equality for all, and a student of many French philosophers — including Montesquieu, Rousseau, and possibly even Voltaire — San Miguel came to excoriate the Revolution's celebration of the principle of equality, and its destruction of the "received notions and ideas of subordination . . . which [before the Revolution] had made the French people happy."[94] Meanwhile, some creoles who would later reject it embraced the Revolution, while others would reverse the process. In 1800, for example, the *alcalde ordinario* of Pátzcuaro filed a report on a dance in a neighborhood known as "la Francia," which was attended by "many people of both sexes," and which spilled out into the streets as partygoers shouted "Viva la Francia! Viva el Arbol de la Libertad!" and other even more "scandalous" propositions. One of the eyewitnesses, a violinist/barber, said that the people who knocked on his door to get him to play were "gente decente," and he named some of Pátzcuaro's wealthy residents. The *alcalde* who reported this incident so disapprovingly was Lic. Nicolás de Michelena, who just nine years later would shift ideological gears and join a conspiracy to overthrow Spanish rule in Mexico.[95] In short, while it is not clear whether Pérez Calama's politico-literary salon ever came into being, it *is* clear that the open and probing political atmosphere he so eagerly sought — with attendant ambiguity and back-tracking and side-switching and mind-changing — existed in Valladolid by the turn of the century. It would take an obvious challenge to a group clearly self-defined as American to turn this intellectual ferment into an ideological direction, but the ferment itself was an essential first step toward clarification and action.

Conclusion

The collection of cities and villages and haciendas that made up the intendancy of Valladolid was not really a coherent political entity at the turn of the century. After 1805, as I will argue in chapter 2, elites (and others) living in the intendancy did begin to imagine themselves as citizens of a state (the state of Michoacán) and a nation, but before then, their self-consciousness, their identity, was much more powerfully shaped by other factors.

They thought of themselves as leaders in an economy that was expanding and whose potential for continued expansion seemed great. That is, some of the very things that made the late eighteenth century a world of trouble for non-elites — high prices, rising rents, loss of access to land, falling wages — gave the wealthy the confidence to remodel their houses, plant more crops, build new storehouses that would enable them to wait out low-price cycles, invest in irrigation systems, open up new lands and buy new haciendas, expand commercial networks. The problems of which they were acutely aware seemed either fixable (high taxes), or so chronic and time immemorial as to dull the perception that there might be an alternative (the shortage of credit), or to be improving (poor roads and communications, high transport costs, low rates of profit), or temporary (unpredictable and uneven supply networks, which they attributed, only partially correctly, to the interruption of shipping caused by Spain's involvement in European wars), or unfortunate, but ultimately unimportant in their own lives (the grinding poverty of the vast majority).

They thought of themselves as part of a social world whose boundaries were generous but not ambiguous or confusing, a world in which there was a satisfying, comforting blend of hierarchy and status consciousness on the one hand, and inclusivity and mobility on the other. There was room for Spaniards as well as creoles, for the *gente decente* as well as for the titled nobility, for the marginally well-to-do as well as for the fabulously wealthy, and even for the occasional illegitimate child of "good" parents, or for the brilliant or successful not-quite-white. They were well aware of the enormous gap between themselves and the *pueblo;* it was, in fact, this gap that allowed for the relatively high degrees of mobility and accessibility within what Abad y Queipo consistently described as the "upper two-tenths" of the population. There was such a difference, in other words, between the urban or urban-oriented middle classes and the Indians and castas of the rural villages that the differences between the wealthy and the merely respectable melted away.

They were beginning to be forced to assume an identity on one side or the other of the great intellectual divide that was emerging in the second half of the century. Those who were receptive to the new ways of thinking about the world — rationalist, secular, individualist — that broke like a tidal wave over Mexico suddenly felt themselves part of a global group of like-minded people. Intellectually, at least, they were linked as never before to places they had probably never visited: Paris, London, Boston, Washington. Those who were frightened or offended by the new currents of thought gravitated toward each other, but not with great self-assuredness. If the dominant tone of thinking about one's chances for economic success, or one's social position, was complacent and self-satisfied, the dominant tone of thought where abstract issues of philosophy and history were concerned was considerably less certain, more questioning — just as Pérez Calama had hoped would come to pass when he proposed the formation of a literary salon in Valladolid in 1787.

One of the great abstractions of the day that might be expected to have come up repeatedly at the meetings of the salon (or even over the billiard table) was the relationship between the New World and the Old, between America and Europe. But it seems likely that for most provincial elites the shining example of political liberalism and nationalism presented by the United States at the time of its independence did not have much local resonance. Most elites at the turn of the century thought of themselves in a political sense as reasonably contented and valued vassals of a remote king. In many ways, of course, the influx of "enlightened" ideas around the desirability of a freer, less hierarchical society and a freer, less monopoly-oriented economy, which many of them embraced, implied the desirability of a freer, more autonomous political system. But that notion remained mainly implicit — at least until 1805.

The Huarte Sons and Sons-in-Law
in the Wars for Independence

The wars for independence put the Huarte family, like many others, at generational odds with itself. The patriarch, Isidro Huarte, as a highly visible and widely resented Spaniard, had much to fear from the Hidalgo Revolt, with its demands for the death of *gachupines*. As Hidalgo approached Valladolid, Huarte fled to Mexico City, where he spent the early years of the insurrection, leaving the Michoacán enterprises to the care of his two eldest sons, José Antonio, a priest, and Isidro, a lawyer. Neither of the sons was entirely pleased to shoulder this burden. José Antonio later wrote that his own interests (by now he was running the hacienda of Guadalupe more or less on his own account) had suffered during the rebellion because he had to obey his father's command that he protect the family mercantile interests before his own. "Perhaps I would not have lost so much," he wrote, "if I had been able to defend my property, as others who escaped without serious harm were able to do, especially since priests were treated by the insurgents with great consideration."[1]

Two of Huarte's sons-in-law, Agustín de Iturbide (m. Ana Huarte) and Pascual Alzúa, (m. Carmen Huarte) took an active role in putting down the rebellion. Iturbide, as a colonel in the Spanish army, directed many counter-insurgent operations, apparently with some relish—though he was, of course, in the vanguard of the second and successful push for independence in 1821. Alzúa played a much more minor role in undermining the insurgency, serving as a prosecutor in a case of pro-Morelos conspiracy in Valladolid in 1813.[2]

At the opposite end of the political spectrum, the youngest of Huarte's sons by Ana Manuela Muñiz, Joaquín, sided openly with the insurgents. Fifteen years after the outbreak of the Hidalgo Revolt, trying to make the case that his co-heirs should shoulder part of a 3,000-peso fine that Comandante Torcuato Trujillo levied against him for his participation in the insurrection, Joaquín claimed that he had joined the rebels only the better to protect the Huarte business interests. The arbiters of the claims upon the Huarte fortune, however, disagreed; no matter how unjust Trujillo's action might have been, it was nonetheless caused, they agreed, not by Joaquín's attempt to defend the family but by his decision in favor of the rebels.[3] Another son, Manuel Huarte, later married the daughter of an insurgent, José María Izasaga, but he was too young to have taken sides during the insurgent decade.[4]

The political sympathies of the other Huarte children fell somewhere in between the counterinsurgency of their brothers-in-law Iturbide and Alzúa and the proinsurgency of their brother Joaquín. None of the Huarte sons or sons-in-law were a part of the independence-minded Valladolid conspiracy of 1809 (which was led by their family rival, Mariano Michelena), and they came down squarely on the side of independence only after the insurgency had faded. Still, it is clear that Isidro and Ramón Huarte had credentials with and sympathy for the movement for independence well before Iturbide's scheme made it easy for almost all creoles to embrace the idea. As a member of the Valladolid *ayuntamiento* in 1810, for example, Isidro spoke up in favor of creole rights even in the context of that overwhelmingly Spanish-born body; a few months later, as Hidalgo approached Valladolid, he was one of the three men the city council sent to arrange for terms of the city's surrender, presumably because he was thought to be acceptable to the rebels.[5] After independence, as we will see, he firmly established his liberal credentials in a long career as a public servant. Ramón, meanwhile, was elected to the second *ayuntamiento constitucional* of Valladolid in 1820, an institution which was, in its own words, dedicated to the "free elections" and "democratic principles" enshrined in the recently reinstated 1812 Spanish constitution.[6]

The Huarte family serves, in many ways, as a microcosm of elite responses to the insurgency. Two of the patriarch's sons-in-law were loyalists, though both "converted" to the cause of independence late in the decade. One of the sons joined the insurgency. But the rest of this second generation of Huartes seems to have been part of an ambivalent middle, with sympathy for both political autonomy and the peculiar proclerical liberalism articulated by Hidalgo and Morelos, but materially wounded by the economic collapse that attended the insurgent wars, and not inclined to rush into a movement for independence over which they had only limited influence. This upper-class ambivalence would carry over into the post-independence period, complicating their struggle to gain control of the process of state-building.

CHAPTER TWO

Imperial Crisis, Economic Collapse, and Political Realignment: From the Consolidación de Vales Reales to Independence, 1804–21

The conventional view of the upper classes' role in Mexican independence swings on their fear of the "masses," from whom they were divided by a vast gap in wealth and income, by culture and race, and by centuries of legislation that embraced the principles of hierarchy and separate treatment for different social and ethnic groups. Naturally nervous about any political program or philosophy that advocated breaking down the legal and economic barriers between whites, *castas*, and indigenous peoples, or between rich and poor — the argument goes — they were terrified by the programs, social composition, and violent methods of the popular rebellion that broke out in 1810 and appalled by the destruction of their own property that the insurgency brought in its wake. All this caused them (temporarily) to put aside their grievances against Spain and Spaniards, with whom, after all, they shared important qualities that they did not share with the foot soldiers of the Hidalgo Rebellion: whiteness, education, and property ownership. In other words, elites shrank from associating with the insurgency, no matter how much, before 1810, they may have talked a fine line on the merits of autonomy. When independence did come, it was spearheaded by conservatives, even reactionaries, who feared resurgent political liberalism in Spain after 1820.

There is no doubt that rejection of revolutionary ideals and horror at the spectacle of armed and impassioned *castas* motivated some elites to help Spain put down the rebellion. Moreover, it seems clear that over the course of the insurgent decade, well-to-do creoles rediscovered some of the fundamental commonalities of interest that they shared with rich Spaniards. But for most this common ground was located on a complex terrain, and not just in blind fear of the insurgency. In fact, wealthy creoles joined the insurgency in fairly large numbers, and in many cases they promoted, not rejected, cross-class alliances, even accepting the leadership of non-elites. Though many were no longer active supporters of the insurgency by 1815, this seems to have been more because of splits within the movement that rendered it increasingly ineffective than because of fear of its excesses. Meanwhile, those who had initially opposed the insurgency were experiencing disenchantments of their own, especially with the manner in which Spanish officials handled the counterinsurgency. Thus, it appears that in Michoacán — which was, admittedly, from Spain's point of view "the most obstinate province in the Kingdom" — genuine reactionaries were a small minority, and most elites eventually supported at least some goals of the insurgents and many goals of the liberal 1812 Spanish constitution.[1] This in turn permitted the formation of a tenuous and shallow cross-class consensus in 1821, under the leadership of Agustín de Iturbide, that led directly to independence.

The Politics of Independence

As early as the first generation after the conquest, "Spaniards" born in America felt they were different from Europeans.[2] What was bound up in that sense of difference changed markedly over the centuries, but the general direction of change was from a diffuse, vague feeling of unjust disinheritance mixed with deep ambivalence regarding the "other" Americans (the indigenous population), to a more focused, prideful patriotism. This patriotism was sharpened in the eighteenth century by the creoles' need to defend themselves against the "evidence" of American inferiority offered up by European "scientists," and against *visitador general* José de Gálvez's preference for Spaniards over creoles when it came to who was to govern and administer New Spain.[3]

But creole self-consciousness seems to have reached a temporary peak in the 1770s, followed by a decline in intensity. As David Brading observes, the 1771 protest by the Mexico City *ayuntamiento* against Gálvez's policies was the "last grand statement of the traditional themes of creole patriotism in New Spain" for decades.[4] Though ten years later another strong creole rebuttal of European anti-Americanism was published — the Jesuit Francisco

Javier Clavijero's *Historia antigua de México*, written from his exile in Italy — its full impact was not felt until after independence, when it finally became available in Spanish.

There are several possible explanations for the diminished vigor of creole patriotism in the 1780s. First, even before Gálvez's death in 1787, the most virulent state-sponsored anti-Americanism had passed, and creole office holding had begun to trend upward once again. As we have seen, both the intendancy system — which gave the provincial upper classes, including creoles, greater informal access to political power — and the expansion of the military, which was quite open to creole officers, had helped ease the sting of Gálvez's policies. Finally, beginning in 1792, when yet another round of expensive European wars began, creole ties to the embattled mother country were reinforced by natural sentiment and by official propaganda and concerted efforts to secure American loyalty (and financial aid).

In short, there is every indication that in the 1780s, 1790s, and early 1800s all but the most politically liberal, U.S.-inspired Michoacanos were loyal to Spain and committed to the colonial system. In 1784 one prominent creole in Valladolid, asked to comment on a proposal to set up workshops to provide work for the poor, warned that promotion of local manufacturing could lead to the "imponderable evil" of loosening ties with Spain. Worse, he continued, economic self-sufficiency could lead to "an ill-fated independence of another sort."[5] After the onset of war with France, when Spain, needing American silver more than ever, put out the call for voluntary loans, the wealthy of Michoacán responded. In 1792 rich Vallisoletanos, including both Spaniards and creoles, donated the staggering sum of 85,912 pesos to build a 74-cannon warship. In 1793 another impressive collection was taken up, again from both Spaniards and creoles.[6]

In light of this record of voluntary donation to the Crown, it was with disbelief that in early 1805 elites in Michoacán first got word of the Consolidación de Vales Reales, the royal decree requiring those who had borrowed pious funds (that is to say, most property owners) to redeem their debts and to lend that money to the Crown. Having freely and generously supported the Crown as individuals and as members of corporations, well-to-do Michoacanos — again, both creoles and peninsulars — were stunned that the Crown should choose such an insulting and destructive means of raising more funds.

Obviously, they were forced to conclude, the king did not comprehend what he was asking of American property holders; he did not understand how different was America from Spain. The petitions (or "representations," as they were called) sent to him by various groups from Michoacán all proceeded from the assumption that once he was informed and educated he would suspend the decree. The strong, clear evocation of difference between Spain and New Spain that is a key part of the representations thus began as a rhetorical device, as a part of the structure of protest.[7] Its ultimate effect, however, was not only to revive but to go well beyond the American self-consciousness and patriotism of the 1770s.

Several of the representations began by acknowledging that in Spain, where the Consolidation had been in effect since 1798, it had had mixed but mainly positive results. This was true not only from the point of view of the Crown, whose revenues were enhanced, but from that of property owners, whose numbers had grown, as much of the property held in mortmain by the church (the bulk of ecclesiastical wealth on the peninsula) was sold off. The 1804 decree extending the Consolidation to Mexico was phrased in such a way as to make it seem that the king beneficently desired his vassals the world over to gain the advantages already enjoyed by his Spanish subjects.

But in New Spain, unlike on the peninsula, the petitioners pointed out, the pious funds owned very little property; instead most of their wealth was in the form of mortgages on privately owned real estate. To force owners to pay off these debts was to ensure that the vast majority would have to sell or cede the affected property. But because virtually everyone would be in the same situation, there would be no buyers for the property, and the result would be the financial ruin of the colony. Furthermore, also in contrast to the situation in Spain, the church was the only lending institution in the Americas, and if it no longer had funds to lend — which would be the immediate effect of the legislation — the already inadequate circulation of capital in New Spain would cease for all intents and purposes, and everyone, even those not affected directly by the decree, would suffer. Moreover, in Mexico there was far less capital in circulation than there was in Spain, but more capital was needed in order to maintain a store or to cultivate the land and to support a respectable lifestyle. This made the consequences of removing church capital from circulation all the more onerous in America.[8] In general, then, the problem — which was, of course, unresolvable — was that "the great distance that separates us from Madrid makes it difficult [for the king] to know the facts of the situation; and the facts are of absolute necessity for good government."[9]

These lengthy and fervid supplications fell on deaf royal ears. From the Crown's point of view the Consolidation had much to recommend it: it not only raised much-needed funds, but it served at the same time to undercut the power of the church, a project squarely in line with late Bourbon anticlericalism. Four years later the measure was still in effect. By then, we may presume, at the very least the nearly 700 signers of the five Michoacano representations, and probably the thousands more who were directly and indirectly touched by the decree, had become accustomed to, and in some cases persuaded by, the logic and some of the language of autonomy. If Spain did not understand America, could not be persuaded to try to understand America, and could not be trusted to pass laws that did not hurt America disproportionately, then at least theoretically Mexican self-government, if not full independence, was the next step.

The Conspiracy of 1809

The leap from adopting the logic of autonomy to embracing the actuality of independence, however, was enormous, and no matter how much the Consolidation and the lack of satisfactory official response to their protests alienated provincial elites, it is impossible to suppose that without a full-fledged crisis of authority it would have been taken any time soon. But that crisis did come in 1808, when Napoleon's army invaded the peninsula, Charles IV abdicated, and his heir Ferdinand VII was imprisoned. In August of that year Dr. Manuel de la Bárcena gave (and the city council quickly published) an impassioned speech in the Valladolid cathedral, urging his listeners to stand fast with Spain, with whom "we Spaniards who inhabit America" share common blood, language, customs, and most of all religion.[10] Ferdinand, he almost pleaded, will be, must be, a better ruler than his inept father with his treacherous advisers; we must rally round the son, even though he is unproven and the task of defeating Napoleon seems insurmountable. The unspoken alternative to loyalty — independence — would open a Pandora's box of evils: "a volcano," he warned ominously, "begins when just a bit of sulfur fermenting in the hidden depths of the earth catches fire, and the fire grows until there is an explosion, destroying everything in its path."[11] But the very burden and tone of his message suggests that he feared Pandora's box was already open.

And indeed it was, if not by August then soon after. Just a month after Bárcena delivered this sermon to his Michoacán audience, events in Mexico City ratcheted up tensions already high from the accumulated resentments of the Consolidation debacle and the uncertainty around the question of who legitimately ruled Spain (and Spanish America). Viceroy Iturrigaray, himself caught up in the chaos of the moment, sided with the creoles of the Mexico City *ayuntamiento* who wanted to form a junta in Mexico City to rule in Ferdinand's place. A group of nervous peninsulars viewed this action as tantamount to a declaration of independence and arrested Iturrigaray in September.

This coup had the immediate effect of bringing to the foreground what had been, for elites, a dimension of the Spain-America split submerged for decades: the rivalry between creoles and peninsulars.[12] The organized opposition to the Consolidation had been a joint project involving both creole and peninsular elites. But from 1808 on, in Valladolid and elsewhere, politics swirled around mutual distrust and antagonism between "europeos" and "americanos." The shift was reflected in an exchange in the Valladolid city council in May 1809 concerning the election of a representative for New Spain to the Junta Central in Cádiz. Though the majority of the council favored submitting a list of candidates that included both creoles and peninsulars, the lone creole, Lic. Isidro Huarte, argued that the *vocal* must be someone born in America. Only an American would enjoy the full trust of *all* the people of New Spain, and furthermore (he continued somewhat perversely) since the Real Orden specifically asked that only "zealous Patriots" be nominated, and since the dictionary suggested a meaning for "patricio" that linked it to natality, it was clear that the order intended that America send an American. Though Huarte was extremely diplomatic in his insistence, agreeing that, in a loose sense of the word, longtime residents of the Americas could be considered "patriotic," his willingness to bring up the subject at all in this thoroughly peninsular setting is striking, and suggests that creole-peninsular tensions ran strong in the city.[13]

Indeed, the situation in the intendancy of Valladolid was especially volatile. In 1809 the deaths of both the well-liked intendant, Felipe Díaz de Hortega, and the scarcely arrived new bishop, Mariano Moriana y Zafrilla, left the city and the province without strong official leadership, at a time when, as we have seen, strong official leadership at the regal and viceregal levels was also missing. Meanwhile, another severe drought dried municipal water supplies to a trickle and created a dangerous corn and meat shortage, just when the arrival in 1808 of the first regiment of infantry to quarter down in Valladolid meant that there were more mouths to feed.[14] The city councils of both Valladolid and Pátzcuaro tried to alleviate conditions by importing corn, but prices were extraordinarily high. The Valladolid *ayuntamiento* contracted to purchase 3,000 *fanegas* of corn from outside the province at 30 reales the *fanega*, some three to four times the price that had been in effect during the past decade or so.[15] In Pátzcuaro the city council borrowed 12,000 pesos from private citizens for the same purpose.[16] But famine in the countryside had driven a large vagrant population into the cities, and the efforts of the *ayuntamientos* were inadequate.[17] The presence of so many newly arrived soldiers and hungry and homeless men, women, and children in their cities must have added a new dimension, and a certain urgency, to the elites' preoccupation with the uneasy political situation.

All this was presided over by an interim intendant, the *asesor* José Alonso de Terán. Perhaps recognizing the weakness of his own authority, Terán chose not to exercise it gratuitously; his strategy, in fact, seems to have been, where possible, to ignore what was going on around him. This must not have been easy to do. It is clear from the statements of dozens of witnesses that rumors and plots were almost openly discussed on street corners, over store counters, and in scarcely encoded letters that circulated throughout the province. The creoles, it was said, planned to send all the *gachupines* (except priests) back to Spain, and if the peninsulars resisted, to kill them. For their part, the *gachupines* planned to kill the "leading creoles," and had organized secret military training exercises to that purpose in a vacant lot across from the house of the Conde de Sierragorda.[18]

It is difficult to know how seriously these rumors were taken. Though one of the "leading creoles," Lic. Nicolás de Michelena, claimed not to believe that his peninsular "friends" were plotting his assassination, another creole leader, Capt. José María García de Obeso, testified that he asked his wife's brothers to sleep at his house to help defend the family against attack.[19] Decades later Nicolás's brother Mariano also recalled a sense of danger: by September 1809 the Spaniards had taken measures "to spy on us and to intimidate us, threatening us and forming a united front against us. We met regularly to compare notes and to discuss the means by which to defend ourselves."[20] These creole-led "discussions" were held at the houses of García de Obeso and Lic. Nicolás de Michelena, who were, with Mariano Michelena, the leaders of the Valladolid conspiracy of 1809.

All three of these men, along with most of the others implicated in the conspiracy, were members of the provincial elite. Mariano Michelena, the man whom Alamán called the "soul" of the Valladolid conspiracy, was an *alferez* of the Regimiento de la Corona and, with his brother and co-conspirator

Nicolás, owner of the vast sugar and indigo hacienda of La Parota, near Urecho.[21] Nicolás was a *licenciado*, a *subdelegado* for Zamora, and owner in his own right of a modest hacienda near Pátzcuaro. José María García de Obeso, like Mariano Michelena and six other elite conspirators, was a military officer, and he was also in charge of his wife's inherited hacienda and his recently deceased father's mercantile operations.

As Table 2.1 shows, at least 20 and possibly 24 of the 36 men named in connection with the conspiracy were wealthy. In addition, 5 of the non-elite participants were employed by either García de Obeso or one of the Michelena brothers, and all of the others (with the exception of the Indian *cacique*, Pedro Rosales) seem to have been *gente decente*, non-elite chiefly by virtue of their very modest wealth and their subordinate occupational positions vis-à-vis the others. José Antonio Morraz owned a tannery.[22] Fray Vicente Santa María was a well-respected intellectual who lectured regularly at the seminary.[23] Camilo Camacho — who, according to slightly different criteria, might be considered elite — owned a bakery and administered the splendid hacienda of San Bartolomé; he may have been a nephew of the owner of a vast cattle hacienda (Canario, owned by Andrés de la Piedra, which was Camacho's second name), and he was a friend of several of the wealthy participants, alongside whom he had been educated at the Tridentine Seminary.[24]

Nonetheless, despite its overwhelmingly creole elite character, there were both rhetorical and real bridges built between this group and the true non-elites, the mulattoes and castas and Indians of the province, especially those in and around Valladolid. To appreciate the significance of the creoles' discursive overtures to their "fellow Americans," it must be recalled that just four years earlier the fulcrums of elite identity, as expressed in the petitions against the Consolidation, were class and residence. There had been no community of interest on this issue between rich Americans and poor Americans; the key element of commonality was that property holders living in America (no matter *where* they were born) perceived themselves as victimized by "bad government" from across the Atlantic. By 1809, however, in the wake of the arrest of Viceroy Iturrigaray and against a backdrop of building centuries-old creole patriotism, place of birth took precedence. Creole elites, drumming up support for their project to overthrow colonial rule, went out of their way to identify — metaphorically — with the Indians against the *gachupines*. García de Obeso put it most bluntly in a conversation with the Indian *cacique* Pedro Rosales: "nosotros somos Yndianos Yndios, todos somos unos, yo también

TABLE 2.1
Participants in the 1809 Valladolid Conspiracy

Economic elites (n = 20)

Military officers: Capt. José María García Obeso; Alferez José Mariano de Michelena; Capt. José María Abarca (also *subdelegado* for Pátzcuaro); Capt. Mariano Jaso; Capt. Mariano Quevedo; Capt. Manuel Muñíz; Capt. Ruperto Mier; Capt. Juan Bautista Guerra.

Licenciados: Nicolás Michelena (also *subdelegado for Zamora*); José Antonio Soto y Saldaña; José María Izasaga; Antonio Castro

Clerics: Br. Manuel Ruiz de Chávez y Larrina, cura Huango; Br. Manuel de la Torre Lloreda, cura Pátzcuaro; Dr. Antonio María Uraga, cura Maravatío; Lic. José Maria Zarco, prebend; Br. Ignacio Arevalo, cura Acámbaro; Br. José Antonio Jiménez.

Other: Francisco Ruiz de Chávez y Carillo (nephew of Br. Manuel Ruiz de Chávez y Larrina; family owns hacienda de Irapeo); and his brother, Mariano Ruiz de Chavez y Carillo.

Economic status uncertain (n = 4)

José de Villar. May be related to Emérito de Villar, who owned a small hacienda near Zacapu.

Martín de Navarrete. May be related to Manuel Martínez de Navarrete, the "patriotic" poet from Zamora who died in 1809.

Luis Gonzaga Correa. *Subdelegado* for Zitácuaro and administrator of the hacienda de Jaripeo (owned by Br. Miguel de Hidalgo).

Lic. Antonio Cumplido. May be related to a relatively wealthy mercantile family with same surname; in 1822, however, figured among deputies named to the constitutional congress of the Empire who needed financial aid in order to make the trip to Mexico City.

Non-elites (n = 12)

Mariano Peguero; Fray Vicente de Santa María; Camilo Camacho, bakery owner and administrator of the hacienda de San Bartolomé; José Antonio Morraz, owner of tannery; Romualdo Carnero; Feliciano Carrillo, clerk for García Obeso; Lorenzo Carrillo, administrator of Mariano Michelena's mining interests in Ozumatlán; Rafael Solchaga, administrator of Nicolás Michelena's hacienda de Comiembaro; José Maria Jaurrieta, administrador of García Obeso's *obraje*; Pedro Rosales, Fiscal de la Santa Cruzada, Indian cacique; Manuel González (el Puruandireño), renter of a rancho; Ygnacio Montero, second sergeant.

SOURCES: ANM, AHPJ, AHMM, AHSM, AHCP, Vega Juanino, López de Lara, "Cuaderno tercero de la causa. . . ."
NOTE: I define "economic elites" as those with personal or family wealth of over 20,000 pesos, and "non-elites" as those with personal or family wealth of under 5,000 pesos.

soy Yndiano" (loosely, "we are all Americans and Indians, we are all as one, I too am an Indian").[25] Manuel Abad y Queipo, writing in May of 1810 (less than four months before the outbreak of the Hidalgo Rebellion), warned that this rhetorical alliance, based on nothing but birthplace, would result in a ruinous insurrection: "Eight-tenths of the population are Indians and *castas*, who own scarcely any property, not even their homes, and find themselves in a state somewhere between abject and miserable. . . . But [still] they side with the American Spaniards against the European Spaniards, only because the latter are foreigners." They must be given a reason to side with the Spaniards, he continued, urging yet once again the abolition of Indian tribute and the removal of a mercantile tax that bore heavily on small businesses run by the poor.[26]

But it is clear that the alliance between the creole leaders of the Valladolid conspiracy and Abad's "eight-tenths" went beyond the rhetorical. In fact, if the conspiracy were to succeed, it was necessary that Indians join the cause. Repeatedly, potential creole adherents were assured that the movement would garner the support of the indigenous population by quickly declaring the abolition of tribute and the *cajas de comunidad*.[27] And it seems that in Valladolid and elsewhere in the province there was a more or less formal agreement between creoles and Indians that the latter would rise up on a prearranged signal from the former.[28] The crucial intermediary was Pedro Rosales, a *cacique principal* who had contacts and influence throughout the province by virtue of his role as a *fiscal* for the Santa Cruzada. We know that Rosales was asked by García de Obeso to get the governors of the Indian *barrios* around Valladolid to turn out their people in the plaza across from García's house on December 22 at ten o'clock in the morning. We can probably assume that this late-in-the-game contact was not the first between García de Obeso and Rosales.[29]

There are also hints of some organized links between the conspirators and the non-Indian "plebe" of Valladolid. The most direct suggestion comes from a question Terán asked the Franciscan Fray Antonio Seguí during his post-conspiracy investigation, regarding "someone who promised to have the Negroes of the Barrio de la Columna ready to rise in insurrection."[30] (Seguí responded that he knew nothing of this.) There is also the testimony of a blacksmith who claims to have been recruited to make 50 to 100 knives "to be delivered to the poor" in time for the insurrection.[31] In any event, it seems likely that the creoles were counting on the "plebe," just as they were counting on the Indians — and probably with good reason, as the anti-Spanish sentiments of the former do not seem to have been at all ambiguous.[32] This sentiment was, perhaps, something of a constant in the late eighteenth century, given the simmering tensions between the rural and urban poor and the Spanish merchants who made fortunes selling to them.[33] But much evidence points to a sudden sharpening of these tensions on the feast day of the Virgin of Guadalupe — the American saint — on 12 December 1809, when large numbers of rural people traditionally came to the city for the festivities and there mingled with "léperos" and other poor urban dwellers. Probably having had a good bit to drink, they taunted Spaniards by reciting insulting verses and spread rumors about Spaniards having poisoned the drinking water, as well as about the alleged Spanish plot to kill the leaders of the creole "party" the next day.[34]

The Valladolid conspiracy — and there apparently was a relatively elaborate plan, which was burned the night before the leaders were arrested — was denounced before it could be put into effect. García de Obeso and Fray Vicente Santa María were quickly arrested; the arrests of Lic. Nicolás and Mariano de Michelena, Br. Manuel Lloreda, Camilo Camacho, Manuel González, and Pedro Rosales followed shortly thereafter. A renegade attempt on the part of Lic. José Antonio Soto y Saldaña to incite the urban poor and the Indian communities after García de Obeso's arrest came to naught. Several witnesses heard him shout as he rode through the neighborhoods of the city on horseback that "the moment has arrived! Now that the soldiers are distracted [by the arrests], we must take up our weapons!" But despite one report that as many as 40 men rode with him, faces covered, he was unable to jump-start the rebellion, and he fled the city.[35] In May, the Michelena brothers and García de Obeso were exiled from the province.

But less than five months later, after a similar conspiracy in Querétaro was also denounced, Br. Miguel de Hidalgo, like Soto y Saldaña, decided to try to start the revolution without his coconspirators. This time the effort was successful.

Hidalgo in Michoacán

When word reached Terán, the interim intendant, of the uprising led by Hidalgo, he called an emergency session of the Valladolid city council. Though the full dimensions of Hidalgo's campaign were not yet appreciated, the mostly peninsular councilmen found plenty to chill them in the reports of looting and pillaging of European-owned stores and homes. They nervously agreed to send two-thirds of the troops stationed in Valladolid to Celaya and/or Querétaro to help defeat the rebels. Within days, however, came the doubly shocking news that *gachupines* had been not just robbed and occasionally murdered, but executed en masse in Guanajuato, and that Hidalgo had turned south toward Valladolid. The city council held another meeting even more frantic than the last to discuss their next step. The question of whether or not the Europeans ought to stay or flee was, naturally, debated with passion, some arguing that flight was the prudent course of action, and others objecting that the departure of the Spaniards would demoralize the Americans who remained. There was also some difficulty deciding which officials ought to command the defense of the city, since, it was pointed out, almost all of the top military hierarchy of Valladolid had been compromised in the conspiracy of 1809. On these issues, it was decided that the Europeans must stay and that the defense of the city should be entrusted to Prebend Agustín de Ledos, who was named Comandante de la Caballería (and whose qualifications for such a position are a mystery), and to a socially distinguished retired militia captain, Juan Antonio Aguilera, who was named Comandante de Urbanos.[36]

In preparation for the attack the troops that had departed for Querétaro were hastily recalled. Blacksmiths melted down the bells of the cathedral to fashion lances and *media lunas*. The causeways into the city were demolished and roads blocked. The wrought-iron balconies of some houses were removed to prevent access through the second stories, and to be melted down for weapons. Women and children prepared to go to the convents for protection. The Spanish population busied itself making wills and either burying valuables in the patios of houses or turning them over to American friends for safekeeping.[37]

As Hidalgo's army approached, and as word came that royalist reinforcements from Mexico City had been captured in Acámbaro, panic spread. When Aldama reached Indaparapeo, only a day's march from Valladolid, with Hidalgo less than a day behind in Zinapécuaro, many Europeans began to flee by whatever road they thought safest. Among those who tried to escape were Terán and Abad y Queipo. Terán's group was captured in Huetamo, and he was brought back to Valladolid and later executed. Abad, who took a different road, made it safely to Mexico City, although not without mishap: his convoy was attacked twice by insurgents, despite the presence of 400 escort troops.[38]

After the departure of the Europeans yet another emergency meeting of the city council and other influential citizens of Valladolid was called on 15 October 1810. It was presided over by a wealthy and well-connected creole named José María Anzorena, whom Hidalgo later appointed as intendant. Aldama had sent word that if the city did not surrender he would enter "a sangre y fuego."[39] The consensus of the meeting was that all previous plans to defend the city should be abandoned and that representatives of the church, army, and city council should go to Indaparapeo to meet Hidalgo and offer him the adherence of the city. The church representative, Lic. Sebastián de Betancourt, later described the meeting with the revolutionaries in despairing language. He said that he tried to convince Aldama that it was wrong to persecute the Europeans, that "these men live with us, have creole wives and creole children." Aldama, he reported, replied that if his own (Spanish) father came to Mexico, he would arrest him, too, a "scandalous" reply that Betancourt said "filled [his] heart with grief."[40] The representative of the city council, Lic. Isidro Huarte, then tried to convince Hidalgo not to bring into the city the 20,000 "indios" that were part of the army. Hidalgo and Allende refused. Thus the three men — Betancourt, Huarte, and Capt. José María Arancivia, the representative of the army — returned to Valladolid, having accomplished only the surrender of the city under an impossible-to-enforce promise that looting would be foresworn. Two days later, on 17 October, Hidalgo entered Valladolid.

According to Alamán, Hidalgo's followers fell on the houses of the most prominent Spaniards, destroying what they could not use, carry off, or drink. At one point Allende allegedly had to fire into the crowd, resulting in some deaths, in an attempt to contain the mayhem.[41] Looting, sacking of houses and stores, and much consumption of liberated *aguardiente*, sherry, and imported French wine continued for three days (Hidalgo is said to have accused the Europeans of poisoning the liquor, since many died after drinking it, but Betancourt believed the deaths were due just to "excess.")[42] Betancourt, who no doubt reflected the sentiments of many others, called the episode "three days of horror and fear in which everything was confusion and disorder. I cannot find words to describe it."[43] (As we shall see below, there is considerable question as to whether things seen from the insurgent point of view were nearly so chaotic and randomly violent as the elite-authored accounts have it.)

In early November Hidalgo returned to Valladolid from his aborted assault on Mexico City, and, despite his failure, he was received with enthusiasm by a city still controlled by his appointees, including Anzorena.[44] Hidalgo now ordered the execution of the hundreds of Spaniards imprisoned in the city. On 13 November the first group of 40 Spaniards were taken from the prisons, told they were being sent to Guanajuato, and executed just outside Valladolid. The next day news came of the insurgent victory in Guadalajara, but even as Hidalgo made preparations to join forces with his western division the second group of some 44 Spaniards were killed. Most of the victims were not from Valladolid but from small towns or the countryside, and their names were not even known by the Valladolid eyewitnesses later consulted by the Crown and by contemporary historians. Of the peninsular elite of Valladolid, Pátzcuaro, and Zamora, it would appear that most escaped, with some important exceptions, including the intendant Terán; several members of the Jaso family, owners of the vast hacienda of Guaracha; Regidor Juan Bautista de Arana, a wealthy merchant; Teniente Hilario Norma, stepfather of Ruperto Mier, one of the 1809 conspirators; Manuel Valdovinos, a prominent merchant and hacendado; the brothers Manuel and N. [probably Francisco Ignacio de] Sierra, Valladolid merchants; and the brothers Manuel, Domingo, and Toribio Ortiz de la Torre, Pátzcuaro merchants.[45]

Anzorena continued to govern Valladolid as Hidalgo's appointee after the army left for Guadalajara, with an eye toward the redistributive justice that the times seemed to demand. Landlords whose renters refused to pay rent pleaded with Anzorena to enforce their contracts; he declined.[46] Store merchandise from Spanish-owned stores was auctioned off by Anzorena's order (later, in the few cases where possession of "stolen" goods could be determined, those who bought such merchandise had to return it or pay the original owners for it).[47] Betancourt describes an eerie scene in which the doors, windows, cabinets and display cases from the Spanish-owned stores were thrown into the plaza, where they were set afire; the flames, he writes, reached higher than the surrounding houses.[48] Insurgent justice was not always carried out, however: Anzorena halted the executions of Spaniards, allegedly when the prior of the convent of San Agustín confronted him with the head of one of the victims found in a ditch on the Augustinian hacienda of Itzícuaro.[49] After that there are no reports of other deaths or even much looting for over a month.

In late December, however, the approach of the royalist army forced Anzorena and other Hidalgo appointees to flee. Then, with new leadership from among their own ranks, the crowds demanded that the 160 or so Spaniards still imprisoned in the ecclesiastical jail be turned over to them.

Alerted to the rebels' plan to storm the jail, on Christmas night several creole military officers and priests quietly transferred the prisoners to various convents around the city.[50] Nonetheless, in the riot the next day, three of the Spaniards were killed, and a creole priest (ironically, the brother of an active supporter of the insurgency), who was trying to prevent the crowd from attacking the prisoners that had been moved to the ex-Jesuit convent, also lost his life.[51] In the end the death toll in Valladolid from October through December was at least 87 civilians, at least seven stores were ransacked (one source says over fourteen), and at least 400,000 pesos were taken from the church and private individuals (one source says 700,000, and another 1,200,000).[52] It was not as bloody as Guanajuato, but it was certainly enough to impress upon the elite, both those who stayed and those who fled, the power and anger of the *pueblo*.

After Hidalgo

ECONOMIC COLLAPSE, 1810–15

When the royalist troops retook Valladolid in January, 1811, the city entered another phase: for the next five or six years it became a semideserted, much-attacked (though never again conquered) garrison town.[53] One contemporary, Juan José Martínez de Lejarza, reported that in 1811 the city's population fell from some 25,000 inhabitants to below 3,000; as late as 1815 another fixed the city's population at only 3,800.[54] The new intendant, Manuel Merino, asked in 1813 to submit a report to the viceroy on the state of the intendancy, politely responded that he could not comply with such a request, since "for more than two years the insurrection has kept us [in Valladolid] isolated, deprived of all relationship and all commerce with the rest of the province."[55] Alamán observed that for eight months in 1812 and 1813 the city received no word of events in the rest of the colony, so effectively had the insurgents closed off communications.[56] Epidemic disease, however, did manage to get in; Valladolid was ravaged by typhoid in 1813 and still had not recovered when Morelos launched an almost-successful attack on the city in December.[57] In 1815, the year when scarcity and depopulation were perhaps at their worst, Alamán reported that "the miserable state to which the city had been reduced" caused the government to send the intendant and other royal employees to Querétaro, leaving behind only a tax collector charged with the task of paying the troops. This move, of course, set off another round of emigration.[58]

Instead of being burned, sacked, and looted, the city crumbled from within under the equally destructive impact of widespread poverty and abandonment. Several of the buildings sold in the late 1820s, when the urban real estate market finally began to revive, were described as "totally destroyed," "uninhabitable," or as nothing more than the lot where a house used to stand. There are no surviving sales tax records for any district in the province before 1817, but it is clear that commerce had come almost to a halt. There were continual complaints about the scarcity of money due to the destruction of the mines, hoarding, and capital flight, as well as to the commercial paralysis. In 1812 the guardian of the minor children of Lorenzo Vásquez decided to sell a house belonging to them for a very low price. He defended his decision by stating that "it is not easy at present, nor will it be any easier in the foreseeable future, to find a buyer who will offer more, or even as much, since it is well known that money grows scarcer every day. Even the wealthy lack funds for their businesses and for their daily needs."[59] Records of urban house sales suggest that he was indeed lucky to find a buyer: total sales of real estate in Valladolid between 1811 and 1819 averaged only 7,800 pesos a year, compared to 36,000 pesos in the previous decade, and the average number of transactions was 17, compared to 58 from 1800 to 1810. The worst years were 1815 to 1819, when total sales averaged only some 3,500 pesos a year in fewer than 12 transactions.[60] Contemporary laments about scarcity of funds in Valladolid are also borne out by the statistics on loans generated from notary records: loans and cash advances fell off from 135,000 pesos a year from 1800 to 1810 to a negligible 7,700 pesos a year from 1811 to 1819.[61] The copper coins used to try to alleviate the problem of cash shortages were evidently counterfeited widely, and none of the measures taken to eliminate falsification was successful.[62]

In other urban areas, the collapse was, if anything, even more complete. No important town besides Valladolid escaped recurrent, alternating, and destructive occupations by insurgents and their royalist pursuers. Government troops under Calleja were responsible for the razing of the eastern town of Zitácuaro and eleven nearby Indian towns, in punishment for their service to the insurgent cause. It is harder to establish blame in the burning and sacking of dozens of other towns, including Pátzcuaro, Ario, Tacámbaro, Uruapan, Apatzingán, Coalcomán, Los Reyes, Peribán, and Tepalcátepec in the south;

Angamacutiro, Zacapu and Puruándiro in the north; and Zamora, La Piedad, Tangancícuaro, and Tinguindín in the west.[63] Martínez de Lejarza, in his district-by-district litany of depredation, observes that most regions were victimized by both sides.[64]

Outside the cities the cycle of property destruction by attack, abandonment, and cessation of exchange also prevailed. Whereas during the short-lived Hidalgo Rebellion Spaniards of all socioeconomic levels, and not the creole elite, had been the targets of the insurgent army, in the countryside in the aftermath of the 1810 Rebellion the properties of creoles known to be royalist sympathizers were also targets of the rebels (more on this phenomenon follows below). And what the guerrilla armies of Morelos and other leaders did not ransack for food and supplies or destroy in a selective scorched-earth policy, their counterinsurgent pursuers finished off, stripping villages, haciendas, and ranchos of horses, food, and arms, destroying forges that could be employed in the construction of lance points and other weapons, and burning towns and houses from which the inhabitants had fled.[65]

Evidence of the destruction of haciendas is contained in numerous kinds of documents, especially wills, estate divisions, tithe records, and debt compositions. These sources yield the names of 58 haciendas (40 owners) whose productive capacity — animals, seeds, dams, aqueducts, irrigation canals, tools, account books, warehouses, fences, mills, outbuildings — was severely reduced if not completely destroyed. In addition, at least eight other haciendas served as troop headquarters for extended periods during the war; it is probably safe to assume that the adverse impact of the occupation was substantial. Finally, another twenty haciendas are known to have produced no revenue for their owners during most of the insurgent decade. This may have been because of destruction, although it is also possible that the fruits of the properties were confiscated by the insurgents or the royalist armies and that actual destruction was minimal. Given the haphazard nature of documentation, these are clearly far from all of the haciendas that were abandoned by their owners or put out of working order during the war, considering that at the height of their power the insurgents controlled some three-quarters of the province's districts.[66] But the value of these 86 haciendas alone is quite impressive: well over 5 million pesos, probably at least a quarter of the value of rural property in the province.[67]

Haciendas devoted to livestock raising were the most obvious losers, since generally the land itself was unimproved and worth very little. The financial losses could be very nearly complete in these cases. Juan Basilio Leiva, for example, noted in 1821 that before the rebellion he ran 3,000 head of cattle on his *estancia* of San Antonio (Churumuco); but "now that I have regained possession of the estate, my *caporal* and *vaqueros* tell me that there may be perhaps 50 head. Likewise, of 500 or so mares, 200 some horses, and over 100 mules, they only left me 104 mares."[68] On sugar-producing haciendas the losses were also significant. Expensive copper equipment was melted down, mills and other important outbuildings burned, cane seedlings destroyed, and mules required to plant and to power the *trapiches* carried off. On cereal-producing haciendas the greatest losses were hydraulic systems and the confiscation of plow animals, without which estate cultivation was almost impossible. This is a point made repeatedly by Martínez de Lejarza, who opines that the cereal producers, because of the loss of oxen and transport mules, were in worse shape than the sugar producers, though he is quick to say that all were suffering.[69]

The haciendas that were destroyed included some of the wealthiest in the province, a predictable pattern given the insurgent propensity to seek out locations that were (generally) lightly defended but likely to provide supplies and additional manpower. Also predictably, many of these valuable haciendas were the sugar, rice, livestock and indigo-producing estates of *tierra caliente*, a part of the state controlled by the insurgents for most of the period. Indeed, almost all of the most valuable hacienda complexes in the hot country took heavy losses during the insurgency.

These included the haciendas of Pedernales, owned by the prominent Spaniard Agustin Barandiarán, said to have been "annihilated" by belligerants on both sides; Laureles, near Zitácuaro, already in receivership before the revolution; and Canario, owned by the insurgent sympathizer/leader Andrés de la Piedra, which was a frequent headquarters for the rebel army.[70] The hacienda of Puruarán, co-owned on the eve of the rebellion by Bishop-elect Manuel Abad y Queipo and Pedro Vélez, a Spaniard and *regidor* of the Valladolid city council, had been the scene of an important 1814 battle between Morelos and Iturbide and was "reduced to ashes."[71] The Augustinian hacienda of Taretan was also severely damaged, its ranchos of Acúmbaro, Potrerillos, and Tahuejo sacked and burned. The renter of Potrerillos noted that the worst damage was not done to his property until 1819, when rebels "fell on my rancho, taking all of the sugar I produced that year, as well as all my tools, account books, money, and supplies . . . the rancho was totally ruined."[72]

An unusually specific accounting of losses is given by Mariano Michelena, the owner of the haciendas of La Parota and San Juan, in 1822. Before the revolution, witnesses agreed, the two haciendas sowed annually 60 *fanegas* of indigo, 210 *arrobas* of rice, and fifteen *fanegas* of corn; they planted 3,000 *tareas* of sugar cane; harvested 80 *arrobas* of tamarind; and had 50 watermelon patches, and groves of banana, coconut, and orange. These enterprises were kept going with 880 mules, 180 oxen, 40 horses, and 450 hogs. Structures included two chapels (one of which was new and very well appointed), a costly main house on La Parota and a less valuable one on San Juan, a store, several mills, an expensive *casa de calderas* on each hacienda, *purgars*, *panocheras*, *galeras formeras*, various outbuildings to house tools and equipment, and eight miles of fence. The 1810 crop (valued at 29,850 pesos), the livestock (21,267 pesos), the structures (29,073 pesos), and the tools and equipment (2,324 pesos), were lost during the insurgency; these losses amounted to just under half of the total value of the estate. What remained was worth less than the amount of the debts on the property.[73]

The largest highland haciendas did not fare much better than those of *tierra caliente*. According to its historian, the mammoth complex of Guaracha-la Mula in the western district of Zamora, valued at over 500,000 pesos in 1808, was in ruins.[74] The hacienda of Coapa, between Valladolid and Pátzcuaro, was said in 1820 to be in a state of "total abandonment," its movables stolen and its outbuildings, storehouses, and fences torn down.[75] The owner of the hacienda of San Bartolomé in the valley of Indaparapeo, Josefa Lavarrieta, reneged on a debt in 1822, citing the "notorious" heavy losses the hacienda had suffered during the insurrection.[76] The hacienda of Bellasfuentes near Puruándiro was occupied soon after 1810, and as late as 1819 parts of it, at least, were still in rebel hands. Its frustrated owner, Br. Juan José Pastor Morales, wrote in 1820 that "the state of deterioration and ruin of the hacienda is well known."[77] One of the two large haciendas in central Michoacán owned by Mexico City residents, Queréndaro, which belonged to the Conde de Heras — Sebastián de Heras y Soto — was reported in 1826 still to be a "cheerless ruin."[78] Even in the eastern highlands, where specific evidence of destruction, as opposed to occupation by the rebels and requisition of crops, is not as readily available as it is for other parts of the province, there are nonetheless strong indications of widespread property destruction. In an 1828 document, the church, never one to underestimate the capacity of a district to tithe, reasoned that the minimum bid for the district of Maravatío should be no higher than 9,000 pesos, compared to the 25,000 pesos for which the right to collect the tithe was auctioned in 1810, in light of the great destruction the district experienced during the wars.[79]

The picture of general devastation that emerges from this discussion of the largest producers is accurate and perhaps even understated for the more modest haciendas, as well. The Augustinians, for example, heard an emotional plea for an extension of a rental contract from the renter of their small hacienda of Itzícuaro near Valladolid, in which he detailed the care with which he had nurtured the hacienda since he first rented it in 1795, and lamented the "cruel and inexcusable sackings" that the hacienda suffered beginning in 1811, which, he says, continued until the hacienda was "absolutely destroyed." (The Augustinians refused to allow him the extension, and forced him to agree to pay 791 pesos in back rent as well as the value of the movables he had signed for in 1795.)[80] The hacienda of Charahuen, near Pátzcuaro, was also "completely ruined," and its owner, Domingo Larragoiti, in the absence of any income from the property that he had had the bad luck to purchase in 1809, claimed that he was forced to sell silver ornaments and tableware in order to survive.[81] In 1826 the owner of the small hacienda of Aguacate in Tarímbaro, just north of Valladolid, noted that since 1810 there had been no income from the hacienda, and that after the "absolute sacking" of the hacienda by Albino García in 1812 the property was completely deserted, and it was still abandoned these fifteen years later.[82]

Statistics generated from notary and other legal records reveal an unsurprising near-shutdown of markets for the sale and rental of haciendas. In the decade and a half after 1810 there were very few buyers for property at any price: total sales of large rural properties averaged less than 5,500 pesos a year. In fact, only five sales took place in the fourteen years from 1811 to 1824, and all of the properties sold were quite small; clearly the owners of the formerly great haciendas either were not yet prepared to give up, or (more likely) could find no one willing or able to assume much agricultural debt. The impression of a ravaged agricultural sector at the estate level is confirmed by the data on rentals of haciendas: the average rent in the two decades before the Hidalgo Rebellion was over 3,200 pesos, but in the fifteen years after 1810 it fell to 1,150 pesos.

Even those whose property was not destroyed found themselves caught in the vortex created by the virtual cessation of commerce and credit, as people to whom they had sold goods on credit or extended advances, or for whom they had served as cosigners, could not meet their obligations. Payment of in-

terest to the church and to individual creditors ground to a halt. Of seven outstanding debts owed to the church-run hospital in Pátzcuaro, for example,
only one was up to date in its interest payments as late as 1827.[83] Using just
the 21 cases in which the church allowed favored and/or particularly devastated borrowers to restructure their debts, ecclesiastical institutions lost over
350,000 pesos in interest between 1810 and 1835, and this was only a small
fragment of the whole.[84] Many delinquent debts were considered unrecoverable, especially those extended by individual lenders, which, unlike ecclesiastical loans, frequently carried no mortgage. The inventory of Guadalupe
Sánchez's estate in 1816, for example, showed that besides her inn and store
in Zinapécuaro, she had accounts receivable of 18,279 pesos. But only 6,732
pesos were collectable.[85] Even the estate of Pascual Alzúa, one of the most astute merchants of the late colonial period, contained 82,199 pesos (some 38
percent of his financial assets) in lost or doubtful debts.[86]

The personalized and intricately intertwined credit system that prevailed
before 1810 also brought other problems, as the routine favor of cosigning a
mortgage obligation for one's associates turned into a nightmare. Domingo
Torices, for example, had served as cosigner for Manuel Valdovinos in a debt
to Diego Valero, no doubt assuming that like most commercial loans, this one
would be repaid promptly and expeditiously. To further secure the loan,
Valdovinos mortgaged his residence. But when Valdovinos was killed during
the insurrection and his haciendas were sacked and burned, his widow was
forced to sell the house for much less than the sum of claims against it.
Valero, who only recovered 657 pesos of his 4,000-peso claim, then sued the
fiador, Torices, for the balance, and Torices was forced to mortgage his wife's
hacienda in order to fulfill his obligation.[87] In an even more drawn-out and
far-reaching case, the descendants of one cosigner were saddled with a debt
of almost 30,000 pesos thirteen years after the death of the borrower. In 1800
Mariano de Escandón, the Conde de Sierragorda, recognized 20,000 pesos on
his magnificent residence in Valladolid that he promised to donate to a fund
that his brother-in-law, Melchor Noriega, was setting up to establish a *mayorazgo* for his son, the conde's nephew. His cosigner was Captain José María
Peredo, a prominent Valladolid landowner. After the conde's death in 1814
interest payments on the debt ceased, as his estate, which he had left to the
"benefit of his soul," was thrown into confusion by the events of the period
and by the absence of a clear heir to supervise its management. No buyer was
found for his property, and it was not until 1827, by which time all the principals had long since died, that the estate was finally sorted out. The three

children of the cosigner, Peredo, were forced to assume the debt — which now, with back interest, amounted to 29,700 pesos. It fell to one of the children, Faustino Peredo, to take over the house and the major responsibility for the debt; he was later forced to declare bankruptcy.[88]

These multiple, reverberating blows to the economic interests of the propertied classes led average personal wealth among the elite to tumble from a 1790–1810 average of more than 90,000 pesos to approximately 75,000 pesos in the two decades after the Hidalgo Rebellion, of which an uncertain but probably relatively high proportion was composed of overvalued (still being based on pre-1810 appraisals) property and unrecoverable debts.[89] In other words, the real drop in elite wealth was probably more on the order of 30 to 35 percent.

SIGNS OF REBUILDING, 1815–21

The magnitude of the economic collapse should not, however, obscure the fact that, as is usually the case, wars made for high prices, and high prices made for a certain, strained success for a handful of well-positioned and nervy entrepreneurs, both farmers and merchants. Information on prices during the insurgency is scattered, but in general it confirms what logic tells us: the disruption of production and distribution meant that urban consumers paid dear for what they needed. The tithe collector in Zamora noted that maize was selling for an astronomically high four pesos/*fanega* in the city in 1813, in part because there were no *fleteros* to bring it from the insurgent-controlled areas where much of the maize the city depended on was grown.[90] A similar difficulty in contracting for mules and drivers was mentioned by the tithe collector at Charo in 1817, from whom all but eight *costales* of his small maize collection (229 *costales*) were stolen by the insurgents because he had no means to transport them to nearby urban markets.[91] And as late as 1819 the tithe collector for the *tierra caliente* district of Ario wrote that more than half of his maize could not be sold "on the outside" because of the "risks of the road"; he was forced in effect to sell it back to the producers at a low price.[92]

The earliest to exploit these difficult market conditions and take advantage of high prices were royalist officers or rebel leaders, emboldened by their numbers and position and good information about troop movements, and inspired in some cases as much by the need to finance their military operations as by the prospects of personal gain. Alamán describes the provisioning of the Guanajuato silver mines during the early years of the rebellion:

The lack of communications caused the price of everything needed to process silver ore [in the formerly flourishing province of Guanajuato] to rise to exorbitant levels; salt from Colima which used to sell for 12–14 pesos the *carga*, now sold for 140 pesos, and so with the rest. Nor could it have been otherwise, since everything had to be transported in convoys, which were a great source of speculation for the *comandantes*, who confiscated everything that was not sent by this means.[93]

Alamán offered Iturbide as an example of a speculator who used his military position to create artificial shortages that only he could ease, specifically mentioning Iturbide's confiscation on his way back from Ario of the cargoes of some mule drivers carrying *piloncillo* and *petates*.

On the rebel side, Morelos tried to prohibit the sale of grains and meat by his officers to the enemy or to enemy pueblos, but such strictures were not effective, and indeed, profits earned in commerce between the rebels and the royalists, according to Archer, were crucial to the insurgent cause.[94] Padre Torres ran a huge operation between the *tierra caliente* of Michoacán and the cities of the Bajío, selling products from these territories to the royalists; in northern Michoacán insurgents were engaged in rustling and selling cattle near Zacapu.[95]

But as the insurgents were pushed farther and farther back from the cities after 1814, and as the risks of trade eased a bit civilian merchants quickly moved to take advantage of still-high prices. In Valladolid in the late 1810s over 150 individuals regularly paid sales tax on goods they brought into the city. The vast majority traded in only one or two items that they had produced and/or marketed: salt, shoes (*zapatos de baqueta*, sold exclusively by Indian traders), cacao, and so forth. There were only twenty or so storeowners, most of whom dealt in foreign imports when they could get them, as well as in domestic goods brought in from other parts of Mexico. At the lowest level of established storeowners were men like Cayetano Gómez, a young and relatively insignificant merchant who would later become Michoacán's first millionaire (and marry one of Isidro Huarte's granddaughters). Gómez paid sales tax in 1819 on *aguardiente* de Castilla, tallow, sugar (imported from the state of Mexico), rapeseed oil, almond extract, and bulk cotton. A slightly older and better-established merchant, Antonio de la Haya, sold 294 pesos of *chile seco* from Acámbaro, 456 pesos worth of *panos de Querétaro*, an additional 1,152 pesos worth of goods imported from Querétaro, 61 pesos worth of domestic olive oil, and 4,456 pesos in foreign imports. At the top of this mercantile hierarchy the well-connected Eugenio Garay sold almost 20,000 pesos worth of imported European goods, which arrived in five cargoes from Veracruz, where he had purchased them, and only 1,735 pesos of domestic goods.[96]

The potential profits to be earned in commerce were, predictably, extremely high. In 56 shipments of goods to merchants in Valladolid, Pátzcuaro, and Uruapan from 1817 to 1821, the average gross profit (the difference between what the merchants had paid for the shipment in Mexico City, Veracruz, or other point of origin, and the amount for which the sales tax assessors reckoned they could sell those goods at the point of destination) was 54 percent. (By contrast, the average profit on 180 shipments sent to Valladolid and Pátzcuaro in the two decades before the Hidalgo Rebellion was 42 percent, and the average profit in the 1780s was only 23 percent on 107 shipments.)[97] Almost one-fifth of the shipments posted profits of over 100 percent, and profit on individual items could be much higher. In 1820, for example, Francisco Iturbe purchased in Veracruz and sold in Pátzcuaro various items, including a large crate of codfish on which he made a profit of 238 percent, three dozen *panuelos de madrón* on which his profit was 200 percent, and one barrel of imported *aguardiente* on which he made a 212-percent profit. Royalist officer Felipe Robledo did even better with red wine, which he purchased at 6 pesos the barrel and sold for 45; *fierro platino*, on which he made a 500-percent profit; Malaga sherry, which he purchased at 8 pesos the barrel and sold for 45; and Havana beeswax, on which the profit was 220 percent.[98] In part, of course, these gross profits were absorbed by transportation costs, which were higher after 1810 than they had been before. But it nonetheless appears that those lucky enough to get their cargoes through were handsomely rewarded for their efforts.

None of this should be taken to mean that the commercial climate was anything like exuberant. First, the volume of commerce in Zamora, Pátzcuaro, and Valladolid was much lower than it had been before the wars. In Valladolid, for example, sales tax receipts indicate that total volume of trade in the decade before 1810 averaged about 680,000 pesos a year. In 1817 the volume of trade was only about 140,000 pesos, and by 1819 it had climbed only about halfway back to pre-1810 levels, at roughly 350,000 pesos.[99] In Pátzcuaro trade averages of about 275,000 pesos a year in the decade before 1810 fell even more sharply than they did in Valladolid, to about 90,000–100,000 pesos in 1818, 1819, and 1820.[100] And, of course, those totals were in inflated, wartime prices.

Second, given the uncertainties of transport during the height of the insurgency, the safest way to transport goods long distances was to convoy, and
convoys were expensive. This meant that the reduced volume of trade was
concentrated in fewer hands than it had been during the pre-1810 period. In
Valladolid from 1801 to 1809, for example, the top ten merchants controlled
36 percent of the nonlocal trade. In 1819, however, the top ten merchants
controlled 53 percent of that trade. Furthermore, close examination of the
sales tax registers reveals that large merchants often paid the *alcabala* in the
name of smaller merchants, perhaps acting as commissioned transporters of
others' merchandise, and so may have been even more powerful than the
numbers suggest.

If the continuing uncertainty of the political situation and the general public insecurity created serious new problems but also new opportunities for
merchants, the same was true (though to a more limited extent) for farmers.
As in commerce, viewed from the sectoral perspective, the prospects of success in agriculture were much reduced. But from an individual perspective
they might be enhanced.

Again, high prices encouraged many hacienda owners and renters to
strain every nerve to return to production. The best data are for maize. The
average price of maize before the rebellion was around ten to eleven reales. In
Zamora, for which we have the most complete price runs after 1810, the first
two years of the rebellion did not affect the price of maize very much: in 1811
maize sold for 11rr and in 1812 for 13rr. But in 1813 the price rose to 32rr,
where it remained for another year. In the end the average price of maize in
Zamora during the insurgent decade (1811–19) was 20rr.[101] Data does not
exist for other locations for the years before 1816, but after that date similarly high prices seem to have prevailed throughout the state: in seventeen isolated observations for the late insurgency (1816–19), across a wide geographical cross-section of the state, the average price of maize was 21rr.[102]

For other commodities price information is scantier, but the general trend
of high post-1810 prices seems to apply. The price of sugar, for example, the
key crop for many of the state's commercial farmers, rose from 16rr/*arroba*
before 1810 to 27rr during the insurgency, when sales tax records show that
sugar was actually being imported from the state of Mexico.[103] The price of
piloncillo rose even more dramatically, from 9 pesos/*carga* before 1810 to 22
pesos/*carga* in the decade after.[104] Wheat prices rose during the insurgency,
but not nearly so much as did those of corn and sugar, while the price of beef
went up by about 40 percent.[105]

For hacienda owners and renters the path to advantage from these high prices was not quite so clear as was that for merchants. Even under the best possible circumstances (their haciendas had not been destroyed during the rebellion, and they were close enough to markets that transport was not prohibitively risky), if they wanted to return to production on the hacienda account, they faced formidable obstacles. At the very least they must pay high wages in order to attract a labor force to clear abandoned fields, plow and prepare soil, and rebuild granaries and storehouses and fences, before they could think of planting, much less of harvesting and of arranging for the transport of their crops. Most of them were not in a position to pay this kind of wage bill.

The best interim solution was to turn over production on their haciendas to tenants and sharecroppers.[106] Because they usually did not have to generate enough income to pay wages to employees outside the family, these small producers could absorb the immediate costs of restoring some of the productive capacity of long-idle or destroyed haciendas. On the hacienda of Casablanca in Maravatío in the late 1810s, for example, 63 percent of the wheat and 100 percent of the maize was produced by sharecroppers or tenants. Likewise, on the haciendas of La Huerta and Las Piedras (also in the Maravatío district) in 1820, tenants produced all the maize (though the owners did raise all the wheat the haciendas produced).[107] In the district of Tuxpan not a single hacienda owner tithed: all tithers for 1817 were hacienda tenants.[108] Hacienda dependents were also the sole or main producers in the cases of the haciendas of La Goleta, San Miguel Ocurio, Camémbaro, and Salitrillo in 1817 and Santa Rosalía in 1819.[109] On the hacienda of Chamuco, owned by Manuel Sáenz Santa María, a Mexico City resident who died around 1817, the administrator of the hacienda left the property completely in the hands of dependents, who managed to increase maize production from 275 *fanegas* in 1817 to almost 2,000 *fanegas* in 1820, and wheat from 125 *cargas* to 210 *cargas*.[110]

In some areas, particularly in the grain belt nearest Mexico City, the role of tenants and sharecroppers in aiding the transition to significant production on the hacienda account was short-lived. The Retana family, for example, owners of the huge hacienda of Tepústepec, moved quickly to reclaim their position as the main producers of both wheat and maize. In 1816 tenants and sharecroppers had harvested 18,500 *fanegas* of maize compared to the hacienda's 1,790, and in 1817 and 1818 they produced roughly 9,400 *fanegas* to the hacienda's 1,600. Beginning in 1819, however, the hacienda began to

step up its own activities, harvesting 580 *cargas* of wheat while increasing
maize production from 1,500 to 4,120 *fanegas* over the next two years.[111]
This increase in direct production was almost certainly at the expense of some
of the tenants and sharecroppers. Encroachment on the lands previously
given over to tenants may also have characterized management of the hacienda of Pateo-Paquisihuato, owned by Agustín Tapia. On these haciendas
in 1817, Tapia produced about 220 *cargas* of wheat, and 15 tenants produced about 900 *fanegas* of maize. By 1820, though, the hacienda produced
over 80 percent of the maize, and its wheat production had increased dramatically to 1,240 *cargas*, probably as a result of taking over fields earlier let
to tenants for maize production.[112]

The Insurgency and Elite Politics to 1815

In terms of the economic interests of wealthy Michoacanos, then, the direction of change after 1810 is somewhat less relentlessly downward spiraling
than is often thought. That is, although it is certainly true that the economic
collapse was devastating and pervasive, it carried within it the seeds of its
own early, tentative reversal. The same is true of elite political alignments
and loyalties, which are rather more complex than the straightforward story
of conservative backlash in the face of popular insurgency that is usually
told.

It is important to begin with the realization that in Michoacán elite ad-
herence to the insurgency was if not commonplace then certainly not re-
markable. We have already noted Joaquín Huarte's decision to side with the
insurgents. Other elites who joined Hidalgo and/or Morelos included Lic.
José María Izasaga; Capt. Manuel Muñiz; Lic. Antonio de Castro; Br.
Manuel Ruiz de Chávez y Larrina; Capt. Ruperto Mier; and Lic. Antonio
Cumplido (all of whom were also implicated in the 1809 conspiracy); José
María Anzorena, Hidalgo's appointed intendant, an *hacendado* and a
Caballero Maestrante de la Real Ronda; the five Rayón brothers of
Tlalpujahua; Benedicto López, a well-to-do Zitácuaro hacendado; the
cousins Br. Juan de Dios Romero Soravilla and Juan de Foncerrada y
Soravilla, sons of two sisters who co-owned the hacienda of Uruétaro (one
of whom was imprisoned for eight months for her support of the revolu-
tion); Lic. Francisco Solórzano y Abarca, son of the owner of the rich sugar
hacienda of Tomendan; Manuel Manso, who had purchased the small ha-

cienda of Chaparro in 1797; and José Ignacio Piña de Ibarrola, favorite nephew of a wealthy creole canon.[113]

Other wealthy Michoacanos served the insurgency not as *caudillos* but as advisers and propagandists. At least eight members of the cathedral chapter were sympathetic to the rebellion, including the Conde de Sierragorda, who may have been a member of the Guadalupes (a secret pro-independence organization), and certainly was one of the delegates to the Congreso de Chilpancingo in 1813.[114] Another member of a distinguished Valladolid family, Dr. Antonio Lavarrieta, as parish priest in Guanajuato had been instrumental in reducing the sentences of the leaders of the 1809 conspiracy, and in 1810 supported and "spoke the language of" the revolution (though when arrested he denied any motives for his contact with Hidalgo other than to secure decent treatment for *gachupino* prisoners).[115] As we shall see in more detail below, by some accounts Valladolid was full of what the frustrated Crown called "insurgentes domésticos," spies and subversives, many of whom were well-to-do creoles and even Spaniards.[116] They may even have included a nun in the convent of Santa Catarina, a sister of Mariano Michelena, who, it is said, received and passed on messages from her exiled brother to revolutionaries in the city of Valladolid. The royal officials discovered the system and confined her to her cell until she could be executed the following day. But, according to one report, "God heard her prayers, and sent her a powerful fever that carried her away before such a terrible fate could befall her and the convent."[117] In all, of the 150 to 200 wealthy households in the province at the time of the Hidalgo Rebellion, I estimate that at least one-third had one or more relatively close family members who served the insurgents.

One of the factors that seems to have shaped elite participation in the insurgency is kinship; certain family names crop up again and again among the insurgent leaders. One cluster of elite insurgents centered around the López Aguado name. José María Anzorena's mother was a López Aguado; the Rayón brothers' mother — who is said to have allowed one son to be executed rather than compromise her family's ideals — was a López Aguado; Lic. Francisco Solórzano y Abarca's grandmother was a López Aguado.[118] This group was linked through José María Anzorena's wife Mariana Foncerrada y Ulibarri to three more insurgents or supporters, Juan de Foncerrada y Soravilla, his cousin Juan de Dios Romero Soravilla, and Dr. Antonio Lavarrieta, whose sister Josefa was married to Bernardo Foncerrada, Juan de Foncerrada y Soravilla's natural father.

Another cluster of well-to-do insurgents has Mariano Quevedo, the 1809 conspirator, at its core, though I have been unable to document Quevedo's own participation in the insurgency.[119] His sister Josefa, who was married to Regidor Benigno Antonio Ugarte, raised the orphaned insurgent Manuel Villalongín. His cousin María Loreto Peredo was married to the brother of the insurgent Miguel Zincúnegui; and another cousin, Faustino Peredo, was married to Carlota Izasaga, who was probably related (although it is not clear precisely how) to the insurgent Lic. José María Izasaga. Faustino and María Loreto Peredo's father, José María, was a cosigner and business associate of the insurgent sympathizer, the Conde de Sierragorda. And Quevedo's natural daughter, Dolores, grew up to marry Francisco Ruiz de Chávez, son of the nephew of the insurgent priest Br. José Manuel Ruiz de Chávez.[120]

Another link among many rebellious elites was economic marginality and/or financial difficulties. Even before the outbreak of the revolution, pocketbook issues had often helped shaped political action. The presumed fragility of New Spain's economy, and the damage that could be done to it and to property owners if the Crown did not relent, had been key themes in the protests against the 1804 Consolidation, and the precarious financial circumstances of the leaders of the 1809 conspiracy bore evidence that the protesters were right. Mariano and Lic. Nicolás de Michelena's troubles came from overextension during the economically exuberant years after their father's death in 1787, when they inherited his sugar-, rice-, and indigo-producing haciendas of La Parota and San Juan in Urecho. In 1800, the reader may recall, they had entered into an unexpectedly profitable partnership with Isidro Huarte, which seems to have emboldened the Michelenas to expand operations even further. In 1809 mortgages on the haciendas amounted to half the value of the property. Worse, the price of sugar was falling, and the man to whom the hacienda had been rented in 1805 had initiated a lawsuit against the Michelenas, claiming that "in order to make the rest of the world think that they were great lords," they had forced him to sign a rental contract stating that he would pay twice what they privately assured him would be the true rent. Later they had insisted on the rent specified in the contract, and he sued on grounds of deception. Ominously for the Michelenas, he was defended by Lic. Isidro Huarte, the son of their former partner.[121]

The situation of the other leader of the conspiracy, José María García de Obeso, was even more desperate. In 1809 García de Obeso, the son of a prominent Spanish merchant-financier who had died in 1805, was still trying to sort through the complicated affairs of his father's estate; Gabriel García de Obeso had left assets of some 100,000 pesos, but claims on his estate amounted to over 95,000 pesos.[122] And what was true of all three of the leaders was also true of many of the participants, almost all of whom had significantly fewer assets than either the Michelenas or García de Obeso, but, proportionately, equally burdensome debts.[123]

Some of the same patterns prevailed when it came to elite involvement in the insurgency; that is, insurgent elites tended to be financially troubled and, like the conspirators, were somewhat less well-to-do (with notable exceptions) than were those who either joined the royalists or remained on the sidelines. On paper, one of the wealthiest and most socially distinguished of the insurgent elites was José María Anzorena. Anzorena's haciendas in Apatzingán, San Antonio Catzundangapeo and Santa Gertrudis de las Huertas, were appraised at 92,496 pesos in 1802, and he lived in one of the principal houses of Valladolid, worth an impressive 27,033 pesos in 1782. Both of these properties, however, belonged to his wife, Mariana Foncerrada; furthermore, they were heavily mortgaged, the hacienda for more than half of its value. He himself had inherited only a house, which was sold in 1797 for 12,500 pesos, all but 500 pesos of which was pledged to creditors.[124]

Also possessed of somewhat shaky or circumscribed wealth was Lic. Mariano Escandón, the Conde de Sierragorda. Escandón was one of the most conspicuous consumers of Vallisoletano society, with personal effects valued at a staggering (for Valladolid) 22,358 pesos, including over 3,000 pesos in paintings and sculpture, almost 4,000 pesos in glass and glassware, over 2,800 in furniture, and 853 in timepieces. He was, according to urban lore, a great lover of rare animals and kept many rare specimens in his palatial house in Valladolid, including (surely apocryphally) an elephant. Yet his estate was relatively small, consisting only of the house and its contents, and it was burdened by debt. After Escandón's death in 1814 his residence was foreclosed upon and auctioned off to pay its debts, though no doubt income from the *mayorazgo* and his prebend protected him from undue suffering during his lifetime.[125]

José Ignacio Piña de Ibarrola's social status was also unquestionable, but he had no parental inheritance to speak of, and his future was dependent on his somewhat eccentric uncle and aunt, Lic. José Antonio López de Piña and his sister Rita López de Piña, who had an unsettling history of revising their wills.[126] Lic. Francisco Solórzano y Abarca was in a similar position: as one of the seven children of his father's second marriage Francisco stood to inherit considerably less than his half brother, Ignacio Solórzano Treviño, who took over the hacienda of Tomendan that constituted the bulk of the estate.[127] Also in a difficult financial situation was the leader of the 1810 Rebellion, Br. Miguel de Hidalgo, whose hacienda of Jaripeo near Tajimaroa, appraised at 44,000 pesos in 1804, was mortaged for 30,000 pesos.[128] Ruperto Mier's paternal inheritance was sizable (a bit over 10,000 pesos), but his stepfather, whom his mother had tried to divorce, seems to have squandered much of what she had received in community property after the death of his father.[129] The worldly goods of Br. José Manuel Ruiz de Chávez and his nephews Mariano and Francisco Ruiz de Chávez were represented mainly by the hacienda of Irapeo, whose debts amounted to more than half of its value.[130]

But if the wealth of these individuals was compromised, at least their assets were fairly substantial. Most of the other elite insurgents were more marginal in the degree of their wealth and/or the depth of their connections to elite society.[131] The orphaned Manuel Villalongín's parents had lost the hacienda of Atapaneo to bankruptcy.[132] Juan de Foncerrada y Soravilla, the son of Bernardo Foncerrada, had inherited little from his natural father, who by law was forced to leave his substantial estate, including the magnificent hacienda of San Bartolomé, to his legitimate daughter. Foncerrada y Soravilla was also unlucky in his marriage to Mariana García de Obeso, sister of José María, since her inheritance was as devastated by their father's financial problems as was his own.[133] Br. José María Morelos owned more property than either of these men — chiefly in the new two-story residence he had just built — and his education was excellent, but his social background was barely middle class; moreover, the house had been embargoed in June of 1810, three months before the Hidalgo Rebellion broke out.[134] There was a host of other borderline or marginal elites, many of them *licenciados* or parish priests in positions roughly equivalent to that of Morelos, that is, with minimal personal wealth and undistinguished social background, but with an education that gave them connections to more established and better-heeled elites.[135]

The number of active loyalists among the provincial elite is much smaller than the number of known insurgents and sympathizers, though in part that may be a function of post-independence historical writing, which has tended to glorify the heroic insurgents and to ignore the names of the royalists unless they can be described as particularly brutal or bloody. A surprisingly small proportion of the local peninsular elite (as opposed to the government officials and royal troop commanders brought in from the outside) enthusiastically supported the "buena causa." Those who did included ten members of the church hierarchy and a fair number of Spanish-born merchants, almost all of whom were also military officers: Manuel Valdovinos, who was killed early in the fighting; Capt. Juan Antonio Aguilera, who was brought out of retirement to command the defense of the city against Hidalgo; Capt. Pedro Celestino Negrete; Capt. Felipe Robledo; Capt. Juan N. Oviedo; Capt. Pascual Alzúa; and Capt. Agustín Barandiarán. In part, these small numbers owe to the fact that there simply was not much of a Spanish population left in the province: most of the Spaniards who were not killed in the early stages of the insurrection fled to Mexico City until the danger in Michoacán had at least partially passed.

The qualities that made royalists out of creoles are intriguing but more elusive, since there are relatively few people known to fit that category in Michoacán. One unstartling pattern does suggest itself: they were somewhat wealthier as a group than were the insurgent elites, and their financial situations were less precarious. Presumably they had more to lose in a destructive war and were willing (at least at the outset) to go to war to stop a war. Among the staunchly loyal creoles was Dr. Angel Mariano Morales y Jaso, a member of a wealthy Zamora family, on whose hacienda of La Mulacita debts amounted to less than 10 percent of the property's value, an unusually low level.[136] José Mariano Torres Guerrero, another creole royalist, felt financially secure enough in 1809 to give his only son 20,000 pesos, to go along with the 9,300 pesos the boy had inherited from his grandmother, in order that he might contract a marriage of which José Mariano very much approved. His wealth (really his wife's inheritance) rested on haciendas in the Zacapu region, including the hacienda of Zipimeo, an overnight stop on the road to Zamora. Unfortunately, no more recent data are available, but in 1797 Zipimeo was worth over 70,000 pesos and was mortgaged for only 17,000 pesos.[137]

In some cases, too, the successful careers of the creole royalists depended, or were thought to depend, not only on preservation of peace but on preservation of the colonial system. This is fairly obvious in the case of the several creole military officers who stayed loyal to the Crown: Cor. Agustín de Iturbide, Cor. Angel Vélez y Solórzano, Capt. Felipe González Castañón, Capt. Juan José Gómez de la Puente, and Capt. Nicolás Menocal y Salceda, all of whom were not only wealthy but also financially stable, with the possible exception of Vélez y Solórzano.[138] It is also perhaps the case for two young creole merchants who were just getting started in a previously peninsular arena, Cayetano Gómez and Fernando Román, both of whom eventually succeeded brilliantly in spite of (and perhaps in part because of) the risks of trade in the midst of an insurrection.[139]

Still, relative wealth and financial security also characterized many creoles who publicly embraced neither cause, so we must assume that among creole royalists loyalty derived from more than just an absence of financial desperation. Though there are no texts produced by creole royalists in Michoacán during these years that might give us special insight into the more ideological factors that may have figured into their decisions to fight for Spain against so many of their countrymen, we can probably assume that they responded to the same kinds of buttons pushed by anti-insurgent propagandists in Mexico City. Some of them were convinced that with the promulgation of the liberal 1812 Constitution in Spain, Mexico's best chance for the good, progressive government that had been lacking under the inept and despotic Charles IV was not to break with Spain but to stay loyal. Spanish propagandists, including the oratorically adept archdean of the Valladolid cathedral, Dr. Manuel de la Bárcena, did everything they could to encourage this line of thought among peasant rebels as well as among elites.[140] Others, coming from the opposite end of the ideological spectrum, saw a movement to break away from Spain as almost matricidal; they feared the breakdown of order in the fullest sense of the word, that is, not only in terms of public security but also in terms of social hierarchy, and they were convinced that the insurgents were godless, that only Catholic Spain could protect religion in America. These diverse points of view would, of course, reappear in shifting rhetorical form throughout the early post-independence period.

If we assume that in the early aftermath of the Hidalgo Rebellion most of the wealthy peninsulars who stayed in or later returned to Michoacán were generally sympathetic (for whatever reasons) to the Spanish cause, and we add to this group the known creole royalists, it seems likely that somewhere around one-third of the elite households in Michoacán were, at least before 1815, relatively firm and sometimes quite active supporters of the Crown. Recalling that the number of wealthy households with insurgent sympathies was also about one-third of the total, this means that the remaining one-third, most of them creoles, were ambivalent from the outset. For a variety of reasons this ambivalent center would grow substantially after 1815.

Elite Politics After 1815

I have painted a picture of elite political alignment that emphasizes family loyalties, economic position, and financial circumstance as keys to understanding why some creole elites joined the insurgency and why others, exposed to the same "enlightened" ideas and also dismayed by royal policies since 1804, did not. But as the early successes of the insurgent armies were reversed by a stepped-up counterinsurgent program, the commitment of the insurgent elites to the cause, and indeed their willingness to think of it as a single cause, were severely tested.[141] A small number of well-off insurgents turned on the movement entirely and joined or aided the royalists (Ruperto Mier, Manuel Muñiz, José María Vargas, Ramón Rayón).[142] Others, less dramatically, accepted offers of amnesty from the royal government (Br. Marcos Castellanos, Lic. Ignacio Rayón, Dr. Sixto Verdusco, Lic. Mariano Tercero, Br. Juan Pablo Anaya).[143] If these were the reactions of most surviving elite insurgents we can probably assume that an even larger number of quiet sympathizers and fence-sitters distanced themselves from the insurrection as it became more marginalized and more fragmented.

In addition to the dead-end political future that further complicity with the insurgency seemed to portend by 1815, it is logically attractive to assume that creole insurgents and other sympathizers soured on the movement because of its negative effect on their own economic interests. It is surely true that no property owners were unscathed by the insurrection. As we have seen, even hacendados and merchants whose businesses were not sacked and looted by rebels or counterinsurgents found it difficult to generate income after the outbreak of the rebellion, because of the breakdown of distribution systems and capital and labor markets. But I have found little evidence to suggest that this was the indiscriminate war on property that the government and some elites portrayed it to be (see, for example, the elite-authored descriptions of rampant drunkenness and random, chaotic violence after Hidalgo entered Valladolid, excerpted earlier in this chapter). Instead, it appears that insurgents usually spared the property of other insurgents, and that royalists were the special target of rebel looting and sacking, just as rebel towns and individuals were the special target of the counterinsurgents.[144] This was in keeping with Morelos' rejection of an anonymous 1812 call for class war (though Alamán, cleverly, later attributed it to him), in which both the peninsular *and* the creole elites were cast as the enemy, and in which the author urged that all large haciendas, stores, and mines ought to be destroyed no matter the owner.[145] It is often said that Morelos' directives regarding protection of the property of insurgents or partisans were ignored by those in the field, and indeed it is hard to imagine that this was not sometimes the case, but I have turned up some evidence to suggest that they were followed, and almost none indicating that they were not.

Unfortunately, most of the evidence that insurgents were not mindlessly anti-elite, but instead made calculated decisions about how much and what to take from whom, is quite indirect. I have found one statement that appears to confirm preferential treatment for creole insurgent sympathizers. One of the 1809 conspirators and the nephew of an insurgent, Mariano Ruiz de Chávez, noted in 1818 that the previous year he himself had collected the tithe on his hacienda of Irapeo, since any tithe collector would have been in danger of his life. He was able to collect 233 *fanegas* of maize, but on his way back to Valladolid was compelled by the rebels to hand over 26 of them. This, he says, he did willingly and almost gratefully, since he was allowed to keep most of the maize, whereas a Spaniard or a royalist might have lost his life and would almost certainly have had to hand over the entire collection.[146]

Beyond this the evidence consists of an apparent pattern of insurgent-owned haciendas coming through the wars relatively intact, and a clear pattern of elite *belief* that Americanness and at least political neutrality, if not outright sympathy with the rebels, conferred a sort of immunity from insurgent assault. On the first point, as far as can be determined, no insurgent's haciendas were attacked by the rebels except for those owned by Mariano Michelena, and even here witnesses were careful to attribute the blame to both "Americanos" and "the troops known at that time as those of the King." Of course this may be a case of rebel bands simply refusing to follow Morelos' instructions about sparing the property of partisans, but it is worth pointing out that Michelena was not an insurgent leader in Michoacán, and that having been exiled from Mexico because of his leadership of the 1809 conspiracy he was in Spain fighting *for Spain* against the French, a fact that may not have set well with some of the insurgents.[147] Royalists were apparently primarily responsible for stripping the hacienda of Canario, owned by the rebel leader Andrés de la Piedra, which seems to have been the only other insurgent-owned hacienda to have been destroyed. Others certainly suffered losses (Tipitaro, owned by José María Abarca; San Antonio and Santa Gertrudis, owned by José María Anzorena), but apparently not so much as some of their neighbors. Tipitaro, for example, was sold by Abarca in 1826 for 120,000 pesos, just 10,000 pesos less than he had paid for it in 1801, suggesting losses due more to abandonment than to sacking.[148] Though the haciendas owned by the Anzorena family were burdened with heavy debts the family managed to hold onto them until 1896, which probably would not have been possible if they had been too badly damaged in the wars.[149] Meanwhile, Lic. José María Izasaga's hacienda of Rosario in Zacatula, an area crisscrossed repeatedly by insurgent armies, was worth almost twice as much in 1834 as it had been in 1808, a most unusual phenomenon, but one that seems also to have characterized the hacienda of Tomendan, owned by the insurgent Lic. Francisco Solórzano's brother. It was worth 97,000 pesos in 1792 and 132,544 pesos in the mid-1830s.[150]

Beyond this, there is no doubt that Spaniards and royalists *thought* that the rebels would treat creole-owned property more respectfully than they would that of Europeans, and hurried to entrust Americans with their valuables, to commission creoles to carry on their businesses (see below for some examples), and in some cases even to put their haciendas or houses into creole hands legally by use of timed sales and other devices.[151] An interesting variation on this scheme occurred in 1819, when the royalist owner of a rancho still occupied by rebels faked the sale of the property to someone whose political affiliation was presumably more neutral, with the proviso that as soon as the rebels vacated the property, he would again be the rightful owner.[152]

Thus it seems likely that the eventual creole withdrawal of support from the insurgent cause had less to do with horror at insurgent excesses, resentment of insurgent destruction of their property, or rejection of insurgent goals, than with the fact that by 1815 the insurgency was no longer a viable movement. Put another way, there was still the strong possibility that under the right circumstances elites might embrace a rejuvenated or reconstituted movement emphasizing the goals that most attracted them: independence, local autonomy, national religion, civil equality (including abolition of slavery and special rights and obligations for Indian peoples), and greater educational opportunity, not just at the primary level but for professionals (doctors, lawyers, pharmacists, notaries, and so on). For the moment, however, and especially from early 1815 on, the insurgency counted fewer and fewer elites among its numbers.

But the distancing of the creole elite from the insurgency was by no means the only factor driving political repositioning. Indeed, one of the most striking features of elite realignments over the decade was not renewed lip-service loyalty to Spain on the part of former insurgents or waverers, but growing disenchantment with and alienation from Spain on the part of many previously loyalist or neutral creole *and* peninsular elites, a reaction to what they considered to be excessive fiscal demands from the Crown, abusive treatment from the troops, and inadequate defense of their interests.

The episcopal hierarchy, whose behavior before and during the insurrection already indicated a certain willingness to part company with an increasingly anticlerical Crown, was given further grounds for discontent in the insurgent decade.[153] During his occupation of Valladolid Hidalgo had carried off almost all the funds in the bishopric's strongboxes, and there was no way to replenish them, since income flows from the tithe and debt service ceased almost entirely. But as part of the nearly impossible task of raising money locally for the city's defense, one of the intendant's first targets was naturally the treasury of the bishopric. To comply with royal demands, the Cathedral Chapter had to solicit loans at interest rates as high as 8 percent, sell real estate (if it could find buyers), and virtually stop paying its personnel.[154] It even went so far as to melt down many of its silver ornaments in order to pay the troops who guarded the city.[155] There was a limit to how much could be squeezed from clerics or from ecclesiastical institutions that remained wealthy on paper, but that, in reality, like all landlords and creditors during this period, commanded but a tiny fraction of their former income, but this did not stop the troop commanders and the intendant from testing those limits.

The other obvious source of funds was the city's merchants, but, like the church, their assets existed largely on paper in the form of IOUs and other credit obligations. What came into their coffers was quickly pounced upon, leading to a cycle of mutual mistrust and recriminations as merchants tried to hide their income and royal officials tried to seize it. In December 1815 the intendant once again turned to the merchants "de mayor proporción" for funds, because there were none in the treasury. He called a meeting at which all in attendance complained that they were in no position to support the troops, since for all intents and purposes commerce was nonexistent, though in the end most of them grudgingly pledged their daily sales to the government to meet the troops' salaries.[156] The merchant-dominated city council petitioned the viceroy for relief at least twice, to no avail. An 1817 petition displayed unusual bitterness about the "pensiones, préstamos, y contribuciones contínuas" imposed on them for military expenses, while there was chronic lack of support from the treasury.[157]

The meager resources that could be extracted from the usual sources (church and merchants) and the unwillingness/inability of the viceregal treasury to contribute, meant that the *ayuntamientos*, which were responsible for supporting the troops that protected their cities, had to levy substantial new taxes on households. In Pátzcuaro, monthly "contributions" were demanded on a more-or-less sliding scale based on income. The wealthiest households (mainly merchants) paid 30 pesos a month, several others paid between 10 and 20, 23 more were charged between 1 and 6 pesos, and the rest of the population, including the Indian *barrios*, paid under a peso.[158] In Valladolid each head of household was levied two and a half *reales* a week.[159]

These financial sacrifices seemed especially obnoxious in light of the fact that the behavior of the troops — both officers and soldiers — was arrogant, high-handed, and deeply antagonizing. Any corn brought to the city by private sellers was commandeered by the troops, who paid for it with chits that the sellers then had to try to redeem from the cash-poor city council. This meant that either the seller lost when the city could not pay, or the city lost when the sellers charged the army inflated prices for which the *ayuntamiento* was held responsible. But when the troops were begged to serve as escorts for tithe collectors or city warehouse officials looking to purchase corn on site, they refused.[160] Troop commanders even required the city council to supply citizen-janitors for the barracks.[161]

Even as early as 1813 the testimony of a witness in a treason case gives the impression that some well-to-do residents of Valladolid were so disgusted that if they were not actively supporting the rebels they were at least willing to socialize with people who were, and to join in taunting (in verse) the troops on whom the protection of the city depended. Among the eleven accused conspirators were several members of the Valladolid elite, including the "ringleader" Prebend Martín García de Carrasquedo, whose prominent family owned the hacienda of Guaparatío just outside of Valladolid. They were charged with being "addicts of the Party of Insurrection and emissaries of its leaders," with bribing soldiers to desert and join the rebels, and with sponsoring dances and "diversions" in which songs praising Morelos and other rebel leaders were performed to the applause of the attendees.[162] Besides the elites named as conspirators were numerous others who attended what seems to have been an almost constant round of thinly disguised pro-insurgent parties held in the decaying and besieged city. These included the canon José María Zarco, licenciados José María Ortiz Izquierdo and Pedro Navarro, and other priests, merchants, and notaries.[163]

Significantly, the names given by witnesses in this conspiracy hearing included not only those of wealthy creoles but also those of several Spaniards and/or royal officials. Referring to some of those who requested that a march be performed that began "valiant soldiers of Sr. Morelos . . . ," the witness named a lieutenant colonel in the royal army, an *alferez de la Corona*, a royal notary, "and many [more] officials."[164] Peninsulars were also numerous among the merchants who in 1815 and 1817 resisted the intendant's demands for more contributions, petitioned the viceroy for tax relief, and pleaded that the Crown curb the actions and demands of the Spanish troops. Indeed, over half the merchants who were asked to attend the meeting called by the intendant in 1815 or who signed the 1817 petition were Spaniards.[165]

This was not quite the same Spanish mercantile elite as the one that had dominated commerce before the insurrection, which had included many men who had not yet put down roots in the province and whose ranks were now thinned by death and flight. Among the older, settled generation of Spanish merchants signing the petitions were Isidro Huarte; Capt. Juan Manuel Cabello, a partner of Huarte's somewhat reclusive but savvy son-in-law, Pascual Alzúa; Manuel González Movellan of Pátzcuaro, one of the leading merchants in that city; Benito López, a merchant/speculator; Lázaro Morales of Zamora, a prominent merchant born in Havana and a son-in-law of Victorino Jaso, owner of the huge hacienda of Guaracha; Domingo Torices, a merchant who had married Josefa Lavarrieta, owner of the rich hacienda of San Bartolomé; and José Manuel de Olarte, a merchant turned miner and sugar hacendado. The majority of these men had creole wives and children and had lived in Michoacán for decades. For the most part, though, they still adhered to the traditional patterns of partnership, operating either on their own or in association with their peninsula-born relatives, usually sons-in-law or brothers or nephews. A partial exception is Huarte, whose interests were so wide-ranging that he concluded several partnerships with creoles, although his primary association was with his Spanish son-in-law and former *dependiente*, Alzúa.

Gradually supplanting this older generation, however, was a younger generation of Spaniards with very close business (as well as family) ties to creoles. To a limited extent the process of recruiting creole partners had begun even before 1810, as "europeans" were ever more widely vilified among their clientele. But after the Hidalgo Rebellion an American partner or associate became almost a necessity. Fernando Moreira and Vicente Domínguez, for example, both Spaniards, had a company in Angamacutiro at the time of the insurrection. Moreira fled to Valladolid, leaving behind an 18,000-peso business — consisting of imported merchandise, commodities, his house, his mules, and accounts receivable — which the partners tried to salvage by sending Domínguez's creole son, Lic. José Domínguez, to oversee the business.[166] Pedro de Arana, a brother of Juan Bautista de Arana, who had been executed early in the insurrection, sent the creole Lic. José María Izasaga to try to liquidate his accounts in Zapotlán el Grande (though Izasaga, he complained, instead of carrying out this commission, joined the rebellion).[167]

Representing this younger generation of Spaniards at the 1815 and 1817 meetings were Pascual Alzúa, whose other partners — besides his father-in-law Isidro Huarte — included the creoles Antonio Anciola and Ignacio Montenegro, later his son-in-law;[168] Eugenio Garay, whose business partner was the creole Cayetano Gómez, another son-in-law of Alzúa;[169] Antonio de la Haya, a merchant who had accompanied Bishop San Miguel to Michoacán as a young man, studied at the seminary along with many creoles, and married into the creole González de Cosío family;[170] Gaspar Alonso de Ceballos, whose business and personal associates included the creoles José María García de Obeso, José Manuel del Río, Mariano Michelena, Juan José Martínez de Lejarza y Alday, and Agustín de Iturbide;[171] and Francisco Iturbe, who was connected by marriage to leading creole families, and whose principal partner, Ignacio Arriaga, was a creole.[172] By 1815 the patriotism of both of these generations of Spaniards was already stretched thin. When in 1821, six years after the execution of Morelos, the economic conditions under which they had to operate had still not substantially improved, they held the royal government at least partially responsible. After Iturbide declared Mexican independence not a single one of these Spaniards chose to leave Mexico and return to Spain.

In addition to the Crown's inability to restore order (much less prosperity), the annoying arrogance of its military officers, and its constant demands for local funds, there was another reason that noninsurgent, formerly loyal provincial elites, both Spaniards and creoles, became increasingly alienated from Spain. This was Ferdinand's refusal, upon being restored to the throne in 1814, to honor the 1812 Constitution. The promulgation of this fairly progressive constitution had given many noninsurgents a good reason to remain loyal. Dr. Manuel de la Bárcena expressed this attitude in an 1813 sermon that praised the constitution for striking "a perfect balance between individual rights and authority." "It is necessary," he reasoned, "that society have laws which . . . protect the weak against the strong, and assure to all life, liberty and property." Under the constitution the king would enforce these laws, but they would be formulated by the "nation," that is, by the parliament (Cortés). Perhaps most important to his listeners, he lauded the constitution for "erasing the Atlantic" ("ya no hay Atlántico") by giving equal rights to citizens on both sides of the ocean, no matter their place of birth.[173]

But with Ferdinand's rejection of the constitution in 1814 people like Bárcena were deeply dismayed. Spain had survived the terrible legacy of Charles IV and Godoy only because of its warriors, its extraordinary Cortés, and its "divine" constitution, Bárcena sermonized in 1820. When Ferdinand was restored to the throne in 1814 it was like a miracle: "Spain now lacked nothing to reassume its rightful place in the world, except Ferdinand's oath of loyalty to that document." But this he refused to give, and for six years he governed in the absolutist manner of his forebears. "Would that the years from 1814 to 1820," Bárcena continued, "could be stricken from the book of time, because during these years the glory of Spain has been eclipsed."[174]

Less than a year after he delivered this sermon Bárcena left behind his slim hope that Ferdinand's at-gunpoint conversion to constitutionalism in 1820 was at all genuine, and he jumped the Spanish ship, opting for independence. So, for different reasons, did many other elites, but all could agree with Bárcena that the time had come for Mexico to assert its "right" to independence, which he likened to a child's right to grow up and live apart from its parents. Repudiating his own argument that the 1812 Constitution had "erased the Atlantic," he now observed that "over two thousand leagues of distance [between Spain and America] are a huge obstacle that not even the wisest government can surmount." Among many things, distance made a mockery of the representative government provided for in the constitution, since it required American delegates to leave their homes and families for three years, whereas peninsular delegates could go back and forth to Madrid three or four times a year without having to give up anything. And on closer reading he was no longer satisfied that other features of the constitution suited America as well as he had originally thought: he particularly condemned its "unjust" exclusion from citizenship of mulattoes, which he said comprised one-third of the population of New Spain.[175]

Here and in his 1820 sermon Bárcena thoroughly anticipated the program of the "Liberator," Agustín de Iturbide, whose advisor Bárcena remained throughout Iturbide's short period of ascendancy.[176] Iturbide's vague "guarantees" — independence, union (which was most often read as equal rights for both peninsulars and Americans, but which could also be seen as guaranteeing equality among whites, Indians, and mulattoes) and religion — were, by 1821, acceptable to most elites, both former royalists and former insurgents.[177] As Bravo Ugarte puts it, "to nationalists, the plan offered Independence. To traditionalists, it offered Religion, the Union of Mexicans and Spaniards, and Monarchy. To liberals, it provided for a constitution."[178]

Conclusion

This view that the Plan de Iguala was essentially a hodgepodge with a little something for everyone assumes that it was designed to appeal to still-polarized elites.[179] But as we have seen, by 1821, there was considerable — though not total — agreement on all of the main features of the Plan (except for Iturbide's idea that monarchy was the best form of government for independent Mexico — precisely the thing that would be his downfall). By 1815 something like a new consensus among both creoles and peninsulars on the appropriateness of independence had emerged out of the chaos and disruption of the early insurgency.[180] The process by which this consensus was reached was multifaceted. First, some creole elites who had initially joined the insurgency pulled away from it as the movement became more marginalized and more factionalized after Morelos' execution in early 1815. Second, both creoles and peninsulars grew more and more disillusioned with the royal government's effectiveness, judgment, and fairness, a shift in attitude that began with the Consolidation and gathered steam during the counterinsurgency. Third, many progressives — again, both creoles and peninsulars — who had seen the 1812 Constitution as an answer to their desire for more decentralization and local autonomy were antagonized by Ferdinand's rejection of the constitution in 1814 and unconvinced by his ungracious acceptance of it in 1820. Finally, underlying the first three realignments, the peninsulars who chose to remain in America in 1810 tended to be those for whom both family and, increasingly, business ties to creoles were especially strong. For provincial elites, then, the mutual animosity between Americans and Europeans that had surfaced in 1809 and 1810 began to dissipate as the number of Europeans declined and as those who remained were more American in their outlook and interests than were Spaniards as a group before 1810.

This was not the same common ground sought by the authors of the 1805 petitions protesting the Consolidation, but because it was based on the increasing perception that Spain could not effectively govern or understand America, it was similar. While the protesters against the Consolidation, however, had failed to exploit this commonality to achieve their goal (to overturn the decree), in 1821 Agustín de Iturbide succeeded in tapping into it to achieve his: independence.

PART TWO

In the Aftermath of Independence: Building the State and Rebuilding the Economy

The Huarte Children After Independence:
Political Power and Economic Powerlessness

To the extent that the political sympathies and inclinations of Lic. Isidro Huarte Muñiz and his brother Ramón can be detected during the insurgent decade, they were marked by the same ambivalence exhibited by many of their generational peers. Not really pro-insurgent (like their brother Joaquín) and not really counterinsurgent (like their brother-in-law Agustín de Iturbide), they mainly stayed on the sidelines. But after 1820 they moved easily to the forefront of the political scene. Ramón, as president of the politically progressive 1820 Valladolid *ayuntamiento*, was named interim intendant in 1821 when the incumbent died; this position was transformed into a sort of protogovernorship (his official title was "Intendente Jefe Político") after Iturbide declared independence later that year. In this capacity he presided over the Michoacán Provincial Deputation's seconding of the federalist Plan de Casa Mata in 1823, which would be used to force Iturbide, his own brother-in-law, out of office.[1] He remained at the head of the state government until the state constitution was in place and a governor could be elected (that is, until 1825), and afterwards he served as *comisario general* for the state until the mid-1830s. Meanwhile his brother, Isidro, was elected in 1824 to the congress that wrote the state's constitution, and Isidro continued to hold positions in the state congress, the national congress, and the senate for almost two decades.

Like many of their peers, in the late 1820s and early 1830s both Ramón and Isidro set aside their early preference for federalism in favor of Anastacio Bustamante's (and Lucas Alamán's) mildly centralist and conservative politics. Ramón was in a particularly ticklish position in 1830 and

1831. As *comisario general* for the state he found himself in the anomalous position of being the sole support of his sister-in-law, Dolores Domínguez, while her husband, Juan José Codallos, led the federalist rebellion known as the War of the South against the government of which he, Huarte, was a part. Huarte was probably one of the "influential persons in Morelia" who tried behind the scenes to save Codallos's life after he was captured in 1831, but he did so anonymously.[2] The awkwardness of his position may, in fact, have driven him from politics; although he lived until the mid-1840s he seems not to have held any public office after 1835.

Isidro, on the other hand, weathered the shift from outspoken federalist to supporter of the centralist Bustamante and emerged in the 1840s with his reputation as a committed liberal intact. Huarte's contribution to the federalist state constitution of 1825 was substantial, but by the end of the decade he, like many others, had become disillusioned with the federal system; he was one of the senators who declared the federalist Vicente Guerrero "morally unfit to govern," and in 1836 he signed the Bases y Leyes, which decreed the replacement of the federal system with a centralist state.[3] But at his death in 1843 he was eulogized by Michoacán's liberal governors for his generosity (he left his roughly 100,000-peso estate to the state to be used to establish a men's hospice) and ideological correctness.[4]

It is difficult to judge whether Isidro and Ramón's involvement in state politics exacerbated the financial difficulties that plagued not only their family but much of the late-colonial upper class. Many public servants did make the connection, submitting letters of resignation that blamed their deteriorating economic circumstances on the fact that they did not have enough time to devote to their financial affairs because their public obligations consumed so much of their energy.[5] But while Ramón did see much of his patrimony slip away, Isidro's net worth may even have grown after independence. Besides, preoccupation with matters of government was by no means a prerequisite for financial hardship; many others, including almost all of the other Huarte children, suffered losses in the decade or so after independence.

The 1820s and early 1830s were trying times for everyone, but for the Huarte children they were made worse by the long-livedness of their father. Isidro Huarte must have been nearly 80 years old when he died in 1824, but his life as he knew it — that is, as an aggressive and active entrepreneur — had ended in 1810. Afterwards, too old and too stunned by the Hidalgo Rebellion to move easily with the times, his behavior became a perverse contradiction of his pre-1810 business practices. A man who had always been a key source of loan capital was forced into the highly unusual position of borrowing (on three occasions in 1820 and one in 1821).[6] Having dominated the commercial scene in Valladolid before 1810, and having had a hand in practically every type of economic activity in the province, from cotton to indigo to sugar to livestock to European imports to urban real estate to estate agriculture (although the only area in which he had not shown a great deal of interest was that of his own haciendas), Huarte scarcely concluded a business transaction in the last fifteen years of his life.

As long as he was alive, however, he refused to relinquish control over his still vast but now languishing enterprises. Though well before his death (in fact, before 1810) three of his sons were put in charge of the haciendas that they would eventually inherit, Huarte still had the last word on their management, and the profits from the haciendas were pooled together with the profits from the house's mercantile activities. For their subsistence the children each had an account with the firm on which they would draw; several of them thus consumed their inheritances in small bits and pieces before their father's death. Partly as a result of this, despite the fact that their inheritances on paper were impressive (50,000 pesos for each of the children of his marriage to Ana Manuela Muñiz, and about 14,000 pesos for the children of the third marriage), his children found it difficult to know how, precisely, to resurrect good fortune from the shattered ruins of post-1810 Michoacán.

Only two of the Huarte siblings ended up with fortunes in the upper ranks of the economic elite: Carmen Huarte, whose husband Pascual Alzúa was Isidro Huarte's principle business partner and whose estate at his death was worth about 250,000 pesos, and Lic. Isidro Huarte, whose estate amounted to some 100,000 pesos. Both Alzúa and Isidro Huarte, however, struggled after 1810. Alzúa's net worth was about the same or perhaps a bit less at his death than it had been in 1808 when Carmen died, and Isidro, after making a stab at rebuilding his hacienda of Urundaneo for direct production, gave up and turned it over to some 126 tenants.[7]

The other children fared much less well. Before his father's death Joaquín frittered away much of his maternal inheritance in small purchases and cash advances at his father's store; as a result he only inherited two houses, the small hacienda of Sindurio, and another hacienda, Sacapendo, which was burdened to its full value by debt. Combined, the net value of these properties was about 25,000 pesos. In 1826 he traded Sindurio to the Augustinians for the rancho of Tepacua, near Sacapendo, apparently in order to consolidate his holdings, but in 1829, despite having invested about 2,700 pesos in improvements, he was forced to cede Sacapendo back to its creditors. A year later he rented the adjacent hacienda of Naranjos from its bankruptcy court. This flurry of activity did not, however, rescue him from a slow slide that ended with his premature death in 1833. By the time his son Francisco reached adulthood in 1843, his inheritance had been whittled down to about 10,000 pesos, represented by the fully encumbered rancho and two houses in Morelia.[8]

Ramón's estate at his death in the early 1840s was also much reduced, amounting to about 12,000 pesos, all in urban real estate: a modest inn with an adjacent house, which he had inherited from his father, and the house he lived in, next door to his father's own main residence.[9] José Antonio's estate was a still paler reflection of his inherited wealth than was his younger brothers'. In 1836 he sold the hacienda of Guadalupe — which he had inherited at a value of 50,000 pesos — for just 33,455 pesos, of which only 16,275 pesos was free and clear. By the time he made his will in 1840 he only had 11,000 pesos left, and by 1844 he had only 8,000, having donated some of his capital to his nephew Francisco Huarte Guerra and his half-brother Mariano Huarte Alcántara. He instructed his executors to give away the rest to four women who had lived in his house and had helped him, but by the time he died in 1852, having outlived all of his siblings except Ana (m. Iturbide), he had virtually no estate at all: all he had left was his modest residence, which was mortgaged for more than it was worth; furniture and household goods worth 200 pesos; clothing worth 15 pesos; and 20 pesos worth of religious images.[10]

There is not much information about Teresa Huarte's wealth at death, since she left the country for New Orleans when her third husband, a Spaniard, was expelled in 1827, but it appears that she was unable to preserve even the modest inheritance she had extracted from her father's estate after he had deducted the costs of the lawsuit he waged to try to prevent her second marriage.[11] Ana Huarte's financial affairs after the 1824 execution of her husband, Agustín de Iturbide, also are not known, though she clearly managed to maintain a respectable position in Philadelphia society after his death.[12]

The Huarte Muñiz children's difficulties after independence were not, of course, unusual among this generation. For those born after 1760 but before 1780 or so, the Hidalgo Rebellion was a great personal (as well as national) watershed. They were old enough to be deeply aware of (one might even say paralyzed by) the profound differences between the ripe exuberance of the late colonial economy and the grim realities of the post-1810 economic collapse. Many of them, trying to do things the way their fathers had but burdened with bad debts and destroyed, heavily indebted property, were unable to adjust to the new conditions of doing business. Moreover, most of them were neither young enough nor old enough to avoid distracting involvement in the busy politics of the period from 1805 forward, even if they wanted to. In this respect the Huarte children and their spouses may have been a bit unusual (it is hard to see how a family with such enormous pre-1810 political power could have failed to be in the middle of politics afterwards), but they were not alone. In part, the price they paid for participating — on either side — in shaping the post-independence state and national governments in the 1820s and 1830s was that they were unable to focus on exploiting the economic opportunities inherent in a period of such profound change. That would be the role of the next generation.

CHAPTER THREE

Celebrating Too Soon:
Euphoria and Disillusionment in the
1820s and Early 1830s

After the ravages of the insurgent decade it may seem absurd to suggest that Mexico gained its independence too easily, but there is certainly a sense in which the patched-together but near-universal consensus in 1821 around Iturbide's "three guarantees" blinded victorious creoles to the difficulties of both nation building and economic reconstruction. Moreover, for another half a decade after independence the sentiment that the end of colonial rule alone had put Mexico on the right track was fed by the fact that the consensus held up, buoyed by an encouraging rebound in agricultural production and mercantile activity. It even survived Iturbide's own downfall in 1823.

But by the late 1820s the very nature of the still-limited economic advances increasingly belied the rhetoric employed to preserve the cross-class alliances of the independence era. That is, to the extent that the rebuilding process had taken hold, it was by means of the sort of business arrangements (including a strong local role for Spanish merchants and a strong national role for foreign merchants) that, along with high commodity prices, gave new life to many of the old, pre-1810 grievances of the popular classes. The result was a renewal of pressure on the political system in the form of riots, rebellions, and banditry. And complicating the situation was the fact that while economic conditions had indeed improved, the beneficiaries were not, for the most part, the people who had owned land when the wars for independence had broken out. In fact the opposite was true: the slow but sure demise of the former landowning elite began to show up in the form of bankruptcies and forced sales of property in the late 1820s, and it continued through the 1830s. In the end, Mexico's, and Michoacán's, failure to thrive, especially after early glittering expectations had been raised, would lead desperate politicians, many of whom were hacendados suffering grave economic reverses, to change the political system from federalism to centralism in the mid-1830s.

Encouraging Signs . . .

THE ECONOMY

In Michoacán, as elsewhere, independence was greeted with elation, in the full expectation that things could only get better from now on. William Hardy, who arrived in Zinapécuaro in 1826 as the town celebrated the first anniversary of the swearing to the new state constitution, wrote that this was "a period of general festivity, when all the province of Valladolid appears to be of one mind. Bull-baiting, dancing, and feasting are the sole objects, and, in this respect, we were fortunate in arriving at a time, which gave us an opportunity of witnessing a feeling so general."[1] Later he described a joyous and well-attended ball held in Valladolid to commemorate the same event, at which "the supper table was laid out with a profusion of flowers and viands of all descriptions, with emblems on the sweetmeats in the shape of little paper flags, curiously cut out, with patriotic verses on them."[2]

A theatrical comedy troupe made plans in 1823 to visit and entertain Valladolid, a city that six years earlier even suppliers of basic goods could not reach.[3] Within a few years the Sociedad de Amigos Protectora del Teatro purchased two houses that were torn down in order to make room for a proper theater for the state capital, built at the staggering cost of 36,000 pesos. The first production featured the famous actress Amada Plata.[4] The 1827 *Memoria de Gobierno* proudly observed that where peace and security were concerned, "Michoacán has no cause to envy any other state. We have had an almost uninterrupted period of tranquillity [since independence], and if our citizens still suffer, like the citizens of all the other states, from occasional minor attacks [from highwaymen], they are certainly no worse than in the so-called good times before 1810."[5] An 1823 contract renewing the rental of the large rancho of Coincho expressed the hopes of many: for the past three years the rancho had "suffered the inconveniences and losses common during the years when public security was still not established," but now, "by the grace of God, a solid peace has arrived," and the renter was poised and ready to begin the necessary repairs.[6]

This renter's decision to resume cultivation on his hacienda was part of a general upward trend in agricultural production whose early indications had been detectable in a few parts of the state as early as 1817 (see chapter 2). By 1822 Martínez de Lejarza's careful survey of the state suggests that a painful recuperation was already underway in most areas. In Zitácuaro, despite the fact that sugar mills, haciendas, and whole towns had been destroyed, agriculture was "beginning to recover its former splendor."[7] Mule drivers with goods — especially cotton, salt, and indigo — from the coastal districts had reappeared in large numbers in the trading town of Uruapan.[8] In Tlalpujahua, he wrote, though haciendas had typically lost two-thirds of their livestock, they had begun the process of restocking.[9] Marked improvement was also noted in Parangaricútiro, Jiquilpan, La Piedad, and Puruándiro, especially the latter, which because of its climate, strategic location, and "enlightened and prosperous populace," was experiencing a vigorous recovery, rebuilding its destroyed residences and churches, reestablishing trade, and reviving its production of shoes and leather goods.[10] In 1827 the state government, while lamenting the still-sluggish pace of commercial exchange, noted that sugar cane products, rice, indigo, cotton, *aguardiente*, wheat, and chile were again being marketed out-of-region. The only traditional "export" missing was livestock, but even here the *Memoria* noted significant improvement.[11] A grand scheme was approved in 1826 not only to reopen the iron works at Coalcomán in the coastal mountains but to develop the whole region through colonization projects, land grants, and port development.[12]

By 1823 the church was busily signing tithe contracts with intrepid potential collectors, admittedly only in the northern and western districts, and with rather high commissions of 10 to 12 percent. Church records indicate that in 1825 tithe pledges reached approximately 115,000 pesos and rose to 140,000 pesos by the end of the decade, not all that distant from the approximately 200,000 pesos the church received from the tithe each year before 1810.[13] In Pátzcuaro, although wheat production levels in 1824 were still only at about 20 percent of 1804 levels, corn production had returned to at least 70 percent of pre-1810 levels.[14] And on some haciendas, pre-1810 levels of income had already been attained and even surpassed by the mid-1820s. On the former Jesuit hacienda of Queréndaro, for example, the value of agricultural production rose from around 24,000 pesos at the turn of the century to some 32,000 pesos in the 1820s.[15] Sales tax records yield a similar picture of tentative recovery, implying total statewide trade of 1,350,000 pesos a year by 1826, compared to 2,000,000 pesos in the decade before

1810.[16] These data reveal an economy that was far from vigorous but also far from the state of near-total collapse in which it had been mired during the previous decade.

"NUESTRO SISTEMA FELIZ"

Accompanying this promising start toward economic reconstruction was a near-complete public agreement on the principles and ideals that should shape the new republican institutions. Those who took part in establishing the most visible of these institutions — a free press and a state congress — spoke the same language: newspaper editors and state legislators differed among themselves only in the shadings of their frequently reiterated commitment to the principles of individual freedom, equality, and private property.[17] Those for whom these principles did not embody political perfection were, temporarily, quiet.[18]

The ubiquity with which liberal individualism and political openness were embraced is especially easy to observe in the debates of the state congress, whose most striking symbolic act came in 1828 when the deputies voted to honor the insurgent priest José María Morelos by changing the name of the state capital from Valladolid to Morelia.[19] Deputies elected to the first three congresses (1826–27, 1828–29, and 1830–31) who argued for some restrictions on individual rights or some exceptions to the rule of absolute equality did so apologetically and with much qualification. In a debate over whether or not city council members should wear a special sash, for example, congressmen on one side of the issue staked out the purest libertarian ground: in "our truly free system," they proclaimed, absolutely any distinction that set one individual apart from others was to be abhorred. Others, wishing to argue that some sort of badge of authority was useful and convenient, scrambled nonetheless to embrace the ideal of "republican equality" and to make sure that no one thought they were endorsing the colonial government's strategy of creating empty honorifics as a sop to individual ego.[20] Similarly, in various discussions around the balance between individual rights and the general good (e.g., should Indian communities without access to firewood be *required* to plant trees? does the government have the right to destroy two bunkers and confiscate a small cache of rifles found on private property?), all speakers felt it necessary to proclaim their devotion to the sacred principle of personal freedom of action before gingerly establishing a position that fell somewhat short of a full and complete defense of individual rights.[21]

Even the debates in the state congress least concerned with abstract ideals and most with power and jurisdiction were couched almost invariably in terms of whether a certain law or decree was sufficiently or insufficiently "liberal." For example, a proposed law allowing prefects to suspend members of the city councils was dismissed by Br. Manuel de la Torre Lloreda as "illiberal."[22] Another proposal, which would have permitted prefects to force into towns, haciendas, or rancherías "people who were suspicious by virtue of living in remote areas and serving no useful purpose," was widely denounced as "contrary to individual liberty." One of its chief critics, Br. Juan José Pastor Morales, owner of the rich hacienda of Bellasfuentes, pointed out with dripping irony that the president of the Republic (Guadalupe Victoria) had spent much time living alone in the mountains.[23]

The legislators were enamored of the language and slogans and icons of liberalism and democracy, but they also had faith in the power of liberal democracy to transform a colonial system that since 1805 they had come to see as tyrannical, corrupt, growth-inhibiting, and unresponsive, into a new and more perfect system of government (often referred to as "nuestro sistema feliz").[24] This faith was reflected in the near-unanimous passage of a series of laws grounded in liberal economic and social principles. For example, the ability of the city councils to regulate and restrict local commerce (and, effectively, grant monopolies) was eliminated in an 1825 law; from now on, retailers could operate whenever and wherever they chose.[25] Also designed to stimulate freer trade was a new system of direct taxation based on income and property, the *contribución directa*, which was meant to take the place of burdensome and consumption-discouraging indirect taxes, especially sales taxes.[26] A law providing for the division of communal property held by Indian villages was passed, on the grounds (as we shall see in more detail shortly) that as individual property owners the "miserable" indigenous population would be converted into model citizens.[27] The democratic ideal of public education was embraced, and a system of teacher training using the Lancaster method was authorized in 1827, easing the path for the middle classes to acquire a professional education or degree as the legislature provided for the establishment of schools of medicine and law and programs to graduate pharmacists and notaries.[28] There were even some tentative steps taken in the direction of expanded government control over what would eventually emerge as the most powerful obstacle in the path of creating a liberal society, the church, though the association of the despised colonial government with anticlericalism, as well as the "heroic" behavior of many priests in the wars for independence, fairly effectively prevented the post-independent governments in the 1820s from picking up where the late Bourbons had left off.[29]

It is worth examining in some detail two lengthy debates carried on in the state legislature, both of which, in different ways, illustrate the difficulties that the deputies experienced when, lightly armed with liberal principles, they came up against the realities of the post-independent world. The first of these issues was of enduring interest and importance in Michoacán and indeed in all of Mexico. It concerned legislation requiring Indian villages to divide their common lands among the individual members of the community. The *reparto de tierras* first came up for discussion in December 1826. As always, the eloquent speeches made both for and against the proposed law were anchored by liberal principles.

Francisco Aragón opposed the law on the grounds that it was "unjust, impolitic, and impractical," and his argument embraced the liberal ideals of social and economic equality, public schooling, and yeoman farms (as against both communal lands and too-large haciendas). Both experience and reason tell us, he orated, that if we divide village holdings those who mainly benefit will be the owners of neighboring lands, who will find ways to acquire them at very little cost. This aggrandizement of estates is condemned by all political economists. Furthermore, it is impossible to give everyone a perfectly equal plot of land, and in any event some communities begin with much better land than others; thus the law inevitably produces violations of the principle of equality. Finally, if the *reparto* goes forward, what will become of the schools whose teachers are paid from community funds, which often come from renting out the commons?

Manuel González agreed, adding that though several villages had requested division of their lands, a close reading of the petitions reveals that they all made the same points in the same order, and might even have been written by the same hand, suggesting that they were forged by an ambitious speculator taking advantage of the gullibility and ignorance of the villagers. Beyond this, he said, the proposed solution to the problem of grasping non-Indians buying up the newly-divided land — that the Indians be forbidden from selling the land they receive for a certain number of years — is a violation of their individual rights as property owners. In sum, division of community lands before the Indians are educated enough to administer them and to recognize when they are being taken advantage of will do more harm than good.

The case in favor of dividing community lands was made by Agustín

Aguiar, a wealthy landowner from the Zamora region, who portrayed village-oriented Indians as albatrosses on economic growth, and as susceptible to "outside" forces fomenting unrest and even rebellion. The choice is between two imperfect alternatives, he began, but he chose *repartimiento* as the least imperfect. If we allow the Indians to continue to hold lands in common, he argued, they will remain in their present state of misery, isolated, and refusing to interact with other citizens of the state. This isolation can only produce two results, both evil. The first is that they come to think of themselves as the only owners of *all* the lands of the Republic, to the exclusion of their fellow citizens (a position that some "malicious ignoramuses" have tried to persuade them to take). The second and more likely possibility is that their isolation will prevent them from assuming high office or position, which will in turn perpetuate their sense of inferiority and their resentment. As long as they are held apart, or hold themselves apart, from the rest of the nation, they will never be a true part of that nation. They may even become the blind instruments of ambitious foreigners who, promising them a return to the glory days of Moctezuma and Caltzontzin, would lead them into rebellion. This is not fantastical, he added: look at the detestable recent events in Sonora, in which the Mayos and Yaquis have risen up under like circumstances. Moreover, if we do not require the division of pueblo lands, they may decide to divide them themselves, which would be a terrible disaster, since the *repartimiento* would be engineered by the *principales*, and would be bloodily contested by those whom these old men have cruelly tyrannized, in the way that the vile agents of the Spanish government encouraged them to do.

On the other hand, if the government presides over the distribution of lands, many good things will result. First, the measure will create a large number of individual property holders, and all the experts agree that the best and most effective way to consolidate free, public institutions is to ensure that the largest possible number of individuals has a stake in the system. The *reparto*, then, converts into our best friends a people that might otherwise be our worst enemies. By causing them to interact and mix with us, this measure will mean the demise of the odious label "Yndios," which still lingers despite our valiant attempts to bring about equality. Let us not be fooled by the pretexts of compassion and beneficence embraced by opponents of the law; these are the same pretexts that the Spanish government employed, to the perdition of those who supposedly benefited. We ought to follow the opposite path. We ought to recognize only the distinctions of virtue and merit, not blood and birth; if we do, we will create a new race of free citizens, all equally committed to defend our freedom and our glorious Independence. He concluded by quoting Humboldt's own conclusion to his *Political Essay*: "Above all I hope I have persuaded [Mexicans] that the future well-being of the white race is intimately linked to that of the bronze race, and that there can be no lasting happiness in the Americas as long as this humble people does not partake of all the benefits of progress and civilization."[30] The vote was nine in favor of the *reparto*, three against.

This debate, many of whose arguments would be repeated over the next 30 years and beyond, typified the ambivalence of the upper- and middle-class legislators toward the Indian population: they saw themselves as redeemers who ostensibly hoped to make indigenous peoples part of the nation, but in the same breath they revealed their fear that the Indians were at best too fundamentally different from the rest of the population for this to happen, and at worst were liable to actively disrupt the formation of a successful nation.

The second issue — that of whether or not to outlaw bullfighting — reflected not only a similar attitude toward the vast majority of the state's population (that is, that the people had to be protected from their own worst instincts), but also the process by which the idealism of political elites in the early post-independent years gave way to recognition of the limits on their ability to legislate a liberal society. The abolition of bullfighting, "this barbaric custom whose violent nature stands in contradiction to the enlightened century in which we fortunately live," seemed a perfect way to advertise to the world the break from a colonial system that pandered to the worst instincts of the plebe without making much effort to raise him up.[31] But it turned out to be a more complicated issue than it seemed on the surface. Manuel Ruiz de Chávez began the January 1826 debate by speaking against the "absolute extinction" of bullfighting. First, he argued, who is to say that if we outlaw this terrible sport the common people will not turn to even more immoral and noxious diversions? Second, men who have tested and honed their courage by bullfighting served the nation well during the Revolution, and we may need such men in the future to defend the *patria*. Why not, he argued — bowing to the seemingly irrefutable argument that the violence of bullfighting was a national embarrassment — allow the fights to go on with dehorned bulls, which could be used as plow animals as well? This curious compromise was supported by Lic. Isidro Huarte and Br. Pablo José Peguero, who added that although it was true that bullfighting was barbaric, it was impolitic to try to outlaw such an ingrained custom.

In support of outright abolition, José María Navarro disagreed that in the absence of bullfighting people would turn to even worse spectacles; there were, he opined (rather unrealistically), plenty more edifying types of entertainment, such as the theater. In any event, no diversion could be more degrading to humanity than bullfighting was. As for the argument that bullfighters are good soldiers, he continued, nothing could be farther from the truth: they are barbaric assassins and just as violent as the sport in which they excel. His position was seconded by Joaquín Domínguez, Manuel González, and Mateo Echaiz, and in the end, abolition won the day.[32]

By 1828, however, the refined sensibilities of the deputies had come up against the practices of the people of the state. In October Ignacio Villavicencio and Juan Gómez de la Puente proposed that the law be revoked. They held fast to the position that barbarism endangered the liberal society that they all desired, but argued, rather weakly, that perhaps bullfighting wasn't *so* barbaric after all, since the slain bulls *were* used to feed people. Besides, it was a "national" custom, and the law was flouted "in all the ranchos and haciendas and even the towns of the state." Citing Montesquieu's dictum that cultural habits cannot be easily uprooted or attacked head on, they convinced their colleagues to back down and rescind the law.[33]

. . . and Discouraging Signs

This was only a minor example of a broad, uneven move in the late 1820s away from the earlier vision of a shining society of free and equal citizens going about their business with no interference from the government. By 1827 the tenor of the debates had begun to change. Concerns about growing political unease and lawlessness and even rebellion intersected with the gathering realization that the earlier optimism about the economy and the political system had been premature. It was becoming clear that even under the most benign political conditions, many landowners — including several deputies — were going to lose their homes and haciendas.

The decline of the old landowning class was not a result of liberalism or federalism so much as it was a product of the church's policies of debt management, which allowed debtors to continue to pile up back interest for years and even decades in the usually vain hope that they would eventually resume debt service, thereby preserving the church's original capital.[34] But the still-new federal system — so very different from the centralized, exclusionary colonial system — was more visible and easier to blame for the political and economic problems that were beginning to emerge as the early post-independence optimism faded. Maybe in retrospect, many people thought, a less generous, less democratic approach to nation building would have been more appropriate for a country in which so many were illiterate and unpropertied; maybe the franchise itself did not make people responsible voters or citizens. As the political situation worsened and the true enormity of the economic task ahead became clear, these considerations began to overwhelm the liberal, reformist tendencies among state legislators. Slowly the language and the substance of the debates began to deemphasize freedom and equality and to emphasize instead the need for government to find a way to secure peace and tranquillity. For the time being this meant plugging some of the loopholes in the constitutional protection of broad individual rights through which "troublemakers" passed. Later it would mean reconsideration of the federal system itself.

The events that inspired the move away from "liberty" and toward "order" had begun in 1827, when nearly six years of relative tranquillity in Michoacán ended with a rebellion mounted by the Civic Militias of Tarímbaro and Tiripitio. Joined by a handful of other militias the rebellious units reached the outskirts of Valladolid in late October. As elsewhere in Mexico in 1827, the chief demand of these "poor and poorly armed *campesinos*" was the expulsion of Spaniards from the state.[35] The hatred of Spaniards, which had always been particularly strong among the rural and urban poor, and which had taken political shape during the wars for independence, had bubbled back to the surface. The newly organized state militias served as an institutional focus for this sentiment, and the York-rite lodges, among whose members military officers were numerous, provided much of the leadership. In the Valladolid rebellion, four *yorkinos* apparently played key roles: General Vicente Filisola, a former *iturbidista*, First Adjutant Ignacio Vásquez (who was associated with the Tarímbaro militia), Vice-Governor José Salgado, and Canon Martín García Carrasquedo.

The rebellion opened a wedge between elites and popular groups, and their tenuous alliance during the insurgency, the Iturbide regime, and the early years of the Federal Republic now fractured. This alliance had been based in 1821 on mutual acceptance of Iturbide's vague guarantees (Independence, Union, and Religion); later, it revolved around agreement on the ideals of republicanism, federalism, and representational government. But throughout the insurgency and the early Republic it had also been based on the threat posed by common enemies: Spain and Spaniards. By the late 1820s,

however, agreement on the danger posed by Spaniards was no longer universal. For creoles — either old families trying to put their lives back together
after the disasters of the last fifteen or so years, or ambitious new men trying
to take advantage of flux and uncertainty in the new post-independent environment — it was increasingly convenient and even essential to act in commercial association with Spanish capitalists, as we shall see in more detail in
chapter 4. The very decision to stay in (or, in a few cases, to immigrate to)
Mexico was, for most creole elites, sufficient evidence of these Spaniards' acceptance of Mexican independence and loyalty to the new nation. Any
doubts about the unseemliness of embracing the "enemy" were eased by the
fact that the Spaniards' capital and expertise were much needed after the capital flight, property destruction, and immobilization of credit during the insurgent decade. And in any event, as we have seen, the construction of the
Spaniard-as-enemy had been, from the elite point of view, late and short-
lived, lasting at most from 1808 to 1815.[36] For well-to-do creoles, except for
that brief span, the real enemy had been Spain, not Spaniards.

But for many of the poor, for whom the most important enemies were
Spaniards they encountered almost daily, it must have seemed that the sacrifices they had made for independence were going for naught. Spaniards who
had fought against them as counterinsurgents and had switched over to
Iturbide at the last moment continued to head up the army, and in some cases
the very same Spanish merchants who had overcharged and underpaid them
before 1810 were now in cahoots with creoles with whom peasants and urban
workers had been allied during the insurgency and the Iturbide movement.

The demand for expulsion, so angrily expressed by the populace, ham-
strung the state congress, which had made a point of proclaiming its devotion
to the interests of the popular classes but which had also made a point of proclaiming its devotion to the principles of equality and protection of property
rights and individual freedom for all citizens, including Spaniards. As one anguished congressman asked, how could the legislature proceed against them
as a group without even a single trial having been conducted?[37]

In the end, however, it did not much matter which principles were invoked, since the reality was that by early November 1827 there was virtually
no military support for Governor Lic. Antonio de Castro's position that the
state must not negotiate with the expulsion-minded rebels. Faced with a military challenge almost literally on their very doorstep, the only thing the legislature could do was to frame a law with as many exemptions as possible.
The 1827 law of expulsion, then, applied only to Spaniards under age 60 who

were unmarried, or did not live with their wives, or were not "good parents" to their children. But an attempt by some deputies to give them longer than 30 days to get their affairs in order was rejected: to let them stay any longer than absolutely necessary would be to further inflame an already angry *pueblo*.[38] Even the knowledge that Castro would resign as governor if congress passed the expulsion law did not sway the deputies. Castro made a half-hearted attempt to face down the rebels, who were camped near the city, but even his personal bodyguard abandoned him along the way. He then made good his resignation in an action that symbolized the growing rift between well-to-do creoles and popular groups: a wealthy former insurgent resigned the governorship rather than accede to the demand to — as the rebels saw it — finish the work of independence.

The 1827 expulsion bought the congress and the state no respite from political turmoil, however. Its many categories for exemption fed the belief on the part of the popular classes that they were being appeased, not satisfied.[39] Continuing *pronunciamientos* and tension led the legislature to propose various broad vagrancy laws and in 1829 to pass another, stricter law of expulsion. The reasoning of the deputies was similar to what it had been in 1827: "these poor men [Spaniards] find themselves between two extremes: expulsion, or death at the hand of a pueblo that detests them." Admitting that their expulsion would further decapitalize Mexico when it could ill afford it, the deputies decided that the peace they hoped (in vain) would surely follow the expulsion would be worth it.[40] But by 1829 other events had intervened to polarize elites and popular groups, so that even this strict expulsion law was not enough to prevent further unrest.

These events began in Mexico City in late 1828. First, there was a revolt by a portion of the military with *yorkino* leadership (the so-called Acordada Revolt), demanding that the relatively radical former insurgent and fellow *yorkino*, Vicente Guerrero, be elevated to the presidency in place of the moderate president-elect Manuel Gómez Pedraza. The rebellion was successful: Gómez Pedraza left the country, and Guerrero became president. Second, in the wake of the Acordada Revolt, there was an assault on the Parián market — an area in the center city where wealthy merchants, many of them Spaniards, maintained retail outlets — by what the propertied classes saw as an uncontrolled and uncontrollable mob, typical, they thought, of Guerrero's supporters. If, even before these incidents, elites had begun to draw away from their former unreserved support of liberal and democratic principles, afterwards upper class rejection of Guerrero, who stood for many of the things they had embraced in the warm glow of the immediate post-independence years, was almost unanimous. Finally in late 1829, just months after a feeble Spanish attempt to reconquer Mexico had been turned back, a handful of military officers, including Vice President Anastacio Bustamante, took thinly veiled action against Guerrero in the form of the Plan de Jalapa, which provided for the recall of officials against whom, through their city councils, a majority of the public had expressed dissatisfaction. Guerrero, with few supporters in the capital, capitulated and left Mexico City. Bustamante became president, and Lucas Alamán, whose centralizing politics were well known, became his chief adviser.

The Plan de Jalapa was accepted, even welcomed, in most parts of Mexico, but in Michoacán the state's leaders went to work against it almost immediately. The governor, José Salgado, who had assumed the office when Castro resigned in protest of the 1827 expulsion, was among the few prominent public officials in all of Mexico who sided with Guerrero and pledged to work to reinstate him and other officials deposed by the plan. A majority of the congress supported him. But the Morelia *ayuntamiento* (whom Salgado branded "a reunion of criminals"), led by Manuel Alzúa, with the former Valladolid conspirator Mariano Michelena in the background, managed to drive Salgado (whom the *ayuntamiento* called "that nefarious *yorkino*") out of town in the dead of night, and out of office. This was the first strong assault on the federal system in Michoacán, but it was hardly the last.[41]

In the wake of the actions of the Morelia *ayuntamiento* and events in Mexico City, supporters of Guerrero — mostly from a background similar to that of the poor sharecroppers, tenants, and Indians who had made up his army in his old, insurgent days — took up arms. By the summer of 1830 Michoacán was a principal battleground of the so-called War of the South, which was centered in the same parts of the state where the insurgency had flourished for so long: the coast, the coastal mountains, and the *tierra caliente* of the Balsas-Tepalcátepec river basin.[42] Led in Michoacán by Ramón Huarte's brother-in-law and a former counterinsurgent officer, Juan José Codallos, and by an unreconstructed insurgent, Gordiano Guzmán — in a last gasp of the cross-class alliances that had been so important in the 1810s and early 1820s — the federalist rebels occupied Uruapan, Tacámbaro, Apatzingán, and Aguililla in the southern part of the state, and Jacona, Zamora, and Jiquilpan in the west. Morelia was once again threatened, but the rebels were turned back on the outskirts of the city.[43] The governor's report to the legislature in 1831 noted sadly that no progress should be expected in the near future, given the "great havoc not only in the South and the East, but also in the North and West, inflicted by invading bands of rebels."[44] The rebellion quieted after July 1831, when Codallos was captured and executed, but a small band of men operating in the Apatzingán-Aguililla area continued to harass the exportation of sugar, *piloncillo*, indigo, rice, and tropical fruits from parts of the central-western *tierra caliente*.[45]

If the public consensus around the form of government (federalism) and the guiding principles of that government (liberalism) had begun to unravel in 1827, the war completed the process. The scorn and venom heaped upon the leaders of the rebellion, especially by the newly founded centralist newspaper *El Michoacano Libre*, was unprecedented. Codallos — despite his connection to the Huartes — was vilified as "perverse, inhuman, criminal, and bloodthirsty," the "apostle of anarchy," the "víbora de Michoacán."[46] The rebels were "cannibals" and "sybarites" poised to deflower virgins and violate their mothers. Given this characterization of the federalist "hordes," it is no wonder that after Gral. Pedro Otero turned back Codallos' attack on Morelia in December 1830 and then chased him to Tacámbaro, the city's leading citizens and corporations greeted him as a liberating hero. A beautiful maiden, Casimira Dávalos, a member of a wealthy Zamora family, crowned him with a laurel wreath on behalf of the Cathedral Chapter, the same body that was known as dangerously radical during the period of the insurgency.[47] The real target of the speechmakers and the press, however, was the federal system, which many elites had decided was too weak to guarantee the predictable investment environment that they so desperately desired as they tried to save themselves from the quagmire of the post-1810 economic depression.

The erosion of support for the federal system was not only trumpeted maniacally in the hyperbolic centralist press but also surfaced more subtly in the debates of the state legislature. The first stages, as we have seen, consisted of drawing away from the relatively pure liberalism of the period 1824–27: in 1827 the congress tentatively began to substitute for the oratorical motifs of "liberty" and "equality" those of "order" and "security." But the trend is especially notable beginning with the "second" Third Congress (elected in July 1830 to replace the original Third Congress, which was deposed under the terms of the Plan de Jalapa). A minor but illustrative example of the shift is to be found in an April 1831 debate over the titles by which members of the new Junta Inspectora of schools would be addressed. In the mid-1820s the consensus had been that no title at all other than "citizen" was needed, but by 1831 the speakers assumed the desirability of some honorific, merely de-

bating whether it should be the extravagant "Excelencia," or the more restrained "Ylustre." In a similar discussion in 1832 one speaker even argued,
disingenuously, that "the pueblo is so used to such distinctions that much as
we dislike them, we must accommodate ourselves to custom."[48]

Rather than formulating sweeping plans to reform society these deputies
wanted to patch up a federal system that they almost all admitted had failed
in key respects, and that was under attack from the "enemies of the system."[49] There was much discussion, for example, of ways to get around the
"ineptness" of the *ayuntamientos* in small towns. A successful federal system
depended on "responsible" city council leadership, but, they complained, it
was hard to find enough qualified persons to serve anywhere except in
Morelia, especially since the congress frowned on close relatives monopolizing the council positions.[50] This position was echoed in the governor's
Memoria de Administración for 1833–34, which sent an initiative to the congress asking it to reduce the number of *ayuntamientos* in light of the fact that
so many city council members could not even read, much less write. "Now is
the time that without rejecting admirable theories, we should act on the basis
of the facts; we should take into special consideration who we are, without
losing sight of what we ought to be."[51] In a similar vein, tightened suffrage requirements and stiff property requirements for elected officials were discussed
(though mostly rejected) as a means to disenfranchise and marginalize those
without good moral principles (maturity, rootedness), while salvaging some
semblance of democracy:

> How can Michoacán have a wise and just administration, capable of
> realizing the full potential of our favorable geographic position and our
> many natural resources, if the electoral basis of such an administration
> is the suffrage of an immense majority . . . which completely lacks the
> education and knowledge to exercise the franchise with prudence? We
> believe that if the State is to survive, it is necessary to reform the part of
> the Constitution dealing with political rights, restricting them to those
> who give society certain guarantees. . . .[52]

Moreover, though some items on the liberal agenda still found favor with this
congress and the one that followed (1832–33), the deteriorating condition of
the state treasury prevented them from being realized or even from being
promoted with much enthusiasm. The project to establish primary schools
throughout the state had faltered, with only 12 of the 32 schools mandated
by an 1831 law having been established by 1835.[53] There was tinkering with

sales tax laws and rates in an attempt to promote a freer flow of trade, and there was talk of eliminating one state-run monopoly, the tobacco monopoly, but in general liberalizing reforms were minuscule because most of them were either too expensive or cost the state revenues that it could ill afford to lose. Almost as soon as the tobacco monopoly *was* abolished in 1833, for example, there was talk of reinstituting it, since the loss to the state treasury was so great.[54]

The only real advances of the liberal agenda in the 1830s occurred during the period in Michoacán politics that coincides with the Gómez Pedraza regime at the national level, from early 1833 through mid-1834. But by this time the themes invoked by the reformers in speeches and debates had less to do with the need to promote liberty and equality — as in the earlier period of ascendant liberalism — than with the need to combat the "enemies of the system." For the leaders of this liberal surge, the key "enemy" was the church, an institution that had largely escaped the attentions of previous reformist congresses, and their assault on the church was so controversial and so vigorously contested that the net effect was to produce a backlash that ensured the triumph of centralism.

This brief period of radical liberalism in Michoacán began when a January 1833 uprising brought down Governor Diego Moreno, an extremely wealthy hacendado from Zamora. Moreno was replaced by the man he himself had replaced in 1830, José Salgado (though there were to be ten different governors in 1833 alone), and the Fourth Congress was replaced by a fifth.[55] The new liberal regime was challenged immediately: in May 1833 congressional anticlericalism provoked the so-called "pronunciamiento de Morelia," directed by Comandante Ignacio Escalada (whose Plan de Escalada was also known as the Plan de Religión y Fueros) and Col. José de Ugarte, a member of a wealthy Valladolid family. Governor Salgado was imprisoned, and the congress fled across the state border to Celaya, Guanajuato. When it returned and Salgado was reinstated, far from deterred, the congress took up where it had left off. For the next year (until another centralist rebellion finally toppled the national government), the congress continued to attempt to weaken the church in almost every aspect of its powerful and multifarious role in Mexican life.

The most telling and explosive exchange came in March 1834, when a proposal was introduced to "severely punish" the "criminal conduct" of the bishop and other churchmen who "only want to erect on the ruins of the Republic the throne of aristocratic tyranny." (Their "crime" was that they refused to accept national laws abolishing the civil obligation to tithe and claiming the right of ecclesiastical patronage for the Mexican nation.) To the tentative objection of Nicolás Menocal that perhaps it was unwise for Michoacán to go so far out on this particular anticlerical limb, Francisco Santoyo replied that for Michoacán to be in the vanguard on this issue would be a "glorious" means of "reclaiming the rights of the Nation and sustaining the Democratic Government that its enemies are trying to tear down by any vile means the process requires, the better to oppress the citizenry." Lic. Gregorio Ceballos then pushed the envelope even further when he argued that the proposed bill was a good one because it would help rescue a pueblo mired in fanatic and excessive devotion to the church. This occasioned an outraged response from Menocal, among others, who defended religion as the key to social stability.[56]

The language with which the anticlerical measures were promoted, perhaps as much as the measures themselves, alienated the moderates in the congress and, presumably, in the city and state. The bishop of Michoacán, José Cayetano de Portugal, whether wittingly or unwittingly, perfectly manipulated the anticlericalism of the state (and national) congresses to inflame the public. Refusing to bend to its dictates, he chose exile from the province, an exile that he took up on foot, walking to Mexico City from Morelia. The wealthy citizens of the city, upon hearing this news, sent their carriages flying after him, but he declined to accept their offers of transportation. Instead he traveled on foot the whole long way to the national capital, and was met and greeted by hundreds, even thousands of faithful, as his legend grew in inverse proportion to that of the heartless liberal deputies.[57]

In May 1834 the radical national government collapsed when its titular head, Antonio López de Santa Anna, gave an approving nod to a centralist *pronunciamiento*, the Plan de Cuernavaca, that sent the de facto president, Santa Anna's radical Vice President Valentín Gómez Farías, out of the country. A month later a similar plan was pronounced in Morelia, headed by Comandante Isidro Reyes and, once again, Col. José de Ugarte.

The last moments of the federal system were presided over by the Sixth Congress (which convened for the first time on 22 December 1834), a group composed evenly of federalists and centralists, to judge by the ties in voting that occurred along the way when the subject of a change of system arose.[58] Though this congress did debate in unusually lengthy sessions an impressive number of broadly important issues (taxation, the police and the criminal justice system, the old problem of whether local justice should be delivered by the widely hated *jueces de letras* or by the *alcaldes*), its defining debate was over the question of whether to cast away the federalist system in favor of centralism.

The form taken by this debate changed slightly over the months between May and October of 1835, but it chiefly revolved around what action should be taken in response to the increasing number of initiatives being sent to the Congress by the state's *ayuntamientos*. Those who wished to reform, not abandon, the federal system were in a difficult position, since the key institutions of federalism had been the *ayuntamientos* — but most of them had declared in favor of centralism.[59] Thus, ironically, supporters of the *cambio* could wrap themselves in the mantle of democracy, while those who tried to protect the federal system found themselves in the uncomfortable position of having to reject these petitions, with their hundreds of signatures, which even they acknowledged represented the "voice of the people." Their strategy was to delay acceptance of the verdict of the pueblo by various means: refusing to include the words "the will of the people must be respected" in instructions to the state's senators; insisting that the only legal petitions were those sent directly to the legislature, and not to the governor or the National Congress; demanding that the petitions be confirmed as having emanated from actual meetings of the various *ayuntamientos*; arguing that the number of people represented by the petitioning *ayuntamientos* was not a majority of the state's population; and so on.[60] They also debated the change of system on its merits. One argument presented in favor of centralism, for example, was that the problem of corruption would be eased by the fact that where 100 honest public employees might be needed in a federalist system, in a centralist system only 10 would be required. (To this Lic. Manuel Alvirez pointed out sarcastically that if that was so, perhaps Mexico should go back to being a monarchy, in which case only one honest person would be needed.)[61] In general, however, the proponents of centralism had an immense advantage: no one could claim that the last eleven years had been a success. One of the petitions, from the town of Huaniqueo, put it this way:

> [The Federal System] deceived us, with its brilliant, false facade. Under this terrible regime we expected to be free, and we have come to be slaves. We hoped to secure political regeneration, but we have lost everything. We imagined the system of 1824 as a beacon of light to show us the way, but it turned out to be nothing but a shady collection of execrable, corrupting rites. Our sacred religion, whose dignity and

splendor we thought would be protected by a government that calls itself
free, has instead been the object of cruel persecutions. In sum, the incal-
culable evils of all sorts that, like locusts, plague this beautiful country
are the results of [federalism].[62]

Or as Br. Antonio de la Peña put it, "the people would rather be happy than
sovereign."[63]

The most dramatic day of the debate was August 13, when José de Ugarte
had to be persuaded to take his seat after angrily threatening to separate from
the legislature if the "will of the people" were not recognized. (This was probably taken as a threat of armed revolt, since Ugarte had already led two con-
servative/centralist rebellions.) A stalemate was finally broken when Vicente
Sosa, who had not been in attendance earlier and was brought in to break the
tie over a procedural issue, suggested that the population figures in the latest
census could be matched up with the *ayuntamientos* who had petitioned in
favor of the *cambio*, to ascertain once and for all whether a majority of the
state desired a new system. The congress adjourned until later that night
while a count was produced. When the figures seemed to show that at least
219,000 out of the state's population of 422,472 favored change, the federalist deputies ran out of ammunition and allowed themselves to be convinced
that a change in government was desired by the majority, and not just by
those who wanted better means to keep the pueblo quiet. Some of the centralists began talking soothingly about how it was now time to join together,
and one of the federalists, Antonio García Rojas, set the tone when he said
that he had opposed the state's taking an officially pro-centralist position because he was unconvinced that this was the will of the majority, but that he
had now changed his mind. On August 14 the congress, reaching the consensus that we can probably assume was by now widespread in the broader
community of elites, unanimously passed a resolution stating that "a considerable majority of the state's population is not satisfied with the Federal
System, on which they blame their suffering," and asking the National
Congress to take the measures it deemed necessary to guarantee "peace, stability, order, and liberty."[64] In effect, the congress had acquiesced to a political change that would soon result in its own extinction.

In sum, by 1835 a new consensus was in place. It had been building since
as early as 1827, based on the increasingly common belief that federalism was
not an appropriate system of government at this stage in Mexico's history —
that lawmakers ought to focus on "who we are," to repeat Isidro García

Carrasquedo's words, temporarily leaving aside the issue of "what we ought to be."[65] Many men who had been early supporters of independence and had used the language of liberalism and federalism to build bridges to the popular classes now became part of the movement to tear down the system they had helped to put in place. García Carrasquedo himself, for example, was the brother of the radical *yorkino* priest Martín García Carrasquedo and editor of the liberal *El Astro Moreliano* in the 1820s, but he now made the case for a *cambio de sistema* by urging deputies who were worried about the apparent fact that the "privileged classes" (by which he meant the church and the army) were leading the centralist effort, to remember that priests and soldiers had always served the best interests of the nation. He pitched the change of government, then, as a natural historical transition, rather than an abrupt about-face:

> Are not the immortal names of the priest Hidalgo and the soldier Allende engraved on the tree of liberty? Did not a multitude of churchmen and military men flock to fight beneath the banner of the nation? Was it not the clergy and the army who helped us to break the chains that bound the two worlds, so that the Eagle of Anahuac could rise again and show itself to the world as sovereign, free and independent? . . . Were not the soldiers of Jalisco the ones who proclaimed the federation? Did not the wise priest and the intrepid soldier help sustain the federal system?[66]

There are two possible explanations for the apparent switch in the political alignments of those — like the former insurgents Ramón Rayón, José María Izasaga, Antonio Cumplido, and Pablo José Peguero — who turned from promoting revolution to taking an active stance against it, or those who, like García Carrasquedo, turned from supporting a moderately liberal federalism to supporting a moderately conservative centralism.[67] One is that the creole elites of Mexico were fundamentally conservative — that their true goal in the wars for independence had been to seize power for themselves but never to bring about real social change. In effect, out of either cynicism or self-delusion, they had posed as liberals. The other is that the shift in alliances represents a response to events and behaviors and tendencies that, perhaps naively, they had not foreseen when they embraced liberalism and federalism before and after independence. Close examination of the debates in the state congress suggests that the second explanation takes us further; it is impossible to read the debates of the mid-1820s without coming away with the impression that they reflect genuine support of the principles of liberalism and federalism and equality, if not always of unadulterated democracy. It is clear that in these early years the deputies believed that the greatest threat to their project of liberal nation building came from outside the country (Spain) and from those few within the country who retained a fondness for colonial habits and ways; it did not occur to them that their allies among the popular classes would, as they saw it, turn on them. Similarly, it is impossible to read the debates of the late 1820s and early 1830s without concluding that what they saw as the ungratefulness of the poor, the uneducated, the Indians had caused their faith in liberal federalist solutions to come undone.

The Decline of the Old Elite

But the loss of faith in federalism on the part of wealthy politicians was also inspired by the personal misfortunes of many of their social class. The almost exclusively Spanish mercantile elite before 1810 had been decimated by death and flight, but the late colonial landowning elite was not much more fortunate; though a handful of hacendados managed to take advantage of high commodity prices to bring their properties back into consistently profitable production, many more, by the end of the decade of the 1820s, were beginning to succumb to the pressures of debt, property destruction, and capital shortages.

One common response to the immense challenges of hacienda ownership in the post-independence period was to retire from direct cultivation and to become a landlord. Twenty-three hacienda rental contracts (not including rentals of church-owned haciendas) were notarized in Valladolid and Pátzcuaro in the 1820s, compared to just eleven in the decade from 1800 to 1809. Almost invariably the low rents the owners were able to command reflected considerable property destruction. In 1829, for example, Dr. Francisco de la Riva rented out the hacienda of La Huerta (near Valladolid), which had helped make his father's fortune, for 1,500 pesos a year, after it had suffered losses of over 50,000 pesos during the wars.[68] Another formerly active owner who gave up after 1810 and rented his hacienda was Felipe Robledo. The property — which he had purchased in 1794 and 1798 for over 200,000 pesos — had been devastated during the insurrection against which Robledo, as a royalist officer, had fought. When the wars were over, discouraged by the destruction of his property and by anti-Spanish sentiment, Robledo moved his family to Mexico City and later north to Zacatecas, and began renting out the hacienda in 1823 for a mere 3,000 pesos a year, implying (according to contemporary formulas for capitalization) that it was worth only about 60,000 pesos.[69]

But others did not have the relative luxury of being able to get by on reduced rental income. The key problem was that in large part the impressive investments in their haciendas that many elites had made during the pre-1810 period had been financed by borrowing. The average hacienda in Michoacán before 1810 carried debts that amounted to over 40 percent of the value of the estate (although there was much variation). Simple arithmetic thus suggests that the loss of half the value of an hacienda during the wars (a proportion of loss that, as we have seen, was not uncommon) brought the level of debt close to 100 percent of the post-1810 value of the property. Many owners in these circumstances could not meet even the most reduced debt-service requirements. Though ecclesiastical creditors (who held the vast majority of rural debt) preferred not to foreclose and tolerated nonpayment of interest for years and even decades, this self-interested leniency on the part of the church served only to prolong the inevitable.[70] By the late 1820s cessions and semiforced sales of heavily indebted property were occurring at unprecedented rates.

Urban properties, of which most hacendados owned several, were usually the first to go. In Valladolid at least 22 elite-owned residences (those valued at 2,000 pesos or more) were ceded before 1830, most of them in the late 1820s. The most spectacular of the urban property cessions was the residence of Juan José Martínez de Lejarza, across from the cathedral. As was true in many cases, Lejarza's problems resulted not so much from damages to the family's property as to the fact that a significant portion of his father's estate consisted of debts owed by others whose projects and enterprises had collapsed: never-to-be-collected debts included 30,000 pesos owed by Pedro Otero y Dovalina of Guanajuato, and 40,000 pesos owed by a general in the Spanish army. In 1817, noting that he and his father had always acted on behalf of the Conde de Heras in his business interests in Michoacán, Lejarza conceded that he had recently been forced to spend on daily expenses some funds belonging to the conde. It was impossible to repay these sums, which amounted to almost 4,000 pesos, because of the present state of his affairs; he could only promise to pay when his situation improved. Having witnessed the crumbling of his considerable patrimony (while at the same time going through a divorce serious enough to break up the marriage of his wife's sister to a member of another wealthy Valladolid family), Martínez de Lejarza died in 1824 at the age of 39, just after completing the statistical analysis of Michoacán that I have often consulted. The deputies of the state congress even debated whether they should help pay for his funeral. Two years after his death his executor ceded his residence, part of which had already been sold off by Lejarza himself to raise cash, in payment of a 19,750-peso debt.[71]

Some members of the old colonial upper class were not quite strapped enough to cede property outright but were too financially beleaguered to hold onto all their properties. One solution was to sell off some less-productive real estate. In 1827 Antonio Olarte, heir of one of Valladolid's leading merchants, sold two houses in Valladolid in order to liberate the hacienda of La Sanja, also part of his uncle's estate, which was threatened with foreclosure; these contiguous houses were among the priciest in the city, selling for a combined 28,000 pesos.[72] Lorenzo González de Cosío sold his home on the plaza in 1829 for 10,500 pesos; he did not lose money, since he had only paid 9,000 pesos for it in 1798, but service on its debt of 8,800 pesos must have consumed nearly all the rental income it produced.[73]

Similar patterns of cession and semiforced sale obtained in the rural sector. As in the case of urban property, cessions of rural properties were much higher in the 1820s than they had been before 1810. There were at least nine cessions of large rural properties during the 1820s, far more than would occur in a typical decade during the colonial period, and most of them came about not when the church foreclosed but when the owners essentially gave up trying to bring the property back into production. This was the decision made by the owners of the hacienda of La Goleta, the well-connected Ortiz de la Huerta family of Valladolid. José Nicolás Ortiz de la Huerta's estate was worth over 93,000 pesos at the time of his death in 1810, and the debts on the haciendas and the house amounted to only 38,863 pesos, a heavy but not intolerable debt for an expanding hacienda to carry.[74] In 1816, however, the eldest son, José Joaquín, was forced to beg his creditors for a loan extension and interest rate forgiveness, because of

> the terrible consequences of the present rebellion and the notorious damages that the enemy has inflicted on my property and the property belonging to the estate of my father, especially the hacienda of La Goleta, which because of its proximity to the city and its ability to supply the needs of the loyal citizenry, has been the special target of their rage.[75]

José Joaquín went on to say that the hacienda had been sacked since the beginning of the revolution. In 1810 the rebels had taken most of the livestock and tools, and he was able to save only the oxen, which he moved to a different pasture, only to lose them to a rebel raid shortly afterwards. With great difficulty he managed to bring in a crop until 1814, when the rebels administered the coup de grace to the hacienda, burning warehouses containing 600 to 700 cargas of wheat, then worth between 12,000 and 14,700 pesos. He himself was captured by the insurgents and held for ransom, and the family was forced to leave the hacienda and flee for their lives. For a short time royalist troops had protected the hacienda, but now, he stated, he could "no longer avail myself of that service." He argued that the hacienda was worth more than enough to cover its debts if the city were to be secured so that the hacienda could be worked. If, on the other hand, the creditors exercised their option to foreclose, it would mean the "total ruin of my family."

This request for leniency in 1816 was granted, but in 1823 Ortiz was forced once again to appear before a court of creditors. He called witnesses who observed that although in 1820 the hacienda began to function again, a killing frost in 1822 had caused the loss of the wheat harvest, and in 1823 the crop was lost to rain because Ortiz had run out of money to finish rebuilding the storehouses. Again it appears that the creditors voted leniency, but by 1828, with many members of the family now living in Mexico City where they had fled during the insurrection, Joaquín gave up and ceded the hacienda (and the house in Valladolid) to the church.[76]

José Génaro Pérez Llera experienced a similar dramatic plunge in fortune. Pérez Llera, another member of an old creole family, had his principal wealth in his hacienda of Naranjos, in the Zinapécuaro/Acámbaro region. In 1805, after numerous improvements, the hacienda was worth over 80,000 pesos and was mortgaged to about half its value. In the revolution, however, all the movables, outbuildings, and fences were destroyed completely; only the lands remained, and they were rented in 1820 for a mere 1,000 pesos a year. Pérez Llera died in 1821, and his heirs ceded the hacienda to its creditors, who continued to rent it for a decade before selling it.[77]

Besides the unusually large number of cessions of rural property in the 1820s, the insurgent wars and accompanying depression also contributed to desperation sales of all or part of many haciendas. Unlike the church, which patiently held onto most of the property it acquired in cession until a buyer could be found who would agree to cover the original capital, many individual heirs or owners in the 1820s were unable or unwilling to wait until property values recovered. In 1820, for example, the nieces and nephews of Lic. Matías Antonio de los Ríos complained bitterly to the executor of his estate about delays in selling the hacienda of Chapultepec. Although he tried to convince them that the hacienda, still under occasional assault from the rebels, could not presently command nearly as much as it was worth, they nonetheless insisted on selling as soon as possible. They even rejected the first proposal by a potential buyer because he offered no down payment, stating that they needed money immediately.[78]

Many other large land sales during the 1820s were motivated to some degree by desperation. Manuel Diego Villavicencio, for example, was compelled to sell his hacienda of Vallenuevo, which had been burned by the rebels, for only 4,500 pesos in order to pay his sister's inheritance, which his brother-in-law, also strapped for funds, had demanded.[79] Barbara Guinea sold her hacienda of Capirio in 1829 under financial pressure; its price was 11,500 pesos "given its miserable state," and its debt was 9,000 pesos.[80] The hacienda of Aguacate was sold to Br. José Antonio Huarte in 1826 for only 5,828 pesos, with its debts amounting to 4,440 pesos. As a selling point the sellers stated that the hacienda had produced nothing since 1810, and that for this reason it was eligible for debt forgiveness from the church.[81] An interesting (because of the identity of the buyers) example of a case in which part of an hacienda was sold to cancel debts is the large chunk of the hacienda of Siranga that was sold by the estate of Inocencio Díaz Barriga to the Indians of the village of Yguatzio for 2,400 pesos. The property was described by the sellers as free from encumbrance, but the village soon discovered that it was mortgaged to the Indians of the village of Tzintzuntzan for 600 pesos, a debt that Díaz Barriga's executor had neglected to mention. (In 1827 the Indians successfully demanded that they be reimbursed for the 224 pesos that they had paid toward redemption of the debt.)[82]

The rate of cession of both urban and rural property slowed in the 1830s. Where some 5.6 elite-owned residences had been ceded each year in the late 1820s, there were about 2.8 cessions a year in the early 1830s. From about 1.5 hacienda cessions a year from 1824 to 1829, the rate fell to about 1 a year in the early 1830s. On the other hand, the rate of forced or semiforced sales (sales of haciendas with debt of at least 60 percent of the purchase price), did not diminish appreciably over the period, with over half of the haciendas sold in the 1830s fitting this description.

Several of the haciendas ceded in the 1830s had been owned by people who either died or abandoned the property in the 1810s and 1820s. The church or other creditors had, for one reason or another (inefficiency, a large backlog of ceded rural and urban properties, lack of a buyer willing to assume the mortgage), declined to foreclose earlier. The hacienda of Milpillas, for example, whose owner had died in 1817, was not ceded by the heir (who lived in Spain) until between 1830 and 1832, and was not sold until 1840.[83] In another case, the hacienda of Coliseo in Zamora was abandoned in 1829, when its owner died, but it was not ceded until much later and was not sold until 1849, by which time unpaid interest on its 28,163-peso mortgage equaled the amount of the mortgage itself.[84] In the same year (1849), the Spanish heirs of Francisco González de Alles finally ceded the hacienda of Nacimiento (La Piedad) to one of its creditors. Interest on the hacienda's 19,000-peso mortgage had not been paid for forty years.[85]

The majority of cessions and forced sales during the 1830s and early 1840s, however, took place after owners had gone some distance toward restoration of the hacienda's productivity but still had not been able to reduce debts or resume regular interest payments. One such case is the 1836 cession of the hacienda of La Parota, owned by Mariano Michelena. Michelena returned from exile abroad soon after independence to find that, like many, his family hacienda was so destroyed that it could not cover the debts it reported. He tried to relieve some financial pressure by turning over an annexed hacienda to one of his creditors, but other creditors, particularly the hardnosed Augustinians of Pátzcuaro (who held the original mortgage on La Parota dating from 1778, when Michelena's father had purchased the property) were also clamoring for payment. Michelena was forced to call a *concurso de acreedores* in 1824, before which he (or more precisely his representatives — he was once more out of the country, serving as ambassador to Great Britain) argued that if La Parota and the contiguous hacienda of San Juan were sold now, more than half of the creditors would lose their capital, because the debts were so many, the destruction so great, and the value of property in general so low. He proposed that the haciendas (which technically belonged to his father's estate) be adjudicated to him and that he serve as *habilitador* — that is, that he invest the sums necessary to make the hacienda profitable and to enable it to service its debts, in return for which the other creditors would allow his credit to take first precedence.

The convent objected to this plan on the grounds that Michelena was underestimating the capital and time necessary to rebuild, and also that the 1,500 pesos a year that Michelena proposed to pay himself was excessive. Michelena responded that if the convent did not think that *he* could find the money to rebuild, where was the convent to raise such funds, given the "almost total destruction of America" and the fact that the chief source of income for the convent was precisely the interest from La Parota? He added that he would forego his proposed 1,500-peso salary. The convent was still not convinced that Michelena's proposal was the best alternative — it had had unhappy experiences with neverending *habilitaciones* in the past — but in fact the convent had little other choice, and the Michelena plan was adopted.[86]

Things went fairly well in the beginning. Michelena's renter, on his instructions, planted coffee and cacao, which had never been cultivated on the estate (or even in the region), and focused on indigo production rather than on the sugar that had been the mainstay of the hacienda before 1810.[87] Late in the 1820s, as a result of "revolutions and other causes," Michelena again fell behind in interest payments. But in an 1829 letter to Manuel Eduardo de Gorostiza, he was still relatively optimistic:

> I have retired to this city [Morelia] to see if I can halfway repair my properties, which the renter left in chaotic state upon his death, without planted fields or serviceable *oficinas*, and compromised to more than 20,000 pesos. This situation . . . has me "bien molido," but I still have not lost patience.[88]

By 1836, however, even if he had not lost patience, his creditors had. Michelena met with them once again in order to arrange for the adjudication of the hacienda to the Augustinians (though not before accusing the convent of "criminal" concealment of assets in its appraisal of the property). The appraised value of the hacienda was only 106,606 pesos, more or less the same as it had been in 1824.[89]

More common than this case, in which La Parota was foreclosed upon against the will of Michelena, were cessions or semiforced sales that took place after the death of an owner whose attempts to revive the property had been largely ineffective, so that the heirs were more than willing to sell or cede. For example, it was not until after the 1831 murder of Angel Vélez, one of the heirs of the heavily damaged hacienda of Puruarán, apparently at the hands of his tenants, that the remaining heirs agreed to rent out and eventually sell the hacienda.[90] In the meantime, at least according to detailed hacienda records from 1832 through 1834, the creditors received a bit here and a bit there, enough to keep them from foreclosing, but less than their full due.[91] Vélez had actually restored Puruarán to a rather high level of productivity, considering its losses in the wars, and, at least during the four-year period from 1831 to 1834, its income averaged a fairly healthy 24,500 pesos annually. But the owners simply did not have the capital or the will to continue the struggle that Angel alone among them had been willing to wage. In short — for a variety of reasons ranging from inefficiency on the part of creditors to those creditors' self-serving desire to give the owner a chance to turn things around — the process of shakeout of heavily damaged, overindebted, and/or undercapitalized haciendas dragged on for many years. So, therefore, did the decline of many old landowning families.

Conclusion

The major themes treated in this chapter — the demise of both the old colonial elite and the new federalist system — come together in the personal histories of many wealthy politician/hacendados during the 1820s and 1830s. There were numerous senators, congressmen, state deputies, and other public servants who were associated with the insurgency and/or federalism, but ended by joining the movement to change the political system from federalism to centralism. In each case their dissatisfaction with the political status quo had a personal dimension: they had been unable to revive their haciendas after independence (or their initial successes were ephemeral), for reasons that they increasingly blamed on the "continual revolutions" that plagued the state.

The most prominent of these men was Mariano Michelena, the former 1809 conspirator whose battle to save his family hacienda, La Parota, ended in the same year that the 1836 Bases y Leyes of the Central Republic, which he helped to frame, became the law of the land.[92] Francisco Romero Soravilla, brother of one insurgent and half-brother of another, also joined the centralist movement, serving twice on the junta departamental del Estado during the centralist period; meanwhile, his hacienda of Uruétaro, worth about 18,000 pesos, had accumulated debts of over 24,500 pesos.[93] Ignacio and Mariano Anzorena, sons of the Hidalgo-appointed intendant José María Anzorena, played important roles in the centralist administrations (Ignacio in the national congress and senate and Mariano as a member of the junta departamental and a government appointee). Their family hacienda, San Antonio de las Huertas, was already deep in debt even before the War of the South closed it down in the early 1830s.[94] Antonio Manso Ceballos, son of another insurgent leader (Manuel Manso), served as governor during the centralist period, even as his small inherited hacienda of Chaparro continued to deteriorate.[95] And in one of the most striking about-faces of the period, the wealthy state deputy Br. Juan José Pastor Morales, who had firmly champi-

oned the purest liberalism in the mid-1820s and in 1828 had designated as
the executor of his will the *yorkino* governor José Salgado, now, on his
deathbed in 1838, replaced Salgado with Lucas Alamán, the architect of the
centralist Republic, and Lic. Mariano Rivas, the rector of the seminary and
the editor of the rabidly antifederal newspaper *El Michoacano Libre*.[96]
The periodic raids staged by federalist rebels on his huge hacienda of
Bellasfuentes, located in the Zacapu-Pátzcuaro-Puruándiro triangle, an area
whose terrain consistently made it a favorite retreat of insurgents, were surely
a factor in his change of heart.[97]

But formerly wealthy politicians whose fortunes — like those of other hacendados — were faltering by the late 1820s were not the only political actors
to embrace the idea of a *cambio de sistema*. In fact, from one-half to two-
thirds of the deputies to the state congress between 1825 and 1835 were *not*
wealthy men, but men with distinctly middle-class backgrounds and occupations, whose ranks had increased significantly in the 1820s as a direct result
of independence.[98] The number of lawyers, for example, was already much
greater by the late 1820s than it had been under the closed judicial system of
the colonial regime, when only a handful of provincial *abogados* were li-
censed to appear before the *audiencia*. Journalism, with the advent of a relatively free press, was an entirely new occupation in the provinces, and the appearance of professional schools, especially the school of medicine, boosted
the number of physicians, notaries, pharmacists, and teachers. Perhaps the
most important factor in the postindependence expansion of the tiny colonial
middle class, however, was the increased opportunities for middle-class men
to rent or purchase parts or all of the haciendas formerly owned by the old
hacendado class.

The voting behavior of the middle-class legislators was not markedly different from that of their wealthier colleagues, and there were no important
cleavages along lines of wealth or income during the congressional debates of
the late 1820s and early 1830s. This alignment continued during the debates
over federalism. Although the dissatisfaction of the middle classes with the
federal system was not so much rooted in personal loss as in the threat that
political unrest posed to their recent gains, the effect was the same: both the
old hacendados and the new landowners and professionals agreed that the
time had come for a change. After 1835, then, many men who had worked,
sometimes a bit awkwardly, within the frameworks of liberalism and federalism in the 1820s were now prepared to work within the frameworks of centralism and conservativism — again, as we shall see in chapter 4, often with

more caution than real enthusiasm. Among them were some of the wealthiest and most successful men of the early republican period: men from old families like Manuel Alzúa, Lic. Isidro Huarte, Juan Gómez de la Puente, Nicolás Ruiz de Chávez, and Antonio Anciola, and new men like Vicente Sosa, Fernando Román, Cayetano Gómez, Lic. Onofre Calvo Pintado, and Lic. Juan Manuel Olmos. Put another way, though the old elite was in decline, the new men who were taking their places were not their political antagonists, and a rough political consensus among the *hombres de bien*, including both the wealthy and the merely respectable, would prevail through the 1830s and into the 1840s.

Financial Revival in the Third Generation: Manuel Alzúa Huarte and Cayetano Gómez (m. Dolores Alzúa Huarte)

Like others of their generation, Carmen Huarte and Pascual Alzúa's children, born around the turn of the century, were not old enough at the time of the Hidalgo Rebellion in 1810 to feel the same crushing sense of catastrophe that their parents had experienced in its aftermath. Perhaps because of this they and their spouses were able to adjust to post-1810 political and economic conditions if not with easy aplomb, then more successfully (in general) than their parents. Their adaptability, the fact that they had no memory of happier times, and their coming of age at a propitious point in the economic cycle (when there was enormous upside potential by virtue of how far the economy had fallen off since 1810), allowed this generation to spearhead the economic recovery of the 1820s and 1830s and to reap its rewards in the 1840s and 1850s.

Pascual Alzúa's only male child by his first marriage, Manuel, had started out in business with his father, along with another junior partner, Antonio Anciola — like Manuel, a second-generation merchant. Second-generation merchants were a rare breed in the colonial period, but the decision for a son to follow a father into trade, rather than into more "gentlemanly" professions, was one of the adjustments to post-1810 conditions that had been made. Until Pascual's death in 1827 the partners shunned agricultural investments, as he had always done. But less than two years later, Manuel Alzúa and Anciola formed a company to run the sugar-producing hacienda of Acúmbaro when its renter, who had borrowed almost 18,000 pesos from Alzúa to rebuild the property, found that he needed still more infusions of cash to earn a profit.[1] In 1832 Alzúa purchased another hacienda, the grain- and chile-producing hacienda of Andocutín, whose current owner had gone heavily into debt in the process of trying to rebuild. Since the original owner's death in 1819, a priest named Primo de Gastaneta had spent almost 17,000 pesos reconstructing a dam, rebuilding fences, and so forth. Alzúa paid 45,700 pesos for the property and within a year had spent another 30,000 pesos stocking it with cattle.[2]

Two years later, in 1835, Alzúa began to rent the property that came to be the core of his estate: the sugar-producing hacienda of Puruarán.[3] He apparently requested detailed records of the hacienda's costs and production for the four previous years in order to be sure that the high rent (9,000 pesos a year) was justified. Those records indicate that although the hacienda was grossing between 23,000 and 33,000 pesos a year, it was showing only a small profit, averaging under 2,000 pesos a year. Only about 1,800 pesos a year were being spent on maintenance and supplies. (The purchases included mules, machetes, wire, nails, shingles, lime, lead, plows, sugar molds, iron, copper, steel, and rope.) The owners were almost certainly not meeting their interest obligations, and well over 80 percent of the hacienda's cane was processed into *piloncillo* instead of into the more profitable sugar or *aguardiente*. Clearly there was room for improvement.[4]

Unfortunately, there are no similar records after the hacienda had been under Alzúa's management for a few years. The only change that Alzúa made of which we can be sure was to invest whatever was necessary in equipment to produce sugar rather than *piloncillo*.[5] Otherwise, it is only possible to infer that Alzúa had made changes that left him satisfied with the hacienda's profitability, since in 1849 he was finally able to resolve some particularly complicated questions of ownership and to purchase the hacienda.[6] By the time of his death in 1861 he had increased its value from some 180,000 pesos to around 380,000 pesos, and he had paid off most of its debts.[7]

Despite his heavy investments in agriculture, Alzúa maintained an interest in trading cotton along the Pacific coast, as his father and grand-father had done. The details of this business are not known, but it was obviously an operation of considerable significance, to judge by the fact that when Alzúa and his Colima partner dissolved one incarnation of the company in 1853 and re-formed it by merging with an Acapulco business-man, the new partnership was capitalized in the impressive amount of

100,000 pesos. In 1862, after Alzúa's death, the partnership was dissolved, having more than tripled this original capital over the ten years of its existence.[8]

Alzúa never married, and when he died he left most of his substantial fortune to his many nieces, nephews, and half-siblings. There were two immense legacies, one of 50,000 pesos to his aunt Ana Huarte (Agustín Iturbide's widow) and one of 130,000 pesos to his nephew Juan de Dios Gómez Alzúa. The bulk of the rest of his estate — over 120,000 pesos — was distributed, according to his detailed instructions, to various relatives.[9] Clearly he anticipated that the sum of these various legacies, some 300,000 pesos, was roughly the net value of the hacienda of Puruarán. The rest of his real assets (a rancho in San Luis Potosí, another Morelia house, a house in Maravatío and several more in San Miguel Allende, a linseed oil factory, two small haciendas on the Acapulco coast, several lots in Morelia, and a *cría de cerdos* in the *barrio* of Guadalupe), was distributed to relatives, dependents, and servants.[10]

Alzúa obviously found ways to succeed in the difficult postindependence period, especially by taking advantage of depressed property values and overextended owners to acquire haciendas with intrinsic worth (e.g. Puruarán, with its splendid soil, water supply, and climate for sugar production, and its good location relatively near markets; or Andocutín, with its central location near Acámbaro and its proven capacity to support a large livestock population, probably a good proportion of which were mules that Alzúa used in the coastal trade), and then using capital earned in trade to revive those properties. But Alzúa, it must be recalled, had the advantage of having inherited a mercantile operation that had been tightly (if unimaginatively) managed by his father. More impressive, because he had no inherited assets and no family connections (at least until his marriage), was the career of his brother-in-law, Cayetano Gómez de Soria.

Gómez was born in 1791 or 1792 in Maravatío to a respectable family with little or no property. (In the mid-18th century an Acámbaro resident named Luis Gómez de Soria owned three small haciendas in the Celaya region, but it seems clear that the relationship was quite distant, and no other landowners of this surname show up in any of the late colonial records.)[11] The Gómez family moved to Valladolid when Cayetano was an infant, and his father's occupation there is unknown. An older brother was an official of the Colecturía de Animas in Valladolid, and a cousin owned a transport

Figure 2.   Dolores Alzúa y Huarte de   Figure 3.   Cayetano Gómez de Soria.
            Gómez.

company and gave piano lessons on the side, but Cayetano and his brother
José María decided to go into trade. José María failed (and was supported
by his brother all his life), but Cayetano succeeded brilliantly.[12]

Gómez began like most creole merchants: trading heavily in the early
stages of his career in local and regional goods and later adding trade in
imported merchandise, purchased through Mexico City wholesalers. He
did not figure in a list of prominent *vecinos* in 1815, but by 1818, the date
of his marriage to Dolores Alzúa, he listed assets of 5,000 pesos.[13] In 1825
Gómez took his first step beyond simple trade and entered into a partnership with the Spaniard Eugenio Garay to rehabilitate the sugar-producing
hacienda of Santa Efigenia (perhaps inspiring his brother-in-law Manuel
Alzúa's similar step four years later). There are a few surviving details concerning this business enterprise; we know, for example, that the partners
increased sugar production from 1,650 *arrobas* a year in 1825 to 4,500
arrobas in 1826, to 9,200 *arrobas* in 1827, and to 10,300 in 1828, the last
year for which production figures are available. At prevailing prices the

1828 crop would have been worth at least 25,000 pesos. Of course we
do not know how much profit there was in this, but it is probably safe
to assume that the books of the Santa Efigenia company (whose partners
included not only Gómez and Garay but also the widow of the previous
owner) showed very little profit. Instead, Garay and Gómez most likely
charged against the company the loans they, as *refaccionarios*, made to it,
and sold themselves sugar from the hacienda at prices that were as low as
they could justify. In any event, we can presume that by whatever combination of sugar profits and lenders' profits, Gómez and Garay were not losing
money, since the *refacción* was continued until at least 1841.[14]

Gómez's business affairs in enterprises other than Santa Efigenia were
also working out well: by the mid-1830s he had established partnerships
with three other merchants, Ignacio Sandoval, Cayetano Villavicencio, and
Agapito Solórzano (all of whom, especially Villavicencio and Solórzano,
were very successful in their own rights somewhat later). He also acted as
a supplier to many other small retailers throughout the state, to whom he
sold merchandise on credit, a phenomenon that was particularly common
in the 1830s.[15] About this time, Gómez claimed that he had loaned the
national government some 100,000 pesos, apparently on behalf of the
Morelia Augustinians.[16] Despite this capital drain, in 1831 he paid 20,000
pesos for one of the premier pieces of urban real estate in Morelia, an
imposing residence on the corner of the Plaza Mayor and the *calle real*
(the seller was his partner Eugenio Garay, who had moved to France after
the expulsion of Spaniards in 1829).[17] And in 1834 he found cash for a
down payment of 34,275 pesos on the rich grain- and chile-producing
hacienda of San Bartolomé in the Indaparapeo valley northeast of Morelia,
for which he paid 200,000 pesos. When the nearby hacienda of Quirio
went on the market three years later, Gómez bought it too, for 34,505
pesos. Also by 1837, Gómez had rented the small sugar-producing hacienda
of Zinzongo (Ario), no doubt to complement and expand the business centered in nearby Santa Efigenia.[18]

Seven years after he purchased it, Gómez's hacienda of San Bartolomé
made a vivid impression on Fanny Calderón de la Barca, who spent two
nights there in late 1841. She described the hacienda as a "vast and beautiful property," adding that there was "a generous, frank liberality apparent
in everything in this hacienda . . . nothing petty or calculating. . . . The
house is one of the prettiest and most cheerful we have seen yet; but we
passed a great stone building on the road, which the proprietor of San

Bartolo is having constructed for one of his family, which, if it keeps its promise, will be a palace when finished."[19]

Her experience at San Bartolomé inspired Señora Calderón de la Barca to wax eloquent about the "great landed proprietors of old family, who live on their own estates, engaged in agricultural pursuits and entirely removed from all the party feeling and petty interests of a city life." "It is true," she went on, that

> the life of a country gentleman here is that of a hermit, in the total absence of all society in the nearly unbroken solitude that surrounds him. . . . Nothing can exceed the independence of his position, but to enjoy this wild country life he must be born to it . . . if he can spend the day in riding over his estate, in directing his workmen, watching over his improvements, redressing disputes and grievances, and can sit down in the evening in his large and lonely halls, and philosophically bury himself in the pages of some favorite author, then his time will probably not hang heavy on his hands.[20]

In fact, of course, a less apt description of Cayetano Gómez's background and lifestyle could scarcely be imagined. Far from retreating to his haciendas to live a life of contemplation, Gómez continued not only to increase their productivity but also to expand his other business dealings. In 1840, even as his mercantile operation, the largest in Morelia, was grossing around 150,000 pesos a year, he founded and directed a large and profitable textile mill in Colima, appropriately called San Cayetano, which was built at a cost of 100,000 pesos.[21] And in 1842 Gómez expanded his sugar interests beyond Santa Efigenia and Sinsongo by renting the Augustinian hacienda of Taretan for 8,000 pesos a year.

To this point in their careers, that is, to about 1840, Gómez and Manuel Alzúa displayed an economic style that was quite similar to that of Isidro Huarte, Alzua's grandfather and Gómez's wife's grandfather. Like Huarte, they took an extremely aggressive approach to agricultural investment and commercial expansion, and they adhered closely to Huarte's basic principle of careful diversification, with an eye toward investing in new enterprises that would complement the old, for example raising mules on one's hacienda for use in long-distance trading. Also like Huarte, they attempted to secure the family fortune by means of monopolizing or at least dominating distribution of key commodities. While they showed somewhat more interest in agriculture than Huarte had done — each of them purchased one large hacienda and one smaller one, and they clearly saw these haciendas as essential complements to their other business interests — the core of their business empires remained their mercantile and speculative activities. That would change over the decade of the 1840s, a decade that they entered having found ways to turn the great risks and great opportunities of these uncertain times to personal advantage, and that would leave them even more materially successful than Isidro Huarte had been.

A New Elite, a New "System," and Old Habits of Mind: Politics, Economics, and Society in the 1830s and Early 1840s

In retrospect, the state congressmen and other public officials who supported the *cambio de sistema* in 1835 must have realized that they had panicked too soon. Even as the federal system was being dismantled, signs of life in the economy — which had been masked by unrest, rebellion, and the bankruptcies of many hacendados in the late 1820s and early 1830s — began to multiply and grow more visible. In fact, if anything, by triggering new federalist rebellions in the late 1830s the *cambio* slowed the processes of building and rebuilding that legislators had hoped it would speed up. But despite these new disruptions, all statistical measures and much anecdotal evidence indicate that the reconstruction of haciendas and commercial networks proceeded apace. The old colonial landowners continued to lose ground (though at a slower pace as the decade of the 1830s went on), but a new generation of landowners and merchants was increasingly successful, sometimes astonishingly so. These men, whose background was almost invariably middle class, found ways to exploit the very conditions that still drove many of the old owners into financial crisis, especially by purchasing heavily indebted haciendas at figurative fire sales. In the end they fashioned a relatively powerful, if not especially inclusive, economic recovery.

As their growing economic power led these new men to positions of political power in the state (now technically the "department" of Michoacán), they came to chafe under many of the restrictions of centralist rule, and to push policies and programs that in many ways resembled those advanced during the Federal Republic. In fact, in Michoacán, the differences between the politics and political styles of the Federal Republic and the Central Republic were not as significant as the similarities. Politicians in both periods shared a belief in the need to privatize Indian lands and advance free trade, among other legislative concerns, and both periods were characterized by a political culture that could be vicious but was at the same time curiously gentlemanly, cautious, and pragmatic, placing more importance on effective administration than on ideologically inspired activism. These were qualities that suited the emerging economic recovery and the men who engineered and benefited from it.

Reviving the Hacienda Economy

One of the most important factors energizing both new owners and those of the old hacendado class who could muster the wherewithal to rebuild and replant in the 1820s and 1830s was the continued historically high price of commodities. Relatively strong and systematic evidence on prices from tithe records suggests that despite the complaints of some unhappy producers caught up in temporary local gluts caused by transportation difficulties, weather-related abundance, or currency shortages, prices of maize, livestock, sugar, chiles, and beans were generally comparable to or higher than the inflated prices of the 1800–09 decade — a decade during which high commodity prices had driven hacienda expansion, shifts in land use toward greater production on the hacienda account, and capital investment in irrigation, warehousing, and fencing.[1] The average price of maize in the 1820s and 1830s was 11 reales/*fanega*, almost exactly the same as the average for the decade 1800–09.[2] Cattle commanded an average of 5 to 6 pesos/head in the pre-1810 period, and almost 10 pesos in the 1820s (2 pesos higher than during the insurgency). The price per head fell slightly in the 1830s but was still well above the pre-1810 level.[3]

Prices for *tierra caliente* crops in the 1820s and 1830s also remained high. Sugar rose from 16rr/*arroba* before 1810 to 23 reales in the 1820s and remained relatively high at 19rr in the 1830s.[4] The price of *piloncillo* rose from 9 pesos/*carga* before 1810 to an average of 12 to 13 pesos in the 1820s and 1830s.[5] In response to these prices, production increased steadily on six of the largest sugar haciendas, from under 5,000 *arrobas* in 1821 to almost 30,000 *arrobas* in 1828.[6] Only wheat, an important commercial crop of the *tierra fria* hacendados, failed to sustain pre-1810 prices in the 1820s, falling from an average of 7.45 pesos/*carga* before 1810 to just over 6 pesos in the 1820s and 1830s.[7]

The notion that some producers in both the cereal and the sugar zones were willing and able to rebuild quickly in response to demand and high prices conforms with H. G. Ward's otherwise puzzling observation that in Tlalpujahua in 1827 it had been difficult to find 150 mine workers because of the dispersal of the population, and hard to feed them because of the "total ruin" of neighboring haciendas. But ten months later, he reported, all that had changed: there were 1,200 workers, a population of 5,000, and they were abundantly supplied with food.[8] For all the inefficiency and low productivity of premodern agricultural technology, its advantage in situations such as these was that "total ruin" could be relatively easily repaired if there was an incentive to effect such repairs (and in this case, no doubt, if there was credit available). This was even true to a certain extent on sugar haciendas, which were "modern" and had large capital requirements only by comparison to the grain-livestock/tenant-sharecropper complex characteristic of the highlands.

PATTERNS OF MANAGEMENT: SHARECROPPING, TENANCY, ADVANCE CONTRACTS, AND RURAL PARTNERSHIPS

The strategies that hacendados used to bring their properties back into production were fairly limited and were by no means universally successful. The cereal/livestock producers of the *tierra fria* had an especially difficult task, given the destruction of herds and the relatively low price of wheat (their two main cash generators). The most successful managers were those who experimented with new crops, especially chiles, but the labor requirements of chile production were beyond many haciendas. The more common means of bringing cereal-producing haciendas back into production was to continue the sharecropping strategy of the late 1810s. Domingo Torices, who managed the rich but shaken hacienda of San Bartolomé for his wife, abandoned corn production to sharecroppers in 1822 in order to concentrate on wheat, traditionally the hacienda's big moneymaker.[9] Detailed tithe records in the 1820s show that many other haciendas also had substantial *arrendatario* populations, though it is usually impossible to compare their numbers to those of the pre-1810 period (and thereby to confirm an increase in dependent production after 1810) for lack of such detail in the late colonial records.[10]

Sharecropping and cash tenancy were better than idle haciendas that produced no income at all, and, as is argued in chapter 2, they were a good, temporary way to get overgrown fields back into condition, to get fences and outbuildings repaired, and to settle a potential labor force on or near the hacienda. But they were certainly not ideal; in fact, several documents leave the strong impression that they were strategies of last resort. This attitude is quite clear in Joaquín Ortiz de la Huerta's 1823 petition for debt relief. An interrogatory asked witnesses: "Is it true that Joaquín Ortiz de la Huerta has lacked funds with which to repair his hacienda, and that he has therefore had to give out his lands to renters and sharecroppers?" All of the witnesses agreed that this had indeed been the case, and several noted that the arrangement had led to a vicious cycle: since Ortiz had been forced to turn to renters and sharecroppers, his income was so reduced that he could not afford to finance repairs internally, thus delaying the day when he could reclaim his lands for his own use.[11] This belief, that small-scale cash and share tenancy were undesirable options forced upon elites by the combination of capital shortages and property destruction, was echoed by the Augustinians of Pátzcuaro in 1831. It had become necessary, the convent noted with obvious regret, to give out the lands of their hacienda of Sanabria to sharecroppers, because the convent did not have the funds to purchase mules, cattle and oxen; as a result of the sharecropping agreements, they said, the harvests were poor and were sometimes lost altogether, "as often happens in these cases."[12]

Share and cash tenancy, then, were one means of adjusting to changed economic conditions after independence, but for owners who were serious about rebuilding and returning to direct production, they were at best an interim measure. Moreover, they did not help much when cash-poor and heavily indebted owners needed to make significant investments in repair, restocking, and reequipping. These hacendados needed strategies to compensate, at least partially, for the continuing weakness of financial markets. Levels of notarized lending remained abysmal: an average of only about 21,000 pesos a year was available in Morelia in the 1820s, a figure that climbed to just 28,000 pesos a year in the early 1830s, to 39,000 pesos a year in the late 1830s, and to 50,000 pesos in the early 1840s — still a far cry from the 135,000 pesos a year that had been available in the decade before the Hidalgo Revolt.[13]

The agonizingly slow recovery of loan markets can be traced directly to the financial weakness of the church. Church lending, which had always made up a very large chunk of total pre-1810 lending, still suffered mightily from the shaky financial situation of many of its debtors, the old elite. Even after a program of debt composition, which was designed to enable hacendados whose property had been destroyed during the insurrection to resume debt service at a lower rate, was put into place in the mid-1820s, it continued to cost ecclesiastical personnel a great deal of trouble to collect interest on pre-1810 debts, not to mention to secure new sources of loan capital.[14]

This meant that hacendados, desperate for funds to rebuild and restock, had to turn to individual lenders, not to the church. Moreover, they had to find ways to avoid paying the crippling interest rates (by some reports, as high as 12 to 40 percent, depending on whether or not there was adequate equity to secure the loan) that straight loans commanded. One solution was to generalize what had been a relatively restricted practice during the colonial period: cash advances, to be repaid in kind. Advances of cash by merchants to agriculturalists were not new, of course; Isidro Huarte, among others, had used this mechanism to gain control of production on many more haciendas than he owned or rented. But before 1810 the church had been the first choice of hacendados with good credit who needed to borrow small to middling sums: enough, say, to cover a bad harvest or to build a fence. And to the extent that the church filled these needs, it was unnecessary to sell one's future harvests in advance — for invariably low prices — in order to acquire working capital. After 1810, however, the church's virtual absence from loan markets moved cash advances from the margins to the center of the credit scene. For many cash-poor hacendados the advance contract was the only way to gain access to operating expenses, necessary tools and supplies, investment capital, future credit, and distribution networks.

The use of advance sales, whose heyday was the decade of the 1830s, was more widespread among sugar producers and ranchers than among cereal producers.[15] From the point of view of the investors, sugar's still-high price in the 1830s and its relatively low bulk made it a more attractive risk than grains were. From the point of view of the owner/producers, the capital requirements of a return to large-scale production were heavier for *tierra caliente* producers than for *tierra fría* growers, who used institutions like sharecropping and tenancy to help make the transition from wartime devastation to resumed production on the hacienda account. These options were not so readily available to planters: the low population density in the hot country, and the (in most cases) ample lands possessed by Indian communities, meant that it was hard to attract tenants and sharecroppers. Furthermore, sugar and also indigo production required relatively high skill levels and a large, disciplined, full-time work force, neither one of which was fully compatible with tenancy and sharecropping. (In fact, one of the adjustments made by sugar planters was to produce *piloncillo* instead of sugar, since it was a less refined and therefore less labor-intensive product.)[16] The difficulties of the situation were explained in detail by Mariano Michelena. In 1822 he stated that his hacienda of La Parota could be repaired fully in six to eight years, but that to do so would require a large investment; his creditors thought it would take at least 20,000 to 30,000 pesos. Success, moreover, was absolutely dependent upon assiduous care of the plants that could only be provided by a large labor force. A modest investment of 2,000 pesos or even of as much as 6,000 to 8,000 pesos, he noted, would allow the haciendas to produce only a "very small" crop with an equally small net profit, and that only after two years.[17]

But some cereal producers also utilized the advance contract. In fact, by the early 1840s, the balance of advances seems to have shifted toward cereal producers, who were beginning to recover land from sharecroppers and tenants and to make the sort of major capital investments in their properties that many sugar producers, by this time, had already made. Fray Mucio Valdovinos, for example, administrator of the Augustinian hacienda of San Nicolás, drew regularly on an account with the Morelia merchant Vicente Rionda, and paid his bill in maize and hogs.[18] José María Ibarrola accepted a 2,500-peso advance from Manuel Alzúa which he agreed to repay with 5,000 *fanegas* of maize — a very low price — delivered to Alzúa's Morelia *expendio*.[19] In 1840 Santiago Ortiz, renter of the hacienda of Itzícuaro, borrowed 973 pesos at no interest from a Morelia merchant to buy seed, prepare land, and pay workers; the loan was to be repaid with 973 *fanegas* of maize.[20]

In sum, the use of cash advances in the 1830s (especially in the *tierra caliente*), and sharecropping and tenancy in the *tierra fría* beginning in the late 1810s and continuing through the 1820s, served much the same purpose: to bring fields back into production with as little cash outlay as possible being made on the part of the owner. In both systems the degree of disadvantage for the dependent partner hinged primarily on the terms he was able to negotiate, though it is clear that there was much more flexibility in the negotiations between merchant and hacendado, who were usually social equals, than between hacendado and sharecropper. If the merchant purchased the whole harvest in advance, then unless the money was used to carry out major improvements (new buildings, equipment purchase, irrigation systems) that would still be there next year, the hacendado was back in the same dependent position come next planting time. If, on the other hand, the hacendado managed to stretch out the repayment over several years, earmarking only a portion of each harvest for the merchant/speculator, it might be possible to sell the rest of the harvest at prices that would in turn reduce or eliminate the need to sell *al tiempo* the next year.[21] A sharp falloff in advance contracts in the 1840s and 1850s suggests that this was not entirely unrealistic.

Another form of adjustment to the changed economic climate after 1810 was the *compañía de campo*. In the 1820s and 1830s many of these partnerships resembled advance contracts quite closely, in that one partner (the "capitalista") supplied capital or goods, and the other, who was usually desperate for working funds and supplies, contributed land and/or labor. Nicolás Menocal, for example, lacking the resources to work his hacienda of Chachalaca, took on a partner (Mariano Ojeda) with whom he had previously negotiated advance contracts. Ojeda agreed to minister in weekly installments whatever was needed to run the hacienda. After the (sugar cane) harvest was sold, Ojeda's credit would be privileged (that is, paid before any others), and anything left over would be fifty-fifty.[22]

But by the late 1830s there was a subtle change in the character of most rural companies, away from the stark inequality between partners that characterized many of the earlier agreements. The partnership formed in 1839 between José María Solórzano Iriarte and Manuel Acha in an hacienda that they rented from a third party, for example, was capitalized with 12,000 pesos from each partner, including 2,400 pesos in the *tienda de raya*, which Solórzano managed and in which he had a 50-percent interest.[23] José Dolores Arceo contracted his third agricultural partnership with Ricardo Villaseñor in 1838 (the other two, formed in 1830 and 1834, were still ongoing in 1839). The partners contributed equally to foment the western hacienda of Platanal, which they rented from María Gertrudis Jaso.[24]

As with advance contracts, most agricultural partnerships were formed to work the highly commercial sugar and/or cattle haciendas in the *tierra caliente*. Usually the amounts invested by the "capitalista" were left vague (the arrangement was simply that he would supply funds as needed), though in cases in which one partner's contribution was specified the range was enormous, from 925 pesos to the 47,900 pesos that Fernando Román put into a partnership with Agustín Elorza that ran over a three-year period from 1836 to 1839 on Román's own hacienda of La Huerta. Most of the companies seem to have been fairly successful, though none so much as the contested Román-Elorza partnership. In an 1839 lawsuit Román admitted that the company's profits totaled 66,400 pesos over a three-year period, for a handsome net return of almost 50 percent a year. Despite these fabulous profits (or perhaps because of them), Román tried to break the contract, accusing Elorza of everything from cowardice in the face of the rebel presence in the region, to mismanagement of herds (the death rate among cattle, he said, was excessive), to failure to follow appropriate crop-management procedures (harvesting the rice too late, for example), to unskillful marketing practices (Elorza held out for too high a price for the rice and thus failed to sell the whole crop, and he sold on credit to customers with notoriously bad credit records). Elorza responded indignantly to all these accusations, blaming some losses on Román's "frugality," which was "carried to such an extreme that it could be called something altogether more meaningful," and claiming that Román had understated profits by some 22,000 pesos. The total net return according to Elorza was over 60 percent a year.[25]

These partnerships, and also the advance-sale arrangements discussed above, brought merchants and agricultural producers into an even closer relationship than they had enjoyed before 1810, and in the process they seem to have given the rural economy an essential stimulus that, even if it did not compensate fully for the absence of low-interest ecclesiastical loans, then at least financed the recovery of productive capacity on an increasing number of haciendas. It is easy to find producers whose demise these arrangements merely delayed, but it is also clear that some producers were able to use the services of an *habilitador* or a merchant-partner for a year or two and then dispense with them. This was possible largely because many external conditions — weather, prices, wages — proved favorable to producers in the 1830s: prices generally remained equal to or higher than they had been before 1810, wages seem to have come back down to pre-1810 levels, and the weather was cooperative.

The biggest problem facing landowners (aside from the capital scarcity that had occasioned the advance sales and rural partnerships in the first place) was the endemic political unrest of the 1830s, both before and after the *cambio de sistema*. Still, though the federalist rebellions no doubt slowed the process of recovery by bringing on commercial and administrative disruption that was widespread at times, the damage to the state's economic base seems not to have been great, certainly not by comparison to that suffered during the insurgency. After the War of the South, for example, tithe officials, in discussions regarding the minimum acceptable bid for each district in the 1833 tithe auction, observed that most districts — specifically Cuitzeo and Puruándiro in the north, Maravatío and Zinapécuaro in the east, Pátzcuaro in the center, La Piedad, Zamora, and Tinguindín/Jiquilpan in the west, and even Zitácuaro and Tacámbaro in the southeastern *tierra caliente* — had not suffered during the "last revolution." As a result, the minimum bid in these districts was set at or above 1828 levels. The only districts in which the church officials conceded that there were significant losses were Morelia, the small coastal districts of Pungarabato and Coahuayana, the central-western *tierra caliente* districts of La Huacana, Uruapan, and probably (they did not have good information yet) Ario and Apatzingán. They noted that even in substantially affected Uruapan, although one tithe collector had petitioned to be released from his contract because of the war, another person was willing to enter the same bid and take his place.[26] The *Memoria de Administración* in 1834, despite a gloomy assessment of state politics, was even more upbeat than the tithe directors about the situation of agriculture. Maize production, it reported, was adequate to feed the state and was more than keeping up with population increases; the livestock population had almost completely recuperated to pre-1810 levels; and the recovery of sugar plantations had been "incredible." Noting that new sugar-producing lands were being opened up in the district of Zacapu, the *Memoria* expected that this trend would continue, and it attributed the recovery to merchant "speculators."[27]

Statistics generated using notary records and other legal documents confirm that the rural economy improved steadily in the 1830s. The average price of an hacienda or large rancho climbed to 32,000 pesos, an increase of around 30 percent over the previous decade, and almost three-quarters of the average during the pre-Hidalgo period. Hacienda rents rose sharply in the 1830s to almost 2,000 pesos, from 1,200 pesos in the 1820s. Even sugar haciendas, which bore the brunt of both of the rebellions of the 1830s, seem to have come back strongly by the early 1840s, when sales tax records indicate that total production was virtually the same as it had been in the decade before 1810.[28] In short, by 1840 the rural sector in Michoacán was functional, if not yet thriving: the market was fluid and prices were jerkily increasing, most haciendas were back in operation, and a handful even exceeded pre-1810 levels of capitalization.

The New Landowners

Who were the owners who brought the hacienda economy back to life? In some cases they were late colonial elites who made successful adjustments to post-1810 conditions. For example, it is clear that José Guadalupe de la Piedra, whose livestock haciendas of Canario and Chirapitiro had been sacked by royalist armies in punishment for his insurgent sympathies, had plentifully restocked them by his death in 1841: the inventory of his estate shows cattle worth an impressive 53,000 pesos.[29] Eusebio Olavarrieta's hacienda of La Magdalena, in the western part of the state, also flourished. Olavarrieta rented out the hacienda, which had been worth 91,696 pesos in 1806, for 8,500 pesos a year in 1839, implying a value of some 170,000 pesos.[30] Juan Gómez de la Puente found time in between his frequent stints in the state legislature to build back his inherited hacienda of La Calera after significant losses during the insurgency.[31]

Other late colonial landowners enjoyed success not on their family haciendas but on others. Lic. Martín García Carrasquedo, the radical prebend and later archdean of the Morelia Cathedral, gave up on his family hacienda, Guaparatío, after his father died in 1819. Martín and his brother Isidro rented out the hacienda for a paltry 1,000 pesos a year in 1833 and for 1,115 pesos a year in 1842, implying that it had lost some 30,000 pesos in value since 1804, when it had been appraised at 50,000 pesos. But both of the brothers were quite active in purchasing and renting *other* haciendas. Martín, for example, bought the small haciendas of Arindeo el Chico in 1824 and Aguacate in 1826, adding a third contiguous property in 1827. With these three purchases he formed the hacienda of Santa Cruz. In 1839 he bought another property, the hacienda of San Isidro Ceniza, whose value he increased by 10,000 pesos within five years while paying off almost all of its debt. Meanwhile, he had begun to rent the cereal hacienda of Huandacareo from the Cuitzeo Augustinians, which his brother Isidro later purchased during the first stage of the Reform.[32]

Still others turned to trade as a way to accumulate capital to revive their family haciendas, a career direction (from hacendado to merchant) that almost never occurred during the colonial period, when creoles would have found it impossible to break into the Spanish merchants' near-monopoly on sources of supply. Joaquín Teobaldo Ruiz's inherited hacienda of Cuisillo was reduced during the insurrection from a value of about 20,000 pesos to one of no more than 7,000 pesos, but by Ruiz's death in 1836 the land and structures alone were worth 11,500 pesos, and movables were appraised at another 5,600 pesos. This improvement had been made possible by using proceeds from Ruiz's three stores in Morelia, established after independence.[33] Another hacendado-turned-merchant was María Josefa del Corral, one of the few women who was a senior partner in a mercantile operation. The twice-widowed, once-divorced María Josefa managed to hold onto the hacienda she had purchased in 1806 (with her share of the *gananciales* from her marriage to the merchant Juan de Mier y Terán) in large part by using proceeds from a store that she had established in the trading town of Santa Clara after her second husband's death at the hands of the insurgents in 1810. At her own death in 1830 the store assets made up over half the value of her estate.[34]

But if part of the recovery of the hacienda economy owed to the efforts of old families who restored their (old or new) properties to pre-1810 levels, the rest of the story, of course, is that of the efforts made by those who purchased the properties that so many of the old elites could *not* maintain. Put another way, the properties that were the object of the cessions and forced sales of the late 1820s and early 1830s eventually (though often later rather than sooner) passed into the hands of people with some combination of access to capital, ambition, and good luck to accomplish what the strained and sometimes traumatized former owners could not. And far more often than not, these were men with middle-class and not upper-class backgrounds.

Not infrequently, a troubled hacienda had to go through several hands before a new owner was able to make a go of it, as the case of the hacienda of El Rincón on the outskirts of Morelia amply demonstrates. This hacienda, whose main buildings are today the Club Campestre of Morelia, was purchased in 1814 by the man who had rented it since 1808, Mariano Figueroa, for approximately two-thirds of its appraised value. Figueroa, who was born in the small town of Panindícuaro and whose father was either an hacienda administrator or a large tenant, had high hopes that he would continue to benefit from extremely high grain prices and from the protection of royal troops, as he had done in the early years of the insurgency, and that he would be able to pay off the mortgage within three to four years. Indeed, the next year, in 1815, he felt confident enough to purchase a large and valuable house in Valladolid at auction for the bargain price of 9,150 pesos. Befitting his new status as a landowner and owner of one of the principal houses in the city, he served in the 1810s and early 1820s as *procurador general* and *regidor* of the city council.[35]

At this point, however, his luck began to turn. He never managed to pay off a peso of the debt he had assumed on purchase of either the hacienda or the house, and he fell farther and farther behind in interest payments. As he put it, after the royal troops were withdrawn in 1815,

the unexpected duration of the insurrection and the continuous sackings of movables and destruction of out-buildings by the belligerents in
those bloody struggles left me with absolutely no means of deriving an
income from the hacienda. Instead, I had to use my own funds to repair
the property and to make some — but not all — payments on its debts,
a fact which I deeply regret.[36]

In 1821 he tried renting out half of the hacienda but was only able to command a rent of 1,000 pesos, less than half of what he owed each year in interest. By 1826 his wife, on her deathbed, stated that her small paternal inheritance had been entirely consumed for expenses. In that year Figueroa was
forced to sell El Rincón for the amount of its debt, 46,253 pesos. He died
bankrupt in 1833, owing over 7,000 pesos in back interest on the hacienda
and the house.[37]

But Figueroa was not the only owner of El Rincón whom the hacienda defeated. Francisco Basurto Murillo, the man to whom Figueroa sold it in 1826,
had to turn it over to his creditors in 1828, and the next buyer, Francisco
Sánchez, was forced to sell it to Cayetano Martínez in 1832, at no profit.
Martínez, like his three predecessors, was unable to keep up with the interest
payments and ceded it back to the court of creditors in 1835, who sold it yet
once again later that year to Buenaventura Ortiz de Ayala, a tenant on his
brother Manuel's small fraction of the hacienda of Cuto (Manuel had been
Mariano Figueroa's partner when he first rented El Rincón in 1808). This
fifth sale in twenty years was the charm. Ortiz de Ayala was finally able to
make a success of the hacienda, and his direct descendants still owned El
Rincón at the time of the 1910 Revolution.[38]

Although the turnover of owners on the hacienda of El Rincón was unusually rapid, the history of this property illustrates several aspects of the general history of estate agriculture during this period. First, of course, it reflects
the great odds against prospering, even on an hacienda that was favorably situated on the outskirts of the capital city and that had proven its ability to earn
profits during the pre-1810 period and afterward. Second, since all five purchasers of the hacienda during this period were men of middle-class background, it is a good example of the potential for upward social mobility
among the provincial *gente decente*. Because the already-landed were generally unwilling and unable in a still-fragile investment environment to risk their
depleted financial assets in new enterprises (and in fact were in many cases
busily divesting themselves of burdensome, often very heavily indebted prop-

erties), there was space open for new men in the rural sector. They were able to move into positions of ownership because this was a buyer's market; owners and creditors were so anxious to move property that they even abandoned the requirement for a down payment. Mariano Figueroa, for example, was ostensibly required to pay 10,000 pesos down when he purchased El Rincón, but this amount was merely a combination of the credits he had already accumulated and an unfulfilled promise to redeem the rest within a few years — and the next four purchasers of the hacienda were not required to make any down payment at all. Thus by the mid-1820s the elements required to permit significant involvement in hacienda agriculture by people who were not already wealthy (a reversal of the late colonial trend, when most haciendas were purchased by capital-rich merchants) were beginning to fall into place: a relative abundance of properties for sale or rent on extremely advantageous terms, a scarcity of qualified (by pre-1810 standards) or willing elite buyers, and little or no requirement for a down payment or deposit.

The dimensions of upward social mobility among the middle class are perhaps best appreciated by considering the profiles of the 52 individuals who purchased haciendas in Morelia, Pátzcuaro, and Zamora during the years 1811 to 1839 (see Table 4.1). Of this number, only nine had family backgrounds of wealth and/or hacienda ownership. The most striking feature of this population, then, was its distinctly middle-class social origins. Predictably (as the history of the hacienda of El Rincón suggests), many of the 43 middle-class hacienda purchasers failed: over one-third (fifteen) were unable to hold onto their properties and had to sell them within a few years for scarcely more and in some cases less than the original purchase price. Six more buyers held on during their lifetimes to at least part of the properties they had purchased, but cannot be said to have prospered. Miguel Ortiz, for example, purchased the hacienda of Chapultepec (which he had previously rented) in 1826 for 32,041 pesos, but in 1839 he was forced to cede back to the sellers almost half of the estate; in 1849 his heirs sold another part of the estate, and in 1858 they sold off the rest.[39] In a similar case, Miguel Baca bought the hacienda of Quinceo in 1837 for 37,000 pesos but had to cede it back to the seller, who then resold it in 1841 to Br. Estevan Cabezas, Baca's uncle. Cabezas died shortly thereafter, leaving the property to his nephew, and although Baca was able this time to hold on to the estate, he was not able to improve it substantially nor to reduce its debt; in 1849 Baca himself appraised it at the same 37,000 pesos for which he had purchased it over a decade earlier, and it was still mortgaged for 32,000 pesos.[40]

TABLE 4.1
Profile of Hacienda Buyers, 1811–39

	Non-elites	*Elites*
Improved dramatically	10	0
Modest success	12	8
Failures, near-failures, or probable failures (unknowns)	21	1
Total no. of individuals	43	9
Total no. of haciendas	46	10

SOURCES: ANM, AHPJ, AHMM, AMHCR, AHCP.

But if almost half of the middle-class aspirants to landownership failed or barely held on, the other 22 had solid and in many cases glittering success, 10 of them more than doubling the value of their purchases in their lifetimes, and the other 12 improving them substantially. About half of the successful middle-class hacienda purchasers were men, like the purchaser of the hacienda of El Rincón, Ventura Ortiz de Ayala, with a background in agriculture; typically they had been renters or hacienda administrators early in their careers. Among them were José María Flores, who served as the administrator of the hacienda of Tipitarillo before he purchased it in a desperation sale in 1826; and Ignacio Marroquín, who rented the hacienda of Presentación from Felipe Robledo for fourteen years, beginning in 1823, before he bought it from the Robledo family in 1837. While he rented the property he increased the value of its land and structures from an implied value of 60,000 pesos at the time of his initial rental contract to the 75,000 pesos he paid for it in 1837. By his death in 1841 the hacienda was worth some 120,000 pesos.[41]

Despite the success of these and other hacienda buyers with a background in agriculture, the most spectacular examples of upward social mobility are to be found among men who started out as merchant/speculators and, in a repeat of the late colonial pattern, later diversified into land. The most dramatic case of upward mobility through trade and then agriculture was that of Cayetano Gómez (see the prologue to this chapter). But Gómez was far from the only example of such movement. In fact, the second wealthiest Michoacano at midcentury, Fernando Román, had preceded Gómez in both his mercantile success and his diversification into land. Román had already amassed 18,000 to 20,000 pesos in trade by the time of his 1813 marriage to Dolores Arriaga y Peralta, and he had done it in the early years of the insurgency, since he does not figure among leading merchants of either Pátzcuaro or Valladolid before 1810. By the late 1810s and perhaps even before, he had begun to speculate in sugar as well as to trade in imported merchandise. When he made his first purchase of land in 1821, however, it was not a sugar hacienda, but the cattle-indigo-rice hacienda of La Huerta (Apatzingán), which he bought at auction for an unknown sum. By the mid-1830s, shortly before he entered into the wildly profitably partnership with Agustín Elorza detailed above, the appraised value of La Huerta had doubled to over 100,000 pesos, and by 1850 it had doubled again to over 200,000 pesos.[42]

Meanwhile, Román's obvious desire to dominate, if not to corner, the market on sugar led him to rent the sugar-producing hacienda of La Loma (Tacámbaro) from the Augustinians in 1830 when it became available, even as he continued to advance cash to other sugar producers to be repaid in kind. The management of La Loma was turned over to one of his partners, Juan Ignacio Anciola, who ran the hacienda until Román's death in 1850. In 1841, Román rented another large sugar-producing hacienda, Araparícuaro (an hacienda whose sugar he had purchased in advance for a decade), putting Anciola in charge of it as well. And in 1839 he entered into another partnership with Manuel Ignacio Anaya to manage, at 50 percent of the profits, a third sugar hacienda (La Magdalena, in Los Reyes) which Román rented for a substantial 8,500 pesos a year. The partnerships with both Anciola and Anaya continued until Román's death in 1850, and contributed substantially to his impressive 616,260-peso estate.[43]

Other highly successful merchants who moved into agriculture early in the period were Antonio Sierra and Francisco Plancarte. Sierra, who was born near Uruapan, had started out as an *arriero*, transporting merchandise from the coast, especially Zihuantanejo, to Morelia and Mexico City. He pieced together an extensive *latifundia* in *tierra caliente* by combining relatively small ranchos that he purchased in 1824, 1828, 1836, 1838, 1840, 1845, and 1849. By his death in 1850 his properties — which, like Román's La Huerta, specialized in rice, livestock, and indigo — were worth over 200,000 pesos.[44] Plancarte's entry into agriculture began with the purchase of numerous *solares* in Jacona that produced vegetables, fruits, and wheat for the rapidly growing nearby city of Zamora. In 1834 he bought his first hacienda, Tamándaro, and in 1837 he added the hacienda of La Sauceda; in the late 1840s and early 1850s he continued to acquire land, including various ranchos and the small hacienda of Parandian. By his death in 1854, Plancarte's estate was worth at least 125,000 pesos.[45]

The Mercantile Sector

Since merchants — and not just those who purchased their own haciendas — played an important role in the rebuilding of haciendas during the late 1820s and 1830s, it is perhaps useful at this point to shift the focus of discussion to them. If merchant/speculators, with their new or expanded credit operations, were essential to the recovery of haciendas — especially, during this period, those specializing in out-of-region exports like sugar, *piloncillo*, rice, indigo, and livestock — it is important to know who these men were and how they obtained the capital and/or credit that was required to set the recovery in motion.

As in agriculture, the turbulence of the independence era created opportunities for considerable upward mobility in trade; indeed, though a handful of men from landowning families went into trade after independence, the great majority of the creoles who took the place of the (mainly) departed Spanish merchants after 1810 were poor and came from middle-class (or in some cases, lower-class) origins. One successful creole merchant of distinctly middle-class background was José María Patiño, whose parents were residents of the Indian town of Capula, outside Valladolid (although they came originally from Valle de Santiago, Guanajuato). Patiño brought only 150 pesos to his first marriage, which took place shortly before 1810, and his wife brought only 350 pesos. But by the date of his second marriage in the mid-1820s he had accumulated 6,500 pesos in trade. The precise nature of Patiño's initial foray into commerce is not documented, but his military rank (lieutenant colonel) may have helped establish him.[46] A variation on this pattern is the career of Ignacio Montenegro, born in Tarímbaro in 1789 to a family that came from Jiquilpan. Socially, the Montenegros were elite: Ignacio's grandfather had been a regidor of Valladolid; his sister Susana was married well to Francisco Olavarrieta, and another sister, Ana María, made an excellent marriage as the second wife of Pascual Alzúa. Ignacio himself married Alzúa's daughter, Macaria, in 1827. But the family was plainly poor. Neither Ignacio nor his sisters brought more than their names to their marriages, and they never inherited a peso.[47]

The most impressive social and economic ascent through trade, however, was mounted by Vicente Sosa. Sosa came from a frankly lower-class background: born to an unmarried woman and unrecognized by his father, he had been a sergeant in the royalist infantry in Morelia (a noncommissioned rank). The priest who recorded his 1819 marriage did not use the honorifics "don" and "doña" to refer to either Sosa or his bride, Loreto Sosa, who was also an illegitimate child.[48] But Sosa became a state legislator, one of his sons married a daughter of Cayetano Gómez, and his became one of the largest mercantile houses in Morelia.

Most of the successful, upwardly mobile merchants began by buying a mule or two on credit and then traveling from hacienda to hacienda, purchasing part of the harvest and taking it to markets where, if all went well, it could be sold at profit. Naturally those profits were rather thin, given the small scale of their operations, but they were bolstered considerably by sales of imported merchandise along the way, which they had acquired from Morelia wholesalers on credit (al fiado), a practice that, like advance sales, flourished in the 1830s. They were thus able to combine profits from the sales of imported goods and commodities with savings on transportation costs in order, they hoped, to eventually save enough to make the transition from arriero/merchant/speculator to established merchant. In other words, while some muleteers during this period were employed on a regular basis by major wholesalers to transport cargoes, as in the colonial period, many others were independents. Jean Meyer describes the early career of one of these men, Nicolás Ramírez Valdés, who began as a merchant/mule driver in the western part of the state around Ixtlán in the 1820s. Ramírez, Meyer writes, "crisscrossed the countryside, buying everything he could and transporting it on muleback: hides, cheese, wax, chiles, soap, clothing, combs, etc., visiting small pueblos with his mule team, directing a small army of 'rabatteurs.'"[49] Ramírez came to be a wealthy landowner and urban landlord.

If itinerant or provincial merchants bought manufactured goods on credit from regional (mainly Morelia) wholesalers, how then did these wholesalers acquire their inventory? The key is the unprecedented array of goods available after independence for purchase on credit from commercial houses in Mexico City and Guadalajara/San Blas, and to a slightly lesser extent in Colima, Acapulco, Mazatlán, and Tampico, at prices that were historically low. Occasionally merchants in Michoacán were able to establish direct connections to those foreign houses. The earliest example I have found appears in the 1830 libro de becerro for Zamora, where José Dolores Galván registered a 7,302-peso debt to Bordon, Harrison, and Brown of Guadalajara, the balance from a larger amount that they had loaned Galván for "giros de su comercio."[50] But during the 1830s, while regional merchants benefited from the foreign presence in Mexico City, for the most part they had not yet tapped into the foreign credit line directly.

Instead, most of the relationships between Michoacano merchants and foreign houses during this period were mediated by formerly prominent local merchants, almost invariably Spaniards, who had moved to Mexico City after they were expelled from the state in 1829 and had begun to handle the commercial needs of their friends and associates still operating in Michoacán. One of the three most important was Agustín Barandiarán, formerly a Pátzcuaro merchant and owner of the *tierra caliente* hacienda of Pedernales, who moved to Mexico City in 1829 with his son Evaristo and seems to have established a partnership (whose terms, unfortunately, are not at all clear from Michoacán archives) with the famous Spanish *agiotista*, Pío Bermejillo.[51] The second was Francisco Iturbe, also a Pátzcuaro merchant who had been a partner of Isidro Huarte in the coastal trade and who dissolved his long-standing partnership with Ignacio Arriaga in Michoacán in 1835, though he probably moved to Mexico City earlier, in response to the 1829 expulsion. His son, Francisco, became another famous *agiotista*. In fact, it was no doubt the son with whom much of the Morelia mercantile elite dealt, since the father must have been nearing 60 by the time of the move, though because the names are the same it is not always easy to distinguish between them.[52] The third was Gaspar Alonso de Ceballos, a successful pre-1810 Spanish merchant who also moved to Mexico City from Morelia around 1829. Like the other two, Ceballos maintained close ties to Michoacán, eventually buying three haciendas in the state, where his nephews, Lic. Gregorio Ceballos and Lic. Juan B. Ceballos, were very active liberal politicians beginning in the early 1830s.[53] All three of these men maintained lines of credit with numerous regional merchants, and they were probably not the only ones to do so. Miguel de la Parra of Jiquilpan, for example, had an agent in Mexico City named Miguel Garibay, who was probably related to the Garibay clan in and around Zamora.[54]

The way the regional trade network hinged on the large Morelia houses, which in turn had close relationships to Mexico City houses, can be appreciated by a quick look at the various activities of Ignacio Montenegro during the mid-1830s. Like most large merchants, Montenegro sold a variety of imported items — especially dry goods, but also chocolate, paper, spices, and wax — and speculated in agricultural commodities like *piloncillo*, in which he accepted payment from customers. In 1833 he is recorded as having sold two "partes de efectos" to Juan Guisa, a Puruándiro merchant, for 8,737 pesos, which Guisa agreed to pay off at the rate of 500 pesos a month. Two weeks later a Tacámbaro merchant asked Montenegro to open an account for him so that he could "borrow" effects from Montenegro's store to sell in Tacámbaro. Montenegro himself, meanwhile, had accounts with at least two (and probably more) Mexico City houses, including "Viuda de Echeverría e Hijos," and a French wholesaler.[55]

For Montenegro, as for most Morelia merchants, agricultural speculation was a sizable portion of his business. But one of the most interesting merchants of the period, Mariano Larreátegui, was a retail specialist — in fact, given the size of his inventory, his operation must have been a sort of forerunner of a department store. He did not speculate in agricultural commodities to any significant degree, and he does not seem to have sold goods regularly to provincial or itinerant merchants on commission, although he did form business partnerships with other merchants in which he stocked their stores at cost as his capital investment. He eventually bought an hacienda, but not so much in order to speculate in agricultural commodities as to supply an ill-fated mining enterprise for which he ultimately abandoned his retail business in the early 1840s.[56] Despite the fact that in these respects his career was unconventional, it nonetheless effectively illustrates the freewheeling commercial climate of the period, the extent to which Mexico City credit was available to merchants, and the extent to which ambitious and hard-driving provincial merchants could turn this availability of credit to their own account.

Larreátegui was born in Jiquilpan, in far western Michoacán, to a family that may have had some social position (one man surnamed Larreátegui served on the Zamora city council in the late 1770s), but almost certainly had no landed wealth.[57] Whatever assets the family possessed, in any event, were lost during the insurrection: Mariano's mother's 1844 will states that around 1814 she and her children moved to Valladolid, penniless. Ten years later, she continued, "at the beginning of the year 1824," when Mariano was probably about twenty years old, "with hard work and industry, we began to acquire the capital that my son now manages."[58] Larreátegui's early poverty was confirmed by three Morelia merchants who had helped him to get started. One stated that he "made loans to the [Larreátegui] family and gave them goods on credit, and when Mariano began to work, he had to pay off these obligations because his father had nothing with which to repay them." Cayetano Gómez and Fernando Román also attested to having loaned Larreátegui small sums as *habilitaciones*. Gómez recalled the first amount as having been just 60 pesos; Román remembered that he sometimes gave him 200 pesos with which to operate, sometimes 300.[59]

By 1835 Larreátegui had apparently saved enough and/or established a sufficiently good credit record to move to a new stage in his mercantile career. In August of that year, he formed a partnership with Rafael Amescua. Amescua, the contract provided, would manage the company, and Larreátegui would put up a capital investment of 53,937 pesos (24,000 in accounts receivable and the balance in merchandise). When he established this partnership and bought an expensive house on the Plaza Mayor in Morelia whose lower floor could serve as the store location, he sold over 100 mules, which he no longer needed: now that he was settled and prosperous, he could either hire mule trains or rely on his suppliers to arrange transport of goods.[60]

Larreátegui adopted a very aggressive, even abrasive approach to business, and it paid off, despite numerous confrontations with the authorities and his own employees:[61] by 1840 his store in Morelia had annual sales of around 150,000 pesos, and in 1842, when he relinquished its management to dedicate himself to his mining operations, his books showed merchandise to a value of 332,685 pesos and accounts receivable of 167,615 pesos for a total capital of over 500,000 pesos. Ominously, however, Larreátegui owed 330,261 pesos to creditors in Morelia, Mexico City, Tampico, and Guadalajara. Some of these creditors tried to stop Larreátegui's mining adventure, forcing him to promise to repay his debts to them before he invested a single peso in his mines. But clearly his difficulties in Morelia were not widely broadcast in Mexico City, where he managed to convince a good portion of the Mexico City elite to buy shares in the mine.[62]

Larreátegui was far from the only merchant in Morelia in the 1830s who was in a big way of business. The surprising degree of mercantile liquidity can be appreciated from an 1840 document in which six leading merchants in Morelia agreed to pay a fixed sum each year to the state treasury in lieu of *alcabalas* (in other words, to *igualar*, as was common in the colonial period). The sum would be based on an agreed-upon estimate of the volume of annual business of each commercial house.[63]

The six merchants were, in order of importance: Cayetano Gómez, who agreed to pay the state treasury 10,250 pesos a year; Larreátegui, who paid 9,160 pesos; Vicente Sosa, who paid 8,250 pesos; Vicente Rionda, manager of the Casa de Barandiarán, who paid 6,250 pesos; Ignacio Arriaga, who paid 5,250 pesos; and the partners José María Ibarrola and José María Flores,

who paid 2,000 pesos. In only two cases — Ibarrola/Flores and Larreátegui —
was the *iguala* broken down into its component parts: municipal lighting, city
taxes, goods produced in Michoacán, goods produced in the rest of the
Republic, and imported goods. Fortunately, these two houses were at opposite ends of a spectrum ranging from enterprises with a high mix of agricultural commodities to those dealing mostly in imported goods, so we can fairly
confidently establish a range of total sales for all six houses.

A key business interest of the Ibarrola/Flores company was marketing agricultural commodities: the two men jointly rented the grain-producing hacienda of Coapa, and Flores owned the sugar-producing haciendas of
Tipitaro, San Vicente, and Tipitarillo.[64] Their 2,000-peso *iguala* thus included
a rather large proportion (39 percent) of sales of domestic goods, mostly
commodities from their haciendas, while 45 percent of the *iguala* represented
estimated tax due on sales of imported goods. The remaining 16 percent went
for *alumbrado* and municipal taxes. Because domestically produced goods
paid sales tax at the rate of 6 to 8 percent, and foreign goods at 5 percent, we
can infer that the Ibarrola/Flores company generated between 28,000 and
31,000 pesos a year in sales.[65] The Casa de Larreátegui, on the other hand,
which as we have seen rarely speculated in agricultural commodities, paid
only 9 percent of its tax on sales of domestic goods, while 76 percent of the
total tax was paid on imported goods (with 15 percent for *alumbrado* and
municipal taxes). The total sales generated by the company were thus around
149,000 to 153,000 pesos.

Although two of the four remaining houses — Sosa and Arriaga — did en-
gage in agricultural speculation, they did not rent or own haciendas themselves in 1840, so the mix of goods they sold was more like Larreátegui's than
like Ibarrola/Flores's. Sosa's total sales, then, must have been about 137,500
pesos, and Arriaga's about 87,500 pesos. Finally, Gómez and Barandiarán,
while still engaging in wholesale trade, were also landowners and speculators
and thus can be expected to have had a higher proportion of domestic goods
in the mix of products sold in their Morelia establishments. If we guess, quite
arbitrarily, that half their business was in domestic and half in imported
goods, then Barandiarán's total sales would have been about 85,000 to
96,000 pesos a year, and Gómez's 140,000 to 160,000 pesos a year.

In sum, just six of Morelia's many commercial enterprises, in whose number are not included such prominent merchants as Fernando Román,
Francisco Estrada, and Nicolás Ruiz de Chávez, generated well over 600,000
pesos in trade each year during the late 1830s. The top six merchants in the

decade before 1810, by contrast, paid *alcabala* on only some 160,000 pesos in total sales each year, and the average value of goods sold by *all* merchants in Valladolid was only 544,000 pesos.[66]

Both the 1800–10 and the 1840 figures are, of course, very rough estimates, but there is no escaping the conclusion that the pace of commercial exchange in 1840, compared to that in 1810, was brisk, despite complaints about the sluggishness of trade. A partial explanation of the impressive trade totals for the later period is that a broad market for imported items such as inexpensive dry goods, which were always the most heavily stocked and traded items in any mercantile inventory during the post-1810 period, existed before 1810, but that because of Spanish mercantilism and the related near-monopoly of trade by a relatively few Spaniards, this market was simply not tapped in the way it could be after independence. Merchants' ability to reach wider markets for imported goods and thereby to generate a large volume of business in turn helps to explain where they acquired the capital to play a key role in the revival of estate agriculture in Michoacán.[67]

The Central Republic

Much of this agricultural recovery took place during the centralist decade, which lasted from 1835 to 1846. At the beginning of the period the economic recovery was still very tentative — in fact, the desire to nurture further advances in a still-fragile economy was no doubt one of the factors driving the *cambio de sistema* — but by 1846 it was in full swing. The economic rebound owed nothing, however, to increased stability under the new system. The state congress had reluctantly traded autonomy for the hope that centralism would provide a measure of elusive public "tranquillity," but that hope was quickly extinguished. Within a year after the devastating cholera epidemic of 1833 to 1834 had presented a different kind of threat to the well-being of the state, federalist rebels under Gordiano Guzmán took up arms against the soon-to-be formalized centralist system.[68] At first the rebellion was quite limited in scope, but at its height in 1837 to 1838 it spread throughout the state. Rebel armies occupied Puruándiro and Zacapu in the center-north and Pátzcuaro and Uruapan in the center-south, and armed confrontations took place in Zamora and Tangancícuaro as well as throughout the *tierra caliente*.[69] Tithe officials almost everywhere complained that in 1837 and 1838 the *pronunciados* and/or government troops had carried off their collections.[70] Again an attack on Morelia was repelled, and the federalists were chased into the coastal mountains around Aguililla. Afterwards the rebellion faded, but pockets of unrest remained through 1841.[71] Manuela Morales de Velasco, for example, pleaded for debt forgiveness in 1843 on the grounds that the "revolution" led by Francisco Ronda had looted and destroyed haciendas — including hers — throughout the Pátzcuaro/Zirahuen region in 1840 and 1841.[72] The estate of Br. Juan Jose Pastor Morales also sought and received debt reduction because of "revolutions" in the early 1840s in the region between Pátzcuaro and Zacapu where his hacienda of Bellasfuentes was situated.[73] A petition circulated by distraught Morelia merchants in 1840 referred, hyperbolically, to the state as "the asylum of disorder"; the South, they lamented, was "deserted, totally abandoned; there are only reports of sackings, hostilities, and vexations . . . the rebels seem to be concerned only with their great project to leave families without honor, owners without haciendas, and respectable men of good will (*hombres de bien*) without prospects."[74]

If anything, in fact, the centralist government seemed even less capable than were earlier regimes of securing the peace, not only because it offered the federalist rebels such an obvious target, but because of its extreme fiscal penury. Two liberal reforms enacted in 1833 (abolition of the civil obligation to tithe, which meant that the state no longer received its fraction of the total collection; and elimination of the tobacco monopoly, whose revenues had bolstered the state treasury in the 1820s as they had done during the colonial regime) had reduced revenues to a trickle of much-evaded sales taxes and miscellaneous unpopular taxes on production and property. The salaries of government employees on whom tax collection, administration of justice, and public security rested went unpaid, and the tasks with which they were entrusted went largely undone.[75] What revenues came in were mainly soaked up by the army, which complained nonetheless of being unable to arm, clothe, and feed, much less pay, the rank and file.[76]

The national government was in even worse shape and, desperate for funds, it began making demands upon the former states (now departments) that the former Congress of Michoacán (now the Junta Departamental) considered most alarming. Less than two months after its installation the junta sent a strongly worded *representación* to the National Congress, protesting a forced loan of which Michoacán's share was an "unsupportable" 20,000 pesos. Several points made in this petition are worth noting. The statement began by proclaiming that the junta took seriously its "duty" to promote the well-being of the department. This was a line of reasoning straight out of the federalist era: the junta, intended by the new centralist regime to be a weak, mainly advisory body, fully subject to the national-level institutions, here cast itself not only as the voice of the citizenry and defender of its rights but as a body whose primary loyalty was to the state, not to the nation. The theme of state chauvinism was pursued as the petitioners built their case. Whereas the debates of the federalist congresses had rarely mentioned other states, invoking instead the "good of the nation" as a goal of their own actions, now the junta vigorously pursued what might be called fairness issues, especially singling out the Department of Mexico as having been assigned a disproportionately small quota while poor Michoacán, devastated by wars fought on its soil, was expected to pay more than its fair share. The petition concluded with a bald challenge: the national government *did not have the right* to demand so much from Michoacán, since the decree that authorized a forced loan specifically stated that it must be spread among the states "in the least onerous manner" possible. The 20,000-peso loan must be reduced to no more than 5,000 pesos.[77]

This preoccupation with the injustices visited upon Michoacán by both the national government and the other states/departments carried through the decade of the central Republic. In early 1837 the junta complained about the national law prohibiting the minting of copper coins and providing for the amortization of those in circulation, on the grounds that, first, the tariff establishing the value of a wide range of goods in circulation, which was formulated in Mexico City, did not take into account local price fluctuations, and, second, bordering states had not abided by the law and were damaging Michoacán's economy by their actions and inactions.[78] A month later the junta went against the intention of the national law by approving the Morelia city council's decision to issue 300 pesos worth of local currency in order to substitute for the disallowed copper coins. Signaling symbolically a connection to the radical insurgency and to liberal values, they decreed that the coins should be stamped with the words: "El Genio de la Libertad," in reference to José María Morelos.[79] Undisguised resentment of centralism, juxtaposed against rose-colored memories of the state of affairs before the *cambio*, were expressed in a July 1838 response to the governor's request for approval of a redesigned Secretaría de Gobierno. The junta commissioner wrote:

> I am sorry to have delayed responding to your proposal, but I am in
> the embarrassing position of not being able to agree with the measures
> you suggest. . . . What Your Excellency sees as a minimum number of

employees is the same number that the Third Congress of the then-State of Michoacán designated in a *reglamento* of 30 July 1831. . . . [But] *in 1831 this Department was a sovereign State, its government of more importance than now, and the state of its Treasury very different from its present decadence.*[80] (emphasis mine)

Eventually, given the precarious fiscal situation of the department, the junta was forced to give up trying to implement certain crucial features of the centralist system. For example, one of the linchpins of centralism was to have been a reformed system of justice, in which the allegedly incompetent and corrupt *alcaldes* would be replaced by *jueces letrados*. For elites, the connection between crime, political unrest, and justice administered (or not administered) by *alcaldes* was obvious; indeed, it had been a point of concern well before the imposition of the centralist system. Halfway measures had been approved; under the measures a new official, the *juez de paz* (appointed by the state, but not a proper judge) would take over some of the functions previously assigned to the *ayuntamientos*.[81] But by 1840 the deplorable state of departmental finances led junta members to conclude that an *alcalde*-based system of justice was better than none at all, since even paying the salaries of the *jueces de paz*, much less of all the *jueces letrados* needed in the department, was out of the question, and to continue not to pay them opened them to temptations and to worse corruption than the *alcaldes*.[82] (They were still not willing to allow even the *jueces de paz* to collect taxes, given their "complete stupidity and ignorance.")[83]

A year later, in 1841, the junta moved quickly to support two initiatives submitted by the Junta of Zacatecas and the Junta of Jalisco, which proposed far-ranging revisions of the centralist 1836 Constitution and insisted that the Supremo Poder Conservador — the shadowy, unelected fourth branch of government whose function was to oversee relations between the other three branches — should have nothing to do with the constitutional reform process. Attempting to seize back some of the power they had enjoyed during the federalist period, they demanded that the bodies with the right to determine the desirability of constitutional reforms should be the Juntas Departamentales.[84]

Now that we have taken into account this undercurrent of opposition on the part of the junta members to the centralist government and to centralism itself, it should also be noted that in some ways the rhetoric and actions of the junta, reinforced by the structure of government itself, conform to expectations for a conservative, mainly upper-class body.[85] One dimension of the junta's moralizing elitism was its perfect willingness to regulate the day-to-day lives of the people of Michoacán, a thing from which, for the most part, the liberty-enshrining congresses of the 1820s had shrunk. The junta was set up to advise the governor on actions that should be taken in the far corners of the department, and accordingly its *libros de registro* are full of requests for permission to expend community funds, appeals of prefectorial decisions, and applications for various licenses and exemptions, mainly submitted by the state's *ayuntamientos* and Indian towns. The members of the junta took their job very seriously, producing sometimes-lengthy disquisitions on all aspects of a certain case, and attempting to mediate between the parties involved in order to produce a harmonious outcome. In other words, they slipped easily into a colonial style of governance.

A good example of this controlling impulse was an 84-page set of instructions concerning exactly what should be included in a new statistical survey soon to be carried out.[86] Another was the junta's enthusiastic endorsement of two sets of detailed regulations for Morelia residents, drawn up by the city council, which were to be enforced by a strengthened police force. There was to be no more urinating in the streets and no emptying chamber pots or throwing dirty water out of windows. Dead dogs were to be removed from the city and taken beyond the quarry, and the slaughter of cattle outside the door of the convent of Santa Catarina was prohibited. Garbage collectors must make regular rounds, leaving enough time after they rang their bell for people to bring the trash out to the street. No animals might be watered or bathed in the public fountains, which must be cleaned twice a month. Citizens must request permission from the *jefe del cuartel* to hold a fandango or *baile*, and the custom known as a *velorio* — in which bonfires were lit and people danced and became intoxicated and staged cockfights and roamed scandalously through the streets at night — was prohibited absolutely. Houses must be whitewashed, and anyone who owned a vacant lot in a residential area must build a fence on the street side. Builders must submit plans for new construction and remodeling.[87] Interestingly, the one popular behavior about which the federalist congresses had moralized — bullfighting — escaped censure by the junta, which even supported a plan to build a *plaza de toros* in Morelia.[88] The junta was, presumably, less anxious to present a "modern" face to the outside world than it was desirous of the revenues that a new bullring would bring in. This relative unconcern with Mexico's international stature, especially if imported standards of behavior meant upsetting the popular classes, was also characteristic of nineteenth-century conservatism, though it is more often evoked where popular religion, rather than popular sport, is concerned.

The junta also sounded like a body of conservative thinkers when it came to the orchestration of national and religious celebrations. Even the federalist congresses had spent a good bit of time debating the proper order in which dignitaries should enter and be seated in the cathedral, but their aim had been to diminish as much as possible the hierarchical distinctions implicit in processional formations. The junta, by contrast, was careful to accommodate (and rank) all corporate groups and individuals, not only those named by the federalists (the church, the *ayuntamiento*, the congress, the governor, and the Supreme Court), but also the various levels of army officers, the medical school faculty, the Junta de Fomento, the Junta de Instrucción Pública, the *asesores*, the Promotor Fiscal de Hacienda, the Administrador de Tabacos, the Administrador de Rentas, the Auditor de Guerra, the Tribunal Mercantil, the barracks commanders, the Jueces de Primera Instancia, the Prefect, the treasurer, the *fiscales* of the Supreme Court, and so on.[89]

But in other ways, the predominantly wealthy members of the junta sounded and behaved more like moderate liberals than rigid conservatives.[90] It is especially easy to appreciate the blurred line between conservative and liberal ideology where the indigenous population, and especially communal landholding, were concerned. The conventional wisdom is that conservatives rejected the liberal efforts to redistribute communally held lands among the individual members of the community. But in Michoacán there was considerable overlap between the postures of the junta and the federalist congress of 1827, which framed the original law of *reparto*.

The 1827 law mandating the division of village lands had opened the door to waves of requests on the part of the communities themselves for enforcement of the law, and these requests did not cease with the *cambio de sistema*. The junta responded to all of them, soliciting the opinions not only of the appropriate prefects but of the villagers themselves. In cases in which the community seemed fully in favor of the land distribution, the junta was willing, sometimes even eager, to go along. When the Indians of Tancítaro petitioned for the division of their lands, for example, the prefect worried that in his experience the individuals who received land in these divisions soon sold them to the neighboring ranchos or haciendas for a third or a fourth of their value. But the junta, while agreeing that this was often the case, "could see no reason to deny [these Indians] what so many others had already received," and contented itself with charging the prefect to exercise "indefatigable zeal" in enforcing article 8 of the 1827 law, which prohibited selling, mortgaging, or otherwise alienating the properties for four years after their distribution.[91] The decision to proceed with *repartimiento* was even easier for the junta to make in the case of the Indians of Coyuca. Here the junta was convinced that the elders of the village were resisting the distribution because they wanted to maintain their control over communal lands and to continue to monopolize rents paid by "outsiders who do not belong to the community, to whom they give 'cartas de Yndios' when they are not Indians at all," while widows and orphans and other legitimate *parcioneros* suffered.[92] Similarly, when the elders of the pueblo of Numerán tried to halt the ongoing distribution of common lands, the junta refused to listen to them, citing evidence that the majority strongly desired the division and that the small minority was just afraid of losing its privileged access to village lands and its position of power if the lands were divided equally.[93]

In general, then, the junta supported redistribution of communal lands. But (and this was also in the spirit of the 1827 law) it looked with disfavor on requests by village elders or others to *sell* (as opposed to distribute) part of the communal property. In 1842, for example, the Indians of one Pátzcuaro barrio wanted to sell some of their land to pay for rebuilding their church, and they also asked to increase the rent on other lots that they rented out. The prefect cautioned against approval: "it is not the spirit of piety that motivates the supplicants," he wrote, "but the personal interests of their *apoderados* and a few others." The junta agreed, noting that the solicitations made in the name of Indian communities were often in contradiction to the true will of the majority, whose miserable conditions did not allow them to resist the well-to-do minority. "It is always appropriate in these cases to ascertain independently the opinion of each one of the members of the community, and not just to listen to what the elders say."[94] In a similar case, the Indians of Sahuayo were among those whose lands had been distributed according to the 1827 law, but a few *caballerías* had been set aside to be rented out and the proceeds used to pay the salary of a schoolmaster. In 1837 some *vecinos*, arguing that they had been unfairly excluded from the original distribution, went to the prefect to ask that lands that had been set aside for schools now be distributed, especially in light of the fact that the lands did not produce enough income for the school to function effectively. The prefect called for a vote among the villagers, which turned out 171 in favor of a new distribution and 9 against. He was prepared to carry out the wishes of the majority when an Indian named Rafael

Martínez presented evidence that those who wanted a new distribution had never had a right to village lands in the first place (the reasons were not given); moreover, the lands dedicated to supporting the school had been ceded "irrevocably" and could not legally be alienated. When the prefect confirmed in the archive of Sahuayo that Martínez was correct, he changed his mind, and the junta commission agreed with him, urging the Indians to add additional lands to the school fund so that they would better support the purposes for which they were intended.[95]

A very similar set of conditions applied in the case of the pueblo of Cutzio's 1846 application for distribution of the lands of the village-owned hacienda of Cuenchendio, which had been set aside in 1827 (in the original *reparto*) for the support of a school by mutual consent of all those involved. Now, nearly twenty years later, the pueblo had changed its mind and wished to divide the hacienda lands as well. This the junta was unwilling to do, arguing that the hacienda produced an income of 208 pesos a year, an amount that might well be increased by raising the rent, since it had remained the same since 1823. Deeming this a sufficient revenue to support a school, the junta insisted upon the original purpose of the set-aside.[96] Sometimes the junta's reasons for disallowing sales of communal lands seem motivated by class interests. In April 1838, for example, the community of Ecuandareo had asked permission to sell part of its lands in order to pay for a lawsuit against neighboring haciendas, but the junta recommended denying this permission, on the grounds that the suit was not winnable.[97] But in general paternalism, while not incompatible with self-interest, seems the more powerful guiding principle. This paternalism is clearly evident in one case involving not lands but community funds. Concluding that the government could apply the income from rentals of communal lands to the creation of primary schools (rather than dividing revenues among the members of the community), the junta observed that

> the Indians may be citizens, in the eyes of the law equal to all others, but it should never be forgotten that their old habits, the abject conditions in which they live, their daily preoccupations — all sad consequences of educational neglect — prevent them from understanding their true interests. . . . Which is preferable: a tiny and quickly spent personal income, or the solid and permanent good that will come to Indian families from their children being instructed in the indispensable principles of civility, morality, and religion?[98]

A different sort of paternalism was exercised in a handful of cases involving a variation on the old colonial policy of moving small, isolated Indian
communities to a more central and "civilized" location, a goal with which
many liberals sympathized (see the speech given by Agustín Aguiar, summarized in chapter 3), but which they preferred to pursue by means of *reparto*.
The junta, however, did experiment with forced relocation, noting, in the case
of the proposed *reducción* of the Indians of Puriacícuaro, that the result
would be "security, good order and other benefits of human association."
The junta ordered this particular *reducción* to go forward despite the vigorous opposition of some members of the community, though it did enjoin the
prefect to be sympathetic to the Indians' "natural resentment of the loss of
their houses and their lands, the orchards, magueyes and other crops they
raise, as well as of the expense and labor involved in the move." "The officials in these cases," it continued,

> must develop paternal and protective instincts . . . and must act, as the
> Laws of the Indies say, with evenhandedness, gentleness and moderation,
> treating the Indians who have been relocated so kindly and helpfully that
> those who still live dispersed will voluntarily join the rest. As the use of
> the verb "procurarán" in the *ordenanza de Yntendentes* and in our own
> *leyes patrias* indicates, the official in charge must justify his actions by
> prudent morality rather than rigorous authority.[99]

But in Puriacícuaro, and apparently elsewhere as well, the junta eventually abandoned the notion of *reducción*, with its long legal pedigree, and
yielded, as they had done in the cases of *repartimiento*, to something like democratic pressures. Citing new information in 1843 — three years after the
original order was issued — that it was not just three or four *vecinos* who opposed the move, but "the whole pueblo, or at least a majority," the junta admitted defeat. Though good reasons for a *reducción* still existed, not surprisingly the prefect and subprefect had been unable to convince the Indians
that their best interests would be served by abandoning their homes. The
junta now recommended that the Indians of Puriacícuaro be allowed to stay
put: "we tried every means the law makes available to us to show them the
benefits of *reducción*, and now we can without regret leave these citizens to
exercise their natural stubbornness; their *ilustración* will have to wait for another generation."[100]

By the mid-1840s the problems inherent in a system in which issues concerning Indian communities were decided on a case-by-case, piecemeal basis,

began to surface, and not only because the "democratic will" was so hard to ascertain. In most cases, including some detailed above, the original beneficiaries of the 1827 law of *reparto* had agreed to preserve some commons. Some of these were set-asides to produce revenues for community purposes, and some were uncultivable lands that were especially appropriate to shared use, for example timbered hills, where all the community cut firewood, or marshes, where everyone could run cattle, fish, and gather reeds for basket-making or weaving. But as young adults in the 1840s looked around them and saw that all the arable lands had been either assigned to their parents' generation or set aside for rental to outsiders, leaving them with an inherited fraction of what had no doubt been a fairly small plot to begin with — or worse, with nothing at all if their parents had sold the *terreno* — they began to demand that the remaining commons, too, be divided. In Zacapu problems arose when some members of the community who had not been a part of the original division apparently seized some of the commons, putting up fences and otherwise appropriating lands that were meant to remain open to all. The junta was impatient in this case: the prefect must destroy the fences and ensure the free, common use of the hills, badlands, and *ciénagas*.[101]

But as these problems multiplied, the junta, in frustration, considered the "radical remedy" of carrying out a complete *reparto de bienes*, which would solve the problems by causing the communities "to disappear forever."[102] This would, of course, be the preferred course of action for the liberal governments of the late 1840s and 1850s, and it had been implicit (and at times even explicit) in the debates of the liberal congresses of the 1820s. In the end the junta members decided not to take this route: they clung to the notion that the land distributions could be carried out smoothly if there were closer regulation of the methods employed by the village leaders, whom the junta blamed for the "ruinous and complicated" state in which many communities now found themselves. Their solution, in other words, was more paternalism, more prefectorial oversight. But it is not hard to imagine that a decade later these same individuals could be convinced not only of the utility and virtue of the principle of communal land distribution — which they seem already in the 1830s to have accepted — but also of the need to abolish the communities as corporate entities in order to solve the problems that arose out of halfway distributions.

The second set of issues displaying some convergence between junta representatives and the liberal federalists who both preceded and would follow them in state government concerned fiscal and economic policy. As we have seen, in the federalist congresses of the 1820s and early 1830s the attempts to stimulate the economy and/or shape the direction of economic growth had been largely limited to the commitment to "liberate" commerce from unnecessary restrictions and especially from heavy indirect taxation, chiefly by means of substituting the *contribución directa* for the colonial *alcabala*. Other than these efforts, the role of government in the economy was seen by the federalists as, fundamentally, that of providing a secure environment in which entrepreneurs could operate. (The federalist governments' failure to do so was, of course, a key to their loss of confidence in the system and their acquiescence in the *cambio de sistema*.)

The members of the junta were generally in agreement with these positions, though the dismal state of the treasury in the late 1830s meant that, more than ever, practical considerations — that is, assuring a flow of revenues into departmental coffers — necessarily took precedence over abstract ideals of free trade and low taxes. Both federalists and centralists lamented the public's unwillingness to accept the *contribución directa*, but if, as the (federalist) state secretary Ignacio José Domínguez put it in 1830, the people were not yet "civic-minded" enough to support the *contribución directa*, then indirect taxes must take up the slack.[103] Likewise, the (centralist) junta reluctantly recommended returning to the colonial system of (indirect) taxation, "to which the Nation was accustomed," but it continued to acknowledge the objective merits of direct taxation, and its wealthy supporters continued to rail against the evils of the *alcabala*.[104]

Indeed, if anything the rhetoric in which excessive taxation and other restrictions on free trade were blamed for commercial stagnation and even for political instability was more apparent in the 1830s and 1840s than in the (in other ways) more liberal 1820s. Increasingly, elites seem to have come to the conclusion that the solution to the problem of disorder was not stricter vagrancy laws or military clampdowns (both characteristic of the late 1820s), but economic growth in general and specifically freer and easier trade. A petition signed by 37 Morelia merchants in opposition to a November 1839 law that raised the sales tax on foreign goods expressed this view by holding up the example of England's prosperity and stability that, they claimed, had been assured by lowering taxes and eliminating restrictions on commerce.[105] Though among them were many men who had served the centralist government (Vicente Sosa, Cayetano Gómez, Fernando Román, Antonio Anciola, Nicolás Ruiz de Chávez, Manuel Alzúa) — one of the key demands of the petition was the reinstatement of the old federalist tax, the *contribución di-*

recta.[106] The link between free trade, economic growth, and political stability was also made in an 1845 petition sent by the departmental assembly (the renamed junta) to the national congress, in this case begging the national government to permit international trade through the port of Manzanillo on Michoacán's Pacific coast:

> Surely there would not be in this Department so many idle hands, *disposed to disturb the peace,* if indigo, chocolate, rice, sugar, soap, lard, maize, rebozos, sarapes and other goods were allowed to be exported to destinations in the Republic of Chile, Argentina, Mazatlán, Guaymas, and Baja California.[107] (emphasis mine)

One related difference of emphasis between the centralists of the 1830s and early 1840s and the federalists of the 1820s is that the former, perhaps taking their cues from earlier national initiatives by conservative-centralists to develop strong domestic economic institutions (e.g. the Banco de Avío), were especially interested in promoting internal improvements, especially those designed to stimulate commerce by easing transportation and communication difficulties both within the state and between Michoacán and the rest of the country. Despite the dismal condition of the state (and national) treasuries, the city councils and a handful of individuals, strongly encouraged by the state government, proposed and in most cases carried out a number of public works during the 1830s. In the early part of the decade, under the direction of the quasicentralist third and fourth congresses, a new causeway was built out of Pátzcuaro to give better entry to the *tierra caliente,* and a "magnificent" new bridge was built over the Río Grande in La Piedad, financed primarily by a wealthy, conservative priest named José María Cabadas.[108] This sort of activity increased in the late 1830s, when new roads were planned from Zamora to Jiquilpan, Mexico City to Morelia via Tajimaroa (a route which, it was promised, would save two days' journey), and Zamora to Tangancícuaro.[109] The old road from Mexico City to Morelia via Zinapécuaro underwent important repairs under the guiding hand of a private company (in which the junta bought shares) that collected a small toll to pay for improvements, maintenance, and profits to its shareholders.[110] New bridges were built at Jaripeo (as part of the improvements on the Mexico City toll road), Zinzongo (on one of the major *tierra caliente* roads), and Puruándiro.[111] A canal was opened to divert the Río Duero from Zamora and to prevent the recurrent flooding of that city, and the first of several plans to build a causeway across Lake Cuitzeo was floated, though they were rejected because of the enormous cost involved.[112]

It is tempting to interpret the centralist emphasis on traditionally liberal policies like lowering taxes, improving transportation — the better to promote free trade — and dividing communal lands as ideological inconsistency. But a more appealing explanation of the similarities between the liberal/federalist and conservative/centralist programs is that the members of the juntas and assemblies of the centralist period, many of whom had held public office during the federalist period, were simply not very ideological. Thus, while political debate in both the first Federal Republic (1824–35) and the Central Republic (1835–46) was at times extremely heated, if the debate is closely analyzed it becomes clear that the disagreements were usually over emphasis or timing, within a context of general consensus.

In the early to mid-1820s almost all political actors had accepted the principles of an abstracted, naive, almost libertarian liberalism. By the late 1820s and early 1830s, faith in this sort of liberalism had been undermined by its association with a federal system that was widely viewed as having unleashed forces that it could not control, manifested in outbreaks of banditry, unrest, riot, and rebellion. As a result, a new elite consensus developed around the need to limit and circumscribe the freedoms that had been thoughtlessly assigned to all citizens in the early post-independence euphoria. Eventually this change of thinking led to the change of system in 1835. The *cambio*, then, did not occur without friction, but the disputes that accompanied it derived more from an awkwardly shifting elite consensus than from a fractured one.

This tidelike quality of elite political alignments before the mid-1840s, according to which ideological differences were less important than were shared economic concerns and social similarities, was reflected in the composition of the congress and the state bureaucracy. As we have seen, many of the same people who called themselves liberals in the 1820s became members of the centralist governments of the 1830s and early 1840s. By the same token, many of those who served under centralists were young liberals who would later lead the way back to a federal system. In short, during the 1820s, 1830s, and into the 1840s, there was an almost complete absence of enduring institutional affiliation or loyalty: though the word "partido" was heard frequently, it almost always meant "group" or "side" rather than "party" in any organized sense of the word. A list of government appointees to various commissions in 1842 illustrates the point in a particularly telling fashion. The 40 men named by the governor to fill positions on the juntas of Estadística, Hacienda, Agricultura e Industria, Beneficiencia, Instrucción Pública, Caminos, Política y Ordenanzas Municipales, and Fomento Comercial were socially very much of a piece, including at least 25 members of the economic elite, among them Cayetano Gómez, Fernando Román, Manuel Alzúa, Agapito Solórzano, Francisco Estrada, and Mariano Larreátegui. Ideologically, however, they represented what appears in hindsight to be a quite startling mix — there were men who would soon be closely identified with the liberal party (Melchor Ocampo, Lic. Juan B. Ceballos, Lic. Isidro Huarte, Dr. Juan Manuel González Uruena, and Mariano Ramírez), but also men who would become outspoken conservatives (Lic. Mariano Rivas, Cor. José Ugarte, and Dr. José María Cavadas). We should not be too cynical about *La Voz de Michoacán*'s summary of their shared qualifications: "influence, talent, and patriotism."[113] Assuming that by this the editor meant some fortuitous combination of wealth, power, education, and willingness to serve, his words effectively capture the profile of an ideal public servant before the mid-1840s.

Conclusion

Several historians have noted the relatively close correspondence between the political behavior and social backgrounds of federalists and centralists, which has been one of the themes of this chapter. Most of these scholars, however, have not attempted to make more than a weak, implied link between, on the one hand, nonideological politics practiced by men cut from much the same bolt of cloth, and, on the other, social and economic trends. The reasons for this are thoroughly understandable: they have been reluctant to risk being seen as falling into a trap of economic determinism in which politics is reduced to a pale reflection of competing economic interests, and they have been put off by the practical difficulties of researching both political and economic history. Typically, they have relied on secondary sources and contemporary rhetoric to sketch a quick picture of an economy going from bad (at the end of the insurgency) to worse (usually until the Porfiriato), and the reader has been left to infer that the *hombres de bien* embraced political pragmatism as the only rational (however ineffective) response to the ongoing disaster that was the Mexican economy.[114]

It is certainly true that Michoacán state congressmen, like politicians elsewhere, were eloquently anguished on the subject of how abysmal were the economic conditions in which they had to operate. In 1835, for example, the junta wrote that Michoacán was a place of "imponderable reversals of fortune . . . to which burned-out ruins . . . give sad testimony."[115] Five years later another official pronouncement asserted that "the Revolution has paralyzed commerce, destroyed agriculture, and sown misery throughout the state. . . . *There is not a single fortune that has not been ruined* (emphasis mine)."[116]

But a close look at the aim of these laments suggests that it would be a mistake to take these statements at face value. The specific aim of the first evocation of disaster was to convince the central government to reduce its demand for a 20,000-peso loan from the department. For this purpose, the more miserable the economy could be made to look, the better. In fact, far from suffering "imponderable reversals," most of the members of the junta who signed this particular petition, among them Lic. Onofre Calvo Pintado, Vicente Sosa, Lic. Mariano Rivas, Nicolás Ruiz de Chavez, and Miguel Acha, were doing very well indeed. Calvo Pintado, for example, was to purchase less than one year later one of the two haciendas he would eventually come to own. He paid 4,275 pesos in cash, and in 1837 he paid off another 9,300 pesos; by 1842, well ahead of schedule, he had paid for the hacienda in full. He went on to acquire other properties, and his estate at his death in 1860 was worth over 275,000 pesos.[117] Vicente Sosa had taken over the bankrupted *casa* of Blas González Castañón in 1832 and by 1837 was Fernando Román's partner in the rehabilitation of the hacienda of Araparícuaro; in 1841 his mercantile enterprises were grossing some 137,500 pesos a year in sales, and his excellent financial situation allowed him to purchase a country home on Morelia's fancy east side, to which he could retreat when he wanted a change from the view of the Plaza Mayor accorded by his residence in the fabulous González Castañón house under the Portal de los Mercaderes.[118]

The context of the second statement of utmost wretchedness was a plea to the national government to forswear a proposed tax increase, always a fearsome thing to wealthy men and women. Among the members who signed this statement and who were very much *not* ruined were, again, Vicente Sosa (now doing even better than in 1835), Francisco Plancarte (who had recently purchased two haciendas, after a decade of successful mercantile operations),[119] Juan Ignacio Anciola (whose trade network linking San Blas, Acapulco, the Bajío, and Morelia was thriving),[120] Martin Mier (owner of a modest but lightly indebted hacienda and seven houses in Morelia),[121] Francisco Solórzano (a partner in one of the most successful agricultural com-

panies of the mid-century),[122] and Mariano Castro (who was poised to purchase an hacienda in 1842).[123]

In short, what the 1834 *Memoria de Administración* called the "weeping
and wailing that is the favorite song of *labradores*" should be interpreted with
appropriate skepticism, especially in light of the second major theme of this
chapter: the continued improvement, in fits and starts, of the regional economy, despite the civil wars of the 1830s.[124] In fact, it may be that the lamen-
tations of merchants and hacendados (both new and old) increased, rather
than diminished, as they felt themselves poised to surmount the true economic
catastrophe of the insurgent decade, now over two decades past. That is, they
felt most threatened by adverse government action in the form of increased
taxes and other burdens (imposed by a genuinely impoverished state) not
when they were flattened but when they were on the verge of success. They
used all the rhetorical tools at their disposal — including painting a vivid picture of economic disaster — to be sure that the fragile recovery, from which
they, and not the poor, were primarily benefiting, was protected.[125]

But their construction of this depression was only partly conscious and in-
tentional; in a certain sense, they hid the improvement of the economy and
their own situations even from themselves. In part this was a function of the
passage of time: as the years before 1810 receded from immediacy, they took
on almost mythical proportions. Nothing in the present could compare to
what people had heard or thought they remembered about how prosperous
and stable Michoacán had been before the wars for independence. As Fanny
Calderón de la Barca put it during her trip to Morelia in 1842, "One must
visit these distant cities . . . to be convinced of the regret for former times
which is felt amongst the most distinguished men of the Republic — in fact, by
all who are old enough to compare what has been with what is."[126]

This "regret for former times" prevented them from seeing that the deeply
flawed economy of the present was not so very much more deeply flawed
than had been the late colonial economy, whose problems (high taxes, credit
shortages, poor communications and high transport costs, uneven supply networks, low rates of profit, severely unequal wealth distribution) faded from
memory in the drama of the break with Spain and the economic collapse of
the period 1810–20. But in fact, by 1840 only the situation of credit was still
markedly worse than it had been in 1810, and some problems — for example
supply networks, wealth distribution (at least among the middle and upper
classes) and probably profit rates, both mercantile and agricultural — were a
bit less serious.[127] The hacienda economy of 1840 cannot yet be said to have

been flourishing, but it was very much stronger than it had been in, say, 1825. Meanwhile, it appears that more merchants were selling more goods to a wider consumer population than had been the case in 1810. Still, for contemporaries, the two-steps-forward, one-step-back nature of the postindependent economic advances, while cumulatively impressive from our perspective, must have been hard to appreciate. Instead of seeing the restoration of individual haciendas (or of the economy in general) to pre-1810 levels of production as an achievement worth celebrating, they bemoaned the fact that this was all they had been able to accomplish. Typical of this mentality was Francisco Gutiérrez de la Lama, whose 1846 will noted dejectedly that he had spent his adult life managing his father-in-law's hacienda of Balsas, which was destroyed in the revolution, and that all he had achieved was to repair the damage done by the insurgents.[128]

Sra. Calderón was wrong, however, to leap from comments like these, or from polite expressions of nostalgia for certain aspects of the colonial past (directed, after all, to the wife of the Spanish ambassador), to the conclusion that the elites with whom she socialized desired to turn back the clock.[129] In fact, in a certain sense the self-image of the state was bound up with how much it had suffered in the cause of independence. Foreign visitors, Sra. Calderón included, were regaled with stories of the wars and shown the sites of bloody battles, and they dutifully recorded "the accounts given us by the most respectable persons" of how, for example, "there [was] no city which had fallen off so much since the independence as Morelia,"[130] And even after independence, one congressional deputy proudly orated, Michoacán continued to "make sacrifices and suffer reverses like no other state" in order to preserve that independence.[131] In a perverse way, the worse the state of the state, the more patriotic its citizens could claim to be.

In all this there is, of course, a very powerful core of truth. The wars of the 1830s *had* affected every aspect of peoples' lives, whether directly or indirectly, actually or psychologically. But around 1840 Michoacán entered a period of relative peace and political stability that would last well into the 1850s. With a measure of tranquillity unmatched since the early 1820s, the economic advances gathered steam, and by the mid-1850s it is fair to say that the state's economic recovery was virtually complete. Even under these felicitous (for the wealthy) circumstances, however, as chapter 5 shows, there were good reasons to continue to practice the rhetoric of decline and decay.

PART THREE

Challenging the Midcentury Status Quo: The Liberal Reform

The High Tide of the Gómez Family Fortune

After Cayetano Gómez had rented the sugar hacienda of Taretan (which he would later purchase from the Augustinians during the Reform) in 1842, the structure of his business empire in Michoacán was complete; from then on, he was primarily concerned with improving what he already owned or controlled. At his death in 1858 Gómez's three haciendas — San Bartolomé, Quirio, and Taretan — were worth over 850,000 pesos, more than double their value when he acquired them.[1] These properties, with their stock and equipment, comprised 72 percent of his 1,200,000-peso estate; his sixteen urban properties counted for 9 percent; his textile mill, 3 percent; and his accounts receivable, mainly from sales of sugar, *aguardiente*, and flour from his haciendas, 15 percent.[2] Virtually his only debt was the 200,000 pesos that he recognized to the Augustinians on Taretan, having redeemed all of the debt that he assumed on the purchase of San Bartolomé and Quirio.

Significantly, he had no assets in store merchandise or credit; although he did operate a store on San Bartolomé, he had otherwise withdrawn completely from the marketing of imported goods that had been such an important part of his early career. In part this was a response to the increased number of foreign wholesale suppliers in Mexico City; as early as the mid-1840s there were signs that the dominant role that Morelia merchants like Gómez had enjoyed in the 1820s and 1830s as middlemen for smaller provincial traders was beginning to erode, as these merchants established direct ties to Mexico City houses. But in part his increasingly exclusive focus on his haciendas was a response to the high profits possible in estate agriculture in Michoacán, especially for those who were willing to experiment with new crops — Gómez, for example, had shifted much of San Bartolomé's land from wheat to chile production — and to spend money on plants to process their haciendas' production (in Gómez's case, on flour mills and *aguardiente* factories).

By 1840 Cayetano Gómez and Dolores Alzúa were well settled in their role as heads of the wealthiest family in Morelia and, indeed, in the state. Their children grew up taking for granted the continued expansion of the family's fortune and their own easy superiority. The rector of the Morelia Seminary fawned over the two oldest sons, for example, just as one might expect someone would treat the richest children in the school. "Juan Bautista Gómez," he wrote, "combines a sharp mind with a good memory and a certain brilliance in expressing himself . . . he has better French than most Mexicans, he is well informed in History and Geography, and he draws to perfection; he is training in Architecture, and his taste grows daily more nuanced and sure." Of Juan de Dios, he wrote that "his heart is pure . . . and he is incapable of deception, because his face is the mirror of his soul . . . he is obedient, gracious . . . and inclines strongly to do good."[3] Fanny Calderón de la Barca offers another insight into the boys' gilded childhood. Visiting the family's hacienda of San Bartolomé in 1842, when Juan Bautista was fifteen and Juan de Dios was twelve, she was taken with the carefree exuberance of one of the "young masters":

> . . . he was on the most untractable horse in the hacienda, and away across the fields with his followers, chasing the bulls as he went — he was fishing — he was shooting — he was making bullets — he was leagues off at a village, seeing a country bullfight — he was always in a good humour, and so were all who surrounded him — he was engaged in the dangerous amusement of *colear* — and by the evening it would have been a clever writer who had kept *his* eyes open after such a day's work. Never was there a young lad more evidently fitted for a free life in the country.[4]

When the oldest of the nine Gómez Alzúa children began to marry in the 1840s each child stood to inherit a very considerable sum (it turned out to be roughly 100,000 pesos each). Naturally they could and did make splendid matches; all — with the possible exception of Ignacio, about whose wife's family almost nothing is known — married men and women from socially prominent and usually wealthy families. In 1844, in a wedding that took place on the hacienda of San Bartolomé, María de Jesús Gómez married into the Iturbide family, distant relatives of the emperor's family who had lived in Morelia since the early 1820s. Two months later Juan Bautista Gómez married Jesús González Solórzano, who was related to two of Pátzcuaro's oldest and wealthiest families. In 1846 Juan de Dios Gómez married Josefa Basauri, from a very affluent Guadalajara family, and just a year later Pilar Gómez married Francisco Román, son of Fernando Román, whose own fortune of over 600,000 pesos paled only by comparison to that of Gómez.[5] Josefa Gómez married Santiago Sosa, son of the prosperous Morelia merchant, Vicente Sosa; Cayetano married Paula Solórzano, a daughter of the very successful merchant cum sugar planter Agapito Solórzano; Teresa married Francisco Menocal, of the prominent (though impoverished) sugar-growing family; and Trinidad married Luis Sámano, heir to a considerable fortune left him by Governor Onofre Calvo Pintado.

Gómez's politics throughout his life were distinguished mainly by their studied neutrality. Like everyone else with economic power he had to learn to maneuver in a world of open, diffuse political conflict that he could not always control, as his grandfather-in-law, Isidro Huarte, had seemingly done so easily in the days when he, along with the intendants that he had carefully cultivated, dominated regional politics in the late colony. His brother-in-law, Manuel Alzúa, adapted by actively participating in politics (he served frequently on both the Morelia *ayuntamiento* and in the state congress), where he practiced the art of compromise (he often played the role of peacemaker in those bodies). But Gómez's political beliefs and actions, both during the tumultuous period in which he made his social/economic ascent and in the calmer decades when he consolidated his fortune, were distinguished not just by moderation but by avoidance of political entanglements altogether. He rarely put himself in a position in which he would have to come down strongly on any given issue. He did accept appointment to several positions in the state government, usually as the head of relatively uncontroversial commissions that had to do with economic issues like transportation or internal improvements, but even this was rare. The closest he came to activism was his leadership of the Tribunal Mercantil in the 1840s, during which he defended it against charges that this special court for merchants re-created the *fueros* of the old colonial *consulados*.[6]

He made loans to the government on behalf of the Augustinians, though this practice, which on the surface suggested that he had conservative sympathies, may have been more self-serving than ideological, since the favors

Figure 4.   Cayetano Gómez de Soria and his
grandson, Luis Iturbide Gómez, 1856.

he did for the order were repaid in lowered rent on the hacienda of Taretan.
Moreover, he also made loans to liberals, at least one of whom, Santos
Degollado, considered this an act of friendship more than a business propo-
sition.[7] And his trusted agent in Mexico City was Francisco María Iturbe,
a liberal *agiotista*.[8] In short, he was not easily identified with any political
faction or party, even late in his life, as politics became more ideological
and political positions rigidified.

His successful straddling of political divides is reflected in the political
affiliations of four of his sons-in-law. Two daughters, Pilar and Josefa
Gómez, married men with conservative inclinations: Francisco Román,
whose sister would host the emperor Maximilian when he visited Morelia

in 1864; and Santiago Sosa, whose father, Vicente, sponsored a ball in the emperor's honor. But two other daughters married liberals. Jesús Gómez was married to Dr. Luis Iturbide, who was well known in liberal circles in Morelia in the 1840s and who would refuse to recognize Maximilian's empire in the 1860s. Two of Luis's brothers, Sabás and Andrés Iturbide, would be heroes of the wars of the Reform, and Sabás was a close personal friend of Melchor Ocampo. Meanwhile Teresa Gómez married Dr. Francisco de Sales Menocal (after her father's death), whose brother Manuel was another liberal hero; Menocal also refused to sign the pledge of allegiance to the empire.[9]

In light of all this it is tempting to conclude that Gómez and his wife were typical of many wealthy men and women of this generation: their business affairs led them more and more to sympathize with Mexican liberalism, with its emphasis on fostering progress by means of unfettering commerce, improving transportation, and protecting individual property rights while eliminating corporate property holding (and the church's domination of land via mortgages it had extended many decades earlier). But, like the conservatives, they admired the church as a social and moral institution and saw the patriarchal family — not the individual or the nation — as the core unit of society.

Certainly it is true that the last thoughts of both Gómez and his wife were of God and family. In the explicit hope of avoiding family-fragmenting problems that might arise when his huge estate was divided, Gómez had made a careful plan for the distribution of his property after his death. And when Dolores Alzúa died five years later, by which time the difficulties her husband had envisioned had been greatly exacerbated by the Reform and its aftershocks, she could only encourage her children "never to abandon the religious principles that your father and I have always tried to inculcate; and always to love each other very much, and help each other in difficult times; and never to take your disagreements with each other into the courts."[10] Fortunately for her, she did not live to see the utter collapse of San Bartolomé in the late 1860s, and the bankruptcy of many of her children.

CHAPTER FIVE

The Seeds of Their Own Demise:
Upper-Class Complacency and Middle-Class Discontent in the 1840s and 1850s

The popular rebellions of the late 1830s had faded to sporadic, minor incidents by 1841, and they finally ceased altogether when the federalist chief Gordiano Guzmán joined government troops to fight the invading U.S. army in 1846. This was the same year that the experiment in centralism ended, the 1824 Federalist Constitution was restored, and Melchor Ocampo became governor of the state. With the orderly transfer of power two years later to Lic. Juan B. Ceballos, and the election and (almost) uninterrupted service of three state congresses, relative tranquillity in the countryside was matched by a period of stability in the statehouse and the legislature from the mid-1840s to 1853. By 1849 even state finances were in good shape for the first time in decades.[1]

This was something of a golden age for the men and women who had struggled to restore haciendas and reestablish commercial networks in the difficult 1820s and 1830s. Though success was by no means universal, most of those who had made it this far now reaped substantial rewards. By the mid-1850s property values and rents (both urban and rural) had fully recovered to and in many cases exceeded pre-1810 levels, and the wealthy were wealthier than ever: the average elite estate in the decade of the 1850s surpassed in size that of the decade before 1810 (see Table 5.1). There was still the perennial shortage of capital to contend with, but even here the situation had im-

TABLE 5.1

Average Gross Wealth Among Economic Elites

1790–1810	91,000 (n = 47)
1811–29	75,000 (n = 41)
1830–39	73,000 (n = 25)
1840–49	78,000 (n = 18)
1850–59	144,000 (n = 37)

SOURCE: Appendix 2.

proved: over 100,000 pesos a year were available in Morelia loan markets in the early 1850s, more than twice the average amount available in the 1840s.

By midcentury there is also a sense in which late colonial ways of doing and thinking, severely tested by war and depression, had been revived along with the economy, so that in some ways the early 1850s looked more like the end of the colonial period than either period looked like the 1810s, 1820s, or 1830s. The wealthy — many of whose social and economic background was not one of wealth or position but of impoverished respectability — increasingly married endogamously, consumed conspicuously, and invested confidently, aiming to consolidate their social and economic positions by means of a cautious combination of past practices and present possibilities. For the first time in decades, not only could a fairly large number of people be said to have "succeeded," but they advertised their success with unprecedented (since 1810) panache.

Resentment of the new shimmer to the lifestyle of the wealthy may have fed into the revival of a relatively radical, culturally ascetic liberalism in the 1840s. This liberalism was initially directed against the centralist state and later, after 1846, focused on the church, which the new generation of liberals saw as the prime obstacle to the implementation of their program. But these new liberals were also, more subtly, antagonistic to the wealthy (or, as they put it, to the "aristocracy"), at least to those who threatened — by their support of the church and by their rentier mentality — to allow economic growth to slow. Thus, while some of the wealthy were sympathetic to the goals of the liberals, few of them were outspokenly supportive of the movement, and others, frightened by the prospect of radical alterations to a status quo with which they were, on the whole, quite content, halfheartedly joined the church in its counterattack on liberalism. The main effect on elites of the increasing intransigence of both "parties," however, was to cause them to abandon politics, an arena where they had been dominant, if not always numerically superior, for decades.

Beyond Recovery: The Economy of Michoacán at Midcentury

The signs of returning prosperity were displayed to great effect in the cities, as the 1840s and 1850s were busy with new construction, beautification, and public-health projects. A concerted effort to remake Morelia's downtown along European lines was launched in 1843, when the city completed an 8,000-peso renovation of the plazas on either side of the cathedral (6,000 pesos of which was supplied by private parties). The weekly market was moved out of the Plaza Mayor, trees were planted to demarcate the boundary between the plazas and the street, and obelisks, stone benches, and lined pathways shaped space that had previously been open and unstructured.[2] At about the same time the city installed 60 new streetlamps; moved the public slaughterhouse out of town; built at least two new fountains (including a difficult installation in front of the church of San José, at the crest of the rise on which Morelia was located); began to dredge the Río Grande so that water would no longer collect on the low plains to the northwest; repaired the *calzada* of Los Santos; and started work on a new *calzada* to the south of the city, which was justified on the grounds that the population needed more places of diversion and that merchants needed better access to the city from this direction.[3]

Among the new public buildings of the mid-1840s was a 3,000-seat bullring, constructed in the Indian *barrio* of San Juan on land previously given over to garden plots and huts. The state-of-the-art building cost 26,250 pesos, which the promoters raised in a matter of weeks by offering 75 shares in the enterprise at a cost of 350 pesos each. The inaugural festivities in November 1844, which were said to have netted a fabulous profit of 9,000 pesos, included a hot-air balloon ascension by the Guanajuatan "aeronauta" Benito León Acosta. (Unfortunately for Acosta a strong wind was blowing that day, and he lost control of his balloon as it sped over the rooftops of the city; he had to jump out over the Plazuela de San Juan, and broke his leg. The balloon was last seen over Querétaro.)[4] The new foot traffic and commercial possibilities opened up by the bullring prompted a request from the Indian inhabitants that the community lands be divided among themselves, and a *reparto* took place in 1850. Soon after, either as a result of the efforts of the original recipients or of those of the people to whom they sold the lots, more "formal" houses were built, and the lines of division between the Indian and non-Indian populations of Morelia became even more blurred than before.[5]

During the late 1840s and early 1850s work also began on a men's hospice, to which Lic. Isidro Huarte (who died in 1843) had pledged his estate, and on a progressive new penitentiary, which was designed to rehabilitate prisoners according to the so-called Auburn system, and not simply to lock them away.[6] The Colegio de San Nicolás, shuttered since the wars for independence, reopened in 1847, a year and a half after the church ceded it to the state government.[7] Another new building was a silk factory erected near the convent of San Diego and dedicated with appropriate religious and municipal ceremony before a huge gathering in June 1844. A director and fifteen skilled workers were recruited from France to run the expensive (159,062 pesos) imported machinery, but the enterprise, which was subscribed by virtually the entire Morelia elite and many from other towns, was overambitious and plagued with bad luck (an unseasonal frost killed the mulberry trees on which the imported silkworms were to feed, and one shipment of worms arrived dead). It was forced to close within a year.[8]

The church also embarked on a number of reedification and modernization projects during this period. The tabernacle and all of the altars of the cathedral were renovated between 1844 and 1845, and in 1854, in the same spirit in which space in the surrounding plazas had been redefined a decade earlier, the atrium was separated from the street and plazas by an elegant and costly (42,000 pesos) wrought-iron fence.[9] Late one night in September 1849, after most of the city was safely asleep, 1,200 bodies were exhumed from the pantheon next to the church of San José to make way for a new convent to be occupied by the nuns of Santa Teresa. (The cadavers were reburied in a deep trench nearby.)[10] And in 1853 Bishop Clemente de Jesús Munguía began work on a magnificent new episcopal palace, though like the penitentiary and the hospice it was not finished before the political upheavals of the second half of the decade intervened.[11]

The impression of urban rejuvenation carries through to other towns besides Morelia. Zamora, a backwater during the colonial period, began to emerge as a major commercial center during the years from 1838 to 1853, which Luis González calls a period of "unbridled growth."[12] Its population more than doubled between the 1820s and the 1850s, and by midcentury many of the amenities enjoyed by Morelia residents were in place, including "street lights, comfortable hostelries, beautiful *paseos* . . . and an animated commerce with Guadalajara, Guanajuato, and Morelia."[13] In the 1840s the city began work on a new parish church (still ongoing in the 1860s, by which time the project was said to have cost over 100,000 pesos). A new hospital went into operation in 1841, and in 1849 a new bridge over the Río Duero was inaugurated, permitting year-round coach and carriage service to a city previously cut off by summer flooding.[14] Puruándiro and Ario, which had been devastated during the independence movements, were both said by midcentury to be flourishing commercial centers, larger and more active than they had been before 1810.[15] Maravatío, on the route from Mexico City to Morelia, was described in 1860 as an "important" town with a "pretty plaza, some two-story houses and many very well-made one-story residences." Like Zamora it was served by a new bridge, this one built by the Junta Directiva de la Empresa de Diligencias that operated between Morelia and Mexico City.[16] Imitating the success of the Morelia-Mexico City line, other companies connected Morelia by diligence to Guanajuato (via Cuitzeo), to Pátzcuaro, and to Tacámbaro in the 1850s.[17]

THE HACIENDA ECONOMY

Despite a flurry of enthusiastic investments in manufacturing establishments in the 1840s, in a region with an economic base like Michoacán's the funds to remake the urban landscape ultimately depended on commercial agriculture, that is, on the continued expansion of the hacienda economy.[18] Indeed, contemporaries were quite clear on the link between the two manifestations of "progress." Romero, for example, writes in 1860 of the town of Jiquilpan that after having been burned in 1810 it had begun to be rebuilt "in good taste" in recent years, "now that agriculture is beginning to flourish."[19]

There are several ways to appreciate the dimensions of the recovery of the hacienda economy in Michoacán. Statistics generated from notary and other legal documents suggest that there was a mild slump in land values in the late 1840s, during which time hacienda prices may have been artificially deflated by colluding buyers and sellers in an attempt to evade a new tax on sales of rural property but were also driven down by uncertainty surrounding the war with the United States and by the vigorous attempts on the part of ecclesiastical creditors to dispose of poorly maintained and decrepit property that had been ceded or foreclosed upon much earlier. But by midcentury the hacienda economy of Michoacán entered what might be called a miniboom.[20] In the early 1850s the average price of an hacienda climbed to nearly 43,000 pesos, almost exactly the average during the decade before the Hidalgo Rebellion. Average rents for the period 1850–54 rose from some 2,000 pesos in the 1840s to 3,200 pesos, again, virtually the same as they had been during the pre-1810 period. Impressively, rising prices and rents in the early 1850s combined with a high rate of activity in the markets for rural real estate: an average of almost five haciendas were sold each year from 1850 to 1856, for example, compared to under two in the period 1800–10.

Predictably, in this era of rising land values cessions of haciendas slowed nearly to a halt. It seems that only three haciendas were given up in the late 1840s, and one of them, Etúcuaro, was ceded by Mariano Larreátegui as part of an attempt to come to terms with his multiple creditors after he had increased the hacienda's value from the 34,000 pesos for which he purchased it in 1845, to some 62,500 pesos in 1847.[21] The only hacienda ceded in the early 1850s was Araparícuaro, the long-troubled property of the Menocal family.[22]

The strength of the hacienda economy is also reflected in the evidence of considerable competition at auctions of rural properties, a striking contrast to the 1820s and 1830s, when auctions often drew little or no attention and the buyer was in almost complete control. As early as 1845 five men, armed with *papeles de abono* from already landed patrons, bid seriously on the foreclosed hacienda of Cutio, driving the price up from the initial offer of 16,000 pesos to a final price of 20,000 pesos.[23] When the bishopric decided to sell its principal hacienda, Coapa, in 1853, three individuals bid fiercely for it even though the bidding continued until it sold for a pricey 201,000 pesos.[24] Even after the Reform-related political troubles had begun, Lic. Juan Manuel Olmos, bidding against Lic. Jacobo Ramírez in 1858 for two ranchos, was forced not only to offer 3,000 pesos more than the 8,994 pesos for which the properties had been appraised, but also to go to court to argue that Ramírez's responding bid came after the last strike of the clock and was therefore ineligible.[25]

As the statistics on prices and rents suggest, almost all haciendas for which we have detailed ownership and price histories had been restored by the time of the Reform to pre-1810 levels or, often, beyond. One of the many examples is the hacienda of Calvario, which had rented in 1802 for 5,000 pesos a year. As late as 1836 its owners, the Valdovinos family, could only command a rent of 2,700 pesos, and in 1839, when Carlos Valdovinos bought out his co-heirs, they all agreed that the hacienda was in a "ruinous" state.

Valdovinos expanded the hacienda immediately, purchasing a small part of the contiguous hacienda of Santa Ana in 1840 and adding another larger section in 1841. He must also have made substantial improvements, since the value of the additions to the property is not enough to account for the fact that he was able to rent the hacienda for 3,490 pesos a year in 1841. He went on to add two more ranchos to the property in 1850 (the ranchos of Cosio and Cuisillito), and the complex rented for 5,000 a year in 1852, signaling the full restoration to its pre-1810 value.[26]

Many haciendas, of course, recorded much more impressive gains. Several examples were given in the context of the personal histories of the new elite that emerged in the 1820s and 1830s, discussed in chapter 4; the reader may recall, for example, the dramatic 200–300 percent increases in the value of Cayetano Gómez's haciendas, and the even more spectacular increase in the value of Fernando Román's La Huerta from under 50,000 pesos at purchase in 1821 to over 200,000 pesos in 1850. Other examples include the hacienda of Jongo, which had been in receivership since well before 1810 (in the hands of Isidro Huarte) and which had suffered further losses during the wars for independence. After Huarte's death it was finally returned to the Pátzcuaro Augustinians, who rented it in 1828 to José Zedeño for 600 pesos a year. When that contract expired in 1837 Zedeño signed on for another nine years at an annual rent of 1,000 pesos, also agreeing to build a new irrigation system, fence the property, and put into operation a new indigo *obraje*. By 1851 the hacienda, now rebuilt right down to a new name — Tepenahua — was rented for 1,800 pesos a year, three times the rent it commanded in 1828.[27] Rent on the hacienda of Chaparro rose from 800 pesos a year in 1843, when the owner died and it was sold, to 1,800 pesos in 1854, under new ownership.[28] The hacienda complex of Tipitaro, San Vicente, and Tipitarillo, which had been sold in 1801 for 130,000, was valued at over 144,000 pesos in 1856, even though Tipitarillo, whose lands alone were worth an additional 35,000 pesos, had been sold off in 1848. When Lic. Juan N. Flores, owner of this complex, commented in 1850 that "it is well known that the value of rural property has increased [in the last two decades]," it is clear that he was not overstating the situation.[29]

Part of the rise in property values during this period was due to hacienda owners' increasing willingness to risk sizable sums in livestock, seed, tools and other easily damaged or confiscated movables. In the decade before the Hidalgo Rebellion movables had constituted an average of 27 percent of the total value of inventoried haciendas, while the *casco* — that is, the improved

TABLE 5.2

Movables as a Percentage of Appraised Value of Haciendas

	Casco (land and structures)	Movables
1800–10	73%	27% (n = 11)
1810–29	81%	9% (n = 6)
1830–39	72%	28% (n = 5)
1840–49	68%	32% (n = 7)
1850–56	57%	43% (n = 13)

SOURCE: ANM, AHPJ, AHMM, AHMCR, AHCP, AGN.

land — was about 73 percent of the total. In the 1810s and 1820s, predictably, the value added to inventoried haciendas by movables went down to 9 percent, despite the fact that land values were very low, while the prices of livestock and seeds were historically high. In the 1830s the pre-1810 ratio between *casco* and movables was reestablished, but because property values had not yet fully recovered the peso investment in movables remained well below that of the pre-1810 period. In the 1840s the trend toward higher proportional investments in movables continued, and in the 1850s — by which time, as we have seen, property values had regained pre-1810 levels — only 57 percent of the average inventory was fixed capital, while 43 percent was represented by portable capital (see Table 5.2).

Moreover, it is clear that hacendados were also increasingly willing to invest in improvements to the *casco* itself — improvements like dams, irrigation systems, mills, and fences, though the custom of lumping together unimproved land and improvements in post-1810 inventories makes this pattern difficult to quantify. On *tierra caliente* haciendas the largest capital investments continued to be in the service of cane production and processing. In 1860 Romero commented that the sugar-producing regions around Taretan, Ario, and Los Reyes had grown rapidly as a result of the presence of numerous *ingenios* and *aguardiente* factories, "which employ many hands."[30] One of the most elaborate of these was a "magnificent" factory built in 1853 near Ario, with capacity for producing not only *aguardiente*, its main business, but also thread, cloth, and flour. This may have been the elaborate installation on the hacienda of Pedernales, which had cost its owners over 10,000 pesos to

build, but it may also have been part of the mammoth 110,000-peso investment in improvements and movables made on the hacienda of Tejamanil by
two Guanajuato-born renters in the early 1850s.[31]

By midcentury most large haciendas in the *tierra fría* seem to have built (or
rebuilt) not only flour mills and storehouses but in some cases also *molinos
de aceite* (present on numerous western haciendas, where linseed was grown)
and sawmills.[32] Investments in hydraulic systems were even more widespread, though they were generally more costly. Sometimes water-powered
processing capabilities and irrigation systems came into conflict. José Serrano,
for example, who owned a large flour mill on the hacienda of Paquisihuato
in eastern Michoacán, brought a successful lawsuit in 1853 against his neighbor, Mateo Echaiz, whom he accused of opening an irrigation ditch above his
mill, which left the mill without sufficient water to operate.[33] Disputes aris-
ing from increasing investments in hydraulic systems are also reflected in two
other suits, one brought by Carlos Valdovinos, owner of the hacienda of
Calabozo, against his neighbor María Ignacia Castro de Pérez Gil, whose new
dam on her hacienda of Santa Cruz (Tarímbaro) threatened to flood his
wheatlands; and the other by Vicente Estrada, who accused his neighbors, the
owners of the hacienda of Queréndaro, of changing the course of the Río de
los Naranjos, causing him to lose his chile fields.[34] In other cases hacendados
were able to arrive at mutually satisfactory compromises when it came to
competition over water. The executor of Antonio Chávez's estate, for example, agreed to pay 200 pesos a year to the owner of the hacienda of San
Joaquín Jaripeo for the right to divert enough water to irrigate ten *cargas* of
sown wheat, and he further agreed to dig his ditches below the point at which
the water powered a sawmill on Jaripeo.[35]

Investments in *tierra fría* haciendas in the 1840s and early 1850s probably
exceeded those in the *tierra caliente* properties — which had already been the
beneficiaries of considerable investment in the 1830s — as sugar hacendados
and other hot-country producers bought and improved haciendas in the cereal zone in order to diversify their business interests. Agapito Solórzano, who
had been mainly invested in sugar haciendas since the 1830s, balanced this
ongoing interest with the purchase of the huge grain-producing hacienda of
Coapa in 1853.[36] Fernando Román, whose activities previously had been in
the sugar, rice, and indigo haciendas of the *tierra caliente*, in 1842 rented a
southern Bajío hacienda from the Augustinians for the staggering sum of
11,000 pesos a year. In addition, he agreed to spend at least 9,000 pesos for
repairs and improvements. This operation was run by his son-in-law, Félix

Malo, and its main function — like that of a section of the hacienda of Villachuato that was rented and managed by another son-in-law, Manuel Malo (Félix's brother) — was to supply Román's *tocinería* in Mexico City, appraised at 41,200 pesos at midcentury.[37] The decision to diversify could also work the other way, of course; take for example Cayetano Gómez's rental and eventual purchase of a sugar hacienda (Taretan), after he had started out by buying the cereal/livestock haciendas of San Bartolomé and Quirio. But since the bulk of mercantile capital had gone into the *tierra caliente* haciendas in the earlier period, the direction of diversification now led, more often than not, to the purchase and improvement of *tierra fría* haciendas in the north.

Many of the large capital investments in movables and productive capacity were made by the agricultural companies that had been an emerging part of the rural economy in the 1830s and that continued to play a significant, indeed increasing, role in the 1840s and 1850s. At least 44 business partnerships were concluded in Morelia and Pátzcuaro between 1840 and 1860, and, as in the 1830s, almost all of them had some connection to the hacienda economy. Some, known as *compañías de comercio* or *compañías de comercio y del campo*, were formed to speculate in agricultural commodities and to trade in imported goods. "Magaña y Compañía," for example, operated the haciendas of Pedernales and La Loma, as well as two stores in Morelia, "El Tuliapán" and "La Luz del Día," in the late 1840s and early 1850s.[38] Others were *compañías de campo*, more purely rural companies in which the partners either rented an hacienda from a third party, worked an hacienda belonging to one of them, or, more rarely, bought jointly and then operated an hacienda, perhaps selling off part of it to raise working capital.[39] Only one company formed in the 1840s and 1850s clearly fit the profile — common in the 1820s and 1830s — of an arrangement between a desperate, capital-poor hacendado and a mercantile partner to whose advantage the contract operated. This was the 1858 partnership between Mariano Soravilla, owner of the very heavily indebted haciendas of Remedios and Uruétaro, and the merchant Vicente Sosa, who was to invest/spend up to 10,000 pesos a year in Soravilla's haciendas. But even here the fact that the company paid Soravilla 4,000 pesos a year to rent the haciendas made this a less exploitative arrangement than most of those that were in effect during the earlier period.[40] The rest of the rural companies were clearly intended not to rescue or take advantage of struggling hacendados but to exploit and if possible monopolize the production of already successful or at least very promising haciendas — usually *not* those mired in debt.

In 24 partnerships for which the initial capitalization of the company is known, the average was a substantial 18,700 pesos, though this included two companies capitalized for 100,000 pesos; without these extreme outliers the average falls to a still fairly impressive 11,300 pesos.[41] Most agricultural companies were simple partnerships, involving one *capitalista* and one *industrial*, with the profits being split fifty-fifty. *Compañías de comercio*, with a tendency to be involved in many different aspects of business enterprise in Michoacán, were more likely to involve at least three partners, one of whom usually committed more capital than the others. In 1854, for example, Francisco Medal de la Mora, Manuel Castañeda, Enrique Sagarminaga, Urbano Cabada, and Francisco Lerín formed a *compañía de comercio* to be called "Castañeda y Compañía." Mora invested 15,149 pesos, against 2,370 pesos for Castañeda and 1,500 pesos each for the other three.[42]

In only fourteen cases is all the necessary information available to piece together a return on capital. The average annual return (not compounded) in these businesses — two of which recorded losses — was 14 percent, with seven mostly agricultural companies averaging 19 percent and seven *compañías de comercio* 9 percent. This meant, of course, that the *capitalistas* in the agricultural companies only derived a return of around 9.5–12.5 percent on the money they put up, after turning over one-half or one-third of the profits to their *industriales*, and the investors in the commercial companies earned even less, between 4.5–6 percent. On the other hand, we should keep in mind that these are net profits, so that any capital borrowed by the company after it came into existence, any interest paid on it, and any rent paid — in short, any expenses — had been calculated before the profits were determined. The five most successful businesses earned annual rates of return of around 24 percent, so that even when split with an *industrial*, the rate of profit (at 12–16 percent) was attractive.

The generally unspecialized nature of the business partnerships formed during this period — epitomized by the construction of "compañías de comercio y del campo" — points up the continuing importance of the connection between hacienda agriculture and trade in manufactured goods as well as in agricultural commodities. Some additional insight into this tight relationship comes from an 1846 lawsuit brought by an hacendado, Cayetano Villavicencio, against a merchant, Agustín Luna.[43]

Villavicencio had sold 96 *cargas* of rice to Luna on credit in November 1843 (note that this was a buyer-pays-later arrangement, the reverse of the cash advances of the 1830s). Three years and five months later Luna still had not paid up, and Villavicencio took him to court, where Luna argued that he was not required to pay the full amount since Villavicencio had caused him damages: when his (Luna's) mules had arrived at the hacienda of Los Bancos to take delivery of the rice, it had not been winnowed; in fact, his drivers had had to wait for several days while Villavicencio "borrowed" rice from his neighbors in order to fill the order. The delay caused Luna to arrive eight days late to the fair of San Juan de los Lagos, where he had intended to market the rice, with the result that he could sell it for no more than the same 8 pesos/*carga* that he had agreed to pay Villavicencio. Still worse, he lost the opportunity to use the money he earned from the sale of the rice to speculate on other items, because (he said) there was nothing left to buy. At the height of the fair, he went on, rice had sold for as much as 12 pesos/*carga* in cash, and for 1 to 2 pesos more if exchanged for merchandise or other goods.

Luna claimed that it had cost him 548 pesos to transport the rice from Apatzingán to San Juan. If this was not an exaggeration designed to enhance his case, it means that if he had managed to sell the rice for what even he admitted was the highest possible price, 14 pesos/*carga* (1,344 pesos), the 576-peso gross profit on the rice (after paying Villavicencio 768 pesos) would have left him with a measly net profit of 28 pesos after freight costs.[44] But his plan had been to trade the rice for 1,344 pesos worth of goods, which he then hoped, no doubt, to sell in central Michoacán at something like a 50-percent gross profit, for around 2,000 pesos. Assuming that the 548 pesos in freight charges represents something close to round-trip costs (since his mules and drivers had to return to Michoacán whether they carried merchandise with them or not), the barter of rice for goods at San Juan and the sale of the bartered goods at his store in Santa Clara would have given him a profit of around 700 pesos, with no initial investment of cash other than that needed to equip his mules and pay his drivers.

As it happens, Luna was a prominent merchant — in fact it was said that he was the most important *arriero* of his time — and so we can suppose that he had a great deal more business at San Juan de los Lagos than is described in this document. In fact it is unlikely that Luna would bother to go to a major trade fair with less than 10,000 pesos worth of agricultural commodities and other Michoacán-produced goods, which he would hope to trade for 15,000 pesos worth of merchandise.[45] He would then, in a perfect world, sell this merchandise in Michoacán for 22,500 pesos (another 50-percent profit). His gross profit on the trip would be 12,500 pesos; and his net profit, if the freight costs from Los Bancos to San Juan and back are a good indication, would be well over 5,000 pesos. By making this circuit (or like ones, perhaps to Tampico or Tabasco or Guadalajara or Durango) several times a year, it was possible for him to earn less than the hoped-for 50-percent profit, pay sales taxes (from which the trade fair purchases were exempt), absorb some bad debts, and still manage to increase his roughly 7,000-peso inheritance to a fortune of almost 140,000 pesos, which was the value of his estate at the time of his death.[46]

Of course it is also true that Luna would not be paid 22,500 pesos in cash for the goods he sold in Michoacán. Some of the goods might be sold in his retail establishment in Santa Clara del Cobre, but most would probably be sold either directly to hacendados or to smaller merchants who would buy on credit. Two financial tools made all these transactions possible. One was the simple account book, in which retail customers would buy goods on credit, or small provincial merchants would buy merchandise on credit from larger houses. This operation was ubiquitous across time and space in Michoacán, and needs no elaboration here. The other was the *libranza*, a sort of transferable IOU.

Libranzas had been in use since colonial times, but in Michoacán they became essential elements of the commercial system in the 1840s and 1850s, probably for two interrelated reasons. One was that the economy had finally recovered sufficiently to give rise to large and stable commercial houses, which were necessarily at the core of a successful financial system based on acceptance of paper. The other was the growing influence of foreign firms, accustomed to far more sophisticated banking environments in their home countries than they encountered in Mexico, who demanded the acceptance of commercial paper as a condition of doing business.

As the use of *libranzas* become more widespread, the previously crippling scarcity of cash and even, to some extent, the continuing shortage of loan capital, became less important. Hacendados could now open accounts with large houses whose reputations were such that their paper was virtually as acceptable as cash, and could pay their expenses (usually purchase of merchandise, but sometimes rent or purchase of land) by issuing *libranzas* against these accounts.[47] From time to time they would liquidate their balances, paying with *libranzas* issued by their own customers. In time *libranzas* came to circulate almost like money, being endorsed over to different people numerous times before they were "cashed."[48]

The proliferation of *libranzas* was both a result of the recovery and a contributor to it. In the 1830s the precarious nature of the economy and the continuing political disturbances had made complicated transactions in paper, involving multiple parties from all over the Republic, most unappealing. As a result, large landowners could not capitalize their haciendas without sacrificing much of their potential profit to merchants willing to advance them cash. With the relative tranquillity of the 1840s and the return to at least pre-1810 levels of production on most haciendas, however, a shift in the center of gravity of the credit system benefited both merchants and hacendados. Instead of paying for a crop in advance, merchants now preferred to buy on credit: this allowed them to make strings of trades like those envisioned by Agustín Luna in the case detailed above, without committing cash resources up front. Hacendados, for their part, preferred to "sell now, collect later" because they could command higher commodity prices if they gave buyers time to pay.[49] And of course the higher the prices they commanded, the more profitable their haciendas, and the more the recovery of the hacienda economy gathered steam.

The role played in the expansion of the system of credit by large commercial houses in Morelia, Pátzcuaro, Zamora, and Puruándiro was crucial, but ultimately, and increasingly, the stability of the system rested on the geographically widening reach of foreign houses in Mexico City, Tampico, Guadalajara, Colima, and Veracruz.[50] Growing competition among foreign houses led them to seek a more direct role in regions like Michoacán, which had not attracted much interest in the early post-independence years because of political turmoil and the relative lack of mineral wealth.[51] As we saw in chapter 4, in the 1830s Michoacán merchants were most often connected to foreign houses indirectly, through Spanish-born friends, relatives, and associates who had relocated in Mexico City after being expelled from the state. By the 1840s, however, virtually all merchants operating in Michoacán, including (indeed, especially) relative newcomers whose main business was usually retail, had often-sizable accounts with foreign houses. More and more young merchants getting started bypassed the established regional firms in favor of buying their merchandise directly from foreign houses, on account. Before 1840 the merchant who came closest to fitting this profile was Mariano Larreátegui, whose career is detailed in chapter 4, but even Larreátegui got his start in Michoacán with goods supplied on credit by Cayetano Gómez, Fernando Román, and other large Morelia merchants, and at the end of his career his Morelia creditors still far outnumbered foreign merchants. But by midcentury it was not unusual for the majority of a merchant's debt to be held by outsiders. Zamora merchant Baltasar Mendes, for example, had no debts to regional firms but owed 86,379 pesos to numerous foreign merchants in Mexico City, Colima, and Guadalajara in 1854.[52] In 1851 Rafael López, like Mendes a new merchant, owed 37,816 pesos to 14 foreign merchants and just 8,767 pesos to 20 Morelia creditors, and in 1857 Vega y Compañía owed all but about 6,000 to 7,000 pesos out of its total debt of 55,641 pesos to 25 different foreign merchants.[53]

It is interesting to note that Governor Juan B. Ceballos, the nephew of one of the Spanish-born intermediaries between foreign houses and Michoacán merchants in the 1820s and 1830s (Gaspar Alonso de Ceballos), used his 1849 *Memoria de Administración* to call attention to important (and, he thought, positive) changes in the way commerce was organized:

> Commerce no longer is governed by the same old rules as before; now success comes from individual effort and shrewdness . . . not just from having access to huge capital resources against which small merchants cannot compete. Commerce is no longer a sure means for a few capitalists to get rich with very little work, acquiring their goods from the same sources at the same prices and colluding to set the prices they will charge consumers. Now it is driven by hard work and astute calculations . . . now it is fairer and more open to all those with the talent and will to succeed.[54]

Documentary insight into the relationship between the new Michoacán merchants and foreign houses comes (unfortunately) mainly in the wake of the political and commercial disruptions of the late 1850s, so that the way these merchants interacted in more tranquil times is a bit hard to pinpoint. But one aspect of the new mercantile climate in the 1840s and 1850s seems clear: foreign merchants were less lenient creditors than local merchants, and far less so than the formerly dominant church, especially after the mid-1840s, when the recurrent and deepening national debt crisis began to have a directly negative impact on some of the largest Mexico City firms. Several of these firms had been engaged in the increasingly dangerous practice of speculating in the public debt since the 1820s, and they had, in the main, earned strong profits.[55] But by the late 1840s, as the government ran out of national properties with which to guarantee its debt, and as the quarrels between Mexican-born and foreign *agiotistas* over exemptions from forced loans and other arbitrary government exactions intensified, the fragile balance between reward and risk swung toward the latter, and several large moneylending houses went under.[56] These bankruptcies inevitably reverberated among other

Mexico City mercantile houses, even if they were not government creditors, and, ultimately, among provincial merchants, who were not only aggressively courted in order to bolster sagging bottom lines but were held to almost impossibly high standards of loan/merchandise repayment.

In Morelia by the late 1840s *libranzas* that were not paid the moment they were due were immediately "protested," the first step toward judicial intervention.[57] Provincial merchants or hacendados who did not regularly liquidate their accounts were hauled before the courts in a flash. Even some Morelia houses got into the spirit: Agapito Solórzano, for example, referring to a new 1853 bankruptcy law, pressed Ramón Ochoa in July 1854 either to pay him the 944 pesos he owed for livestock Solórzano had sold him on credit just two months earlier, or to declare bankruptcy.[58] The reader will recall that it took Cayetano Villavicencio over three years (from 1843 to 1846) to press charges against Agustín Luna for nonpayment in a similar case. The seemingly unreasonable impatience of foreign creditors was occasionally lamented in legal documents. When Francisco Zincúnegui borrowed 2,000 pesos from the Juzgado de Testamentos in 1853, he stated that the reason for the loan was to cover a debt incurred by his son Antonio to creditors who were "especially demanding."[59] And when Magaña y Compañía was forced in 1856 to cede the company's assets to one of its (Spanish) creditors the notary went out of his way to record the common belief that the problem was not with the skill of the principals or the excellent prospects of their main business, the hacienda of Pedernales, but with the creditors' lack of patience and confidence.[60] One contemporary put it rather less delicately: "the retailer is a tributary of the importer, and belongs body and soul to the vampire who allows him to open a running account."[61]

The ready credit offered by foreign merchants to willing provincials, and the tight leashes that tied these locals to the foreigners, surely played a part in a trend whose first flickerings can be detected in the mid-1840s. This was the decision by several successful Michoacán merchants to withdraw from trade in imported merchandise, in favor of agriculture and agricultural speculation. Ignacio Arriaga, for example, abandoned the import trade altogether in 1844, when he sold his store for 23,244 pesos and rented the storefront in his house to the buyer. Three years earlier he had rented the hacienda of Tejamanil in partnership with José María Bocanegra, an arrangement that ended in 1847 when Bocanegra bought the hacienda, but in the meantime he had rented the sugar hacienda of Santa Efigenia from its creditors in 1843, and this now became the focus of his energies.[62] Another merchant who left trade altogether was José María Ibarrola, who sold his store and rented out its location in 1845; ten years earlier he had rented the hacienda of Coapa from the bishopric, and Coapa now became his sole business operation.[63] As we have seen, though he was the most prominent merchant in Morelia in 1840, Cayetano Gómez's estate at his death in 1858 contained no store effects at all, and the same is true of Francisco Estrada: his early career was built on trade, but he sold his store in 1848, and his 1852 estate included no mercantile interests.[64]

Similarly, there was a tendency for business partnerships that had centered on trade to shift into agriculture, and sometimes out of trade altogether. Castañeda y Compañía, for example, sold its store in 1857 for 27,038 pesos and rented the hacienda of Tepenahua; later the company rented the hacienda of Urundaneo as well.[65] In 1847, after four years in trade, Magaña y Compañía rented and three years later bought the sugar hacienda of La Loma; in 1854 the company bought the hacienda of Pedernales. When the company ran into trouble in 1856, the solution — agreed to by all parties — was to sell off the two retail establishments and concentrate on the haciendas.[66] Zacanini, Losano y Compañía is another partnership that began purely as a trading company but in 1850 sold its retail outlet, a year after it had bought one-fourth of the hacienda of Corralejo near Pénjamo in 1849; three years later it purchased the hacienda of Turicato in *tierra caliente*.[67]

Social Mobility and Elite Consolidation

The movement out of trade and into agriculture suited several different needs on the part of elites who had spearheaded the rebuilding process of the 1820s and 1830s. Most superficially, some may have come to believe that trade, especially retail trade, was no longer an appropriate occupation, now that they had "arrived." To the extent that this attitude prevailed, it was a relatively recent innovation. Antimercantile snobbery does not seem to have been a powerful factor in the late colonial period, when even the most aggressively land-acquiring merchants rarely gave up trade, and although it is true that their sons rarely followed in the father's footsteps, they typically preserved the family connection to trade in the next generation by marrying their daughters to merchants. Instead, it was probably linked to the post-independence arrival of English travelers whose disdain for "shopkeepers" cannot have escaped the attention of their Mexican hosts. Bullock, for example, commenting on the social "scene" in Zamora, wrote that in provincial towns

> a shopkeeper naturally enough enjoys a much higher position socially than in highly-civilized countries like England and France. . . . The Mexicans are not yet sufficiently advanced in civilization to attach any kind of social disability to the calling of a tradesman. They still look upon him in the light of the public benefactor which he really is, and entertain towards him feelings of wonder and gratitude, analogous to that which children feel towards any one who, bringing curiosities and pretty things among them, makes a gratuitous display of them.[68]

But, more fundamentally, the decision to shift resources and energies out of trade was rooted in the improving prospects of hacienda agriculture in the 1840s and 1850s. As we have seen, good profits were possible in a variety of rural enterprises, and land values were increasing accordingly. But land ownership and agricultural entrepreneurship offered more than just acceptable profits and appreciation of rural assets. As it became more and more difficult to carve out an independent niche in the distribution of imported merchandise, as provincial merchants became more and more dependent on foreign suppliers, the best ways for elites to solidify their hard-won wealth and status were to be found in the rural sector.

The avenues to consolidation of elite economic power in the rural sector were several. Some pursued what economists call vertical integration, that is, control of different stages of the production and processing of raw materials. For example, Cayetano Gómez financed the operations of several manufacturers of *aguardiente*, in return for which they agreed to purchase their cane juice exclusively from his sugar haciendas, and he did the same with bakers, who were expected to buy their flour from his hacienda of San Bartolomé.[69] In a vertical integration that worked the other way he loaned money to cotton growers in order to assure a regular supply of raw materials for his textile factory in Colima.[70] His brother-in-law Manuel Alzúa had agreements with cotton textile manufacturers, whom he supplied with cotton that he purchased in his trading activities on the Pacific coast.[71] And, as we have seen, Fernando Román's two sons-in-law managed large cereal-livestock haciendas in the Puruándiro region, which supplied the *tocinería* that Román owned in Mexico City.[72]

Much more commonly, however, elite consolidation involved horizontal integrations, that is, purchase of additional land on the part of those who already owned at least one hacienda. Sometimes, as we have seen, landowners bought additional haciendas that allowed them to diversify the structure of their wealth; for example, sugar (or rice, or indigo) producers might purchase cereal-producing estates, and vice versa. Others were more intent upon buying properties adjacent to or near their core haciendas. In some cases the aim was to gain a useful resource (water, forest, pasture); in other cases it was to rid themselves of troublesome neighbors (usually Indian villagers). Sometimes these enlargements were accomplished in one or two dramatic moves, for example Tomás López Pimentel's 67,000-peso purchase of the hacienda of Santa Clara, which he added to his wife's already huge hacienda of Queréndaro (Zinapécuaro); or José María Bocanegra's addition of the hacienda of Tanzo to his Zicuirán (Ario); or Rosa María de la Fuente's purchase of the hacienda of Los Cerritos, contiguous to her half of an inherited hacienda, San Sebastián (Los Reyes).[73] But more frequently the additions were made in small increments, often of parcels of land originally assigned to Indians in the various *repartos* of the 1830s and 1840s. Francisco Estrada, for example, noted that he had purchased so many of these Indian-owned parcels that he could not even remember who had been paid and who had not.[74] The list of land sales by Indians to Mariano Villaseñor in (mostly) amounts of about 20 pesos occupied 46 pages in the 1839 notary register for Jiquilpan.[75] Francisco Alvarez's hacienda of San Diego (Acámbaro) was formed exclusively of *terrenos* purchased from Indians, as was (apparently) Francisco Plancarte's hacienda of Jauja (La Piedad).[76] In 1854 Octaviano Igartúa rented a parcel from two members of the community of Tangamandapeo, bordering some lands he had already bought from the same community.[77]

Whatever the motivation or mechanism, a pattern of increased purchase of land by already landed elites was clear in the 1840s and 1850s, as a profile of hacienda purchasers during the period 1840–56 indicates. The reader may recall that a similar profile covering the period 1811–39 yielded a striking picture of middle-class ambition and ascendancy: over 80 percent of the 56 haciendas or large ranchos sold during these years had been purchased by men who had not previously owned any land or inherited any appreciable wealth — that is, had not been part of the late colonial elite. In the 1840s and early 1850s, however, only about half of the 71 transactions involved previously landless purchasers (see Table 5.3). Put another way, access to landownership for renters, administrators, and other aspirants did not cease, but it

TABLE 5.3

Profile of Hacienda Buyers, 1840–56

	Non-elites	*Elites*
Improved dramatically	6	16
Modest success	19	7
Failures, near-failures, or probable failures (unknowns)	16	7
Total no. of individuals	41	30
Total no. of haciendas	36	35

SOURCES: ANM, AHPJ, AHMM, AHMCR, AHCP, AGN.
NOTE: Does not include purchases of haciendas in the first stage of the Reform, beginning in September 1856.

narrowed noticeably, while the landed elites added to their domains and expanded and diversified their interests.

If we approach the question of social mobility using data comparing wealth at marriage to wealth at death, the picture is similar. Over one-quarter of the eventually wealthy couples who married between 1810 and 1839 had been penniless and had enjoyed no prospect of inheritance at the time of their marriages. But in the 1840s and 1850s the percentage of initially poor, eventually wealthy marriages fell to 14 percent, suggesting that the opportunities for upward mobility for this generation were somewhat more limited than they had been for their parents.

It is true that the relative failure of poor couples marrying in the 1840s and 1850s to become wealthy over the course of their marriage had in part to do with the collapse of the economy in the wake of the Reform, a phenomenon that is the subject of chapter 6. This crisis altered the career trajectory of many of the upwardly mobile, just as the midcentury recovery had been responsible for the relative success of many middle-class marriages in the earlier period. The fact that this study uses gross rather than net wealth as the criterion for economic "eliteness," however, means that even if an individual's assets were severely compromised by debt at death he or she would still be included among the elite; in other words, those who began their ascent in the 1840s or 1850s and lost ground in the wake of the post-Reform crisis would still, in all cases short of outright bankruptcy, be considered to have achieved

TABLE 5.4

Amounts Brought by Husband and Wife to Households
That Eventually Became Wealthy, 1810–59

	Date of marriage	
	1810–39 (n = 74)	1840–59 (n = 56)
Both < 1,500 pesos	26%	36%
Both ≥ 1,500 pesos	26%	14%
Husband ≤ 1,500, wife ≥ 1,500 pesos	9%	2%
Wife ≤ 1,500, husband ≥ 1,500 pesos	39%	48%
Average wealth brought by husband	10,000 pesos	19,300 pesos
Average wealth brought by wife	4,800 pesos	4,600 pesos

SOURCES: ANM, AHPJ, AHMM, AHSM, AHCP.
NOTE: For convenience I have used the symbols "≥ for "at least" ("greater than
or equal to") and < for "under" ("less than").

elite status. A more compelling interpretation of this data is that fewer members of the middle class were able to get a "toehold" in the 1840s and 1850s
than could those of the earlier generation, in part because the newer generation's way was blocked by the already wealthy, who were busy consolidating
their own positions by some of the means discussed above. This interpretation is given additional weight by evidence suggesting that the wealthy were
also, more frequently than in the past, consolidating their positions by marrying each other. As Table 5.4 shows, in 36 percent of elite marriages in the
1840s and 1850s both partners brought or stood to inherit at least 1,500
pesos, compared to just 26 percent in the 1810–39 period.

Not only were there more elite-consolidating marriages in the 1840s and
1850s than there had been before, but they were also more visible, involving
some of the wealthiest families of the period. The Gómez children's marriages
in these decades, for example, were all flashy, sure-to-be-remarked-upon
unions, especially the marriage of Pilar Gómez to Francisco Román, which
brought together the two wealthiest families in Morelia. And in what must
have been an even more emblematically elite-consolidating set of marriages in
the 1840s and 1850s, Francisco Román's three sisters married three sons of
Félix Malo and Ana María de Valdivieso, the daughter of the fourth Marqués
de Aguayo.[78]

Prosperity and relative stability no doubt made these Morelia weddings, as it made the everyday lifestyles of the rich and powerful, more elaborate and more luxurious than were those of the earlier period. The image of carriages, occupied by the fashionable ladies and gentlemen of Morelia society, wending their way the ten miles or so from the city to the hacienda of San Bartolomé for Jesús Gómez's 1844 marriage to Luis Iturbide, appropriately symbolizes the turning of the tide from the turbulent 1830s to the generally secure 1840s.[79] Such a parade of wealth outside the safe confines of the city would have been unthinkable a decade or even five years earlier.

The champion of midcentury ostentation, however, was Francisco Velarde, *el burro de oro*, whose hacienda of Buenavista (near the border with Jalisco) was famous at midcentury for its "bacchanals."[80] The hacienda residence was described by one slightly disdainful but nonetheless impressed English visitor:

> I found myself in a court-yard, the walls of which were covered
> with glaring frescos in the worst possible taste and style, representing
> mythological subjects. Into this court-yard most of the rooms opened,
> on the principle of a Roman or Pompeian villa, which the architect had
> evidently aimed at reproducing. Nor was the attempt by any means un-
> successful, for the whole house was characterized by an air of solidity
> and elegance, unsurpassed by any with which I had yet met in town or
> country in Mexico. Indeed, but for the vile and profuse daubing on the
> walls, one could have imagined that one was wandering in some luxuri-
> ous villa at Pompeii or Herculaneum.[81]

By every indication, the Morelia elite was considerably more discrete than Velarde was. To judge by his estate inventory, Cayetano Gómez's homes must have been well appointed but not flamboyantly so: the total value of his household furnishings and goods was 13,111 pesos.[82] Fernando Román's household was appraised at a surprisingly modest 4,634 pesos and Nicolás Ruiz de Chávez's at 6,005 pesos, while Francisco Estrada's was appraised at only 2,450 pesos. In each of these cases the money spent on household decor and personal effects was under 2 percent of the individual's total wealth, the bulk of which was comprised of income-producing property.[83] Nonetheless, it seems clear that in a calmer age and with their own social ascent well behind them, midcentury elites felt freer to enjoy and display their wealth than had their 1820s and 1830s counterparts, when the cultural ideals of simplicity and equality inspired by early post-independence liberalism had made a good fit with the perilous political and economic times.

The cultural asceticism associated with liberalism had not disappeared, however. In fact the failure of the conservative governments of the late 1830s and early 1840s to build lasting support for their leading personalities, and their ideology of centralizing, suffrage-limiting government, had left room for a new generation of liberals to articulate a vision that, if it differed in some respects from that of the independence-era liberals, was no less insistent on the virtues of egalitarianism and self-sacrifice and no less disparaging of "aristocracy." Time and again in the liberal rhetoric of midcentury, "aristocrats" came in for special opprobrium, often being compared unflatteringly with the miserable and the poor. The 1850 *Memoria*, for example, began by noting the "apathy and lack of civic responsibility that characterize not only our humble poor, but also our most prominent classes."[84] In the 1820s almost all proposals to the state congress had been judged on the basis of how "liberal" or "illiberal" they were; similarly, from the late 1840s through the early 1860s, the worst that could be said of a person or an institution or a piece of legislation was that it was "aristocratic."[85] That the wealthiest men and women at midcentury often had quite modest social backgrounds, and that they were relatively restrained in the celebration of their success and good fortune (compared to the late colonial generation), did not reassure those who believed that Mexico's political and economic future depended on the sort of radical social and economic reforms that a self-satisfied, comfortable, consolidating elite would be unlikely to embrace.

Politics in the 1840s and 1850s

Chapter 4 argues that despite its belligerent surface during the first three decades or so after independence, politics in Michoacán fundamentally lacked the sort of bitterness that leads to notions of revenge; lacked the resources — during a long depression — to reward; lacked the power — during a shaky political period — to punish; and to a considerable extent even lacked a substantive ideological dimension. One observer, writing around midcentury, looked back upon the early years of Mexican independence as a period of "enlightened fraternity."[86] A clichéd exaggeration to be sure, but probably not a statement that even the most blindly nostalgic could have made about the period after 1842.

In a certain sense the turning point — the point at which the previously narrow ideological spectrum broadened into openly warring camps, and at which the qualifications for office came to depend much more clearly on party loyalty and shared ideology than on social position and "patriotism" — occurred as soon as the centralist government installed in 1835 demonstrated itself to be no more capable than the federalists had been of safeguarding the peace and replenishing the treasury. The weakness of the national government was embarrassingly exposed in the Pastry War (1838); and even before this, in Michoacán, the federalist revolts beginning in 1836, along with the increased demands on the state by an arrogant national government, were (as we have seen) enough to cause many tepid supporters of the *cambio* to have second thoughts soon after the new system was put in place.

But general dissatisfaction did not become a call for radical change until 1842, when Santa Anna closed down the congress he himself had called (to which Michoacán, along with other states, had elected a number of liberals) because it leaned toward a restoration of federalism, and then tried to close down its replacement when it, too, proved too independent.[87] These events caused despair among liberals who had to this point continued to think they could work within the framework of centralism to regain some measure of popular, representative, republican government, and caused some of them (often referred to as "puros") to adopt a more radical, more intransigent position. But Santa Anna's inconsistencies also alienated the most conservative conservatives, who increasingly feared that anything short of dictatorship or monarchy would be incapable of both keeping the peace and keeping undesirable agendas (anticlericalism, democracy) off the national table.

This radicalization of politics was, of course, speeded along and intensified by the dispute over Texas policy and by the impending war with the United States.[88] By the time Santa Anna, having alienated just about every faction in the country, was removed by the reactionary Mariano Paredes in January 1845, the battle lines were well drawn. And when Paredes himself was removed in a coup in August 1846 the coup makers were as determined to restore the federal system and use it to effect dramatic reforms as the conservatives (at the core of whose movement was the church, the main target of much liberal reformism) were to prevent them from so doing.

Unsurprisingly, then, with the return of federalism as a result of the 1846 coup, the practice of politics became sharper, more partisan, more confrontational. The deputies to the 7th, 8th, and 9th congresses in Michoacán displayed an unprecedented feistiness. Several men who were elected to the 7th Congress in 1846 refused to serve on openly ideological grounds. Among them was the future archbishop of Mexico and conservative stalwart, Lic.

Pelagio Antonio Labastida, who resisted all attempts by his fellow deputies to force him to attend by arguing that he had sworn allegiance to the Bases Orgánicas (1843) and could not in good conscience serve under a different constitutional system.[89] Indeed, for their entire term the liberal deputies had great difficulty obtaining a quorum, given the unexcused absence of so many conservatives.[90] Gone, for the most part, were the days of effusive praise for one's opponent's oratory and erudition and apologies for the inadequacies of one's own contribution to the debate. Deputies attacked each other verbally on the floor of the congress, accused each other of treachery, questioned each other's motives, refused to allow each other to speak.[91]

The liberal administrations of Melchor Ocampo and Juan B. Ceballos did nothing to discourage this sort of partisanship. Within days of the 7th Congress's installation, the new deputies listened as the governor drew a picture of sharp differences between the centralists and his own party:

> [Before the revolution of 4 August] the government was uncertain, vacil-
> lating, mysterious; it was engaged in constant battle with the press, with
> the traditions of liberty, and with the country's desire for independence;
> it utterly lacked the confidence of the nation. . . . [But now] the govern-
> ment is decisive, firm, and open; it is in accord with the press and
> with the principles of liberty and independence; it enjoys the absolute
> confidence of the people, whose sovereignty has been restored to its
> proper place of central importance.[92]

Even more pointedly, in 1850 Governor Juan B. Ceballos told his listeners that the keenest threat to the state's current calm was not the Indian population — which he believed was unlikely to follow the rebellious example of the "casta primitiva" of the Sierra Gorda, the Yucatán, and the southern part of the state of Mexico — but the "retrograde faction that wants to return us to the era of absolutism, even at the cost of our independence." Though this "party that calls itself 'conservative' has been defeated," he added propheti-cally, "its very impotence makes it all the more stubborn; the fact that it cannot win legally may cause it to pursue its ends illegally, by promoting rebellion."[93]

LIBERAL REFORMISM

Before we can begin to understand the awkward position of the wealthy in this new and suddenly much more complex political environment, it is im-portant to step back and sketch, very briefly, the differences between midcentury liberalism and early postnational liberalism. Taken separately, many of the programs and policies advocated by the midcentury liberals were quite similar to those of the 1820s (in fact there were times when the need for a new law to replace one drafted in the 1820s was questioned).[94] But together they formed an all-or-nothing ideological package that had tight doctrinal coherence, whose different elements could not easily be separated from the whole. Where the earlier reformers had justified their proposals primarily by loose appeals to unquestioned, abstract principles (democracy, private property, individual liberty, and self-interest), and these principles had provided the link between their various initiatives, the midcentury liberals saw each element of their program as intimately connected to the others. The thread tying them together was the need to strengthen and preserve the nation, a cause that was, of course, made far more urgent by the events of 1846 to 1848, when Mexico suffered the loss of one-third of its territory and legitimately feared a U.S. takeover of the rest.[95] And the corollary to that axiomatic goal was the need to diminish the power of the church; in fact the assault on the church was the cornerstone of the midcentury reform program in a way that had been only hinted at (and that had been quickly rejected) during the brief period of radical reformism in 1833 to 1834.

Midcentury liberals saw the church as the nation's rival for the sympathies and loyalty of the *pueblo*, and they now sought to cast themselves, instead, as the true champions of the people. To a significant extent the numerous public works that transformed the urban landscape in the late 1840s and early 1850s were designed, as the governor's *Memoria* put it, to "provide to the pueblo the best testimony that the government is concerned for their well-being and wants to help them."[96] Juan B. Ceballos took great pride in recounting the roads that had been improved, and the bridges, jails, cemeteries, aqueducts and fountains that had been constructed during his administration. He also created the Junta de Inspección de Beneficiencia Pública, designed to oversee the establishment of government-run asylums, hospices, hospitals, and orphanages, and thus ultimately to take over the charitable activities of the church. "Is it not the Government, after all," asked Ceballos's advisor Santos Degollado in his speech to Congress asking for authorization for the new junta, "that is the legitimate guardian of the poor?"[97]

Liberals also sought to counter the church's influence by expanding the number of free public schools and, to a certain extent, changing their mission. Schools were to be not only means of improving literacy rates, as before, but centers of nationalist propaganda. Introducing his proposal for a new law governing primary education, Dr. Juan Manuel González Urueña began by arguing that "the first and most pressing requirement of a Nation constituted under a system of popular representative government is that the masses be aware of their rights and their obligations, that they understand the ties that bind members of a society together, and that they recognize the authorities who govern and lead them."[98] In order to infiltrate, as it were, out-of-the-way villages in which the local priest had provided heretofore the only ongoing connection to the world outside, it was proposed that the criteria for selecting teachers and establishing schools be relaxed.[99] Teachers should be free to start their own schools without having to pass a special examination, and local authorities should only require that they exhibit "good religious and civil behavior."[100] In the course of debate, even the first part of this minimal requirement was eliminated: as Francisco Sendejas put it, "good religious conduct is very difficult to evaluate, since there are many hypocrites who put on a show of piety but have corrupt hearts; it is enough to require a good civil record — the rest is of no importance."[101]

Indeed, many liberals did not really want teachers whose good behavior might be characterized as "Christian" rather than "civic-minded." The local political influence of parish priests had been demonstrated recently when they organized a blizzard of initiatives sent to congress by the state's *ayuntamientos* protesting an anticlerical executive order.[102] A similar initiative campaign against the federal system in 1835 may also (some liberals suspected) have been orchestrated by the church and carried out by the church's local representatives.[103] Now they wanted teachers on the ground, so to speak, to counteract the influence of the priests, teachers who could tell the people "what system was best for them," who could warn them not to follow, in their ignorance, the "empty promises" of the clerical party.[104]

But for liberals priests represented more than just negative moral and political influences at the local level. Since independence the church had been visibly engaged in a battle for recognition as a sovereign power, separate from the state — something that the liberals, for whom the nation had become all-important, could not abide. Under the colonial system the state had enjoyed the right of patronage, that is, the right to name bishops, members of the cathedral chapters, and even priests if it so desired, a right that had been granted soon after the discovery of America in return for Spain's willingness to finance the Christianization of the Americas. With Mexico's independence from Spain the church had fiercely resisted transfer of patronage rights to the new nation, arguing that its special subordination had been to the *Spanish* state, not to just any state. The impasse prevented the naming of new bishops in Mexico until 1831, which in Michoacán meant that the diocese was bishopless for over twenty years. Even then the issue was not entirely resolved; the church still displayed great willingness to protest or reject laws that did not suit it.[105]

Under the liberal administrations of the late 1840s and early 1850s the conflict over sovereignty burst once again onto center stage. The first occasion was the national executive decree of January 1847, which allowed ecclesiastical property to be mortgaged or sold for up to 15 million pesos in order to finance the war with the United States. This was the clearest attempt yet to subject the church to the state, and it put the deputies to the congress in a bind. Though some of them stood squarely with the church, calling the decree an "unjust, unconstitutional threat to state sovereignty" (because it was a federal law), and an "antieconomic invitation to sedition," others agreed with José María Manso Ceballos that even if this particular law did not meet with everyone's approval, it was important to assert in principal the government's right to occupy clerical property if necessary.[106] But this ambivalence had largely disappeared by a year later, when the church's unpatriotic behavior (not only its unwillingness to help finance resistance to the U.S. invasion but also its earlier collaboration with Paredes on the search for a European monarch to rule Mexico) had sufficiently annoyed some of the wavering deputies that they were cheerfully willing to pass another piece of anticlerical legislation, a bill that would force the church to pay sales taxes and municipal taxes on the sale of the tithed goods.[107]

One of the arguments in favor of taxing the tithe, expressed by the fiery Francisco Sendejas, was that the proceeds of the tax would go to alleviating poverty and to supporting the hospices that the government was so keen to promote. Charity, he went on, was supposed to be the work of the church, but instead of helping their miserable parishioners, most priests, with the connivance of the "so-called ecclesiastical authorities," abused them by charging exorbitant fees for their services, while they themselves lived in luxury.[108] This seems to have been the first mention in post-independent Michoacán of an issue — excessive sacramental fees — that Melchor Ocampo would seize upon as the best means yet to force the church to bend to the will of the government, as well as to impress upon the pueblo the extent to which the government, and not the church, had its best interests at heart.

Ocampo's entry into the debate over ecclesiastical fee schedules, in the form of his much-publicized exchange with an anonymous "cura de

Michoacán," came in March 1851, over a year and a half after the congress
had first asked the bishop for a list of these fees with an eye toward forcing
their reduction.[109] Though the church's foot-dragging was most irritating, the
immediate spur to Ocampo's first *representación* was probably the direct
challenge to state sovereignty laid down less than two months earlier by Lic.
Clemente de Jesús Munguía during the ceremony installing him as bishop of
Michoacán. Munguía had shocked everyone by refusing to take the oath of
allegiance to the constitution and laws of Mexico, which included recognizing the right of patronage.[110] Ocampo and the anonymous priest (probably
Lic. Agustín Dueñas, one of the deputies who had refused to serve in the liberal congress of 1846) kept up their polemic through November 1851, but by
August the congress had already agreed to give the church just 30 days to propose its own reforms of the fee schedule. After that they would rescind the
civil obligation to render fees for baptism, marriage, and burial. Some
deputies had argued for a less inflammatory phrasing of the order, but as Lic.
Juan Ortiz Careaga observed, without a specific date by which the church
must come up with a new *arancel*, there would be more endless delays.[111]

By this time, then, the tension between the liberals and the church over
moral and political issues — as local as the qualifications for schoolteachers
and as national as the right of patronage — was probably powerful enough in
its own right to provoke the series of events that began to unfold early in
1853, with the conservative coup that drove the liberals from power. But the
attack on the church also operated in the economic realm. Indeed, important
strands of the liberal reform program were connected to each other by the
fact that they all hinged on diminishing or eliminating the church's economic
power.

The liberals believed that Michoacán's most pressing economic problems
stemmed from the church's pivotal role in the hacienda system. The issue was
not so much outright ecclesiastical land ownership (they knew that the
church owned relatively few properties in the state), as the ecclesiastical mortgages that burdened virtually all privately owned haciendas.[112] One of the
many terrible legacies of the colonial era, the liberal governors pointed out
year after year in the *Memorias* they presented to congress, was a pattern of
huge landholdings, formed at the time of the conquest. These vast tracts had
been "passed down from generation to generation almost intact," they argued (forgetting or ignoring the notorious instability of land ownership in the
colonial period and especially in the late eighteenth century).[113] This accu-

mulation of huge properties in the hands of proprietors who used them inefficiently, making a profit by "tyrannizing" and underpaying their workforce rather than by increasing productivity, was the "great defect of our agricultural system."[114]

The problem, as the liberals saw it, was that even if these owners *wanted* to subdivide their haciendas this would have been impossible, since ecclesiastical mortgages burdened most of them almost to the full value of the property. Each year, after the owners paid the staggering interest on their debts, they had only a small profit left over, if they were lucky. Naturally they could not afford to invest in improvements or to purchase new equipment that would make them more productive and would lift agriculture in Michoacán out of its present state of stagnation and degeneration and put it on the track of progress. In fact, many owners just gave up and rented out their properties. But this, too, was intrinsically bad for agriculture, because renters were never willing to sink money into permanent improvements; they just wanted to exploit the property for the short time it was in their possession.[115] Ecclesiastical mortgages on haciendas, then, were a fundamental cause of major deficiencies in Michoacán's agricultural system.

Moreover, outside the hacienda economy there were also problems for which the church was held at least partly responsible. The misery in which the indigenous population lived owed in part, liberal dogma asserted, to the fact that the poor were not encouraged to strive to produce more or to produce differently, but rather to accept the status quo: if their crops failed it was God's will, not the fault of their own obsolete techniques and timeless habits.[116] Moreover, one of the most retrograde features of the state's agriculture was the landholding village, which kept "a good part" of the state's best lands out of circulation and out of private hands.[117] The church bore considerable responsibility for the perpetuation of this intolerable situation, since many a village clung to these lands in order to support its priests and its rituals.[118]

The ramifications outside of the rural sector of such a backward, undercapitalized agricultural system were profound, liberals argued. Neither heavily indebted hacendados nor impoverished subsistence farmers could support a system of taxation based on property or wealth; instead the state was forced to collect commerce-stifling indirect taxes. As a result commerce stagnated, and the state's revenue base was not large enough to allow it to build the roads and ports that would be necessary to truly stimulate trade. In short, the church blocked economic as well as political progress at every turn.

BUILDING THE CASE FOR REFORM

As we have seen, beginning in 1810 and continuing into the early post-independence years, creole insurgents/reformers sought and received support from the popular classes for their cause. In large part they accomplished this by emphasizing the difference between Spaniards and all Americans, whether rich or poor. At midcentury the invasion of Mexico by the United States (in many ways an even more attractive common enemy than Spain) offered a similar opportunity to develop cross-class alliances, and for a brief period in Michoacán the government attempted to do so. Ocampo issued impassioned calls for money, arms, and volunteers for the Batallón Matamoros de Morelia, and drew responses from all sectors of society, from the 4,000 arti-sans and campesinos who showed up at the former Jesuit convent in April 1847, willing to take up arms against the invaders, to the Junta Patriótica de Señoras convened by Dolores Alzúa (Cayetano Gómez's wife) to organize do-nations of clothing and supplies.[119]

But the fighting was over within months, and the internal recriminations and scapegoating in the wake of the disaster began. This process does not ap-pear to have been so divisive and agonizing in Michoacán as it was in Mexico City, but it was nonetheless obvious that the war alone would not build bridges between the rich and the poor. Nor, after the end of the war, did the liberals try to do so. Instead they showed themselves quite willing not only to foster partisanship (as we have seen) but actually to promote awareness of class differences. What were they trying to accomplish?

It might be inferred from their antiaristocratic and antihacienda rhetoric, and from their programs of public works and free public education, that, like the independence-era reformers, the midcentury liberals wished to enlist the popular classes in their reformist mission. In a certain sense this was true, but not if it meant accepting the more unacceptable predilections of the poor, es-pecially their notorious religiosity. While some of the Indian and mestizo poor (especially, perhaps, in areas like the coastal mountains and part of the *tierra caliente*, where the presence of the church had been weak historically) would be drawn to some of the liberal promises and goals (individual land ownership, education, municipal autonomy, popular elections, abolition of the draft and compulsory personal service), for others the centerpiece of the reformers' pro-gram — the demolition of the power of the church — was a cause that was not likely to go over well no matter how many asylums the government sponsored or how many teachers they brought in to emphasize loyalty to the nation.

Recognizing this, the liberals did not spend much rhetorical energy identifying themselves with the unreconstructed poor, despite the care with which these liberals distinguished themselves from the rich. Though they acknowledged the "essential nobility" of the Mexican poor, they saw it as submerged, waiting to be released by the liberal reforms: "*If our people had the advantage of education*," Ocampo wrote, "they would be as commonsensical and prudent as the German, as scrupulous as the Englishman, as energetic and generous as the Spaniard, as cultured as the Frenchman, and as hardworking as the North American, but without his infamous thirst for riches (emphasis mine)."[120] It was virtually impossible to make common cause with the indigenous population until they had been made, by several important criteria, no longer Indians; that is, until their primary allegiances to the village and the church, rather than the nation, were eliminated (through education and removal of undue clerical influence) and they became private landholders (through the *reparto*). Unlike the independence-era creoles (or, later, the Porfirian liberals), the midcentury liberals did not even wish to associate their cause with dead Indians by constructing a national identity around images of a glorious Aztec past; their anticlericalism and egalitarian impulses made it uncomfortable for them to hold up for admiration a society like that of the Aztecs that had revolved around state religion and rigid social hierarchies.[121] Ocampo, comparing the invading "Yankees" with the sixteenth-century Spanish conquerors, noted that "at least Cortés brought a civilization superior to that of our [Indian] ancestors."[122] In short, the liberals would identify with and court a future, idealized poor (educated, ambitious), but their reforms had to come first.

Part of the liberals' unwillingness to align themselves with the poor and the Indian population, then, was philosophical. But the absence of *indigenista* spirit was also grounded in day-to-day experiences with Indian villagers. Despite the fact that there were no serious native uprisings in the state, the 1840s and early 1850s were years when Indians seemed more quarrelsome than ever, aggressively disrupting the very haciendas of which the liberals most approved: those that were being worked intensively by owners or renters willing to experiment with new crops and new activities, buy new equipment, and invest large sums in increasing production. Hacendados went to court against the indigenous villages and *barrios* of La Piedad, Capula, Jesús del Monte, Jesús Huiramba, Gerahuaro, Tacámbaro, and Indaparapeo, alleging in every case that the Indians had illegally occupied their lands and in individual cases that they had assaulted hacienda employees (La Piedad), quarried stone on hacienda lands without permission (Jesús del Monte), torn down a new fence and impeded its reconstruction (Jesús Huiramba), and prevented the transport of lumber (Indaparapeo).[123] Meanwhile, hacendado aggression against Indian possessions was alleged by the community of San Salvador Atecuario, which claimed that the owner of the hacienda of Etúcuaro, among others who shared the village's boundaries, had been encroaching bit by bit on their lands, "with the clear intent of dispossessing them altogether."[124] Similar suits were brought by the communities of La Piedad, Tarímbaro, Santa Catarina, and Cuitzeo.[125]

One of the most revealing cases of tension between villagers and hacendados is to be found in an 1847 lawsuit brought by the Indian community of Indaparapeo against the owner of the hacienda of Naranjos, Francisco Estrada, one of the most successful of the middle-class men who had purchased haciendas in the 1820s and 1830s. The suit described the community's chronic and escalating problems since 1840, when Estrada ordered the removal of trees from a dense forested area that had always been claimed by the pueblo. By 1844 Estrada was calling the forest his own, telling the Indians "in the most threatening and insulting way" that they must leave, that they had no right to be there. This, the Indians said, they refused to do. Finally, in December 1846, the matter came to a head. Estrada had set up a sawmill in the disputed territory, and the Indians apparently responded by building a fence of nopal to prevent the removal of the timber. In February 1847 the majordomo of the hacienda, Domingo Silva, stabbed the Indian Mariano Andrade with a knife. It was this "barbarous act" that brought about the lawsuit. The presentation of the Indians' case concluded with the hope that there were, somewhere, authorities who would punish the "evil actions of ambitious men," and who would enforce the laws that protected the property rights of citizens.[126]

Estrada's lawyer responded angrily, and his words effectively capture the liberals' frustration with the Indians' control of land resources they were convinced could be put to better use by private owners (like themselves):

> It is well known in our Republic, where land is distributed so unevenly and where Indian communities possess so much of it, that the individual landowner unlucky enough to share a boundary with one of these communities lives in eternal conflict with them, suffering incessant claims and litigation born of the almost proverbial imbecility of these *comuneros*. . . . Sr. Estrada has been a victim of these abuses.[127]

In short, the midcentury liberals distanced themselves from both the rich and the poor, evoking in rhetoric a third, middle class where before there had been only two: the *hombres de bien* and the *clases humildes*. The concept of this "new" class was promoted almost exclusively by members of it: the only wealthy advocates of midcentury liberalism in Michoacán were Ocampo himself, who owned an inherited hacienda (Pomoca, an anagram of his name); the Ceballos brothers (Juan Bautista and Gregorio, who had inherited several haciendas from their uncle); and the Iturbide brothers (Manuel and Luis, the latter married to one of Cayetano Gómez's daughters).[128] The other prominent liberals were squarely middle class, mainly professionals. Naturally enough, their reformist program — while meant to save everyone, even those who did not want to be saved — would provide the clearest benefit for people like themselves, who were neither rich nor poor, who aspired to land ownership, who embraced the bourgeois values of hard work and thrift, who looked abroad to rationalist philosophies, and not to the church, for inspiration, and who were prepared to take advantage of the freed-up factors of production (Indian and church land, church capital) that their reforms promised to bring about. Put another way, the thoroughgoing reforms of the social and economic order that they envisioned were designed in large part to make more room for themselves in a world presently dominated, as we have seen, by established elites.

The problem, of course, was that these middle classes represented a very small proportion of the state's population; the liberals' natural constituency was not large enough for them to push through far-reaching reforms by pointing to their program as an expression of the "will of the people." Since they were not inclined to suffer the messy compromises entailed in developing cross-class alliances, liberals had to find ways both to convince others to join them on their own terms and to make it harder for people to stand in their way. From the beginning they set out to accomplish both of these goals.

DENYING THE OPPOSITION

The defeat of the first federal republic in 1835 had come at the hands of one of the institutions that the federalists had earlier seen as a key to Mexican democracy, the *ayuntamientos*. The 1824 Constitution guaranteed the *ayuntamientos* the right to submit proposals for laws and decrees, and it was the avalanche of *ayuntamiento* initiatives in favor of centralism — suspiciously alike in their reasoning and even their wording — that had finally convinced the last federalist congress that the majority of the people desired a change in the system of government.

The midcentury liberals were not prepared to cave in to the same kind of pseudodemocratic (as they saw it) pressure. One of the most consistent themes of the governors' reports to congress from 1846 to 1852 was the need to reduce the number of *ayuntamientos* and the number of officials serving in each one, even if this required a "loose interpretation" of the state constitution.[129] The congress went even farther, narrowly approving a reform (or as its backers put it, a "clarification") of the state constitution intended to prevent the *ayuntamientos* from "abusing" the right to present initiatives:

> The *derecho de iniciar* shall be understood to be limited to areas of which the submitting corporations have special knowledge; so that the Supreme Court can only propose projects of law or decrees that concern the administration of justice, and the *ayuntamientos* can only do so in matters that concern the police, public security, public works, transport and public health.[130]

Upon José Manso Ceballos' objection that this was unconstitutional, that the constitution specifically gave the *ayuntamientos* the prerogative to submit initiatives, Dr. Juan Manuel González Urueña replied that the right was not really being taken away; it was just that the intention of the framers was being explained more fully and the councils given better guidelines to follow, so that they could not be used as dupes by political "factions" looking for a "veneer of legality" to cover their machinations.[131]

The liberal governors' desire to curb the power of the *ayuntamiento*, in order to deny the conservative opposition a means of exercising power even when they were out of office, was matched by their desire to strengthen executive power. Year after year the governor sent *Memorias* to Congress pleading for more power than the "wretchedly small" sphere of executive action allowed by the constitution, and recounting cases in which greater flexibility would have been able to avert disasters.[132] A typhoid epidemic in some towns north of Morelia, for example, spread quickly because the governor first had to beg congress for money before he could act; a tense situation in the southern prefecture that could easily have erupted into widescale violence could not be addressed by the governor except in an advisory capacity, making it appear that the government lacked the energy and resources to keep the peace.[133] Moreover, only the executive was capable of taking on mammoth and complex tasks that required a sure hand and direct action, for example the organization, editing, and codification of the welter of laws dating from the early colonial period that were still on the books and that slowed the administration of justice to a crawl, so that criminals walked the streets and civil cases dragged on forever.[134]

Predictably, congressional liberals were more ambivalent about the expansion of executive power than they had been about the reduction of the power of the *ayuntamientos*. In 1848 the congress defeated a proposal that the government be given "extraordinary power" to raise a militia, arguing that this was the role of congress, not of the executive.[135] Roughly a year later several deputies again objected to a government proposal for a new vagrancy law, on the grounds that the law "trampled" on the constitution by allowing the executive branch to encroach on territory properly reserved for the judiciary.[136] When a broader project of constitutional reform came up soon afterwards, the language of debate was even more incendiary. "The project to reform the constitution makes the Executive into a Dictator!" one deputy fumed.[137] When Deputy José Manso Ceballos objected that this was a gross exaggeration, the sarcastic response was that

> It is true, as Sr. Manso says, that the Executive cannot exactly be called a "dictator," since his terrible power and influence in the formation of laws and their publication is disguised; but he can impose punishments and perform other functions of the judiciary merely by calling them 'corrective actions;" he can dispose of public funds at his discretion; and he can remove from office at will not only bureaucrats but officials as high as the Prefects; in sum, his power nullifies that of the other branches of government, which are left with only the appearance of function and purpose.[138]

Even small concessions to the executive, Manuel Elguero argued in a similar debate, would "open the door to greater abuses, to the point that the Government might even claim the power to reverse decisions made by the courts. It is easy to see the abyss into which this might lead."[139]

Nonetheless, some deputies agreed with the governors that the executive needed to be strengthened, even if this meant cutting into the congress's own sphere of power. Among them was Manuel Alzúa, who had been a leader of the movement to defeat an earlier expansion of executive power but who now observed that even if the project to reform the constitution was not perfect, there was no real danger of creating a too-strong executive; most of the proposed changes would just streamline the government and make it possible for the governor to combat "enemies of the system," not rearrange power in any important ways.[140] (Alzúa, who usually voted with the more moderate liberals and conservatives in the congress, may here have been reassured by the fact that the conservative statesman and intellectual Lucás Alamán shared the liberal opinion that the power of the executive needed to be strengthened and that the number of local officials needed to be reduced and their power circumscribed, even if it meant a loose reading of the constitution.)[141]

Most of the congressional debates on the issue of executive power ended in ties or at least in very close votes. Clearly it was not going to be easy for the government to convince certain liberals, for whom the most important feature of the 1824 Constitution was its recognition of one's right to do as one pleased as long as it did not offend the rights of others, that the new proposals offered sufficient guarantees of personal liberty or congressional prerogative.[142] It would takes decades, of course, for liberals to fully accept the substitution of a strong and active executive for the old ideal of government as "night watchman"; even Benito Juárez, in his role of restorer of the republic after the French Intervention, would be sharply criticized for his use of dubiously constitutional means to strengthen the presidency. But the liberals of the late 1840s had already started down this path, seeking the power they needed to push through far-ranging reforms.

CONSTRUCTING ECONOMIC DEPRESSION

The second liberal strategy for gaining support for their program operated in the less nitty-gritty realm of public discourse and consisted of an effort to portray Michoacán's (and Mexico's) problems as so staggering and so fundamental that they could only be addressed by means of radical reforms. Though some of these problems were of a moral or political nature, liberals focused most fundamentally on social and economic changes, without which progress on any front was impossible.

A typical evocation of the crying need for reform began with a glowing description of the state's bountiful natural resources. "Michoacán," began Ocampo in his first address to congress in 1846,

> is the land of eternal spring. . . . Its flora is among the richest in the
> world; its soil can support not only all the plants in the plant kingdom,
> but contains all of the most useful mineral products. Of silver, copper,
> gold, lead, and tin, the state has plenty; also cotton and indigo, chocolate

and vanilla, sugar cane and coffee, rice and bananas, corn, wheat, beans, chiles, barley — in short everything that the civilized world needs and demands, our state produces in perfect abundance.[143]

But, he continued, "Michoacán is poor." He went on to elucidate the defects of the state's agriculture, most of which we have already examined in a different context: undercapitalization, overindebtedness, poor systems of distribution, technological backwardness, communal ownership. "Mexico must completely reorganize its society," Ocampo concluded.[144] In much the same vein, Juan B. Ceballos wrote in his 1849 address: "in the excellence of its climate, the variety of its plant life, the abundance of its pasturelands, the extent of its fertile valleys, the magnificence of its forests, and the wealth of its mineral resources, Michoacán is the most privileged state in the Republic," but it suffers from problems that "inevitably lead to the decay and ruin in which the whole Republic now finds itself."[145] The only solution was, of course, the package of liberal reforms.

"Many deny that Mexico is in such a terrible state; many are content with things as they are," Ocampo wrote, and indeed, conservatives looked around them and saw a Mexico different from the Mexico of the liberals.[146] "As far as the alleged poverty of the nation is concerned," Alamán wrote, "it has been greatly exaggerated."[147] If, for Ocampo, agriculture was "miserable, decadent, and backward," for Alamán it was "thriving," "more prosperous than ever."[148] Ocampo thought it would be impossible for property values to rise without major reforms in the land tenure and mortgage systems; Alamán, however, observed that property values had already risen and that there was no reason to expect them not to continue to climb.[149] For Ocampo independence from Spain had been a glorious event; the abysmal state of things at midcentury did not mean that independence had been a mistake but merely that the leaders of independent Mexico had not lived up to the vision of the founding fathers, especially of Hidalgo.[150] For Alamán, "general prosperity" reigned not because of independence but despite it, and things surely would have been even better with "calm and good government," of the type Mexico had enjoyed before independence.[151] For Ocampo, as we have seen, the most pressing order of business was to diminish ecclesiastical power — this was the key to all the other social and economic reforms he envisioned. For Alamán the church represented the only glue that held the nation together; if anything, it should be strengthened rather than the reverse.[152] The institutional targets of his program were not the church but the executive, the congress, and the states, for which he proposed a variety of generally centralizing and antidemocratic reforms.[153]

From the perspective of the late twentieth century, there does not seem much doubt that Ocampo and the liberals had a more "modern," structural understanding of Mexico's problems. Time and again, their analysis, which linked together the themes of technology, transportation, capital development (including human capital, by means of education), progressive taxation, property rights, wealth, and land distribution, rings true. Alamán's sunny view of Mexico's economy seems naive in comparison; though it is surely the case that the economy needed political stability, which Alamán thought to bring about with his narrow institutional reforms, that is far from all that was required.

But, as we have seen, Alamán's picture of the *trajectory* of economic change from 1810 to midcentury is closer than Ocampo's to the reality in Michoacán. Things *were* better at midcentury than they had been; property values *were* rising; individual wealth among the propertied classes *was* increasing. The liberal view that the economy was spiraling downward, getting worse all the time, simply did not capture the reality of the Michoacán that Ocampo governed. But it was important to the liberals that things be made to *seem* terrible, else the case for radical reforms — which Ocampo saw as necessary — fell to the ground. Put another way, Mexico's economic history since 1810, along with many other midcentury issues, was politicized; the ongoing, indeed worsening, economic depression was, in large part, a political creation of the liberals, born of the need to justify radical social and economic reforms.

Elite Political Alignments

The place of the Michoacán elites in this politically charged climate is ambiguous. On the one hand, Alamán's view of Mexico was really a view of *their* Michoacán; it was a place of increased wealth for the wealthy, of rising hacienda values, of sumptuous houses in the cities, of more theaters and more carriages in the streets than ever before (to use some of Alamán's measures of prosperity).[154] Like Alamán, most elites admired the church and feared that the "docile" *pueblo* that Alamán described, with its "deep religious sentiments," would be angered and aroused by any attack on the church.[155] But other aspects of conservative ideology — for some, centralism, and for most, perhaps, the conservative antipathy to republican institutions — were less appealing. At the same time, many of them approved of key elements of the liberal program: its taxation policies, its emphasis on education, its promotion of agriculture and free trade, its commitment to division of Indian community lands and abolition of the landholding village as a corporate entity, its promise to ease their burden of indebtedness to the church. But we may presume that they did not appreciate its anti-elite rhetoric (including strong language about the desirability of breaking up large landholdings), its anticlericalism and occasional hint of impiety, or its constant refrain of "remaking" or reforming a socioeconomic status quo that they cannot have seen as nearly so terrible as the liberals' portrait of it made it out to be.

The notion that most elites were ambivalent about their relationship to the two political parties, neither fully sympathizing with nor embraced by either, is supported by an 1849 petition that was signed by over three hundred men, including almost all wealthy Morelianos. Published under the title "Documentary Proof of Fraud and Irregularities in the [recent] Elections, Published to Make Manifest the Behavior of the False Liberals who have Defamed Truth and Justice before the Citizens who Desire Order and True Liberty," the petition demanded that 28 electors, all of them well-known liberals, be excluded from the Junta del Estado that would choose new state and national officials, on the grounds of electoral fraud.[156] The past elections, they argued, had left the "principal classes of the State" without anyone to represent their interests.

> When we speak of 'classes' we do not refer to those with *fueros* and special privileges, but to those whose property, thought, and morals are on the most solid footing . . . , those without whom society cannot progress; those who for many years have been almost indifferent [to politics], busy with their businesses and their families, avoiding these [political] battles; but who now awaken from their lethargy . . . as they see powerful threats to the interests of morality, order ("los intereses morales y conservadores"), property, family, political and civil liberty, and individual security.[157]

Because the petition was directed against the "false liberals" in power who had organized the election, and because it used the word "conservador" in an approving manner, it is easy to leap to the conclusion that the signers of the petition had made their choice for the conservative party. But on close scrutiny this does not appear to have been entirely the case. Although some who signed the petition *were* well-known conservatives, including twelve who would be active in drumming up support for Maximilian's empire (which was sponsored by the conservative party) in 1864, other important conservatives did not sign.[158] Furthermore, several moderate liberals *did* sign: among them Dr. Juan Macouzet, José María Celso Dávalos, José María Sámano, Justo Carreón, Manuel Cárdenas, José Vallejo, Fermín Ortega, Francisco Menocal, and Francisco Zincúnegui.[159]

The signatures were organized by sector and block of the city and were often accompanied by detailed descriptions of the way that voting fraud in their particular *cuartel* was carried out. At the end of the document, however, there were appended six signatures of men who, for various reasons, had not signed along with other individuals in their districts when the petition originally circulated. Now, they said, they wanted to be sure their names were added "in order to prevent the *organs of the conservative Party* from inferring from the absence of our signatures that we do not support the petition, since the advocates of such a *renegade cause* never allow the slightest misstep to go unchallenged (emphasis mine)."[160]

Thus it seems that the majority of the Morelia elite (with the exception of the upper clergy, most of whose names were conspicuously absent from the petition), saw themselves as fitting somewhere in between the radical liberals and the radical conservatives. In other words they continued to pick and choose issues that suited their needs from both sides of the ideological spectrum, as they had always done. But their failure to fully align with either party ultimately drove many of them to the political sidelines over the next two decades.

The End of the Second Federal Republic and the Last Santa Anna Dictatorship

The hard-fought battles between fairly evenly matched (at least in congress) factions came temporarily to an end in early 1853. Out of the so-called "revolution of Guadalajara" of September 1852 came the call for Santa Anna to return once again from exile to replace the liberal President Mariano Arista. This call was seconded in Zamora by "el burro de oro," Francisco Velarde, and in La Piedad by Francisco Cosío Bahamonde, who denounced the liberals' "impious principles," and their "alarming attacks on landowners."[161] When Arista and his vice president, Juan B. Ceballos (the former governor of

Michoacán), were both forced to resign, the liberal governors also began to fall, including Ocampo in Michoacán. Bahamonde's forces entered Morelia, and possession of the governorship fell to the old conservative war horse, General José de Ugarte. Ocampo retreated to the hacienda of San Bartolomé where, it is said, he stayed for several days with a friend, perhaps Juan de Dios Gómez, Cayetano's second son.[162]

In late January 1853 ten members of the state congress met secretly in the residence of Lic. Francisco Figueroa to determine their next course of action. All of the deputies approved of issuing a statement to the effect that congress was dissolving itself entirely against its will, but Manuel Alzúa voted against a companion proposal recommending that the congress refuse to recognize the new order of things. Another meeting was called later the same day, by which time events had been proceeding so rapidly that some of the propositions of the morning session no longer made sense, while new ones seemed called for. Alzúa did not attend this meeting, during which the deputies who were present agonized but produced no new statements. Two days later, when they met again, there were not enough deputies present to make a quorum, and on 29 January President Figueroa again had to cancel the session for the same reason: three deputies claimed to be sick, while another had fled the city. Under these circumstances the seven deputies in attendance agreed to set down "for posterity" in the congressional *Actas* the "insuperable difficulties" that prevented them from keeping the congress in session, "as written testimony that they had no choice but to disband."[163] The tone of utter dismay and fear in these scribblings (they literally *were* scribbled; obviously there was no scribe present to record the proceedings in standard penmanship) comes through clearly, but so, too, does a sense of determination. It is not hard to envision these men and others like them supporting another revolution less than two years later, one that would drive Santa Anna from power for the last time and install a reformist regime that would finally set into law the central tenets of the liberal agenda.

Conclusion

The main themes of this chapter have been the final stages of the midcentury economic recovery in Michoacán and the early stages of the liberal reformist movement. The link between the two seems, at first glance, to be almost paradoxical: just when the damage to the economy from the wars for indepen-

dence had been more or less repaired, state finances were in surplus for the
first time ever, and the public and private trappings of prosperity were everywhere evident, liberal ideologues proposed an extremely divisive program of
reforms that, if enacted, were almost certain to plunge the country into another round of destructive wars. What were they thinking? One of the most
notable features of the long, slow economic recovery had been the extent to
which it was led by middle-class men and women for whom the late colonial
society and economy had made only limited room. Why, now, were the almost exclusively middle-class leaders of the Reform willing to risk war and
instability, seemingly jeopardizing their own chance to take advantage of the
growth of the economy?

It would be difficult, and in any event unsatisfyingly simplistic, to try to establish a direct or causative connection between the midcentury economic recovery and the resurgence of liberal reformism. Nevertheless, without dis-
counting the importance of the war with the United States (1846–48) as a
catalyst for liberal disillusionment, some of the social and economic patterns
discussed in this chapter allow us to infer a complement to this traditional explanation for the timing of the Reform.

Essentially, by midcentury it must have become clear to everyone that the
"recovered" economy was closer to a re-creation of the late colonial economy
than to a "modernized" economy that had undergone important structural
changes. The distribution of land and the size of haciendas, the distribution
of wealth, the proportion of the population living in the cities and in the
countryside, the daily wages paid to unskilled laborers, the strong role played
by foreigners in commerce, the system of transport — all of these had changed
relatively little. There is some evidence to suggest that agricultural profitability on some large, aggressively managed estates may have been higher at midcentury than before the wars for independence, but higher profitability does
not necessarily mean higher productivity, and even if it did in some cases, it
is very clear that higher productivity had not yet translated into higher wages
and lower commodity prices.[164] This was not an economy that was obviously
poised to move much beyond recovery; there were limits to its potential for
expansion.

Moreover, those who had prospered in the recovery were now older and
showing signs of complacency. The middle-class men and women who had,
in the 1820s and 1830s, taken over haciendas, mercantile houses, and professions from the thinned and dispirited late colonial elite, and who had employed innovative strategies for success (reducing debt; reaching new mar-

kets; diversifying production; experimenting with new crops and new retail products; modernizing operations; promoting professional and elementary education), were now the established elite. They had reached the point at which their primary interest was in consolidating and protecting what they already had. The principles to which they adhered in this effort were surely dictated as much by circumstance as by instinct: hierarchy, monopoly, privilege, and exclusivity had long pedigrees in Mexico, but they were more than just force of habit or cultural reflex. They made a certain kind of sense in an economy and society that had a weak state, weak institutions (except for the church, and even its economic power was much reduced from its glory days during the colony), and extremely weak capital, labor, and commodity markets. Full legal equality, open competition, and political inclusivity were theoretically attractive, but a bit frightening to those with a lot to lose.

This left the next generation of ambitious and activist middle-class men and women little room to maneuver. Put another way, their own upward mobility was blocked, not so much by a specific class of landowners or merchants (though the marriage patterns and habits of consumption of the established elite may have grated on some nerves), but by the "backwardness" of commercial intercourse and especially of that great potential source of wealth in Michoacán, agriculture. Their futures could not be assured without relatively radical changes in the status quo designed to enlarge the pie: removing the Indian communities, the church, and the rentier landlords as obstacles to the free movement of property; building railroads to permit access to national markets; and establishing a banking system that would extend credit on an impersonal basis. Liberal ideology in the 1840s and 1850s offered not only this economic program but also a vision of a strong nation with a strong executive committed to its implementation. Put another way, this is not a case of "the" middle class, or even "the" middle classes, attempting to defeat "the" aristocracy in the political arena — both the social groups involved and the political movement itself are far too complex to be reduced to such a crude formulation. But it does not seem unreasonable to suppose that perceptions of the limited nature of the recovery on the part of those who had not benefited dramatically from it, combined with the perception that those who *had* benefited were not likely to act in ways that would make it easier for the next generation to follow in their footsteps, may well have given rise to resentments that the disastrous war with the United States fanned into flames.

From Riches to Rags:
The Gómez Alzúa Children After the Reform

Cayetano Gómez and Dolores Alzúa's children were part of the generation that came of age in the late 1830s, the 1840s, and early 1850s, during the economic recovery. They were well aware of the dismal economic conditions that had prevailed during their parents' young adulthood, if for no other reason than that there were numerous lingering economic problems and pockets of still-severe dislocation. But their own formative experience (or at least that of the six oldest children) had been one of a steadily improving climate in which families like theirs could flourish.

This background did not prepare them for the political and economic wrenches of the Reform, which were compounded by the timing of their father's death in 1858. Even if Cayetano Gómez had died when times were tranquil there would have been inevitable difficulties in bringing about the smooth transfer of his 1,200,000-peso estate to his widow and nine children. Gómez himself had acknowledged this and had made a careful plan for the distribution of his property after his death, but doing so was no easy task. Three of the possible options for dividing the estate, Gómez reasoned, were deeply flawed. To parcel out the largest property, San Bartolomé, among the heirs was not prudent, since its warehouses, barns, mills, housing, and other outbuildings would be impossible to divide, but without them the profitability of the hacienda would plummet. Possession of the hacienda in common, the second possibility, was dangerous because it could too easily lead to familial discord. A third option, to sell the hacienda at auction, was unacceptable since there were few buyers who could afford such an expensive property, and none of them would be likely

to offer more than two-thirds of its appraised value in the uncertain political climate of the late 1850s. The only solution was for Juan de Dios, the
second-oldest son and the one heir who could already cover large portions
of the *legítimas* of his co-heirs, to take sole responsibility for the hacienda.[1]
The other two haciendas would go to Juan Bautista (Taretan) and Cayetano
(Quirio), both of whom would also recognize some amounts to their co-
heirs, though not to the same extent as Juan de Dios would.

    This plan, however, soon fell apart. Caught up in cash-flow problems
that accompanied their father's death, the wars of the Reform, and the
forced redemption — as one of the Reform measures — of a large part of
the 200,000-peso debt on Taretan (acquired from the Augustinians under
the Lerdo law just two years earlier), Juan de Dios and Juan Bautista began
to borrow in order to cover their short-term obligations. Naturally, many
individuals were more than willing to lend capital that would be secured by
some of the finest agricultural properties in Michoacán. Over the next few
years Juan Bautista borrowed about 63,000 pesos and Juan de Dios over
215,000 pesos, some of which was for the stated purpose of repaying
earlier debts.[2] Still, instead of retrenching until the wars were over or
until they had unburdened themselves of most of their obligations to their
co-heirs, both brothers followed the example that their father had set during his early career: they took risks, trying to invest and speculate their way
out of trouble. Juan Bautista bought an hacienda near Morelia, La Goleta,
and built a state-of-the-art *aguardiente* factory on Taretan; Juan de Dios
also bought another hacienda, invested in one flour mill, and rented
another one.[3]

    Juan de Dios's already-complex affairs were further complicated when
his childless uncle, Manuel Alzúa, died in 1861, naming him as the executor
of *his* estate, which included the rich sugar hacienda of Puruarán in *tierra
caliente*. Alzúa's bequests were precise and involved; Juan de Dios was
instructed to set up trusts for many of his less-fortunate relatives as well as
to pay out some large sums to others.[4] All of this leveraged Puruarán nearly
to the full extent of its value. Moreover, Alzúa's death triggered the dissolu-
tion of his trading partnership with Fermín Huarte in Colima and Juan de
Alzuyeta in Acapulco; when the accounts were squared the Alzúa estate
owed Huarte 50,000 pesos, which Gómez had to guarantee on unfavorable
terms because he could not pay in cash.[5]

    Even though Alzúa left him a huge legacy (130,000 pesos), Juan de Dios
simply was not able, in the current political climate, to effectively adminis-

ter two of the largest, previously unencumbered but now heavily indebted, haciendas in the state. His mother, realizing the gravity of the situation, made allowances for Juan de Dios — she pardoned some of his debts to her and left him, in her will of 1863, a larger portion than that received by any of his siblings.[6] In addition, his brothers Juan Bautista, Cayetano, and Ignacio all cosigned notes for him. But none of these measures could rescue him. By 1864 some of the claimants on Alzúa's estate were complaining that Puruarán had been severely neglected; that Juan de Dios had rendered no accounting or inventory of the estate in over three years; that there was no new planting in 1864; that part of last year's cane harvest had not been milled; that necessary maintenance work had not been done; that store credit with the merchants of Tacámbaro — impeccable while Alzúa was alive — had been lost; and that Juan de Dios, who had been characterized as such a sunny and guileless child (see the prologue to chapter 5), was sharp and sullen toward concerned creditors who tracked him down at San Bartolomé. Lawsuits were initiated, and some of Juan de Dios's urban property was ceded in payment.[7] Finally, in late 1864, with Juan de Dios effectively in bankruptcy, a *concurso de acreedores* was formed, and the decision was made to sell off the lands of San Bartolomé. Over the next seven years 34 of the approximately 40 fractions into which the hacienda was divided were sold to some 25 people for a total of over 480,000 pesos.[8] Juan de Dios was allowed to keep around 100,000 pesos worth of the property, in the hope that he would be able to pay off a more-or-less equal amount of debts, but eventually he and his heirs lost these lands as well. After his death in 1882 his widow and children began ceding mills, outbuildings, and land, until finally, in 1891, they had nothing left of the hacienda that had formed the dazzling centerpiece of their grandfather's vast estate.[9]

Several things conspired to bring about Juan de Dios's spectacular fall. First was the unfortunate timing of his father's and uncle's deaths in 1858 and 1861, during the Three Years' War and the enactment of the Reform in Michoacán. Second was the inappropriateness, in light of these difficult circumstances, of Alzúa's and the elder Gómez's inheritance strategies — which immediately overburdened with debt both of the haciendas that formed the cores of their estates. Third was Juan de Dios's decision to take on new ventures before he had come close to assimilating his inherited property and obligations. Finally there is some evidence that the Reform government of Michoacán during these years, headed by Epitacio Huerta, made a special effort to target the Gómez family, perhaps even going out of its way to nudge along the collapse of its inherited fortune. Among the people from whom Juan de Dios and Juan Bautista, as executors of their father's estate, had borrowed money was Lic. Onofre Calvo Pintado, who made the loans in his capacity as the executor of the estate of Juan José Pastor Morales. Because Pastor Morales, the owner of the hacienda of Bellasfuentes, had left his fortune in part to his soul and in part for public works, the Reform government considered his estate to be the property of the state. Shortly after Calvo Pintado's death in 1860 the state government began demanding that all debts belonging to the Pastor Morales estate be redeemed — including even the Gómez debts, whose term had not yet expired.[10] The Gómez brothers, already strapped for cash (in fact, the loan from the Pastor Morales estate had probably been contracted precisely because the brothers were experiencing cash shortages), could not comply. Desperate, Juan de Dios asked his friend, Santos Degollado, the prominent liberal politician from the 1840s and early 1850s, to intercede on the family's behalf to ensure that the debts to the Pastor Morales estate would not be called before they were due, but apparently Degollado was unable to prevent the Huerta government from acting "arbitrarily" and with "injustice," as he later put it.[11] Perhaps even in the absence of the hostility of the Huerta government Juan de Dios would have found it impossible to digest the huge burdens thrust upon him by his father's and uncle's deaths, but the antagonism certainly did not help.

Predictably, Juan de Dios Gómez's bankruptcy had repercussions within the family, especially for his siblings whose inheritances were secured by the now-fragmented and alienated San Bartolomé. His brother Cayetano was perhaps the hardest hit. In 1859 Cayetano had cosigned two notes for Juan de Dios, one for 40,000 pesos and one for 51,000 pesos. When Cayetano did not make a 29,000-peso installment payment on the second note, due in September 1864, the creditor took him to court. Against his vigorous protests, the court ordered that Cayetano's hacienda of Quirio, which was appraised at 92,874 pesos, be auctioned to this creditor at the standard two-thirds of its value. After Gómez was forced to pay court costs, sales taxes, back interest, and fines, he was left with only 8,872 pesos. He never recovered from this blow. In 1876 he was forced to cede two diligences and 27 mules with which he had earned a living transporting people to and from Pátzcuaro; this property, worth 1,600 pesos, and a share in the estate of his uncle Manuel Alzúa designated for "poor relations" were his only assets. All this was despite Cayetano's having made what must have appeared at the time to be an excellent marriage in 1862 to Paula Solórzano, one of the daughters of the wealthy merchant/landowner, Agapito Solórzano. But Agapito was having his own financial difficulties as a result of the Reform, having been forced to redeem almost 50,000 pesos on his haciendas of Coapa and Araparícuaro, and his daughter's relatively modest (6,772 pesos) inheritance was not enough to save her husband from the vortex of Juan de Dios's bankruptcy.[12]

Also severely damaged by Juan de Dios's failure was Josefa Gómez, who had married Santiago Sosa, the son of the wealthy merchant Vicente Sosa, in February 1858, six months before her father's death. Like her older brothers, Josefa and her new husband were very aggressive investors almost from the moment of Cayetano *padre*'s death. In November 1858 Santiago entered into an ill-fated agricultural partnership with the owner of the haciendas of Remedios and Uruétaro, in which Sosa lost most of his 20,000-peso investment. But he plunged ahead, renting the hacienda of Atapaneo in 1863 from the heirs of Gregorio Ceballos and agreeing to pay 38,500 pesos to their creditors, most of which was forced redemptions of ecclesiastical debts as a result of the Reform laws. By 1864 Sosa was in bankruptcy, and Josefa was forced to cede part of her inheritance, which she had invested in movables on the hacienda her husband had just rented, to one of his creditors. In the meantime Josefa had purchased the sugar ha-cienda of Tomendan from Agustín Solórzano in late 1859, but seven years later, stating that she could not pay interest or taxes on the hacienda, she took on a *refaccionario* (the firm of Ruiz y Erdozain, which also ran the huge hacienda of Guaracha, near Zamora). In 1874 she sold Tomendan to one of the partners, Ignacio Erdozain (by now married to Josefa's niece, Guadalupe Román Gómez), clearing 37,500 pesos, all that was left of her inheritance. What became of Josefa and her husband after they gave up Tomendan is unclear, but things do not seem to have gone well. An 1894 magazine article decried the Sosa family's demise, observing that Santiago's brother José María, once a fine poet, now was forced to live in a shack out-side of Morelia and beg, blind, for his food.[13]

Rivaling Juan de Dios, Cayetano, and Josefa for the dubious honor of the most vertiginous fall was their sister Pilar, whose husband experienced his own dramatic bankruptcy. Pilar had made what was on the surface of things the most glittering marriage of any of the Gómez children, to Francisco Román, whose inheritance — at 104,000 pesos — actually ex-ceeded hers. When Francisco's father, Fernando Román, died in 1851, two

of his sisters, Josefa and Francisca, divided the massive hacienda of La
Huerta in Apatzingán between them, and Francisco took over the mercantile branch of the family fortune, including the house under the *portales* in
which their store, Ciudad de París, was located. In 1859, just a year after
Cayetano Gómez's death, however, Francisco sold the store and bought out
his sisters' interests in La Huerta, paying them 100,000 pesos each. He later
claimed that he had so thoroughly devoted himself to agriculture that he
did not even maintain a retail outlet for selling the indigo, rice, sugar, corn,
and wheat from his own haciendas. This claim seems fairly clearly to have
been an attempt to keep the Tribunal de Comercio at bay after he began the
slide into bankruptcy, but the fact that he could make even a weak case for
having left commerce behind suggests that he had indeed given up the trade
in imported goods, especially clothing, in which his emporium had specialized before the Reform. Shortly afterwards Román began requesting loan
extensions at ever higher rates of interest. Under these circumstances it is
very difficult to understand the motivation behind his purchase in 1864
of the cereal- and chile-producing hacienda of Calvario, to the north of
Morelia — though it is worth reemphasizing that in this seemingly reckless
behavior he was not alone, since Juan de Dios, Juan Bautista, and Josefa
Gómez de Sosa had also charged ahead into new ventures even as the foundations of their inherited fortunes were crumbling. Calvario did generate
a stronger cash flow than La Huerta, which was located in distant
Apatzingán, and transporting goods to market during this period of dangerous roads was certainly easier from Calvario than from La Huerta. But it
still seems to have been ill-advised to take on an additional 90,000 pesos
in debt when Román's 100-odd creditors were already knocking at the door
to collect a staggering 724,511 pesos, which he owed them. In any event,
by March 1865 Román was officially bankrupt, and his assets were taken
over by his *concurso de acreedores*. In 1866 he was forced to cede his house
under the *portales*. In 1869 he ceded the hacienda of Calvario. In 1873
he ceded what was essentially her original half of La Huerta back to his
sister Francisca. Finally, in 1885, a year after Pilar's death, the *concurso*
on her husband turned over the ranchos of Agua Nueva, Las Joyas, Santa
Rita, and Marfil, all part of the former La Huerta, to the Román Gómez
children. The value of these ranchos, at 58,085 pesos, was all that remained
of Pilar's inheritance from her father and Francisco's from his.[14]

Two of the younger Gómez children were less than thoroughly successful, though they were not so flattened by the post-Reform depression as

were Juan de Dios Cayetano, Josefa, and Pilar. Little is known of Ignacio Gómez's career, beyond that he lost some, though perhaps not all, of his inheritance when he cosigned a note for Juan de Dios in 1864.[15] Teresa Gómez, like her sisters, married a socially prominent man, Dr. Francisco Menocal, but Menocal did not bring much by way of an inheritance of his own: his family had clung to the formerly great sugar hacienda of Araparícuaro for decades after 1810, only, finally, to be forced to cede it in 1851. After such a struggle with this property, it is a bit of a mystery why the couple used Teresa's inheritance to repurchase the hacienda in 1873. In any event, they had no better luck with it the second time around than they had the first; the record contains a long string of advance sales and loans taken out using the hacienda as collateral. In 1894 Teresa's heirs sold Araparícuaro for an amount that barely covered its debt.[16]

The youngest daughter, Trinidad, married Luis Sámano. The Sámano family was only modestly prosperous, but Luis, for reasons that remain a mystery, was one of the two heirs of Lic. Onofre Calvo Pintado (the other was Soledad Antia, an illegitimate daughter of Antonia Antia). When Calvo Pintado's estate was finally sorted out in 1865, and some 40,000 pesos in former ecclesiastical debts were redeemed, Luis took the hacienda of Guadalupe, in Tarímbaro, which he was able to hang on to for the rest of his life (he died in 1900). But he and Trinidad went through a period during which that outcome was in doubt. In 1876, in the wake of the bank-ruptcies of his brothers-in-law Juan de Dios and Cayetano, who owed him a combined 50,000 pesos, Luis voluntarily turned over his property to his creditors until his own debts were paid, some of them by property cession. After these measures were taken, however, he was able to regain the hacienda and his shares in the bullfight arena in Morelia, which provided the family with a respectable income. Trinidad, meanwhile, received the old family residence on the corner of the Portal de Matamoros and the *calle nacional* (formerly the camino real) in Juan de Dios's bankruptcy; here Trinidad and Luis, and later their daughter María and her family, lived until 1938, when they sold the home to a company that remodeled it for use as a hotel, today the Hotel Virrey de Mendoza.[17]

The most successful of Cayetano Gómez's daughters was María de Jésus, who married Dr. Luis Iturbide, an astute businessman and careful liberal politician (Maximilian's advisors described him as "excellent in all re-spects" despite the fact that he had refused to serve the empire and had resigned his post as *consejero departmental* with the French Intervention).

Iturbide was a member of a completely different branch of the family from Mexico's first emperor, but his father's decision to move the family from Durango to Valladolid in 1822 surely had to do with the fact that he expected their shared surname to be a plus in Agustín de Iturbide's hometown. Indeed, despite what appears to have been an almost complete lack of financial expectations, Luis's sisters also made good matches among Morelia's elite when they began to marry in the 1840s.

Like his brothers-in-law, Luis Iturbide had ambitious plans for his wife's inheritance, but the couple executed these plans somewhat more prudently than the other Gómez children and their spouses seem to have done. To begin with, unlike some of the others, who rushed to buy haciendas soon after their father died, Luis had already edged into hacienda ownership six years before Jesús came into her inheritance: in 1853 he had loaned María Loreto Caballero, who owned the small hacienda of La Noria in Tarímbaro, 12,126 pesos; to repay him she agreed to give him usufruct for five years and first option to purchase if she decided to sell. In 1856 he did buy the hacienda, probably for the amount of the 1853 loan. For three decades he added to the hacienda, bit by bit, as *terrenos* that he could afford to pay for on the spot became available; in 1893, when he sold La Noria to his son Felipe, he listed seventeen transactions, including the original 1856 purchase and several purchases/cessions from Juan de Dios Gómez, by means of which he had built the hacienda. Jesús, meanwhile, did purchase an hacienda — Quinceo — quickly, in 1859, but like La Noria it was a relatively modest property; moreover, when the Reform government demanded that she redeem the 24,816-pesos the hacienda owed to the church, Luis had the cash to do so, in full, in 1861. In short, Jesús and Luis survived the difficult transition associated with the death of her father in large part because they started with small investments and built on them, rather than purchasing an already huge and thriving hacienda and going into debt to do so. Another important factor contributing to the family's success may have been that Luis Iturbide, as a leader of the liberal movement in the state, was untouchable in a way that the politically neutral Juan de Dios Gómez was not. The difference between the fates of Jesús Gómez de Iturbide and most of her siblings is epitomized by the fact that when in 1868 her sister Pilar Gómez de Román was forced to cede the family's luxurious residence in the Portal de Iturbide, across from the cathedral, Jesús was able to buy it. When Jesús died in 1905, eleven years after she and Luis celebrated their *bodas de oro* in Mexico City, where they had moved a year earlier, this magnificent residence was sold to the Banco de Michoacán for a pricey 55,000 pesos.[18]

The eldest son, Lic. Juan Bautista Gómez, was the only other one of the children besides Jesús who came close to fulfilling the expectations that his parents' wealth inspired, though his was certainly not an easy road. In 1844 Juan Bautista married Jesús González Solórzano, who was descended from one very old Michoacano family (the Solórzanos) and one fairly old family (the González Movellan), but who possessed little in terms of capital assets. Some of her cousins on the Solórzano side, however, had a long history of sugar hacienda ownership and investment, and Juan Bautista seems more or less from the time of his marriage to have been "in training" under Ignacio Solórzano, who administered Cayetano Gómez's sugar hacienda of Taretan. Like Juan de Dios, Juan Bautista had to find a way to manage significant debt after his father died (he owed over 80,000 pesos to his siblings and 200,000 pesos to the Augustinians and later to the government from the purchase of Taretan). Though it is unlikely that he thought so at the time, he may have been fortunate in the long run that the Reform government forced him to redeem the debt to the Augustinians, because by 1867 he had reduced the mortgage on Taretan from 200,000 pesos to 37,174. It had cost him — as we have seen he had had to borrow considerable sums at high rates of interest, partly in order to comply with the laws of the Reform and partly to try to bail out his brother, and he was unable to hold on to the hacienda of Goleta that he had somewhat rashly purchased in 1859 — but in the end he emerged in a relatively strong financial position. Perhaps weary of the struggle, in 1870 he hired a commissioned administrator to manage his assets, which for the purposes of the *refacción* he estimated at 486,595 pesos, and he moved to Mexico City.[19]

The experience of the Gómez children in the wake of the Reform was an exaggerated version of the experience of other elites. While the rate of bankruptcy among the nine Gómez Alzúa children, at over 50 percent, was much higher than that of the general elite population, the difficulties that all of them endured, of adjusting from the relatively prosperous and certainly elite-friendly decade before the Reform to the economic depression of the post-Reform period, were typical. Many others, like the Gómez children, faced forced redemption of ecclesiastical debts, creditor-induced fragmention of their haciendas, subtle and sometimes not-so-subtle persecution at the hands of the Reform government, and heavy borrowing at high interest, and yet managed to survive with at least part of their fortunes intact.

Those who did avoid bankruptcy began, around the mid-1880s, to see the light at the end of the tunnel of the post-1860 depression, and many of their children would be the beneficiaries of an economic boom in the 1890s and 1900s that would make the period of midcentury prosperity pale by comparison.

CHAPTER SIX

Elites and the Reform: Economic Retreat and Political Marginalization, 1854–85

Santa Anna's harsh dictatorship, beginning in 1853, and his willingness to sell Mexican territory to the United States in the humiliating Gadsden Purchase, soon alienated even some of those who had supported his eleventh return to the presidency. By early 1854, across Mexico and in communities of exiles in the United States, liberals, ousted from power just a year earlier, were resurgent. They retook national power in 1855 under the banner of the Plan de Ayutla and in that year began to institute the thoroughgoing reforms advocated by many of their leaders for a decade.

These reforms had powerful and mainly negative short-term economic effects, but in the long term they produced at least some of the changes that liberals hoped would pave the way for increased investment in Mexico on the part of both domestic entrepreneurs and foreigners. For the wealthy the Reform and the wars it occasioned brought almost universal reverses of economic fortune, and in some cases financial ruin, but a majority managed to hang on to a core of assets that their children would see explode in value in the late Porfiriato.

As political actors, however, elites in the wake of the Reform lost ground that they were never truly to regain, or at least came to exercise power in much more oblique ways than before. Having practiced a largely nonideological politics in the first half of the century, they lacked the commitment and passion seemingly required by both liberalism and conservatism in the late

1850s and 1860s. Only after both the conservative party and the more radical representatives (especially Epitacio Huerta) of liberalism in Michoacán had been defeated in the late 1860s did a moderate form of liberalism, entirely acceptable to most elites, emerge triumphant. But even then the wealthy did not resume an active political role in the restored Republic or, for that matter, the Porfiriato; instead they were content to be courted on relevant issues by the moderate liberals, who increasingly resembled an almost professional caste of politicians.

Michoacán Around 1870

A traveler returning to Michoacán in 1870 after an earlier visit at midcentury would find the state and its capital city much changed — mainly, it must have seemed, for the worse. Although in retrospect it is easy to see that many of the changes were early hints of the massive transformations that Michoacán, and Mexico, would experience later in the century (and that most provincial elites would come to embrace with enthusiasm), at the moment they must have looked like evidence of an experiment in reformism gone terribly wrong.

The first thing a returning visitor would notice was the deterioration in the condition of the Mexico City-Morelia road. New bridges, new passes blasted through mountains, and good road maintenance had cut what in 1800 had been a six- or seven-day trip down to only three days by the early 1850s.[1] These improvements, most of which dated from the mid-to-late 1840s, had been inspired by the emerging realization that Michoacán urgently needed to be better integrated into national (and international) economic life, and they had been financed by a combination of private investment, user fees, and state subsidies, all made possible by the relative prosperity and stability of the period.

By 1870, however, diligence passengers had to endure predawn departures, late-night arrivals at the designated stopovers, and bone-rattling bumps even to make the trip in four days. One traveler described how the carriage "came down with a great thud each time the mules, straining themselves to the utmost, succeeded in dragging its unwieldy body over some apparently insuperable block of stone." After an agonizing climb, he continued, they were "whirled down the descent in a succession of wild bounds from rock to rock."[2] Clearly maintenance of the road, which had always been susceptible to washouts and rock slides during the rainy season, had been almost completely deferred during the nearly constant round of wars that had plagued the country since the mid-1850s.

Another difference between the 1850s and the 1870s was less obvious, though it was more far-reaching in its implications. This was the fact that many of the largest haciendas in the state had been divided into smaller, and sometimes much smaller, units. Because the main house at the hacienda of Tepetongo, on the border between Mexico and Michoacán, was in good repair, many exhausted travelers stopping there for the night would not guess that the vast hacienda that surrounded it had been split into seven parts that were soon to be sold to different buyers.[3] Even the more radical fragmentation of Juan de Dios Gómez's hacienda of San Bartolomé (see the prologue to this chapter), through which the diligence also passed, would probably have gone unnoticed by its passengers. And of course no casual traveler could have guessed that this trend toward fractionalization of large haciendas would continue through the 1870s and well into the 1880s.

No doubt returning visitors were aware that in 1870 there was less mercantile traffic sharing the roads with the carriage than there had been in the relatively bustling early 1850s. But it was only upon arrival in Morelia that the vague impression of commercial sluggishness must have come into clear focus. "Trade in Morelia there is none," wrote Bullock in 1865, and by 1870 the situation had grown much worse.[4] The Mexico City newspaper *El Siglo XIX* noted in September 1868 that in Morelia there was "as much peace and stability as one could want, but unfortunately, commerce, that life-giving force, is . . . as quiet as the political scene." The writer went on to paint a picture of warehouses full of goods for which there was no demand,

> merchants languishing at their desks with their pens behind their ears,
> occasionally recording in their account books the disastrous story of
> their profits and losses . . . shuttered stores, bankruptcy proceedings,
> desperate pleas for loan extensions, businesses run by the owners' credi-
> tors, protests of non-payment, falsified signatures on commercial docu-
> ments, porters sleeping on the street corners, muleteers praying in the
> cathedral.[5]

This was not much of an exaggeration. Many of the finest stores in the city were closed or up for sale: in just four years, between 1866 and 1869, at least eighteen mercantile establishments went out of business or began the process of liquidation.[6] For the nine for which precise figures of indebtedness are available, the accounts payable (but unpaid) totaled over 500,000 pesos;

it is likely, then, that Morelia's mercantile deficit to Mexico City and other commercial capitals (Colima, Tampico) was close to 1,000,000 pesos. If we add to these mercantile bankruptcies property cessions (both rural and urban), forced sales, and mercantile bankruptcies outside of Morelia, at least 80 individuals and/or companies — representing at least one-third of the state's wealthy families — lost a significant part of their fortunes during the 1860s.

Heightening the impression of decay created by this mercantile paralysis was the condition of the city's many churches, convents, and colleges, which had been neglected, abandoned, willfully destroyed, or converted haphazardly and incompletely to secular use. The cathedral had been stripped of what was estimated to be some 25,000 pounds of silver.[7] The church of the Third Order of Franciscans, located just to the south of the cemetery of San Francisco, had been torn down, as had the chapel of the Hospital of San Juan de Dios.[8] The seminary, across from the cathedral, had been closed and the building occupied by the state government.[9] The tithe offices and warehouses had been sold to a German investor who, somewhat optimistically in light of the economic collapse, had begun to convert them to a hotel.[10] Many convents were being used as barracks: Santa Catarina, on the *calle nacional*, San Agustín, El Carmen, La Merced.[11] Santa Teresa also served as a barracks for several years, until in 1869 it became a women's jail and a men's hospice, while the convent of Las Rosas became a women's hospice.[12] The convent of San Francisco was acquired by a Belgian who gave part of it over to a masonic lodge, a move which so infuriated some of the pious that in 1871 they rioted for two days in protest.[13] The block of buildings formerly occupied by the Juaninos and their Hospital de San Juan, just across from the cathedral, was now the site of various warehouses and mercantile establishments, an iron foundry, and a steam-powered mill, and the new state-run public hospital had been temporarily housed well out of town in the convent of San Diego. It was later moved to the convent of Capuchinas in 1867.[14]

Because these ecclesiastical structures and properties were among the most prominent features of the city's architecture, their disrepair, combined with the obvious slackness in trade, might have made for a picture of pervasive inactivity had it not been for the fact that both local and state governments were forging ahead, where funds permitted, in the long-interrupted project of remaking Morelia in the image of a progressive, secular city. Thus, alongside the deteriorating churches and convents, there were numerous ongoing construction projects. Six new city streets — still raw, unpaved, and largely unimproved in 1870 — had been cut through the former gardens and orchards of the convents of San Agustín, San Francisco, Santa Catarina, and El Carmen. Along some of these streets house lots had been distributed, and new houses and other structures were going up. Félix Alva's "Hippodrome," for example, a large wooden structure with a conical roof in which popular theatrical productions and cockfights were held, was built along the *calle nueva de San Agustín*, a street cut through the convent's orchard, which the Augustinians, anticipating expropriation, had sold to the *ayuntamiento* in 1856.[15] House lots along the *calle del Tapón*, which bisected the former *huerta* of San Francisco, were sold in 1859 under protest from the Franciscans.[16] In 1861 eight lots in a new block created by the *calle nueva de Monjas*, which ran north from the *calle nacional* through the orchard of Santa Catarina, were distributed, mainly to liberal war heroes.[17] New streets also crisscrossed the *bosque* of San Pedro, which had been acquired by the city government from the Indians of the *barrio* of San Pedro, and some 26 lots were given out to individuals who promised to build a "solid house in good taste" that was, in the spirit of democratic forthrightness, open to public view, and not hidden behind high walls.[18]

Later, in 1868, a public debate (which one historian calls an early sally in the Franco-Prussian war) was carried on between Othon Welda, baron of Brackel (Prussia) and Guillermo Wodon, baron of Sorinne (Belgium), over the manner in which the rest of the San Pedro forest should be reformed. Welda accused Wodon of presenting a plan that was "out-of-date" and "derivative of Versailles," and argued instead for a more "modern" and "tasteful" style of landscape architecture after the English Victorian model. Despite this criticism, Wodon's project won the approval of the *ayuntamiento*, but all that seems to have been accomplished by 1870 was the construction of two isolated *glorietas*, one a low, grassy hill planted in flowers and surrounded by seven stone pedestals on which additional flowers could be placed on holidays, and the other a small rose garden with a "rustic" fountain and a spot for a statue of America, yet to arrive.[19]

Several major construction projects were initiated by the *ayuntamiento* but had to be suspended for lack of funds. A new bridge, meant to complement the long-awaited drainage of the marshlands to the north of the city (which was itself to be accomplished by diverting the Río Grande), was only partly complete when the whole project was put aside in the early 1870s.[20] In 1869 an ambitious reconstruction of the Colegio de San Nicolás, which was a shambles after more than three years of use during the French occupation as a barracks, was called off, apparently after the job had been partially concluded using stones and other materials from the pile of rubble that used to be the church of the Third Order.[21] Material from this church was also used to carry out the only major construction project that was actually completed by 1870: the reedification of the city theater, now called the Teatro Ocampo, modeled by its Polish architect after the Teatro de la Concordia in Venice.[22] Other projects never got much past the drawing board, including street paving (to eliminate the huge potholes in which filthy water collected), new systems of garbage collection and sewage disposal, prison reform (the new penitentiary building, begun in the 1850s, had never been finished), and a new water supply to supplement or, better yet, replace the old aqueduct.[23] Besides the Teatro Ocampo, the only government initiative that seems to have been more or less fully realized was a program of tree planting along the *calle nacional*, the *calzadas*, and the *plazas*.[24] The 1868 *ayuntamiento* put in some new gaslights, but many of these were destroyed in the 1871 *cristero* riot.[25]

A similar pattern of progress frustrated by penury obtained where the state government was concerned. Only a few kilometers of a proposed road from Morelia to Colima were completed, as were about 1,000 meters of the long-anticipated *calzada* over shallow Lake Cuitzeo, which would have greatly lowered freight costs between Michoacán and markets in Guanajuato and Zacatecas and Durango.[26] A project to dredge and widen the Balsas River never got past the planning stage, though it effectively prevented governor Justo Mendoza from considering an 1868 proposal by an Englishman, Edmund Stephenson (whose pushy insistence apparently annoyed Mendoza), to build a railroad that would have connected northern Mexico to the Pacific coast through Michoacán and thus, finally, have provided an inexpensive means of transporting the highly commercial products of the *tierra caliente* to broader markets.[27]

The contrast between the half-finished projects initiated by the reformist state and city governments, and the half-destroyed buildings formerly used by the church, was probably less apparent at the time than it is in the telling. Both contributed to an overall impression of instability, unease, transition — perhaps because they were both manifestations of the same process. Indeed, not only the crumbling ecclesiastical property and the overambitious government projects, but also the fragmented haciendas, the mercantile collapse, the spate of personal bankruptcies, even the bad roads, can be traced back to the particular nature of the Reform in Michoacán, and the particular nature of the resistance to it.

The Reform in Michoacán

All of the major laws of the 1856–57 Reform caused a furor in Michoacán: the creation of a civil registry for marriages, births, and deaths; the proclamation of religious tolerance; the *Ley Juárez*, which abolished most military and ecclesiastical privileges; the *Ley Iglesias*, which regulated sacramental fees; and the *Ley Lerdo*, which required corporations (including not only the church but also the city councils and Indian communities) to dispose of their real property. But it was the Lerdo law that had the most immediate impact. Decreed in June 1856, the law was already being applied in Michoacán by early July, and by the end of 1857 over 800,000 pesos worth of church-owned property, as well as most of the haciendas, ranchos, and *solares* owned by city councils and state agencies (e.g. the men's hospice), had been sold.[28] (Privatization of Indian community lands did not begin so quickly, in large part because dividing lands among villagers — as the earlier history of *repartimiento* clearly showed — was a cumbersome, controversial, and expensive process in the best of times, and in this case it was further delayed by the outbreak of civil war. In Morelia, only around 7,200 pesos worth of Indian lands were sold between 1856 and 1859.)[29]

Despite this massive property sell-off, the Lerdo law was less immediately disruptive than might be supposed. In the first place, the law merely accelerated an already well-established trend toward property divestment on the part of the church. Partly in anticipation of the law, and partly because the economic recovery beginning in the 1840s had made it possible to market property acquired in cession and foreclosure since the 1820s, the church had already sold off almost one million pesos worth of haciendas and houses between 1840 and 1856, more than was alienated in the two years after the 1856 Lerdo Law went into effect.[30]

Second, people who rented corporate properties had the first option to purchase them, and in Michoacán the vast majority took advantage of this provision of the law. Even most well-known conservatives — presumably at some psychic cost — participated in this phase of the Reform, perhaps having convinced themselves or having been convinced that they were safeguarding the property for the church in the expectation that the Lerdo law would eventually be overturned.[31] Since the sale price was determined by capitalizing rent at 6 percent, and since the whole price (less sales tax) could be taken as a mortgage at 6 percent interest, in effect nothing was changed except the technicalities of ownership. Thus, although there was a flood of properties

TABLE 6.1

Rural and Urban Property Sale Prices, 1850–84

	Average price of haciendas	Average price of houses sold in Morella
1850–54	42,600 (n = 25)	891 (n = 690)
1855–59	45,800 (n = 25)	823 (n = 676)
1860–64	40,650 (n = 31)	737 (n = 801)
1865–69	32,750 (n = 46)	574 (n = 1,013)
1870–74	26,200 (n = 29)	562 (n = 790)
1875–79	19,500 (n = 20)	408 (n = 939)
1880–84	31,500 (n = 46)	616 (n = 913)

SOURCES: ANM, AHPJ, AHCP, AHMM, AHMCR, ANCM, AGN.

onto the market, there were ready buyers for virtually all of them, and there was no immediate depression in property values (see Table 6.1).

In the third place, though the church suffered a serious blow to its cherished independence from the state, its material interests were not damaged much at all, in that it was well compensated for the expropriations. That is, it gave up real property but gained an equivalent amount of financial assets in the form of mortgages on its former properties. Indeed, Melchor Ocampo was unhappy with the extent to which the law actually left the church better off than before, because it still received the same income (now interest, instead of rent), but had no upkeep costs. "If their insolence and spirit of domination had not been superior to all economic consideration," he wrote, "the clergy would have accepted without a murmur the decrees that so benefited them."[32]

Beginning in 1859, however, the second, radical stage of the Reform entirely changed the relationships of economic power between church, state, and individual. Angered by the clergy's intransigence (including Pope Pius IX's bizarre threat to excommunicate anyone who swore allegiance to the 1857 Constitution), and desperately in need of funds literally to battle back after being expelled from Mexico City in 1858 by a conservative takeover, the liberal government took new steps to strip the church of its worldly goods and possessions, a course of action that "puros" like Melchor Ocampo had favored all along. New federal laws now mandated the nationalization of *all* church wealth.

This included, of course, property not already alienated under the Lerdo law.[33] In Morelia alone sales and adjudications of nationalized church property from 1859 forward amounted to over 400,000 pesos.[34] Roughly one-third of this was property used by the church in its day-to-day activities: convents, orchards, schools, the tithe offices, the hospital, the ecclesiastical prisons, and so on. The other two-thirds were income-producing properties (houses, *mesones*) that either had not been sold during the first stage of the Reform or had not been sold legally, that is, the sales had not been properly registered with the civil authorities. These properties passed into private hands in two ways. First, people could "denounce" a property as belonging to the church (or illegally belonging to another individual) and thereby gain the right to purchase it from the government for two-thirds of its appraised value. Alternatively, the government itself could assign or sell church property to its creditors or allies, often in repayment of debts or services rendered. Juan Bautista Espejo, for example, received the episcopal palace and jail in 1863 in repayment of a loan to the government of some 40,000 pesos (though Espejo had predictable difficulty realizing anything close to this amount — the jailhouse was eventually sold for 7,000 pesos, but not before his heirs ceded the palace back to the government in payment of accumulated property taxes.)[35]

Though the symbolic value of the closure of the convents and the government occupation of the seminary and the Hospital of San Juan de Dios was enormous, a far greater blow to the church's economic power during this second stage of the Reform was the expropriation of its financial assets, including the mortgages created under the Lerdo law. As it turned out, this legislation was also a blow to most property owners with ecclesiastical debts, since the financially strapped wartime government was not prepared to content itself, as the church had done for centuries, with the income provided by interest and gradual amortization. Nationalization meant that these debts were to be redeemed as soon as possible.

The alienation of church capital took three basic forms in Michoacán. First, debtors could transfer their ecclesiastical debts to a civil organization such as the city council, the Colegio de San Nicolás, the Fondo de Instrucción Primaria, or the public hospital, at a reduced interest rate (usually 3 percent). Second, they could redeem their ecclesiastical debts on very favorable terms, usually 10 percent down, with the balance to be paid (over a relatively short period of time, generally three to five years) in a typical combination of 30 percent cash and 70 percent government bonds.[36] Since bonds could be acquired in Michoacán, as elsewhere, at much less than face value (5 to 10 percent), an individual could usually redeem his or her ecclesiastical debts for less than 50 percent of their value, and sometimes for considerably less. If the debt supported a chaplaincy, disentailment usually required the debtor to pay half the value of the debt directly to the chaplain.

The third form of nationalization of capital assets went into effect when property owners could not or did not make arrangements to redeem or transfer their own debts. In these cases a second party was permitted to redeem the debts, on generally even easier terms than the owners themselves enjoyed (that is, rarely was more than a 10-percent down payment required, and the full balance was often payable in bonds). Having satisfied the government, this person then gained the right to collect both interest and principal from the original debtor. In 1859, for example, Félix López redeemed a 36,000-peso debt on the hacienda of Itzícuaro, which Juan Campero Calderón had contracted when he purchased it from the Augustinians in the first phase of the Reform. Because Calderón had neither redeemed nor transferred this debt, López was allowed to buy the mortgage from the government for 10 percent down, the balance to be paid in bonds within one year, almost certainly making his total cash outlay less than 7,000 pesos. Calderón would then, theoretically, have owed López the full 36,000 pesos, though often the individual who redeemed the debt agreed to cancel it for less than the face value of the mortgage, especially if he was not willing to go through the process of foreclosure.[37] If López agreed to accept in payment, say, 18,000 pesos (and the agreements usually cut the debts just about in half), he would still more than double his cash investment. In a variation on this theme, if an individual did not redeem his own debts, the government could adjudicate them to someone of its own choosing, as in the case of the 8,000 pesos in pious debts that were awarded to the daughter of General Ignacio Zaragoza.[38]

Short-term Effects of the Reform

All of these means of nationalization were designed with two purposes in mind, besides the obvious aim of disempowering the church. The first was to raise money for the liberal government quickly, money that was desperately needed to defeat the conservative armies and regain Mexico City. The second was to make the terms of the nationalization so palatable that even moderate liberals and conservatives who were squeamish about this frontal attack on the church might be willing to go along. The government succeeded only to a limited extent in attaining its first objective. Figures from the state treasury reports up to 1862 indicate that of slightly more than 3,000,000 pesos in church wealth nationalized during 1859, 1860, and 1861, the state realized in cash and promissory notes less than 1,000,000 pesos.[39]

We have already seen the lengths to which the government went to achieve its second goal. The terms of the nationalization in Michoacán had, at first glance, something for everyone. For the property owner with some cash with which to make a down payment, or who at least had someone from whom he could borrow that amount, direct redemption offered a means of unburdening property at a very low cost. For individuals without the ready resources to make a down payment, transferring their debts to a civil agency such as the hospital allowed them to pay about half the interest they had been paying to the church and gave them (they thought) at least five years to redeem, with the possibility that a more conciliatory future government might not require redemption at all.[40] Even the government's creditors received some payment for their loans and services; if it was not always as much as they were owed on paper, it was at least better *than* paper in an era when loaning money or offering one's services to any government was not always a voluntary act for which one could reasonably expect any compensation.

But there is every indication that despite the best intentions of lawmakers to soften the impact of replacing the lenient church with more demanding creditors, the second stage of the Reform would have had a very disruptive effect on the economy of Michoacán even if it had been executed in the most peaceful of times. Accompanied by a bitter and destructive civil war (1858–61), and followed by a long struggle against foreign occupiers (1862–67), it was devastating. For most property owners, especially under these circumstances, the requirement to redeem even a modest fraction of their ecclesiastical debts was no less burdensome than a similar requirement had been at the time of the 1804 Consolidation. As a result, despite the seemingly favorable terms of direct redemption, I have identified very few individuals who took advantage of them until they were absolutely compelled to do so. Instead, most debts were transferred to a civil organization, and those that were not were redeemed by second parties — often, if not invariably, liberal partisans, public servants, and military leaders. In Morelia the rights to collect well over one million pesos in ecclesiastical debts were adjudicated to second parties, some of whom made a business of not only redeeming debts but also foreclosing on the mortgaged properties when the original debtors did not pay up. Indeed, several of the bankruptcies and losses of assets during the 1860s and 1870s can be traced directly to the Reform.

Both poor and rich were affected, the more so because the 1856 Lerdo law had substantially increased the ranks of those who owed money to the church and other corporations, especially among the urban poor who had purchased their shacks and *cuartos* in the first stage of the Reform. María Epigmenia Landín, for example, was a widow who before 1856 had rented a plot of land from the city council, upon which she and her husband had constructed a hut where the family lived. When the Lerdo law gave them the opportunity to buy the plot, they did, agreeing to recognize its price of 75 pesos at 6 percent, or 4.50 pesos a year, the same amount as they had paid in rent. In stage two of the Reform, however, the 75-peso principal was redeemed by a second party, who then demanded it of the widow. She could not, of course, begin to come up with such a sum on her own and had to borrow it from yet a third party, whose demands she was even less able to meet. In 1869 she ceded the plot to her creditor, who paid her 10 pesos for the hut and built a few more like it, after which he sold the property in the same year for 250 pesos.[41]

Several elites who had purchased properties during the Lerdo phase of the Reform also lost them in the second stage, though in most cases the consequences were not as devastating as they were for the poor, who lost homes and lands they had rented (in some cases) for decades. Agustín Luna, for example, ceded the hacienda of Santa Rosalía, which he had acquired under the Lerdo law, because he was unable or unwilling to redeem its 22,000-peso debt, but he still died a wealthy man in 1876.[42] Similarly, Lic. Antonio del Moral lost the small hacienda of Coincho, which he had purchased in 1856, when Antonio Reynoso redeemed its 15,000-peso debt in 1859 and Moral refused to make payments to Reynoso, to whom the government adjudicated the hacienda soon thereafter. For Moral the hacienda of Coincho was a small loss that he could easily absorb; it was apparently more important to him to make a moral statement in favor of the church than to hang on to a property that he did not really need.[43] A much more significant blow was that levied by the 1867 auction of the ex-Augustinian hacienda of Huandacareo, which took place when its Lerdo purchaser could not redeem the debt he had originally transferred to the Hospital Civil. Isidro García Carrasquedo had rented Huandacareo for many years, and it was an important complement to his hacienda of San Isidro Ceniza, which bordered Huandacareo; the loss of one of their haciendas did not bankrupt the family, but it set them back considerably.[44]

Generally more painful were the effects of the Reform on families who had owned properties longer than the three to five years since the Lerdo law had come into effect; in fact, for several of them, the second stage of the Reform was a disaster. The hacienda of Irapeo had been in the Ruiz de Chávez family for generations when in 1861 the government demanded redemption of ecclesiastical debts that the family had earlier transferred to the Hospital Civil. They did not have the funds to comply, and two of the siblings were forced to immediately sell their shares in the hacienda to their sister Guadalupe, whose husband, Miguel Estrada, liberated the entire hacienda of debt "at great personal sacrifice," using 28,755 pesos of his own money. The widow of the fourth sibling, Dolores Quevedo de Chávez, was eventually forced to do the same (though not before Estrada initiated a lawsuit against her).[45] In another case the Patiño family had to surrender rental income from their hacienda of Guaparatío for seven years and seven months in order to repay General Porfirio García de León, who had redeemed the debts on Guaparatío; two years later they gave up and ceded the hacienda to the government, which then adjudicated it to García de León.[46] When the state government demanded that the conservative General José de Ugarte redeem the 28,675 pesos that his hacienda of Colegio owed the Hospital Civil, he did so by borrowing 9,000 pesos, which he agreed to repay with 1,000 *cargas* of wheat at 5.50 pesos and 1,400 *fanegas* of corn at 2.50 pesos. This meant that even if his crop had been bountiful enough to allow him to make the payment in commodities — which it evidently was not — he would have lost some 4,600 pesos in potential profits, since wheat was selling in the open market at that time at 8 pesos/*carga* and corn at 4 pesos/*fanega*. If he could not make payment in wheat and corn, according to the terms of the loan he was obligated for the 13,600 pesos that the creditor would have received in the market — the equivalent of a 50-percent interest rate. What role this burden played in Ugarte's financial troubles is not precisely clear, but, having rented it for most of the decade of the 1870s to one of his creditors at a well-below-market rate, his children sold the hacienda in 1879, stating that they were lucky to receive anything at all from the sale, since the hacienda's debts exceeded its value.[47]

The unsettling effects of the Reform, however, did not end at this swallowing up of the cash-poor of all income levels. It also initiated a drain of capital from the state, for many of the individuals who acquired church property or the rights to collect ecclesiastical debts owed by Michoacanos were not themselves residents of the state. The rents, interest, and principal that were

TABLE 6.2
Alienation of Corporate Wealth
Notarized in Morelia, 1856–80

Adjudications of capital		
In-state	823,000	(69%)
Out-of-state	377,000	(31%)
Total	1,200,000	
Adjudications of property[a]		
In-state	704,500	(63%)
Out-of-state	413,500	(37%)
Total	1,118,000	
Transfers to civil organizations		
In-state	950,000	(100%)
Out-of-state	0	
Total	950,000	
Grand totals:		
In-state	2,477,500	(76%)
Out-of-state	790,500	(24%)
Total	3,268,000	

SOURCES: ANM; Mexico, Secretaría de Hacienda,
Memoria . . . 1857; Bazant, *Alienation*.
[a]Includes property owned not only by the church but also
by the city council and by the state of Michoacán.

paid to these out-of-state residents like Amilcar Roncari, a U.S.-born Mexico City resident who alone redeemed 146,608 pesos on ten haciendas in eastern Michoacán, may have stayed within the Republic, but in few cases was it reinvested in Michoacán.[48] Table 6.2 summarizes the alienation of corporate wealth recorded in the capital and shows that by one means or another at least 24 percent fell into the hands of outsiders; for the whole state the proportion may have been closer to 30 percent.[49]

It is almost impossible, however, to separate the effects of the Reform pure and simple from the effects of the wars that the church and the conservative party waged to turn back the reformist project. Indeed, as we have seen, the second phase of the Reform came about in response to the first of these wars (though something like it would no doubt have superseded the halfway measures of the first phase under any circumstances), and the manner in which the second-phase laws were put into effect in Michoacán was directly related to the need to raise money to fight a war. Thus while the radical measures of the 1859 Reform precipitated some collapses of family fortunes, the wars exacerbated the Reform's depressive effect on commerce and property values and ended up causing far more business failures and bankruptcies than can be directly linked to the Reform. Similarly, while the Reform was responsible for some drain of capital out of the state, decapitalization of the regional economy was also an effect of the wars, as local capitalists and property owners were pressed to contribute a significant portion of their income to one side or the other, much of which left the state to pay for weapons, ammunition, and clothing.[50]

Forced loans against merchants were the primary means of raising funds quickly during the Three Years' War.[51] Four years later, during the French Intervention, when the liberals had only a roving seat of government, landowners became the easiest targets. Ignacio Solórzano, for example, the owner of the sugar hacienda of Tomendan, was forced to loan 4,211 pesos to the empire and 16,780 pesos to the republican armies, for which he was given receipts; much more, he noted, was simply extorted.[52] Gregorio Jiménez stated that 19,200 pesos worth of cattle on his rich hacienda of Villachuato (near Puruándiro) were consumed by the republican armies during the fight against the empire, 2,970 pesos in mules and 5,400 pesos in horses were commandeered, 9,000 pesos in maize for forage were taken, and 3,500 pesos in cash were handed over.[53] Bullock reported that the administrator of the hacienda of Guaracha, which he visited in 1865, was "periodically carried off by the Chinacos [republicans], and dragged about, until he [was] ransomed." He continued,

> This vicarious suffering on the part of his administrador is a great saving to the proprietor; for where they would ask 10,000 dollars for the ransom of the owner, they will let the administrador free for 1,000 . . . [though] after my departure, Don Carlos was carried off to the *Tierra Caliente*, and not released till he had paid a ransom of nearly 6,000 dollars.[54]

In sum, many of the short- and medium-term economic effects of the Reform were negative. By flooding the market with heavily mortgaged prop-

erty (in the first phase) and then selling the mortgages for less than 50 percent
of their value (in the second), the Reform contributed to a two-decade slump
in the prices of both rural and urban real estate after 1860 (see Table 6.1). By
allowing favored second parties to purchase ecclesiastical and municipal
mortgages in exchange for a small cash payment to the government, the
Reform was at least partially responsible for an unprecedented bankruptcy
rate in the 1860s and a very high rate in the 1870s. By diverting money to
out-of-state creditors it intensified a shortage of cash that seems to have been
a constant feature of nineteenth-century Michoacán.[55] And by eliminating the
church's admittedly inadequate lending function without putting anything in
its place (not until 1882, with the establishment of a Monte de Piedad in
Morelia, did Michoacán have another lending institution, and it was 1898
before the first bank opened in the state), the Reform contributed to very high
interest rates (consistently in the range of 12 to 24 percent until the turn of
the century), and made it extremely difficult for new property owners to
make the sort of productivity-enhancing investments that had been at the core
of the reformers' hopeful expectations.[56] Finally and perhaps most inevitably
(given the clerical hierarchy's arrogant intransigence), by attacking the
church — the nation's most entrenched institution, unparalleled in its ability
to arouse passion and emotion among both its defenders and its opponents —
the Reform touched off two decades of war, unrest, and political uncertainty.

These factors came together to generate a deep and lengthy economic depression that was in many ways similar to the post-1810 depression: in both,
property values fell, interest rates soared, commerce slowed, bankruptcies
skyrocketed. There were important differences, however. First, there seems to
have been a less striking and less enduring increase in commodity prices during the wars of the late 1850s and mid-1860s than during the insurgency and
the early 1820s, when extraordinarily high prices had helped make commerce
(which almost always involved speculation in agricultural commodities) very
profitable for those merchants who had not fled to Europe or at least to
Mexico City. Perhaps even more significant, it is clear that after the wars of
the Reform and Intervention were over, commodity prices fell to levels not
seen for decades and stayed low at least through the decade of the 1870s (see
Table 6.3).

In part this pattern of low commodity prices seems to owe to the second
difference between the post-1810 and the post-Reform depressions: in the latter, property destruction during the wars was not nearly as powerful a factor
as in the former. There was very little fighting in Michoacán during the Three

TABLE 6.3
Commodity Prices, 1810–84

	Maize (reales/fanega)	Wheat (pesos/carga)	Sugar (reales/arroba)
1810s	20	7.70	28 (n = 9)
1820s	11	6.30	23 (9)
1830s	11	5.60	20 (12)
1840s	12	5.50	15 (9)
1850–54	12	6.85	16 (4)
1855–59	10.5	5.25	17 (8)
1860–64	14	5.00	19 (29)
1865–69	16 (16)	6.90 (4)	17 (13)
1870–74	9.5	3.60	14.5 (16)
1875–79	12	5.20	12 (10)
1880–84	11	5.20	17 (16)

SOURCES: Sugar prices are from notarized contracts and inventories in the ANM, AHPJ, AHMM, AHCP. Maize and wheat prices are from tithe data (AHMCR), except for 1865–69, which is from contracts and inventories since there is no tithe data for these years. For 1790–1850, tithe data is from Morelia, Puruándiro, Maravatio, Zamora, Tacámbaro and other miscellaneous locations; for 1860–84, only data from Morelia were used.

Years' War (in fact, brigades from Michoacán, not being needed within the state, helped the liberal cause in other parts of the country), and while there were many skirmishes in Michoacán during the French Intervention, both sides seem to have resisted the sort of scorched-earth policies that were common during the insurgency in favor of keeping alive the productive capacity of haciendas, the better to be able to demand periodic loans and supplies. The republican armies, for example, demanded almost 5,000 pesos in 1865 and 1866 from Francisco Román's hacienda of La Huerta, but the cash flow generated during this same period amounted to almost 90,000 pesos.[57] As this case and many others suggest, agricultural production did not diminish, nor did distribution networks become disrupted enough for merchant-speculators to count on high prices to prevail over a relatively lengthy period. The wars of the late 1850s and 1860s did succeed, however, in cutting off supply sources of imported goods for merchants (whose numbers did not dwindle, as had happened in 1810), even as their demanding foreign creditors in Mexico

City and elsewhere (see chapter 5) put the screws to them to pay off their out-standing balances. The result was that the post-Reform depression was much harder on merchants than the post-1810 depression, with all its terrible con-sequences, had been; around two-thirds of the bankruptcies of the 1860s in-volved merchants, a rough inversion of the rate of merchant versus land-owner bankruptcy after 1810.

This does not mean, however, that landowners were immune to the effects of the post-Reform depression. They suffered not only from the fact that prices for what they produced were generally low (or were high only for brief and unpredictable periods), but also from the drop in the value of their rural and urban real estate, as the market struggled to absorb the large amounts of new property in circulation as a result of the Reform. Land and housing val-ues had plummeted after 1810, too, but it was mostly from a combination of property destruction and risk aversion, and not because of a sudden increase in the number of available properties. Moreover, as we have seen, just at the time that they had to contend with falling commodity and real estate prices, landowners either had to come up with extra cash to pay off their debts to the government (formerly to the church), or they had to find a way to fend off de-manding new creditors who had purchased their ex-ecclesiastical mortgages from the government.

But in the end the difficult adjustments to post-Reform realities brought about many of the results desired by the reformers, albeit neither as quickly nor as painlessly as they had hoped. Thirty years after the laws of the Reform went into effect the economy was more specialized, capital and property cir-culated more freely, land was more subdivided and less debt-burdened, and agriculture was probably at least marginally more profitable than before the Reform. These basic changes were crucial antecedents to the dramatic for-eign-investment-led economic boom of the late nineteenth and early twenti-eth centuries.

Long-term Effects of the Reform and the Wars of the Reform

THE STRUCTURE OF TRADE

Since the late colonial period, as we have seen, wealthy merchants in Morelia had had multiple functions: they purchased imported merchandise at trade fairs and in Jalapa, Acapulco, Mexico City, or, later, Tampico and Colima; they maintained at least one retail establishment in Valladolid/Morelia, where they offered more or less over-the-counter credit and small loans; they served as wholesalers for smaller merchants or hacienda storeowners located throughout the province, to whom they often sold merchandise on credit as a way of extending their net of influence; they advanced cash, supplies, and merchandise to hacendados; they purchased agricultural commodities on speculation and marketed them, often outside the province/state; and they sometimes provided minimal banking services, for example accepting deposits and paying interest on them, and clearing *libranzas* and other paper for a small fee. With independence many aspects of this system were altered, but its essential structure was not: Spanish merchants were replaced in Michoacán by young creoles and their Spanish suppliers by (mainly) non-Spanish Europeans, but the role of the large mercantile houses in Morelia remained much the same. By the late 1840s, as we see in chapter 5, there were signs of more thoroughgoing changes to come: Mexico City merchants were establishing direct connections to many small provincial merchants, and some Morelia merchants were abandoning trade in favor of agriculture. But at the time of the Reform the Morelia houses, if not as all-important as they had been in the past, were still key actors in regional commerce.

This diminishing but still significant regional dominance enjoyed by the large merchants of Morelia came to an end during, and in large part because of, the post-1860 depression. As small retailers with relatively low volumes of business, pressed by their panicky wholesale suppliers in Mexico City, started to fold in staggering numbers, they brought down with them the larger mercantile houses of Morelia to whom almost all of them were still heavily indebted. In ten detailed bankruptcy proceedings from the 1850s and 1860s Morelia creditors still held over 50 percent of the debt of the troubled enterprises (though two decades earlier the figure might well have been 90 percent or more). Each additional bankruptcy placed more pressure on the large houses, since virtually the same Morelia creditors were named in every proceeding.

In the end the entire system collapsed. Replacing it was a new structure of trade in which the role of foreign importer/wholesalers in Mexico City was far more important to trade in Michoacán than it had ever been, and the Morelia intermediary/wholesaler as a central feature of the trade network was practically eliminated. In ten commercial bankruptcy proceedings from 1870 to 1910 the presence of Morelia creditors was nominal, usually less than 5 percent, while Mexico City establishments held the vast majority of the provincial mercantile debt.

The growing importance of foreign-owned Mexico City firms was felt not only in terms of the structure of wholesale supply but also in the social composition of the retail merchant group in Morelia. In the 1850s not a single important merchant in Morelia had been born outside Mexico, and most were native Michoacanos. By the late 1860s foreigners were running several stores that were apparently branches of Mexico City retail establishments, for example, "Las Fábricas de Francia," "El Puerto de Liverpool," and "El Palacio de Cristal," though Mexican nationals still dominated retail trade. By 1874, however, four of the nine "principal" Morelia merchants were foreigners, and by the mid-1880s four of the five merchants specializing in apparel — the most lucrative field — were foreigners.[58]

None of this meant that Mexicans stopped selling imported goods. It was just that their function was now more or less purely retail. Among the store-owners most often mentioned by contemporaries as having well-stocked emporia in central locations around the Plaza Mayor in the late 1860s and 1870s, for example, were José María Infante, Benito Barroso, Ireneo Alva, Febronio Retana, Silviano Murillo, and Silvano Milanés, none of whom had any interest in agriculture either as landowners or as speculators. Though all had comfortable lifestyles, they were too far removed from the sources of supply for their profits to enable them to accumulate great wealth. Typically their estates at death included a respectable but not fabulous residence, store merchandise, and minor credits — in other words they were squarely middle class, not elite as we have defined it.[59]

In a slightly different category were Plácido Guerrero and Atanacio Mier. Guerrero owned the general store cum sewing machine agency "El Ferrocarril" in the 1870s, but in 1876 he also acquired one of the fractions of Juan de Diós Gómez's hacienda of San Bartolomé and parlayed it into a modest fortune.[60] Like Guerrero, Mier's wealth qualified him as a member of the lower ranks of the elite, though he did not really earn his fortune in retail sales: his family had figured among the lower economic elite for three generations. He used his 2,730-peso paternal inheritance, based mainly in his share of the hacienda of Camémbaro near Pátzcuaro, to set up a flourishing state-of-the-art pharmacy in the ground floor of their family residence in Morelia. When he retired in 1908 he sold the business to his sons for 36,000 pesos.[61]

The only truly wealthy, native-born retail merchants in Morelia after 1870 whose careers more or less replicated the late colonial and early post-independence pattern — in which successful retail merchants became Morelia wholesalers and then, relatively late in life, landowners — were the brothers Epifanio and Gabino Oseguera, Agustín Luna, and Ramón Ramírez. Having grown wealthy from over a decade of commodity speculation and sales in his Santa Clara store, Luna used his mercantile fortune to purchase the hacienda of Sinagua in 1852 for 34,288 pesos (it was worth almost 150,000 pesos when he died in 1876), although in a slight departure from the norm, he bought Sinagua three years *before* he opened his Morelia store.[62] In another twist on the typical career pattern of earlier generations, Ramón Ramírez, who opened "La Mina de Oro" in Morelia in 1862 when he was 23 years old, bought his first hacienda just a decade later; thus, although he did not sell the store until 1895, hacienda agriculture became the main focus of his energies at an unusually early age.[63]

Like Luna, the Oseguera brothers made their first fortunes in retail trade outside of Morelia (in their case, in Ario) before moving their base of operations to Morelia.[64] Despite the increasingly specialized nature of commerce in the capital, or perhaps in part because of it, it seems to have remained possible to accumulate substantial capital in retail trade in the smaller towns of the state. Indeed, virtually all of the native-born elites who got their start in retail trade after 1860 did so outside of Morelia: Rafael Ramírez, for example, in Puruándiro; Antonio Tena in Panindícuaro; José María Tena in Cuitzeo; Feliciano Vidales in Taretan; Francisco Camorlinga and Francisco Farías in Uruapan.[65] This is probably because in settings where there was less competition, merchants could charge their customers enough to give them the strong profits that the Morelia retailers could no longer command, so that they could absorb the relatively high prices that Mexico City merchants charged them. But even here the trend over time was for foreign retailers to gain market share and for the native-born to turn to other investments. After 1870 the proportion of the state's future-elite who started out as merchants dropped from over one quarter during the half-century after independence to around one in ten.[66]

THE STRUCTURE OF CREDIT

The demise of the large regional mercantile houses in Morelia meant more than just a change in the way that retailers were supplied with goods and credit. Other functions previously performed by the Morelia mercantile elite were distributed among more specialized businessmen. The 1870s, for exam-

ple, saw the emergence of the *casa de empeño*, a sort of pawnshop that offered small cash loans at scandalously high interest rates, sometimes as high
as 12.5 percent a month.[67] The public horror over these rates led to the establishment of the Monte de Piedad, which performed essentially the same
service, lending small amounts in Morelia beginning in 1881 at the "reasonable" annual rate of 12 percent, though this institution did not entirely sup-
plant the pawnshops.[68] In the 1870s several businessmen began to specialize
in clearing *libranzas* and lending larger sums than the *casas de empeño* did at
not-quite-so-high rates of interest: in Morelia, for example, there was the
Spaniard José Oruña, and in Maravatío, Leandro García.

The role that large merchants had once played in extending agricultural
credit and marketing hacienda production was substantially taken over by
still another group. Even before the collapse of the Morelia retail houses a
new class of speculators had begun to emerge, whose aim in business was not
to sell textiles and brandy and make loans to farmers on the side but to serve
more or less exclusively as middlemen between producers and the market.
Men like Francisco Grande, Manuel María Solórzano, Juan Basagoiti, and
Gustavo Gravenhorst — who were neither retailers nor landowners (at least
until much later in their careers) — handled huge volumes of sugar and grains
in the 1860s, 1870s, and early 1880s, sometimes acquired by means of advance purchases (when the hacendado needed working capital), and sometimes by means of on-site purchases of an hacendado's entire crop at the time
of harvest. Table 6.4 shows the rapid expansion of speculative purchases during the 1860s, a pattern that continued through the 1870s and 1880s.
Though commodity prices were relatively low for much of this time, most of
the speculators were able to wring profits out of seasonal price fluctuations
by warehousing commodities until they were out of season, then releasing
them on the market — a time-honored technique, honed during this period by
men who usually had no other important sources of income.[69]

This trend had some advantages for producers. For one thing, the supply
of agricultural credit was no longer inexorably linked to the unpredictable
and narrowly based retail trade, which had provided earlier generations of
merchants with much of their profit and hence much of the capital that hacendados could borrow. For another, since speculators made their profit on
volume, in order to gain access to an hacendado's entire crop they often had
to offer some enticements, usually a share of the profits above a certain
amount. Manuel María Solórzano, for example, loaned Octaviano Ortiz
15,000 pesos in 1873, which Ortiz was to pay with 10,000 *arrobas* of sugar

TABLE 6.4
Speculative Transactions in Morelia, 1800–1910

Date	Average number of transactions per year	Average annual peso volume
1800–10	1.8	14,400
1811–29	1.1	3,000
1830–39	4.9	8,200
1840–49	4.0	6,400
1850–59	3.3	9,600
1860–69	12.3	70,600
1870–79	7.9	37,200
1880–89	9.3	32,200
1890–99	3.4	18,200
1900–10	1.3	28,500

SOURCE: ANM.

at the low price of 12rr. But any profit over 3rr/*arroba* was to belong to Ortiz; in effect Solórzano had agreed to limit himself to a 25-percent profit, while assuming a considerable degree of risk (since the crop was not even harvested yet).[70]

The Reform seems, in the long run, to have had a positive effect on the levels of general lending. This was surely related to the fact that while in the short run the Reform triggered some bankruptcies and (with its accompanying wars) put the brakes on economic activity, ultimately the redemption of former ecclesiastical debts demanded by both government and second-party creditors forced capital to circulate more frequently than it had in the past, when the church had simply collected interest on its outstanding loans — even those that were long overdue — without pressure to amortize. As Table 6.5 shows, loan capital was available in Morelia throughout the 1860s, 1870s, and 1880s in *relative* abundance, at least compared to the post-1810 depression. Even at the nadir of the depression in the 1870s levels of lending were not much below those of the relatively prosperous early to mid-1850s.

By removing the church as a mortgageholder on the haciendas of Michoacán and replacing it with individual creditors, the reformers also smoothed the way for credits against haciendas or urban properties themselves to circulate, almost like *libranzas*: by the early 1880s notaries were reg-

TABLE 6.5
Loans Notarized in Morelia, 1800–84

Date	Amounts	Date	Amounts
1800–10	135,000	1850–55	105,000
1811–24	11,000	1856–59	39,000
1825–29	23,000	1860–64	158,000
1830–34	28,000	1865–69	140,000
1835–39	39,000	1870–74	93,000
1840–44	50,000	1875–79	84,000
1845–49	45,000	1880–84	140,000

SOURCE: ANM.
NOTE: Includes only loans and cash advances; does not include commercial credit (buyer pays later), cession of credits, liquidation of accounts, obligations assumed upon purchase of businesses or property, obligations to one's co-heirs as a result of estate division, subrogations, or protests of *libranzas*.

istering dozens of these transfers of credits (not included in Table 6.5), as the original creditor sold them to a third party who would then collect against the original debtor. This no doubt made for some anxiety on the part of indebted property owners, at least in the early stages of the phenomenon, since they had lost control over to whom they owed money. But in the end it made for an increased willingness to lend, because the potential lender knew that if he needed cash before the terms of the loan specified that it must be repaid, he could always sell the credit to someone else.

None of this is to say that capital was available in anything like sufficient amounts, a fact that was reflected in the continuing high interest rates. In a typical case, former-governor Epitacio Huerta borrowed 9,000 pesos from a Mexico City resident in 1879 and found himself unable to pay the standard 12-percent annual interest. When it looked in 1882 as if he might lose his hacienda because he could find no one who would loan him enough to cover the earlier debt, two Frenchmen living in Morelia offered Huerta 16,500 pesos at 2 percent a month.[71] In general, however, given the absence of banks (without which there was not much hope for a truly adequate supply of capital), the system of credit seems to have been somewhat sturdier than it had been earlier in the century.

AGRICULTURE

The Reform policies that forced capital to circulate more freely — directly, by government insistence on redemption of former ecclesiastical debts, and indirectly, by allowing second-party creditors to demand repayment of principal — also had a salutary effect on agriculture in the long run by reducing the debt burden of most haciendas. This was, of course, one of the fondest goals of Melchor Ocampo, who had consistently identified ecclesiastical mortgages, and not ecclesiastical landowning, as the most malevolent dimension of the church's strong economic role (see chapter 5). Even in the face of low commodity prices, the reduction in the amount of gross profit that had to be devoted to interest service meant that many hacendados, after they absorbed the initial blow of forced amortization, had more disposable income each year than before. This was income they could invest in improving their operations if given good reasons for doing so, for example broader markets and/or higher prices, both of which would be possible with a rail link to the rest of the Republic — another project of the reformers.

The reformers also hoped and expected that privatizing Indian community lands would increase agricultural productivity. In a certain sense they were right: though we may deplore the human cost of legislation leading to the loss of these lands, the liberals' complaints about their low productivity were probably on target more often than not. It was not, however, private ownership per se that would improve the situation (as liberal rhetoric had it), but private owners with access to capital for good seed, relatively sophisticated tools and equipment, irrigation systems, and other improvements — and these were not, in most cases, the original Indian *parcioneros*. More research on this subject would be welcome, but until that becomes available the classic example of a trade-off between productivity and community well-being in Michoacán remains Paul Friedrich's spare and powerful treatment of a massive drainage project near Pátzcuaro in the 1890s, which generated huge increases in the peso value of what the lands produced but whose effects on the small indigenous community of Naranja were disastrous.[72] (The other effect of the separation of indigenous peoples from their traditional lands — an increase in the wage labor supply and the concomitant lowering of wages — does not seem to have been an essential ingredient of capitalist growth in Michoacán, where there were rarely complaints about a lack of workers, even in the *tierra caliente*, where many of Friedrich's dispossessed Naranjeños went to work.)

The sale of church-owned haciendas to individuals probably had less direct effect on productivity than did the privatization of Indian lands. This was in part because there were too few of them to make much difference; in part because in most cases the church had already invested in basic irrigation facilities, fencing, and so on, so that the uses to which these haciendas were put under private ownership were not dramatically different than before; and in part because the renters of ecclesiastical haciendas generally had access to capital. Nevertheless, the value of some former church haciendas increased substantially. To the extent that something other than the general increase in land values in the late nineteenth century was responsible, however, it was less likely to have been the benefits of private ownership than the benefits of subdividing huge and inefficient properties into smaller units. This was a phenomenon that prevailed not only on some of the largest ecclesiastical properties but also on many privately owned estates: between 1860 and 1890 at least thirty-eight large haciendas in Michoacán were subdivided and sold to over three hundred individuals. Hacienda fractionalization offers a good illustration of the general rule that the Reform was intensely disruptive in the short run but stimulative in the long run.

In most cases in the late 1860s and 1870s fractionalization was made necessary by the economic downturn.[73] A spectacular example, of course, was the fragmentation of Juan de Dios Gómez's hacienda of San Bartolomé as a result of his bankruptcy, in which property worth over 580,000 pesos was distributed among some 30 people (see the prologue to this chapter). Equally dramatic was the dismemberment of the huge hacienda complex of Guaracha-Cojumatlán west of Zamora in 1861 and 1862, when its owner, Antonia Moreno, who had allegedly lost a fortune at cards, auctioned off Cojumatlán to some fifty bidders.[74] Similarly, the sprawling hacienda of Coapa, which in 1853 had been sold by the church to Agapito Solórzano for 201,000 pesos, was auctioned in 1877 to one of Solórzano's Mexico City creditors, Tirso Sáenz, for 190,000 pesos. Sáenz then divided the hacienda into four parts, most of whose different owners also spun off ranchos over the next decade or so.[75]

But most cases involved somewhat smaller haciendas and/or fewer buyers. In one of several subdivisions with a direct link to the Reform, Cristóbal Orozco was forced to sell two ranchos — for 14,000 pesos and 12,480 pesos — from the already once-divided hacienda of Zipimeo, because he could not redeem ex-ecclesiastical debts of almost 30,000 pesos. Subdivision allowed him to shift the vast majority of his ecclesiastical debts to these two ranchos and thereby to reduce his own debt to a manageable amount. His daughter and her sons (Antonio P., Manuel N., and José Alberto Carranza), saw the value of the remaining lands of the hacienda soar in the late Porfiriato.[76] In another case, Miguel Orozco and Amado Montaño, co-owners of the hacienda of Etúcuaro, began in 1862 to sell and cede ranchos belonging to the hacienda in order to pay their debts. One rancho was donated to Lic. Mariano Huarte in payment of 12,650 pesos they had owed him since 1854; another was sold for 8,236 pesos to Benigno Pérez Gil, three to Félix Alva for 10,000 pesos, and several more to José María Rodríguez for 16,000 pesos. The next year they ceded two more to pay debts of 2,300 pesos and 12,000 pesos. Even these measures did not entirely free the hacienda, however, and in 1870 Orozco was finally forced to turn over his half to Montaño. But here the bleeding stopped. Although the value of what remained of the original hacienda had not significantly increased by the time of Montaño's death in 1879, his heirs eventually reaped the benefits of the much-earlier subdivision, since they were able to hold on to the property until at least 1910. By that time its value had appreciated considerably.[77]

As these examples suggest, one of the most immediate benefits of fractionalization was to give hacienda owners a chance to resolve their debt problems without losing the entire estate, a process that was made easier — indeed, encouraged — by an 1857 law that specifically gave owners the right to subdivide both their property and the debts on that property.[78] Before the Reform, though it was certainly not unheard of for large estates to be split up, the church (as the main creditor on most haciendas) seems to have discouraged it, preferring to keep intact the estate that served as collateral for the loan. Since the church did not demand much of its borrowers, this system worked adequately in good times, but in bad times the result was that owners were often forced eventually to cede the entire property after years of nonpayment of interest built the debt to staggering proportions. This is, of course, precisely what happened during the 1820s and 1830s. But with the new law in effect, overburdened hacienda owners could and did save part of their haciendas by selling off nonessential ranchos. Later, in the 1880s, this strategy to avoid foreclosure would metamorphose into a strategy to raise capital that could be used to improve the core of the estate or to purchase expensive productivity-enhancing machinery.

Beginning in the mid-1880s some land speculators even made a business of buying up haciendas and subdividing them, an endeavor for which they were praised in the press, which claimed that the smaller units were "better cultivated and more productive [than the hacienda in its original incarnation] because they required less capital for effective exploitation."[79] Was it true that fragmentation led to greater productivity? Without focusing a research project specifically on this problem, it is difficult to establish unequivocally that the smaller units that resulted from the subdivision of huge estates were more productive or more profitable, or even that they appreciated in value faster than did undivided properties: while the value of virtually all of the subdivided properties did eventually increase substantially, this could be said of almost all rural properties in the state in the late Porfiriato. But logic suggests that in most cases the individual parts of formerly huge haciendas, administered separately, were more efficient than the whole had been. Among other things, while a few haciendas were divided into very small parts (e.g. the hacienda of San Juan de la Viña in Tacámbaro, from which 29 *terrenos* were sold for an average of just over 200 pesos each), in most cases the ranchos that were spun off were large enough, at an average value of 11,500 pesos, to give their owners most of the advantages of economies of scale, but not so large as to be unwieldy.[80]

Moreover, fragmentation had the effect of making land available to a group of—on the whole—highly motivated agricultural entrepreneurs. But because the post-1860 depression was not characterized by the same sort of collapse of old landowning families as had occurred during the post-1810 depression, nearly half of the purchasers of hacienda fragments were already part of the economic elite. Feliciano Vidales, for example, had already purchased three haciendas and had been ceded the formerly magnificent hacienda of La Parota in payment of a 5,000-peso debt by the time he bought a fraction of the ex-Augustinian hacienda of Taretan from Juan Bautista Gómez in 1881 for 25,000 pesos. In 1908 this rancho, now known as the hacienda of Tahuejo, was conservatively appraised at 200,000 pesos.[81] Cayetano Gómez's old partner, Ignacio Solórzano, purchased a chunk of Juan Bautista Gómez's Taretan for 32,000 pesos in 1880 and made it into a showplace for agricultural progress: his daughters sold what was by then known as the hacienda of Zirimícuaro for 328,000 pesos in 1910.[82] And the Errejon brothers—Juan de Dios, Ramón, Rafael, and Simón—who had inherited a modest hacienda in Indaparapeo from their father Antonio, each expanded their inherited tracts by purchasing parts of the adjoining hacienda of San Bartolomé.[83]

This pattern, in which a certain amount of upward social mobility was made possible by hacienda fragmentation without (in the main) completely displacing the original owners, was reinforced by the process of nationalization and privatization of corporate property during the Reform: here, too, new landowners were created without massive turnover among the extant class of owners, who under the Reform laws suffered financial reverses and loss of assets but in most cases not outright bankruptcy. Obviously not all purchasers of church and community properties were successful, but given the relatively easy terms under which they acquired these properties, many were. Juan Campero Calderón, for example, who had bought the hacienda of Itzícuaro from the Augustinians in 1856 and whose debt to the order was later redeemed by a second party, came through that difficult time with the hacienda intact. His sons not only held onto the hacienda and saw its value increase, but they became active in Morelia and state politics — in short, they were able to join the elite as a direct result of the Reform policies.[84] Perfecto Méndez Garibay, a small Zamora merchant, bought one of the many ranchos sold in 1856 by the city council in conformance with the Lerdo law and later traded it for the hacienda of Tamándaro, which, much improved, formed the core of his 56,000-peso estate at his death in 1897.[85] Antonio Alvarez took advantage of both newly available church and Indian community land, buying the hacienda of Pilón (Uruapan), formerly dedicated to a pious work, at auction from the government, and purchasing the adjoining rancho of Lagunita from the Indians of Apo; the resulting property rented for an impressive 4,000 pesos a year in 1885.[86]

Many of the "new" men who became a part of the elite as a direct result of the Reform laws were active liberal partisans. Indeed, it is fair to say that vigorous support of the Reform was almost a prerequisite for acquiring the properties that the Reform made available. Among the officeholders and military men who took advantage of legislation they had helped frame and defend was the governor during the second phase of the Reform, General Epitacio Huerta. The former Augustinian hacienda of Chucándiro, near Cuitzeo, had been purchased under the Lerdo law by its renter, Basilio Páramo, but because the sale was never approved by the civil authorities, Huerta was permitted by law to "denounce" the property in 1860, purchasing it for 74,000 pesos (mostly paid in bonds). In 1863 he bought section two of the hacienda of Bellasfuentes (where his family had been tenants), which was also nationalized during the Reform, at a value of 78,818 pesos. In the meantime he had acquired three church-owned houses in Morelia and formed a partnership with his comrade in arms, Mariano de Jesús Gordillo, to redeem ecclesiastical capitals on the hacienda of Botello (Gordillo later bought him out and assumed full ownership of the hacienda). He also had a less formal partnership with Manuel Cárdenas to redeem debts on large urban properties in Morelia.[87]

Huerta was perhaps the most brazen of the liberals to benefit personally from the Reform, but there were many others who did so also. Lic. Francisco W. González, later a confidante of Juárez and secretary to Gral. Nicolás Regules, followed Huerta's lead by denouncing the hacienda of Cuaracurio, which had been sold to its renter, Mariana Ortiz, in 1856; despite her protestations it was adjudicated to him in 1860.[88] Francisco Velarde's fabulous hacienda of Buenavista was seized and later acquired at auction by a liberal captain, José María Martínez Negrete.[89] Octaviano Ortiz, who published the liberal newspapers in Morelia, paid 15,000 pesos (again, mostly in bonds) to acquire the most prized piece of Morelia real estate made available by the Reform, the property of the Hospital of San Juan de Dios, which looked out onto the Plaza de San Juan and the cathedral; he also purchased an entire block in the Indian *barrio* of San Juan.[90] The hacienda of Bellasfuentes was divided into five sections and adjudicated to General Epitacio Huerta; General Porfirio García de León; Coronel José Guadalupe López; Luis G. Obregón, a Mexico City liberal; and the Macouzet brothers, who had loaned over 27,000 to the liberal cause.[91]

This does not mean that conservative sympathizers who purchased church property in the Lerdo stage of the Reform were universally unable to hold on to those properties. But the liberals in control of the state government often found ways to make property ownership for these individuals so trying that they gave up the struggle. They were made to jump through legal hoops in order to prove ownership and/or to register their purchases with the civil authorities, and they were forced to redeem their ecclesiastical debts as soon as the law allowed, either directly to the government or to favored individuals the government had allowed to denounce and redeem these debts. Of course, the government now wielded power over everyone who was formerly indebted to the church or who had purchased property that was formerly mortgaged to the church — not just conservatives — and in this sense, though it did not reap the financial windfall it had hoped for as a result of the Reform, it did substantially increase its economic power by taking on the church's former role of creditor and dispenser of fiduciary favors.

The Beginning of the End of the Post-Reform Depression

By the mid-1880s there were finally clear signs in Michoacán that the worst of the post-Reform economic collapse had passed. Hacienda prices rose from an average of 23,500 pesos in the 1870s to 31,400 pesos in the early 1880s, and the pace of sales almost doubled, increasing from under five a year to over nine. Hacienda rents rose in similar proportions, from 2,400 pesos a year in the 1870s to 2,800 pesos in the early 1880s, and here, too, the number of rental contracts each year just about doubled. Loans notarized in Morelia improved from an average of 88,500 pesos a year in the 1870s to 140,000 pesos in the early 1880s. Urban real estate prices went up about 30 percent. Corn prices stayed about the same, but the more commercial crops — wheat and sugar — both saw their prices rebound in the late 1870s and early 1880s.[92]

One family's experience from roughly 1840 to 1885 nicely illustrates the rhythms of change during this period. José María Domínguez had rented the hacienda of San Simón Cuiringuaro near Pátzcuaro for many years and had finally managed to save enough money to buy it in 1851, paying 20,000 pesos in cash and accepting ecclesiastical debts of over 27,700 pesos. But the laws of the Reform hit hard; by the time José María died in 1861 he had been required to redeem 17,300 pesos of the ecclesiastical debt, and he had had to borrow to do so; he died with 30,000 pesos in debts. His widow, Josefa Montaño, was forced to sell several ranchos from the hacienda in order to meet her creditors' demands, and to pay off the remainder of the debt the family had to make "enormous sacrifices and endure a multitude of difficulties . . . , vexations, and humiliations, including imprisonment . . . during the long period when war unsettled the country."[93]

In 1885, however, they began to "try to save" the hacienda, by which they meant that having paid off almost all of their debts they could now focus on rebuilding the property. Probably not coincidentally, even as the Domínguez family recorded their deposition, the rail link between Morelia and Pátzcuaro, which would finally provide them with inexpensive access to the world of exchange outside the state, was nearing completion. This may have been the single most important source of their cautious optimism. But another significant factor, no doubt, was that in 1885, for the first time in 25 years, a governor (elected in 1881) served out his full term in office, and a new governor had been elected who seemed capable not only of soothing, co-opting, or terrifying into submission the still-warring liberal factions in the state, but also of neutralizing (at least to a certain extent) the Catholic opposition. As a result of both the arrival of the railroad and the arrival of political stability, in 1885 Michoacán was poised to resume the economic expansion that had been interrupted but ultimately (for better or worse) put on a faster track by the Reform.

The Struggle to Define and Control the Reform: Politics from 1854 to 1885

The political history of Mexico during this period is cluttered and complex. A rebellion against Santa Anna's last dictatorship brought the liberals to power in 1855, and they presided over the first phase of the Reform in 1856 and the writing of a new constitution in 1857. But in 1858 conservatives managed to close down the congress and take over Mexico City. President Comonfort resigned, and the next in the line of succession to the presidency, Benito Juárez, escaped to the north and prepared to wage war to regain the capital city and the nation. This war, known as the War of the Reform or the Three Years' War, ended in liberal victory in 1861, but a year later Mexico was invaded by a French occupation force. Though initially turned back at the Battle of Puebla by the liberal army, the French remained in Mexico for five years, a period of more or less constant guerrilla warfare aimed at evicting the foreigners, deposing the emperor Maximilian, and restoring the republican system. Maximilian was defeated and executed in 1867, but it was almost fifteen years before Mexico clearly entered into a period of relative political stability and national consolidation. All the presidential elections before 1880 were bitterly contested, and there were numerous military challenges to the constitutionally ordained succession of power, including the Tuxtepec Rebellion, which brought Porfirio Díaz to the presidency in 1876.[94]

Political changes in Michoacán roughly paralleled this course of events at the national level, though here, unlike in most of the rest of the country, the liberals' control of state government was not seriously threatened from 1855 until the arrival of French troops in 1864. Once settled in, however, the French were relatively secure in their hold on the state. The roving liberal government was run on a shoestring, and republican guerrilla bands were not able to do much more than stage quick attacks on haciendas and isolated towns, only to withdraw after they had seized enough money or supplies to keep themselves going for a bit longer. In fact the empire was never really defeated in Michoacán; instead the imperial troops were withdrawn from the state in 1867 in order to support Maximilian's futile last stand at Querétaro.

After republican government was reestablished in 1867 the contest to control the state was waged for the most part at the ballot box and in the press, but the elections were extremely bitter and hard-fought, and they were punctuated by *cristero* riots (most notably in Morelia in 1871) and rebellions (between 1874 and 1875, in the center-western part of the state), as well as by challenges to national political figures centered elsewhere but with adherents in Michoacán. These challenges included the 1869 anti-Juárez rebellion that began in San Luis Potosí, and Porfirio Díaz's 1871 Plan de la Noria. Things did not calm much after the Tuxtepec Rebellion in 1876; by 1878 the struggle for power had already forced three Porfirian governors out of office.[95]

Over the long period from Ayutla (1854) to the beginning of Díaz's second term in office (1884), what constituted a "liberal" or a "conservative" or a "patriot" was redefined constantly and inconsistently, most notably (but far from exclusively) during the French Intervention, when the conservatives imported a liberal prince to rule the country. Beginning almost from the outbreak of the Ayutla Rebellion the infighting among groups all calling themselves "liberal" was endemic; it made the victory over Santa Anna more difficult than it should have been, given the widespread dissatisfaction with his regime; it consistently undermined the stability of the liberal governments beginning in 1858; it allowed the French to occupy the state with relative ease; and it dogged the governors of the state well into the 1880s, with one "liberal" governor forced out by a group of "liberal" congressmen as late as 1878.[96]

The differences among the feuding groups of liberals were partly ideological. That is, there were clearly some liberals who were more radical or "puro" than others: generally they were more intensely anticlerical (the defining ideological issue before the French Intervention), more wedded to a republican system of government (the defining issue during the Intervention), and less willing to compromise and less forgiving in victory (the defining issue after the restoration of the Republic) than the so-called moderates. Indeed, both the "puros" and the "moderados" seemed at times almost to ignore the genuinely reactionary (and not insignificant, even after 1867) remnants of the conservative party, which continued to fulminate against all liberals from the pages of the Catholic press, from the Catholic social associations, and (when they could get away with it) from the pulpits.[97]

But ideological differences alone do not account for all of the factionalism among liberals. Instead, from the early days of the Ayutla Rebellion, there were divisions within liberal ranks over what might be called political style or culture, some of which may have stemmed from personality differences, but most of which seem to have had at their core actual and constructed class differences between the urban, middle-class liberal party stalwarts and the rural, working-class men who formed and (mainly) headed the liberal army.

To illustrate the point we may begin with the ideology and social composition of the leadership of the revolution of Ayutla in Michoacán. Spearheading the movement against Santa Anna were middle-class (and a smattering of elite) politicians like Santos Degollado, Gregorio Ceballos, Miguel Silva, and Melchor Ocampo, who had been active politically since the mid-1840s. These men were all ideologically-correct liberals: their anticlericalism was beyond dispute, and their credentials had been reinforced over a decade or more of government service. They assumed, as we see in chapter 5, that the enactment of their program of education, privatization of corporate lands, and drastic curtailment of both ecclesiastical privilege and presence would eventually create allies among the rural poor — Indians, hacienda workers, owners of marginal ranchos, tenants, and sharecroppers — but they envisioned themselves, it is clear, as fully in control of the process of winning over the hearts and minds of the citizenry. Florencia Mallon characterizes the program of a similar group in Puebla as "in effect, a version of the white man's burden," and that seems an appropriate encapsulization of the Michoacán liberals' view of themselves in relation to the rest of the potential adherents to their cause.[98]

These lawyerly liberals (though Silva was a medical doctor and Degollado was a notary and an accountant, the vast majority of the urban liberals were *licenciados*) were confronted with a dilemma in 1853, then, when Santa Anna's last and harshest dictatorship made it necessary to mount a military — and not just an ideological or electoral — challenge to him. The situation demanded acceptance of allies from among the armed bands organized by sometimes opportunistic rural leaders, often rancheros or muleteers who had expertise with horses and weapons and had contacts and potential followers across a relatively wide geographical space. Many of these men had a strong commitment to at least some core liberal ideals, especially anticlericalism (though one has the clear sense that their anticlericalism was directed against priests more than against the principle of church property ownership, say, or against ecclesiastical birth registry). But they did not, could not, have the same commitment to the middle-class liberals' political style. This was a style that was verbally aggressive but not much given to dramatic action; it had been refined over decades of editorializing, speechifying, campaigning, debating, maneuvering, and meeting in committees, none of which had involved the largely poor and uneducated rural leaders.

The quintessential example of what Romero Flores calls the *soldado del pueblo* was Epitacio Huerta, a tenant on the hacienda of Bellasfuentes, a captain in a National Guard unit organized by his father (who had fought in the insurgency) in nearby Coeneo in response to the U.S. invasion of Mexico, and an early adherent to the Ayutla movement.[99] Ideologically, as he demonstrated during his first stint as state governor from 1858–61, he was as "pure" as any of the old liberal guard: among other things, he presided enthusiastically over a nationalization of church property that met all of Ocampo's standards of thoroughness. But there was no love lost between him, or others with similar backgrounds (Manuel García Pueblita, Porfirio García de León, Nicolás Romero, Rafael Rangel, Eutimio Pinzón, the Picazo brothers, Mariano de Jesús Gordillo), and the middle-class politician/intellectuals like Degollado, Ceballos, Ocampo, Silva, Justo Mendoza, or Rafael Carrillo. In fact, Silva and 25 others publicly registered their horror at the tactics of some of the Ayutla revolutionaries in October 1854:

> We judge the revolution not for its proclamations, but for its actions. . . . And what we see in Michoacán are bands of men, some having more principles than others, but all engaged in pillaging haciendas and pueblos [and] in scandalizing the citizenry. . . . We cannot approve of a rebellion that counts among its proselytizers criminals of every sort who steal, commit sacrilege, murder, arson, and other excesses.[100]

The gap between the political culture of the old liberal politicians and the new liberal *caudillos* was papered over long enough at the outbreak of the Three Years' War in 1858 for the state congress to turn over all executive, legislative, and judicial power to Huerta — who had emerged as the strongest of the military leaders within the state — thus creating a "legal dictatorship."[101] Huerta, for his part, later stated that he tried to surround himself with "persons who had previously figured in the liberal party, in order that they might enlighten me with their wisdom and ideas."[102] But things quickly degenerated. In mid-1859 Huerta seized a pretext to call for a new *jefe* to replace Degollado, now minister of war and commander-in-chief of the federal army, a move that infuriated Huerta's growing number of opponents and caused

them to accuse him of acting solely out of "personal ambition."[103] Also in
1859 several of the old liberals (Justo Mendoza, Pascual Ortiz, Manuel
Alvires) launched a newspaper, *La Constitución*, in opposition to Huerta's *La
Bandera Roja*.[104] These same men would later support their fellow *licenciado*,
Rafael Carrillo, against Huerta in the bitter 1861 election for governor.
Mendoza, along with Lic. Anselmo Argueta, and Cor. Manuel Menocal — obviously having second thoughts about the wisdom of granting Huerta unlimited power — also tried to reconvene the defunct state congress in 1859, an ef-
fort that resulted in Huerta's exiling them from the state.[105]

What had Huerta done to antagonize his ideological compatriots among
the middle-class, urban liberals? Partly the problem was the intersection between national events in 1858, which led to the state congress's panicky decision to dissolve itself and vest virtually all power in the governor, and the
personality of that governor: authoritarian, devious, and, to judge by the constant evocation of unnamed "enemies" in his 1861 *Memoria*, slightly para-
noid. That is, a man with dictatorial tendencies was given dictatorial pow-
ers — a recipe for offending even those who before Ayutla had argued in favor
of more executive power.

Huerta seemed almost to go out of his way to take actions that were
bound to be seen as arbitrary and excessive. His decision to strip the cathedral of its silver, for example, was criticized by a much wider population than
just the church and the conservatives, as he himself noted (rather proudly) in
his 1861 *Memoria*. Though he professed to be a believer and merely to want
to "purify" the church, many people saw his actions as going well beyond the
anticlerical to the sacrilegious, an important distinction for many liberals. At
the very least, many of them thought, his actions constituted a grotesque
abuse of power.[106] These accusations were hardly blunted by Huerta's boast
that he did not really need the silver to support the war effort; instead, he continued, he wanted to teach the church and the population at large a lesson in
how far he, as the "hand of authority," was willing to go to enact his program
of reform.[107] When the church refused to turn over the 90,000-peso loan that
Huerta demanded, and also refused to allow Cayetano Gómez to pay it on
the church's behalf, it played into Huerta's hands. Stationing troops all
around the cathedral and sending patrols into the streets to keep people in
their houses, his soldiers broke down the doors to the sacristy, and for the
next four to five days methodically removed the gold and silver objects used
to celebrate the mass, the silver crucifixes, the crown and nails from an image
of Our Lord of the Sacristy, the jewels adorning the Virgin de la Soledad, and

the silver plate covering the balustrades, pulpits, and choir grill, for which purpose Huerta had rounded up all the silversmiths in the city.[108]

This was not the style in which even the most vigorously anticlerical middle-class liberals would have gone about "teaching the church a lesson." But perhaps even more antagonizing to them was Huerta's decision to close down the seminary (where many of them including Melchor Ocampo, Luis Iturbide, Manuel Teodosio Alvires, Justo Mendoza, Rafael Carrillo, and Antonio Florentino Mercado had been educated) seven months after he had had the cathedral stripped.[109] Here, too, Huerta's actions were seen as overreaction at best, and at worst as antiliberal, in the sense that the liberal program had always been very pro-education. Though many liberals agreed that under the rectorship of the nationally famous conservatives Clemente de Jesús Munguía (1843–50) and Pelagio Antonio de Labastida (1850–58) the seminary had taken a conservative turn, and they were perfectly willing to deny individual seminary students their degrees, many were, as Huerta himself observed, strongly opposed to shutting down what they saw as one of the institutional "splendors" of the state.[110]

Why did Huerta behave in office in ways that, despite his lack of schooling and political experience, he must have known were bound to alienate his ideological allies? At the very least we can assume that he did not care, but it is more likely that he saw such antagonism as a positive advantage, not a liability: his efforts to construct a popular base for himself and for radical liberalism in a certain sense depended on seizing the mildly anti-elite rhetoric of the middle-class liberalism of the 1840s and early 1850s, and running with it.

A typical attempt to exaggerate the common-man roots of his liberalism, as opposed to those of the middle-class liberals, was his assault on the reputation of Santos Degollado, a man with whom Huerta was at first friendly, but whom he soon recognized as one of his chief rivals for the affections of the Michoacano public. In April 1861 Degollado finally decided to respond in print to accusations leveled by the Huertista press in Morelia that he was the lackey ("vergonzante tinterillo") of the richest family in Morelia, the Gómez clan, and that he had helped them to evade or at least deflect the effects of the laws of the Reform.[111] (See the prologue to this chapter for details of the case.) Clearly the "insults and slanders" of the Huertista newspapers (including a paper aimed at a working-class readership, *El Artesano Libre*) were intended to imply that while Huerta's radical liberalism treated the rich like any other citizens, the liberalism of the middle-class lawyers and politicians, however rigorously anticlerical and republican it might be, could not help making exceptions for the rich because of the close family ties and social relationships that bound them together. Indeed, even Degollado admitted this when he noted in his own defense that he had helped the Gómez brothers because their father, Cayetano, had helped his own family during the hard times of the Ayutla Rebellion.[112]

While he was in complete control of the state Huerta saw to it that the contest between the urban middle-class politicians and the largely uneducated military *caudillos* was conducted mainly behind the scenes; he resolved the problems that arose from active opposition to his regime by censoring, cowing, or exiling his opponents. But with the victory of the liberal armies in 1861 he had to find a way to triumph at the ballot box. The elections, which pitted Huerta against Lic. Rafael Carrillo for the governorship, were very closely fought, but Huerta came out the winner. Apparently he had succeeded in his effort to paint himself as the champion of the people, and his middle-class opponents as the friends of the "privileged classes."

Over the next couple of years the middle-class liberals became more and more desperate to regain their position; in early 1863 they even recruited one of Huerta's former military allies, General Manuel García Pueblita, to rebel against Huerta in Zitácuaro. President Benito Juárez, concerned that the split within the party had reached such a stage, and sympathetic to the middle-class liberals, appointed a new governor, Santiago Tapia, to replace the divisive Huerta. The anti-Huerta faction of the liberal party in Morelia thus won an important victory, and it was soon to win another: the French Intervention changed the balance of power in Michoacán in ways that eventually cleared the field for them to regain leadership of the party.

The liberal disarray made French victory in Michoacán relatively easy. Once the state was occupied, everyone, including the former military and political leaders of the liberal party, had to decide whether (one), to participate actively in the attempt to depose the French; or (two), to refuse to sign a pledge of allegiance to the empire and to retire from public life; or (three), to support and/or serve the empire. After the Republic was restored in 1867 most of those who had taken the third course of action were considered deeply suspect by all of those who had made other choices, though their sheer numbers made it impossible to completely ostracize or punish them — in Morelia alone almost 2,000 people had signed the act of allegiance.[113] Some of them, pointing to the fact that Maximilian was himself a liberal and in his visit to Morelia in 1864 had even come dressed as a *chinaco*, continued to call themselves "liberals" after 1867 and maintained that they had been so all along.

The men who took the first course of action — active loyalty to the republican cause — enjoyed, naturally, a superior moral position upon the fall of the empire. But during the occupation itself it was immensely difficult to hold this group together, since, as before, it was deeply heterogeneous, being composed of both middle-class politicians and military leaders with rough, rural backgrounds, who were often at odds with each other. Governor Juan B. Caamaño, for example, even went so far as to execute republican guerrillas who disobeyed his orders to cease their activities. (In one case that took on the dimensions of a popular myth, Caamaño ordered Refugio Salguero, who had attacked a Semana Santa procession in Zamora, to be shot, but Salguero managed to intoxicate the priest who came to give him last rites, and dressed in the priest's clothes to escape. The moral of the story — prissy liberal governor is less admirable than renegade folk hero — is clear.)[114] On the part of both politicians and *caudillos* there were numerous defections to the empire, including, late in the Intervention, that of Governor Caamaño.

But where the balance of power between the politicians and the *caudillos* before the Intervention had slightly favored the latter, after the Intervention the reverse was true, primarily because the most important popular/populist leader of the pre-Intervention period, Epitacio Huerta, had been captured at Puebla and imprisoned in France. This left Nicolás Regules, a Spaniard who did not seem to aspire to the sort of political prominence that Huerta craved, as the most important military leader in the state; his only competition was Vicente Riva Palacio, who operated in the eastern part of the state but whose main sphere of influence was the state of Mexico.

Even if he had not been absent from the scene, however, Huerta's support might well have begun to shift and diminish, as Juárez's profile in the national resistance movement increased. As we have seen, Juárez had already made one move against Huerta, replacing him as governor with Santiago Tapia in 1863; relations between the two deteriorated further when Huerta accused Juárez of doing less than his utmost to secure Huerta's (and other prisoners') release from imprisonment.[115] Especially from afar, Huerta could not easily criticize Juárez and also maintain his support within the state. As a result it wavered; some of his former supporters went over to Juárez (e.g. Lic. Francisco Wenceslao González); and at least two of them (Lic. Bruno Patiño and Lic. Antonio Rodríguez Gil) were compromised by agreeing to serve as Maximilian's emissaries in the emperor's last-ditch attempt to convince liberals in Michoacán to support him in return for his pledge to uphold the laws of the Reform.[116]

Thus, almost by default, the post-Intervention leadership of the liberal party fell to the middle-class *políticos*. Justo Mendoza, whom Huerta had exiled from the state eight years earlier, became governor in 1867, and seven *licenciados*, one doctor, and one merchant-industrialist were elected to the state assembly. After his release from prison Huerta was successfully marginalized; he did surface in 1869 when he joined an anti-Juárez *pronunciamiento* centered in San Luis Potosí (a move that cost him over 40,000 pesos when the Juárez government seized every last chicken on his hacienda of Chucándiro), and again in 1871 when he seconded Díaz's Plan de la Noria, but he was never again a force to be reckoned with in Michoacán politics.[117]

With Huerta out of the picture, Mendoza, who had opposed Huerta as being too extreme, became the leader of the "radicals," though "radicalism" now implied not so much anticlericalism — after all, the major anticlerical reforms proposed in the 1850s were already largely realized, thanks, ironically, to Huerta — as an unforgiving stance toward former collaborators.[118] Mendoza's chief task in the early days of his administration was, in fact, to be sure that all of his appointees were "immaculate" republicans and patriots.[119] Meanwhile the "moderates," who rallied in 1867 and 1871 behind Bruno Patiño, advocated a more conciliatory stance toward those who had not actively worked to restore the Republic, and even in some cases toward those who had signed the act of adhesion to the empire.[120] They pointed out that many of those who served the empire had done so very reluctantly (e.g. Lic. Antonio del Moral, who tried four times to resign the position to which Maximilian appointed him), and that the liberal Maximilian had disdained to employ genuinely conservative men (e.g., José de Ugarte, whom Maximilian's advisors criticized for lacking the necessary "spirit of moderation and impartiality" and for having seized "arbitrarily and illegally" former clerical properties from those to whom they had been adjudicated).[121]

But the most important point for our purposes is that the split within the liberal party after 1867 no longer had a significant class dimension; both "radicals" and "moderates" drew support from essentially the same middle/upper-class social strata. Put another way, there was no focal point for a genuinely popular, non-middle-class liberalism in Michoacán after 1867. Popular activism came instead to be oriented toward a restoration of some measure of the church's power or at least visibility, most notably during the *cristero* riots in Morelia in 1871 and the *cristero* uprisings of 1874–75, which the consistently anticlerical Huerta helped to put down. Porfirio Díaz's

Tuxtepec rebels in 1876 briefly linked up with this *cristero* activism; in fact Huerta, who was the Tuxtepecanos' first choice as governor of the state, was removed from office by Díaz once he found out that Huerta had helped to defeat the *cristeros*. But they were not a strong enough force in the state to force Díaz to take them into account once he had consolidated his hold on national power; instead Díaz focused his energies on finding ways to neutralize the internecine feuding within the liberal party, for it was this factionalism that most threatened the stability of his regime in Michoacán.

By 1890 he had more or less accomplished this feat, mainly by means of shrewd appointments to the governorship. His strategy was to allow different factions relative freedom of press and speech to state their positions and identify their candidates, and then to appoint someone else — in two cases, from outside the state — whose instructions were to co-opt and placate these positions and individuals insofar as possible. The selection of a candidate to replace Pudenciano Dorantes as governor in 1885 was a classic example of this approach. The "radical" liberals proposed for the governorship Coronel José Vicente Villada, who had been a guerrilla warrior against the Intervention, while Dorantes favored as his successor Lic. Manuel de Estrada, a very controversial choice because of Estrada's support of the empire.[122] Tensions ran even higher after the assassination of Luis González, the editor of the newspaper *El Explorador*, which had opposed both Dorantes and Díaz; González was the nephew of Lic. Francisco W. González, an old liberal and Juarista, and the friend of many others, including Manuel Alvires González, Angel Padilla, and Gabino Ortiz.[123] Díaz settled matters by appointing General Mariano Jiménez, an old friend from Oaxaca. Jiménez successfully courted the *rojos*, appointing some of them to plummy offices (Lic. Pascual Ortiz to the Regency of the Colegio de San Nicolás, Félix Alva to the *prefectura* of Morelia, Lic. Macedonio Gómez to a chair at San Nicolás, Lic. Francisco W. González to Promotor Fiscal).[124] Meanwhile he consolidated his army support by naming soldiers "accustomed to military campaign" to be prefects in most of the state's districts, while at the same time reorganizing the system of *acordadas* to provide "vigilance" and bring order to the disorderly countryside.[125] By the end of Jiménez's term in office *La Libertad* observed that many people who had earlier disagreed with the government were now part of it, and although it was partly wishful thinking on the part of this semi-official newspaper to boast that "opposition to the government does not exist in Michoacán," in a relative sense the statement was true.[126]

Elites in Politics

Most wealthy Michoacanos stayed on the political sidelines during the period before the restoration of the Republic. I have identified only about 25 economically elite families with ties to the liberals in the 1850s, and far fewer held leadership roles. This does not mean, however, that most elites were conservatives; in fact even fewer wealthy Michoacanos were closely identified with the conservatives during these years than with the liberals, and when they were it was as likely to be because of family ties to the church hierarchy as because of genuine enthusiasm for conservative ideology. Instead, as is argued in chapter 5, elites found parts of both the liberal and the conservative agendas attractive — the conservative defense of the church appealed to many, but so did the liberals' promises to promote agricultural progress by all means possible, to abolish the landholding village, and to promote education. The vaguely anti-elite rhetoric of the liberals in the 1840s and early 1850s may have alienated some elites, but so, too, did the shrill and implicitly unpatriotic diatribes of the church. All this meant that in Michoacán a significant proportion of the wealthy were ambivalent about liberalism; they would not lead the midcentury charge to bring about dramatic social reforms, especially since they were generally prospering under existing conditions, but under the right circumstances they could probably have been expected eventually to accept them.

Elite tolerance for liberalism was severely tested during the years that the Reform was actually enacted, however. Even though many elites welcomed the Ayutla challenge to the stifling Santa Anna dictatorship in 1854, the *soldado del pueblo* leadership of the rebellion may have given them pause, and it is fair to suppose that the vividly uncompromising nature of Huerta's anticlericalism — convents emptied, nuns figuratively turned out into the street, churches torn down, sacred objects seized — was widely deplored. Moreover, the short-term economic consequences of the Reform, as we have seen, did nothing to encourage elites to link their fortunes to the liberal party: the Reform profoundly disrupted the state economy, and it dealt a serious blow to the fortunes of many elites by forcing them to redeem their ecclesiastical debts. From 1858 until the French Intervention, then, the period when liberalism in Michoacán was shaped and defined by Huerta, elites previously sympathetic to liberalism backed away, some of them even turning in 1864, along with conservatives, to Maximilian. The refined Hapsburg prince was a moderate whom they could easily envision as a sort of Mexican Pedro II, especially if he could be trusted to follow through on his promise during his visit to Morelia to replace most of the foreigners in his government with Mexican nationals. From the list of Morelia adherents to the empire alone, I have identified 75 wealthy individuals, representing about 60 families, around a quarter of whom had been loosely associated with liberalism before the Intervention: they included Angel and Luis Alzúa, whose uncle Manuel had been named to the first Reform cabinet after the fall of Santa Anna in 1855; Manuel Cárdenas, who had only three years earlier been elected to the state congress as a liberal; Antonio and Pedro Gutiérrez, whose brother-in-law, Antonio Balbuena, Ocampo had named as his executor; Lic. Fermín Ortega, who had been a liberal activist in the 1840s; and Cristóbal Orozco, who had served the liberal cause for years but went over to the conservatives (allegedly because he needed his conservative grandfather, José María Torres, owner of the hacienda of Zipimeo, to loan him money to cover a gambling debt).[127]

Roughly another quarter of the elite signers of the pledge of allegiance to the empire were well-known, longtime conservatives, among them the Estrada brothers (Manuel, Vicente, and Miguel) and several of their children, owners of multiple haciendas around Morelia; Atanacio, Justo, Martín, Luis, and Jesús Mier, whose family owned an hacienda in Pátzcuaro; Antonio and José María Plancarte, who owned haciendas in Zamora and whose uncle was the famous conservative bishop, Pelagio Antonio de Labastida y Dávalos; and Francisco Román, whose sister, Francisca, was a lady-in-waiting to Carlota and entertained and housed Maximilian when he visited Morelia. (Unrepentant at the end of her life, when Francisca listed her assets she placed special emphasis on a portrait of the emperor Maximilian, which she left to her nephew Salvador).[128] The depth of the other half of the elite signers' devotion to the conservative cause is unknown, but for many the decision to sign must have been as much pragmatic as principled: they did not expect the ragtag republican armies of Michoacán to be able to oust the numerous and disciplined French army; they were not sure that they trusted those republicans — were they somehow to win — not to repeat what were from their point of view the disasters of the Huerta years; and they feared that if they did not sign they might be punished.[129]

By 1867, however, it appears that a majority of elites in Michoacán was prepared once again to accept liberalism. The reasons have everything to do with Epitacio Huerta's brief, blazing hold on power in the state. Huerta's inflexibility gave rise to vigorous opposition and ultimately to his marginalization at the hands of the middle-class liberals. Nonetheless, both his blinderson rigor in enforcing the laws of the Reform *and* his subsequent marginalization were necessary components of the elites' slow resolution of their ambivalence toward liberalism and their eventual embrace of it. It was precisely Huerta's scorched-earth attack on the church that made it impossible for conservatives during the Intervention to restore the status quo ante, even if the liberal Maximilian had consented to such an effort (which he did not). At the same time, Huerta's extreme behavior in that effort made the middle-class liberals, even when they called themselves "radicals," seem reasonable and acceptable. When these "radicals" took power in 1867 the choice for all but the handful of implacably conservative elites was between these "radicals" and the equally acceptable middle-class "moderates." Both of the true extremes — Huerta's popular liberalism and the conservatives' reactionary clericalism — had been effectively eliminated.

In power, the liberals made it even easier for the wealthy to accept liberalism by focusing on relatively uncontroversial, indeed greatly desirable projects from the elite point of view. Significantly, Justo Mendoza's first "state of the state" report to the legislature in 1869 contained only one page of discussion of church-state relations — in which he pointed out that he had ordered government officials "not to give the slightest cause for complaint from the religious communities, always to respect religious sentiment, and to allow expressions of that sentiment as long as it does not subvert public order or third-party rights."[130] But he devoted over eleven pages to proposals for "material improvements," including the opening of the Pacific port of Maruata, the dredging of the Río Balsas, and the telegraph. He also dwelled lovingly on his modest industrial policy, which led to the establishment of several textile factories in the state (in the process turning his back on his fellow liberals' pre-Reform antagonism to any sort of protection or special treatment for industrialists), on his plans for lowering taxes, and on the crying need to abolish "these strange conglomerations that call themselves [Indian] communities," which he planned to make a top priority of his administration.[131] Though the pitiful state of the treasury prevented most of these projects from being completed expeditiously, they at least advertised the fact that liberalism was more than anticlericalism. Even the brief anticlerical interlude (1873) during Sebastián Lerdo de Tejada's presidency, when some of the laws of the Reform not already incorporated into the 1857 Constitution were elevated to constitutional status (among others, full separation of church and state and complete freedom of religion, moves that were supported by the *lerdista* liberals of Michoacán: Rafael Carrillo, Justo Mendoza, Luis Iturbide, Manuel and Aristeo Mercado), did not dramatically hurt the liberals' efforts to woo elites. While some elites (Francisco Menocal, Herculano Ibarrola) came out strongly against Lerdo's actions, the rural *cristeros* were even more outraged, and they expressed their anger in uprisings that included attacks on haciendas. This in turn caused some elites who might otherwise have strongly opposed Lerdo's actions to mute their criticism, not wishing to ally themselves with property-destroying popular groups. When liberal armies put down the *cristeros*, hacendados even owed a certain debt to them.

By 1876, when Porfirio Díaz mounted his second and successful bid for the presidency, elites in Michoacán were well on the way to accepting the sort of "order and progress" liberalism that Díaz espoused, and with which they were already familiar. In fact, Díaz's particular political genius was not that he satisfied most elites — who generally prospered during his regime, especially after 1890 — nor even that he found ways to manage and defuse the feuds within the ranks of liberal politicians (as noted above), but that he was able to secure the acquiescence of many of the urban and rural poor. The key was his relaxed posture toward the church, a position that is sometimes depicted as pandering to the church but that was in truth a means to a much more important end: putting an end to the rural unrest that had been stirred up by priests and inspired by liberal anticlericalism. In short, he managed to re-create the multiclass support last enjoyed in Mexico by Iturbide at the time of independence, though Díaz's three guarantees — Order, Progress, and Religion — were more symbolically potent, more realistic, and easier to keep in balance than Iturbide's. And he managed to keep them in rough balance for at least 25 of his 35 years in office.

Epilogue:
The Porfirian Boom and the Patriarch's Great-Great Grandchildren

The generation to which Cayetano Gómez and Dolores Alzúa's grandchildren belonged was deeply affected by the post-Reform depression, which almost invariably caused at least the partial loss of their patrimonies. Juan de Dios Gómez's children, for example, grew up on the part of San Bartolomé that he had been allowed by his bankruptcy court to keep, but these lands diminished over time, and they and their mother, Josefa Basauri, were forced to cede the last of them in 1891. I have not been able to determine what became of his sisters, but José Gómez Basauri was employed by the millionaire hacendado Ramón Ramírez as the administrator of the hacienda of La Huerta in Apatzingán. (In 1898 *La Libertad* informed its readers that Gómez had issued invitations to the inauguration of a new machine to clean and process rice.)[1] Meanwhile, José's cousin, Francisco Román Gómez, the son of the bankrupted former owner of La Huerta, also worked as an administrator on someone else's hacienda: the hacienda of Conguripo in La Huacana, owned by Felipe Iturbide Gómez, another cousin.[2] Three of Francisco's five sisters — Luisa, Angela, and Soledad Román Gómez — never married; they lived comfortably, though not luxuriously, in a small Morelia house on income from the ranchos that their mother, Pilar Gómez, received in her husband's bankruptcy.[3]

TABLE 7.1
Hacienda Sales and Rentals, 1870–1910

	Hacienda sales			Hacienda rentals	
	Average price of haciendas	Avg. annual vol. of activity	Avg. annual no. of transactions	Average rent	Avg. annual no. of transactions
1870–79	23,500	115,000	4.9	2,400	3.6
1880–89	28,400	244,000	8.6	2,600	7.2
1890–99	24,500	267,250	10.9	3,000	6.0
1900–10	47,600	943,290	19.8	4,700	8.6

SOURCES: ANM, AHPJ, AHMM, AHMCR, AHCP, AGN.

Society and Economy in the Late Porfiriato

But it is fair to say that this generation was shaped as much if not more by the powerful economic boom that began to build around 1880 and reached its peak shortly after the turn of the century as by the post-Reform depression. As chapter 6 argues, the groundwork for the Porfirian expansion was laid during the Reform, but the turning point in the depression did not come until the early 1880s, when the Porfirian governors finally succeeded in securing a measure of public tranquillity, and when the railroad reached Morelia (1883) and Pátzcuaro (1886). Even then, what we look back at and identify as the beginning of a "boom" looked more like a period of slightly anemic prosperity until two factors came together in the late 1890s: a spurt of railroad construction that finally connected the important cities of Zamora, Zitácuaro, and Uruapan to the national rail system in 1897, 1898, and 1899 and the belated establishment of a banking system, the first element of which — a branch of the Bank of London — began operations in Morelia in 1898.

The statistics used throughout this study help to quantify the expansion. Hacienda prices and rents roughly doubled between the 1870s and 1910 (with most of the inflation coming after the mid-1890s), while the volume of sales quadrupled, reflecting the continuing increase in the fluidity of the land market — and especially the market for ranchos and small haciendas — that had been set in motion by the Reform (see Table 7.1). The capital market of Morelia increased almost six times during the same period (see Table 7.2).

TABLE 7.2
Loans Notarized in Morelia, 1870–1910
(Annual average, in pesos)

	Private	Institutional[a]	Total
1870–79	88,500	—	88,500
1880–89	155,000	3,000	158,000
1890–99	133,000	15,000	148,000
1900–10	364,500	170,000	534,500

SOURCE: ANM.
NOTE: Includes only loans and cash advances; no commercial credit, cessation of credits, liquidation of accounts, obligations assumed upon purchase of businesses or property, obligations to one's co-heirs as a result of estate division, protests of *libranzas,* or subrogations.
[a]Loans from the Monte de Piedad from 1881 to 1900; bank and Monte de Piedad loans after 1900.

The prices of maize, wheat, cattle, beans, and rice rose between two and three times.[4] Though sugar prices actually fell slightly, production more or less doubled, while production of wheat, the crop that most clearly benefited from the arrival of the railroad, increased four-fold.[5] The livestock industry flourished, with the introduction of new technologies for preserving meat, the rapid growth of urban demand, and the conversion of pasture to farmland in other regions of the nation that were cashing in on the growing opportunities for export of commercial crops.

Less dramatic than the boom in property values and commercial agricultural production, but still impressive, was the expansion of manufacturing and processing capacity: breweries, distilleries, match factories, soap factories, sophisticated textile mills, hydroelectric generating plants, and flour mills proliferated. Sawmills were set up across the state as lumbermen mowed down forests to supply the railroads with timber for fuel and railroad ties.[6] The long-dormant mining industry was revived as foreign investors reworked the old colonial silver and gold mines near Angangueo and Tlalpujahua, while the Rothschilds, among others, poured capital into the copper mines of Inguarán in the south.[7] Accompanying all this were the trappings of urban modernity: streetcars, electric lights, civic beautification, suburban parks, potable water systems, automobiles, telephones and telegraphs, luxury hotels, restaurants with French cuisine. Wealthy Morelians could plan their wedding banquets around a bewildering array of imported specialty foods that even today are not to be found on the city's grocery shelves. The facades of downtown mansions were gussied up in what passed for a French style, especially in the wake of Luis MacGregor's much-envied remodel of Josefa Gómez de Sosa's old house (now the state congress) in 1899. (One young man is said to have whiled away his hours admiring this house. So great, the story goes, was his admiration for its "arquitectónica moderna" that when a friend told him straight-faced that Sr. MacGregor had moved to Mexico City and taken his house with him, he fainted.)[8]

There was to the long-awaited prosperity a frenetic quality, an exuberance bordering on a collective mania to make money, to invest, to speculate, to buy at any price. In the vanguard of this exaggerated optimism were the new banks, which acquired early on the habit of confidently and unrealistically appraising the assets of potential borrowers at values far above even the rising market prices for real estate. The hacienda of Huandacareo, for example, was sold in 1910 for 250,000 pesos — five times its 1867 price — but it had been appraised two years earlier by the Banco Nacional de México at a surreal 730,503 pesos.[9] Similarly, Francisco Madrigal of Zamora borrowed almost 93,000 pesos from the Banco Nacional, the Banco de Jalisco, and the Banco de Guanajuato, but in 1909, when he was forced to cede the hotel and clothing store that had guaranteed the loans, they offset less than 27,000 pesos of the debt.[10]

In this consistent overvaluation the banks were almost certainly motivated by a sincere if naive belief in undeterable progress, in the unlimited capacity of the economy to continue to grow in great leaps and bounds, leading appraisers to base their property valuations on potential rather than market value. For example, when Juan B. Paulín applied for an extension of a 40,000-peso loan from the Banco Nacional in 1908, the appraisers filed this report:

The hacienda [of La Goleta] has its own railroad station, 2790 hectares, and its land is for the most part very suitable for the production of corn and beans. There are at present 1500 hectares under cultivation. We believe that the hacienda *could* harvest annually:

8,000 hectoliters of corn at 2.50 pesos: 20,000 pesos
500 cargas of wheat at 13.00 pesos: 6,500 pesos
100 cargas of beans at 10.00 pesos: 1,000 pesos
Camote, chile, straw, misc.: 3,000 pesos
There are alfalfa fields which *if cared for* are enough to maintain
    a herd which *would* produce an additional 5,000 pesos
The limestone and sand deposits *could* produce 1,500 pesos

TOTAL 37,000 pesos
The annual costs of producing this amount *should not* exceed
   12,000 pesos
Net profit 25,000 pesos
Capitalized at 10%, the value of the hacienda is 250,000 pesos
                                                    (Extracted; emphasis mine)[11]

Whether or not Paulín used his loan to increase production along the lines envisioned by the appraisers depended entirely upon his own initiative, another
factor that the banks, in many cases, overestimated.

Also exemplifying the turn-of-the-century self-confidence were foreign
businessmen with names like Rockwood Puffer or Herman Schrumpf who
came to Morelia in much-publicized visits, lodged at fancy hotels, were feted
by city officials, and announced plans to invest unheard-of sums in projects
of awe-inspiring scale. The dimensions of the schemes hatched by the North
American Beef Company or the San Antonio Land and Cattle Company to
breed, fatten, slaughter, and pack beef made those who grazed a mere 5,000
or 6,000 head of cattle and then drove them to Mexico City for slaughter appear antique in their limited expectations.[12] The air was full of ideas about
how to get rich quick — the giddiness is palpable even after its manifestations
were reduced to legalese — some of which were tossed aside nearly as quickly
as they were committed to paper. A plan to manufacture turpentine, for example, was presented to the state government by a North American dentist,
James A. Rogers, and his partner Julius R. Ambrosius, who promised to invest at least 50,000 pesos in the factory; later the same year the company was
dissolved with no profit.[13] Another North American, Santiago Murray — one
of the most hapless individuals who ever determined to make his fortune in
Mexico — invested in a factory to manufacture organs, a lumber mill, a silver
and copper mine, and an electric company, none of which, so far as the record
shows, ever amounted to anything.[14] Not so his compatriot Santiago Slade,
an engineer from Georgia who married into a wealthy Uruapan family and
whose descendants still live in Michoacán. Between 1899 and 1909, Slade
formed at least four companies, each of which was apparently more successful than the last. The first was capitalized with 18,000 pesos, the second with
48,000 pesos, and the third with 100,000 pesos. The fourth was originally a
lumber business, to which Slade added a government contract to build a railroad between Zamora and Zitácuaro, and another contract to set up a state
lottery, on the basis of which the Banco Nacional gave him a 250,000-peso
line of credit.[15]

The strong foreign flavor to much of the economic activity of the late nine-teenth and early twentieth centuries should not imply that wealthy Michoacanos were passive spectators. Many elites were actively involved in the new infrastructural and industrial projects: though foreigners were almost exclusively responsible for building the railroads, jump-starting the mines, and establishing the banks in Michoacán, locals were important coinvestors in the banks, and for the most part they owned and operated the streetcar systems, the telephones, the textile factories, and the electric companies.

But most of all they poured money into their haciendas, especially after the banks made loans available in relative abundance: they purchased expensive new equipment (threshers, dredgers, plows, pumps, turbines); they actively pursued new ways to use the railroads to get their products to distant markets; and they practiced new techniques of crop rotation and crop selection, for example planting alfalfa in fallow fields to renew the soil and switching to fashionable export crops like coffee or oranges instead of maize. The percentage of the value of haciendas represented by movables (livestock, seed, and equipment) in the first decade of the twentieth century, at roughly 40 percent, was the highest it had been since the 1850s, when movables had constituted about 43 percent of the value of inventoried haciendas.[16] These investments apparently paid off in a historically high rate of return on hacienda agriculture. Though rates of profit are still notoriously difficult to establish, there are clear signs that they were on the increase. First, the profits earned by partnerships established after 1880 indicate that agricultural companies, which had earned average compounded returns of around 24 percent in the period 1810–79, earned an impressive 37 percent in the period 1880–1910, while mercantile profits remained almost exactly the same (see Table 7.3). Second, banks and other lenders in the first decade of the twentieth century determined the value of an hacienda by capitalizing its rent or net income at 10 percent, compared to 6 percent at the time of the Reform and 5 percent in the colonial and early national periods. If we assume that changes in the customary rate of capitalization roughly parallel changes in the actual rate of profit, which certainly seems reasonable, then agriculture may have been in the neighborhood of twice as profitable in the Porfiriato as it had been a century earlier.

In all this activity agricultural entrepreneurs derived moral ammunition from the press, which regularly published articles excoriating "unprogressive" hacendados who neglected to increase production or raise the wages of the peons, while praising others for Goldbergian plans as certain to excite their contemporaries as to horrify a modern environmentalist.[17] (One writer, for example, described the birds, clear water, and ducks of Lake Pátzcuaro as sym-

TABLE 7.3
Business Partnership Profitability, 1810–1910
(Compounded)

Type of Partnership	1810–1879	1880–1910
Mercantile	17% (n = 14)	16% (n = 20)
Agricultural	24% (n = 11)	37% (n = 15)
Industrial	—	9% (n = 10)

SOURCES: ANM, AHPJ, AHMM, AHCP.

bolic of the backward-looking attitudes and "lamentable complacency" that still characterized much of the populace. But luckily, he continued, Domingo Narvarte, owner of the hacienda of Charahuen, was installing steam engines to pump water from the lake to his hacienda, the better to power his new sawmill.)[18] They sheltered under the same philosophical umbrella (positivism) as did the Díaz government, defining progress in strictly material terms and cheerfully, perhaps sincerely, assuming that social good would eventually flow from personal enrichment. Given this shared disposition, it should come as no surprise that the state government and the legislature (which had lost most of their earlier distrust for each other in light of the fact that all members of both bodies owed their positions to Díaz) went out of their way to support "forward-looking" elites, whether natives or foreigners — men who, in turn, came to count on exploiting their connections with government officials and lawmakers in order to increase and protect their wealth.

At the same time, by the turn of the century other local elites — even some of those whose early careers were models of entrepreneurial ambition — showed signs of tiring of the pace set by wave upon wave of foreign investors in the economy and began to exhibit nostalgia for what they imagined as gentler and more aristocratic days. And with some frequency they not only wrote wistful poems and newspaper articles but acted in ways that reinforced their sense of themselves as a privileged and distinct group, above the fray. They married their children to other wealthy individuals, closing the door to the sort of upward social mobility by marriage that had characterized Michoacán society since the colonial period. They joined exclusive clubs, paying 1,000 pesos for the privilege.[19] And, perhaps most important, they transformed themselves into *rentiers*, distancing themselves from the hustle and bustle of making money.

This is not to say that they were not prospering: whether they leased their lands or sold them and loaned out the proceeds, the income from rent or interest during this period of steep appreciation in the value of rural property was sufficient to make possible, for the first time since independence, a delightful and apparently secure existence. In fact, the easy rhythms of this lifestyle made them relatively immune to the criticisms of the Díaz circle of economic advisers, who were frustrated to see Mexican landowners reject or abandon the kind of aggressive, risk-taking, productivity-enhancing behavior that they saw as necessary if Mexico were to continue to progress. No wonder that the Díaz regime rained favors on foreign businessmen (and the native-born entrepreneurs who followed their lead) like the North American Slade, or the Spaniards Eduardo and Alfredo Noriega, who were responsible for transforming the Zacapu marshes into prime farmland by means of massive capital investments in drainage projects.[20] These men, by virtue of their immigration to Mexico in the first place, were self-selected to meet the standards of ambition and risk-willingness that liberals since Ocampo had articulated.

The Huarte Family in the Fifth Generation

The fifth generation of Huarte descendants displayed many of these general tendencies among elites. For example, like most Michoacán-born elites, Cayetano Gómez and Dolores Alzúa's grandchildren spurned careers as merchants, but, like others of their class, several had a stake in infrastructure or industry. Manuel Gómez González owned the streetcar concession for Morelia, which cost him 50,000 pesos but earned a respectable 9 percent return annually.[21] Pilar Iturbide Gómez's husband, Joaquín Macouzet López, owned and ran the Fábrica de la Paz, a textile factory in Morelia.[22] Three of Francisco and Felipe Iturbide Gómez's children married into families with infrastructural and industrial interests: the Osegueras (owners of the fabulous Hotel Oseguera in Morelia and of a state-of-the-art distillery) and the Vidales (owners of the lucrative textile factory, La Providencia, in Uruapan).[23]

But, as was true of most of this generation, hacienda agriculture was at the core of their economic interests. Despite their diversification into other sectors, the Oseguera and Vidales fortunes remained anchored in agriculture: Joaquín Oseguera and his sons owned the haciendas of Puruarán and Cahulote (formerly owned by Manuel Alzúa), having made their initial fortune renting the sugar haciendas of Tipitarillo, Otates, and Tepenahua; and Feliciano Vidales and his sons owned the haciendas of San Marcos, Santa Catarina, and La

Parota, having originally rented part of nearby Taretan.[24] With the exception of Luis and Francisco Iturbide Gómez, who followed the career path of their father and became doctors, all of María de Jesús Gómez and Luis Iturbide's sons were agricultural entrepreneurs. Eduardo Iturbide Gómez owned a major fraction of the hacienda of Coapa until he sold it in 1894 to Luis MacGregor; José Iturbide Gómez bought and sold three haciendas in the 1890s and 1900s; and Felipe Iturbide Gómez owned the haciendas of La Noria and Conguripo.[25] Their brothers-in-law, José del Moral and Nicolás Menocal, were also owners of large haciendas (Uruétaro and Zicuirán).[26]

Several members of the fifth generation married foreigners — the first generation to do so since the colonial period — reflecting Michoacán's opening up to the outside world and the accompanying influx of foreign fortune seekers. Juan Bautista Gómez González and his sister María married children of the French bookseller, Eugenio Maillefert, and José Iturbide Gómez and Elena Menocal Gómez, too, married men and women of French descent. But this generation also cemented ties to the emerging local bourgeoisie, especially by means of their children's marriages, which generally took place in the 1890s and 1900s. Table 7.4 illustrates how the sixth-generation marriages connected their fifth-generation parents to some of the wealthiest new families in the city and state, most notably the Osegueras and the Vidales, both of whose patriarchs (contemporaries of the fifth generation) were self-made men who had started out in a small way of business during the post-Reform depression.[27]

True to their grandfather Cayetano Gómez's careful political neutrality, most of the men of this generation avoided politics; even Luis Iturbide's sons and sons-in-law mainly stayed out of the limelight, despite Luis's own history of involvement with the liberal party. Though Francisco Iturbide Gómez did serve three terms in the state legislature, the most politically active of this generation was Teresa Menocal Gómez's husband, Nicolás Menocal, who was a state deputy for twelve years running. Menocal clearly benefited from his position as one of the Díaz faithful when he was allowed to purchase the vast hacienda of Zicuirán from the Pudenciana Bocanegra Trust, whose administration had been taken over — with somewhat dubious legality — by the state government.[28]

Finally, like the rest of the Michoacán elite, the Gómez descendants divided into those (like Nicolás Menocal) who associated themselves, often formally, with foreign businessmen, and those who opted for a less engaged style of business. Juan Bautista Gómez Alzúa had been the first in the family to retire from active participation in managing his properties (in the early 1870s) and to turn them over to a commissioned administrator. His example was followed by his son Juan Bautista Gómez González, who was described as a "ro-

TABLE 7.4

Kinship Networks in the Fifth and Sixth Generations of the Iturbide Family

The fifth generation (married in the 1870s and 1880s)

Pilar Iturbide Gómez	m.	Joaquín Macouzet López
Dolores Iturbide Gómez	m.	Manuel Macouzet López
Francisco Iturbide Gómez	m.	Soledad Macouzet López
Paz Iturbide Gómez	m.	Luis Macouzet López
Concepción Iturbide Gómez	m.	José del Moral Peredo
Felipe Iturbide Gómez	m.	Soledad del Moral Peredo
Juan Macouzet López	m.	Concepción del Moral Peredo

The sixth generation (married in the 1890s and 1900s)

Adrian Iturbide Macouzet	m.	Clara Osequera Vidales
Jesús Iturbide Macouzet	m.	Joaquín Oseguera Vidales
Catalina Iturbide del Moral	m.	Joaquín Oseguera Herrera
Elena Iturbide del Moral	m.	José Elguero Videgaray
Javier Iturbide Macouzet	m.	Adela Lama Macouzet
Ignacio Lama Macouzet	m.	Angela Videgaray Luna
Concha Macouzet del Moral	m.	Alfonso Videgaray Luna
Pablo Macouzet del Moral	m.	María Videgaray Luna
Manuel Macouzet Malo	m.	Debora Macouzet Malo
Debora Macouzet Malo	m.	Crescencio Oseguera
Carmen Macouzet Malo	m.	Feliciano Vidales Ortega

SOURCES: ANM, AHSM, IBARROLA.

mantic," and by his grandson Eugenio Gómez Maillefert, a diplomat with a "certain air of aristocratic disdain."[29] Eugenio's cousins, the poets Alfredo Maillefert Vidales, Alfredo Iturbide Chávez, and José Ortiz Vidales also epitomized the peculiar combination of romanticism and modernism that was so much a part of the *fin de siècle*.

But others in the family besides Menocal acted fully in the other spirit of the age, an almost boosterish belief in progress. Eduardo Iturbide Gómez, for example, was one of the most successful of his generation in riding the boom, and his son, Eduardo N. Iturbide, was even more agile, wheeling and dealing with the likes of the Terrazas-Creel family of Chihuahua and with his brother-in-law, Julio Limantour (brother of Díaz's Minister of Finance).[30] Another prominent player in the late Porfirian boom in Michoacán was Salvador Vallejo, who was married to Ignacia Macouzet López, through whom he was linked by marriage to all of the Iturbide Gómez siblings (see Table 7.4).[31]

Toward Revolution

Until shortly after the turn of the century these two elite economic styles not only coexisted but to a considerable extent coexisted to their mutual advantage. The *rentiers* benefited from the fact that ambitious locals and foreigners bid up the prices of their property, allowing them to retire on its income, and, moreover, often left their properties dramatically improved, with irrigation systems and other permanent improvements that were not there before. Even if they did not sell or rent out their entire hacienda and withdraw from direct cultivation, the rise in commodity prices allowed them to enjoy a higher income with the same or even less effort than before, say, 1895.

Meanwhile, entrepreneurs benefited from these rental agreements that allowed them to exploit an hacienda's natural resources (pasture, forests, virgin soil) and then move on, without the burdens of ownership. Foreign agricultural capitalists, especially (e.g., the Indart brothers, the Basterrechea brothers, the Noriega brothers, Dante Cusi, and dozens of others), seem to have found it at least as desirable to rent as to own. Moreover, if some growers were not as interested as they were in improving productivity, it meant that prices for their own production stayed relatively high, while wages for their workers remained relatively low. In short, the only truly unambivalent champions of the principle that every hacienda owner ought to be hotly in pursuit of maximum profits on his/her own hacienda were the national and state governments and the pro-government press.

But five years into the twentieth century it was becoming clear that the growth that had seemed so unstoppable over the past decade, and that had made room for all economic styles among provincial elites, was in jeopardy. The troubles first arose in connection to the increasing difficulties Michoacán had feeding its population, a fact reflected in the persistent shortages of corn and extremely high corn prices after 1900 and especially after 1905 (see Tables 7.5 and 7.6). There had been weather-related production crises (the first of which led the government to import corn from the United States to

TABLE 7.5

Prices of Corn in the Plaza of Morelia

Year	Price (pesos/fanega)	Year	Price (pesos/fanega)
1882	2.62 to 2.75	1905	4.35
1889	2.50	1906	4.80
1897	2.75	1907	3.80
1902	3.75	1908	4.80
1903	3.20	1909	6.30
1904	2.30	1910	6.70

SOURCES: *Revista comercial*; *El Derecho Cristiano*, May 16, 1889; *La Libertad*, September 21, 1897; and beginning in 1902, a monthly report in *Periódico Oficial del Estado de Michoacán* entitled "Lo que consumen en el Hospital Civil." For a comparison to maize prices earlier in the century, see Table 6.3.

satisfy demand in Michoacán) in 1891 to 1892, 1895 to 1896, and 1901 to 1902, but beginning in 1906 there was virtually no respite from an uncommon series of droughts and/or damaging torrential rains (1906–07, 1908, 1909–10).[32]

As the dimensions of the problem — as much a product of the assault on Indian communal lands and of the arrival of the railroad, which made wheat a more attractive commercial crop than corn for many *tierra fría* hacendados, as of the weather — became clear, criticism of "unprogressive" hacendados, who opposed the importation of corn and held back supplies in order to keep prices up, gathered steam. In 1902, for example, *La Libertad* published an article with the title "Su majestad el maíz," in which the author drew a sharp distinction between the government and the "hombres de negocio" on the one hand, and the "feudal lords" ("señores feudales") on the other. "There are many hacendados," he asserted, "who are not eager to open up new lands for cultivation or to irrigate their fields; there are even occasions when they refuse to purchase water from enterprises that offer it at a low price," because they want to keep prices high. "This situation," he continued, "must not be tolerated; we must democratize agriculture, and bring down the feudal lords by means of competition that will oblige them to expand their production and lower their prices."[33]

TABLE 7.6

Corn Production in Michoacán, 1808–1905

	Total fanegas[a]	Fanegas per capita
1808	2,000,000–3,700,000	6 to 11
1851	2,900,000–5,300,000	6 to 10
1872	2,200,000–4,200,000	3 to 6
1895	2,076,000	2.4
1897	3,036,000	3.4
1899	3,348,000	3.7
1900	2,324,000	2.6
1901	2,509,000	2.7
1902	1,990,000	2.1
1903	2,192,000	2.3
1905	2,829,000	2.9

SOURCES: Romero, p. 29; *Boletín de la Sociedad Mexicana de Geografía y Estadística*, 1:56, 117; Bureau of the American Republics, p. 151; Mexico, Secretaría de Fomento, *Anuario estadístico*, 3:722–723; 7:298; 8:376; 9:431; 10:306; 11:477.
[a] 1 fanega = .908 hectoliters.
NOTE: The figures for 1808, 1851, and 1872 were given by the authors in terms of *fanegas* of seed planted. Using as guidelines the Secretaría de Fomento, *Memoria . . . 1865*, p. 49, which stated that corn yields in Mexico varied from 100 to 400 fanegas per fanega of seed; the *Boletín de la Sociedad de Geografía y Estadística* 1:117, which stated that in Michoacán in 1872 yields varied from 150 to 400 per *fanega*; Busto, 1:5, who noted that the most common yield in Mexico was 150 to 1, a ratio also cited by Humboldt, p. 257; and taking into account the probable propensity in these sources to overestimate yields, I have used the 150:1 ratio as the upper range, and 80:1 as the lower range. See also Brading, *Haciendas*, pp. 65–66, for a discussion of the problem of estimating yields.

Even though the distinction between the two groups was probably nowhere near as clear in actuality as it was in the author's rhetoric — that is, even the most entrepreneurial hacendados may have had some misgivings about a potential drop in the price of corn (Eduardo Noriega, the Spanish capitalist who was responsible for draining the Zacapu marsh and who regularly sold corn to the government to relieve shortages comes to mind), it appears clear that the foreign and local bourgeoisie were increasingly resentful of their insufficiently enlightened fellow hacendados, whom they saw as threatening not only continued progress, but, now, continued (relative) social tranquillity, as corn shortages led to popular rumblings and outbreaks of violence. For their part, the less aggressive landowners no doubt disliked being lectured to and bullied with vague threats of "democratizing" agriculture (shades of the anti-hacienda and anti-elite liberal rhetoric of the 1840s and early 1850s), and if some nativism did not play into their feelings, it would be astonishing.

But despite the increasing rancor of the debate over "progress," for elites it was the world crisis of 1907 that most clearly exposed the fragility of the Porfirian boom. The depression was particularly painful in Mexico because the country had switched to the gold standard in 1905. This meant that the buffer of a depreciated silver currency, which had made imports more expensive and exports more lucrative for over a decade and a half, could no longer shield the economy from the booms and busts of the international economy. Ill luck dictated that the first of these cycles should be a depression. Poor planning and an ill-advised laissez-faire attitude toward the development of the banking system in Mexico, however, made things even worse.

In Michoacán, except for a brief and unsuccessful experiment with a promotion or mortgage bank (the Banco Refaccionario de Michoacán), there were no credit institutions in the state designed to issue long-term, low-interest loans to new enterprises or projects. Instead there were only the more profitable commercial banks, set up to offer relatively high interest (8 to 10 percent), and short-term (six months) credit. These banks of issue were the only institutional sources of large amounts of loan capital for the innovating landowners and industrialists who, with their good social and political connections, were the favorite clients of the banks. Even though their ambitious plans for the money they were borrowing meant that there was no possibility that the loan would be repaid within six months, the unspoken solution was for the allegedly short-term loans to be extended indefinitely for another and yet another term.

The 1907 world crisis, however, put a quick and painful end to this practice. As the commercial banks began to call their short-term loans in order to cover liabilities in a shrinking economy, they found that they had not only overextended themselves by loaning too much on the basis of too little, but also that their debtors, who had come to think of their loans as made if not in perpetuity then at least for a good deal longer than the six-month period they had cynically agreed to, could not comply. There were 35 known bankruptcies among elites in the 1900s — the most since the 1860s — almost all of which resulted from the pressures caused by the crisis in general and banking policies in particular. In booming districts such as Zamora the bankruptcy rate was particularly high.

Some of these failures were spectacular, though none more so than that of the Spaniard Juan Basagoiti, who had been intimately involved in the economy of Michoacán (as a lender, speculator, hacendado, textile factory owner, Spanish consul, and founder of a firm called the Industrial Company of the Future) since the 1870s.[34] Basagoiti owed well over 300,000 pesos to the Banco del Estado de México, the Banco Nacional de México, and the Banco Alemán Transatlántico, and his heirs (he died in 1905) were forced to cede their home in the Portal de Iturbide, their controlling shares in a textile factory, and the hacienda of Turicato. The Revolution of 1910 intervened before they were forced to give up their other haciendas, but that seems to have been inevitable; even Basagoiti himself, as is evidenced by his 1905 will, did not expect to be able to hold onto them.[35] The collapse of his roughly 700,000-peso fortune made it the most dramatic since the falls of Francisco Román and Juan de Dios Gómez in the 1860s.

Even those who were not personally touched by the banking crisis and the wave of bankruptcies it occasioned must have begun to question the assumption that progress was forever and to talk openly about grievances (the close ties between the state government and foreign capitalists, for example, or the monotonous regularity of Governor Aristeo Mercado's reelection since his first term beginning in 1891) that until now they had not, perhaps, even articulated to themselves. Previously ineffectual opposition groups (students at the Colegio de San Nicolás; liberals unhappy with Díaz's conciliatory posture toward the church; Catholics who were also unhappy with Díaz because they claimed he had not gone far enough to reinstate the church) grew bolder.[36] In other words, for many elites the end of Porfirian prosperity and confidence in the Díaz regime came several years before the Revolution of 1910. When Francisco I. Madero, with his call for political reform, gave elites someone to rally around whose background was much like their own, many of them did so.

In fact, virtually all of the early leaders of the Revolution in Michoacán were wealthy or at least well-connected men. Salvador Escalante, who headed the Madero Revolution in Michoacán, was married to Elena Plancarte, a member of two of Michoacán's most venerable elite families, the Plancartes and the Dávalos (her grandfather, Francisco Plancarte, was one of the most successful hacendados and entrepreneurs of the mid-nineteenth century, and her great-uncle was the conservative archbishop Pelagio Antonio de Labastida y Dávalos). Elena's cousin, Carmen Plancarte, was married to Eduardo Iturbide Gómez; her sister was married to Gabino de Jesús Oseguera; one aunt was a Menocal, and another was an Igartúa, of the wealthy Zamora clan. Escalante's own grandfather, José Antonio Pérez Gil, had been a vice governor of the state and owned the hacienda of Santa Cruz in Tarímbaro.[37]

Dr. Miguel Silva González, who was elected governor in 1912 and later fought with Pancho Villa, was the son and grandson of governors and hacendados. Lic. Primitivo Ortiz, Silva's opponent in the 1912 elections on behalf of the Partido Nacional Católico, was married to Susana Vidales, Feliciano's oldest daughter.[38] Ortiz was a cousin of another revolutionary (and later, briefly, president of the Republic), Ing. Pascual Ortiz Rubio, a partisan of Obregón, whose family had owned the hacienda of El Rincón, outside of Morelia, for three generations. Lic. Julio Ramírez Wiella was a *silvista* (a supporter of Miguel Silva's campaign for governor), whose mother owned the haciendas of Cutio and El Sauz, in Ario.[39] Rafael Elizarrarás, another *silvista*, owned the Farmacia Central, one of the largest drugstores in Morelia, and was in the process of divorce from Dolores Flores Anciola, the daughter of the owner of the rich hacienda of San Vicente (Nuevo Urecho), Lic. Juan N. Flores.[40] It is surely fair to say that few of them expected or desired that the movements they led in 1911 and 1912 would set off a popular revolution in which all social groups in the state and the Republic would play a part. But at the same time it is not possible to argue that the revolution came upon them suddenly and by complete surprise; they, like their ancestors in 1810, had a hand in making it what it was.

Conclusion

This book set out to question whether the grand cyclicality conjured up by the striking parallels between the lives of the wealthy on the brink of the wars for independence and those of their great-great grandchildren's generation 100 years later should define the rhythms of Mexican history in the nineteenth century. I have tried throughout the study to underline the changing texture of life for the wealthy and powerful over the course of the century, but here it may be useful to highlight the most important of those changes by addressing two questions of fundamental historiographical importance: what difference did independence make? And what difference did the Reform make?

What Difference Did Independence Make?

For decades historians assumed that the beginning of national life was inherently meaningful. Beginning in the 1960s, however, this seemingly natural and almost automatic periodization came under attack from scholars who argued that independence brought no changes of real importance. Instead, basic "structures" (class structure, Mexico's "dependent" position in the international economy, the structure of land tenure, and so on), and the social relations associated with those structures, remained essentially the same, as did many other deep-seated beliefs, behaviors, and relationships. "Modern" Mexico, some of them suggested, cannot really be said to have come into being until the late nineteenth century (the date 1880 often crops up); when capitalist social relations began to dominate internally, Mexico became integrated into the world economy on different (though still dependent) terms, the political system stabilized around the Díaz dictatorship, and Mexico opened up culturally to the rest of the world. Even then the extent of true structural change remained limited.

My close examination of Michoacán in the late colonial and early modern periods suggests that, as is so often the case, both understandings of the significance of independence have merit. On the one hand, there is no doubt that beginning with the push toward independence, processes that had been in motion for decades were sent into reverse, long-held assumptions about the proper relationship of individuals to God, King, and each other were shaken deeply, and in short everyone's lives (not just those of the wealthy) changed mightily. For prosperous merchants and landowners the wars that began in 1810 set off a catastrophic economic depression that had deep and lasting social, economic, and institutional repercussions: the fall of most old landowning families (which carried with it the potential for unprecedented upward social mobility for well-positioned members of the middle classes); the erosion of the economic and to a certain extent the political power of the church; the collapse of mercantile networks and financial structures. The struggles for independence also produced important political reconfigurations among elites, and inspired many non-elites whose previous political activism had been very localized and short-lived to take up arms and join in broad conflicts.

Moreover, independence itself brought tremendous changes. With Spain's virtual monopoly on supplying Mexico with trade goods at an end, the country was invaded by new foreign merchants and inundated with cheap foreign goods, all of which had the effect of reestablishing mercantile networks on quite different (broader and deeper, though also, in an unstable period, more fragile) terms than before. Moreover, the enduring weakness of the church's lending power called forth new and creative ways of doing business that, in general, made it easier for new men to gain access to credit, property, and a measure of prosperity, or at least economic opportunity. Institutional power was rather suddenly located in new places (congresses, state governments, the army, state courts, the press), and exercised by many more people, including some whose professions had been previously restricted or nonexistent, for example newspaper writers, congressmen, prefects, military leaders, and lawyers.

Legal equality among citizens was established, which as a practical matter meant, among other things, the abolition of slavery, Indian tribute and, soon, of titles of nobility and the privileges associated with them. It also meant, at least temporarily, that all male citizens were permitted to vote. Newspapers cropped up everywhere. Political discourse, being more open, was more heated, and here, too, many more people participated in shaping it, not only in the approved contexts of election campaigns, congressional debates, and battles between rival newspapers, but by means of riot, rebellion, and *pro-nunciamientos*. The results of all this were Mexico's notorious political instability and, at times, a complete breakdown of mundane mechanisms of administration like tax collection and prosecution of criminal misconduct, a far cry from the (relatively) stable and efficient late Bourbon administrations.

On the other hand it is equally true that many things changed very little. Spanish laws and legal codes — the Spanish system of justice — largely remained in place, so that in most respects the ways business was conducted, wealth was passed on to heirs, criminals were tried and punished, taxes were collected, and corporate and individual rights were protected were the same as before independence. There were no massive demographic shifts out of rural areas into cities; there was no real industrialization or any other dramatic change in the way wealth was produced; there was no profound alteration in modes of transportation (though the opening of additional ports after independence did add some new routes of mercantile circulation). There were still a very few rich people and a lot of poor people, with a relative handful in between. Wages and prices remained about the same, after an upward spike during the insurgency. Though there were numerous attempts to improve productivity (agricultural and otherwise) by use of new technologies or new methods, these cannot be said to have been widespread or consistent, and they were undermined by the continuing temptation to boost profits in tried-and-true fashion by keeping expenditures, especially wages, low. Corporate entities (the church, the Indian villages) continued to own property that, by and large, did not enter the market (although on the part of both there was more divestment of property before the Reform than has usually been thought). There were still no impersonal, institutional sources of credit other than the church — and to call the church an "impersonal" source of loan capital was stretching the point.

In short, at the levels of legal culture and social and economic structure, the changes brought about by economic collapse and political independence were far from revolutionary. Moreover, by the 1840s some combination of

conscious intention and unconscious instinct had led the survivors and beneficiaries of the post-1810 economic depression to think and behave more like
their grandparents' generation than like their parents'. In large part, of
course, these behaviors resurfaced because by midcentury the economy was
strong enough to support an increase in conspicuous consumption, elite-consolidating marriages, and general complacency. If we were to plot measure-
ments of social and economic change important to elites (personal wealth,
land prices, rents, loan capital, urban property values) on a graph, most of the
lines would drop off steeply in 1810 and then would begin gradually to rise
around 1825, gathering steam after 1840 until the 1810 point was more or
less regained at midcentury.[1]

Rather than dismiss all this as an illustration of the truism that different
theoretical frameworks lead historians looking at the same period to different conclusions, it seems helpful to make both the presence and absence of
change work to explain the most significant political event in nineteenth-century Mexico: the Reform. There is a sense in which it was neither change nor
sameness that provoked the new political movements that began to develop
in the late 1840s, but rather both together, in dynamic counterpoint to each
other. Put another way, structural change is not the only sort of social and
economic change that can influence political alignments and practices.

If we take as a starting point that the Reform movement was led by
(mainly) men whose background can best be described as middle class — a
point that has been made by many historians and one that this study sup-
ports — the key question becomes: why did these individuals act the way that
they did at midcentury? What were their motivations? The answer suggested
by the evidence from Michoacán is that the sudden and rather striking possibilities for upward social mobility during the 1810s, 1820s, 1830s, and early
1840s (when 83 percent of hacienda purchasers and virtually all successful
merchants had no inherited wealth or close family connections to the
wealthy) fed the expectation among middle groups that intelligence, risk-willingness, ambition, and hard work would be rewarded in republican
Mexico — where before 1810 the rewards for similar traits and behaviors had
gone to Spanish immigrants. To a considerable extent, of course, the idea that
anyone (or at least anyone who was not a plebeian or a manual laborer)
could be successful, could join the ranks of the elite, was implicit in the liberal ideologies that were gaining adherents in the late colonial period. It was
not until after 1810, however, that the theoretical promise of liberalism was
accompanied by the actual experience of upward mobility, made more dra-

matic and in fact made possible by the downward mobility of so many of the late colonial landowning families.

But at the same time the fact that the process of rebuilding after independence had led most clearly to the re-creation of something like the pre-1810 economy — and not to a markedly more open and flexible economy, fully capable of self-sustaining growth — meant that there was a limit to the extent to which the following generation, the generation that came of age in the 1840s and 1850s, could be accommodated. In other words upward mobility for the first post-independence generation had been possible mainly because of the collapse of the old elite after 1810, not because of basic alterations in the structure of economic opportunity. Now a new generation of middle-class men and women was faced with the prospect that they could not achieve similar success unless they either displaced those who were presently in positions of wealth and power, or, alternatively, effected dramatic changes that would expand their access to land and capital currently immobilized and/or unavailable.

It was out of this realization — that fundamental changes in the order of things were necessary if they, as individuals (and, they thought, Mexico as a nation, after the disastrous war with the United States), were to prosper — that the idea of a "middle class," distinct from both the idle, unproductive poor and the idle, unproductive rich, was born. This small, newly (and still embryonically) self-conscious group was willing to make common cause with the progressive rich and the progressive poor, but only on their own terms. In sum the middle classes' perception of the need for reform came out of the lack of fundamental changes in post-independent Mexico, and of the fear that midcentury Michoacán was coming to look more and more like late colonial Michoacán, a place where established elites were content with a status quo that made some room for middle-class individuals but could not allow for a high degree of social mobility. But their sense of themselves as deserving and capable and central to the future of the nation would not have been possible had it not been for the political and economic changes that *did* occur after independence, which not only increased their numbers (because of the emergence of new sources of employment for educated men in the state government, press, schools, and courts), but also, and perhaps more important, increased their expectations of economic success and their visibility as a group, even to themselves. It was, then, a sense of mission tinged with resentment, born of a perception of opportunities closing off, that drove the midcentury reformers.

What difference did the Reform make?

These liberal reformers had high hopes that they could deeply and positively change Mexico's economic prospects, social structure, and political stability. They saw their goals (promoting a free national market, expanding and empowering the middle class, strengthening the scope and authority of government at all levels, but especially the national state) as fully intertwined, but it makes some sense to analyze separately the socioeconomic and the politico-cultural results of the Reform and of the contested process of putting the reformist program into place.

ECONOMY AND SOCIETY

The key question in evaluating the long-term socioeconomic impact of the Reform is: would the midcentury economy, in some ways stronger than it had been on the eve of the Hidalgo Rebellion, have evolved on its own in the directions desired by the reformers? Could the economic reforms contained especially in the Lerdo law have come about without provocative anticlericalism, which had the immediate effect of plunging the country into civil war and foreign intervention and delaying the very changes that the reformers thought so essential? After all, the church's economic power had already diminished significantly since 1810, and considerable divestment of ecclesiastical property had already taken place; isn't it reasonable to assume that even without the Reform such divestment would have continued until ecclesiastical property holding was negligible? Furthermore, might not politicians less obsessed than the midcentury liberals by the need to take on the church have made a first priority of some relatively uncontroversial but important steps to protect property rights and stimulate enterprise: laws to facilitate formation of limited liability corporations, a modern patent law, a body of mortgage credit law designed to protect long-term investments, a comprehensive commercial code, the abolition of internal tariffs? Instead, these legal-institutional innovations, often pointed to as key ingredients in the Porfirian growth spurt, were not put in place until the late 1880s and 1890s.[2] Finally, might not the need to compete with aggressive agricultural capitalists like Cayetano Gómez have led eventually to the sort of broad-scale improvements in agricultural productivity that always precede industrialization?

On balance, I think that the answer to the question of whether major structural changes in the pre-Reform economy could have come about uneventfully is negative. First, the church might very well have continued to divest itself of its real property, but without being forced by the Reform to do so it would never willingly have permitted the nationalization of its financial assets. And, as Ocampo well understood, it was in its capacity as a mortgage holder that the church exerted the most deleterious effect on the rural economy. Its time-honored practices of discouraging both amortization and subrogation — which almost guaranteed very high levels of debt on properties that could not easily be subdivided — held down reinvestable profits (as interest payments soaked up income), kept land markets from attaining the fluidity they might have had if subdivision had been a realistic possibility (thereby also standing in the way of the creation of a class of small property holders), and inhibited the emergence of crucial new institutions of credit, that is, banks. Also, in less obvious ways, the strength of the church discouraged the foreign investment that was necessary to build a system of cheap rail transportation, the first step in developing a national market. Potential U.S. and northern European investors were, perhaps, primarily put off by the instability of Mexico's political system, but anti-Catholic sentiment on their part should not be underestimated.

The question then becomes whether the Reform was successful in eliminating the obstacles to economic growth associated with the church and, secondarily, the landholding villages. That is, did the Reform free previously immobilized factors of production and create the preconditions for economic growth in the Porfiriato? First, let us consider land. As argued in chapter 6, the Reform does seem to have had the desired effect of promoting greater circulation of land in smaller units. Though the breakup of the largest haciendas, both privately owned and church owned, was, in the 1860s and through most of the 1870s, a function of financial hardship rather than of purposeful and profit-minded subdivision, the laws passed by the reformers to ensure that indebtedness did not stand in the way of subdivision clearly encouraged the process.

But the new "yeomen" created directly and indirectly by the Reform were not nearly so numerous nor so initially successful as the reformers had hoped they would be, and, in what must have been a disappointing (though not, perhaps, a thoroughly unexpected) development, they seem scarcely to have included any former members of Indian communities. In fact, the Lerdo law and later liberal legislation regarding the landholding villages probably had relatively little impact on the ongoing trend toward disentailment of Indian communal lands. It is true that the post-1867 liberals made the abolition of the landholding community a key rhetorical point, but ultimately the villages that wished to divide their lands did so at their own pace, as they had been doing since 1825, and those that did not wish to divide their lands managed to hold onto them until they became valuable enough for creoles or mestizos to covet them. That is, disentailment rarely promoted progress for indigenous peoples, as the liberals had hoped, but economic growth almost always promoted disentailment.

Still, despite the failures of the *reparto* to transform villagers into yeoman farmers, "in some measure, the liberal goal of creating a solid, loyal, liberal yeomanry was met" (to use Alan Knight's words), mainly through the breakup of large church-owned and privately owned haciendas and through sales of village holdings to outsiders.[3] New men were not so ubiquitous among purchasers of haciendas in the period 1855–85 as they had been in the 1820s and 1830s, but they were still a substantial minority. Perhaps more important, they completely dominated the market for small to medium ranchos and large *terrenos* (under 5,000 pesos), which even a cursory glance at the notary registers for these years will demonstrate to have circulated at a much faster rate after 1880 than before 1855.[4]

Chapter 6 also argues that the Reform, by forcing property owners to amortize church-held mortgages, ultimately stimulated the circulation of capital, though its short-term effect was the opposite: the capital represented by ecclesiastical mortgages temporarily shrank when the reformers tried to make paying off nationalized debts less painful by reducing the amount of debt that had to be paid off in cash. But in the long run forced amortization not only fed the process of subdivision of large and often-inefficient haciendas, but enhanced agricultural profits. Moreover, freeing mortgage debt from the policies of the church enabled the mortgages themselves to circulate, something that would never have been sanctioned by the church but that had the effect of encouraging lending. The greatest failure of the Reform in this area was that it did not lead earlier to the development of a banking system, something that does not seem to have been high on the list of the reformers' priorities. The reasons for and implications of this glaring omission from their program would make an interesting topic of further research.

The factor of production on which the Reform clearly had the least impact in Michoacán was labor. This is related, of course, to the point made above, that is, that the Reform (as separate from the eventually speeded-up economic growth that was arguably its end result) did not appreciably accelerate the ongoing disappearance of the landholding village. As village lands passed into the hands of creole or mestizo hacendados or rancheros, in a relatively steady but also relatively slow process since the late 1820s, it is certainly true that the labor supply available to work or sharecrop on haciendas or, potentially, to work in manufacturing, expanded. But high wages and scarce labor were not bottlenecks on most haciendas (there were some exceptions in the *tierra caliente*) or in industrial development, at least not until very late in the Porfiriato, when out-migration seems to have become a factor.[5] Thus, freeing supplies of labor "immobilized" in villages was not so crucial to economic growth in Michoacán as was freeing immobilized property and capital. In fact, the expansion of the labor supply, by keeping wages low despite some fairly impressive improvements in agricultural productivity by the 1890s, may have hindered economic growth by limiting consumption and impeding the creation of local markets for manufactured goods.

Any discussion of the economic effects of the Reform in Michoacán must acknowledge the singlemindedness with which the post-1867 governments pushed the building of railroads in the state. Although the railroad did not reach Morelia until 1883, this was in fact surprisingly early, considering that Michoacán, never the wealthiest or most productive of regions, had slipped in national importance since the colonial period. The fact that Morelia was in the first wave of cities connected to the national capital was, then, a tribute to the state's liberal tradition and the perseverance of its leaders. This post-1867 agenda was, of course, logical, in that liberals had called attention to Michoacán's devastating isolation from national markets even during a period of relative prosperity (the 1840s and 1850s). In the late 1860s and 1870s, when conditions in the state really *were* deteriorating, the emphasis on internal improvements is unsurprising. Still, the liberals in the 1870s saw what the late-colonial elites did not: that Michoacán's topography and its out-of-the-way geographical position presented enormous obstacles to continued growth, which had to be overcome if there was to be any possibility of increasing the size of the middle class.

This does not mean that the railroad was an easy solution to Michoacán's economic problems. While connection by rail to the rest of Mexico led to a quadrupling of wheat production in the highlands, it did so at the expense of maize, which often had to be imported; moreover, the failure to extend the railroad quickly to the *tierra caliente* left Michoacán's sugar producers well behind those of the rapidly modernizing state of Morelos (though this was a situation that was probably inevitable given their much greater distance from large markets), and caused what was traditionally the most liquid and savviest group of agricultural capitalists in the state, the sugar planters, to lose ground vis-à-vis wheat farmers. All the same, the railroad was closely and clearly associated in fact and in the minds of contemporaries with the rise in property values, agricultural production, and general affluence of the late Porfiriato. And the liberals in power took credit for it; the liberal spin on the condition of the economy by the 1890s resembled that of the conservatives in the 1850s: things were not perfect but they were improving, while the Catholic press in the 1890s sounded much like the liberals of the 1840s and 1850s in their stinging criticisms of the Porfirian economy and in their calls for reform.[6]

The liberal victories in the Three Years' War and the war of the French Intervention, which succeeded in eliminating the conservative party as a viable opponent and dealt a blow to public acceptance of the church's temporal power, also had economic consequences. By establishing the supremacy of civil power the Reform cleared the way for the consolidation of the national state that can be said to have begun under Juárez in 1867 and was carried to fruition by Porfirio Díaz. The Díaz dictatorship, in turn, was able to provide the sort of political stability that encouraged foreign investment in railroads and in other important infrastructure.

POLITICS AND NATIONAL IDENTITY

While there is no doubt that a key goal of the midcentury reformers was to replace loyalty to the church with a sense of duty to and identification with the nation, it seems clear that in Michoacán their primary political goal was to build an effective and efficient apparatus of government, and not to foster nationalism. To use Brading's phrase, they were more interested in state-building than in nation-building. Moreover, the means by which identification with the nation was to be achieved were not those usually associated with nationalism: liberals could not lavish praise on the virtues of the common man because they saw the defining characteristics of the *gente humilde* as too bound up with Catholicism, and they could not appeal to a glorious national history because its most remarkable moments were linked to the successes of the almost equally unacceptable Aztecs, Spaniards, or priest-led independence movements.[7] In other words, in the years leading up to the 1856 Reform the nation was celebrated not for itself but as the antichurch, as a substitute for the church. Instead of holding up for admiration the quintessential, ordinary Mexican as a symbol of what was great about the nation, the liberals hoped to create a new Mexican Everyman by changing the material conditions in which the popular classes lived, by giving them new interests that only a strong nation could protect, and by exposing them to new ideas through the schools, thereby making it logical and natural for them to think of themselves as "Mexicans," rather than, say, as Catholics or Michoacanos or Patzcuarenses. The pre-Reform liberals, then, wanted to transform the masses rather than to transform liberal rhetoric.

But by 1867 things had changed. The liberals had become not just the champions of reform but the leaders of an army that had twice triumphed over the church and the conservatives. This experience *did* transform the way liberals thought about and presented their agenda, in two ways: by making unrelenting anticlericalism no longer necessary (since the church was not only defeated but was also discredited), and by giving them heroes who were not only not priests or Spaniards or Indians but who were linked directly to the liberal cause. Thus, despite the fact that many popular groups in Michoacán resisted liberalism (especially the numerous indigenous communities that followed General Ramón Méndez, an Indian from Ario, into the conservative/French camp), the wars inspired the liberal party publicly to trumpet virtues that it had relegated to unimportance before the Reform. This was especially true, of course, of patriotism during the recent wars, which became almost a litmus test for public office. But the liberals also felt freer, in the wake of their victory over the church, to appropriate and mythologize the patriotism of priests during the independence wars and, under Díaz, symbolically to accept the spiritual leadership of the defanged Catholic church. These were themes that had appeal across class lines, as opposed to the appeals pitched narrowly at the middle class before the wars. In time, liberal definitions of patriotism came to include entrepreneurship as well as direct service to the government: elites who invested in their haciendas or in mines or railroads or banks were helping to build the new liberal state as much as military leaders had done. The more discursively inclusive liberal approach, then, in the hands of the moderates who dominated the state after 1867, while not entirely eliminating antiliberal sympathies within the state (witness the *cristero* rebellions of the 1870s and, later, the 1920s), did help Díaz to govern, almost unchallenged, for over 30 years.

Having achieved, by the mid-1880s, the thing that had eluded almost all previous national governments — stability — the liberals' other preoccupation, economic progress, became a driving force. This preoccupation, which was only slightly reshaped by the positivist-influenced *científicos* in the late Porfiriato, led them in turn down roads that eventually undercut the very thing they had succeeded in building and capitalizing on during and after the midcentury wars: the sense of nation. The leading liberals, from Díaz on down, were so intent on courting the foreign investment that would enable Mexico to "catch up" with the rest of the world that their actions necessarily diminished the still-tenuous perception that the citizens had a primary loyalty to the nation, for the leaders of the nation were not behaving as if their primary loyalty was to their own citizens. Even the railroad came to take on a negative connotation of intrusive foreign exploitation: *El Derecho Cristiano* wrote in 1889 that the "railroad so far has brought nothing but trouble, and in fact has caused complete disequilibrium in the established order of commerce in the country; the railroad has come to be not a two-way street, as we were led to believe, by means of which foreign wealth flows to us, but the tentacles of an enormous octopus that swallows our soul."[8]

The liberals might have avoided the nationalist backlash, however, if they had been able to follow through on their pre-Reform pledge to use schools to inculcate the values of liberal nationhood. But by 1910, despite many years of state budget surpluses, there were only 344 primary schools in Michoacán—an increase of just 125 over the whole course of the Porfiriato—serving only some 27,500 children, perhaps 10 percent of those eligible for the "compulsory" and free system of schools mandated by Epitacio Huerta in 1858.[9] In Mexico City the effort to promote nationalism had tended toward the public spectacle and the public monument (for example, the "murals of stone" along the Porfirian-built Paseo de la Reforma), but in Michoacán few similar efforts were made.[10] People who had developed "nationalist" instincts, then—and they included men and women from all classes—felt increasingly betrayed by their own government, while the schools, potentially the most effective weapon with which to counterbalance the perception of the government as *vendepatria*, were allowed to languish.

The Reform in Michoacán in Historical and Historiographical Context

The writing on Mexican politics and national identity in the period before and after the Reform has generally not connected well to the scant literature on the socioeconomic causes and effects of the liberal movement. The former tends to see the Reform as an almost fully political phenomenon, springing from the political disasters of the post-independence period and especially the war with the United States, and dominated by often-inappropriate ideas imported from Europe. Where an economic dimension to the Reform is noted, it is as a complement to the general picture of decline; indeed, much of the literature on the nineteenth-century economy agrees that at midcentury Mexico was in the middle of a downward economic spiral that was scarcely affected by the Reform one way or the other. The thrust of most writing about the economic effects of the Reform has been either to emphasize its failures (the failure to create a large rural middle class, the failure to produce much revenue for the liberal cause, the failure to invigorate the unproductive hacienda system, and the failure not only to improve the economic fortunes of the Indian population, but also to provide any sort of substitute for the social and economic support formerly provided by the now-extinct Indian communities), or to suggest that its effects were limited, that nothing much changed, and that the Mexican economy continued to deteriorate.

This study, by contrast, suggests that neither the timing nor the long-term effects of the Reform can be fully understood unless it is placed in a context of economic cyclicality, specifically the strong economic upturn in the decade or so before the Ayutla Rebellion. As we have seen, it is that upturn that gave the reformers a context in which their program seemed real and necessary to a sufficient number of middle-class people to make their movement succeed after several earlier experiments in liberal reformism had failed. The midcentury economic recovery also shaped the nature of post-1867 politics, whose dominant characteristic was the choice made by the middle-class liberals to swallow their earlier anti-elite rhetoric and ally themselves with the wealthy landowners (and a smattering of industrialists) who had survived the Reform with a substantial portion of their wealth intact. If Michoacán had been as depressed and overburdened with debt before the Reform as conventional wisdom has it, these landowners would have suffered the same eclipse that had decimated the ranks of the hacendado class after 1810. But because of hacienda agriculture's relative strength before the Reform, hacendados were in a position to benefit from the reforms instituted by the liberals, and, in the long run, they did. The post-Reform depression, then, was not merely a continuation of an earlier depression but an almost completely different cycle that severely tested, but did not break, the wealthy landowning classes. It should be seen as part of a long and difficult process by means of which at least some of Ocampo's hopes for a more productive, more profitable, more commercial agricultural system were realized.

The fact that the middle-class liberals who took power in 1867 found it expedient to seek the acquiescence and approval of the temporarily weakened but not destroyed landowning class allowed landowners, in turn, to withdraw from direct participation in politics for the first time since independence, since they were assured of political influence without having to take on the responsibilities of governance and administration. Of course the centerpiece of the elite-courting policies of the post-1867 liberals — a vigorous program of internal improvements — also squared fully with the project to expand the economy to the benefit of the middle class, but there is a clear sense in which both the rhetoric and the policies of the Restored Republic and the early Porfiriato were meant to nurture the growth of an aggressively capitalist class.

But as the Porfirian regime grew stronger and more self-confident it became less and less attentive to the psychic and material needs of the Mexican-born wealthy, not only in its blatant catering to foreign investors but in its cavalcade of criticism of (some) domestic entrepreneurs for not being more like the foreigners, for being, essentially, insufficiently bourgeois. And it was true that as the post-Reform depression eased (in the 1880s), and then mutated into the helter-skelter race for wealth of the last decade of the Porfiriato, many elites *did* resume the "aristocratic" habits of mind and behavior that had always infuriated the liberals but that were submerged during the periods of depression (the 1820s and 1830s, and the 1860s and 1870s). During the boom of the first decade of the twentieth century, just as during the more modest boom of the 1840s and early 1850s, the political alliance between the middle groups and the hacendados broke down along just these lines. It is impossible to generalize about the political sympathies of a decidedly heterogeneous elite, which was deeply split over the question of whether or not the boisterous and ambitious foreign investors should be models for the behavior of the Mexican upper class. But it should not surprise that the leaders of the Revolution of 1910 in Michoacán were grandchildren of wealthy men who had dominated politics in the first half of the nineteenth century, and children of wealthy men who had sat on the political sidelines since the Reform. This was, after all, the political history of many well-to-do families in the late Porfiriato, a history that, like Mexican history itself, was given shape and direction by the Reform.

Inventoried Wealth at Death, 1800–1910

This appendix consists of a series of tables showing the inventoried wealth at death of members of the provincial elite. It includes only individuals with gross assets of more than 20,000 pesos for whom detailed information about the nature of their wealth at death is known. Almost invariably, this information comes from estate inventories, but I have also used a few detailed wills or other accountings that were made shortly before death (see "Sources" after Appendix Table 1.10). Represented here, then, is only a fraction of the economic elite, which I estimate — according to the following reasoning — to number around 250 heads of household in the state at any given moment. A list compiled by the state government in the early 1840s for the purpose of establishing forced loan quotas names some 200 individuals who owned property worth more than 20,000 pesos, while an 1889 property registry lists 165 owners of *rural* property in this range. These two lists, then, square reasonably well, given that in 1889 we might expect another 35 or so individuals to own *urban* property worth more than 20,000 pesos. To this estimate of 200 property owners, however, we must add a certain number of merchants or industrialists who did not own enough property to qualify them as economic elites, but whose residences and financial assets combined to push their assets into the 20,000 peso and above range. If we assume that there were at least 50 such individuals in the state, we arrive at an estimate for the entire economic elite of 250. AHCE, Actas, Caja 25, exp. 1, "Actas de sesiones secretas," 4 September 1842; AHCE, Actas, Caja 25, "Actas públicas," 25 June 1843; "Noticia de la propiedad rústica del Estado y producción de la misma," in *Memoria de la administración pública del Estado de Michoacán . . . 1889.*

APPENDIX TABLE 1.1

Wealth at Death of Michoacán's Elite, 1800–1810

Name	Value of land and structures	Movables[a]	Cash and credits	Urban real estate	Factories and mills	Store merchandise	Personal effects	Total
1. Aguilera, Juan Antonio	50,000	30,000	145,367	17,000	—	—	5,000	247,367
2. Arandia, Ventura	—	30,580	41,367	6,551	—	—	3,085	81,583
3. Betancourt, Br. J. M.	8,281	5,712	—	3,606	1,100	—	2,986	21,685
4. Díaz de Hortega, Felipe	—	—	18,166	—	—	—	17,853	36,019
5. González de Bustamante, M.	18,500	6,762	10,443	—	—	—	392	36,097
6. Orovio, Ma. Josefa	28,607	30,311	4,926	11,076	—	1,077	3,303	79,300
7. Ortiz de la Huerta, J. N.	72,740	1,000	9,897	9,565	—	—	—	93,202
8. Peredo, José María	54,726	106,190	19,186	55,260	—	—	4,244	239,606
9. Pérez Busta, José Cipriano	—	—	—	3,000	—	17,000	—	20,000
10. Ramos, Ma. Concepción	—	16,768	3,956	21,715	—	3,913	471	46,823
11. Soriano, Antonio	—	—	—	14,304	—	9,000	—	23,304
12. Tapia, Antonio	—	550	6,340	12,193	—	—	1,349	20,432
13. Valdes, Ma. Josefa	55,053	34,371	4,392	4,452	—	2,125	3,154	103,547

[a]Where there is no separate account of movables on an hacienda or other rural property, this usually means that the value of the movables has been included in the category "Value of land and structures."

APPENDIX TABLE 1.2

Wealth at Death of Michoacán's Elite, 1811–29

Name	Value of land and structures	Movables[a]	Cash and credits	Urban real estate	Factories and mills	Store merchandise	Personal effects	Total
1. Alday, Ma. Josefa	12,010	7,089	836	9,250	—	—	3,801	32,986
2. Alzúa, Pascual	—	—	115,505	32,983	—	94,590	7,452	250,530
3. Bárcena, Br. Juan de la	25,427	2,339	17,387	9,300	—	—	1,396	55,849
4. Botello, Br. Joaquín	7,000	—	26,500	2,300	—	—	—	35,800
5. Corral, Santos	—	—	44,187	—	—	4,328	—	48,515
6. Escandón, Mariano	—	—	—	35,859	—	—	22,358	58,217
7. Espinoza de los Monteros y Plata, Juan Manuel	—	896	—	22,430	—	—	2,642	25,968
8. García Carrasquedo, D.	61,000	7,374	—	10,000	—	—	—	78,374
9. González Castañón, B.	—	—	38,160	18,395	—	1,371	1,096	59,022
10. Huarte, Isidro	124,373	—	306,103	84,833	—	73,321	27,844	616,475
11. Larragoiti, Domingo	30,159	—	6,424	14,364	—	—	1,096	52,043
12. de los Ríos, Matías A.	29,701	2,340	—	7,902	—	—	—	39,943
13. Sámano, Mariana	46,681	7,948	—	2,200	—	—	908	57,737
14. Sánchez, Ma. Guadalupe	—	2,495	19,310	7,719	—	2,049	2,749	34,322

[a]Where there is no separate account of movables on an hacienda or other rural property, this usually means that the value of the movables has been included in the category "Value of land and structures."

APPENDIX TABLE I.3

Wealth at Death of Michoacán's Elite, 1830–39

Name	Value of land and structures	Movables[a]	Cash and credits	Urban real estate	Factories and mills	Store merchandise	Personal effects	Total
1. del Corral, Ma. Josefa	18,330	—	57,684	11,380	—	—	706	88,100
2. García de Obeso, José Ma.	—	—	64,243	21,055	—	—	—	85,298
3. Lavarrieta, Josefa	—	—	60,000	14,566	—	—	21,609	96,175
4. Manzo Ceballos, Antonio	13,250	8,220	2,200	—	—	—	574	24,244
5. Molina, Francisco	—	—	9,764	12,000	—	2,624	(incl. in store)	24,388
6. Muñiz, José María	—	22,910	28,948	7,171	—	—	1,137	60,166
7. Ponce de León, Trinidad	22,543	3,075	14,153	—	—	—	305	40,076
8. Ruíz, Joaquín Teobaldo	11,508	5,889	9,978	6,119	—	8,116	958	42,568

[a]Where there is no separate account of movables on an hacienda or other rural property, this usually means that the value of the movables has been included in the category "Value of land and structures."

APPENDIX TABLE 1.4

Wealth at Death of Michoacán's Elite, 1840–49

Name	Value of land and structures	Movables[a]	Cash and credits	Urban real estate	Factories and mills	Store merchandise	Personal effects	Total
1. Campusano, Joaquín	—	—	27,715	26,459	—	5,847	7,542	67,563
2. Gómez Puente, Juan	27,799	9,976	10,707	9,112	—	—	2,311	59,905
3. Luna, Juan Bruno de	8,000	—	—	25,425	—	—	—	33,425
4. Muñiz y Soto, Ramón	—	—	33,807	2,837	—	—	75	36,719
5. Ortiz de Ayala, J.	19,488	—	—	300	—	11,553	400	31,741
6. Páramo, Norberto	14,171	4,955	—	6,800	—	—	1,076	27,002
7. Piedra, José Guadalupe	72,389	53,343	5,357	5,100	—	—	532	136,721
8. Quevedo, Mariano	47,524	7,317	3,562	—	—	—	699	59,102

[a] Where there is no separate account of movables on an hacienda or other rural property, this usually means that the value of the movables has been included in the category "Value of land and structures."

APPENDIX TABLE 1.5

Wealth at Death of Michoacán's Elite, 1850–59

Name	Value of land and structures	Movables[a]	Cash and credits	Urban real estate	Factories and mills	Store merchandise	Personal effects	Total
1. Alzúa de Montenegro, M.	—	—	8,087	17,881	—	2,218	3,433	31,619
2. Chávez, Antonio	28,481	27,560	15,565	30,532	800	—	2,904	105,842
3. Estrada, Francisco	89,500	49,766	22,712	16,000	300	—	2,450	180,728
4. García Carrasquedo, Martín	27,317	15,442	12,641	10,513	—	—	1,305	67,218
5. Gómez, Cayetano	857,321	—	178,538	106,703	37,950	—	13,111	1,193,623
6. Macouzet, Juan	—	3,000	38,975	15,638	—	—	5,373	62,986
7. Maldonado, Mariano	—	—	626	20,125	—	791	5,133	26,675
8. Martínez, Concepción	44,050	2,887	260	—	—	—	—	47,197
9. Mier, Martín	24,085	28	4,406	10,038	—	—	443	39,000
10. Parente, Tomás	2,600	5,153	10,220	17,827	—	—	605	36,405
11. del Río, Joaquín	39,764	21,316	14,306	6,386	—	—	3,319	85,091
12. Román, Fernando	114,693	72,736	338,354	39,330	41,200	5,314	4,634	616,261
13. Ruiz de Chávez, Nicolás	185,146	95,301	54,876	33,468	—	—	6,005	374,796
14. Soravilla, Francisco	60,420	15,844	—	7,000	—	—	—	83,264
15. Zacanini, Antonio	69,902	—	72,914	29,628	600	36,828	3,858	213,730

[a]Where there is no separate account of movables on an hacienda or other rural property, this usually means that the value of the movables has been included in the category "Value of land and structures."

APPENDIX TABLE 1.6

Wealth at Death of Michoacán's Elite, 1860–69

Name	Value of land and structures	Movables[a]	Cash and credits	Urban real estate	Factories and mills	Store merchandise	Personal effects	Total
1. Castañeda, Ramón	—	—	24,000	—	—	—	552	24,552
2. Castrejón, Micaela	18,794	—	—	7,536	—	—	—	26,330
3. Chávez de Macouzet, S.	—	—	17,891	—	450	1,670	200	20,211
4. Chávez, Rafael	1,320	24,804	7,825	1,000	—	—	—	34,949
5. Losano, Ignacio	83,500	12,126	—	6,865	—	19,629	—	122,120
6. Maciel, Jesús	—	1,008	17,233	5,500	—	—	39	23,780
7. Magaña, Juan	38,620	5,872	14,607	8,433	—	—	330	67,862
8. Romero, José Guadalupe	—	—	34,457	9,737	—	—	14,032	58,226
9. Valdes, José María	—	1,350	21,427	12,083	—	—	1,910	36,770
10. Villaseñor, José Antonio	—	5,879	6,385	7,800	—	300	44	20,408

[a]Where there is no separate account of movables on an hacienda or other rural property, this usually means that the value of the movables has been included in the category "Value of land and structures."

APPENDIX TABLE 1.7

Wealth at Death of Michoacán's Elite, 1870–79

Name	Value of land and structures	Movables[a]	Cash and credits	Urban real estate	Factories and mills	Store merchandise	Personal effects	Total
1. Arriaga, Francisco	52,095	—	—	1,000	—	—	—	53,095
2. Barrera, Génaro	47,764	—	—	5,621	—	—	991	54,376
3. Bocanegra, Ramón	50,984	59,150	30,172	—	—	—	—	140,306
4. Cabellero, Juan Clímaco	105,932	—	2,254	5,000	—	—	—	113,186
5. Campusano, Buenaventura	—	—	38,375	41,401	—	7,851	682	88,309
6. Cañedo, Ramón	41,900	22,637	3,400	6,300	—	7,628	757	82,622
7. Elguero, Manuel	—	—	1,674	8,622	14,247	—	—	24,543
8. Errejón, Antonio	71,611	6,358	28,170	8,140	—	—	510	114,789
9. Flores, Juan N.	86,110	—	43,855	10,044	—	—	7,755	147,764
10. García, Francisco	168,078	19,205	323,712	30,800	—	20,133	3,733	565,661
11. García, Miguel	4,433	3,728	15,688	10,708	—	1,849	399	36,805
12. Garibay, María Concepción	19,094	28,587	10,445	4,000	—	1,497	733	64,356

(continued)

Wealth at Death of Michoacán's Elite, 1870–79 *(continued)*

Name	Value of land and structures	Movables[a]	Cash and credits	Urban real estate	Factories and mills	Store merchandise	Personal effects	Total
13. Grande, Francisco	67,000	—	20,482	26,000	—	—	1,573	115,055
14. Larrauri, Lorenzo	68,095	4,984	—	5,660	—	—	323	79,062
15. López Verdusco, Francisco	18,222	6,047	360	1,950	—	125	—	26,704
16. Luna, Agustín	146,787	—	22,602	21,000	—	800	2,887	194,076
17. Pérez Gil, José María	3,750	9,247	—	14,464	—	—	—	27,461
18. Piedra, Juan Bautista	27,900	17,061	10,363	—	—	120	—	55,444
19. Sánchez, Vicente	163,718	10,098	12,361	14,608	—	—	4,859	205,644
20. Torres Ortiz, J. M.	7,956	4,134	6,345	3,150	—	—	—	21,585

[a]Where there is no separate account of movables on an hacienda or other rural property, this usually means that the value of the movables has been included in the category "Value of land and structures."

APPENDIX TABLE 1.8

Wealth at Death of Michoacán's Elite, 1880–89

Name	Value of land and structures	Movables[a]	Cash and credits	Urban real estate	Factories and mills	Store merchandise	Personal effects	Total
1. Aguiar, Agustín	35,500	2,000	22,534	5,200	—	—	—	65,234
2. Anaya, Ramón	—	—	57,470	6,000	—	—	—	63,470
3. Antia, Antonia	51,843	21,974	—	1,000	—	—	862	75,679
4. Díaz Barriga, J. M.	25,336	8,965	7,394	2,035	22,100	—	—	65,830
5. Echaiz, Jesús	40,000	1,559	60	—	—	242	—	41,861
6. Erdozain, Ignacio	300,000	27,607	—	12,000	—	—	—	339,607
7. García, Luis G.	25,900	3,317	20,681	—	—	—	300	50,198
8. González, Alejandro	37,603	10,892	33,826	—	—	—	1,396	83,717
9. Gutiérrez, Antonio	26,702	7,756	1,979	7,431	—	—	181	44,049
10. Hegarat, Juan	—	—	76,697	—	—	8,643	—	85,340
11. Jiménez, Marcos	—	160	1,700	6,865	—	12,436	245	21,406
12. Lascano, Guadalupe	25,000	600	—	2,500	—	—	80	28,180
13. Mendoza, Cipriano	12,000	4,500	3,830	9,700	—	—	415	30,445
14. Montes, Felipe de Jesús	30,000	9,855	8,669	5,723	—	—	479	54,726
15. Mora de Anaya, Antonia	—	—	22,172	—	—	—	—	22,172
16. Ortiz de Sánchez, Jesús	95,589	3,764	6,056	—	—	—	394	105,803
17. Oviedo, Juan N.	16,000	—	—	7,998	—	—	—	23,998

(continued)

Wealth at Death of Michoacán's Elite, 1880–89 *(continued)*

Name	Value of land and structures	Movables[a]	Cash and credits	Urban real estate	Factories and mills	Store merchandise	Personal effects	Total
18. Rodríguez, Vicente	14,633	14,094	35,548	5,300	3,044	—	83	72,702
19. Sandoval, Pedro	35,638	3,830	14,690	888	—	—	424	55,470
20. Solórzano, Ignacio	71,666	40,773	238,834	25,000	2,476	—	—	378,749
21. Verdusco, Mariano	31,600	—	2,000	11,900	—	—	500	46,000

aWhere there is no separate account of movables on an hacienda or other rural property, this usually means that the value of the movables has been included in the category "Value of land and structures."

APPENDIX TABLE 1.9
Wealth at Death of Michoacán's Elite, 1890–99

Name	Value of land and structures	Movables[a]	Cash and credits	Urban real estate	Factories and mills	Store merchandise	Personal effects	Total
1. Alvarez de Méndez, Jesús	20,636	2,670	—	12,428	—	9,703	—	45,437
2. Chavolla, Francisco	55,000	27,786	12,239	4,367	—	1,479	—	100,871
3. Coria, Espiridión	16,248	18,819	3,192	10,660	5,090	—	3,755	57,764
4. Dávalos, Arcadio	51,870	34,940	—	9,190	—	1,500	—	97,500
5. Dávalos, Nicolás	100,000	—	30,000	12,478	—	—	170	142,648
6. Elorza, Cristóbal	14,118	24,168	40,119	1,388	—	—	144	79,937
7. Errejón, Juan de Dios	8,650	4,426	15,497	2,150	—	—	1,233	31,956
8. Errejón, Simón	92,190	5,770	131,317	26,318	—	—	1,286	256,881
9. Estrada, Concepción	22,008	11,246	8,000	19,074	—	—	2,670	62,998
10. Fernández, Francisco	5,250	—	35,034	3,500	—	—	339	44,123
11. García, Andrés	119,432	52,459	1,089	9,843	—	1,054	134	184,011
12. García Cambrón, Rafael	11,626	7,736	4,337	10,628	—	3,832	—	38,159
13. García Zapata, José	43,150	18,905	235,433	45,131	—	2,657	3,758	349,034
14. Igartúa, Octaviano	60,450	8,694	9,095	—	—	—	1,455	79,694
15. Jiménez, Epifanio	101,940	25,420	40,856	16,350	—	—	—	184,566
16. Loaiza de Pérez Gil, J.	19,600	1,000	16,129	3,787	—	—	—	40,516
17. Macouzet, Juan	65,000	8,444	136	—	—	—	767	74,347

(continued)

Wealth at Death of Michoacán's Elite, 1890–99 *(continued)*

Name	Value of land and structures	Movables[a]	Cash and credits	Urban real estate	Factories and mills	Store merchandise	Personal effects	Total
18. Marván, Alcibíades	3,000	—	6,500	3,250	—	17,651	—	30,401
19. Méndez, Hermenegildo	16,500	7,238	4,250	4,300	—	—	—	32,288
20. Méndez Cano, Miguel	79,106	17,317	32,667	9,520	—	—	4,100	142,710
21. Méndez Garibay, Perfecto	26,122	9,740	7,000	6,800	6,000	—	350	56,012
22. Menocal de Luna, C.	20,000	27,430	18,757	—	—	—	2,427	68,614
23. Montaño, Rafael	38,150	210	245	7,300	7,135	—	2,893	55,933
24. del Moral, Antonio	183,333	3,961	3,571	20,390	—	—	3,971	215,226
25. Moreno, Calixto	31,460	—	10,009	28,962	—	—	—	70,431
26. Mota, Antonio P.	—	—	6,715	23,605	—	—	—	30,320
27. Oseguera, Joaquín	—	148,263	124,396	144,600	—	—	7,457	424,716
28. Pérez, Juan Mucio	—	—	3,308	9,000	27,522	27,708	—	67,538
29. Pérez Gil, José Antonio	5,000	—	9,889	17,694	—	—	450	33,033
30. Reynoso, Antonio	5,998	—	10,450	4,500	—	—	113	21,061
31. Rubio, Juan Bautista	7,275	—	3,635	12,907	—	—	1,362	25,179
32. Ruiz Valle, Ramón	—	—	4,555	18,336	—	—	393	23,284
33. Treviño, Antonio	96,500	107,669	14,811	41,772	—	—	—	260,752
34. Valladares, Jesús	70,670	28,154	35,410	—	5,066	—	—	139,300
35. Vidales, Feliciano	110,000	180,336	93,845	42,885	50,000	21,567	1,993	500,626

[a]Where there is no separate account of movables on an hacienda or other rural property, this usually means that the value of the movables has been included in the category "Value of land and structures."

APPENDIX TABLE 1.10
Wealth at Death of Michoacán's Elite, 1900–1910

Name	Value of land and structures	Movables^a	Cash and credits	Urban real estate	Factories and mills	Store merchandise	Personal effects	Total
1. Aguiar, Dolores	19,750	—	273	1,400	—	—	501	21,924
2. Amescua, Román de Jesús	23,000	3,220	33,199	5,000	—	—	848	65,267
3. Arciga, José Ignacio	—	—	276,250	92,167	—	—	12,672	381,089
4. Arriaga, Luis	53,963	2,020	—	14,578	—	—	—	70,561
5. Bocanegra, Antonio	67,890	29,496	—	3,500	2,036	128	—	103,050
6. Bris de Errejón, Pilar	—	—	10,000	16,625	—	—	1,480	28,105
7. Díaz de Torres, Rita	15,070	—	18,570	36,355	—	—	451	70,446
8. Espinosa, Francisco	24,227	3,275	12,918	8,089	6,000	1,796	164	56,469
9. Gómez de Sámano, Trinidad	30,000	4,693	45,399	21,000	—	—	—	101,092
10. Guerrero, Plácido	—	—	77,328	19,189	—	—	800	97,317
11. Haristoy, Francisco	—	—	40,208	2,800	—	—	—	43,008
12. Higareda de Sierra, Jesús	58,251	19,685	—	600	—	—	190	78,726
13. Hiribarne, Cayetano	80,030	—	—	—	—	215	—	80,245
14. Hiribarne, Juan	—	—	58,268	42,684	—	—	200	101,152
15. Landeta, Juan Bautista	202,532	—	18,752	10,600	—	—	4,000	235,884
16. Martínez, Angel	5,500	5,795	2,600	15,900	—	—	—	29,795
17. Mejía, Miguel	112,000	1,040	—	—	—	—	—	113,040

(continued)

Wealth at Death of Michoacán's Elite, 1900–1910 (continued)

Name	Value of land and structures	Movables[a]	Cash and credits	Urban real estate	Factories and mills	Store merchandise	Personal effects	Total
18. Morfín, José María	—	—	12,541	5,900	24,531	—	1,000	43,972
19. Núñez de Monge, Dolores	—	—	24,223	24,387	—	—	2,082	50,692
20. Orozco de Camorlinga, A.	—	—	13,250	8,615	—	51,343	558	73,766
21. Ortiz de Gutiérrez, María	—	—	26,000	5,000	—	—	—	31,000
22. Ortiz Huerta, Francisco	—	—	—	22,400	—	—	1,507	23,907
23. Oseguera, Crescencio	94,000	12,000	—	9,000	—	—	1,354	116,354
24. Piñon, Ignacio	3,324	—	—	17,752	—	—	—	21,076
25. Ramírez, Ramón	468,839	—	317,277	44,983	—	9,565	2,625	843,289
26. Reyes, Epifanio	65,564	—	26,000	21,000	7,800	—	—	120,364
27. Sámano, Luis	32,740	11,123	22,649	6,000	—	—	—	72,512
28. Santoyo, Isidoro	139,942	—	8,220	2,500	—	—	214	150,876
29. Solórzano, Francisco	28,500	3,555	1,200	1,900	2,100	—	736	37,991
30. Solórzano, Manuel María	95,000	55,000	—	28,000	—	—	—	178,000
31. Vallejo de S., Loreto	66,400	144,481	28,579	40,000	—	2,696	—	282,156
32. Vélez, José	44,865	—	3,971	20,434	—	—	—	69,270

[a] Where there is no separate account of movables on an hacienda or other rural property, this usually means that the value of the movables has been included in the category "Value of land and structures."

SOURCES FOR APPENDIX TABLES 1.1 TO 1.10

APPENDIX TABLE 1.1 (1800–1810)

1. Juan Antonio Aguilera: ANM, Aguilar, 1810, 3 October.

2. José Ventura de Arandia: AHMM, 1808, "Inventarios formados a los bienes que quedaron por fallecimiento de D. Ventura Arandia."

3. Br. José Manuel de Betancourt: AHCP, Leg. 65-B, 1800–09, exp. 3, no title, inventory dated 1803.

4. Felipe Díaz de Hortega: AHMM, 1809, "Inventarios formados a los bienes del Sr. Felipe Díaz de Hortega, Intendente Corregidor que fue . . ."

5. Mariana González de Bustamante (m. Francisco Gutiérrez de la Madrid): AHCP, 65-B, 1800–09, exp. 3, "Inventarios y aprecios de los bienes que quedaron por muerte de Da. Mariana González de Bustamante," 1805.

6. María Josefa Orovio: AHCP, Leg 65-B, 1800–09, exp. 4, testament of María Josefa Orovio (m. Capt. Joaquín de Monasterio), 1802.

7. José Nicolás Ortiz de la Huerta: AHMM, 1816, "Expediente formado sobre esperas pedidas por D. Joaquín Ortiz de sus acreedores."

8. José María de Peredo: AHMM, 1808, "Autos de inventarios a bienes del difunto Capitán José María Peredo."

9. José Cipriano Pérez de la Busta: ANM, Montaño, 1809, 8 November.

10. María Concepción Ramos: AHCP, 66-C, 1800–09, exp. 1, "Año de 1807. Inventarios de Doña María Eusebia de la Concepción Ramos."

11. Antonio Soriano: ANM, Montaño, 1805, 30 January.

12. Antonio Tapia: AHMM, 1810, no title, inventory of estate of Antonio Tapia.

13. María Josefa Valdes (m. Eusebio de Olavarrieta): AHCP, leg. 66-C, 1800–09, exp. 3, "Inventarios de los bienes que quedaron por muerte de Da. María Josefa Valdes," 1806.

APPENDIX TABLE 1.2 (1811–29)

1. María Josefa Alday, viuda de Agustín del Río: AHCP, Leg. 71-C, 1820–29, no title [has 1825 on front page, but concerns inventory of goods dated 1827.]

2. Pascual Alzúa: AHMM, 1830, "Cuenta de hijuela de división y partición de los bienes que quedaron por muerte de D. Pascual de Alzúa y de su primera mujer Da. María del Carmen Huarte."

3. Br. Juan de la Bárcena: AHMM, 1822, "Inventarios formados por memorias extrajudiciales a los bienes que quedaron por fallecimiento del Pres. Br. Juan de la Bárcena."

4. Br. Joaquín Botello, cura de Huango: AHMCR, Autos Testamentarias, Leg. 35 (1689–1853). Will of Br. José María Sierratagle [alvacea de Botello], dated 27 November 1821.

5. José Santos del Corral: AHMM, 1820, no title, inventory dated 4 May 1820.

6. Lic. Mariano de Escandón, Conde de Sierragorda: AHMM, 1815, "Inventario de bienes del Lic. Mariano Escandón . . ."

7. Juan M. Espinosa de los Monteros y Plata: AHMM, 1818, testament and inventory.

8. Dionisio García Carrasquedo: ANM, Aguilar, 1817, 8 August.

9. Blas González de Castañón: AHMM, 1817, "Inventarios formados a los bienes que quedaron por fallecimiento del Regidor Blas González Castañón . . ."

10. Isidro Huarte: AHMM, 1824, testament and inventory.

11. Domingo Larragoiti: AHCP, Leg. 68, exp. 3, testament and estate inventory.

12. Lic. Matías Antonio de los Ríos: AHMM, 1820, testament and inventory.

13. Mariana Sámano, v. de Sebastián de Odriosola: AHMM, 1819, "Autos de las haciendas de Andocutín y la Bartolilla."

14. María Guadalupe Sánchez: AHMM, 1816, "Testamentaria de Da. Maria Guadalupe Sánchez mujer legítima de Salvador Dueñas . . ."

APPENDIX TABLE 1.3 (1830–39)

1. María Josefa del Corral: ANM, Iturbide, 1831, n. d.

2. José María García de Obeso: AHMM, 1839, "Cesión de bienes que para pago de los acreedores del finado Capt. José María García de Obeso hizo su viuda Rafaela de la Riva."

3. María Josefa Lavarrieta: ANM, Rincón, 1837, 20 September.

4. Antonio Manzo Ceballos: ANM, Valdovinos, 1838, apéndice.

5. Francisco Molina: AHCP, Leg. 73-E, 1820–29, inventory of estate of Francisco Molina, dated 1835.

6. José María Muñiz: AHMM, 1835, "Estado en que se hayan los bienes de la Testamentaria que es a mi cargo, como alvacea de mi finado esposo D. José María Muñiz," and AHPJ, 1838, Primero Civil, Leg. 1, "Autos formados sobre el fallecimiento intestado de Doña Guadalupe Soto, viuda que fue de D. José María Muñiz."

7. María Trinidad Ponce de León: AHMM, 1833, "Hijuela y cuenta de partición de los bienes de la finada Da. María Trinidad Ponce de León."

8. Joaquín Teobaldo Ruiz: AHMM, 1836, testament and inventory.

APPENDIX TABLE 1.4 (1840–49)

1. Joaquín Campusano: ANM, Rincón, 1840, 3 August.

2. Juan Gómez Puente: ANM, García, 1848, 20 July.

3. Juan Bruno de Luna: ANM, Valdovinos, 1840, 29 January.

4. Ramón Muñiz y Soto: ANM, Valdovinos, 1844, n. d.

5. Joaquín Ortiz de Ayala: ANM, García, 1848, 8 February.

6. Norberto Páramo: ANM, Alvarez, 1847, 10 October.

7. José Guadalupe de la Piedra: AHMM, 1841. "Autos de inventarios formados a los bienes . . . de D. José Guadalupe de la Piedra."

8. Mariano Quevedo: AHPJ, 1840, Primero Civil, Leg. 1, "Autos sobre inventarios de los bienes que quedaron por fallecimiento de D. Mariano Quevedo."

APPENDIX TABLE 1.5 (1850–59)

1. Macaria Alzúa de Montenegro: ANM, García, 1851, appendix.

2. Antonio Chávez: AHMM, 1855, "Expediente instruido a instancia de D. Esteban García, alvacea del finado D. Antonio Chávez, sobre facción de inventarios . . ."

3. Francisco Estrada: AHMM, 1852, "Inventarios a bienes de D. Francisco Estrada."

4. Martín García Carrasquedo: AHPJ, 1851, Primero Civil, Leg. 1, "Juicio de Testamentaria del Sr. Martín García de Carrasquedo."

5. Cayetano Gómez: AHMM, 1858, "Resumen general de todos los bienes pertenecientes a la Testamentaria [de Cayetano Gómez] y que existen tanto en esta Ciudad y en la de Colima como en las jurisdicciones de los pueblos de Yndaparapeo, Tarímbaro, Taretan, y de la Villa de Charo."

6. Juan Macouzet: AHPJ, 1860, Civil, "Cuenta de alvaseasgo y partición de los bienes del finado Dr. Juan Macouzet."

7. Mariano Maldonado: AHPJ, 1850, Primero Civil, Leg. 1, "Promovido por el Br. Francisco Maldonado sobre facción de inventarios a bienes de la Testamentaria de D. Mariano Maldonado."

8. Concepción Martínez de Landeta: ANM, Laris, 1899, appendix.

9. Martín Mier: AHPJ, 1864, "Testamentaria del Sr. D. Martín de Mier."

10. Tomás Parente: ANM, León, 1865, appendix.

11. Joaquín del Río: AHCP, leg. 95-D, Protocolo de 1856, n.d. (follows 20 November 1856).

12. Fernando Román: ANM, García, 1851, 6 March.

13. Nicolás Ruiz de Chávez: ANM, Valdovinos, 1856, 4 December.

14. Francisco Soravilla: AHPJ, 1854, Primero Civil, Leg. 1, "Promovido por el curador de la menor Doña Rosario Soto contra D. Mariano Soravilla . . ."

15. Antonio Zacanini: AHMM, 1857, mistakenly attached to an unrelated document entitled "Curaduría ad bona de la menor Doña Socorro Chávez."

APPENDIX TABLE 1.6 (1860–69)

1. Ramón Castañeda y Tresguerras: ANM, León, 1866, appendix.

2. Micaela Castrejón: ANM, Victoria, 1896, 14 December (Pátzcuaro).

3. Socorro Chávez de Macouzet: ANM, León, 1866, appendix.

4. Rafael Chávez: AHPJ, Civil, 1862, "Cesíón de bienes que hace D. Rafael Chávez para pagar a sus acreedores."

5. Ignacio Losano: ANM, Huerta, 1867, 12 February.

6. Jesús Maciel: ANM, Alvarado, 1880, 26 May.

7. Juan Magaña: ANM, Pérez, 1862, 4 December.

8. José Guadalupe Romero: ANM, Larís, 1902, appendix.

9. José María Valdes: ANM, León, 1866, appendix.

10. José Antonio Villaseñor: ANM, Huerta, 1866, 11 April.

APPENDIX TABLE 1.7 (1870–79)

1. Francisco Arriaga: ANM, Larís, 1893, 23 October.

2. Génaro Barrera: ANM, Huacuja, 1879, 1 October (Pátzcuaro).

3. Ramón Bocanegra: ANM, Huerta, 1877, 24 and 29 September.

4. Juan Climaco Caballero: ANM, León, 1876, appendix.

5. Buenaventura Campusano: ANM, Huerta, 1880, appendix.

6. Ramón Cañedo: ANM, Registro de Hipotecas de Maravatío, 1878, 10 April.

7. Manuel Elguero: ANM, González, 1873, appendix.

8. Antonio Errejón: ANM, González, 1873, appendix.

9. Juan N. Flores: ANM, González, 1872, 26 September.

10. Francisco García: ANM, Haro, 1880, 6 February.

11. Miguel García: ANM, Alvarado, 1879, appendix.

12. María Concepción Garibay (m. Luis Verdusco López): ANM, Haro, 1882, 16 January (Zamora).

13. Francisco Grande: AHPJ, Civil, 1875, "Testamentaria [del Sr. Francisco Grande], promovida por el Lic. Manuel Grande."

14. Lorenzo Larrauri: ANM, Larís, 1895, appendix.

15. Francisco López Verdusco: ANM, Haro, 1881, 12 November (Zamora).

16. Agustín Luna: ANM, Huerta, 1879, 1 October.

17. José María Pérez Gil: ANM, Huerta, 1888, 4 February.

18. Juan Bautista Piedra: ANM, Huacuya, 1888, 13 April.

19. Vicente Sánchez: ANM, Alvarado, 1878, appendix.

20. José María Torres Ortiz: ANM, Huerta, 1878, appendix.

APPENDIX TABLE 1.8 (1880–89)

1. Agustín Aguiar: ANM, Haro, 1880, 13 July (Zamora).

2. Ramón Anaya: ANM, Alvarez, 1880, 4 December.

3. Antonia Antia de Sámano: ANM, Ruiz Durán, 1900, appendix.

4. José María Díaz Barriga: ANM, Victoria, 1884, 29 June (Pátzcuaro).

5. Jesús Echaiz: ANM, Torres Pallares, 1896, 19 February (Maravatío).

6. Ignacio Erdozain: ANM, Gutiérrez, 1904, appendix no. 2.

7. Luis G. García: ANM, Haro, 1907, 14 May (Zamora).
8. Alejandro González: ANM, Victoria, 1885, 13 May (Pátzcuaro).
9. Antonio Gutiérrez: ANM, Maciel, 1892, 6 August (Tacámbaro).
10. Juan Hegarat: ANM, Gutiérrez, 1890, 17 May; Ibarrola, 1898, 23 May.
11. Marcos Jiménez: ANM, Maciel, 1886, 19 June (Tacámbaro).
12. Guadalupe Lascano: ANM, Peredo, 1899, 27 September (Pátzcuaro).
13. Cipriano Mendoza: ANM, Victoria, 1886, 2 October (Pátzcuaro).
14. Felipe de Jesús Montes: ANM, Haro, 1883, 28 June (Zamora).
15. Antonia de la Mora de Anaya: ANM, Alvarez, 1889, 29 April.
16. Jesús Ortiz de Sánchez: ANM, Huerta, 1886, appendix.
17. Juan N. Oviedo: ANM, Huerta, 1892, appendix.
18. Vicente Rodríguez: ANM, Díaz, 1895, 29 October (Uruapan).
19. Pedro Sandoval: ANM, Alcocer y Piña, 1894, 13 September (Pátzcuaro).
20. Ignacio Solórzano: ANM, Huacuja, 1888, 17 March.
21. Mariano Verdusco: ANM, Haro, 1891, 6 June (Zamora).

APPENDIX TABLE 1.9 (1890–99)

1. Jesús Alvarez de Méndez: ANM, Ruiz Durán, 1907, 17 January (Uruapan).
2. Francisco Chavolla: ANM, Saavedra, 1895, 6 June (La Piedad).
3. Espiridión Coria: ANM, de la Pena, 1894, 22 May (Uruapan).
4. Arcadio Dávalos: ANM, Haro, 1905, 1 July (Zamora).
5. Nicolás Dávalos: ANM, Haro, 1898, 27 May (Zamora).
6. Cristobal Elorza: ANM, Larís, 1898, appendix no. 1; Larís, 1898, 9 May.
7. Juan de Dios Errejón: ANM, Gutiérrez, 1899, appendix.
8. Simón Errejón: ANM, Gutiérrez, 1903, appendix no. 2.
9. Concepción Estrada: ANM, Larís, 1894, appendix.
10. Francisco Fernández: ANM, Larís, 1899, appendix.
11. Andrés García: ANM, Gutiérrez, 1893, appendix.
12. Rafael García Cambrón: ANM, Torres Pallares, 1893, 3 November (Maravatío).
13. José García Zapata: ANM, Estrada, 1897, appendix.
14. Octaviano Igartúa: ANM, Haro, 1896, 25 January (Zamora).
15. Epifanio Jiménez: ANM, Haro, 1906, 16 August (Zamora).
16. Joaquína Loaiza de Pérez Gil: ANM, Larís, 1896, appendix.
17. Juan Macouzet: ANM, Huerta, 1900, 16 November.
18. Alcibíades Marván: ANM, Mancera, 1900, 2 November (Maravatío).
19. Hermenegildo Méndez: ANM, Haro, 1892, 21 June (Zamora).
20. Miguel Méndez Cano: ANM, Haro, 1902, 21 August (Zamora).
21. Perfecto Méndez Garibay: ANM, Haro, 1899, 7 January (Zamora).
22. Concepción Menocal de Luna: ANM, Larís, 1897, appendix.

23. Rafael Montaño: ANM, Larís, 1895, appendix.
24. Antonio del Moral: ANM, Huerta, 1893, appendix.
25. Calixto Moreno: ANM, Gómez, 1893, 30 October.
26. Antonio Primitivo Mota: ANM, García, 1898, 16 March.
27. Joaquín Oseguera: ANM, Huerta, 1889, 5 July.
28. Juan Mucio Pérez: ANM, Ruiz Durán, 1907, 14 June.
29. José Antonio Pérez Gil: ANM, Larís, 1896, appendix.
30. Antonio Reynoso: ANM, Angeles, 1898, 28 May.
31. Juan Bautista Rubio: ANM, Larís, 1894, appendix.
32. Rafael Ruiz y Valle: ANM, Gutiérrez, 1902, 3 November.
33. Antonio Treviño: ANM, Uribe, 1898, 13 October (Uruapan).
34. Jesús Valladares: ANM, Uribe, 1901, 8 February (Uruapan).
35. Feliciano Vidales: ANM, Gutiérrez, 1898, 18 June.

APPENDIX TABLE 1.10 (1900–1910)

1. Dolores Aguiar: ANM, Larís, 1902, appendix.
2. Roman de Jesús Amescua: ANM, Haro, 1908, 11 June (Zamora).
3. José Ignacio Arciga: ANM, Larís, 1901, appendix.
4. Luis Arriaga: ANM, Huerta Cañeda, 1909, 11 August (Pátzcuaro).
5. Antonio Bocanegra: ANM, Larís, 1902, appendix.
6. Pilar Bris de Errejón: ANM, Barroso, 1909, appendix.
7. Rita Díaz de Torres: ANM, Gutiérrez, 1908, 14 May.
8. Francisco Espinosa Ramírez: ANM, Haro, 1909, 8 October (Zamora).
9. Trinidad Gómez de Sámano: ANM, Gutiérrez, 1904, 19 July.
10. Plácido Guerrero: ANM, Gutiérrez, 1907, appendix.
11. Francisco Haristoy: ANM, Gutiérrez, 1903, appendix.
12. Jesús Higareda de Sierra: ANM, Ruiz Durán, 1910, 16 April (Uruapan).
13. Cayetano Hiribarne: ANM, Cano, 1910, 9 April.
14. Juan Hiribarne: ANM, Angeles, 1910, 11 January.
15. Juan B. Landeta: ANM, Gutiérrez, 1910, appendix.
16. Angel Martínez: ANM, Uribe, 1905, 25 August (Uruapan).
17. Miguel Mejía: ANM, Cerrato, 1908, 11 August.
18. José María Morfín: ANM, Gutiérrez, 1906, 17 November; Gutiérrez, 1907, 7 January.
19. Dolores Núñez de Monge: ANM, Larís, 1905, appendix.
20. Antonia Orozco de Camorlinga: ANM, Ruiz Durán, 1901, 26 April (Uruapan).
21. María Ortiz de Gutiérrez: ANM, Barroso, 1906, 18 March.
22. Francisco Ortiz Huerta: ANM, Gutiérrez, 1906, appendix no. 1.
23. Crescencio Oseguera: ANM, Cano, 1910, 13 January.
24. Ignacio Piñón: ANM, Larís, 1906, appendix.

25. Ramón Ramírez: ANM, Cano, 1909, 22 September and 13 October.

26. Epifanio Reyes: ANM, Larís, 1902, appendix; Díaz, 1896, 23 March (Uruapan); Laris Contreras, 1892, 14 December.

27. Luis G. Sámano: ANM, Ibarrola, 1900, appendix.

28. Isidoro Santoyo: ANM, Larís, 1901, appendix.

29. Francisco Solórzano y Solórzano: ANM, Alcocer, 1904, 1 September (Pátzcuaro).

30. Manuel María Solórzano: ANM, Larís, 1903, 3 December and appendix.

31. Loreto Vallejo de Solórzano: ANM, Larís, 1905, appendix.

32. José Vélez: ANM, Cano, 1910, 31 May.

Inventoried and Estimated Wealth at Death, 1800–1910

This appendix consists of a series of tables that include not only individual wealth for which we have detailed information in the form of inventories, but also estimates of wealth that derive from other sources and methods. Usually these estimates have been inferred from the portions received by the individual's heirs and/or spouses, but occasionally I have reached an estimate based on knowledge about the market value of the individual's property, when it seems clear that this property constituted the vast majority of his or her wealth. All averages are rounded.

Inventoried and Estimated Wealth at Death of Michoacán's Elite, 1800–1810

Name	Gross assets	Assets after debts	Assets after debts as a percentage of gross assets
Aguilera, Capt. Juan Antonio	247,367	239,367	97%
Ayala, Teresa de	54,460	31,841	58
Arandia, José Ventura	81,583	41,346	51
Barandiarán, Ignacio	158,390	71,406	45
Betancourt, Br. José Manuel	21,685	8,923	41
Betancourt, Ma. Ana	25,000	—	—
Caballero, Andrés	49,000	38,840	79
Caballero, Juan Ignacio	—	120,000	—
Calvillo, Antonio	51,000	35,000	69
Cordero de Torres, Andrés	45,100	31,372	70
Cuevas, Lic. Joaquín de	29,418	—	—
Dávalos, Diego José	61,000	54,200	89
Díaz de Hortega, Int. Felipe	36,019	31,019	86
Farías Corral, Diego	31,112	16,137	52
Fernández Agreda, Br. Juan Manuel	31,500	31,500	100
Foncerrada, José Bernardo	310,000	235,000	76
García de Obeso, Gabriel	136,253	11,671	9
Gómez Maya, José Gregorio	70,171	50,126	71
González Venero, Br. Juan	23,000	—	—
González de Bustamante, Mariana	36,097	23,529	65
Guedea, Br. José Ignacio	46,000	32,000	70
Guinea, Julian Gerónimo	35,000		
Herrero, Miguel de	110,386	71,986	65
Hidalgo, Br. Miguel de	44,000	14,000	32
Ibarrola, Francisco Javier	—	52,696	—
Isasaga, Juan de	50,000	—	—
Isasaga, Agustín de	—	22,000	—
Iturria, Ma. Antonia	38,743	0	0

(continued)

Inventoried and Estimated Wealth at Death of Michoacán's Elite, 1800–1810 *(continued)*

Name	Gross assets	Assets after debts	Assets after debts as a percentage of gross assets
Jaso, Francisco Victorino	550,000	450,000	82%
Jaso, José Antonio	152,000	133,000	87
López de Piña, Lic. José Antonio	110,000	100,000	91
Martínez de Lejarza, Juan José	—	289,804	—
Martínez de Mendana, Eugenio	74,845	65,452	87
Michelena, Juan Manuel de	220,575	116,000	53
Mier y Terán, Juan de	—	110,000	—
Monasterio, Joaquín de	40,000	15,000	38
Monroy, Pedro de	—	25,000	—
Orovio, Ma. Josefa	79,300	48,062	61
Ortiz de la Huerta, José Nicolás	93,202	85,452	92
Peredo, Capt. José María	239,606	152,242	63
Pérez de la Busta, José Cipriano	20,000	20,000	100
Ponce de León, José María	—	28,000	—
Pimentel, José María	20,000	—	—
Ramírez de Prado, Antonio	25,416	—	—
Ramos, Ma. Concepción	46,823	41,549	89
del Río, Agustín	—	39,813	—
de la Riva, Francisco	100,000	—	—
Ruiz, Francisco Antonio	25,000	22,000	88
Ruiz de Chávez Larrina, Nicolás	85,000	38,000	45
Sagasola, Ignacio	49,000	37,000	76
Salceda, Pedro Antonio	274,088	180,000	66
San Miguel, Bishop Fray Antonio	—	28,000	—
Soriano, Antonio	23,304	13,304	57
Tapia, Antonio	20,432	6,946	33
Tapia, Simón de	—	125,000	—
Valdes, Ma. Josefa	103,547	61,603	59
Valdovinos, Manuel de	85,000	17,000	20
AVERAGES	90,700	78,100	64

APPENDIX TABLE 2.2

Inventoried and Estimated Wealth at Death of Michoacán's Elite,
1811–29

Name	Gross assets	Assets after debts	Assets after debts as a percentage of gross assets
Abarca de León, José María	120,000	73,379	61%
Alday, Josefa	32,986	4,957	15
Alday, Lic. Miguel de	27,000	27,000	100
Alzúa, Pascual	250,530	238,655	95
Arana, Pedro de	47,523	38,137	80
Arriaga, Ignacio	59,914	47,914	80
Bárcena, Br. Juan de	55,849	47,377	85
Bárcena, Dr. Manuel de la	36,000	11,600	32
Botello, Br. Joaquín	35,800	35,800	100
Castañeda, Ventura de	35,000	5,000	14
Celaya, Br. Manuel	27,016	27,016	100
Corral, José Santos	48,515	46,394	96
Escandón, Lic. Mariano de	58,217	—	—
Escobar, José Gregorio	34,686	—	—
Espinosa de los Monteros y Plata, Juan M.	25,968	—	—
García Carrasquedo, Dionisio	78,374	56,274	72
González Castañeda, Juan José	25,700	22,000	86
González Castañón, Blas	59,022	6,542	11
Herrera, Pedro	25,000	15,100	60
Huarte, Isidro	616,475	607,000	98
Iturbide, Agustín de	93,000	—	—
Iturbide, José Joaquín	100,000	75,000	75
Jiménez, Mariano	76,400	—	—
Larragoiti, Domingo de	52,043	27,918	54
de la Madrid hermanos	50,000	37,000	74
Martínez de Lejarza, Juan José	72,500	53,000	73
Menocal, Cor. Francisco	—	30,000	—
Morales, Lázaro	51,000	36,000	71
Navarro, José	67,745	6,400	9

(continued)

Inventoried and Estimated Wealth at Death of Michoacán's Elite,
1811–1829 *(continued)*

Name	Gross assets	Assets after debts	Assets after debts as a percentage of gross assets
Olarte, José Manuel de	139,000	66,000	47%
Pérez Llera, José Génaro	20,000	0	0
Ponce de León, Francisco	30,000	20,000	67
de los Ríos, Lic. Matías Antonio	39,943	24,330	61
Ruiz de Chávez, Ma. Ignacia	28,900	19,900	69
Sámano, Mariana	57,737	6,237	11
Sánchez, María Guadalupe	34,322	29,460	86
Solórzano, Br. Lázaro	40,000	28,000	70
Soto y Saldaña, Ignacio Fco.	25,000	—	—
Torres, José Mariano de	55,000	15,000	27
Velásquez Gudino, Ma. Antonia	80,000	80,000	100
Vélez de las Cuevas Cabeza de Vaca, María de la Luz	72,000	72,000	100
Vélez y Solórzano, Angel	187,000	71,200	38
AVERAGES	74,900	55,700	63

APPENDIX TABLE 2.3
Inventoried and Estimated Wealth at Death of Michoacán's Elite, 1830–39

Name	Gross assets	Assets after debts	Assets after debts as a percentage of gross assets
Corral, María Josefa del	88,100	65,874	75%
Domínguez, Lic. Pablo	124,000	42,840	34
García de Obeso, José María	85,298	0	0
González Cosío, Juan	50,000	38,000	76
Guedea, Br. Rafael	115,000	37,275	32
Isasaga, Ignacio	52,000	20,000	38
Jiménez, Ma. Ignacia	194,611	194,611	100
Larragoiti, Manuela	26,000	—	—
Lavarrieta, Ma. Josefa	96,175	96,175	100
Manzo Ceballos, Antonio	24,244	—	—
Mendes, Mariano	—	60,000	—
Molina, Francisco	24,388	15,530	64
Muñiz, José María	60,166	—	—
Muñoz, Br. Salvador	100,000	63,800	64
Peredo, Faustino	49,500	9,000	18
Peredo, Ma. Loreto	60,729	45,729	75
Ponce de León, María Trinidad	40,076	36,656	91
Ponce de León, Mateo	65,000	42,300	65
Ramos, Feliciano	49,000	49,000	100
Retana Lascano, José María	343,606	308,606	90
Ruiz, Joaquín Teobaldo	42,568	22,872	54
Ruiz de Chávez, José Manuel	44,200	39,000	88
Ruiz de Gaona, Ma. Ignacia	30,000	6,000	20
Solórzano Solar, José María	25,000	21,800	87
Solórzano Treviño, Ignacio	—	219,000	—
Velasco, Bacilio	20,000	—	—
Villavicencio, Manuel Diego	22,000	22,000	100
AVERAGES	73,200	63,300	65

Inventoried and Estimated Wealth at Death of Michoacán's Elite, 1840–49

Name	Gross assets	Assets after debts	Assets after debts as a percentage of gross assets
Campusano, Br. Joaquín	67,563	58,772	87%
Cevallos, Gaspar de	—	114,250	—
Gómez de la Puente, Juan	59,905	49,498	83
González Aragón, Mariano	20,000	6,000	30
Huarte, Lic. Isidro	110,000	91,283	83
Ibarrola bros. (Antonio, Mariano)	—	40,000	—
Iturbe, Francisco	—	112,000	—
Larragoiti, Antonio	20,000	3,000	15
Luna, Br. Juan Bruno de	33,425	3,300	10
Marroquín, Ignacio	75,000	30,200	40
Martínez, Luis	98,500	40,200	41
Morales, Bishop Angel Mariano	105,000	—	—
Moreno, Diego	300,000	200,000	67
Muñiz y Soto, Ramón	36,719	36,719	100
Olavarrieta, Eusebio	170,000	—	—
Ortiz de Ayala, Joaquín	31,741	19,797	62
Páramo, Norberto	27,002	19,938	74
Parra, Miguel de la	—	180,000	—
Piedra, José Guadalupe	136,721	—	—
Quevedo, Mariano	59,102	—	—
Solórzano Ugarte, Luis	—	36,000	—
Talavera, José Eugenio	22,100	21,000	95
Villalón, Dolores	31,613	17,937	57
AVERAGES	78,000	56,850	60

APPENDIX TABLE 2.5

Inventoried and Estimated Wealth at Death of Michoacán's Elite, 1850–59

Name	Gross assets	Assets after debts	Assets after debts as a percentage of gross assets
Acha, Juan de Dios	—	67,431	—
Alzúa Montenegro, Macaria	31,619	30,130	95%
Anzorena y Foncerrada, Mariano	38,000	15,700	41
Aviles, Mariano	70,000	58,900	84
Bocanegra, José María	133,500	104,000	78
Caballero, Isidro	—	72,669	—
Castrejón, Timoteo	100,357	82,293	82
Chávez, Antonio	105,842	97,782	92
Dávalos y Tompis, Nicolás	285,300	173,700	61
Estrada, Francisco	180,728	173,660	96
Flores, José María	149,550	75,402	50
García Carrasquedo, Isidro	122,664	72,664	59
García Carrasquedo, Br. Martin	67,218	47,935	71
Gil de Hoyos, Francisco	26,250	—	—
Gómez, Cayetano	1,193,623	981,126	82
González Herrera, Juan	30,000	5,000	17
Ibarrola, Mariano	—	20,000	—
Igartúa, Manuel	46,000	—	—
Izasaga, Lic. José María	35,850	—	—
Lambrano, Francisco	—	42,553	—
Larreátegui, Mariano	139,600	30,000	21
Luna, Simón	—	28,946	—
Macouzet, Dr. Juan de	62,986	62,986	100
Magaña, Juan José	67,916	31,048	46
Magaña, Vicente	—	25,000	—
Maldonado, Mariano	26,675	23,843	89
Martínez, Ma. Concepción	47,197	7,712	16
Michelena, Mariano	120,000	89,240	74

(continued)

Inventoried and Estimated Wealth at Death of Michoacán's Elite, 1850–1859 *(continued)*

Name	Gross assets	Assets after debts	Assets after debts as a percentage of gross assets
Mier, Martín	39,000	25,776	66%
Ortiz de Ayala, Buenaventura	104,000	78,300	75
Parente, Tomás	36,405	—	—
Patiño, José María Lino	—	45,500	—
Plancarte, Francisco	125,000	—	—
del Río, Joaquín	85,091	54,028	63
del Río, José Manuel	68,401	58,401	85
Román, Fernando	616,261	538,448	87
Romero, Mariano	36,425	28,225	77
Romero Soravilla, Francisco	83,264	31,189	37
Ruiz de Chávez, Nicolás	374,796	317,705	85
Sierra, Antonio	220,000	—	—
Silva, José María	90,000	62,700	70
Valenzuela, Ramón	30,000	6,600	22
Villavicencio, Cayetano	141,526	134,400	95
Zacanini, Antonio	213,730	94,562	44
AVERAGES	144,450	102,500	66

APPENDIX TABLE 2.6

Inventoried and Estimated Wealth at Death of Michoacán's Elite,
1860–69

Name	Gross assets	Assets after debts	Assets after debts as a percentage of gross assets
Alzúa, Manuel	—	266,666	—
Anciola, Juan Ignacio	84,093	—	—
Calvo Pintado, Lic. Onofre	274,350	99,518	36%
Campero Calderón, Juan	—	57,500	—
Cárdenas, Manuel	152,000	0	0
Castañeda, Ramón	24,552	24,552	100
Castrejón, Micaela	26,330	26,330	100
Celá, Mariano	—	50,000	—
Cevallos, Lic. Gregorio	106,923	44,946	42
Chávez, Rafael	34,949	9,108	26
Chávez de Macouzet, Socorro	20,211	20,211	100
Cuevas, José María	—	144,000	—
López, Domingo	30,000	30,000	100
Losano, Ignacio	122,120	85,820	70
Maciel, Lic. Jesús	23,450	20,027	85
Magaña, Juan José	67,862	21,981	32
Mora, Francisco	45,000	22,500	50
Orozco, José María	—	37,600	—
Retana, Silverio	91,700	25,000	27
Romero, José Guadalupe	58,226	14,336	25
Saavedra, Pedro	25,353	16,121	64
Salceda, Félix María	74,807	74,807	100
Sierra, Manuel	95,000	30,000	32
Torres, José María de	100,000	48,000	48
Valdes, José María	36,770	36,770	100
Villamil de Gil, Dolores	28,095	28,095	100
Villaseñor, José Antonio	20,408	20,408	100
Zincúnegui, Francisco	30,400	8,900	29
AVERAGES	67,600	50,500	62

APPENDIX TABLE 2.7

Inventoried and Estimated Wealth at Death of Michoacán's Elite, 1870–79

Name	Gross assets	Assets after debts	Assets after debts as a percentage of gross assets
Arriaga, Francisco	53,095	30,000	56%
Balbuena, Antonio	37,596	0	0
Barrera, Génaro	54,376	18,463	34
Bocanegra, Ramón	140,306	99,570	71
Caballero, Juan Climaco	113,186	110,880	98
Campusano, Buenaventura	88,309	88,309	100
Cañedo, Ramón	82,622	72,922	88
Coria, Luis	20,078	20,078	100
Cortes, Antonio Homobono	93,000	26,500	28
Díaz Barriga, Miguel	—	37,400	—
Echeverría, Pedro	100,340	17,320	17
Elguero, Manuel	24,543	19,400	79
Elizondo, Gerónimo	—	83,300	—
Errejón, Antonio	114,789	—	—
Flores, Lic. Juan N.	147,764	127,673	86
García, Francisco	565,661	513,300	91
García, Miguel	36,805	29,090	79
García López, Rafael	36,205	34,601	96
García de Garibay, Francisca	26,000	26,000	100
Garibay, Ma. Concepción	64,356	45,706	71
Grande, Francisco	115,055	87,768	76
Jaso, Epifanio	—	24,414	—
Jiménez, José María	65,000	20,000	31
Jiménez, Pedro	—	51,000	—
Larrauri, Lorenzo	79,062	66,549	84
López Verduzco, Francisco	26,704	—	—
Luna, Agustín	194,076	138,845	71
Montaño, Amado	35,247	—	—
Ochoa, Claudio	—	318,442	—
Patiño, Miguel	35,000	30,000	86

(continued)

Inventoried and Estimated Wealth at Death of Michoacán's Elite,
1870–1879 *(continued)*

Name	Gross assets	Assets after debts	Assets after debts as a percentage of gross assets
Pérez Gil, José María	27,461	18,981	69%
Piedra, Juan Bautista	55,444	—	—
Reynoso, Ignacio	40,000	31,500	79
Rubio de Tello, Carmen	—	31,425	—
Sánchez, Vicente	205,644	137,819	67
Secada de Amescua, Ma. de los A.	30,739	30,739	100
Solórzano, Agapito	368,700	108,925	29
Tena, Antonio	89,714	57,984	65
Torres Ortiz, José María	21,585	21,585	100
Ugarte, Cor. José de	54,000	0	0
Verduzco, Zacarías	32,715	22,715	69
Victoria, Juan	37,943	34,755	92
AVERAGES	92,000	69,300	69

Inventoried and Estimated Wealth at Death of Michoacán's Elite,
1880–89

Name	Gross assets	Assets after debts	Assets after debts as a percentage of gross assets
Aguiar, Agustín	65,234	22,100	34%
Alcazar, Francisco Dario	67,700	27,700	41
Anaya, Ramón	63,470	59,684	94
Antia, Antonia	75,679	69,181	91
Backhausen, Daniel	36,000	28,000	78
Bárcena, Félix	26,503	—	—
Díaz Barriga, José María	65,830	50,325	76
Echaiz, Jesús	41,861	41,861	100
Erdozain, Ignacio	339,607	267,000	79
Estrada, Vicente	—	96,000	—
García, Luis G.	50,198	—	—
Gómez, Juan de Dios	81,200	0	0
González, Alejandro	83,717	77,315	92
Gutiérrez, Antonio	44,049	44,049	100
Hegarat, Juan	85,340	81,667	96
Jiménez, Marcos	21,406	21,406	100
Juárez, Ignacio	60,000	—	—
Lascano, Guadalupe	28,180	14,000	50
Mendoza, Cipriano	30,445	13,459	44
Montaño, Manuel	25,053	—	—
Montes, Felipe de Jesús	54,726	43,531	80
Mora de Anaya, Antonia	22,172	22,172	100
Ortiz, Br. José Antonio	143,113	140,098	98
Ortiz de Sánchez, Jesús	105,803	51,553	49
Oruña, Eustaquio de	92,083	63,125	68
Oviedo, Lic. Juan N.	23,998	23,998	100
Rodríguez, Vicente	72,702	72,702	100
Sandoval, Pedro	55,470	51,653	93
Segura, Lic. Luis G.	110,800	57,500	52
Solórzano, Ignacio	378,749	214,146	56
Valdes, Justo	—	36,750	—
Verdusco, Mariano	46,000	—	—
Verduzco, José Dolores	25,000	—	—
AVERAGES	78,100	62,600	74

Inventoried and Estimated Wealth at Death of Michoacán's Elite, 1890–99

Name	Gross assets	Assets after debts	Assets after debts as a percentage of gross assets
Aldrete, Gregorio	—	160,000	—
Alvarez de Mendes, Jesús	45,437	26,852	59%
Anciola, Cruz	185,000	185,000	100
Anzorena Aguirre, José Mariano	40,000	18,000	45
Arias, Antonio	29,098	29,098	100
Cerda, Antonio	21,433	—	—
Chavolla, Francisco	100,871	70,680	70
Coria, Espiridión	57,764	57,764	100
Dávalos, Arcadio	97,500	64,180	66
Dávalos, Nicolás	142,648	130,196	91
Díaz Barriga, Diego	35,500	10,500	30
Elorza, Cristóbal	79,937	79,929	100
Errejón, Juan de Dios	31,956	30,889	97
Errejon, Simón	256,881	—	—
Estrada, Concepción	62,998	62,998	100
Estrada, Miguel	175,000	155,300	89
Fernández, Br. Francisco	44,123	23,678	54
Flores, Urbano	35,000	0	0
García, Andrés	184,011	180,000	98
García Cambrón, Rafael	38,159	32,268	85
García Zapata, José	349,034	332,919	95
Guerra, Filomeno	41,088	33,828	82
Hernández de Farías, Benedicta	—	40,000	—
Igartúa, Octaviano	79,694	63,965	80
Jiménez, Epifanio	184,566	—	—
Loaiza de Pérez Gil, Joaquina	40,516	27,000	67
Macouzet, Juan	74,347	29,248	39
Magaña, Marcelino	50,000	45,000	90

(continued)

Inventoried and Estimated Wealth at Death of Michoacán's Elite,
1890–1899 *(continued)*

Name	Gross assets	Assets after debts	Assets after debts as a percentage of gross assets
Marván, Alcibíades	30,401	24,459	80%
Méndez, Hermenegildo	32,288	21,942	68
Méndez Cano, Miguel	142,710	134,392	94
Méndez Garibay, Perfecto	56,012	52,012	93
Menocal de Luna, Concepción	68,614	45,614	66
Mercado, José María	42,390	39,543	93
Montaño, Dr. Rafael	55,933	55,933	100
del Moral, Lic. Antonio	215,226	197,721	92
Moreno, Calixto	70,431	67,431	96
Mota, Dr. Antonio Primitivo	30,320	26,876	89
Ochoa, Domingo	51,168	51,168	100
Oseguera, Joaquín	424,716	387,166	91
Oviedo, Lic. Manuel	85,720	77,520	90
Patiño, Francisco	65,000	29,800	46
Pérez, Juan Mucio	67,538	55,000	81
Pérez Gil, Dr. José Antonio	33,033	32,857	99
Plancarte, Luis	220,240	25,800	12
Reynoso, Antonio	21,061	21,061	100
Rubio, Lic. Juan Bautista	25,179	2,605	10
Rubio, Miguel	29,303	25,201	86
Ruiz Valle, Ramón	23,284	23,284	100
Treviño, Antonio	260,752	233,350	89
Treviño, Lic. Macario	20,855	4,145	20
Valladares, Jesús	139,300	—	—
de la Vega, Ramón	72,000	—	—
Vidales, Feliciano	500,626	444,000	89
AVERAGES	101,300	81,000	77

Inventoried and Estimated Wealth at Death of Michoacán's Elite, 1900–1910

Name	Gross assets	Assets after debts	Assets after debts as a percentage of gross assets
Aguiar, Dolores	21,924	17,384	79%
Amescua, Br. Román de Jesús	65,267	65,267	100
Amesquita de Treviño, Pilar	59,700	31,800	53
Arciga, Archbishop José Ignacio	381,089	363,448	95
Arriaga, Luis	70,561	63,564	90
Basagoiti, Juan	650,000	0	0
Bocanegra, Antonio	103,050	9,050	9
Bocanegra, Pudenciana	182,500	182,500	100
Borbolla, José	68,000	63,000	93
Bris de Errejón, Pilar	28,105	26,937	96
Campero Calderón, Rafael	30,000	—	—
Cárdenas Vallejo, Manuel	32,316	0	0
Castro, Lic. José María	180,000	174,335	97
Díaz Barriga, Dr. Rafael	130,000	130,000	100
Díaz de Torres, Rita	70,446	70,446	100
Espinosa, Francisco	56,469	56,469	100
Gómez de Sámano, Trinidad	101,092	90,267	89
Guerrero, Plácido	97,317	92,658	95
Haristoy, Francisco	43,008	43,008	100
Higareda de Sierra, Jesús	78,726	78,726	100
Hiribarne, Cayetano	80,245	80,245	100
Hiribarne, Juan	101,152	101,152	100
Landeta, Juan Bautista	235,884	235,884	100
Luna de Reynoso, María	35,200	—	—
Martínez, Angel	29,795	29,745	100
Mejía, Miguel	113,040	7,000	6
Morfín, José María	43,972	42,212	96
Núñez de Monge, Dolores	50,692	50,692	100
Orozco de Camorlinga, A.	73,766	52,351	71

(continued)

Inventoried and Estimated Wealth at Death of Michoacán's Elite,
1900–1910 *(continued)*

Name	Gross assets	Assets after debts	Assets after debts as a percentage of gross assets
Ortiz de Gutiérrez, María	31,000	31,000	100%
Ortiz Huerta, Francisco	23,907	—	—
Oseguera, Crescencio	116,354	73,941	63
Piñon, Ignacio	21,076	20,576	98
Plancarte, Dr. José Antonio	194,440	194,440	100
Ramírez, Ramón	843,289	780,574	92
Reyes, Gral. Epifanio	120,364	35,364	29
Rionda, José María	34,000	30,000	88
Sámano, Luis	72,512	72,512	100
Santoyo, Isidoro	150,876	106,524	71
Solórzano, Francisco	37,991	31,191	82
Solórzano, Manuel María	178,000	159,056	89
Solórzano, Teresa	300,000	175,000	58
Torres, Hesiquio	70,446	—	—
Torres Ruiz, Francisco	39,928	29,928	75
Vallejo de S., Loreto	282,156	278,656	99
Vélez, José	69,270	6,599	9
Veyan, Luis	289,400	210,000	73
Vidales, José María	175,000	—	—
Vidales, Salvador	107,138	29,231	27
AVERAGES	130,000	100,500	78

APPENDIX TABLE 2.11
Summary of Appendix Two

Period	Avg. gross wealth	Avg. assets after debts	Avg. pct. of gross assets comprised by assets after debts[a]
1800–1810	90,600 (47)	78,100 (49)	64% (39)
1811–29	74,900 (41)	55,700 (36)	63% (35)
1830–39	73,200 (25)	63,300 (23)	65% (21)
1840–49	78,000 (18)	56,850 (19)	60% (14)
1850–59	144,450 (37)	102,500 (38)	66% (31)
1860–69	67,600 (22)	50,500 (29)	62% (23)
1870–79	92,000 (36)	69,300 (38)	62% (32)
1880–89	78,100 (31)	62,600 (27)	74% (25)
1890–99	101,300 (52)	81,000 (49)	77% (47)
1900–1910	130,000 (49)	100,500 (44)	78% (44)

SOURCES: ANM, AHCP, AHMM, AHMCR, AHPJ, AGN, ANMC
[a]Cases where both are known.

AGN   Archivo General de la Nación.

AHMCR   Archivo Histórico Manuel Castañeda Ramírez (Casa de Morelos)

AHMM   Archivo Histórico Municipal de Morelia

AHCP   Archivo Histórico de la Ciudad de Pátzcuaro

AHPJ   Archivo Histórico del Poder Judicial [de Michoacán]

AHSM   Archivo Histórico del Sagrario Metropolitano [de Morelia]

ANCM   Archivo de Notarías de la Ciudad de México

ANM   Archivo de Notarías de Morelia

BL   Bancroft Library manuscript collection

CL   Coleción Lafragua

INTRODUCTION

1. For the Porfiriato, the number of studies with a strong political economy dimension is greater, in part because of the stability of the period, and in part because of the importance placed in the late nineteenth century on data gathering and statistics. See Haber, *Industry and Underdevelopment*; Wasserman; Saragoza; Meyers; Coatsworth, *Growth Against Development*; Holden; Wells; Joseph; Miller; Tortolero Villaseñor; and in a certain sense (though it is much more than "political economy"), Knight, *Mexican Revolution*.

2. Walker; see also Cardoso; Harris.

3. For example, Potash; Costeloe, *Church Wealth*.

4. Tenenbaum, *Politics of Penury*; Stevens; Meyer Cosío; Tenenbaum, "Banqueros sin bancos"; Carmagnani.

5. Hale, *Mexican Liberalism*; Hale, *Transformation of Liberalism*; Brading, *Prophecy and Myth*; Brading, *Origins of Mexican Nationalism*; Brading, *First America*; Tenorio-Trillo; Guerra; Costeloe, *Primera república*.

6. Mallon; Thomson, "Agrarian Conflict"; Thomson, "Popular Aspects of Liberalism"; Thomson, "Montaña y Llanura"; Thomson, *Patriotism, Politics, and Popular Liberalism*; Guardino; Lira; Pastor; Garavaglia and Grosso; Thomson, *Puebla*; Brading, *Miners and Merchants*; Brading, *Haciendas and Ranchos*; Cerruti; Voss; Olveda; Tutino.

7. See the journals published by the Colegio de Michoacán (*Relaciones*) and the Universidad Michoacana (*Tzintzun*); and, to name just a few that have been very useful in the preparation of this manuscript, Tavera; Vega Juanino; Herrejón Peredo; Sánchez Díaz, *El suroeste . . . 1821–1851*; Sánchez Díaz, *El suroeste . . . 1852–1910*; Tapia Santamaría; Durán Juárez and Bustin; Juárez Nieto, *La oligarquía*; Guzmán Pérez and Juárez Nieto, *Arquitectura, comercio*; Moreno García, *Haciendas de tierra*; Uribe Salas; Pérez Acevedo.

8. On the figure of 20,000 pesos as a "cut-off" for eliteness, see the excerpt from an 1833 article in *El Indicador de la Federación*, which defines the wealthy as those with assets of at least 25,000 pesos, reprinted in Reyes Heroles, 2:110; and "Representación a nombre de los Labradores y Comerciantes de Valladolid de Michoacán," p. 62.

9. The most influential proponent of this view of Mexico's nineteenth-century economic decline is Coatsworth, whose brilliantly short and sweet 1978 interpretation of Mexico's nineteenth-century economic trajectory in the *American Historical Review* (parts of which are expanded in his 1990 "La decadencia de la economía mexicana, 1800–1860"), set the agenda for all economic histories of the nineteenth century. For a short review of the historiography of the post-1810 depression, see Chowning, "Contours." The careful reader will note that I do not fundamentally disagree with Coatsworth's assessment of the Mexican economy before 1880 as structurally different from that of the post-1880 period. Coatsworth is making very broad generalizations about the economy, while I am more interested in capturing its ups and downs, even if they do *not* add up to "structural" changes. It is for this reason that I have taken pains not to locate the economic recovery of midcentury along an inevitable path leading to capitalism. What seems to me most interesting about the recovery, in fact, is the ways that it may have altered the perceptions that the already wealthy of one generation and the not-yet wealthy of the next had of each other and that, in so doing, it may have had a profound effect on political relationships and thinking.

PROLOGUE

1. This account is drawn from the following: Martínez de Lejarza; *Inspección ocular*; Ajofrín; Humboldt; Hardy; Ward; Calderón de la Barca; Wheat; Lyon; Bullock; Jasso Espinosa; De la Torre; Ramírez Romero; *La Lira Michoacana*, pp. 73–77, 91–93, 100–01, 131–32, 148–49, 278–79, 286–87, 294–95, 301–02, 309–11, 375–76, 431–32, 480, 503–04, 547–48, 571–72.

2. Hardy, p. 26. It is perhaps worth noting that the foreign travelers almost invariably overestimated the distances they had traveled during the day.

3. Humboldt, 4:6 and 2:6.

4. Bullock, pp. 190, 192, 208–09.

5. Martínez de Lejarza, p. 45.

6. Hardy, p. 34.

7. Martínez de Lejarza, pp. 46–47; Ajofrín, p. 150.

8. Ramírez Romero, p. xxi.

9. Hardy, p. 40. For example, Dr. Manuel de la Bárcena owned a house and orchard worth 2,000 pesos; Lic. Juan José González de Castañeda owned the *quinta chica*, which he rented for 600 pesos a year; Lic. Sebastián de Betancourt had a house and garden in the *calzada* of Guadalupe; Notario Oficial Mayor del Juzgado de Capellanías Lorenzo Vásquez had a house in the *barrio* de Guadalupe, bordering the convent of San Diego; and Lic. Manuel García Cubilano owned a house lot and garden worth 6,000 pesos next to the aqueduct at the entrance to the *calzada* of Guadalupe in the *barrio* of San Pedro. ANM, José María Aguilar, 1826, 31 October; Montaño, 1809, 1 February; Birbiescas, 1804, 13 March; Montaño, 1807, 6 May; Aguilar, 1810, 7 February.

10. Ramírez Romero, p. 84.

11. De la Torre, p. 164; Lyon, 2:73.

12. De la Torre, pp. 164–66; Calderón de la Barca, p. 587; Lyon, 2:73–74; Hardy, p. 43; *La Lira Michoacana*, p. 146.

13. De la Torre, p. 37.

14. ANM, Aguilar, 1811, 22 November; Correa, 1792, 20 December; Rincón, 1839, 17 January; Montaño, 1805, 26 January.

15. ANM, Aguilar, 1814, 25 January; Joaquín Aguilar, 1826, 27 October; Marocho, 1809, 20 April; Marocho, 1809, 17 November; Marocho, 1808, 11 June; Aguilar, 1804, 9 May; Valdovinos, 1833, 16 October; Marocho, 1810, 15 December; Montaño, 1808, 28 July; Aguilar, 1793, 26 November; José María Aguilar, 1826, 29 November.

16. ANM, Aguilar, 1795, 22 May; Ramírez Romero, p. 323.

17. ANM, Correa, 1775, 27 April; AHMM, "Inventario de los bienes del Lic. Mariano Escandón, Conde de Sierragorda," January 1815.

18. ANM, Montaño, 1809, 24 July.

19. ANM, Aguilar, 1822, 4 September; Laris, 1897, 24 September; Montaño, 1805, 27 May.

20. De la Torre, p. 77; Pastor and Frizzi, p. 185.

21. ANM, Arratia, 1782, 17 June; Valdovinos, 1834, 29 November; Montaño, 1808, 23 December; Aguilar, 1821, 9 March.

22. ANM, Correa, 1783, 7 January; Rincón, 1835, 23 January.

23. Ramírez Romero, p. 93.

24. Ramírez Romero, pp. 89–105. See also Silva Mondujano, *La catedral*, and Brading, *Church and State*, p. 184.

25. Morin, p. 162.

26. Morin, p. 154.

27. AGN, Historia, vol. 135, exp. 16, 1805, "Un individuo de Valladolid . . . hace acusaciones contra el Regidor Alcalde Provincial D. Ysidro Huarte, íntimo amigo del Yntendente de la Provincia. . . ."

28. Lyon, 2:77.

29. AGN, Historia, vol. 135, exp. 16, 1805, "Un individuo de Valladolid. . . ."

30. *La Lira Michoacana*, p. 286.

31. Juan González Castañón's new residence in the Portal de Matamoros, for example, had three stores, and Regidor José Santiago de los Monteros y Plata's house on the Portal de las Dulceras also had three *locales* — two stores and a billiard room. ANM, Montaño, 1808, 23 December; AHMM, 1818, "Testamentaria de D. Juan Espinosa de los Monteros y Plata."

32. The other owners were three canons of the cathedral, a lawyer (Lic. Matías Antonio de los Ríos, who owned two contiguous houses next to the Casas Consistoriales), and a government official (the postmaster and sales tax collector for Cuitzeo, Ignacio Soto y Saldaña).

33. ANM, Correa, 1802, 25 October.

34. Besides the 21 houses around the plaza mayor, there were 44 other houses with values of at least 5,000 pesos. Churchmen owned 32 percent of these houses; unmarried women 16 percent; hacendados who were not also merchants 18 percent; and government officials 9 percent. I was unable to identify the occupations of three (male) owners.

35. ANM, Arratia, 1772, 27 January; Valdovinos, 1834, 29 November.

36. ANM, Aguilar, 1801, 14 February; Marocho, 1803, 9 July.

37. Ibarrola, p. 161, says that Vicente Romero y Valle added the second floor in 1779, while Ramírez Romero, p. 191, says it was added by Romero y Valle in 1797. Ibarrola seems to have transposed the last two digits, since the value of the house in 1794 was only 1,200 pesos more than its value in 1748, meaning that a second story was unlikely to have been added before 1794. ANM, Mafra Vargas, 1748, 15 October; Aguilar, 1794, 2 June; J. M. Aguilar, 1827, 8 February.

38. ANM, Arratia, 1787, 25 May; Ibarrola, pp. 239–240.

39. In fact the house sold in 1831 for 31,200 pesos, but the sale was rescinded for reasons that were not given; finally in 1842 it sold for 26,400 pesos. The other two houses around the plaza that were dramatically improved around the turn of the century were the residence of José Santiago de los Monteros y Plata, who in 1790 purchased a house for 10,025 pesos that was valued at 22,430 pesos in 1818; and another house owned by Isidro Huarte, which had been purchased in

1797 for 12,500 pesos and improved in the amount of about 3,500 pesos soon thereafter. ANM, Correa, 1776, 28 June; Aguilar, 1821, 9 March; Aguilar, 1831, 12 November; Valdovinos, 1842, 29 September; Correa, 1790, 15 April; Aguilar, 1820, 23 August; AHMM, 1818, "Testamentaria de D. Juan Manuel Espinosa de los Monteros y Plata."

40. ANM, Aguilar, 1811, 22 November; Aguilar, 1795, 31 July.

41. The 1808 appraisal comes from AHMM, 1808, "Autos de inventarios a bienes del difunto Capt. José María Peredo"; ANM, Mafra Vargas, 1772, 1 February; Marocho, 1804, 24 November; Pérez, 1864, 26 December.

42. Ibarrola, p. 199; ANM, Montaño, 1808, 17 September.

43. These transactions are found in ANM, Montaño, 1805, 25 June through 3 July.

44. On overcrowding and the problem of village lands in this area being taken over by haciendas, see *Inspección ocular*, pp. 22–33, 99–102.

45. *Inspección ocular*, p. 15.

46. Martínez de Lejarza, p. 116; ANM, Prieto, 1823, 24 November.

47. Silva Mandujano, "Pátzcuaro," pp. 21–36.

48. *Inspección ocular*, p. 157; Martínez de Lejarza, insert following p. 96.

49. Martínez de Lejarza, p. 139.

50. *Inspección ocular*, pp. 116–17.

51. *Inspección ocular*, pp. 116–17.

52. *Inspección ocular*, pp. 142–43.

53. González Sánchez, p. 281; Paso y Troncoso, p. 35.

54. *Inspección ocular*, p. 118.

55. *Inspección ocular*, p. 154; Paso y Troncoso, pp. 43–44. On the Tepalcatepec basin, see Barrett.

56. Martínez de Lejarza, pp. 57, 72.

57. Pastor and Frizzi, p. 202.

58. AGN, Archivo Histórico de Hacienda, Alcabalas de Zamora (1808 and 1809).

59. Martínez de Lejarza, pp. 107–13.

60. Martínez de Lejarza, pp. 185, 189.

61. Ortiz Ybarra and González Méndez, p. 65; Pastor and Frizzi, pp. 200–01.

62. Bullock, p. 212.

63. ANM, Aguilar, 1810, 23 August; Aguilar, 1831, 19 November.

64. Bullock, pp. 213–14; ANM, Aguilar, 1813, 10 November.

65. González, *Zamora*, pp. 60, 68; Lyon, 2:64.

66. Ward, pp. 669–70. Also see Hardy, pp. 46–49, who tried following the Río Grande by heading north from Tecacho through Numerán and La Piedad.

67. ANM, Arratia, 1772, 27 January; AHMM, 1827, "Primera cuenta de hi-

juela de los bienes de la testamentaria de D. Ysidro de Huarte hecha por el contador Cd. Ygnacio José Dominguez."

68. ANM, Correa, 1773, 22 October.

69. ANM, Correa, 1778, 30 December; Correa, 1784, 7 February.

70. ANM, Correa, 1787, 1 June; Marocho, 1803, 27 August; AHMM, 1827, "Primera cuenta de hijuela de los bienes de la testamentaria de Ysidro de Huarte. . . ."

71. ANM, Aguilar, 1800, 27 November. See also Marocho, 1797, 20 January; Marocho, 1806, 21 February, for other business partnerships.

72. AHMM, 1827, "Primera cuenta de hijuela de los bienes de la testamentaria de Don Ysidro de Huarte. . . ."

73. AHMM, 1825, "Compromiso hecho por los Ynteresados a la Testamentaria del finado D. Ysidro Huarte, sus reclamos, y el laudo promovido por el Doctor Lama y el Licenciado Tercero, en 24 de septiembre de 1825."

74. There are too many examples of cash advances to be repaid in kind to cite here. Most of them took place after the mid-1790s.

75. ANM, Correa, 1778, 10 March; Correa, 1779, 10 November; Correa, 1780, 8 March; AHMM, 1822, no title, on destruction of the hacienda of La Parota.

76. ANM, Montaño, 1809, 21 June. González's politically prominent descendents include Dr. Juan Manuel González Urueña, Lic. Carlos González Urueña, Lic. Luis González Gutiérrez, and Dr. Miguel Silva González.

77. AHMM, 1809, "Sobre arrendamiento de la Hacienda de La Parota."

78. ANM, Correa, 1802, 13 October.

79. Vega Juanino, p. 135.

80. AHMM, 1824, "Testamentaria e inventario de los bienes que quedaron por fallecimiento de D. Ysidro de Huarte"; AHMM, 1825, Cuaderno 2, "Compromiso hecho por los Ynteresados a la Testamentaria del finado Isidro Huarte. . . ."

81. ANM, Marocho, 1793, 5 January; Aguilar, 1829, 3 August; Aguilar, 1800, 9 September; AHMM, 1825, Cuaderno 2, "Compromiso."

82. AHMM, 1824, "Testamentaria e inventario de los bienes que quedaron por fallecimiento de Ysidro de Huarte."

83. ANM, Arratia, 1781, 4 July; Correa, 1782, 27 April; Correa, 1782, 24 July; Correa, 1784, n.d., follows 30 September; Marocho, 1795, 18 November.

84. AHMM, 1827, "Primera cuenta de hijuela de los bienes de la testamentaria de Don Ysidro de Huarte. . . ."

85. ANM, Correa, 1781, 3 March; AHSM, "Libro de Casamientos de Españoles," 1 November 1804; AGN, Historia, vol. 135, exp. 16, 1805, pp. 275–80, "Un individuo de Valladolid que se nombra Ruperto Verdad en papel de dos de diciembre hace acusaciones contra el Regidor Alcalde Provincial D. Ysidro

Huarte, íntimo amigo del Yntendente de la Provincia, que le disimula sus excesos, y para dar razón con claridad se indican por partes."

86. Mendoza Briones and Terán, "Repercusiones," p. 223; AGN, Historia, vol. 135, exp. 16, 1805, "Un individuo de Valladolid. . . ."

87. Ibarrola, p. 189.

88. ANM, Aguilar, 1832, 7 September.

89. ANM, Marocho, 1808, 23 January; Aguilar, 1810, 20 July; AHMM, 1825, "Compromiso hecho por los Ynteresados a la Testamentaria del finado D. Ysidro Huarte. . . ."

90. AHMM, 1825, "Compromiso hecho por los Ynteresados a la Testamentaria del finado D. Ysidro Huarte . . ."

91. AHMM, 1809, "Sobre arrendamiento de la Hacienda de la Parota."

92. AGN, Historia, vol. 135, exp. 16, 1805, "Un individuo de Valladolid. . . ."

CHAPTER I

1. Annual expenses to maintain the Valladolid cathedral alone came to 28,275 pesos a year, including 3,250 pesos for candle wax. Brading, *Church*, p. 194.

2. There were seventeen different levels of civil administration controlled by the office of the Real Hacienda alone. Franco, p. 258.

3. Lemoine, *Morelos*, p. 103.

4. Morin, p. 166.

5. For some examples of elites who lived on their haciendas, see AHCP, 66-C, 1800–09, exp. 1, 1807, "Inventario de la testamentaria de Da. María Eusebia de la Concepción Ramos"; AHCP, 66-C, 1800–09, exp. 3, 1806, "Inventarios de los bienes que quedaron por muerte de Da. María Josefa Valdes"; ANM, Marocho, 1809, 1 September; Aguilar, 1804, 3 September; Aguilar, 1804, 19 October; Aguilar, 1805, 30 January; Montaño, 1805, 16 February; Montaño, 1805, 8 March. Many more stated that they were resident in the small towns adjacent to their haciendas.

6. Lemoine, *Morelos*, pp. 61–70.

7. Calderón de la Barca, p. 563.

8. BL, M-M 1830:5, Intendant Merino to Viceroy Calleja, "El Yntendente de Valladolid en contestación a orn. de 31 de Marzo informa lo que se le ofrece acerca de Puentes, Calzadas, Canales, y Caminos, Frutos e Industria de aquella Provincia," dated 30 June 1813, pp. 4–6, 8.

9. BL, M-M 1830:5, "El Yntendente," pp. 10–11.

10. Brading, *Church*, pp. 232–34, notes Abad's call for "absolute civil equality of the class of Indians with the class of Spaniards," and adds that for Abad, the "chief cause for the backwardness of Mexican agriculture and the stark contrasts

between rich and poor" was concentration in landownership. Poor roads and mountainous terrain were among many other "contributory causes."

11. *Inspección ocular.*

12. Ajofrín, pp. 145–47.

13. Humboldt, 4:1.

14. Humboldt, 4:3.

15. Pastor and Frizzi, pp. 195–98. Morin, pp. 60–72, shows strong rates of population growth between 1742 and 1792, but especially after 1785–86.

16. Figures for the provincial breakdown for the 1730s and 1761 are from Morin, p. 119. For 1805–09, when the tithe was contracted out, the only option is to rely on the amounts of the tithe auction, which I have extracted from the notary records (the total for the bishopric was 525,375 pesos) compared to Romero's average in 1806–09 of 512,260. Brading, *Church*, p. 217, puts the intendancy of Michoacán's proportion of the tithe in 1787 at just 32 percent, but this does not include the districts in Guadalajara that were assigned to that bishopric shortly thereafter, and which were included in Morin's earlier figures.

17. As with population growth, the strongest increases in the tithe receipts were for the *tierra caliente* districts and the western parts of the province. In the west the tithe auction for the La Piedad/Tlasasalca district increased over 60 percent in just twenty years between 1789 and 1809. In the southern *tierra caliente*, bids to collect the tithe in Apatzingán (not even including indigo, a key crop in the district) increased over 50 percent between 1795 and 1808, and the tithe on cane products in the Tacámbaro/Turicato/Urecho district almost doubled between 1793 and 1805. This is especially impressive in light of the fact that sugar prices and most prices of other hot-country products were essentially stable during this period, so that increases in tithe revenue are especially likely to have reflected increases in production. Even in the relatively densely populated, long-settled highland districts, where the rate of growth might be expected to be slower, there was a fairly significant expansion of revenues, in the range of 30 to 40 percent between the early to mid-1790s and the mid- to-late 1800s, though here inflation in the prices of maize and beef played an important role. ANM, Montaño, 1805, 22 June; Morin, p. 120, 144; BL, M-M 1830:5, "El Yntendente," pp. 4, 5; AGN, Hacienda, Alcabalas de Zamora, various years; *Inspección Ocular*, 18; Pastor and Frizzi, pp. 164, 167; Martínez de Lejarza, insert following p. 96 entitled "Plan que Manifiesta el estado en que se hallaban las fincas de la jurisdicción de Ario antes de la revolución . . ."; AHMM, 1839, "Convenio en arbitradores nombrados por los ciudadanos Fernando Román y Agustín de Elorza . . ."; AHMCR, Diezmos, Valladolid, various years. For commodity prices, see Chowning, "Reassessing," n. 21.

18. BL, M-M 1830:5, "El Yntendente," p. 5.

19. BL, M-M 1830:5, "El Yntendente," p. 5; Pastor and Frizzi, p. 203; Morin,

pp. 143–44; AHCE, Legislatura I, Caja 2, exp. 9, "Memoria del Gobierno, 1827," pp. 22–23.

20. AHMCR, Diezmos, Leg. 877 (Valladolid, 1756–1805), "Cuentas de cargo y data . . . 1800"; Morin, p. 221; González, *Zamora*, pp. 63–64.

21. AGN, Hacienda, *alcabalas* for Valladolid, 1800.

22. Martínez de Lejarza, pp. 139–40; Morin, p. 174.

23. AGN, Hacienda, *alcabalas* for Zamora, 1783, 1788, 1790–93, 1798, 1800, 1805–07; Morin, pp. 173–174.

24. Martínez de Lejarza, pp. 150–67. Muleteer towns included Cotija, Sicuicho, Periban, Tlasasalca, Purepero, Churintzio, Chilchota.

25. Morin, pp. 150–51.

26. Includes all rural properties sold for 5,000 pesos or more. For 1770s and 1780s, n = 24. For 1790s, n = 36. For 1800 to 1810, n = 31.

27. Includes all rural properties that rented for 250 pesos or more. For 1770s to 1790s, n = 29. For 1800s, n = 15. Morin, pp. 273–74 asserts that there was much more prolific renting of plots on haciendas and rising rents in the late colonial period.

28. Good summaries of the relationship between rising prices, rising land values, and falling wages are in Brading, *Haciendas and Ranchos*, chapter 8; and Van Young, "Age of Paradox."

29. ANM, Montaño, 1805, 24 January.

30. On this point, also see Pastor and Frizzi, p. 167.

31. ANM, Correa, 1778, 5 March; Montaño, 1805, 30 July; AHMM, 1809, "Sobre arrendamiento de la hacienda de Parota [to Domingo Arechaga]"; AHMM, 1822, no title, on destruction of the hacienda de La Parota.

32. AHCP, 55-E, exp. 1, "Libro de Becerro [kept by notary José Ignacio Ramírez, 1786–1814]," 3 October 1793; ANM, Valdovinos, 1843, 10 May.

33. The owner of Pedernales, José Ignacio de Barandiarán, bought 35,366 pesos worth of *enseres* from the hacienda of Chupio in 1791; this was only one of his many large purchases of herds. AHCP, 55-E, exp. 1, "Libro de Becerro," 23 October 1798; AGN, Hacienda, *alcabalas* for Zamora, 1791.

34. Morin, pp. 252–54.

35. AGN, Hacienda, *alcabalas* for Valladolid, 1791; ANM, Aguilar, 1817, 8 August.

36. AHMM, 1808, "Autos de inventarios a bienes del difunto Capt. D. José María Peredo."

37. Moreno García, p. 92; ANM, Marocho, 1808, 18 February.

38. ANM, Arratia, 1779, 28 May; Arratia, 1788, 30 October; Marocho, 1806, 5 September. For an inventory of Coapa, see AHMM, 1808, "Inventarios formados a los bienes que quedaron por fallecimiento de D. Ventura Arandia." The inventory was formed because Olarte was worried about the competence of

his administrator's widow; she in turn produced evidence that she was as hard-nosed and profit-minded as her husband had been: AHMM, 1809, "Pruebas de Doña Manuela Arias en los autos seguidos con D. Manuel Olarte sobre mal manejo de la primera en los intereses de la Testamentaria de D. Ventura Arandia." Morin, pp. 281–82, also makes the point that the church often demanded that renters make improvements.

39. AHCP, 65-B, 1800–09, exp. 4, "Testamentaria de Doña María Josefa Orovio . . . 1802"; AHCP 65-B, 1800–09, exp. 3, no title, consists of inventory of effects of Br. D. José Manuel de Betancourt, 1803; AHCP, 65-B, 1800–09, exp. 3, "Inventarios y aprecios de los bienes que quedaron por muerte de Da. Mariana González de Bustamante . . . 1805"; AHMCR, Negocios Diversos, 1805, Leg. 1, "Inventario de la Hacienda de Paquisihuato hecho en febrero de 1805 por muerte de D. Miguel de Herrero . . ."; ANM, Aguilar, 1804, 27 July; AHCP, 66-C, 1800–09, exp. 3, "Inventarios de los bienes que quedaron por muerte de Da. María Josefa Valdes . . . 1806"; AHCP, 64-A, 1800–09, exp. 4, "Autos seguidos por D. Mateo González Movellan contra D. José María Solórzano . . . 1808"; "Inventarios formados a los bienes que quedaron por fallecimiento de D. Ventura Arandia . . . 1808"; AHMM, "Autos de inventarios a bienes del difunto Capitan D. José María Peredo . . . 1808"; AHMM, 1822, no title, on destruction of ha-cienda of La Parota; ANM, Aguilar, 1817, 8 August.

40. Chowning, "Reassessing." For a contemporary comment on the problems of high sales taxes and tithes, see "Representación a nombre de los Labradores y Comerciantes de Valladolid . . . ," in Sugawara, ed., p. 66.

41. ANM, loan transactions from 1780 to 1810; Brading, *Church*, p. 193. The Juzgado's loans from 1780 to 1784 averaged about 87,500 pesos a year, but in 1785 it loaned some 233,000 pesos. Similarly, the cathedral averaged about 26,500 pesos a year in the period from 1780 to 1784, and in 1785 it loaned 98,000 pesos. The loans extended in 1785 were to tide people over, to increase production, and to enable city councils to purchase stores of grain at harvest.

42. ANM, Aguilar, 21 July 1804; Birbiescas, 13 March 1804; Aguilar, 30 April 1804; Aguilar, 24 May 1804; Montaño, 16 March 1804; Aguilar, 21 March 1804; Marocho, 11 June 1804; Birbiescas, 10 July 1804; Marocho, 16 August 1804.

43. "Representación a nombre de los Labradores y Comerciantes de Valladolid . . . ," in Sugawara, ed., p. 68; "Representación contra la Con-solidación del Ayuntamiento de Valladolid," in Sugawara, ed., p. 52.

44. ANM, Marocho, 16 August 1804.

45. "Representación contra la Consolidación del Ayuntamiento de Valla-dolid," in Sugawara, ed., pp. 51–52.

46. Brading, *Church*, p. 225, notes a change in the late colony from the older

church policy of spreading out its loan portfolio among many borrowers to a policy of making larger loans to fewer individuals.

47. Loan transactions in the ANM from 1780 to 1810 show an increased role for private lending, a trend also detected elsewhere; see Greenow, and Lindley. In Valladolid, private lenders began to be an essential element of the credit system after the mid-1780s drought: see Chowning, "Consolidación."

48. AHCP, 64-A, 1800–09, exp. 4, "Autos seguidos por D. Mateo González Movellan contra D. José María Solórzano . . . 1808."

49. ANM, Aguilar, 1813, 4 November.

50. ANM, loan transactions from 1780 to 1810. Includes church and private loans and cash advances, but not liens.

51. Chowning, "Consolidación."

52. See Garner; Coatsworth, "Obstacles," Van Young, "Age of Paradox"; and Morin.

53. Brading, *Church*, p. 230.

54. For discussions of administrative changes after 1786, see Mendoza Briones and Terán, pp. 219–23; Franco, p. 259; Mazín, ed., *El gran Michoacán*, pp. 181–203.

55. AHMM, 1809, "Inventarios formados a los bienes del Sr. D. Felipe Díaz de Hortega, Yntendente Corregidor que fue . . ."; ANM, Aguilar, 1821, 29 May; AHSM, "Libro de Casamientos de Españoles," 8 October 1796, 1 November 1804, and 26 November 1813. For other marriages involving prominent royal officials as principals or *padrinos*, see AHSM, "Libro de Casamientos de Españoles," 21 April 1798, 1 May 1805, 7 December 1807, and 12 May 1808.

56. Mendoza Briones and Terán, p. 224; ANM, Aguilar, 1805, 14 February; Birbiesca, 1804, 11 October; Montaño, 1806, 29 November; Montaño, 1805, 6 April; Aguilar, 1820, 3 October.

57. AGN, Subdelegados 16, 27 June 1803, has a list of the 24 subdelegados of Valladolid and their *fiadores*.

58. This discussion is based primarily on Vega Juanino.

59. Most of these identifications are from ANM, AHMCR, AHCP, AHMM, but several come from Vega Juanino and Ibarrola.

60. The word "oligarchy" is used by Pastor and Frizzi, Franco, and Juárez Nieto.

61. ANM, Aguilar, 1799, 29 August.

62. Brading, *Church*, p. 139; Pastor and Frizzi, p. 173. See Brading, *Church*, chapter 9, for a discussion of the structure of the cathedral chapter.

63. Brading, *Church*, especially chapters 8 and 10.

64. Cardozo Galué, pp. 128–32.

65. ANM, Marocho, 1804, 5 July; Montaño, 1805, 2 January; Montaño, 1805, 15 July; Marocho, 1806, 10. September; Marocho, 1806, 4 October.

66. Vega Juanino, pp. 66–67.

67. ANM, Aguilar, 1805, 30 January; Marocho, 1810, 16 March; Aguilar, 1810, 27 August; Marocho, 1806, 4 October; García, 1850, 25 July; AHSM, "Libro de casamientos de españoles," 1 November 1804.

68. ANM, Montaño, 1809, 11 August; Ibarrola, pp. 265, 223.

69. ANM, Birbiesca, 25 April 1804; Marocho, 23 January 1808.

70. AHCP, 67-D, Protócolo de Ramírez, 19 October 1809.

71. For examples of cross-regional tithe cosigners, see ANM, Aguilar, 1804, 23 May; Birbiesca, 1804, 24 July; Marocho, 1807, 1 October; Montaño, 1809, 24 July.

72. On this point, see also Franco, pp. 261–62.

73. There were scholarships available in the church-run schools, opening this avenue of upward mobility for poor and middle-class young men.

74. "Representación a nombre de los Labradores y Comerciantes," in Sugawara, ed., pp. 70–75.

75. "Representación contra la Consolidación del Cabildo Eclesiástico de Valladolid de Michoacán," in Sugawara, ed., p. 48.

76. "Representación contra la Consolidación del Ayuntamiento de Valladolid," in Sugawara, ed., p. 55.

77. "Proyecto del doctor José Pérez Calama para la realización de tertulias literarias en Valladolid de Michoacán, 1787," reprinted in Cardozo Galué, pp. 133–35.

78. Cardozo Galué; Mazín, *Entre dos majestades*; Brading, *Church*.

79. On curricular and educational reform, see Cardozo Galué, pp. 21–38; Brading, *Church*, chapter 10.

80. Brading, *Church*, p. 11.

81. Brading, *Church*, pp. 167–68.

82. Brading, *Church*, chapter 4; Mazín, *Entre dos majestades*, p. 162.

83. Cardozo Galué, pp. 53–69 and Appendix VI, "Edicto sobre la reconstrucción del acueducto de Valladolid de Michoacán y composición de varias calzadas y caminos de la misma ciudad, 1785."

84. Cardozo Galué, Appendix IV, "Proyecto para el establecimiento de una 'Sociedad de los Amigos del Pais' en Valladolid de Michoacán, 1784," and Appendix V, "Informe sobre el estado de la educación e industria popular en la provincia de Michoacán, 1784." The references to the "sexo mas débil" and to the role of mining in the Mexican economy are on p. 119.

85. Brading, *Church*, p. 232.

86. Brading, *Church*, p. 229.

87. Brading, *Church*, p. 110.

88. Brading, *Church*, p. 245.

89. García Alcaraz, pp. 72–92.

90. On disputes between European-born members of the cathedral chapter, see Brading, *Church*, pp. 196–205.

91. Brading, *Church*, pp. 209.

92. This fissure between creole patriotism and liberalism is analyzed at length in Brading, *The First America*, chapter 25.

93. Brading, *Church*, pp. 240–54.

94. "Un notable escrito póstumo del obispo de Michoacán, Fray Antonio de San Miguel," p. 19; "Carta pastoral de Fray Antonio de San Miguel sobre los males de la Revolución francesa," in Cardozo Galué, p. 137.

95. AHCP, 67-D, exp. 2, 10 January 1800.

PROLOGUE TO CHAPTER TWO

1. AHMM, 1825, "Compromiso hecho por los Ynteresados a la Testamentaria del finado D. Ysidro Huarte...."

2. "Conspiración de Valladolid de 1813," p. 3.

3. AHMM, 1825, "Compromiso hecho por los Ynteresados a la Testamentaria del finado D. Ysidro Huarte...."

4. Ibarrola, p. 193.

5. "Acta de Cabildo de 16 de mayo de 1809," in Herrejón Peredo, ed., pp. 213–24.

6. Mendoza Briones and Terán, "Fin del órden colonial," p. 290.

CHAPTER TWO

1. "Conspiración de Valladolid de 1813," p. 474.

2. On the evolution of creole patriotism, see Brading, *First America*, and Pagden, "From Noble Savages."

3. Brading, *First America*, pp. 450–62, 473–79.

4. Brading, *First America*, p. 483.

5. "Informe sobre el estado de la educación e industria popular en la provincia de Michoacán, 1784," in Cardozo Galué, appendix.

6. Lemoine, *Morelos*, p. 105. See also "Representación a nombre de los Labradores y Comerciantes de Valladolid," in Sugawara, ed., p. 61, for references to other donations.

7. The distinctions drawn by the authors of the petitions is implicit in all of them, and it is made explicit in the following (all in Sugawara, ed.): "Representación contra la Consolidación del Cabildo Eclesiástico," p. 47; "Representación contra la Consolidación del Ayuntamiento de Valladolid," pp. 51, 57; "Representación a nombre de los Labradores y Comerciantes de Valladolid," p. 62; "Representación contra la Consolidación del Ayuntamiento de Pátzcuaro, Michoacán," p. 110. The petition signed by 118 people from

Huaniqueo, Puruándiro, and San Francisco Angamacutiro merely stated that the signers agreed with the arguments made in the other Michoacán representations.

8. "Representación a nombre de los Labradores y Comerciantes de Valladolid," in Sugawara, ed., p. 62.

9. "Representación a nombre de los Labradores y Comerciantes de Valladolid," in Sugawara, ed., p. 62.

10. "Sermón que en la Jura . . . ," p. 22.

11. "Sermón que en la Jura . . . ," p. 23.

12. This point is also made in 1810 by Abad y Queipo, who wrote: "This extraordinary event [the imprisonment of Iturrigaray] . . . dramatically intensified the rivalry and division between *gachupines* and creoles." "Representación a la regencia del reyno . . ." in Hernández y Dávalos, ed., 2:892.

13. "Acta de Cabildo de 16 de mayo de 1809," in Herrejón, ed., pp. 213–24.

14. Mendoza Briones, "Fuentes documentales," in Herrejón, ed., pp. 195–96.

15. AHMM, 1811, "Expediente sobre el adeudo de maíz a Benito López."

16. AHCP, 67-D, Protócolo de Ramírez, 1809, 13 October 1809.

17. Mendoza Briones, "Fuentes documentales," in Herrejón, ed., pp. 189–93.

18. "Cuaderno tercero de la causa," pp. 254, 257–58, 267, 270, 304, 307, 311, 312, 315, 335, 342, 362. On the conspiracy, see also López de Lara in *Boletín del Archivo General de la Nación*, 6:1.

19. "Cuaderno tercero de la causa," pp. 334–35, 364.

20. "Cuaderno tercero de la causa," p. 467.

21. Alamán, 1:315.

22. "Cuaderno tercero de la causa," p. 268.

23. García Alcaraz, p. 89.

24. ANM, Montaño, 1808, 22 January; "Cuaderno tercero de la causa," p. 260.

25. "Cuaderno tercero de la causa," p. 289.

26. "Representación a la regencia del reyno . . ." in Hernández y Dávalos, ed., 2:892–93.

27. "Cuaderno tercero de la causa," p. 322. Some creoles questioned this assurance, arguing that the Indians saw tribute as "just." Moreover, as one pointed out, some Indians, especially those in the eastern part of the province, might even actively oppose the movement.

28. Mendoza Briones, "Fuentes," pp. 192–93, cites a letter from Terán to the subdelegado of Zinapécuaro in which he refers to "a person who has tried to seduce the people [of Zinapécuaro], offering to relieve the Indians of the burdens of tribute and community."

29. García de Obeso was arrested shortly after this meeting took place. Whether Rosales and the Valladolid *barrios* played an important role early in the conspirators' deliberations, or whether their recruitment was part of a despera-

tion strategy once the conspirators were on the verge of being arrested, is not entirely clear. "Cuaderno tercero de la causa," pp. 278–90, 301.

30. "Cuaderno tercero de la causa," p. 298.

31. "Cuaderno tercero de la causa," p. 315.

32. "Cuaderno tercero de la causa," p. 336.

33. Guardino is strong on this point, especially pp. 19–24 and 38–41.

34. "Cuaderno tercero de la causa," pp. 258, 311, 324, 332, 334.

35. "Cuaderno tercero de la causa," pp. 271, 275–77, 309.

36. Romero Flores, *Historia*, 1:429 (following Julian Bonavit's reading of the municipal records); "Defensa del canónigo D. Sebastián de Betancourt..." in Hernández y Dávalos, 3:406; Mendoza Briones, "Fuentes documentales," pp. 195–97.

37. ANM, Marocho, 1811, 26 February; Marocho, 1811, 30 April; Aguilar, 1810, 11 October; Romero Flores, *Historia*, 1:432; Alamán, 1:461–62.

38. Archer, "'La Causa Buena,'" p. 85.

39. "Defensa del canónigo D. Sebastián de Betancourt...," 3:408.

40. "Defensa del canónigo D. Sebastián de Betancourt...," 3:409.

41. Alamán, 1:464.

42. "Defensa del canónigo D. Sebastián de Betancourt...," 3:413.

43. "Defensa del canónigo D. Sebastián de Betancourt...," 3:414.

44. Alamán, 1:498.

45. ANM, Aguilar, 1811, 13 March; Marocho, 1810, 13 October; Birbiesca, 1812, 15 April; Aguilar, 1816, 22 March; Aguilar, 1818, 17 January; "Noticias relativas a la matanza de españoles," 2:520–21; Moreno García, p. 96.

46. "Defensa del canónigo D. Sebastián de Betancourt...," 3:415. Van Young makes a similar point about insurgent justice in his comment on Archer, "Los dineros de la insurgencia," p. 59.

47. ANM, Aguilar, 1811, 16 November.

48. "Defensa del canónigo D. Sebastián de Betancourt...," 3:414.

49. "Noticias relativas a la matanza...," 2:520–21. The story of the severed head being shown to Anzorena was hotly disputed by his sons, reacting in 1850 to Alamán's treatment of their father's role in the revolution. See "Defensa del Sr. José María de Ansorena"; "Contestación del presbítero D. Mucio Valdovinos"; "Respuesta del Sr. D. José Mariano de Ansorena," all in Hernández y Dávalos, ed., 2:528–93.

50. "Noticias relativas a la matanza...," 2:520–21; Alamán, 2:40; Mendoza Briones, "Fuentes," pp. 198–99, "Certificación de méritos de D. Mariano Quevedo," pp. 223–24.

51. Alamán, 2:75.

52. "Noticias relativas a la matanza...," 2:520; Alamán, 2:40–41, 75; Romero Flores, *Historia*, 1:445; "Manifiesto del ayuntamiento de Valladolid," in

Hernández y Dávalos, 5:90; ANM, Marocho, 1811, 30 April; Aguilar, 1813, 19 June.

53. On this period see Alamán, 2:300–09; 3:360–61; 3:578–80; 4:262.

54. Martínez de Lejarza, p. 96; "Representación a Su Majestad en 20 junio de 1815," cited by Fisher, p. 122.

55. BL, M-M 1830:5, "El Yntendente," p. 1.

56. Alamán, 3:173–74.

57. Mendoza Briones, "Fuentes documentales," p. 203.

58. Alamán, 4:462; Mendoza Briones, "Fuentes documentales," p. 209.

59. ANM, Aguilar, 1812, 16 April.

60. ANM, urban property sales in Valladolid.

61. ANM, loans notarized in Valladolid.

62. ANM, Aguilar, 1814, n.d.

63. Archer, "'La Causa Buena'," p. 87; Martínez de Lejarza, pp. 200, 242; Hardy, pp. 46–48; Macías, p. 58; Mendoza Briones and Terán, "El levantamiento popular," 2:273–74; Alamán, 4:116, 540.

64. Martínez de Lejarza, p. 231.

65. Gortari, "La minería," pp. 133–34; Archer, "'La Causa Buena'," pp. 94–95; Alamán, 4:116. On urban and rural destruction, see also Hamnett.

66. Alamán, 4:298.

67. At least approximate value is known for 69 out of the 86 destroyed haciendas, the total of which is some 5,250,000 pesos. In the mid-1850s the value of rural property in Michoacán was estimated to be 10 million pesos, a figure that some contemporaries thought to be only about half its "true" (market) value. If we assume that rural property values had recovered by mid century to pre-1810 levels (see chapter 5), then in a *very* rough way we may estimate the value of rural property in 1810 to have been about 20 million pesos. Romero, p. 147.

68. AHMCR, Diezmos, Varios, Leg. 1, "Cuenta de la administración de diezmos de Churumuco de los años de 1818, 1819, y 1820."

69. Martínez de Lejarza, pp. 101, 111, 207, 216, 231, 235.

70. ANM, Aguilar, 1824, 13 November; Alamán, 4:651; AGN, Alcabalas, Valladolid, "Igualas celebradas en Zitácuaro, 1805"; AHMM, 1823, "Instancia de Da. Josefa Peña Madrazo."

71. "Parte detallado de la acción en Puruarán," 6:258; ANM, J. M. Aguilar, 1825, 14 January.

72. AHMCR, Diezmos, Varios, Leg. 10, "Cuenta del maíz . . . Pátzcuaro"; ANM, Aguilar, 1818, 15 July.

73. AHMM, 1822, no title, on destruction of the hacienda of La Parota.

74. Moreno García, p. 97; ANM, Marocho, 1808, 18 February.

75. ANM, Marocho, 1806, 5 September; Aguilar, 1820, 14 January.

76. ANM, Aguilar, 1822, 15 March.

77. ANM, Aguilar, 1819, 22 January; Aguilar, 1820, 27 November.

78. Hardy, p. 36.

79. AHMCR, Diezmos, Varios, Leg. 9, "Año de 1832. Cálculo que ha formado la Contaduría de Diezmos del Estado de Michoacán para el remate de las Administraciones del Ramo en el quinquenio 1833. . . ."

80. ANM, Aguilar, 1814, 26 April.

81. AHCP, Leg. 68, exp. 3, 1817, "Testamento de D. Domingo Larragoiti."

82. ANM, Joaquín Aguilar, 1826, 10 June.

83. AHCE, Varios, caja 2, exp. 9, "Memoria del Gobierno . . . 1827," Anexo #4.

84. Chowning, "Management of Church Wealth."

85. AHMM, 1816, will of Guadalupe Sánchez.

86. AHMM, 1830, estate of Pascual Alzúa.

87. ANM, Aguilar, 1814, 18 July; Valdovinos, 1837, 3 July.

88. ANM, Montaño, 1808, 13 June; J. M. Aguilar, 1827, 7 June; AHMM, 1841, "Lista de los bienes muebles cedidos a los acreedores de D. Faustino Peredo."

89. Most estimates are from estate inventories or *hijuelas de división*. A few are inferred by other means, e.g. parental inheritances or detailed wills listing assets.

90. AHMCR, Diezmos, Varios, Leg. 22 "Diezmos de Zamora. Año de 1811 [–1827]."

91. AHMCR, Diezmos, Varios, Leg. 18, "Cuenta que presenta al Tribunal de Hacedería el Administrador de este diezmatario [Valladolid] D. Sergio Velasco de los productos del año de 1817."

92. AHMCR, Diezmos, Varios, Leg. 1, "Cuenta del diezmatario de Ario, Santa Clara, y Urecho correspondiente al año de 1819."

93. Alamán, 4:298.

94. Archer, "Los dineros," pp. 52–53; Gortari, p. 134.

95. Archer, "Los dineros," p. 52; ANM, Marocho, 1815, 24 November; see also Timmons, p. 104, on the subject of commerce between insurgents and merchants.

96. AGN, Hacienda, Alcabalas, "Libro Real de Valladolid," 1819.

97. AGN, Hacienda, Alcabalas, "Comprobantes, Guias . . . ," for Valladolid, labeled "varios años"; for Pátzcuaro, 1785, 1788, 1793, 1797, 1798, 1802, 1805, 1806. The profits on domestic imports (commodities and manufactures) were at least as high as were those on foreign imports.

98. AGN, Hacienda, Alcabalas, "Comprobantes," Año de 1821.

99. AGN, Hacienda, Alcabalas, "Libros Reales" for Valladolid, 1801–09, 1817; Alcabalas, Caja 13, Valladolid and misc., "Valladolid, 1818," Foja 81, "Resumen y liquidación general del cargo de Alcabalas de 6%, del 2% de aumento y de la eventual al 8 y 6%. . . ."

100. AGN, Hacienda, Alcabalas, "Libros Reales" for Pátzcuaro, 1800–1809, 1818, 1819, 1820.

101. AHMCR, Diezmos, Varios, Leg. 22, "Diezmos de Zamora. Año de 1811 [–1827]."

102. Prices from inventories and contracts from: ANM, AHMM, AHPJ, AHCP, and AHMCR. Tithe prices are all from AHMCR. For maize, average price based on 35 observations for the period 1810–19.

103. Average sugar prices based on 14 observations for 1800–10; and 10 for 1811–19. AGN, Hacienda, Alcabalas, "Libro Real de Valladolid" for 1819 contains numerous examples of sugar imports.

104. Average *piloncillo* prices based on 6 observations for 1800–10, and 14 for 1811–19.

105. Average calf prices based on 10 observations for 1800–10, and 7 for 1810–19.

106. For a fuller discussion of the advantages and disadvantages of share-cropping, see Chowning, "Reassessing."

107. AHMCR, Diezmos, Varios, Leg. 8, "Cuenta general . . . de Maravatío"; AHMCR, Diezmos, Varios, Leg. 5, "Año de 1820. Quaderno donde constan las semillas . . . Irimbo"; AHMCR, Diezmos, Varios, Leg. 8, "Copias de manifestaciones . . . Maravatío . . . 1819 a 1822."

108. AHMCR, Diezmos, Varios, Leg. 17, "Diezmos de Tuxpan. Año de 1817."

109. AHMCR, Diezmos, Varios, Leg. 18, "Cuenta que presenta . . . D. Sergio Velasco . . . del Diezmatario de Charo . . . 1817"; Leg. 23, "Quaderno primero que contiene las Cuentas de Administración de los Diezmos de Zitácuaro . . . 1817"; Leg. 2, "Colecturía de Coroneo. Memoria . . . 1817"; Leg. 14, "Cuentas de Tiripitío y Santiago Undameo en 1818, 1819."

110. AHMCR, Diezmos, Varios, Leg. 8, "Cuenta general . . . Maravatío"; AHMCR, Diezmos, Varios, Leg. 5, "Año de 1820. Quaderno donde constan las semillas . . . Irimbo."

111. AHMCR, Diezmos, Varios, Leg. 8, "Copia de Manifestaciones . . . Maravatío . . . 1819"; Leg. 17, "Quaderno . . . manifestaciones . . . 1817 . . . Tlalpujahua"; Leg. 24, "Cuentas de Irimbo, 1818–1819"; Leg. 2, "Colecturía de Coroneo . . . 1816."

112. AHMCR, Diezmos, Varios, Leg. 8, "Cuenta general . . . de Maravatío"; AHMCR, Diezmos, Varios, Leg. 5, "Año de 1820. Quaderno donde constan las semillas . . . Irimbo"; AHMCR, Diezmos, Varios, Leg. 8, "Copias de manifestaciones . . . Maravatío . . . 1819 a 1822."

113. Romero Flores, *Historia*, 1:455; Romero Flores, *Diccionario*, pp. 307–08, 311; Ibarrola, p. 127; *Enciclopedia de México*, 9:5373; ANM, Montaño,

1809, 26 April; García, 1843, 27 February; Montaño, 1807, 19 October; Marocho, 1810, 13 October; Marocho, 1811, 9 February.

114. "Relación secreta del brigadier José de la Cruz"; Farriss, appendix (list of clerical participants in the Independence movement); Torre Villar, p. 314; Bravo Ugarte, *Historia sucinta*, 3:21.

115. "El cura Dr. Antonio Lavarrieta pide indulto," 2:371; Taylor, p. 455.

116. "Conspiración de Valladolid de 1813," p. 474.

117. Ibarrola, p. 292.

118. Ibarrola, pp. 30, 43, 123, 127, 451, 453; Romero Flores, *Diccionario*, p. 471.

119. Quevedo was one of those who tried to protect European lives from the mob, after the departure of Hidalgo and Anzorena in late 1810, and was later given a "certificación de méritos" by the *ayuntamiento* in recognition of this service, which suggests that he did not join the insurgency (since the city council would have been unlikely to salute him if he had).

120. ANM, Pérez, 1839, 15 August; J. M. Aguilar, 1827, 7 June; Ibarrola, pp. 370, 497.

121. AHMM, 1809, "Arrendamiento de la hacienda de la Parota a D. Domingo Arechaga"; AHMM, 1822, no title, on the destruction of the hacienda of La Parota.

122. ANM, Montaño, 1807, 2 October; AHMM, 1807, "Inventario y aprecio de los bienes . . . Reg. Gabriel García de Obeso."

123. For example, Lic. José Antonio Soto y Saldaña's father owned a very modest and heavily indebted hacienda (ANM, Marocho, 1804, 13 October). Capt. José María Abarca owned the valuable but debt-laden sugar haciendas of Tipitaro, Tipitarillo, and San Vicente in *tierra caliente* (ANM, Montaño, 1809, 4 November; Joaquín Aguilar, 1826, 20 September).

124. ANM, Arratia, 1782, 17 June; Correa, 1802, 3 February; Aguilar, 1820, 23 August; Ibarrola, pp. 390–91.

125. AHMM, 1815, "Inventario de los bienes . . . del Lic. Mariano Escandón"; Ibarrola, p. 107.

126. ANM, Montaño, 1807, 8 June; Montaño, 1808, 5 March; Marocho, 1811, 9 February.

127. Ibarrola, pp. 452–56.

128. ANM, Aguilar, 1804, 23 June.

129. ANM, Aguilar, 1804, 21 March; Birbiesca, 1805, 15 July; Aguilar, 1805, 26 August.

130. ANM, Aguilar, 1812, 21 July; Marocho, 1807, 16 December; Aguilar, 1819, 12 October.

131. Among the few who were *not* financially troubled was Lic. José María Izasaga, the son of a creole hacendado who was living in Uruapan and who

owned modest but flourishing cattle haciendas near Zacatula (ANM, Marocho, 1808, 16 November).

132. ANM, Aguilar, 1810, 11 October.

133. Ibarrola, p. 124.

134. ANM, Correa, 1801, 17 August; Aguilar, 1810, 22 June; Aguilar, 1823, 14 January.

135. Sources for insurgent names: García Alcaraz; Romero Flores, *Diccionario*; Romero Flores, *Historia*; *Enciclopedia de Mexico*; Farriss; Ibarrola,; Bravo Ugarte, *Historia sucinta*. It is possible (though not likely) that some of the other men I have identified as "not quite elite" were better-fixed financially than I have implied; for several of them I do not have good information such as estate inventories or other indications of their or their families' wealth and property.

136. Fisher, pp. 103–04; ANM, José María Aguilar, 1826, 14 April.

137. AHCP, 67-D, Protocolo de Ignacio Ramírez, 11 December 1809; Ward, 671–2; AHSM, "Libros de Casamiento," 16 December 1812.

138. Ibarrola, pp. 484, 497, 143, 453; Romero Flores, *Historia*, 1:477; ANM, Aguilar, 1819, 10 December.

139. Ibarrola, pp. 157, 404. Another merchant-royalist was Francisco Basurto Murillo, who cooperated with the royal troops in Apatzginán. Romero Flores, *Historia*, 1:633.

140. Guardino, chapter 3.

141. Good accounts of the splits within the Michoacán insurgency are in Romero Flores, *Historia*, chapter 26; *Enciclopedia de México*, "Michoacán," v. 9; and Bravo Ugarte, *Historia sucinta*, pp. 26–38.

142. Romero Flores, *Historia*, 1:478, 621, 633, 626.

143. Romero Flores, *Historia*, 1:608, 640; Bravo Ugarte, *Historia sucinta*, 3:55.

144. Histories of the insurgent decade are full of examples of alleged rebel vengeance on royalists. Just two examples from Michoacán are the sacking of the house of Manuel de la Bárcena, supposedly in retribution for his support of the King, and the sacking of the hacienda of Zipimeo, owned by José María Torres, in retaliation for his having helped some Europeans in Pátzcuaro to escape. Ibarrola, p. 119; Ward, pp. 671–72.

145. "Medidas políticas que deben tomar los jefes de los ejércitos americanos para lograr sus fines . . ." in Alamán, v. 3, Appendix, Doc. num. 19, p. 69; Lemoine, ed., *Manuscrito Cárdenas*, lxvii–lxviii. Lemoine says that the author was a member of the Guadalupes. Abad y Queipo also depicted the insurrection as a war against creole as well as peninsular property: "Dr. Manuel Abad Queypo . . . a todos sus habitantes," 16–17.

146. AHMCR, Diezmos, Varios, Leg. 3, "Charo. Comprobantes de [1817]."

147. AHMM, no title, on the destruction of the hacienda of La Parota; ANM, Joaquín Aguilar, 1826, 16 August and 20 September; Aguilar, 1832, 5 July.

148. ANM, Joaquín Aguilar, 1826, 20 September; Valdovinos, 1843, 10 May.

149. ANM, Montaño, 1807, 24 April; Montaño, 1809, 26 April; Huacuja, 1883, 30 November; Huerta, 1896, 7 September. It is true that Mariana Foncerrada y Ulibarri sought and received reduced interest payments on her church debts in 1824, citing the fact that she had received no income from her haciendas for many years. ANM, Aguilar, 1824, 24 November.

150. ANM, Marocho, 1808, 16 November; Valdovinos, 1834, 5 June; AHCP, Leg. 68, 1810–19, exp. 4, Libro de Hipotecas 1818–53, 14 September 1837.

151. ANM, Aguilar, 1810, 11 October.

152. ANM, Aguilar, 1819, 22 January. In the meantime the temporary owner was allowed to keep whatever was produced on the rancho.

153. The composition of the Cathedral Chapter in 1812 was approximately one-quarter peninsular, three-quarters creole. Nineteen members are listed in Birbiesca, 1812, 3 November, which is well short of the full complement of 27. I can identify one of the missing prebends (Martín García Carrasquedo). I have wills or other sources indicating place of birth for all but 4 of these 20, and I can infer place of birth for 2 of these. One is identified as both European and American in different places. The number of definite Spaniards is 5, and of probable Spaniards, 6.

154. ANM, Birbiesca, 1812, 3 November; Aguilar, 1813, 11 January; Aguilar, 1814, 5 August; Aguilar, 1816, 8 January; Birbiesca, 1812, 14 November; AGN, Hacienda, Alcabalas, Valladolid, 1818.

155. "Manifiesto del ayuntamiento de Valladolid . . . ," 5:90. The church also melted down silver objects to help pay for the pressing needs of the patients in the Hospital of San Juan.

156. AHMM, 1815, "Lista de los Yndividuos citados de orn. del Señor Yntendente Corregidor de esta Provincia para la Junta de hoy."

157. ANM, Aguilar, 1817, 5 July.

158. AHCP, 68, 1810–19, exp. 3, "Lista de los sugetos aquienes se señalan las cantidades con que deven contribuir por ahora cada mes para sostener a los urbanos realistas de . . . Pátzcuaro, impuestos por la Junta de Arvitrios. . . ."

159. Mendoza Briones, "Fuentes documentales," p. 200.

160. Mendoza Briones, "Fuentes documentales," p. 201.

161. Mendoza Briones, "Fuentes documentales," p. 210.

162. "Conspiración de Valladolid de 1813," pp. 469–70.

163. "Conspiración de Valladolid de 1813," pp. 470–72.

164. "Conspiración de Valladolid de 1813," p. 471. The lieutenant coronel was Joaquín Domínguez, whose daughter later married into the Huarte family;

the last name of the *alferez* was Rivero; the royal notary was Ignacio Birbiesca. Ibarrola, pp. 66, 191; ANM, Marocho, 1809, 5 July.

165. ANM, Aguilar, 1817, 5 July; AHMM, 1815, "Lista de los Yndividuos citados. . . ."

166. ANM, Aguilar, 1816, 5 June.

167. ANM, Aguilar, 1818, 17 January.

168. ANM, José María Aguilar, 1827, 14 December.

169. ANM, José María Aguilar, 1825, 8 July.

170. ANM, Joaquín Aguilar, 1829, 2 April; Aguilar, 1804, 4 June.

171. ANM, Marocho, 1806, 17 April; Aguilar, 1822, 8 November; Aguilar, 1824, 21 February; Salomo, 1846, 9 January.

172. ANM, Iturbide, 1830, 11 March; Rincón, 1835, 30 December.

173. Bárcena, "Exhortación que hizo . . . ," pp. 1–4.

174. Bárcena, "Exhortación que hizo . . . ," pp. 3–4.

175. Bárcena, "Manifiesto al Mundo. . . ."

176. The pages of the 1820 sermon in which the Plan de Iguala is prefigured are Bárcena, "Exhortación que hizo . . . ," pp. 6–8. Iturbide even justified Mexican independence using the same metaphor that Bárcena employed in his 1820 sermon: that there comes a time when a nation, like a child, grows up and no longer needs to live under its parents' wings. See Iturbide's statement in Bravo Ugarte, *Historia sucinta*, 3:58.

177. Former wealthy insurgents and/or conspirators who joined Iturbide include: Miguel Zincúnegui, Capt. José María Lino Patiño, Br. Manuel de la Torre Lloreda, and Ramón and Ignacio Rayón. Former royalists who joined Iturbide include Cor. Pedro Celestino Negrete, Cor. Mariano Laris, Capt. Juan José Gómez de la Puente. Romero Flores, *Diccionario*, pp. 597, 472, 311; Ibarrola, pp. 355, 143; Romero Flores, *Historia*, 1:690, 665–66, 609.

178. Bravo Ugarte, *Historia sucinta*, 3:57.

179. Not all creole elites could bring themselves to support Iturbide, who some thought had betrayed the 1809 conspiracy, and who all knew as a bloody-minded counterinsurgent, though they probably would not have supported anyone who proposed that Mexico be governed by a monarch. Among those in Michoacán who stood aside from the Iturbide juggernaut was Mariano Michelena, who would later lead the drive to bring him down.

180. For a persuasive argument that the Plan de Iguala also had a strong appeal for popular groups, see Guardino, especially pp. 74–80.

PROLOGUE TO CHAPTER 3

1. ANM, Aguilar, 1823, 17 March.

2. Romero Flores, *Comentarios*, p. 71; AHCP, Leg. 76–C, 1830–39, "Protocolo de 1831," exp. 2; Archivo de la Iglesia Parroquial de la Inmaculada

Concepción, Córdoba, Veracruz, vol. 11, 1793–98, "Bautismos de españoles y demás gente de razón desde el 3 de septiembre de 1793 hasta el 30 de abril de 1798," 4 July 1795; AHSM, "Libro de Bautismos, 1802–07," 29 September 1808. Details on the Codallos-Huarte connection can be found in Chowning, "Elite Families and Popular Politics."

3. On Huarte's contributions to the federalist constitution of 1825 see AHCE, Actas, Caja 1, exp. 9, 22 April, 25 April, 27 April 1825. For his condemnation of Guerrero and his signing of the 1836 Bases y Leyes, *El Sol*, 15 January 1830 (Riva Palacio, p. 232, urges that because of this action, Isidro Huarte's name should be remembered "al desprecio de nuestros lectores imparciales."); Biblioteca Nacional de México, pp. 3326, 3570.

4. ANM, García, 1843, 5 April; Michoacán, "Memoria que sobre el Estado que guarda en Michoacán la administración pública . . . 1850," p. 28.

5. The archives of the state congress for the 1820s contain numerous resignations on the part of men who had served previously or had been elected to serve, pleading that their business affairs required their full attention; most of these resignations were not accepted by the congress. See for example AHCE, Varios, III Congreso, caja 6, exp. 9, "Renuncia del C. Dip. Juan Anciola [1831]."

6. ANM, Aguilar, 1820, 23 August; Aguilar, 1820, 14 October; Aguilar, 1821, 25 October.

7. AHMM, 1830, "Cuenta de hijuela y division y partición de los bienes que quedaron por muerte de D. Pascual de Alzúa y de su primera muger Da. María del Carmen Huarte"; ANM, Aguilar, 1821, October; José María Aguilar, 1826, 21 November; Valdovinos, 1845, 16 July; Valdovinos, 1844, 22 February; Huerta, 1851, 25 January; Valdovinos, 1856, 22 July. Besides Urundaneo, Huarte also owned two semirural properties (a *quinta* and a summer house) in the *barrio* of Guadalupe, worth a combined 12,000 pesos, and a residence near the convent of La Merced worth over 6,000 pesos.

8. AHMM, 1825, "Compromiso hecho por los Ynteresados a la Testamentaria del finado D. Ysidro Huarte . . ."; ANM, Aguilar, 1829, 3 August; Aguilar, 1829, 28 September; Iturbide, 1830, 25 September; Rincón, 1841, 24 March; Pérez, 1848, 10 April.

9. ANM, Salomo, 1850, 23 March; García, 1845, 20 October; García, 1845, 22 October; Rincón, 1840, 21 August.

10. ANM, Rincón, 1836, 20 December; García, 1840, 8 July; García, 1844, 4 July; García, 1852, appendix at end of register.

11. Ibarrola, p. 190.

12. ANM, Huerta, 1886, 22 November. Of the four children of Huarte's third marriage to Ana Gertrudis Alcántara y Arrambide, two lived all their lives in Morelia, one (Mariano) was a lawyer, and the other (Manuel) became a priest. None was especially successful economically.

CHAPTER THREE

1. Hardy, p. 35.

2. Hardy, p. 42.

3. ANM, Prieto, 1823, 5 November.

4. ANM, José María Aguilar, 1828, 11 February and 16 February; De la Torre, p. 157.

5. AHCE, Legislatura I, Caja 2, exp. 9, "Memoria de Gobierno . . . 1827," 27.

6. ANM, Aguilar, 1823, 19 November.

7. Martínez de Lejarza, p. 136.

8. Martínez de Lejarza, pp. 200–01.

9. Martínez de Lejarza, pp. 117–18.

10. Martínez de Lejarza, pp. 207, 216, 235, 242.

11. AHCE, Legislatura I, Caja 2, exp. 9, "Memoria de Gobierno . . . 1827," 27, 22–23.

12. Sánchez Díaz, *El suroeste de Michoacán*, pp. 80–81.

13. AHCE, Varios III, Caja 6, exp. 8, "Memoria de la Administración Pública . . . 1831," anexo #12; ANM, tithe auctions for 1800–10.

14. AHCE, Legislatura I, Caja 2, exp. 9, "Memoria de Gobierno . . . 1827," anexo no. 3, "Nota de los frutos colectados en los diezmatarios de los departamentos del Norte y Poniente en el año de 1824"; AHMCR, Diezmos, Varios, Leg. 10, "Informes de los curas del diezmatario de Pázquaro . . . [1804]."

15. AHMCR, Diezmos, Varios, Leg. 23, "Cuentas del diezmatario de Zinapécuaro . . . 1819 [–1826]." The key to this hacienda's success seems to have been a new crop — chile — which was scarcely grown in this region in the late colonial period. Chiles of all varieties comprised 37 percent of the total value of production, topping wheat (33 percent) and corn (17 percent). This innovation was also seen on the hacienda of La Bartolilla, where chiles accounted for some 23 percent of the value of production.

16. AHCE, Varios, Congreso I, Caja 2, exp. 9, "Memoria de Gobierno . . . 1827," anexos #7–12; Litle, "Sales Taxes," p. 222.

17. Referring to the strong consensus around liberalism during this period, the conservative Bishop Clemente de Jesús Munguía later called this a period when "rationalist ideas paved the road to social anarchy." ("El sistema ciéntifico entró en nosotros para llanar los caminos de la anarquía social.") Munguía, "Memoria instructiva," p. 417.

18. The following discussions take a broad view of what it meant to be a liberal in Michoacán during this period. For a much more nuanced treatment of the many variations within liberalism, see Hale, *Mexican Liberalism*; Brading, *First America*; and Reyes Heroles.

19. AHCE, Actas, Caja 8, exp. 1, "Actas . . . 1826–1828," 6 September 1828.

20. AHCE, Actas, Caja 1, exp. 9, "April 1825," 27 April 1825.

21. AHCE, Actas, Caja 1, exp. 8, "Actas . . . octubre–diciembre 1824," 23 December 1824; Actas, Caja 3, exp. 6, "Año de 1827," 1 March 1827.

22. AHCE, Actas, Caja 1, exp. 11, "Actas . . . enero–julio 1825," 11 January 1825.

23. AHCE, Actas, Caja 1, exp. 11, "Actas . . . enero–julio 1825," 11 January and 15 January 1825.

24. The phrase appears, among other places, in AHCE, Actas, Caja 3, exp. 6, "Año de 1827," 1 March 1827.

25. Coromina, 29 December 1825.

26. The first debates on the issue are in AHCE, Actas, Caja 4, exp. 2, 20 September 1826. For the text of the law, Coromina, 24 April 1829.

27. Coromina, 18 January 1827.

28. Coromina, 26 September 1827. Exemption from media-anata for students in medicine, surgery, or pharmacy: 25 August 1827; establishment of a Proto-medicato: 31 March 1829; authorization for president of state Supreme Court to grant law degree: 12 May 1829; creation of Catedra de Medicina: 9 November 1829. The emphasis on education carried well beyond the 1820s. The Primer Ley de Educación of 30 May 1831 provided for mandatory public education, and also provided that the poor should attend free and the rich should pay a modest pension. Romero Flores, *Historia*, 1:745.

29. See Coromina, 8 March 1827, for the law creating the Contaduría de Diezmos to oversee tithe collection; 10 April 1828, for law legislating cessation of the *anualidades eclesiásticas*. See also the sometimes-heated debates on the proper relationship between church and state in AHCE, Actas, Caja 1, exp. 2, "Actas . . . 1824," 30 June 1824; Caja 1, exp. 7, "Actas secretas . . . abril–sept. 1824," 19 June 1824; Caja 1, exp. 8, "Actas . . . oct.–dic. 1824," 11 November 1824.

30. The debates over *reparto de tierras* are in Caja 4, exp. 3 (no label), 13 December 1826.

31. AHCE, Actas, Caja 1, exp.11, 23 January 1826.

32. The debates on outlawing bullfighting are in AHCE, Actas, Caja 4, exp. 2, "Año de 1826," 29 December 1825 and Caja 1, exp. 11, 23 January 1826.

33. The debates reconsidering the bullfight issue are in Caja 9, exp. 1, 24 October and 25 October 1828.

34. For more detail on the church's management of debt after independence, see Chowning, "Management of Church Wealth."

35. All accounts of the rebellion rely on Bustamante, 3:120–24. See also Sánchez Díaz, "Los vaivenes del proyecto republicano, 1824–1855," pp. 8–13; and Sims, pp. 90–94.

36. For some of the close connections between creoles and expelled Spaniards, see the notary registers for 1829, especially in the months of January, February,

and March, which contain numerous examples of departing Spaniards arranging for the sale and/or management of their properties by trusted creoles.

37. AHCE, Actas, Caja 5, exp. 3, "1827, libro 2," 8 November 1827. The deputy was Joaquín Domínguez.

38. AHCE, Actas, Caja 5, exp. 3, "1827, libro 2," 8 November 1827.

39. Coromina, 3:64, includes a list of 92 men who were exempted according to the national law of expulsion, dated 20 December 1827: "Lista de los Españoles que como eceptuados del decreto de espulsión por el Ecsmo. Sr. Presidente de la República . . . pueden permanecer en el Estado. . . ."

40. AHCE, Actas, Caja 9, exp. 1, "Actas . . . 1828," 17 February 1829.

41. "Representaciones que el Ayuntamiento de Morelia dirigió al Sr. Vice-Presidente y Cámaras de la Unión," insert in *El Astro Moreliano*, 18 February 1830; *El Astro Moreliano*, 8 March 1830.

42. Good treatments of the War of the South are in Guardino and Olveda.

43. AHCE, Varios III, Caja 6, exp. 8 [1831], "Memoria de la Administración Pública del Estado de Michoacán . . . 1831," 4v. On Codallos, see Chowning, "Elite Families and Popular Politics."

44. AHCE, Varios III, Caja 6, exp. 8 [1831], "Memoria de la Administración Pública del Estado de Michoacán . . . 1831," 1–2.

45. AHCE, Varios III, Caja 6, exp. 8 [1831], "Memoria de la Administración Pública del Estado de Michoacán . . . 1831," 5v, 7v.

46. *El Sol*, 3 May 1830; *El Sol*, 28 December 1829; *El Sol*, 29 December 1829; *El Sol*, 3 January 1830.

47. Bustamante, p. 438. See also the anonymous letter from a Zamora resident, published in *El Sol* (4 December 1830), which makes reference to the narrow escape from an "insolentísima" mob in November 1830 of Casimira's uncle, Diego Dávalos.

48. AHCE, Actas, Caja 14, exp. 2, "Actas . . . abril–junio 1831," 25 April; AHCE, Actas, Caja 18, exp. 3, "Actas . . . octubre 1832–marzo 1833," 31 October 1832. In the 1832 case the deputies were persuaded against the idea of granting themselves colonial-style honorifics by Lic. Isidro Huarte and Lic. Manuel Alvires, not so much on the grounds that distinctions were abhorrent (though Huarte comes close to making this argument), but because under the "present circumstances," they did not want to give ammunition to those who already thought the congress was full of "ideas aristocráticas."

49. AHCE, Actas, Caja 14, exp. 2, "Actas . . . april–junio 1831," 21 April 1831.

50. AHCE, Actas, Caja 12, exp. 2, "Actas . . . octubre 1830–abril 1831," 26 October 1830. It is worth noting that this concern continued to preoccupy deputies in the radical congress of 1833–34 (see AHCE, Caja 20, exp. 3, "Actas . . . marzo 1834–febrero 1835," 22 March 1834) and beyond (see chapter 5).

51. AHCE, Varios, VI Congreso, Caja 1, exp. 12, "Memoria del Estado de la Administración Pública de Michoacán en 1834," 13r.

52. AHCE, Varios, III Congreso, Caja 5, exp. 10, "Causas de degradación en la ciudadanía presentadas al H. Congreso, 22 abril 1831." The most restrictive elements of this and other similar proposals were rejected by the congress. See AHCE, Actas, Caja 18, exp. 3, "Actas ... octubre 1832–marzo 1833," 9 October 1832.

53. AHCE, Actas, Caja 12, exp. 2, "Actas ... octubre 1830–abril 1831," 20 April 1831; Caja 14, exp. 2, "Actas ... abril–junio 1831, 22, 23, 25 April; AHCE, Varios, VI Congreso, Caja 1, exp. 12, "Memoria del Estado de la Administración Pública de Michoacán en 1834," 18r.

54. AHCE, Actas, Caja 14, exp. 2, "Actas ... abril–junio 1831," 3 June and 4 June; AHCE, Actas, Caja 15, exp. 2, "Actas ... junio–septiembre 1831," 16 August; AHCE, Actas, Caja 18, exp. 3, "Actas ... octubre 1832–marzo 1833," 12 October 1832; AHCE, Actas, Caja 15, exp. 2, "Actas ... 21 junio–19 septiembre 1831," 16 August; AHCE, Varios, VI Congreso, Caja 1, exp. 12, "Memoria del Estado de la Administración Pública de Michoacán en 1834," 26v–27r.

55. AHCE, Varios, VI Congreso, Caja 1, exp. 12, "Memoria del Estado de la Administración Pública de Michoacán en 1834," 3v.

56. AHCE, Actas, Caja 20, exp. 3, "Actas ... marzo 1834–febrero 1835," 22 March 1834. Another acrimonious discussion of whether or not the constitution should protect the Catholic religion can be found in AHCE, Actas, Caja 20, exp. 3, "Actas ... marzo 1834–febrero 1835," 10 May 1834.

57. This account is in Romero Flores, *Historia*, 1:759–60. See also "Conducta del reverendo obispo de Michoacán D. José Cayetano Portugal."

58. AHCE, Actas, Caja 21, exp. 3, "Actas públicas ... febrero–agosto de 1835," 13 August 1835. Among the more vocal federalists were Lic. Manuel Alvirez, Lic. Antonio García Rojas, Lic. Juan Manuel Olmos, and Dr. Mariano Ramírez. Among the centralists were José de Ugarte, Br. Antonio de la Peña, Mariano Porto, and Br. Rafael Guedea. Manuel Alzúa, who had led the Morelia *ayuntamiento* in the fight against Salgado in 1830, nonetheless took a moderate position in this congress.

59. AHCE, Varios, VI Congreso, Caja 6, exp. 4, "Pronunciamiento de Pátzcuaro a favor del cambio de sistema de gobierno"; AHCE, Varios, VI Congreso, Caja 7, exp. 17, "Pronunciamiento de Apatzingán en favor de D. Antonio López de Santa Anna y contra D. Valentín Gómez Farías . . ."; AHCE, Proyectos-Acuerdos, VI Congreso, Caja 1, exp. 2, "Cinco iniciativas" (actually contains more than five).

60. AHCE, Actas, Caja 20, exp. 3, "Actas ... marzo 1834–febrero 1835," 1 January 1835, 7 August, 12 August, and 13 August 1835.

61. AHCE, Actas, Caja 21, exp. 3, "Actas públicas . . . febrero–agosto de 1835," 12 August 1835.

62. AHCE, Proyectos-Acuerdos, VI Congreso, Caja 1, exp. 2, "Cinco iniciativas."

63. AHCE, Actas, Caja 21, exp. 3, "Actas públicas . . . febrero–agosto de 1835," 13 August 1835.

64. AHCE, Actas, Caja 21, exp. 3, "Actas públicas . . . febrero–agosto de 1835," 14 August and 17 August 1835.

65. AHCE, Varios, VI Congreso, Caja 1, exp. 12, "Memoria del Estado de la Administración Pública de Michoacán en 1834," 13r. On the emerging political consensus of the early 1830s at the national level, see the excellent short overview by Vázquez, "La crisis y los partidos políticos." Vázquez emphasizes the foreign threat and fear of territorial fragmentation as motives for some moderate federalists to join the centralists. I did not come across any mention of foreign threats in my reading of the state debates; this is perhaps one more difference between politics at the national level and at the state level.

66. AHCE, Varios, VI Congreso, Caja 1, exp. 12, "Memoria del Estado de la Administración Pública de Michoacán en 1834," 31–31v.

67. Romero Flores, *Historia*, 1:762; AHCE, Actas, Caja 15, exp. 2, "Actas . . . 21 junio–19 septiembre, 1831" 9 September; AHCE, Actas, Caja 22, "Actas . . . agosto 1835–octubre 1835," 10 October 1835; AHCE, Actas, Caja 20, exp. 3, "Actas . . . marzo 1834–febrero 1835," 1 January 1835.

68. ANM, Marocho, 1810, 16 March; Aguilar, 1829, 10 July.

69. ANM, Birbiescas, 1804, 18 August; Prieto, 1823, 27 June; Rincón, 1835, 17 March.

70. Chowning, "Management of Church Wealth."

71. ANM, Aguilar, 1813, 16 September; Marocho, 1814, 3 October; Aguilar, 1817, 15 July; Aguilar, 1819, 27 July; Aguilar, 1824, 11 October; Joaquín Aguilar, 1826, 1 August; AHCE, Actas, Caja 1, exp. 7, "Actas secretas . . . abril–sept. 1824," 30 September 1824.

72. ANM, José María Aguilar, 1827, 7 February.

73. ANM, Aguilar, 1798, 18 May; Joaquín Aguilar, 1829, 2 April.

74. AHMM, 1823, no cover, Joaquín Ortiz de la Huerta petitions for debt relief. In 1787 José Nicolás Ortiz de la Huerta had purchased La Goleta for 33,786 pesos, and he had improved it by adding "pedazos de tierra" for 5,350 pesos; an adjoining property for 9,000 pesos; a hacienda house and various outbuildings, including a flour mill, worth 9,300 pesos; and almost thirteen miles of stone fence, valued at 16,364 pesos. The hacienda complex, with its improvements, was thus worth almost 74,000 pesos. In Valladolid the family owned a house on the *calle real* worth some 10,000 pesos, and they had miscellaneous accounts receivable amounting to another 10,000 pesos, for a total estate of some 93,000 pesos.

75. AHMM, 1816, "Expediente formado sobre esperas pedidas por D. Joaquín Ortiz de sus acreedores."

76. ANM, Aguilar, 1815, 27 February; Aguilar, 1829, 14 March; Aguilar, 1829, 2 July; Aguilar, 1829, 11 August; AHMM, 1823, no cover, Joaquín Ortiz de la Huerta petitions for debt relief.

77. ANM, Montaño, 1805, 1 February; Montaño, 1807, 13 April; Aguilar, 1820, 10 January; Aguilar, 1821, 26 May.

78. AHMM, 1820, "Testamentaria del Lic. Mathías Antonio de los Ríos."

79. ANM, Aguilar, 1820, 3 October.

80. ANM, Joaquín Aguilar, 1829, 29 October. The hacienda had been ceded several years earlier to her mother in payment of a debt of 17,777 pesos.

81. ANM, Joaquín Aguilar, 1826, 10 June.

82. AHCP, Leg. 72-D, exp. 3, "Indígenas de Yguatzio demandan a D. Serapio Díaz Barriga," 18 October 1827.

83. ANM, Iturbide, 1830, 12 June; Rincón, 1840, 15 February.

84. AHMCR, Documentos especiales de bienes inmuebles, Leg. 2, Año 1846–48, 11 June 1849.

85. ANM, Salomo, 1849, 10 March.

86. AHMM, 1822, no title, on destruction of the hacienda of La Parota.

87. AHMM, 1822, no title, on destruction of the hacienda of La Parota; AHMM, 1836, "Promovido por el Sr. Gral. Mariano Michelena, sobre la aprovación de la acta de la junta estrajudicial . . . para la entrega de la Hacienda de la Parota."

88. AHMM, 1822, no title, on destruction of the hacienda of La Parota; BL, M-A 26, Mariano Michelena to Manuel Eduardo de Gorostiza, 22 June 1829.

89. AHMM, 1836, "Promovido por el Sr. Gral. Mariano Michelena. . . ." After he gave up on La Parota, Michelena became one of several hacendados to find success managing a different property, in his case the embargoed sugar hacienda of Laureles, near Zitácuaro, which he operated until his death in 1852. *Gaceta del gobierno de Michoacán*, 22 March 1841.

90. ANM, José María Aguilar, 1825, 14 January; Valdovinos, 1833, 17 August; Rincón, 1835, 11 April; *La Voz de Michoacán*, 14 August 1842.

91. AHMM, 1831–34, "Cuentas de cargo y data . . . Hacienda de Puruarán." The hacienda was mortgaged to approximately 116,000 pesos, which meant that it had yearly interest obligations of some 5,800 pesos. The hacienda's records show, however, only 2,800 pesos in 1832 and 729 pesos in 1833 "remitido a Morelia para los censualistas." An additional 6,536 pesos worth of sugar and *piloncillo* was used over the three-year period to pay *libranzas* issued by the owners; these notes may or may not have been used to pay interest. The owners themselves are listed as having received 3,650 pesos over the three-year period in cash or, somewhat more rarely, in chiles, beans, and other effects; again, we do not

know what the owners did with these funds. Finally, 3,900 pesos worth of sugar and *piloncillo* was sold *al tiempo* in 1832, but this was presumably in payment of a new cash advance. Even if we assume, however, that *all* of these sums were applied to interest — which is most unlikely — the total, 17,615 pesos, would barely equal the mortgage interest due, which over a three-year period was 17,400 pesos.

92. Biblioteca Nacional de México, pp. 3326, 3570.

93. *El Filógrafo*, 11 October 1838; Coromina, 8:118–19; AHMCR, Documentos especiales de bienes inmuebles, Leg. 10, "Año de 1845. Cuaderno donde se toma razón de las escrituras de las fincas cituadas fuera de la Capital. . . ."

94. Biblioteca Nacional de México, p. 3570; Coromina, 7:8–9; *La Voz de Michoacán*, 6 March 1842 and 20 March 1842; ANM, Aguilar, 1824, 24 November.

95. Romero Flores, *Historia*, 1:763; ANM, Aguilar, 1831, 17 February; Valdovinos, 1838, 20 August.

96. ANM, José María Aguilar, 1828, 4 June; García, 1845, 9 October; Aguilar, 1831, 19 November; Fernández de Córdoba, 3:141. Additional evidence of Pastor Morales' early and ardent liberalism can be found in the records of the Inquisition case against him in 1794, when he was charged with promoting republicanism and independence; see AGN, *Los precursores ideológicos de la guerra de independencia*, pp. vi–xv.

97. Other wealthy politicians whose fortunes had deteriorated since independence and who accepted (with varying degrees of enthusiasm) the centralist state included Diego Moreno, the owner of the hacienda of Guaracha near Zamora; Juan Gómez de la Puente and Br. José Manuel Ruiz de Chávez, both of whom owned haciendas in the Puruándiro region; Lic. Manuel Diego Solórzano, brother of the insurgent Lic. Francisco Solórzano and owner of a small hacienda near Ario; Dr. Juan Manuel González Urueña, co-owner of a small, ruined hacienda near Apatzingán; and Lic. Antonio de Castro, a former insurgent.

98. The highest proportion of wealthy men was in the constitutional congress elected in 1824, in which eight of the twelve deputies were of the economic elite. In the seven different state congresses, beginning with the one that served in 1826–27 and ending with the one elected early in 1835, the highest proportion of wealthy men was seven out of fifteen (1826–27, 1831–32, 1835) and the lowest was four out of fifteen (1828–29); the others were either five (1830) or six (1830–31 and 1833–34) out of fifteen. Middle-class participation in the city councils of Morelia and Pátzcuaro was also high. See *El Astro Moreliano*, 18 February 1830 and 8 March 1830; AHCE, Varios, Caja 2, exp. 5, "Correspondencia del Ayuntamiento de Morelia . . ." January, 1830.

PROLOGUE TO CHAPTER FOUR

1. AHMM, 1830, "Cuenta de hijuela de división y partición de los bienes que quedaron por muerte de D. Pascual de Alzúa y de su primera mujer Da. María del Carmen Huarte"; ANM, Iturbide, 1829, 24 July.

2. ANM, Aguilar, 1832, 18 August; José María Aguilar, 1825, 16 April; Rincón, 1833, 21 March.

3. ANM, El Rincón, 1835, 6 April and 11 April.

4. AHMM, 1831–34, "Estados mensales de frutas," and "Cuentas de cargo y data de la Hacienda de Puruarán."

5. In 1836, just one year after he began to rent Puruarán, Alzúa borrowed 5,500 pesos from a Morelia merchant/speculator, Nicolás Ruiz de Chávez, which he promised to repay the following year in 4,000 *arrobas* of sugar; he complied with this promise to the letter. We do not know if this was the hacienda's entire production of sugar, but even if it were it was a great deal more sugar than Puruarán had produced before Alzúa rented it, when the average had been less than 500 *arrobas* a year. ANM, Rincón, 1836, 2 September.

6. ANM, Salomo, 1849, 23 April; Salomo, 1849, 15 November; Salomo, 1850, 7 November; García, 1853, 1 December; AHMM, 1849, "A instancia del C. Manuel Alzúa, sobre que se rematen . . . los bienes de la Testamentaria de D. Pedro Vélez Morante . . ."; Huerta, 1888, 18 December. The problems began with the fact that Capt. Pedro Vélez, an unmarried Spaniard, had purchased the hacienda jointly with Bishop-elect Manuel Abad y Queipo in 1799; this meant that in the case of neither owner was there a clear line of inheritance. Furthermore, Vélez and Abad had borrowed a huge sum soon after they had purchased the hacienda, so the heirs of that creditor, as well as the heirs of the original seller, who held part of the mortgage, all had a stake in the fate of the hacienda. By 1849, of course, not only did Vélez's nieces and nephews — some of whom lived in Morelia and had de facto owned the hacienda since Vélez's death in 1810, and some of whom lived in Spain — need to be satisfied, but there was also the tricky question of Abad's heirs, who were ultimately cut out of the proceeds from the sale by reason of having made no contribution to interest payments on the property for 39 years.

7. ANM, Cano, 1869, 30 January.

8. ANM, Valdovinos, 1853, 26 September; Escobar, 1862, 1 August.

9. Forty thousand pesos went to the three living children of Isidro Huarte's second marriage to Ana Gertrudis Alcántara (Francisca, Mariano, and Manuel Huarte); 46,000 pesos to his sister Juana's son, Manuel Oviedo, and his children; 6,000 pesos to his sister Macaria's children, with another 6,000 pesos to the children of one of them, María Montenegro (m. Gregorio Patiño); and 12,000 pesos to the children of his half brothers Ramón and José Alzúa. In addition, he wanted

the interest on 10,000 pesos, as well as a country house in Morelia, to go to a woman named Concepción Odorica, whose relation to Alzúa is not known.

10. ANM, Valdovinos, 1861, appendix at end of register.

11. ANM, Mafra Vargas, 1766, 26 May.

12. AHSM, "Libro de Casamientos," 8 September 1818; AHMCR, Negocios Diversos, Leg. 5 (1806); ANM, José María Aguilar, 1827, 17 July; Valdovinos, 1841, 9 December; Salomo, 1848, 1 January.

13. AGN, Alcabalas, Valladolid, "Libros Reales de Pátzcuaro" for 1817–18; AHMM, 1815, "Lista de los Yndividuos citados . . ."; ANM, Aguilar, 1819, 23 December; García, 1849, 10 April.

14. ANM, José María Aguilar, 1825, 8 July; Valdovinos, 1841, 27 October; AHMCR, Diezmos, Leg. 7, "Ario, Santa Clara, Urecho. Expedientes de dulces, Urecho (1820–35)."

15. ANM, Aguilar, 1829, 7 November; Aguilar, 1832, 14 January; Rincón, 1836, 18 July.

16. ANM, Valdovinos, 1836, 17 February; Valdovinos, 1856, 13 February.

17. ANM, Aguilar, 1831, 10 November.

18. ANM, Valdovinos, 1834, 16 January; Rincón, 1837, 11 August; AHMCR, Libro 268, "Libro en que constan las fincas y capitales pertenecientes al Sr. San José . . . 1837–38."

19. Calderón de la Barca, pp. 561–62.

20. Calderón de la Barca, p. 561.

21. AHMM, 1840, "Sobre igualas celebradas con algunos comerciantes por sus giros de comercio"; ANM, García, 1845, 31 May.

CHAPTER FOUR

1. See, for example, the complaints of the admittedly self-interested heirs of Josefa Alday, who protested in 1827 that the appraised value of effects on her hacienda near Pátzcuaro was too high, because "the lack of markets and trade have debased prices." In the same year the *Memoria de Gobierno* registered a similar complaint: tithe receipts, it pointed out, were reduced because commodity prices were low, and low prices discouraged producers. AHCP, Leg. 71-C, 1827, no title, inventory of estate of Josefa Alday; AHCE, Legislatura I, Caja 2, exp. 9, "Memoria de Gobierno . . . 1827," 23.

2. Average maize prices based on 115 observations across the state during the 1820s and 46 observations for the 1830s, mainly from tithe records.

3. Calves sold by tithe collectors confirm this pattern: from an average of 22rr in the 1800s, the price per head rose to 35rr in the 1820s and fell back to 28rr in the 1830s. Average cattle prices based on 8 observations for 1800 to 1810, 6 for 1820 to 1829, and 9 for 1830 to 1839; average calf prices based on 10 observations for 1800 to 1810, 57 for 1820 to 1829, and 34 for 1830 to 1839.

4. Average sugar prices based on 14 observations for 1800 to 1810, 26 for 1820 to 1829, and 27 for 1830 to 1839.

5. Average *piloncillo* prices based on 6 observations for 1800 to 1810, 44 for 1820 to 1829, and 37 for 1830 to 1839.

6. AHMCR, Diezmos, Leg. 7, 1820–1835, Ario, Santa Clara, Urecho. Ramo de Dulces, Urecho; AHMCR, Diezmos, Varios, Leg. 17, "Diezmatario de Uruapan . . . 1818 [–1827]." In the 1820s sugar from Michoacán was sold in Guadalajara, the trade fair at San Juan de los Lagos, and Querétaro. AHMCR, Diezmos, Varios, Leg. 16, "Cuenta de Tacámbaro del año de 1819"; AHMCR, Diezmos, Varios, Leg. 10, "Cuenta del Maíz, muebles y aprecios colectados en el año de 1828 en el diezmatario de Pátzcuaro, que se aplican a el de 1817 . . . ," see enclosed sugar accounts for 1818; AHMCR, Diezmos, Varios, Leg 10, "Añiles, dulces y semillas de Pásquaro de los años de [18]17 . . . ," 1819.

7. Wheat prices based on 11 observations for 1800 to 1809, 74 for 1820 to 1829, and 34 for 1830 to 1839.

8. Ward, 2:323–24.

9. AHMCR, Diezmos, Varios, Leg. 23, "Cuenta . . . del Diezmatario . . . de Zinapécuaro . . . 1819 [–1826]."

10. AHMCR, Diezmos, Varios, Leg. 26, "Cuentas de Etúcuaro del año de 1823."

11. AHMM, Año de 1823, no cover, Joaquín Ortiz de la Huerta petitions for debt relief.

12. BL, ms. collection, "Libro de Consultas [del Convento de Santa Catarina de Pátzcuaro, 1808–1848]," f. 62 (15 January 1831). See also ff. 58–59 (20 August 1828), for a similar comment regarding the trouble that collecting many small rents caused the convent.

13. "Loans" does not include liens, liquidation of accounts, business transfers, mortgage transfers, goods sold on credit, or *obligaciones* (e.g., one heir recognizing the amount of a co-heir's inheritance). These statistics underreport the availability of credit in the 1830s and early 1840s by an extent that cannot be determined, since two of the ways in which the economy adjusted to changed circumstances after 1810 — cash advances to farmers, which are included here when notarized, and agricultural partnerships — do not always show up directly in the notary records. Still, the very need for new forms of doing business (which are discussed below) testifies to the scarcity of capital and to high interest rates, and so although the availability of loan capital was probably not quite as limited as my statistics suggest, there is no question that weak financial markets were still a significant constraint on growth during this period.

14. For more detail on this point, see Chowning, "Management of Church Wealth."

15. For more detail on this point, see Chowning, "Reassessing Profitability."

16. AHMM, 1831–34, "Estados mensales de frutas de la Hacienda de Puruarán," "Cuentas de cargo y data de Puruarán," and "Estado que manifiesta las operaciones diarias de trabajo de esta Hacienda [de Puruarán] en el presente mes de la fecha. . . ."

17. AHMM, 1822, no title, on destruction of the hacienda of La Parota.

18. ANM, Valdovinos, 1841, 12 May.

19. ANM, Rincón, 1844, 10 October.

20. AHPJ, primero civil, 1840, Leg. 1, "Promovido por D. Carlos Valdovinos pidiendo se libre orden . . . para que le permita trasladar unas fanegas de maíz . . ."

21. The success or failure of sharecroppers theoretically turned on some of the same factors as did the success or failure of hacendados who negotiated advance sale contracts: what share of the crop did they have to give up? Were they able to get a good price for the part of the harvest they were allowed to sell on their own terms? In reality, though, the sharecroppers who succeeded in bringing fields back into production risked losing their contracts, since hacendados might well prefer to farm their newly profitable fields directly.

22. AHCP, 1839, Leg. 75-B, exp. 2, "Protocolo de 1839," 15 March 1839.

23. AHCP, 1839, Leg. 75-B, exp. 2, "Protocolo de 1839," 30 April 1839.

24. ANM, Sierra (Jiquilpan), 17 October 1838 and 15 April 1839.

25. AHMM, 1839, "Convenio en arbitradores nombrados por los Cds. Fernando Román y Agustín Elorza, para decidir las diferencias que les ocurrieron en la compañía que celebraron para el giro de la Hacienda de la Huerta propia del primero."

26. AHMCR, Diezmos, Varios, Leg. 9, "Año de 1832. Cálculo que ha formado la Contaduría de Diezmos del Estado de Michoacán para el remate de las Administraciones del Ramo en el quinquenio . . . 1833 . . . 1837."

27. AHCE, Varios, VI Congreso, Caja 1, exp. 12, "Memoria del Estado de la Administración Pública de Michoacán en 1834," 10–10v.

28. In both periods sugar production was around 300,000 *arrobas* a year. BL, M-M 1830:5, "El Yntendente," p. 4; "Contestación del Administrador Pral. substituto de rentas del departamento al editorial que bajo el rubro de alcabalas, consta en . . . la *Voz de Michoacán* del . . . 25 de enero de 1844" (Morelia, 1844), p. 6.

29. AHMM, 1841, "Autos de inventarios formados a los bienes . . . de D. José Guadalupe de la Piedra."

30. AHCP, Leg. 66-C (1800–09), exp. 3, 1806, "Inventarios de los bienes que quedaron por muerte de Da. María Josefa Valdes"; ANM, Valdovinos, 1839, 18 March.

31. AHMM, 1833, "Hijuela y cuenta de partición de los bienes de la finada Da. María Trinidad Ponce de León"; ANM, Valdovinos, 1845, 1 April; García, 1848, 20 July.

32. ANM, Marocho, 1804, 10 September; Aguilar, 1819, 3 February; Aguilar, 1819, 19 August; Aguilar, 1820, 1 March; Aguilar, 1817, 8 August; Aguilar, 1824, 12 February; José María Aguilar, 1827, 7 February; Rincón, 1836, 8 November; Rincón, 1841, 31 August; Rincón, 1844, 3 February; Pérez, 1850, 14 November; Valdovinos, 1857, 20 November; AHPJ, 1851, Leg. 1, "Juicio de Testamentaria del Sr. Martín García de Carrasquedo."

33. ANM, Rincón, 1836, 9 April; Valdovinos, 1837, 27 June; Valdovinos, 1838, 29 March; AHMM, 1836, "Testamento e inventario de bienes de D. Joaquín Teobaldo Ruiz."

34. ANM, Birbiesca, 1805, 15 July; Aguilar, 1805, 26 August; Aguilar, 1814, 4 October; Joaquín Aguilar, 1825, 6 September; Iturbide, 1831, n.d. (inventory of estate of María Josefa del Corral).

35. AHSM, "Libro donde se sientan las Partidas de Casamientos de Españoles," 13 July 1791; ANM, Montaño, 1805, 21 November; Montaño, 1808, 6 September; Aguilar, 1814, 29 April; Aguilar, 1813, 11 August; Aguilar, 1814, 12 August; Aguilar, 1815, 10 March; Aguilar, 1815, 17 July; AHMM, 1808, "Autos de Inventarios a bienes del difunto Capitan D. José María Peredo"; AHMM, 1825, no cover, statement of Mariano Figueroa regarding the auction of the hacienda of El Rincón.

36. AHMM, 1825, no cover, statement of Mariano Figueroa regarding auction of the hacienda of El Rincón.

37. AHMM, 1825, no cover, statement of Mariano Figueroa regarding auction of the hacienda of El Rincón; AHMCR, Diezmos, Varios, Leg. 19, "Cuentas del Diezmatario de Valladolid del año de 1820"; ANM, Joaquín Aguilar, 1826, 11 March; Joaquín Aguilar, 1826, 18 October; Rincón, 1839, 17 January.

38. ANM, Joaquín Aguilar, 1826, 11 March; José María Aguilar, 1828, 21 May; Aguilar, 1830, 15 February; Aguilar, 1832, 20 October; Rincón, 1835, 17 September.

39. ANM, Aguilar, 1820, 19 September; José María Aguilar, 1826, 3 November; Valdovinos, 1839, 1 June; Cano, 1868, 25 April.

40. ANM, Rincón, 1837, 19 December; García, 1841, 13 November; García, 1849, 8 August; García, 1849, 6 November.

41. AHMCR, Diezmos, Varios, Leg. 10, "Cuaderno perteneciente al Ramo de Dulces, 1818" (contained in "Cuenta del Maíz, Muebles, y Aprecios colectados en el año de 1828 . . . que se aplican a él de 1817)"; ANM, Aguilar, 1826, 20 September; Prieto, 1823, 27 June; Rincón, 1837, 1 August; García, 1847, 24 May.

42. AGN, Alcabalas, Valladolid, "Libros Reales" and "Comprobantes, Guías y Pasos" for Pátzcuaro, 1818–21; ANM, Salomo, 1848, 21 June; Prieto, 1823, 8 March; Rincón, 1833, 7 October; García, 1851, 26 February.

43. ANM, Joaquín Aguilar, 1830, 14 September; Rincón, 1835, 26 October;

Aguilar, 1831, 22 September; José María Aguilar, 1828, 4 November; Rincón, 1842, n.d. (rental contracts for haciendas of Chuen and Araparícuaro); Valdovinos, 1839, 18 March; Salomo, 1849, 26 July; García, 1851, 26 February.

44. ANM, Ruiz (Uruapan), 1881, 22 April; AHMCR, Documentos especiales de bienes inmuebles, 1862, Leg. 8, "Denuncia de capitales ignoradas por el C. Rafael Ahumada, sobre capitales eccos. de la Hacienda del Rosario y los Hoyos"; AHMCR, Diezmos, Leg. 887 (Apatzingán, 1835–63), "Cuentas que presentó el Br. Manuel B. Gutiérrez por los efectos que recibió de la restitución de D. Antonio Sierra . . . 1847,48 y 49"; Sánchez Díaz, El suroeste, pp. 44–46, 94–95.

45. ANM, "Libro de Hipotecas . . . Zamora, 1830–45" (see esp. 1834 and 1837 for hacienda purchases); AHMCR, Diezmos, Varios, Leg. 9, no title, 1837 list of individuals in the state who refused to tithe (Plancarte appears in the Zamora list); ANM, García, 1854, 9 June.

46. ANM, Joaquín Aguilar, 1828, 5 September.

47. ANM, José María Aguilar, 1827, 14 December; José María Aguilar, 1825, 21 September; AHSM, "Libro de Casamientos," 3 February 1827 and 7 July 1822.

48. AHSM, "Libro de Casamientos," 26 November 1819.

49. Meyer, pp. 192–94.

50. ANM, "Libro de Hipotecas de Zamora, 1830–1845," n.d. 1830, Galván debt to Bordon, Harrison, and Brown.

51. When Evaristo Barandiarán was called upon to sign a petition submitted by the Mexico City *ayuntamiento*, of which he was a member, in 1840, an "E." Bermejillo signed for him (Biblioteca Nacional de México, 3947 and 5745). At his 1839 marriage to Josefa Iradi, Evaristo Barandiarán stated that he had lived in Mexico City for ten years (AHSM, "Libro de Casamientos," 12 April 1839). For his continuing interests in Michoacán, see BL, "Libro de Consultas," f. 60 (9 September 1830); ANM, Aguilar, 1829, 13 July; Joaquín Aguilar, 1829, 6 February; Valdovinos, 1835, 14 May; and AHMM, 1840, "Expediente sobre igualas celebradas con algunos comerciantes por sus giros de comercio."

52. AGN, Alcabalas, Valladolid, "Comprobantes" and "Libros Reales" for Pátzcuaro 1817 and 1818, and "Libro Real" for Valladolid, 1820; ANM, Rincón, 1835, 30 December; Iturbide, 1830, 11 March (Francisco María Iturbe as *alvacea* of uncle, Antonio Anciola).

53. AHCP, Leg. 78-E, "Inventario a los bienes que quedaron . . . del Cd. José María Jaurrieta," 28 November 1838; AHMM, 1829, "Papeles sobre expulsion de españoles"; ANM, García, 1841, 4 August; Salomo, 1846, 9 January; Salomo, 1846, 7 May.

54. ANM, Sierra (Jiquilpan), 11 July 1838. Miguel Garibay Verduzco was a grandchild of Diego Antonio Verduzco, owner of the hacienda of Quiringuícharo: *Protocolos notariales del Distrito de Zamora*, p. 32 (9 April 1844).

55. ANM, José María Aguilar, 1827, 14 December; Rincón, 1833, 8 November; Rincón, 1833, 19 November; Rincón, 1835, 14 September.

56. ANM, Valdovinos, 1845, 17 September.

57. ANM, Correa, 1778, 10 July. Larreátegui returned to Jiquilpan in 1829 to marry Eduvige Anaya, probably a relative of Manuel Ignacio Anaya. The latter was active in the Jiquilpan area as an hacienda renter and later came to be administrator of the large sugar hacienda of La Magdalena. ANM, Sierra (Jiquilpan), 20 January 1838, 25 May 1838, and 24 July 1838.

58. ANM, Valdovinos, 1844, 19 February.

59. AHPJ, primero civil, 1838, Leg. 1, "Información promovido por D. Mariano Larreátegui sobre no haber adquirido de sus padres bienes algunos."

60. ANM, García, 1838, 3 July; Valdovinos, 1841, 18 September; Rincón, 1836, n.d. (sale of mules).

61. The associates with whom Larreátegui clashed included Rafael Amescua, whose partnership Larreátegui sued successfully to dissolve in 1837 (three years ahead of schedule), complaining that half of the alleged profits consisted of lost or dubious accounts receivable; Vicente Parra, whom Larreátegui accused of criminal negligence; and one of his Mexico City suppliers: in 1837 he ordered five *tercios* of thread, which were supposed to leave Veracruz and go directly to Morelia, but the documentation carried by the muleteer mistakenly listed Durango and Guadalajara as the cargo's official destinations. This led to the confiscation of the thread, and Larreátegui, in characteristically intemperate language, demanded restitution for the value of the cargo, the fine, the costs and expenses of releasing the confiscated cargo, and damages from his cosigner in Mexico City. Larreátegui also refused to back down from confrontations with government officials. He ran into trouble with the tax collectors in 1839 over sales tax on 250 Havana cigars, and in the same year was accused of declaring only 200 *arrobas* of cacao to sales tax officials, instead of the 283 *arrobas* he actually sold. This accusation of fraud generated a huge lawsuit in 1839. ANM, García, 1838, 3 July; Rincón, 1837, 12 June; Rincón, 1837, 17 July; AHPJ, primero civil, 1839, Leg. 1, "Expediente promovido a instancia del Administrador de Tabacos del Departamento sobre la aprehensión que el resguardo de alcabalas de esta capital hizo de D. Mariano Larreátegui . . ."; AHPJ, primero civil, 1839, Leg. 1, "Juicio verbal celebrado con arreglo al capítulo 50 de la última pauta de comisos. . . ."

62. AHMM, 1840, "Expediente sobre igualas celebradas con algunos comerciantes por sus giros de comercio"; ANM, Valdovinos, 1842, 5 April; García, 1842, 19 November; Rincón, 1843, 3 April; Rincón, 1842, 27 August; CL, "Escrituras de Contrata y de Asociación de los Señores accionistas al Mineral de Guadalupe . . . con el propietario de las minas Providencia . . . , D. José Mariano Larreátegui" (Mexico, 1849); *El Siglo Diez y Nueve*, suplemento al n. 415 del día 30 de noviembre de 1842; CL, "Informe que dió el périto facultativo D. Pablo

Parkman . . . sobre las minas del Mineral del Gallo . . ."; CL, "Comunicado sobre la situación económica de su empresa y ofrecimiento de acciones para la explotación de la mina El Gallo . . ." (Morelia, 1842).

63. AHMM, 1840, "Expediente sobre igualas celebradas con algunos comerciantes por sus giros de comercio."

64. ANM, Aguilar, 1826, 20 September; García 1852, 6 September.

65. Sales tax rates come from "Contestación del Administrador Pral. substituto," p. 6.

66. AGN, Alcabalas, Valladolid, "Libros Reales" for Valladolid, 1800–10.

67. Another part of the explanation may be higher levels of trade in the form of contraband than are contained in official statistics. On this subject, see Mayo.

68. The state government claimed that 17,000 people in the state died during the epidemic. AHCE, Varios, VI Congreso, Caja 1, exp. 12, "Memoria del estado de la Administración Pública de Michoacán en 1834," 14r.

69. El Filógrafo, 5 September 1838; Sánchez, "Los vaivanes," pp. 10–19; and Romero Flores, Historia, 1:764–69.

70. AHMCR, Diezmos, Leg. 889, Ario/Santa Clara/Urecho, 1831–53; Leg. 905, Jiquilpan, 1834–73; Leg. 913, Valladolid 1834–47; Leg. 929, Tacámbaro, Turicato, Caráquaro, 1833–80; Leg. 934, Uruapan/Taretan, 1833–64; Legs. 912 and 914, Puruándiro 1834–63 and 1835–80.

71. Romero Flores, Historia, 1:797.

72. AHCP, Leg. 90-F, exp. 2 [1843], "La Sra. Da. Manuela Morales de Velasco por el capital de 4500 que reconoce la hacienda de Tujacato. . . ."

73. ANM, García, 1849, 20 September.

74. "Segunda esposición . . . ," pp. 3–4, 20–21. The merchants, however, had good reason to paint as bleak a picture as possible: they were trying to fight a tax increase. For more discussion of rhetorical exaggeration of economic disasters, see the end of this chapter.

75. On the miserable and deteriorating state of government finances, see Tenenbaum, Politics of Penury, and Stevens.

76. AHCE, Actas, Caja 22, exp. 5, "Actas . . . octubre 1835–noviembre 1837," 5 April 1837.

77. AHCE, Actas, Caja 22, exp. 5, "Actas de la junta departamental . . . octubre 1835–noviembre 1837, 18 December 1835.

78. AHCE, Actas, Caja 22, exp. 5, "Actas de la junta departamental . . . octubre 1835–noviembre 1837," 1 February 1837.

79. AHCE, Actas, Caja 22, exp. 5, "Actas de la junta departamental . . . octubre 1835–noviembre 1837," 1 April 1837.

80. AHCE, Actas, Unnumbered box shelved between Caja 22 and Caja 23 (hereafter Caja 22-B), "Libro primero de registros," part 1, 30 July 1838.

81. Coromina, 15 May 1837; 19 May 1837; 10 November 1837; 19 December 1837; 20 February 1838; 24 July 1838; 15 November 1838.

82. AHCE, Actas, Caja 22-B, "Libro segundo de registros," part 2, 21 September 1840 and 19 June 1840.

83. AHCE, Actas, Caja 22-B, "Libro segundo de registros," part 3, 15 July 1841 and 30 July 1841.

84. AHCE, Actas, Caja 22-B, "Libro segundo de registros," part 3, 11 August 1841. On the functions of the Supremo Poder Conservador, see Costeloe, *Central Republic*, pp. 104–06.

85. Wealthy individuals were very evident in the composition of the junta. Eleven of the 14 members of the 1837 junta were among the economic elite, as were 8 of the 14 members elected in 1838. The next elections to the junta were not held until 1844, and at that time 10 of 17 members were wealthy. The overwhelming majority of state government appointees were also of the economic elite. In 1842, for example, *La Voz de Michoacán* ran a list of 25 individuals named to various commissions, and 21 of them were wealthy. Coromina, 7:8–9; 8:118–19; *El Filógrafo*, 11 October 1838; *La Voz de Michoacán*, 6 March 1842.

86. AHCE, Actas, Caja 22, exp. 5, "Actas de la junta departamental . . . octubre 1835–noviembre 1837," 20 September 1837.

87. AHCE, Actas, Caja 22, exp. 5, "Actas de la junta departamental . . . octubre 1835–noviembre 1837," 13 September 1837; AHCE, Actas, Caja 25, exp. 4, "Actas públicas de la Exma. Asamblea Departamental . . . enero 1844–noviembre 1844," 28 August 1844.

88. AHCE, Actas, Caja 22-B, "Libro segundo de registros," part 4, 7 April 1842.

89. AHCE, Actas, Caja 25, exp. 4, "Actas públicas . . . [January 1844–November 1844]," 5 July 1844.

90. The thrust of Costeloe's *Central Republic* is also to blur the distinctions between conservatives and liberals, though his emphasis is on their shared class interests, while here I focus more on ideological convergences.

91. AHCE, Actas, Caja 22-B, "Libro segundo de registros," part 2, 23 March 1840.

92. AHCE, Actas, Caja 22-B, "Libro segundo de registros," part 3, 2 August 1841.

93. AHCE, Actas, Caja 22-B, "Libro segundo de registros," part 2, 2 July 1840.

94. AHCE, Actas, Caja 22-B, "Libro segundo de registros," part 4, 7 January 1842.

95. AHCE, Actas, Caja 22-B, "Libro segundo de registros," part 1, 20 March 1839.

96. AHCE, Varios, VII Central, Caja 9, exp. 3, "Consultas y Comunicaciones

que la H. Asamblea Departamental dirige al Supremo Gobierno," no. 69, 13 July 1846.

97. AHCE, Actas, Caja 22-B, "Libro primero de registros," part 1, 6 April 1838.

98. AHCE, Actas, Caja 22-B, "Libro tercero de registros," part 1, 25 June 1842.

99. AHCE, Actas, Caja 22-B, "Libro segundo de registros," part 2, November 1840 (date illegible) (no. 75).

100. AHCE, Actas, Caja 22-B, "Libro tercero de registros," part 2, 3 April 1843.

101. AHCE, Actas, Caja 22-B, "Libro tercero de registros," part 2, 13 November 1843.

102. AHCE, Varios, VII Central, Caja 9, exp. 3, "Consultas . . . ," no. 92, 30 July 1846.

103. BL, ms. collection, "Memoria de la Administración Pública del Estado de Michoacán . . . 1830," p. 14.

104. AHCE, Actas, Caja 22-B, "Libro primero de registros," part 1, 5 September 1838.

105. "Segunda esposición . . . ," p. 16.

106. "Segunda esposición . . . ," pp. 7–8.

107. "Exposición que de nuevo . . .", p. 6.

108. AHCE, Varios, VI Congreso, Caja 1, exp. 12, "Memoria del Estado de Administración Pública de Michoacán . . . 1834," 17–17v.

109. AHCE, Actas, Caja 22, exp. 5, "Actas de la junta departamental . . . octubre 1835–noviembre 1837," 13 April 1836; AHCE, Actas, Caja 22-B, "Libro primero de registros," part 1, 28 June 1838; AHCE, Actas, Caja 22-B, "Libro tercero de registros," part 2, 20 February 1843.

110. AHCE, Actas, Caja 22-B, "Libro tercero de registros," part 2, 18 May 1843; AHCE, Actas, Caja 22-B, "Libro segundo de registros," part 3, 3 May 1841.

111. AHCE, Actas, Caja 22-B, "Libro tercero de registros," part 2, 18 May 1843; AHCE, Actas, Caja 22-B, "Libro tercero de registros," part 1, 14 June 1842; AHCE, Actas, Caja 22-B, "Libro segundo de registros," part 2, 17 November 1840.

112. AHCE, Actas, Caja 22-B, "Libro tercero de registros," part 2, 20 February 1843; AHCE, Actas, Caja 22-B, "Libro segundo de registros," part 4, 20 May 1842.

113. La Voz de Michoacán, 6 March 1842. In another example of the same phenomenon, the future archconservatives Bishop Clemente de Jesús Munguía, Archbishop Pelagio Labastida y Dávalos, Canon José Guadalupe Romero, and Lic. Ignacio Aguilar y Marocho formed a literary club in 1834 in Morelia. Club

members also included the future ardent liberals Melchor Ocampo, Juan B. Ceballos, Agustín Aurelio Tena, and Antonio Florentino Mercado. Romero Flores, *Historia*, 2:126.

114. For a short discussion of the historiography on the post-1810 depression, see Chowning, "Contours."

115. AHCE, Actas, Caja 22, exp. 5, "Actas . . . octubre 1835–noviembre 1837," 18 December 1835.

116. ANM, Rincón, 1836, 20 December; Rincón, 1837, 17 November; Cano, 1865, 30 September.

117. ANM, Rincón, 1832, 6 June; Rincón, 1837, 1 July; AHMM, 1840, "Expediente sobre igualas celebradas con algunos comerciantes por sus giros de comercio"; Rincón, 1841, 28 July.

118. AHCE, Actas, 2:2, no. 58, 14 August 1840.

119. ANM, "Libro de Hipotecas . . . Zamora . . . 1830–45," contains many loan contracts involving Plancarte and also records his 1834 purchase of the hacienda of Tamándaro and his 1837 purchase of La Sauceda. See also his will, García, 1854, 9 June.

120. ANM, González, 1872, 26 September.

121. ANM, Valdovinos, 1833, 19 August; Cano, 1868, 27 May; AHCP, Leg. 68 (1810–19), exp. 4, "Libro de Hipotecas . . . Pátzcuaro, 1818–53," 4 May 1838.

122. ANM, García, 1846, 28 August; AHCP, Leg. 68 (1810–19), exp. 4, "Libro de Hipotecas . . . Pátzcuaro, 1818–1853," 31 August 1837, 14 September 1837, 21 April 1840, 15 March 1841. The company was in the hacienda of Tomendan, which the partners had inherited from their father, Ignacio Solórzano Treviño, and which was worth about 185,000 pesos in 1840, with a mortgage of only 18,700 pesos.

123. ANM, García, 1874, 24 July.

124. AHCE, Varios, VI Congreso, Caja 1, exp. 12, "Memoria del Estado de la Administración Pública de Michoacán en 1834," 10.

125. It should be noted that these tools included the exaggerated style that is also apparent in the popular press. Historians recognize hyperbole when it concerns political factionalism and personalism, but they have been less ready to discount rhetorical excesses regarding the economy.

126. Calderón de la Barca, p. 591.

127. For agricultural profitability, see Chowning, "Reassessing."

128. AHCP, Leg. 85-A (1840–49), Protocolo 1846, 2 September 1846.

129. Costeloe, *Central Republic*, p. 25, makes this point in regard to national elites.

130. Calderón de la Barca, p. 588.

131. AHCE, Actas, Caja 27, exp. 6, "Actas públicas . . . noviembre 1846–julio 1847," 30 April 1847.

PROLOGUE TO CHAPTER FIVE

1. ANM, Valdovinos, 1834, 16 January; Rincón, 1837, 11 August; Valdovinos, 1842, 10 October; Valdovinos, 1856, 3 December; AHMM, 1858, "Resumen general de todos los bienes pertenecientes a la Testamentaria [de D. Cayetano Gómez] y que existen tanto en esta Ciudad y en la de Colima como en las jurisdicciones de los pueblos de Yndaparapeo, Tarímbaro, Taretan, y de la Villa de Charo."

2. AHMM, 1858, "Resumen general de todos los bienes pertenecientes a la Testamentaria [de D. Cayetano Gómez] . . ."; AHMM, 1858, "Cuenta de alvacea . . . [de D. Cayetano Gómez]. . . ."

3. "Alocución con que [el Lic. Mariano Rivas] cerró el año escolar . . . ," pp. 29–30.

4. Calderón de la Barca, p. 562.

5. Ibarrola, pp. 152, 154–55, 171, 405; Van Young, *Hacienda and Market*, pp. 150–54; AHSM, "Libro donde se sientan . . . casamientos," 24 September 1844; 30 November 1844.

6. AHCE, Varios, IX Congreso [1850–51], exp. 1, "Sobre la subsistencia del Tribunal Mercantil."

7. Juárez, 4:385.

8. AHMM, 1858, "Cuenta de alvacea . . . [de D. Cayetano Gómez]."

9. Ibarrola, pp. 197, 225–26, 283.

10. ANM, Pérez, 1863, 15 April.

CHAPTER FIVE

1. AHCE, Actas, Caja 32, exp. 12, "Actas públicas . . . dic. 1849–julio 1850," 7 September 1849.

2. AHCE, Actas, Caja 22-B, "Libro tercero de registros," part 1, 10 June 1842; *La Lira Michoacana*, p. 76; "Noticia estadística de Morelia."

3. AHCE, Actas, Caja 22-B, "Libro segundo de registros," part 2, 25 August 1840, 21 March 1840, and 4 August 1840; "Libro segundo de registros," part 1, 14 March 1839 and 5 April 1839; Michoacán, "Memoria . . . 1850," p. 29; De la Torre, pp. 121–22.

4. De la Torre, pp. 103, 161–62.

5. De la Torre, p. 103.

6. ANM, García, 1843, 5 April; De la Torre, pp. 111, 187.

7. ANM, Salomo, 1845, 21 October; De la Torre, p. 137.

8. Romero Flores, *Historia*, 1:804–05; Bravo Ugarte, *Historia sucinta*, pp. 137–38; Michoacán, "Memoria . . . 1846," p. 16.

9. Romero, p. 42; Ramírez Romero, p. 92.

10. Romero, p. 46.

11. De la Torre, p. 131.

12. González, *Zamora*, p. 81.

13. Romero, part 2, p. 44.

14. González, *Zamora*, p. 88; Romero, part 2, p. 42. Many of the funds to build the new parish church were donated by Martín Raimundo Pardo, who left his entire estate (consisting of two haciendas and a Zamora residence) for this purpose: *Protocolos . . . de Zamora*, Peña, 1846, 8 June.

15. Romero, part 2, pp. 57, 73–74.

16. Romero, part 2, pp. 3–4.

17. Romero, part 2, pp. 61, 76; AHPJ, Civil, 1850, Leg. 1, "Promovido por D. Nicolás Aldayturriaga contra D. Manuel Molina."

18. Heredia Correa, p. 122. Of 37 juntas industriales organized in Mexico in the 1840s, 16 were in Michoacán.

19. Romero, part 2, p. 38.

20. On the new sales tax lowering rural prices, see Michoacán, "Memoria . . . 1850," pp. 48–49. Most of the record number of rural properties that the church sold in the 1840s had been ceded or foreclosed upon decades earlier. In 1847, for example, Santa Catarina sold the hacienda of Sacapendo, which had been ceded to the convent in 1829 (ANM, Aguilar, 1829, 11 August; Pérez, 1847, 26 November); in 1848 the Juzgado sold the hacienda of La Sanja, which it had acquired by cession in 1824 (ANM, Aguilar, 1824, 6 May; García, 1848, 30 August); and in 1845 the *concurso de acreedores* on the estate of José María Sagasola sold the hacienda of Porumbo, which had probably been ceded even before 1810. (AHCP, Leg. 80-G, Año de 1832, Cuaderno 12, no title, concerns fianza for rental of hacienda of Porumbo) In disposing of these properties the church was following a new policy of real estate divestment—motivated in part by fear of government confiscation and in part by the increased willingness of buyers to meet the church's terms in a generally improving climate for agriculture. For more detail, see Chowning, "The Management of Church Wealth."

21. ANM, Valdovinos, 1845, 17 September; García, 1849, 13 January.

22. ANM, García, 1851, 27 December.

23. AHCP, Leg 87-C (1840–49), exp. 7, "Remate de la Hacienda de Cutio," 5 February 1845. For another early example of bidding wars over rural property, see ANM, Sierra (Jiquilpan), 1842, 6 June.

24. ANM, Valdovinos, 1853, 21 October.

25. AHCP, Leg. 97-F (1850–59), exp. 3, 1858, no title page, concerns ap-

praisal and auction of rancho of La Estancia de Chapultepec to Lic. Juan N. Olmos.

26. ANM, Aguilar, 1802, 21 June; Pérez, 1836, 14 March; Valdovinos, 1839, 2 May; García, 1841, 24 February; Valdovinos, 1852, 10 December.

27. BL, ms. collection, "Libro de Consultas [del Convento de Santa Catarina de Pátzcuaro, 1808–1848]," 20 August 1828 and 30 May 1837; AHCP, Leg. 68 (1810–19), exp. 4, "Libro de Hipotecas, 1818–53," 28 May 1851.

28. ANM, Aguilar, 1831, 17 February; Valdovinos, 1842, 26 October; García, 1854, 6 July.

29. ANM, Valdovinos, 1843, 10 May; AHMCR, Documentos eclesiásticos de bienes inmuebles, Año 1850–54, Leg. 3, 1850, "Expediente promovido por el Lic. Juan N. Flores ... para segregar de la Hacienda de Tipitaro, la de Tipitarillo"; AHCP, Leg. 95-D, "Protocolo de 1856," 8 April 1856. For other contemporary comments on the rise in land values, see AHPJ, 1854, Leg. 1, "Promovido por el curador de la menor Da. Rosario Soto contra D. Mariano Soravilla ..."; and AHPJ, 1851, Leg. 1, "Juicio de testamentaria del Sr. Martín García de Carrasquedo."

30. Cayetano Gómez, for example, built a new sugar mill on the hacienda of Taretan soon after he purchased it from the Augustinians in 1856. Romero, pp. 28, 35, 73; AHMM, 1858–59, "Cuenta de alvacea [de D. Cayetano Gómez]. . . ." See also the discussion of improvements in productivity on Manuel Alzúa's hacienda of Puruarán in the early 1860s, achieved by the introduction of new techniques for use of the machines already installed there: AHMM, 1857, cover reads "Información que para justificar en pobreza se rinde por parte del curador de los menores José María and Ma. Gertrudis Rodríguez ... ," but actually contains "Año de 1864. Laudo arbitral [regarding the salary of the administrator of Puruarán]."

31. Romero, p. 73; ANM, Valdovinos, 1856, 25 February; Pérez, 1860, 23 April.

32. Heredia Correa, p. 135; Piquero, p. 184.

33. "Informe a la vista . . ."

34. AHPJ, Leg. 2, 1845, "Promovido por el Cd. D. Carlos Valdovinos pidiendo la suspencíon de una nueva obra"; AHPJ, Civil, 1865, "Interdicto promovido por ... Vicente Estrada contra el dueño de la hacienda de Queréndaro."

35. AHMM, 1855, "Expediente instruido a instancia de D. Esteban García, alvacea del finado D. Antonio Chávez, sobre facción de inventarios. . . ."

36. ANM, Valdovinos, 1834, 18 February; García, 1851, 27 December; Valdovinos, 1853, 21 October; Salomo, 1850, 22 August.

37. ANM, Rincón, 1842, 20 April; Salomo, 1848, 21 June; García, 1851, 6 March.

38. ANM, Valdovinos, 1854, 14 October; Valdovinos, 1856, 7 April.

39. ANM, Salomo, 1849, 22 February. Lic. Antonio del Moral, Antonio Zacanini, and Cruz Vega formed a company to buy the hacienda of Corralejo near Pénjamo. The hacienda was divided into four parts, one of which they planned either to rent or to sell immediately.

40. ANM, Valdovinos, 1858, 25 November; Valdovinos, 1859, 30 December.

41. One was Mariano Larreátegui's 1842 agreement with Miguel Patiño; the other was a company established in 1853 to exploit the Michoacán/Guerrero coast, in which Manuel Alzúa and Fermín Huarte invested 18,000 pesos cash and 32,000 pesos from an earlier company for a total of 50,000 pesos, and Juan de Alzuyeta matched this amount. ANM, Valdovinos, 1842, 5 April; Valdovinos, 1853, 26 September.

42. ANM, Valdovinos, 1854, 29 July.

43. AHCP, Leg. 90-F, exp. 3, "Año de 1846. Arbitraje promovido por los Sres. D. Cayetano Villavicencio, vecino de Uruapan, y D. Agustín Luna, vecino de Santa Clara."

44. The rough accuracy of Luna's freight cost claim is confirmed by an 1861 document putting the cost of transport from La Huerta (in the same district as Los Bancos) to Guanajuato (about the same distance as San Juan de los Lagos) at 6.25 pesos/*carga*, compared to the 5.71 pesos/*carga* claimed by Luna 13 years earlier. AHMM, 1861, "Civil no. 9, promovido por el Sr. Lic. D. José María Cardoso como apoderado del Sr. D. Francisco Román contra el Sr. Lic. D. Francisco Castro."

45. See Forbes, pp. 108–10 for a contemporary description of the fair at San Juan. The author was told by one Mexico City merchant that he sent 300,000 pesos worth of goods to this important fair.

46. ANM, Huerta, 1879, 1 September; Huerta, 1879, 1 October.

47. Ignacio del Corral, for example, paid for his rancho of Buenavista with *libranzas*, and Francisco Plancarte and Antonio Zacanini both accepted *libranzas* in payment of rent on ranchos belonging to their haciendas. AHCP, Leg. 95-D, "Protocolo de 1856," 3 January 1856; *Protocolos . . . de Zamora*, Peña, 1848, 19 June; AHMM, 1857, document whose cover reads "Curaduría ad bona de la menor Da. Socorro Chávez," but that actually contains the estate inventory of Antonio Zacanini.

48. Every time a house cashed or cleared a *libranza*, it profited by charging a small fee for the service. Cayetano Gómez's *casa*, for example, in just nine months (August 1858 to April 1859) made 2,240 pesos from the 2–4-percent fee for clearing some 65,000 pesos in *libranzas*. AHMM, 1858–59, "Cuenta de alvacea [de D. Cayetano Gómez]. . . ."

49. For other examples of buy-now-pay-later arrangements, see *Protocolos . . . de Zamora*, Peña, 1848, 28 November; Peña, 1854, 1 June; ANM, Valdovinos, 1858, 23 January; AHMM, 1855, "Expediente instruido á instancia de D. Esteban García, alvacea del finado D. Antonio Chávez, sobre facción de in-

ventarios . . ."; AHMCR, Documentos especiales de bienes inmuebles, Leg. 11, 1856, "Sobre inventario a bienes de Da. María Antonia Farías."

50. At midcentury there was only one foreign mercantile house established in Morelia, a "branch" of the Mexico City establishment headed by the Spaniard Pío Bermejillo. AHCP, Leg. 68, exp. 4, "Libro de Hipotecas, 1818–53," 2 April 1849.

51. The most productive silver mines in Michoacán were those at Tlalpujahua and Angangueo, but they did not compare to Guanajuato or Zacatecas. Copper was also mined in Michoacán, but its value was considerably lower in foreign eyes than silver's was.

52. ANM, "Libro de hipotecas de Zamora," 1 July 1854.

53. AHPJ, Civil, 1851, Leg. 1, "Concurso promovido por D. Rafael López solicitando de sus acreedores le conceden esperas . . ."; ANM, Valdovinos, 1857, 29 January.

54. Michoacán, Memoria . . . 1849," pp. 16–17.

55. On *agio*, see Meyer Cosío, Tenenbaum, "Banqueros," and Walker.

56. Walker, pp. 184–85 and 219.

57. Walker, p. 123.

58. AHPJ, Civil, 1854, Leg. 1, "Promovido por D. Agapito Solórzano, contra D. Ramón Ochoa, pidiendo se le declare en estado de quiebra, por haberle suspendido el pago de su crédito."

59. ANM, García, 1853, 31 August.

60. ANM, Valdovinos, 1856, 12 March and 7 April. See also AHPJ, 1844, Leg. 1, "Promovido por D. Manuel María de la Sierra sobre sesión de bienes."

61. Meyer, p. 17.

62. ANM, Rincón, 1835, 30 December; Rincón, 1843, 7 June; Valdovinos, 1843, 5 July; Valdovinos, 1844, 26 July; García, 1845, 31 May; García, 1845, 28 June; García, 1847, 12 June; García, 1847, 1 July; García, 1851, 5 June.

63. ANM, Rincón, 1841, 16 October; Valdovinos, 1845, 16 May; García, 1852, 6 September.

64. ANM, Aguilar, 1828, 9 April; Aguilar, 1829, 8 May; Tercero, 1848, 6 February; AHMM, 1852, "Inventarios a bienes de D. Francisco Estrada."

65. ANM, Valdovinos, 1857, 11 August; Cano, 1860, 27 August; Cano, 1860, 10 October; Valdovinos, 1866, 3 November; Cano, 1866, 20 February.

66. ANM, García, 1843, 2 December; García, 1847, 5 November; Valdovinos, 1853, 20 June; Valdovinos, 1855, 22 December; Valdovinos, 1856, 12 March.

67. ANM, Salomo, 1849, 22 February; Huerta, 1850, 6 March; Pérez, 1852, 7 May; Valdovinos, 1857, 19 January; Pérez, 1859, 14 June; AHMM, 1857, on cover is "Curaduría ad bona de la menor Da. Socorro Chávez," but contains inventory and liquidation of estate of Antonio Zacanini.

68. Bullock, pp. 220–21.

69. ANM, Valdovinos, 1841, 27 October; Rincón, 1841, 6 December; Valdovinos, 1861, 6 August; Valdovinos, 1861, 5 September.

70. ANM, Rincón, 1842, 26 September.

71. ANM, Iturbide, 1831, 2 December.

72. ANM, García, 1851, 26 February and 6 March.

73. ANM, García, 1846, 2 September; Valdovinos, 1855, 20 December; Valdovinos, 1856, 3 January; García, 1852, 27 May.

74. AHMM, 1852, "Inventarios a bienes de D. Francisco Estrada." Estrada had also purchased three adjacent or near-adjacent haciendas.

75. ANM, Sierra (Jiquilpan), 1839, 5 June.

76. ANM, Valdovinos, 1857, 15 June; Valdovinos, 1856, 10 June.

77. *Protocolos . . . de Zamora*, Peña, 1854, 12 June. For other references to elite purchases and/or rentals of Indian lands, see *Protocolos . . . de Zamora*, Peña, 1842, 15 October; Peña, 1849, 6 June; Peña, 1849, 1 October; ANM, Salomo, 1850, 24 September; Sierra (Jiquilpan), 1842, 31 August.

78. AHSM, "Libro donde se sientan . . . casamientos," 8 January 1842; 14 May 1849; Ibarrola, pp. 256, 405.

79. AHSM, "Libro donde se sientan . . . casamientos," 24 September 1844; Calderón de la Barca, p. 562; Ibarrola, p. 227.

80. Cerda Hernández, p. 59.

81. Bullock, p. 259.

82. AHMM, 1858, "Resumen general de los bienes [de D. Cayetano Gómez]. . . ."

83. ANM, García, 1851, 6 March; Valdovinos, 1856, 4 December; AHMM, 1852, "Inventarios a los bienes de D. Francisco Estrada."

84. Michoacán, "Memoria . . . 1850," p. 2; see also Michoacán, "Memoria . . . 1846," p. 12; AHCE, Actas, Caja 28, exp. 6, "Actas . . . julio 1847–junio 1848," 17 September 1847.

85. See, for example, AHCE, Actas, Caja 38, exp. 1 "Actas . . . abril–noviembre 1861," 5 June 1861 and 24 June 1861.

86. *La Voz de Michoacán*, 6 March 1842.

87. A good overview and national-level interpretation of these events is Costeloe, *Central Republic*, chapters 7, 8, and 9.

88. On the polarizing effect of the war with the United States on Mexican politics, see Vázquez, and Hale, *Mexican Liberalism*.

89. AHCE, Actas, Caja 28, exp. 6, "Actas . . . julio 1847–junio 1848," 18 August 1847.

90. AHCE, Actas, Caja 27, exp. 6, "Actas . . . noviembre 1846–julio 1847," 7 December 1846; Actas, Caja 28, exp. 6, "Actas . . . julio 1847–junio 1848," 18 January 1848.

91. AHCE, Actas, Caja 31, exp. 3, "Actas . . . enero 1849–julio 1849," 26 March 1849; Actas, Caja 32, exp. 5, "Actas . . . julio 1849–septiembre 1849," 6 August 1849; Actas, Caja 34, exp. 6, "Actas . . . marzo 1851–septiembre 1851," 22 March 1851.

92. Michoacán, "Memoria . . . 1846," p. 4.

93. Michoacán, "Memoria . . . 1850," p. 15.

94. AHCE, Actas, Caja 31, exp. 3, "Actas . . . enero 1849–julio 1849," 21 March 1849; AHCE, Actas, Caja 32, exp. 5, "Actas . . . julio 1849–septiembre 1849," 23 July 1849; AHCE, Actas, Caja 34, exp. 6, "Actas . . . marzo 1851–septiembre 1851," 8 and 11 August 1851. The new *ley de reparto* brought before Congress in 1851, for example, read much like the 1827 one, though there were a few changes. Those that had been made were mainly to take into account the fact that in the intervening decades many villages had already divided their lands. One of these changes aimed to force the communities that had not yet "taken advantage" of the law to do so, providing specifically that Indian elites (who stood to lose much of their power if community lands were divided evenly among villagers) could not impede the *reparto*. There were also controversial proposals to permit cash indemnification on a prorated basis to Indians who could prove that they had not received land to which they were entitled in an earlier division, and to give Indians who had moved to a new village and lived there for five years a right to lands in that village rather than to that in their original community, even if they had already received a parcel of land in an earlier *reparto*. Both proposals were approved, despite the fear that they would result in bureaucratic migraines.

95. Brading calls this an "ideological innovation" in which the earlier " 'possessive liberalism' of Mora was supplemented by an appeal to classical republicanism" and liberal "patriotism," though he seems to fix its appearance later in time, during the Reforma and the Intervention. Brading, "Liberal Patriotism," pp. 28–29.

96. Michoacán, "Memoria . . . 1850," pp. 28–29.

97. AHCE, Caja 28, exp. 6, "Actas . . . julio 1847–junio 1848," 9 August 1847.

98. AHCE, Actas, Caja 28, exp. 6, "Actas . . . julio 1847–junio 1848," 6 September 1847.

99. Michoacán, "Memoria . . . 1846," pp. 3–4.

100. AHCE, Actas, Caja 28, exp. 6, "Actas . . . julio 1847–junio 1848," 15 September 1847.

101. AHCE, Actas, Caja 28, exp. 6, "Actas . . . julio 1847–junio 1848," 15 September 1847.

102. AHCE, Actas, Caja 27, exp. 6, "Actas . . . noviembre 1846–julio 1847," 10 February 1847; AHCE, Actas, Caja 28, exp. 6, "Actas . . . julio 1847–junio

1848," 26 July 1847; "Iniciativa que el mui ilustre . . ."; "Protesta del señor Portugal. . . ."

103. AHCE, Actas, Caja 28, exp. 6, "Actas . . . julio 1847–junio 1848," 26 July 1847.

104. Michoacán, "Memoria . . . 1850," p. 18.

105. On Bishop Portugal's decision to accept exile from the state rather than obey an 1833 law, see chapter 3 of this book.

106. AHCE, Actas, Caja 27, exp. 6, "Actas . . . noviembre 1846–julio 1847," 10 February 1847.

107. Brading, *First America*, p. 655; AHCE, Actas, Caja 28, exp. 6, "Actas . . . julio 1847–junio 1848," 17 September 1847.

108. AHCE, Actas, Caja 28, exp. 6, "Actas . . . julio 1847–junio 1848," 17 September 1847.

109. AHCE, Actas, Caja 32, exp. 5, "Actas . . . julio–septiembre 1849," 20 July 1849; "Representación[es] sobre reforma del arancel de obvenciones parroquiales," and "Un Cura de Michoacán," in Ocampo, *Obras Completas*.

110. Munguía, "Manifiesto"; "Un voto independiente . . ."; "Réplica al folleto . . ." See also the account in Bravo Ugarte, *Munguía*, pp. 53–54. For an earlier debate over whether or not the bishop should be forced to swear loyalty to the constitution, see AHCE, Actas, Caja 15, exp. 2, "Actas públicas . . . junio 1831–septiembre 1831," 2 August 1831.

111. AHCE, Actas, Caja 34, exp. 6, "Actas . . . marzo 1851–septiembre 1851," 8 August 1851.

112. The liberals were partly motivated to push their anticlerical agenda because since the mid-1840s the church had been pursuing a policy of converting real property into ecclesiastical mortgages; this policy allowed the church for the first time since independence to consolidate its economic ties to the provincial elite by putting it in a position to loan to, rather than merely collect from, property owners. See Chowning, "The Management of Church Wealth."

113. Michoacán, "Memoria . . . 1849," p. 14.

114. AHCE, Varios, X Congreso, Caja 2, exp. 3, "Borrador, 1852" (a rough draft of the 1852 "Memoria"), p. 34.

115. Michoacán, "Memoria . . . 1849," pp. 13–15; Michoacán, Memoria . . . 1846," p. 14. The extent to which the Michoacán liberals were influenced by the thought of José María Luis Mora can be seen by comparing this language to Mora's anticlericalism, as summarized by Brading, *First America*, pp. 648–56.

116. Michoacán, "Memoria . . . 1849," p. 13.

117. Michoacán, "Memoria . . . 1846," p. 14.

118. AHCE, Actas, Caja 35, exp. 2, "Actas . . . diciembre 1851–agosto 1852," 18 March 1852.

119. Sánchez Díaz, "Los vaivanes," pp. 21–22; Ocampo, 2:254.

120. Michoacán, "Memoria . . . 1846," p. 12.

121. See Brading, *First America*, pp. 601–02 and 668–71.

122. Ocampo, 2:255.

123. AHPJ, Primero Civil, 1850, Leg. 1, "Civil Ordinario promovido por . . . los Sres. Ponce de Ayimbo contra el común de indígenas del Pueblo de Capula sobre propiedad de tierras"; AHPJ, Primero Civil, 1845, Leg. 1, "Promovido por D. Ventura Ortiz de Ayala sobre despojo de tierras, contra el común de indígenas del Pueblo de Jesús del Monte"; AHPJ, Primero Civil, 1839, Leg. 1, D. "José María Ibarrola, arrendatario de la Hacienda de Coapa y como apoderado de la Sagrada Mitra contra el común de indígenas del pueblo de Jesús Huiramba"; AHPJ, Primero Civil, 1856, ". . . Sres. Rubio y Duranes, condueños de los Montes de los Azufres y cuyo juicio se sigue con los Indígenas de Gerahuaro"; AHPJ, Primero Civil, 1853, Leg. 1, "Yndígenas de Tacámbaro contra el Prior del Convento de Agustinos"; AHPJ, Primero Civil, 1855, "Instruido a instancia de D. Antonio Homobono Cortés, contra el común de Yndígenas de Yndaparapeo, sobre perjuicios por haber impedido el trasporte de maderas."

124. AHPJ, Primero Civil, 1848, Leg. 1, "Común de indígenas de San Salvador Atecuario sobre apeo y deslinde de sus tierras."

125. AHPJ, Primero Civil, 1847, Leg. 1, "Comunidad de Zaragoza [La Piedad] contra Lic. Pedro García"; AHPJ, Primero Civil, 1839, Leg. 1, "Lic. Clemente Munguía, como apoderado de varios indígenas vecinos de Tarímbaro contra D. Ventura González"; AHPJ, Primero Civil, 1839, Leg. 1, "Indígenas del Pueblo de Santa Catarina Morelia sobre posesión de un terreno contra D. Mariano Mota como encargado de las rentas de los propios y arbitrios de Morelia"; AHPJ, Primero Civil, 1856, Leg. 1, "Común de indígenas de Cuitzeo contra el convento de agustinos de Cuitzeo."

126. AHPJ, Primero Civil, 1847, Leg. 1, "Común de indígenas del Pueblo de Indaparapeo contra la Hacienda de Naranjos."

127. AHPJ, Primero Civil, 1847, Leg. 1, "Común de indígenas del Pueblo de Indaparapeo contra la Hacienda de Naranjos." Estrada was one of the hacendados who bought up many Indian-owned parcels, but it is not clear whether these purchases predated the difficulties with the Indians of Indaparapeo, or whether they were part of a partial resolution of the matter as a result of the lawsuit.

128. ANM, Salomo, 1846, 2 November; Salomo, 1846, 9 January. Dr. Juan Manuel González Urueña (whose family owned the modest hacienda of Buenos Aires in Apatzingán), and José María Manzo Ceballos (whose uncle Antonio had owned a small hacienda, though there is no indication that he himself had any landed wealth) did not quite meet the criteria established here for elite status, though they came close. ANM, García, 1849, 3 October; AHMCR, Diezmos, Leg. 887 (Apatzingán, 1835–1863), "Cuentas que presentó el Br. Manuel B.

Gutiérrez por los efectos que recibió de la restitución de D. Antonio Sierra . . . 1847–49."

129. Michoacán, "Memoria . . . 1846," p. 9; Michoacán, "Memoria . . . 1849," pp. 8–9; Michoacán, "Memoria . . . 1850," pp. 9–10.

130. AHCE, Actas, Caja 28, exp. 6, "Actas . . . julio 1847–junio 1848," 26 July 1847.

131. AHCE, Actas, Caja 28, exp. 6, "Actas . . . julio 1847–junio 1848," 26 July 1847.

132. Michoacán, "Memoria . . . 1849," p. 6; Michoacán, "Memoria . . . 1850," pp. 3, 16.

133. Michoacán, "Memoria . . . 1849," pp. 5–6.

134. Michoacán, "Memoria . . . 1846," p. 23.

135. AHCE, Actas, Caja 29, exp. 10, "Actas . . . junio 1848–diciembre 1848," 21 August 1848.

136. AHCE, Caja 32, exp. 5, "Actas . . . julio 1849–septiembre 1849," 25 July 1849.

137. AHCE, Caja 32, exp. 12, "Actas . . . septiembre 1849–julio 1850," 5 September 1849.

138. AHCE, Caja 32, exp. 12, "Actas . . . septiembre 1849–julio 1850," 7 September 1849.

139. AHCE, Caja 33, exp. 9, "Actas . . . julio 1850–marzo 1851," 8 November 1850.

140. AHCE, Actas, Caja 32, exp. 12, "Actas . . . septiembre 1849–julio 1850," 7 September and 10 September 1849.

141. Alamán, 5:932–36; 5:945–46.

142. AHCE, Actas, Caja 32, exp. 12, "Actas . . . septiembre 1849–julio 1850," 10 September 1849.

143. Michoacán, "Memoria . . . 1846," p. 13.

144. Michoacán, "Memoria . . . 1848," p. 5.

145. Michoacán, "Memoria . . . 1849," pp. 12–13.

146. Michoacán, "Memoria . . . 1848," p. 5.

147. Alamán, 5:928.

148. Michoacán, "Memoria . . . 1846," p. 13; Alamán, 5:915, 922, 929.

149. Michoacán, "Memoria . . . 1846," p. 15; Alamán, 5:916.

150. Ocampo, "Discurso pronunciado el 16 de Septiembre de 1852," 2:84–87.

151. Alamán, 5:916. Alamán did believe that independence became inevitable with the Consolidación de Vales Reales, which so profoundly alienated property holders that to remain part of the empire was almost impossible.

152. Alamán, 5:906, 929.

153. Alamán, 5:930–50.

154. Alamán, 5:916–17, 922–23.

155. Alamán, 5:929.

156. "Documentos justificativos. . . ."; See also "Manifiesto que para justificar. . . ."

157. "Documentos justificativos," pp. 9–10.

158. Romero Flores, *Historia de Michoacán*, 2:217–19 has a long though still incomplete list of men who "adhered" to the empire.

159. Macías, p. 205; ANM, Pérez, 1860, 3 December; Cano, 1862, 6 November; Gómez, 1892, 29 October; *El Constitucionalista*, 10 February 1868; Romero Flores, *Historia de Michoacán*, 2:479; Ibarrola, pp. 468, 282–83.

160. "Documentos justificativos," pp. 45–46.

161. *Enciclopedia de Mexico*, vol. 9, "Michoacan," p. 5379.

162. Romero Flores, *Historia de Michoacán*, 2:124–25.

163. AHCE, Actas, Caja 36, exp. 10, "Actas . . . septiembre 1852–enero 1853," 26 January, 28 January, and 29 January 1853.

164. Chowning, "Reassessing."

PROLOGUE TO CHAPTER 6

1. AHMM, 1858, "Cuenta de hijuela [de los bienes de D. Cayetano Gómez]."

2. ANM, Valdovinos, 1859, 2 April; Huerta, 1863, 12 March; Huerta, 1863, 28 March; Huerta, 1863, 1 April; Huerta, 1863, 11 May; Huerta, 1863, 23 July; Huerta, 1863, 27 August; Huerta, 1863, 30 December; Huerta, 1864, 8 April; Cano, 1864, 22 April; León, 1864, 27 June; León, 1865, 2 October; Huerta, 1866, 21 April; Valdovinos, 1866, 13 August; Huerta, 1867, 22 January; Valdovinos, 1867, 3 October.

3. ANM, Valdovinos, 1859, 12 September; Valdovinos, 1858, 17 September; Valdovinos, 1861, 5 September; Cano, 1863, 23 May.

4. ANM, Valdovinos, 1861, appendix.

5. ANM, Escobar, 1862, 1 August.

6. ANM, Pérez, 1863, 15 April.

7. AHPJ, 1864, Leg. 2, no title, concerns court appointment of Lic. Nestor Caballero as "depositario" and administrator of the estate of Manuel Alzúa, replacing Juan de Dios Gómez.

8. ANM, Huerta, 1865, 28 June; Huerta, 1865, 14 August; Valdovinos, 1866, 6 February; Valdovinos, 1866, 21 February; Valdovinos, 1866, 24 February; Valdovinos, 1866, 18 June; Valdovinos, 1866, 31 July; Valdovinos, 1866, 16 August; Valdovinos, 1866, 29 August; Valdovinos, 1866, 5 September; Valdovinos, 1866, 4 October; Valdovinos, 1866, 21 December; Cano, 1866, 4 September; Cano, 1866, 6 September; Huerta, 1866, 4 September; Huerta, 1867, 22 January; Huerta, 1867, 27 May; Huerta, 1867, 19 June; Valdovinos, 1868, 26 February; Valdovinos, 1868, 19 June; Valdovinos, 1868, 30 November; Cano,

1868, 31 July; Valdovinos, 1869, 4 May; León, 1870, 8 February; León, 1870, 4 July; León, 1870, 9 February; González, 1870, 15 July; García, 1870, 17 September; Valdovinos, 1871, 17 March; Valdovinos, 1871, 26 July.

9. ANM, León, 1882, 6 October; Huerta, 1882, 2 December; Huacuja, 1887, 26 February; Laris Contreras, 1891, 9 May.

10. ANM, Valdovinos, 1861, 22 May; see also the debates over how to handle the Pastor Morales estate in AHCE, Actas, Caja 38, exp. 1, "Actas . . . abril–noviembre, 1861," esp. June 1861.

11. Juárez, 4:384–86 ("Degollado rechaza ataques del periódico *Partido Puro*"), dated 27 April 1861.

12. ANM, Escobar, 1860, 30 October; Valdovinos, 1859, 2 April; Huerta, 1863, 27 August; León, 1865, 2 October; León, 1876, 13 February; León, 1876, 31 July; ANMC, Roldán, 1872, 31 December.

13. ANM, Valdovinos, 1858, 25 November; Valdovinos, 1859, 30 December; Huerta, 1862, 7 February; Escobar, 1862, 30 April; Pérez, 1863, 30 October; Huerta, 1864, 4 November; Valdovinos, 1859, 8 November; Valdovinos, 1866, 5 November; León, 1871, 31 July; Valdovinos, 1874, 18 February; Bullock, p. 198; *La Lira Michoacana*, p. 240.

14. ANM, Valdovinos, 1859, 18 October; García, 1851, 6 March; Valdovinos, 1859, 11 June; Valdovinos, 1861, 4 April; Valdovinos, 1869, 18 December; Cano, 1866, 25 October; González, 1873, 9 October; Huacuja, 1884, 11 May; Huacuja, 1885, 27 February; AHPJ, Civil, 1866, "Concurso de quiebra de D. Francisco Román," see especially the interrogatory presented to the Tribunal de Comercio, dated 3 February 1866; AHPJ, Civil, 1865, Varios no. 1, "Balanza de movimiento de las operaciones practicadas en el Libro Mayor de la casa de Francisco Román. . . ."

15. ANM, Pérez, 1864; 31 March.

16. ANM, García, 1851, 27 December; Valdovinos, 1873, 14 April; González, 1873, 20 December; Huerta, 1877, 19 November; León, 1878, 8 June; Huerta, 1880, 20 September; Huerta, 1884, 16 January; Huerta, 1884, 28 November; Ibarrola, 1895, 21 August.

17. ANM, Cano, 1860, appendix; Cano, 1865, 30 September; González, 1876, 17 November; Ibarrola, 1900, appendix; Huerta, 1904, 13 May; Gutiérrez, 1904, 19 July; AHPJ, Civil, 1864, "D. Manuel Castañeda contra D. Luis G. Sámano"; AHPJ, Civil, 1875, "Concurso voluntario de D. Luis G. Sámano"; Ibarrola, p. 162.

18. *El Constitucionalista*, 27 January 1868; *La Libertad*, 22 September 1894; ANM, Iturbide, 1831, 1 July; Valdovinos, 1853, 20 October; Huerta, 1893, 27 October; Valdovinos, 1859, 22 October; Cano, 1865, 27 April; Valdovinos, 1868, 11 April; Barroso, 1906, 18 December.

19. AHMM, 1858, "Cuenta de alvacea . . . [de D. Cayetano Gómez]," ANM, Valdovinos, 1859, 12 September; Valdovinos, 1866, 20 March; Valdovinos,

1867, 3 October; León, 1870, 5 February; García, 1870, 12 February; León, 1871, 4 July; González, 1875, 25 January; Huerta, 1880, 11 March; Huerta, 1881, 2 June; Huerta, 1883, 30 May.

CHAPTER 6

1. Pérez Hernández, p. 39; Alvarez and Durán, p. 7; Bullock, p. 190.

2. Bullock, pp. 190–91.

3. ANM, "Libro de hipotecas de Maravatío, 1870–78," 20 Sept. 1872.

4. Bullock, p. 203.

5. Quoted in Tavera Alfaro, 2:138, 140.

6. AHPJ, 1866, Civil #2, "Concurso en la quiebra mercantil de D. José Revuelta"; ANM, Valdovinos, 1866, 19 November; Cano, 1866, 29 December; Valdovinos, 1867, 18 January; Valdovinos, 1867, 12 February and 6 March; Valdovinos, 1867, 6 May; Cano, 1868, 1 April; Valdovinos, 1868, 21 August; Valdovinos, 1868, 16 December; AHMCR, Libro #324, "Libro en que constan los capitales . . . del colegio de Santa Rosa María"; Valdovinos, 1866, 15 March; Alemán, 1869, 5 August; Tavera Alfaro, 2:141.

7. De la Torre, p. 55; Ramírez Romero, p. 92.

8. De la Torre, p. 111; *La Lira Michoacana*, pp. 76–77.

9. De la Torre, p. 124.

10. ANM, Pérez, 1862, 10 March; Cano, 1863, 30 July.

11. *La Lira Michoacana*, pp. 91, 77; De la Torre, pp. 76, 79, 93.

12. *La Lira Michoacana*, p. 91.

13. Tavera Alfaro, 2:179.

14. ANM, Cano, 1863, 25 November; De la Torre, p. 78; *La Lira Michoacana*, pp. 77, 91.

15. ANM, Valdovinos, 1856, 6 October; De la Torre, p. 160.

16. ANM, Pérez, 1859, 6 July and 23 July.

17. ANM, Herrera, 1861, 11 April, 13 April, 16 April, 22 June, 25 June.

18. ANM, Herrera, 1861, 24 May; De la Torre, p. 167.

19. Tavera Alfaro, 1:187–88.

20. De la Torre, p. 169; Tavera Alfaro, 1:174–78.

21. De la Torre, p. 141; Tavera Alfaro, 1:159.

22. De la Torre, p. 158; Tavera Alfaro, 1:194.

23. Tavera Alfaro, 1:9–146.

24. Tavera Alfaro, 1:144–49.

25. Tavera Alfaro, 1:150–51.

26. Tavera Alfaro, 2:42–44, 2:39–40. Work on the *calzada* did not actually begin until 1873.

27. Tavera Alfaro, 2:44–45.

28. The value and acreage of lands owned by the state's towns and cities var-

ied widely; Zamora, for example, owned at least 29 ranchos, which were sold in accordance with the Reform laws for nearly 100,000 pesos, but Morelia's *ayuntamiento* disposed of land worth only about 30,000 pesos. The 1857 *Memoria de Hacienda* shows around 233,500 pesos in nonchurch corporate property sales; this includes 96,718 pesos from Lic. Isidro Huarte's estate, which were pledged to the *hospicio de pobres* of Morelia. ANM, various transactions in the 1856 registers, including the "Libro de hipotecas del Distrito de Zamora, 1846–61" for 1856; Mexico, Secretaría de Hacienda, *Memoria de Hacienda . . . 1857.*

29. Delays in breaking up village lands were also engineered by the lawyers who represented the communities and presided over the *repartimiento*, because they were keen to keep the properties intact until they were paid for their efforts, often with land formerly belonging to the community. In 1863, for example, the *común* of Santa Ana Maya turned over to Benigno Pérez Gil their rancho of Quinceo to pay him for his services; later they had to sell the rancho of Chamo to pay another 4,191 pesos in honoraria, legal fees and costs, and damages. ANM, Pérez, 1863, 9 February; AHPJ, 1869, Civil, Varios #2, "Arbitraje entre Tomás García y Donanciano López, apoderado de la comunidad de Santa Ana Maya, sobre cuentas del primero." Moreover, when the individual Indian owners began to resell the lands they received, these sales were often arranged extrajudicially (see, for example, ANM, De la Peña (Uruapan), 1885, 2 July), so that the dimensions of the alienation of community property are hard to quantify with any precision.

30. On this ecclesiastical policy of divestment of real property, see Chowning, "The Management of Church Wealth." Over half the sales were of properties that the church had owned "since time immemorial"; the rest had been acquired in cession and foreclosure.

31. See, for example, the case in which the seminary sold two houses to Manuel Estrada with a *pacto de retroventa*, that is, a promise to sell it back at some point. ANM, Valdovinos, 1856, 4 July.

32. Quoted in Sinkin, p. 127.

33. For a comparison between the way that the second stage of the Reform was played out in Michoacán and elsewhere in the nation, see Bazant, *Alienation of Church Wealth*. There was considerable variation from region to region, in light of the fact that Conservatives controlled some areas through much of 1859 and 1860, while governors in Liberal-controlled states were free to enforce the federal decrees more or less as they saw fit.

34. The imperial government compiled statistics on the disamortization process, which were published in the *Memoria de Hacienda* of 1872 to 1873. The table showing property nationalized before March 1866 gives a total for Morelia that is almost three times greater than that which is accounted for in the notary records. The discrepancy may stem from the inclusion in the 1866 figures of what

I have treated as nonecclesiastical property, including the tobacco factory, the 100,000-peso Huarte estate, and the rich hacienda of Bellasfuentes, which was left (somewhat ambiguously) by Juan José Pastor Morales to the benefit of his soul and the public welfare. Also, the "value" of nationalized property in this list is probably the appraisal value and as such is at least one-third higher than market values; the church's nonproductive property (convents, etc.) may have been especially overvalued.

35. ANM, Valdovinos, 1863, 24 August; Laris, 1892, 24 December; Barroso, 1909, 9 July.

36. Epitacio Huerta later defended himself against criticism that he sold off church capital too cheaply by pointing out that in other states only 5- or 7-percent down payments were required. Michoacán, "Memoria en que el C. General Epitacio Huerta . . . ," p. 41.

37. ANM, Valdovinos, 1859, 22 August; for an example of such an agreement, see Valdovinos, 1860, 1 June.

38. ANM, Valdovinos, 1867, 14 November.

39. Bazant, *Alienation*, pp. 162, 246–47.

40. As it happens, in October 1861 and again in September 1862 the state government demanded redemption of at least a portion of the capitals earlier assigned to the Hospital Civil, etcetera. By 1863 most of these capitals had been redeemed in the usual combination of cash (ordinarily 30 percent) and bonds (70 percent).

41. ANM, Valdovinos, 1869, 3 July.

42. ANM, Valdovinos, 1862, 12 June; Huerta, 1876, 28 July; Huerta, 1879, 1 October.

43. ANM, Valdovinos, 1859, 4 August; Valdovinos, 1862, 17 January.

44. ANM, Valdovinos, 1859, 18 November; Valdovinos, 1867, 15 October; Valdovinos, 1867, 25 October; Valdovinos, 1867, 18 November; Valdovinos, 1867, 7 December; Pérez, 1865, 8 February.

45. ANM, Pérez, 1859, 7 November; AHPJ, 1874, Civil, "Hacienda de Irapeo."

46. ANM, Valdovinos, 1860, 12 September; Valdovinos, 1862, 2 December. The Patiño family eventually regained possession of the hacienda, presumably after paying off its debts.

47. ANM, Valdovinos, 1859, 7 November; Valdovinos, 1861, 3 June; González, 1871, 25 February; Huerta, 1879, 21 June.

48. ANM, Valdovinos, 1861, 3 May.

49. Since all debts transferred to civil organizations were owed by in-state residents, and since most of these transactions were notarized in Morelia, the percentage of church wealth sold in Morelia to in-state residents is unrepresentatively high.

50. It was partly to keep money in the state that Governor Epitacio Huerta established a *maestranza* in Morelia to manufacture artillery and military supplies (though this small shop could not come close to supplying all the state's needs). Michoacán, "Memoria en que el C. General Epitacio Huerta . . . ," p. 33.

51. Coromina records forced loans on the *comercio* of Morelia on 22 March 1858, 1 July 1858, 2 August 1858, 9 June 1860, 9 October 1860, and 29 November 1861.

52. AHMCR, Diezmos, Leg. 934 (Uruapan, 1833–64), "Manifestación de los dulces que la Hacienda de [Tomendan] debe al diezmo por los años [1856–74]."

53. AHMCR, "Documentos especiales de bienes inmuebles, Leg. 9, Años 1863, 1864, and 1865," statement by Gregorio Jiménez dated 2 April 1867.

54. Bullock, p. 229.

55. The scarcity of currency and its link to low real estate prices and low commodity prices were remarked upon often in the notary documents, a somewhat unusual phenomenon that underscores the public's feeling of helplessness. The only other period during which emotions showed through legalities was the decade and a half after 1810. See, for example, ANM, Cano, 1865, 11 October; Cano, 1866, 29 December; Valdovinos, 1867, 18 January; Valdovinos, 1867, 12 February; León, 1870, 28 April; León, 1870, 13 July; García, 1872, 3 June; Valdovinos, 1874, 9 April; García, 1874, 24 July; Copias de Testamentos, 1878, f. 8.

56. Rosenzweig, p. 813. Banks had been established in Mexico City and in the north by the late 1880s, and their branches were scattered in many other areas of the country by this time.

57. AHPJ, Civil, 1865, Varios no. 1, "Balanza de movimiento de las operaciones practicadas en el Libro Mayor de la casa de Francisco Román . . ."

58. ANM, Valdovinos, 1867, 6 May; Valdovinos, 1868, 21 August; Huerta, 1888, 7 July; Tavera Alfaro, 2:153; Pérez, p. 392; Mexico, Secretaría de Fomento, *Datos mercantiles*, p. 413.

59. ANM, Valdovinos, 1858, 3 February; Huerta, 1880, 30 December; Huerta, 1886, 7 August; Huerta, 1887, 4 April; Cano, 1909, 25 March; Tavera Alfaro, 2:147. It is interesting to note that several of these more-or-less-pure retail merchants were related to each other: Febronio Retana was Benito Barroso's stepson; Silvano Milanés's sister Jesús was married to one of the Alva brothers; Silviano Murillo's sister Regina was married to Juan Antonio Milanés, Silvano's father. ANM, Escobar, 1860, 30 August; Valdovinos, 1858, 3 February; Ibarrola, 1900, appendix.

60. Tavera Alfaro, 2:152; ANM, Huerta, 1885, 29 January; ANM, Gutiérrez, 1886, 14 December; Gutiérrez, 1907, appendix.

61. AHPJ, 1864, Primero Civil, Leg. 1, "Testamentaria del Sr. Martín de

Mier"; ANM, Cano, 1868, 27 May; García, 1870, 28 March; Gutiérrez, 1908, 17 October.

62. ANM, García, 1852, 22 June; Huerta, 1877, 2 August; Huerta, 1879, 1 October; Tavera Alfaro, 2:153.

63. Pérez Acevedo, pp. 48–49; ANM, García, 1872, 3 June; *La Libertad*, 2 January 1895.

64. ANM, Valdovinos, 1867, 28 August.

65. ANM, Laris, 1897, 20 July; León, 1872, 12 August; León, 1877, 31 January; Huerta, 1879, appendix; Uribe (Uruapan), 1898, 31 August; Gutiérrez, 1898, 18 June; Ruiz Durán (Uruapan), 1901, 26 April; de la Peña (Uruapan) 1896, 9 September; AHMM, 1857, on cover is "Curaduría ad bona de la menor Doña Socorro Chávez," but concerns estate of Antonio Zacanini.

66. This pattern held true for all wealth groups, but it was even more noticeable in the upper ranges of wealth. Of the early to mid-nineteenth-century elite with fortunes of 100,000 pesos or more one-third had started out as merchants, compared to only 14 percent of the later generations; among the wealthiest of the wealthy all but one of the men with assets over 500,000 pesos during the first part of the period had been merchants, compared to three of twelve in the second.

67. ANM, Alvarado, 1873, 20 May.

68. *La Libertad*, 30 May 1899.

69. For some examples of the strong profits that speculative endeavors could yield during this period, and for another treatment of the phenomenon from a slightly different perspective, see Pérez Acevedo, pp. 37–48.

70. ANM, León, 1873, 31 October.

71. ANM, Huerta, 1882, 3 June.

72. Friedrich, pp. 10–18, 43–49. See also Guzmán Avila, "Movimiento campesino."

73. The chief exception was the division of the hacienda of Bellasfuentes, which was taken over as a result of the Reform legislation by the national government, divided into five parts, and distributed to the government's supporters.

74. González, *Pueblo en vilo*, pp. 93–98. For some examples outside of Michoacán, see Bazant, "The Division of Some Mexican Haciendas," and Gómez Serrano.

75. ANM, Valdovinos, 1853, 21 October; Barroso, 1899, 12 May; Cano, 1909, 22 September and 13 October; Canedo (Pátzcuaro), 1909, 11 November; Laris, 1903, 29 April; Huerta, 1880, 2 January; ANMC, Roldán, 1875, 26 July; ANMC, Covarrubia, 1877, 19 August 1877.

76. ANM, León, 1871, 26 July; León, 1871, 12 September; Laris, 1898, 28 November; Ibarrola, 1899, 7 November; Barroso, 1903, 17 January; Cano, 1908, 14 December.

77. ANM, Huerta, 1862, 18 February, 20 February, 21 February, 24 April, 16

June, 7 July; Valdovinos, 1863, 9 June; Valdovinos, 1870, 29 January; León, 1879, 5 September; Cano, 1890, 2 October; Cano, 1909, 12 March. Huarte later sold his rancho, received in payment of a debt of 12,650 pesos, for 3,000 pesos, noting that although it was appraised at 4,485 pesos, its value was diminished by the fact that the rancho surrounded an Indian pueblo that was frequently troublesome: Valdovinos, 1868, 24 July.

78. AHCE, Actas, Caja 37, exp. 1, "Actas ... julio–octubre, 1857," 29 August 1857 and 3 October 1857; Díaz Polanco, p. 46.

79. *El Grano de Arena*, 14 March 1886.

80. ANM, Valdovinos, 1868, 20 March, 23 March, 5 December.

81. ANM, González, 1873, 14 July; Ruiz (Uruapan), 1880, 6 December; Huerta, 1881, 2 June; Cano, 1908, 30 June.

82. ANM, Huerta, 1880, 11 March; Cano, 1910, 19 December.

83. ANM, González, 1873, appendix; Valdovinos, 1866, 6 February; Cano, 1866, 3 September.

84. ANM, Valdovinos, 1856, 4 October; Laris, 1875, 28 June; León, 1875, 14 December; León, 1876, 27 September; Huerta, 1899, 14 November; Laris, 1902, 22 November; *El Regenerador*, 2 January 1877; *El Arnero de Tío Juan*, 10 July 1878.

85. ANM, Haro (Zamora), 1881, 14 February; Haro (Zamora), 1885, 30 April; Haro (Zamora), 1897, 3 November; Haro (Zamora), 1899, 7 January.

86. ANM, León, 1881, 21 December; Huerta, 1882, 20 January; de la Peña (Uruapan), 1885, 2 July.

87. ANM, Valdovinos, 1860, 27 September; Valdovinos, 1863, 24 October; Pérez, 1860, 7 December; Pérez, 1860, 3 December; Cedeño Peguero, pp. 103–13.

88. ANM, Huacuja, 1887, 9 September; Michoacán, "Memoria en que el C. General Epitacio Huerta . . . ," p. 28.

89. Cerda Hernández, pp. 151–53.

90. ANM, Cano, 1863, 25 November; Escobar, 1862, 15 November.

91. ANM, Valdovinos, 1862, 5 December; Valdovinos 1863, 24 October; Alvarado, 1882, 21 January; Cano, 1862, 6 November; Valdovinos, 1863, 4 November and 7 November.

92. *Revista Comercial*, 1 February 1882.

93. ANM, García, 1851, 16 October; García, 1868, 23 November; Victoria (Pátzcuaro), 1889, 10 December; Alcocer y Piña (Pátzcuaro), 1891, 30 January.

94. On national politics during the Restored Republic, see Hamnett, "Liberalism Divided."

95. They were Epitacio Huerta, who was removed after three days; Felipe Neri Chacón, whom Díaz retired because of his persecution of liberals and his

conservative appointments; and Bruno Patiño, who was driven to resign by a majority of the state congress.

96. For splits within the liberal ranks in other parts of Mexico, see Mallon.

97. Bravo Ugarte, *Historia sucinta*, 3:190; Tavera Alfaro, 2:145, 179, 188–90.

98. Mallon, p. 41.

99. Romero Flores, *Historia*, 2:8; Cedeño Peguero, pp. 77–78. There is some confusion regarding the position of the Huerta family on the "hacienda" of Tunguitiro before the Reform. Most authors seem to think that the Huertas owned the property, but in fact it was a section of the larger hacienda of Bellasfuentes, which Huerta bought during the Reform.

100. Aguilar y Marocho, pp. 23–24.

101. Michoacán, "Memoria en que el C. General Epitacio Huerta . . . ," p. 5.

102. Michoacán, "Memoria en que el C. General Epitacio Huerta . . . ," p. 6.

103. Michoacán, "Memoria en que el C. General Epitacio Huerta . . . ," pp. 30–31 and documents 25–32.

104. Bravo Ugarte, *Historia sucinta*, 3:156; Romero Flores, *Historia*, 2:172.

105. Michoacán, "Memoria en que el C. General Epitacio Huerta . . . ," p. 9; *La Bandera Roja*, 28 July 1859.

106. Michoacán, "Memoria en que el C. General Epitacio Huerta . . . ," pp. 63–64; Cedeño Peguero, p. 87.

107. Michoacán, "Memoria en que el C. General Epitacio Huerta . . . ," p. 62.

108. Cedeño Peguero, pp. 86–87; Bravo Ugarte, *Historia sucinta*, 3:102–04; Zamacois, 15:70–72.

109. Rivas, pp. 33–34; Romero Flores, *Diccionario*, pp. 29, 101, 241, 390.

110. Michoacán, "Memoria en que el C. General Epitacio Huerta . . . ," p. 50; AHCE, Actas, Caja 38, exp. 1, "Actas . . . abril–noviembre, 1861," 11 October 1861 and 22 October 1861.

111. Juárez, 4:382–86.

112. Juárez, 4:385.

113. See the partial list in Romero Flores, *Historia*, 2:217–19.

114. Romero Flores, *Historia*, 2:230.

115. Guzmán Avila, "La república restaurada," p. 121.

116. Romero Flores, *Historia*, 2:395, 398–99.

117. ANM, Alvarado, 1878, appendix.

118. There was, however, a short but important burst of strong anticlericalism during the Lerdo regime at the national level in 1873, when Lerdo and his many supporters in Michoacán, including Mendoza and his successor, Rafael Carrillo, pushed to incorporate the laws of the Reform into the constitution.

119. Tavera Alfaro, 1:83.

120. On the post-Intervention split between hardline liberals and liberals who advocated policies of conciliation, see Tavera Alfaro, 1:69–70; 1:79–83.

121. From the *Libro secreto de Maximiliano*, quoted in *El Constitucionalista*, 26 February 1868.

122. Romero Flores, *Historia*, 2:195, 535; *La Sombra de Hidalgo*, 19 February 1885; *El Chinaco*, 4 May 1885.

123. *El Explorador*, 1 March 1885.

124. Romero Flores, *Historia*, 2:539; *El Grano de Arena*, 14 February 1886; *La Libertad*, 3 February 1894.

125. Romero Flores, *Historia*, 2:540.

126. *La Libertad*, 11 August 1894.

127. Romero Flores, *Historia*, 2:144, 172, 176, 194–95, 217–19, 231; *El Constitucionalista*, 10 February 1868.

128. ANM, Barroso, 1903, 21 July; see also her diary account of the emperor's visit in Ibarrola, p. 197.

129. This interpretation of the huge number of adherents to the empire in a traditionally liberal state like Michoacán is advanced in Pérez Acevedo, p. 37.

130. Michoacán, *Memoria . . . 1869*, pp. 61–62.

131. Michoacán, *Memoria . . . 1869*, pp. 37–58. A debate in the state congress in 1851 had pitted Manuel Alzúa, whose interest in the cotton textile industry prompted him to make a strong case for keeping protectionist tariffs in place, against liberal free traders who wanted to abolish them. AHCE, Actas, Caja 34, exp. 6, "Actas . . . marzo 1851–septiembre 1851," 16 July, 18 July and 21 July 1851.

EPILOGUE

1. *La Libertad*, 21 June 1898.

2. ANM, Laris, 1904, 9 September.

3. ANM, Huacuja, 1885, 27 February; Huacuja, 1886, 16 November; Laris, 1892, 14 December; Huerta, 1898, 12 October; Barroso, 1901, 26 January.

4. *Periódico Oficial del Estado de Michoacán*, regular feature entitled "Lo que consumen en el Hospital Civil"; *Boletín de la Sociedad Mexicana de Geografía y Estadística*, 1:116; Busto, vol. 1, Cuadro de agricultura #30 and Cuadro de industria #3; *Cuadro sinóptico informativo de la administración del Sr. General D. Porfirio Díaz . . . hasta 1909*, p. 75; Mexico, Secretaría de Fomento, *Anuario estadístico*, 9:426–552; 10:302–408; 11:402–599.

5. *Boletín de la Sociedad Mexicana de Geografía y Estadística* 1:56, 116–17; Mexico, Secretaría de Fomento, *Memoria . . . de enero 1883 a junio 1885*, 5:803; Mexico, Secretaría de Fomento, *Anuario estadístico*, 2:514, 554; 3:722–23 and 768–69; 7:298, 304; 9:431, 473; 10:306, 339; 11:470, 480; Bureau of the American Republics, p. 163; Melville, p. 61; *La Libertad*, 6 July 1897. Production

figures for wheat (and corn) from Busto have not been included, following John Coatsworth's argument (with which my own figures concur) against its accuracy, in "Anotaciones," p. 175.

6. Many of the forested areas belonged to Indian communities that had managed to avoid extinction in the numerous assaults on communal landholding since the Reform. There is strong evidence to suggest that these communities were coerced into signing contracts with the lumbermen, implying that they did not receive or did not expect to receive the fairly substantial sums promised in these contracts. But private landowners, far less dependent on their *montes* for subsistence, also made deals with the lumbermen and were rewarded with handsome supplements to their income. For some of the lumber contracts, see ANM, *juez de letras* (Maravatío), 1891, 14 October; Barroso, 1901, 12 April; Laris, 1902, 12 May; Laris, 1907, 31 May; Ruiz Durán (Uruapan), 1907, 26 November; Ruiz Durán (Uruapan), 1908, 19 March and 20 March, 23 April, 8 August and 25 August, 24 September, 27 September, and 30 September; Cano, 1908, 28 January and 4 February; Méndez (Zamora), 1909, 1 November. On the coercion of Indian communities, see the excerpt from the archives of Francisco Múgica, in Guzmán Avila, "Inversiones extranjeras," p. 170.

7. Guzmán Avila, "Inversiones extranjeras," pp. 159–68; *La Libertad*, 1 November 1898.

8. ANM, Barroso, 1899, 13 May.

9. ANM, Cano, 1908, 1 August; Cano, 1910, 22 April; Valdovinos, 1867, 7 December.

10. ANM, Méndez (Zamora), 1909, 28 October.

11. ANM, Cano, 1908, 10 April.

12. *La Libertad*, 23 August 1901; ANM, Gutiérrez, 1906, 24 November.

13. ANM, Cano, 1907, 18 May.

14. ANM, Laris, 1893, 20 July; Ibarrola, 1897, 22 June; Laris, 1889, 6 November.

15. ANM, Uribe (Uruapan), 1899, 11 February; Uribe (Uruapan), 1902, 11 March; Cano, 1907, 3 July; Cano, 1909, 18 June; Cano, 1909, 4 June; Cano, 1910, n.d.

16. Percentage for 1900–10 based on 48 sales and inventories.

17. *Periódico Oficial*, 8 June 1905; *La Libertad*, 4 December 1903; *La Libertad*, 3 January 1902; *La Paz*, 28 June 1892; *La Paz*, 6 July 1892; *Pierrot*, 20 July 1890; *El Grano de Arena*, 7 March 1886.

18. *El Católico*, 24 July 1884.

19. ANM, Ortega González, 1906, 11 May; Barroso, 1906, 17 May.

20. In 1900, for example, the government confiscated lands of the "extinguida comunidad" of Zacapu for failure to pay property taxes, and sold them to Eduardo Noriega for 1.12 pesos/hectare. Two months later Noriega resold these

(and other) *terrenos*, which he had promised to drain as part of a massive dese-cation project, for approximately 280 pesos/hectare. ANM, Barroso, 1900, 29 January and 22 March.

21. ANM, Huerta, 1885, 15 October.

22. ANM, Valdovinos, 1873, 12 May; Laris, 1906, 30 January.

23. An advertisement for the "Gran Hotel Oseguera" emphasized its proxim-ity to Morelia's streetcar system; its restaurant, bar, billiard room, and warm water baths; the luxury of its rooms; the fact that French, English, and German were spoken; and the fact that within half an hour of the arrival of the Mexico City train mail addressed to its guests would be specially delivered. *El Estado de Michoacán*, 9 April 1889.

24. ANM, Victoria (Pátzcuaro), 1882, 21 July; Huerta, 1889, 5 July; Huerta, 1890, 24 March; Laris, 1891, 18 June; Laris, 1900, 2 October; González, 1873, 14 July; González, 1877, 17 September; Ruiz (Uruapan), 1880, 6 December; Huerta, 1881, 2 June; Arias (Uruapan), 1886, 11 September; Laris, 1890, 12 September; Gutiérrez, 1898, 18 June.

25. ANM, Barroso, 1899, 12 May; Huerta, 1893, 27 October; Barroso, 1900, 31 October; Laris, 1896, 3 November; Huerta, 1898, 18 May; Huerta, 1898, 22 December; Huerta, 1899, 8 August.

26. ANM, Laris, 1895, 25 June; Laris, 1905, 16 June.

27. For Feliciano Vidales' early poverty, see his grandson's lyrical memoir (Maillefert, pp. 11–12); see also Vidales' agreement with his daughter Susana to equalize her inheritance with that of the children of his second marriage, since he had "pocos bienes" at the time of her mother's death (ANM, Alcalde ordinario de Uruapan, 1880, 16 July). For Joaquín Oseguera, see his will (ANM, Laris Contreras, 1891, 18 June), in which he states that he and his wife had only 1,300 pesos between them at the time of their marriage, and see also the history of his career in Huerta, 1889, 5 July, which notes, among other things, that his son, Joaquín Esteban Oseguera, began keeping the books of his father's business in 1875, when he was about thirteen years old, and also indicates that his wife, Cruz Bocanegra, did not know how to write her name.

28. ANM, Laris, 1905, 16 June.

29. Maillefert, pp. 44, 66.

30. ANM, Laris, 1906, 4 June; Cano, 1910, 22 April; Cano, 1910, 19 December; Brand, p. 183.

31. Guzmán Avila, "Inversiones extranjeras," p. 166.

32. Sánchez Díaz, "Las crises agrícolas," pp. 255–63.

33. *La Libertad*, 3 January 1902.

34. ANM, Huerta, 1871, 11 May; Huerta, 1872, 25 January; Huerta, 1882, 17 August; Gutiérrez, 1889, 8 August; Huerta, 1893, 4 May; Laris, 1900, 23

May; Cortés Rubio, 1900, 29 November. See also Haber, *Industry*, pp. 69–71, for Basagoiti's Mexico City connections.

35. ANM, Gutiérrez, 1904, 7 January; Gutiérrez, 1904, 11 May; Gutiérrez, 1904, 21 May; Gutiérrez, 1904, 19 December; Angeles, 1905, 11 January; Gutiérrez, 1905, 5 April; Gutiérrez, 1905, 20 June; Angeles, 1906, 22 November; Laris, 1907, 19 June; Angeles, 1907, 16 July.

36. Sánchez Díaz, "Los cambios demográficos," pp. 304–05.

37. ANM, Huerta, 1887, 14 March; Huerta, 1890, 16 December; Barroso, 1904, 5 January.

38. ANM, Gutiérrez, 1898, 18 June.

39. ANM, Huerta, 1896, 19 May; Barroso, 1902, 24 May.

40. ANM, González, 1872, 26 September; Laris, 1902, 31 July; Cano, 1908, 7 January.

CONCLUSION

1. For just such a graph, see Chowning, "Contours."

2. Haber, "Assessing the Obstacles," pp. 6, 10–11.

3. Knight, "Peculiarities," p. 121.

4. In any discussion of the Reform's effect on the number of people who by wealth and/or occupation fit into the category of middle classes, it should be noted that while the goal of enlarging the rural middle class was only partly successful, the urban middle class was dramatically expanded by the creation of government jobs: as one critical newspaper editorial put it, "these days all of the Liberals seek to live off the government budget, and almost all of them manage to do so." *El Derecho Cristiano*, 17 January 1889.

5. *El Globo*, 29 August 1889; *La Libertad*, 4 December 1903.

6. *El Explorador*, 31 August 1884; *El Derecho Cristiano*, 17 January 1889; *El Derecho Cristiano*, 31 January 1889; *La Libertad*, 14 April 1894; *La Libertad*, 8 August 1899.

7. Brading, "Liberal Patriotism," p. 40.

8. *El Derecho Cristiano*, 17 January 1889.

9. Rodríguez Díaz, pp. 317–23.

10. Tenenbaum, "Streetwise History," p. 147. See also Tenorio-Trillo.

NEWSPAPERS *(all published in Morelia unless otherwise noted)*

El Astro Moreliano
El Sol
La Voz de Michoacán
El Filógrafo
El Constitucionalista
La Libertad
El Grano de Arena
El Regenerador
El Arnero de Tío Juan
Revista Comercial
La Bandera Roja
La Sombra de Hidalgo

El Chinaco
El Explorador
El Estado de Michoacán
El Derecho Cristiano
Periódico Oficial del Estado de Michoacán
La Paz
La Lira Michoacana. Periódico quincenal de literatura y amenidades
Pierrot
El Católico
El Globo

SECONDARY SOURCES

Abad y Queipo, Manuel. "Dr. Manuel Abad Queipo, Canónigo Penitenciario de esta Santa Iglesia, y Obispo Electo . . . a todos sus habitantes paz y salud en nuestro Señor Jesucristo." Valladolid [Morelia], Michoacán, 1810.
———. "Representación a la regencia del reyno, manifestando el estado de fermentación en que se encuentra la Nueva España y medios para evitar un trastorno." In Hernández y Dávalos, ed., *Colección de documentos*, 2: 891–96.

Aguilar y Marocho, Ignacio. *La familia enferma*. Mexico City: Editorial Jus, 1969. Originally published as *Primer calendario de la familia enferma para el año bisiesto de 1860* in 1860.

Ajofrín, Francisco de. *Diario del viaje que hizo a la América en el siglo XVIII el P. Fray Francisco de Ajofrín*. Mexico City: Galas de México, 1964.

Alamán, Lucas. *Historia de Méjico desde los primeros movimientos que prepararon su independencia en el año de 1808 hasta la época presente*. 5 vols. Mexico City: J. M. Lara, 1849–52.

Alvarez, José J. and Rafael Durán. *Itinerarios y derroteros de la República Mexicana*. Mexico City: J. A. Godoy, 1856.

Archer, Christon I. " 'La Causa Buena': The Counterinsurgency Army of New Spain and the Ten Years' War." In Jaime O. Rodríguez, ed., *The Independence of Mexico and the Creation of the New Nation*, pp. 85–108. Los Angeles: U.C.L.A. Latin American Center Publications, 1989.

———. "Los dineros de la independencia." In Carlos Herrejón Peredo, ed., *Repaso de la independencia*, pp. 39–55. Zamora, Michoacán: Colegio de Michoacán, 1985.

Archivo General de la Nación. *Los precursores ideológicos de la guerra de independencia*. Mexico City: Talleres Gráficos de la Nación, 1929.

Bárcena, Manuel de la. "Exhortación que hizo al tiempo de jurarse la Constitución española, en la catedral de Valladolid de Michoacán. . . ." Mexico City: M. Zúñiga y Ontiveros, 1813.

———. "Manifiesto al Mundo, la justicia y la necesidad de la Independencia de la Nueva España." Mexico City: M. Ontiveros, 1821.

———. "Sermón que en la Jura del Señor D. Fernando VII (que Dios guarde) Dixo en la Catedral de Valladolid de Michoacán el Dr. D. Manuel de la Bárcena . . . el día 26 de Agosto de 1808." Mexico City: Arizpe, 1808.

Barrett, Elinore M. "Land Tenure and Settlement in the Tepalcatepec Lowland," Ph.D. diss., University of California at Berkeley, 1970.

Bazant, Jan. *Alienation of Church Wealth in Mexico: Social and Economic Aspects of the Liberal Revolution, 1856–75*. Cambridge: Cambridge University Press, 1971.

———. "The Division of Some Mexican Haciendas During the Liberal Revolution, 1856–1862." *Journal of Latin American Studies* 3, no. 1 (1971): 25–37.

Bellingeri, Marco, and Isabel Gil Sánchez. "Las estructuras agrarias." In Ciro Cardoso, ed., *México en el siglo XIX (1821–1910): historia económica y de la estructura social*, pp. 97–118. Mexico City: Nueva Imagen, 1980.

Biblioteca Nacional de México, *Catálogo de la Colección Lafragua, 1821–1853*. Mexico City: Universidad Autónoma de México, 1975.

Brading, D. A. *Church and State in Bourbon Mexico. The Diocese of Michoacán 1749–1810.* Cambridge: Cambridge University Press, 1994.

———. *The First America: The Spanish Monarchy, Creole Patriots, and the Liberal State 1492–1867.* Cambridge: Cambridge University Press, 1991.

———. *Haciendas and Ranchos in the Mexican Bajío. León, 1700–1860.* Cambridge: Cambridge University Press, 1978.

———. "Liberal Patriotism and the Mexican Reforma." *Journal of Latin American Studies* 20, no. 1 (1988): 27–48.

———. *Miners and Merchants in Bourbon Mexico.* Cambridge: Cambridge University Press, 1972.

———. *The Origins of Mexican Nationalism.* Cambridge, Eng.: Centre of Latin American Studies, 1985.

———. *Prophecy and Myth in Mexican History.* Cambridge, Eng.: Centre of Latin American Studies, 1984.

Brand, Donald D. *Coalcomán and Motines de Oro.* The Hague: Martinus Nijhoff, 1960.

Bravo Ugarte, José. *Historia sucinta de Michoacán.* 3 vols. Mexico City: Editorial Jus, 1964.

———. *Munguía, Obispo y Arzobispo de Michoacán. 1810–1868.* Mexico City: Editorial Jus, 1968.

Bullock, W. H. *Across Mexico in 1864–5.* London: Macmillan, 1866.

Bureau of the American Republics. *Mexico: A Geographical Sketch, with Special Reference to Economic Conditions and Prospects of Future Development.* Washington, D.C.: Government Printing Office, 1900.

Bustamante, Carlos M. *Continuación del cuadro histórico de la Revolución Mexicana.* 4 vols. Mexico City: Biblioteca Nacional, 1953.

Busto, Emiliano. *Estadística de la república mexicana.* 3 vols. Mexico City: I. Cumplido, 1880.

Calderón de la Barca, Fanny. *Life in Mexico: The Letters of Fanny Calderón de la Barca.* Garden City, N.J.: Doubleday, 1966.

Cardoso, Ciro, ed., *México en el siglo XIX (1821–1910): historia económica y de la estructura social.* Mexico City: Nueva Imagen, 1980.

Cardozo Galué, Germán. *Michoacán en el siglo de las luces.* Mexico City: Colegio de México, 1973.

Carmagnani, Marcelo. "El liberalismo, impuestos domésticos, y el estado federal de Mexico, 1857–1911." *Historia Mexicana* 38, no. 3 (1989): 471–96.

Cedeño Peguero, María Guadalupe. *El General Epitacio Huerta y su hacienda de Chucándiro, 1860–1892.* Morelia, Michoacán: Instituto Michoacano de Cultura, 1989.

Cerda Hernández, Berta G. *Don Francisco de Velarde, "El Burro de Oro:" un hombre de su época.* Mexico City: M. Porrúa, 1975.

Cerruti, Mario, ed. *El siglo XIX en Mexico: cinco procesos regionales: Morelos, Monterrey, Yucatán, Jalisco y Puebla*. Mexico City: Clavos Latinoamericanos, 1985.

"Certificación de méritos de D. Mariano Quevedo." In Carlos Herrejón Peredo, ed., *Repaso de la independencia*, pp. 223–24. Zamora, Michoacán: Colegio de Michoacán, 1985.

Chowning, Margaret. "The Consolidación de Vales Reales in the Bishopric of Michoacán." *Hispanic American Historical Review* 69, no. 3 (1989): 451–78.

———. "The Contours of the Post-1810 Depression in Mexico: A Reappraisal from a Regional Perspective." *Latin American Research Review* 27, no. 2 (1992): 119–50.

———. "Elite Families and Popular Politics in Early Nineteenth-Century Michoacán: The Strange Case of Juan José Codallos and the Censored Genealogy." *The Americas*, 55, no. 1 (1998): 35–61.

———. "The Management of Church Wealth in Michoacán, Mexico, 1810–1856: Economic Motivations and Political Implications." *Journal of Latin American Studies* 22, no. 3 (1990): 459–96.

———. "Reassessing the Prospects for Profit in Nineteenth-Century Mexican Agriculture from a Regional Perspective: Michoacán, 1810–1860." In Stephen H. Haber, ed., *How Latin America Fell Behind*, pp. 179–215. Stanford, Ca: Stanford University Press, 1997.

Coatsworth, John. "Anotaciones sobre la producción de alimentos durante el Porfiriato." *Historia Mexicana* 26, no. 2 (1976): 167–87.

———. "La decadencia de la economía mexicana, 1800–1860." In John Coatsworth, *Los orígenes del atraso: nueve ensayos de historia económica de México en los siglos XVIII y XIX*, pp. 110–41. Mexico City: Alianza Editorial Mexicana, 1990.

———. *Growth Against Development: The Economic Impact of Railroads in Porfirian Mexico*. Austin: University of Texas Press, 1982.

———. "Obstacles to Economic Growth in Nineteenth-Century Mexico." *American Historical Review* 83, no. 1 (1978): 80–100.

"Conducta del reverendo obispo de Michoacán D. José Cayetano Portugal con motivo del destierro que impuso el gobierno. . . ." Mexico City: I. Cumplido, 1833.

"Conspiración de Valladolid de 1813. Auto cabeza de proceso y pedimento fiscal." *Boletín del Archivo General de la Nación* 3, no. 3 (1932): 469–80.

"Contestación del Administrador Pral. substituto de rentas del departamento al editorial que bajo el rubro de alcabalas, consta en . . . *La Voz de Michoacán* del . . . 25 de enero de 1844." Morelia, Michoacán: 1844.

Coromina, Amador. *Recopilación de leyes, decretos, reglamentos y circulares ex-*

pedidas en el Estado de Michoacán. Morelia, Michoacán: Hijos de I. Arango, 1886–1923.

Costeloe, Michael. *The Central Republic of Mexico, 1835–46*. Cambridge: Cambridge University Press, 1994.

———. *Church Wealth in Mexico. A Study of the "Juzgado de Capellanías" in the Archbishopric of Mexico, 1800–1856*. Cambridge: Cambridge University Press, 1967.

———. *La primera república federal de México (1824–1835)*. Mexico City: SEP, 1975.

"Cuaderno tercero de la causa instruida en Valladolid contra las personas que prepararon allí un movimiento revolucionario en favor de la independencia." In Génaro García, ed., *Documentos históricos mexicanos*. Vol. 1. Mexico City: Museo Nacional de Arqueología, 1910.

"El cura Dr. Antonio Lavarrieta pide indulto concediéndosele bajo las condiciones que se expresan." In Hernández y Dávalos, ed., *Colección de Documentos*, 2: 371–72.

"Defensa del canónigo D. Sebastián de Betancourt y León, con un informe de lo ocurrido en Morelia desde el 18 de septiembre al 28 de diciembre de 1810." In Hernández y Dávalos, ed., *Colección de documentos*, 3: 406–23.

"Defensa del Sr. D. José María de Ansorena, escrita por su hijo el Lic. D. José Ignacio, en contestación a la historia de México, por D. Lucas Alamán"; "Contestación del presbítero D. Mucio Valdovinos al Lic. D. José Ignacio Ansorena sobre los asesinatos de Valladolid"; and "Respuesta del Sr. D. José Mariano de Ansorena, a la contestación que dió el presbítero D. Mucio Valdovinos, a la defensa del Lic. D. José Ignacio Ansorena." In Hernández y Dávalos, ed., *Colección de documentos*, 2: 528–93.

Díaz Polanco, Héctor. *Formación regional y burguesía agraria en México*. Mexico City: Ediciones Era, 1982.

"Documentos justificativos de los vicios y nulidades de las elecciones primarias y secundarias de Morelia, publicados para manifestar el mal comportamiento de los falsos liberales y para vindicación de la verdad y de la justicia, ultrajadas por ellos con desprecio de los ciudadanos amantes del órden y de la verdadera libertad". Morelia, Michoacán: Ignacio Arango, 1849.

Durán Juárez, Juan M., and Alain Bustin. *Revolución agrícola en Tierra Caliente de Michoacán*. Zamora, Michoacán: Colegio de Michoacán, 1983.

Enciclopedia de México. Mexico City: SEP, 1987. 14 vols.

"Exposición que de nuevo ha dirigido la Asamblea Departamental de Michoacán a las Augustas Cámaras sobre la conveniencia, la justicia y la necesidad de abrir el puerto de Manzanillo." Morelia, Michoacán: Ignacio Arango, 1845.

Farriss, Nancy. *Crown and Clergy in Colonial Mexico, 1759–1821*. London: Athlone, 1968.

Fernández de Córdoba, Joaquín. "Sumaria relación de las bibliotecas de Michoacán." *Historia Mexicana* 3, no. 1 (July–August, 1953): 134–56.

Fisher, Lillian Estelle. *Champion of Reform: Manuel Abad y Queipo*. New York: Library Publishers, 1955.

[Forbes]. *A Trip to Mexico, or Recollections of a Ten-Months' Ramble in 1849–50*. London: Smith-Elder, 1851.

Franco, Ivan. "Una nota sobre la oligarquía de Valladolid a fines del siglo XVIII." *Estudios Michoacanos* 3, pp. 255–68. Zamora, Michoacán: Colegio de Michoacán, 1989.

Friedrich, Paul. *Agrarian Revolt in a Mexican Village*. Englewood Cliffs, N.J.: Prentice-Hall, 1970.

Garavaglia, Juan Carlos, and Juan Carlos Grosso. "Mexican Elites in a Provincial Town: The Landowners of Tepeaca, 1700–1870." *Hispanic American Historical Review* 70, no. 2 (1990): 255–93.

———. "Propiedad, crédito y desamortización en las haciendas mexicanas (1700–1870): El entorno agrario de Tepeaca." *Siglo XIX* 5, no. 10 (1990): 33–76.

García, Génaro, ed. *Documentos históricos mexicanos*. Mexico City: Museo Nacional de Arqueología, 1910.

García Alcaraz, Agustín. *La cuna ideológica de la independencia*. Morelia, Michoacán: Fimax, 1971.

Garner, Richard L. *Economic Growth and Change in Bourbon Mexico*. Gainesville: University of Florida Press, 1993.

Gómez Serrano, Jesús. *Hacendados y campesinos en Aguascalientes*. Aguascalientes: Centro de Investigaciones Regionales, 1985.

González, Luis. *Pueblo en vilo: microhistoria de San José de Gracia*. Mexico City: Colegio de México, 1968.

———. *Zamora*. Zamora, Michoacán: Colegio de Michoacán, 1984.

González Sánchez, Isabel. *El Obispado de Michoacán en 1765*. Morelia, Michoacán: Gobierno de Michoacán, 1985.

Gortari Rabiela, Hira de. "La minería durante la guerra de independencia y los primeros años del México independiente, 1810–1824." In Jaime Rodríguez, ed., *The Independence of Mexico and the Creation of the New Nation*, pp. 129–61. Los Angeles: U.C.L.A. Latin American Center Publications, 1989.

Grosso, Juan Carlos. "De los borbones al porfiriato: grupos económicos y poder político en Puebla." *Siglo XIX* (1996).

Greenow, Linda. *Credit and Socioeconomic Change in Colonial Mexico: Loans and Mortgages in Guadalajara, 1720–1820*. Boulder, Co.: Westview, 1983.

Guardino, Peter. *Peasants, Politics and the Formation of Mexico's National State: Guerrero, 1800–1857*. Stanford, Ca.: Stanford University Press, 1996.

Guerra, Francois-Xavier. *Mexico: Del antiguo regimen a la revolución*. 2 vols. Mexico City, 1988.

Guzmán Avila, José Napoleón. "Las inversiones extranjeras: origen y desarrollo." In Enrique Florescano, ed., *Historia general de Michoacán*. Vol. 3, *El siglo XIX*, pp. 156–80. Morelia, Michoacán: Gobierno de Michoacán, 1989.

———. "Movimiento campesino y empresas extranjeras: la ciénaga de Zacapu, 1870–1910." In *La cuestión agraria: revolución y contrarrevolución en Michoacán: Tres ensayos*, pp. 27–40. Morelia, Michoacán: Universidad Michoacana, 1984.

———. "La república restaurada: en busca de la consolidación de un proyecto liberal, 1867–1876." In Enrique Florescano, ed., *Historia general de Michoacán*. Vol. 3, *El siglo XIX*, pp. 101–36. Morelia, Michoacán: Gobierno de Michoacán, 1989.

Guzmán Pérez, Moisés, and Carlos Juárez Nieto. *Arquitectura, comercio, ilustración y poder en Valladolid de Michoacán: siglo XVIII*. Mexico City: INAH, 1993.

Haber, Stephen H. "Assessing the Obstacles to Industrialisation: The Mexican Economy, 1830–1940." *Journal of Latin American Studies* 24, no. 1 (1992): 1–32.

———. *Industry and Underdevelopment: The Industrialization of Mexico, 1880–1940*. Stanford, Ca.: Stanford University Press, 1989.

Hale, Charles A. *Mexican Liberalism in the Age of Mora, 1821–1853*. New Haven, Ct.: Yale University Press, 1968.

———. *The Transformation of Liberalism in Late Nineteenth-Century Mexico*. Princeton, N.J.: Princeton University Press, 1989.

Hamnett, Brian R. "Liberalism Divided: Regional Politics and the National Project During the Mexican Restored Republic, 1867–1876." *Hispanic American Historical Review* 76, no. 4 (1996): 659–89.

———. "Royalist Counterinsurgency and the Continuity of Rebellion: Guanajuato and Michoacán, 1813–20." *Hispanic American Historical Review* 62, no. 1 (1982): 19–48.

Hardy, William. *Travels in the Interior of Mexico*. London: H. Colburn & R. Bentley, 1829.

Harris, Charles H. *A Mexican Family Empire: The Latifundios of the Sánchez Navarro Family, 1765–1867*. Austin: University of Texas Press, 1975.

Heredia Correa, Roberto. "Zamora y su distrito en 1844." *Relaciones. Estudios de Historia y Sociedad* 5 (Fall 1984): 121–40.

Hernández y Dávalos, J. E., ed. *Colección de documentos para la historia de la guerra de independencia de México de 1808 a 1821*. 6 vols. Mexico City: 1878.

Herrejón Peredo, Carlos, ed., *Repaso de la independencia*. Zamora, Michoacán: Colegio de Michoacán, 1985.

Holden, Robert H. *Mexico and the Survey of Public Lands: The Management of Modernization, 1876–1911*. DeKalb: Northern Illinois University Press, 1993.

Humboldt, Alexander von. *Ensayo político sobre el reino de la Nueva España*. Mexico City: Porrúa, 1966.

———. *Political Essay on the Kingdom of New Spain*. London: Longman, Hurst, 1814.

Ibarrola Arriaga, Gabriel. *Familias y casas de la vieja Valladolid*. Morelia, Michoacán: Fimax, 1969.

"Informe a la vista, que . . . leyó el Lic. D. Francisco Benites, como patrono del Sr. D. Mateo Echaiz, en el juicio que sobre despojo de aguas, promovió en su contra el Sr. D. José Serrano." Morelia, Michoacán: Imprenta de O. Ortiz, 1853.

"Iniciativa que el mui ilustre Ayuntamiento de Morelia hace al Congreso, pidiendo derogación del decreto de 11 de enero de 1847." Morelia, Michoacán: Tip. de Ignacio Arango, 1847.

Inspección ocular en Michoacán. Regiones central y sudoeste. José Bravo Ugarte, ed. Mexico City: Editorial Jus, 1960.

Jasso Espinosa, Rodolfo. *Grandeza de Michoacán*. Mexico City: B. Costa-Amic, 1969.

Joseph, Gilbert M. *Revolution from Without: Yucatán, Mexico, and the United States, 1880–1924*. Cambridge: Cambridge University Press, 1982.

Juárez, Benito. *Documentos, discursos y correspondencia*. 4 vols. Mexico City: Libros de México, 1972.

Juárez Nieto, Carlos. *La oligarquía y el poder político en Valladolid de Michoacán, 1785–1819*. Morelia: Congreso del Estado, 1994.

———. "Sociedad y política en Valladolid (hoy Morelia), 1780–1816." *Estudios Michoacanos* 3, pp. 229–54. Zamora, Michoacán: Colegio de Michoacán, 1989.

Knight, Alan. *The Mexican Revolution*. 2 vols. Cambridge: Cambridge University Press, 1986.

———. "The Peculiarities of Mexican History: Mexico Compared to Latin America, 1821–1992." *Journal of Latin American Studies* 24, Quincentenary Supplement (1992).

Lemoine Villicana, Ernesto. *Morelos y la revolución de 1810*. Morelia, Michoacán: Gobierno de Michoacán, 1984.

———, ed., *Manuscrito Cárdenas. Documentos del Congreso de Chilpancingo, hallados entre los papeles del caudillo José María Morelos*. Mexico City: Instituto Mexicano de Seguro Social, 1980.

———. "Un notable escrito póstumo del obispo de Michoacán, Fray Antonio de

San Miguel, sobre la situación social, económica y eclesiástica de la Nueva España, en 1804." *Boletín del Archivo General de la Nación* 5, no. 1 (1964): 5–64.

Lindley, Richard. *Kinship and Credit in the Structure of Guadalajara's Oligarchy, 1800–1830.* Ph.D. diss., University of Texas at Austin, 1976.

Lira, Andrés. *Comunidades indígenas frente a la ciudad de México: Tenochtitlán y Tlatelolco, sus pueblos y barrios, 1812–1919.* Zamora, Michoacán: Colegio de Michoacán, 1983.

Litle, Marcela M. "Sales Taxes and Internal Commerce in Bourbon Mexico, 1754–1821." Ph.D. diss., Duke University, 1985.

López de Lara, Abraham. "Los denunciantes de la conspiración de Valladolid en 1809." *Boletín del Archivo General de la Nación* 6, no. 1 (1965): 5–42.

Lyon, G. F. *Journal of a Residence and Tour in the Republic of Mexico in the Year 1826.* 2 vols. Port Washington, N.Y.: Kennikat, 1971 [1828].

Macías, Pablo G. *Ario de Rosales.* Morelia, Michoacán: Gobierno de Michoacán, 1980.

Maillefert [Vidales], Alberto. *Ancla en el tiempo.* Morelia, Michoacán: Universidad Michoacana, 1963 [1940].

Mallon, Florencia. *Peasants and Nations: Mexico and Peru in the Nineteenth Century.* Berkeley: University of California Press, 1994.

"Manifiesto del ayuntamiento de Valladolid, hoy Morelia." In Hernández y Dávalos, ed., *Colección de documentos,* 5: 86–91.

"Manifiesto que para justificar ante la opinión pública su salida de la junta de estado, hacen al público los electores que suscriben." Morelia, Michoacán: Ignacio Cumplido, 1849.

Martínez de Lejarza, Juan José. *Análisis estadístico de la provincia de Michoacán en 1822.* Morelia, Michoacán: Fimax, 1974 [1824].

Mayo, John. "Consuls and Silver Contraband on Mexico's West Coast in the Era of Santa Anna." *Journal of Latin American Studies* 19, no. 2 (1987): 389–411.

Mazín, Oscar. *Entre dos majestades. El obispo y la iglesia del Gran Michoacán ante las reformas borbónicas, 1758–1772.* Zamora, Michoacán: Colegio de Michoacán, 1987.

———, ed. *El gran Michoacán: cuatro informes del obispado de Michoacán, 1759–1769.* Zamora, Michoacán: Colegio de Michoacán, 1986.

Melville, Roberto. *Crecimiento y rebelión: el desarrollo de las haciendas azucareras en Morelos, 1880–1910.* Mexico City: Centro de Investigaciones del Desarrollo Rural, 1979.

Mendoza Briones, María Ofelia. "Fuentes documentales sobre la independencia en archivos de Morelia. 1808–1821." In Carlos Herrejón, ed., *Repaso de la in-*

dependencia, pp. 185–236. Zamora, Michoacán: Colegio de Michoacán, 1985.

Mendoza Briones, María Ofelia, and Martha Terán. "Fin del órden colonial." In Enrique Florescano, ed., *Historia general de Michoacán*. Vol. 2, *La colonia*, pp. 279–300. Morelia, Michoacán: Gobierno de Michoacán, 1989.

———. "El levantamiento popular." In Enrique Florescano, ed., *Historia general de Michoacán*. Vol. 2, *La colonia*, pp. 249–278. Morelia, Michoacán: Gobierno de Michoacán, 1989.

———. "Repercusiones de la política borbónica." In Enrique Florescano, ed., *Historia general de Michoacán*. Vol. 2, *La colonia*, pp. 217–34. Morelia, Michoacán: Gobierno de Michoacán, 1989.

Mexico. Secretaría de Fomento. *Anuario estadístico de la república mexicana*. Vols. 2, 3, 7, 9, 10, and 11. Mexico City: Imprenta de la Secretaría de Fomento, 1894–5, 1899, 1901–03.

———. *Cuadro sinóptico informativo de la administración del Sr. General D. Porfirio Díaz . . . hasta 1909*. Mexico City: Imprenta de la Secretaría de Fomento, 1910.

———. *Datos mercantiles*. Mexico City: Imprenta de la Secretaría de Fomento, 1889.

———. *Memoria . . . 1865*. Mexico City: Imprenta de la Secretaría de Fomento, 1866.

———. *Memoria . . . de enero 1883 a junio 1885*. Mexico City: Imprenta de la Secretaría de Fomento, 1887.

Mexico. Secretaría de Hacienda. *Memoria de Hacienda*. Mexico City: Imprenta de la Secretaría de Hacienda, 1872–73.

Meyer, Jean. *Esperando a Lozada*. Zamora, Michoacán: Colegio de Michoacán, 1984.

Meyer Cosío, Rosa María. "Empresarios, crédito y especulación. 1820–1880." In Leonor Ludlow and Carlos Marichal, eds., *Banca y poder en México, 1800–1925*, pp. 99–117. Mexico City: Grijalbo, 1986.

Meyers, William K. *Forge of Progress, Crucible of Revolt. The Origins of the Mexican Revolution in La Comarca Lagunera, 1880–1911*. Albuquerque: University of New Mexico Press, 1993.

Michoacán. "Memoria sobre el estado que guarda la administración pública de Michoacán, leida . . . en 23 de noviembre de 1846." Morelia, Michoacán: Gobierno de Michoacán, 1846.

———. "Memoria sobre el estado que guarda la administración pública de Michoacán, leida . . . enero de 1848." Morelia, Michoacán: Gobierno de Michoacán, 1848.

———. "Memoria que sobre el estado que guarda en Michoacán la Administración Pública . . . presenta . . . el secretario del despacho . . . en 2 de enero de 1849." Morelia, Michoacán: Gobierno de Michoacán, 1849.

———. "Memoria que sobre el estado que guarda en Michoacán la Administración Pública . . . presenta . . . el secretario del despacho [Francisco G. Anaya] . . . enero de 1850." Morelia, Michoacán: Gobierno de Michoacán, 1850.

———. "Memoria en que el C. General Epitacio Huerta dió cuenta al Congreso del Estado del uso que hizo de las facultades con que estuvo investido durante su administración dictatorial, que comenzó en 15 de febrero de 1858 y terminó en 1 de mayo de 1861." Morelia, Michoacán: Gobierno de Michoacán, 1861.

———. "Memoria leída ante la legislatura de Michoacán en . . . 1869." Morelia, Michoacán: Gobierno de Michoacán, 1869.

———. "Memoria de la administración pública del Estado de Michoacán . . . 1889." Morelia, Michoacán: Gobierno de Michoacán, 1889.

Miller, Simon. *Landlords and Haciendas in Modernizing Mexico: Essays in Radical Reappraisal.* Amsterdam: CEDLA, 1995.

Morales García, Rogelio. *Morelia: hornacina de recuerdos.* Morelia, Michoacán: Gobierno de Michoacán, 1990.

Moreno García, Heriberto. *Guaracha: tiempos viejos, tiempos nuevos.* Zamora, Michoacán: Colegio de Michoacán, 1980.

———. *Haciendas de tierra y agua en la antigua ciénaga de Chapala.* Zamora, Michoacán: Colegio de Michoacán, 1989.

Morin, Claude. *Michoacán en la Nueva España del siglo XVIII: Crecimiento y desigualdad en una economía colonial.* Mexico City: Fondo de Cultura, 1979.

Munguía, Clemente de Jesús. "Manifiesto que el Lic. Clemente de Jesús Munguía electo y confirmado obispo de Michoacán . . . dirige a la nación mexicana, explicando su conducta con motivo de su negativa del día 6 de enero al juramento civil . . ." Morelia, Michoacán: Imprenta de Arango, 1851.

———. "Memoria instructiva sobre el origen, progresos y estado actual de la enseñanza . . . en el Seminario Tridentino de Morelia," [1845]. Facsimile printed in García Alcaraz, doc no. 11.

"Noticia estadística de Morelia, capital del departamento de Michoacán, en la República mexicana." Morelia, Michoacán, 1843.

"Noticias relativas a la matanza de españoles en Valladolid (Morelia)." In Hernández y Dávalos, ed., *Coleción de documentos,* 2: 520–22.

Ocampo, Melchor. *Obras completas.* 2 vols. Mexico City: El Caballito, 1978.

Olveda, Jaime. *Gordiano Guzmán: un cacique del siglo XIX.* Mexico City: SEP-INAH, 1980.

———. *La oligarquía de Guadalajara: De las reformas borbónicas a la reforma liberal.* Mexico City: Consejo Nacional para la Cultura, 1991.

Ortiz Ybarra, Héctor, and Vicente González Méndez. *Puruándiro*. Morelia, Michoacán: Gobierno de Michoacán, 1980.

Pagden, Anthony. "From Noble Savages to Savage Nobles: The Criollo Uses of the Amerindian Past." In Anthony Pagden, *Spanish Imperialism and the Political Imagination: Studies in European and Spanish-American Social and Political Theory 1513–1830*, pp. 99–116. New Haven, Ct.: Yale University Press, 1990.

"Parte detallado de la acción en Puruarán, 20 de enero de 1814." In Hernández y Dávalos, ed., *Colección de documentos*, 6: 258–60.

Paso y Troncoso, Francisco del, ed. *Puruándiro y Urecho*. Mexico City: Vargas Rea, 1945.

Pastor, Rodolfo. *Campesinos y reformas: la Mixteca, 1700–1856*. Mexico City: Colegio de México, 1987.

Pastor, Rodolfo, and María de los Angeles Romero Frizzi. "Expansión económica e integración cultural." In Enrique Florescano, ed., *Historia general de Michoacán*. Vol. 2, *La colonia*, pp. 161–92. Morelia, Michoacán: Gobierno de Michoacán, 1989.

Pérez, Juan E. *Almanaque estadístico de las oficinas y guía de forasteros y del comercio de la república para 1875*. Mexico City: Imprenta del Gobierno, 1874.

Pérez Acevedo, Martín. *Empresarios y empresas en Morelia, 1860–1910*. Morelia, Michoacán: Universidad Michoacana, 1994.

Pérez Hernández, José María. *Estadística de la república mexicana*. Guadalajara: Tip. del Gobierno, 1862.

Piquero, Ignacio. "Apuntes para la corografía y la estadística del Estado de Michoacán," *Boletín de la Sociedad Mexicana de Geografía y Estadística 1*, primero época (1861): 142–237.

Potash, Robert A. *El banco de avío de México: el fomento de la industria, 1821–46*. Mexico City: Fondo de Cultura, 1959.

"Protesta del señor Portugal contra la ley de enero 1847 sobre ocupación de bienes eclesiásticos." Mexico: Imprenta de Torres, 1847.

Protocolos notariales del Distrito de Zamora, 1842–54. Zamora, Michoacán: Colegio de Michoacán, 1983.

Ramírez Romero, Esperanza. *Catálogo de construcciones artísticas, civiles y religiosas de Morelia*. Morelia, Michoacán: Universidad Michoacana, 1981.

"Relación secreta del brigadier José de la Cruz sobre la conducta pública del clero de Valladolid de Michoacán, antes de la insurrección y durante el gobierno insurgente de Anzorena. Enero de 1811," with introduction by Carlos Juárez Nieto. *Anales del Museo Michoacano*, supplement to no. 4 (1992): 51–75.

"Replica al folleto titulado Voto Independiente, en que su autor sienta conceptos subversivos, cismáticos e injuriosos a las leyes, a la Yglesia y a las supremas autoridades de la república, por defender a la negativa. . . ." Morelia, Michoacán: Imprenta de Octaviano Ortiz, 1851.

Reyes Heroles, Jesús. *El liberalismo mexicano.* 3 vols. Mexico City: UNAM, 1959–63.

Riva Palacio, Vicente. *México a través de los siglos: historia general y completa del desenvolvimiento social, político, religioso, militar, artístico, científico y literario de México desde la antigüedad más remota hasta la época actual.* 5 vols. Barcelona: Espana y Compañía, 1887–89.

Rivas, Mariano. "Alocución con que cerró el año escolar de 1834, en el Seminario Tridentino de Morelia." Morelia, Michoacán, 1835. Facsimile in García Alcaraz.

Rodríguez, Jaime O., ed. *The Independence of Mexico and the Creation of the New Nation.* Los Angeles: U.C.L.A. Latin American Center, 1989.

Rodríguez Díaz, María del Rosario. "La educación y las instituciones de enseñanza." In Enrique Florescano, ed., *Historia general de Michoacán.* Vol. 3, *El siglo XIX,* pp. 309–24. Morelia, Michoacán: Gobierno de Michoacán, 1989.

Romero, José Guadalupe. *Noticias para formar la historia y la estadística del Obispado de Michoacán,* reprinted in *Boletín de la Sociedad Mexicana de Geografía y Estadística.* Vol. 9. Mexico City, 1862.

Romero Flores, Jesús. *Comentarios a la historia de México, 1821–1861.* Mexico City: Libro Mex, 1958.

———. *Diccionario michoacano de historia y geografía.* Mexico City: Venecia, 1972.

———. *Historia de Michoacán.* 3 vols. Mexico City: Claridad, 1946.

Rosenzweig, Fernando. "Moneda y bancos." In Daniel Cosío Villegas, ed., *Historia moderna de México.* Vol. 8, *El Porfiriato. Vida económica,* pp. 789–885. Mexico City: Hermes, 1965.

Sánchez Díaz, Gerardo. "Los cambios demográficos y las luchas sociales." In Enrique Florescano, ed., *Historia general de Michoacán.* Vol. 3, *El siglo XIX,* pp. 287–306. Morelia, Michoacán: Gobierno de Michoacán, 1989.

———. "Las crisis agrícolas y la carestía del maíz, 1886–1910." In Enrique Florescano, ed., *Historia general de Michoacán.* Vol. 3, *El siglo XIX,* pp. 251–65. Morelia, Michoacán: Gobierno de Michoacán, 1989.

———. *El suroeste de Michoacán: estructura económico-social, 1821–1851.* Morelia, Michoacán: Universidad Michoacana, 1979.

———. *El suroeste de Michoacán: economía y sociedad, 1852–1910.* Morelia, Michoacán: Universidad Michoacana, 1988.

———. "Los vaivenes del proyecto republicano, 1824–1855." In Enrique Florescano, ed., *Historia general de Michoacán.* Vol. 3, *El siglo XIX,* pp. 7–38. Morelia, Michoacán: Gobierno de Michoacán, 1989.

Saragoza, Alex M. *The Monterrey Elite and the Mexican State, 1880–1940.* Austin: University of Texas Press, 1988.

"Segunda esposición que el Comercio de la capital del Departamento de Morelia hace al soberano congreso, manifestándole la justicia y necesidad de derogar la ley de 26 de noviembre de 1839 que aumentó los derechos de consumo a los efectos estrangeros en las aduanas interiores. . . ." Mexico City: Galván, 1840.

Silva Mandujano, Gabriel. *La catedral de Morelia.* Morelia, Michoacán: Gobierno de Michoacán, 1984.

———. "Pátzcuaro. Sede de la oligarquía del centro michoacano 1750–1780." *Tzintzun* 9 (1988): 21–36.

Sims, Harold D. *La expulsión de los españoles en México, 1821–28.* Mexico City: Fondo de Cultura, 1974.

Sinkin, Richard N. *The Mexican Reform, 1855–1876: A Study in Liberal Nation-Building.* Austin: University of Texas Press, 1979.

Stevens, Donald F. *Origins of Instability in Early Republican Mexico.* Durham, N.C.: Duke University Press, 1991.

Sugawara H., Masae, ed. *La deuda pública de España y la economía novohispana, 1804–09.* Mexico City: INAH, 1976.

Tapia, Juan Antonio de. "Exhortación del Sr. Dr. D. Juan Antonio de Tapia, Dean de la Santa Iglesia de Valladolid . . . a fin de que sus Diocesanos contribuyan conforme a sus facultades para las actuales necesidades de la peninsula." N.p., 1808.

Tapia Santamaría, Jesús. *Campos religiosos y evolución política.* Zamora, Michoacán: Colegio de Michoacán, 1986.

Tavera Alfaro, Xavier. *Morelia en la época de la República Restaurada. (1867–1876).* 2 vols. Morelia, Michoacán: Instituto Michoacano de Cultura, 1988.

Tayloe, Edward Thorton. *Mexico 1825–28. The Journal and Correspondence of Edward Thornton Tayloe.* Chapel Hill: University of North Carolina Press, 1959.

Taylor, William B. *Magistrates of the Sacred: Priests and Parishioners in Eighteenth-Century Mexico.* Stanford, Ca.: Stanford University Press, 1996.

Tenenbaum, Barbara. "Banqueros sin bancos: el papel de los agiotistas en México (1826–1854)." In Leonor Ludlow and Carlos Marichal, eds., *Banca y poder en México, 1800–1925,* pp. 75–97. Mexico City: Grijalbo, 1986.

———. *The Politics of Penury: Debts and Taxes in Mexico, 1821–1856.* Albuquerque: University of New Mexico Press, 1986.

———. "Streetwise History: The Paseo de la Reforma and the Porfirian State, 1876–1910." In William H. Beezley, Cheryl English Martin, and William E. French, eds., *Rituals of Rule, Rituals of Resistance: Public Celebrations and Popular Culture in Mexico,* pp. 127–50. Wilmington, De.: Scholarly Resources, 1994.

Tenorio-Trillo, Mauricio. *Mexico at the World's Fairs: Crafting a Modern Nation.* Berkeley: University of California Press, 1996.

Thomson, Guy P. C. "Agrarian Conflict in the Municipality of Cuetzalán. Sierra de Puebla: The Rise and Fall of "Pala" Agustín Dieguillo, 1861–1894." *Hispanic American Historical Review* 71, no. 2 (1991): 205–58.

———. "Montaña y Llanura in the Politics of Central Mexico: The Case of Puebla, 1820–1920." In Arij Ouweneel and Wil Pansters, eds., *Region, State and Capitalism in Mexico: Nineteenth and Twentieth Centuries.* Amsterdam: CEDLA, 1989.

———. *Patriotism, Politics, and Popular Liberalism in Nineteenth-Century Mexico: Juan Francisco Lucas and the Puebla Sierra.* Wilmington, De.: Scholarly Resources, 1998.

———. "Popular Aspects of Liberalism in Mexico, 1848–1888." *Bulletin of Latin American Research* 10, no. 2 (1991): 265–92.

———. *Puebla de los Angeles: Industry and Society in a Mexican City, 1700–1850.* Boulder, Co.: Westview, 1989.

Timmons, Wilbert H. *Morelos: Priest, Soldier, Statesman of Mexico.* El Paso: Texas Western College Press, 1963.

Torre, Juan de la. *Bosquejo histórico de la ciudad de Morelia.* Morelia, Michoacán: Universidad Michoacana, 1986 [1883].

Torre Villar, Ernesto de la. *La constitución de Apatzingán y los creadores del estado mexicano.* Mexico City: UNAM, 1964.

Tortolero Villaseñor, Alejandro. *De la coa a la máquina de vapor: actividad agrícola e inovación tecnológica en las haciendas mexicanas: 1880–1914.* Mexico City: Siglo XXI, 1994.

Tutino, John. *From Insurrection to Revolution in Mexico. Social Bases of Agrarian Violence, 1750–1940.* Princeton, N.J.: Princeton University Press, 1986.

Uribe Salas, José Alfredo. *La industria textil en Michoacán, 1840–1910.* Morelia: Universidad Michoacana, 1983.

Van Young, Eric. "The Age of Paradox: Mexican Agriculture at the End of the Colonial Period, 1750–1810." In Nils Jacobsen and Hans-Jurgen Puhle, eds., *The Economies of Mexico and Peru During the Late Colonial Period, 1760–1810,* pp. 64–90. Berlin: Colloquium Verlag, 1986.

———. *Hacienda and Market in Eighteenth-Century Mexico: The Rural Economy of the Guadalajara Region, 1675–1820.* Berkeley: University of California Press, 1981.

Vázquez, Josefina Zoraida. "La crisis y los partidos políticos, 1833–1846." In Antonio Annino et al., eds., *America Latina dallo stato coloniale allo stato nazione,* pp. 557–72. 2 vols. Milan: Franco-Angeli, 1987.

Vega Juanino, Josefa. *La institución militar en Michoacán en el último cuarto del siglo XVIII*. Zamora, Michoacán: Colegio de Michoacán, 1986.

Voss, Stuart F. *On the Periphery of Nineteenth-Century Mexico: Sonora and Sinaloa, 1810–1877*. Tucson: University of Arizona Press, 1982.

"Un voto independiente, en la cuestión del juramento del ilustrísimo obispo Lic. Clemente de Jesús Munguía." Morelia, Michoacán: Imprenta de I. Arango, 1851.

Walker, David W. *Kinship, Business and Politics: The Martínez del Río Family in Mexico, 1824–1867*. Austin: University of Texas Press, 1986.

Ward, H. G. *Mexico in 1827*. London: H. Colburn, 1828.

Wasserman, Mark. *Capitalists, Caciques and Revolution: The Native Elite and Foreign Enterprise in Chihuahua, Mexico, 1854–1911*. Chapel Hill: University of North Carolina Press, 1984.

Wells, Allan. *Yucatán's Golden Age: Haciendas, Henequen, and International Harvester, 1860–1915*. Albuquerque: University of New Mexico Press, 1985.

Wheat, Marvin. [Cincinnatus]. *Travels on the Western Slope of the Mexican Cordillera*. San Francisco: Whitten, Towne, 1857.

Zamacois, Niceto de. *Historia de Méjico desde sus tiempos más remotos hasta nuestros días*. Barcelona, 1880.

Cataloging-in-Publication Data

Chowning, Margaret.

Wealth and power in provincial Mexico : Michoacán from the late colony to the Revolution / Margaret Chowning.

p.   cm.

Includes bibliographical references (p.441–456) and index.

ISBN 0-8047-3428-3 (cloth : alk. paper)

1. Michoacán de Ocampo (Mexico)—History—19th century.
2. Michoacán de Ocampo (Mexico)—History—19th century.
3. Elite (Social sciences)—Mexico—Michoacán de Ocampo—History—19th century.   4. Upper class families—Mexico—Michoacán de Ocampo—History—19th century.   5. Huarte family.   6. Gómez Alzúa family.   I. Title.

F1306.C46   1999

972'.37—dc21   99-24871